LAND IN AMERICA

PETER WOLF

LAND IN AMERICA

ITS VALUE, USE, AND CONTROL

PANTHEON BOOKS
NEW YORK

**FOR PHELAN AND ALEXIS,
WHO ARE BEGINNING TO KNOW THE LAND**

Library of Congress Cataloging in Publication Data

Wolf, Peter M
    Land in America.

    Bibliography: p.
    Includes index.
    1. Land use—United States. 2. Real property—
United States. I. Title.
HD255.W64   333.73'0973   80–83622
ISBN 0–394–50437–2

This project is supported in part by a grant from the
National Endowment for the Arts, Washington, D.C.

Grateful acknowledgment is made to Farrar, Straus and
Giroux, Inc., for excerpts from *On Photography* by
Susan Sontag. Copyright © 1973, 1977 by Susan
Sontag. Reprinted by permission of Farrar, Straus and
Giroux, Inc.

Because all copyright acknowledgments cannot be
accommodated on this page, they will be found
beginning on page 575.

Design by Clint Anglin

FIRST EDITION

CONTENTS

v

PART TWO
CHANGING LAND VALUES
IN A CHANGING COUNTRY

CONTENTS

APPENDIX

ACKNOWLEDGMENTS

This project was initially shaped in discussions with Barbara Plumb, my editor, who worked throughout to inspire and to refine this manuscript.

Without early support from Philip Johnson, Professors Vincent Scully of Yale, Robert Gutman of Princeton, Richard Pommer of Vassar, and Dean John Hejduk of Cooper Union, there would be no book, as it was through their helpful recommendations that I was able to obtain financial support for this almost three-year effort. I am deeply grateful for their early confidence.

Because of a much appreciated fellowship awarded by the Graham Foundation for Advanced Studies in the Fine Arts, and an equally appreciated Accomplished Professional Fellowship in Design awarded by the National Endowment for the Arts, I was able to isolate the time needed to research and to begin writing. In addition, a generous six-month leave granted by the trustees of the Institute for Architecture and Urban Studies made final rewriting and editing of this manuscript possible.

Once the manuscript was nearly complete, a variety of experts to whom I am deeply indebted generously gave their professional critique of particular aspects of this work. For comments and assistance I want to thank Professor Paul W. Gates, Professor Emeritus of American History, Cornell University; Marion Clawson, Consultant to Resources for the Future; Tersh Boasberg, president of the National Center for Preservation Law and general counsel to Preservation Action; Antonio Russmann, former executive director of the National Center for Preservation Law; Peter R. Stein, vice-president of the Urban Land Program, the Trust for Public Lands; Frank Steinhauer, a member of the New York accounting firm Milton Rindler & Co.; and David Osborn, the insightful farmer of Wainscott, East Hampton, New York.

For certain specialized, detailed information, criticism, and encouragement at one time or another I thank Joe Milner of Golden Land Realty, Petaluma, California; Renna and John Godchaux, wise observers of the New Orleans scene; Ann Kaufman, managing editor of *Précis;* Nancy Goell, former executive director of the Group for America's South Fork, Bridgehampton, New York; Susan Henshaw Jones, executive director of the New York Landmarks Conservancy; Ken Witty, a producer of the *MacNeil-Lehrer Report* at WNET/13, New York; Dick Netzer, dean of the Graduate School of Public Administration, New York University; Allen D. Manvel of the Brookings Institution; John W. Reps of Cornell

ACKNOWLEDGMENTS

University and Historic Urban Plans; Jean M. Halloran of INFORM; Gregory Andrews at the National Trust for Historic Preservation; Alice Andrews, Larry Rockefeller, and Beth Mullen at the Natural Resources Defense Council offices in New York; Nancy MacKinnon of the Nature Conservancy; and finally, my very old and dear friends Alice and Calvin (Bud) Trillin.

For their generosity in sharing visual material used in this book I am indebted to Jon Barnett, author of *Urban Design as Public Policy;* Sheldon Pollack of the Regional Plan Association, New York; Laurie Beckelman and the Municipal Art Society of New York; The New York City Landmarks Preservation Commission; and Gail McEachern of The Rouse Company. Many other individuals and agencies were of inestimable value in supplying material that made the visual content of this book possible. They are individually acknowledged in the list of credits at the end of the book. For assistance with particularly difficult original visual material I am grateful to Stan Reis for his photographs.

Without the dedicated, long-suffering aid of two full-time assistants through most of the campaign, I could not have endured. To Elizabeth Robertson I am particularly grateful for help with selecting photographs, for general research, and for working intensively with some of the legal material in the manuscript. Elizabeth Nomellini, who started as a neophyte on the project and on the subject itself, ended up after several years as an invaluable combined research assistant, editor, and administrator of the whole endeavor.

Were it not for the graceful and dedicated editing of this manuscript in its final stages by Donna Bass, this book would have been even longer and the text less readable. And finally, for their much appreciated help in converting a messy manuscript into a designed, manufactured, and presentable book, my thanks to a number of others at Pantheon and outside, especially André Schiffrin, Robin Stevens, and Clint Anglin.

INTRODUCTION

Land in America explores a selection of contemporary issues which, I believe, will affect the control, value, appearance, and use of land in America for years to come.

One aim of this book is to caution and inform readers who seek to decide whether to hold, buy, or sell a parcel of undeveloped land. But beyond this is an examination of facts and fictions, links and connections, which, taken together, cast a much wider spotlight on land in America. It is a quest to reveal ways in which particular national trends now set in motion will each play a decisive role in determining how this country looks, how its land is merchandized, and what its future will be.

At certain points along the way—and with considerable trepidation, hurtling along as we are in a turbulent, fast-changing world running out of inexpensive credit and inexpensive energy—I offer predictions. At other times I take the liberty of suggesting ways to redirect certain public policies and private activities which I feel to be misguided because of their adverse impact on the land.

No book for laymen has ever been written about land in America— public and private. And now I know why. Pertinent information is dispersed, vague, and varied. The range of linked, essential considerations is preposterously large. Few archives exist. Relatively few helpful public records are maintained; and the private records that are kept are kept very privately.

Yet today, over half the total national wealth of the United States is tied up in real estate, and over 25 percent of all real-estate value in America is in the land. After equipment and structures, land is the largest single component of national wealth. Three percent of the population owns about 55 percent of all American land and 95 percent of the private acreage, most of it in ranches, farms, and forests. This includes ownership by fewer than six hundred companies and corporations of about 11 percent of the nation's land area, and some 23 percent of all private land in America.

Underlying my own decision to write this book was, most of all, a sense of frustration, as both a land planning consultant and as a teacher. As the former, I found myself time after time undertaking detailed, painstaking research to prove or merely to explain a general point to a planning commission, a town board, or a client. Oftentimes the problem faced by a client landowner or a client community was the result of laws, practices, and regulations which, though neither originally nor specifically intended to affect undeveloped land, had, in fact, become a crucial influence over its future.

In the university classroom, I found an absence of general understanding and of reference sources as to how land in America is owned, how and why it is used as it is, how and why it is transformed as it is; in short, how our contemporary culture influences the use and the potential of the land.

Land, like a magnet, attracts two specific forces in our culture, and always has. One is the personal objective of some to achieve prosperity, indeed to accumulate wealth. The other is the visible, much debated movement toward increased government regulation. When these two powerful forces collide over land-related issues, links are created between public regulatory power and private wealth which reveal our national priorities, which indeed express where power and control reside in our so-called free enterprise system. (Throughout this book, as a shorthand device I use the word "power" to refer specifically to the power of public regulatory authority.) As times change, as the political and social order evolves, the relationship between land, power, and wealth exposes basic priorities in this country.

The American past was characterized by a tradition of protected and implicit links between land, power, and wealth which favored relatively few influential individuals and businesses. In recent years, as a larger proportion of people in America gains economic stability and political influence, more than ever before these connections are questioned, tampered with, altered. Testing occurs on the open land, in suburban communities, in city centers. As a result, significant new initiatives are evident, as I will discuss.

These changes touch the lives of all people living in America, rich and poor, landowner or tenant. When the established links between land, power, and wealth in America are interfered with, citizens of every class and every political stripe take an avid position. In the chapters that follow, their voices are heard. There is much to lose, much to gain.

The future of the land is basic to how much each of us will pay for a place to live. The destiny of cities, the fate of suburbs, the future of the open countryside, the very quality and character of life where each of us lives, is affected. Food costs and supplies; much of the way wood, mineral, water, and recreation resources of our country are managed or mismanaged; private property rights; and the rate and the way that we are taxed—each is involved.

A word about the structure of this book. The first three chapters establish the context and raise issues to which I return. More specifically, Chapter

One is intended to introduce the theme of land as wealth, as value, as a target of investment and speculation. In it I focus on certain myths, mystiques, and misconceptions rampant today which lead to misunderstanding and miscalculation of land as an ideal investment. In all that follows, the theme of land as wealth and value—of land as a commodity —continues as a component for evaluation and analysis. This particular concern becomes especially prominent again in Chapters Eleven through Fifteen.

Chapter Two sets the historical context. Through a series of brief vignettes and short commentaries, the land itself becomes the focus, as well as what has happened on it and to it since white settlement. The remarkable scale and various methods of land acquisition by the federal government, and its varying means of disposal to the private sector, are briefly presented in an endeavor to make our situation as a nation of mixed private property and public ownership of over 30 percent of the land more understandable, and much more vivid.

Chapter Three, the last of the introductory essays, focuses on law. Its aim is to introduce yet another context, that of judicial decisions that have, over the last hundred years or so, significantly modified the relationship between the private landowner and the rights in his possession over privately owned land. In each era it is in the courts, even more than in the legislative annals of America, that the relationship between land, governmental power and private wealth is hammered out. It is in the courts that the contest between land as a commodity and land as a public resource is seen most clearly and witnessed as a telling, ongoing encounter.

Each chapter that then follows endeavors to achieve two goals. One is to explore a single specific subject and its relationship to the future value of land. In working toward this goal I have tried to summarize the obvious points as well as to indicate important ironies and indirect impacts which are rarely discussed and even less often recognized by laymen. The second goal within each of these chapters, as mentioned already, is to further reveal the links between operative public regulatory power, the value of land, and its future as a national resource. A reader inclined to go through all of the material will gain a multifaceted view of this motif, much as a visitor at an amusement park gains multiple, overlapping views of his own form in a mirrored room.

The appendix is intended to assist readers particularly interested in the history of land in America. It provides significant facts, chronologically arranged events, and legislative milestones. Use of the appendix in conjunction with Chapter Two may make this chapter a more comprehensible reading experience. As no single study specifically addresses the fascinating and much neglected history of the buying and selling of this continent, the appendix can also be used as a guide through the maze of general American history books.

This brings me to the bibliography. It too is presented as an aid to further and more informed study. In it, two years of specialized research are summarized. My hope is that this bibliography becomes an effective tool that enables others to save much time in the quest to know more and to say more and to care more about land in America.

Peter Wolf
New York City
January 1, 1980

PART ONE

OVERVIEW: LAND, POWER, AND WEALTH

ONE

THE MYSTIQUE
OF LAND
AS A PRIME
INVESTMENT

In America, land is magic. And it always has been. Success is owning it with a house. Wealth is owning a lot of it, without a house. But in recent years, land all over America has been elevated in stature to nearly mythic heights as the ideal investment. There is a continuing mystique that land

**DUST BOWL FARM,
COLDWATER DISTRICT,
DALHART, TEXAS,
JUNE 1938**

Land, despite complex factors that control its actual value, has always held the promise of security and wealth for Americans. In this photograph by WPA photographer Dorothea Lange, abandoned farms testify to the harsher realities of land ownership in America.

will create wealth. There is a mystique that land, like gold, is a tangible, solid investment that will provide security. There is a mystique that land is not just a hedge against inflation, but maybe the best hedge against inflation. The mystique survives that private individuals still absolutely control their land. These beliefs do not merely exist today; they are rampant, and so often they are wrong.

It is true that the ownership of land is unlike the ownership of anything else. Each piece is absolutely unique. Each piece of land is composed and prepared by an unduplicatable process. And each piece of land is an immutable part of reality—the earth itself. Like nothing else that can be

possessed, land is essential to life. It is the source of all mineral and vegetable and animal substance. It is the surface upon which all people must stand, dwell, move, and build. How remarkable. How astonishing that it can be possessed at all.

Endowed with such attributes and suffused with such a mystique, it is no wonder that the ownership of land appeals to so many people in so many different ways. To some it is a source of wonder and inspiration. To others it has long been seen as a valuable commodity, an entity worth fighting for and most of all one to be bought and sold for profit. Will Rogers advised the whole country: "Buy land. They ain't making any more of the stuff." Marshall Field told prospering nineteenth-century America that land is "not only the best way, the quickest way, and the safest way, but the only way to become wealthy." Margaret Mitchell's Southern plantation owner Gerald O'Hara impressed upon his daughter Scarlet, in *Gone with the Wind,* "Land is the only thing in the world that amounts to anything . . . for 'tis the only thing in this world that lasts, and don't you be forgetting it! 'Tis the only thing worth working for, worth fighting for —worth dying for. . . ."

How seriously should we take Will Rogers' advice today? Is land now, as Field so fervently believed, the "quickest," "safest," and "only" way to become wealthy? Indeed, just how appealing an investment is land in America today, and what are its prospects for the next five to ten years?

FOR THE RECORD: LAND AS AN INVESTMENT DURING THE 1970s

Most researchers believe that land of all sorts all across America increased in value between 1960 and 1975 an average of 6–8 percent per year. When the impact of inflation is removed from these figures, average land values increased, according to general estimates, from 2.5 to 3.5 percent per year over and above the inflation rate.

Since 1975, land value increases have stepped up significantly, and so has inflation. The average acre of farmland during the period 1970–1979 escalated a dramatic 10–20 percent per year depending on location. My guess is that well-located raw land of all types in America over the past five years escalated in value, in current dollars, at a rate of 8–12 percent annually. During this same interval, the Consumer Price Index rose on average about 10 percent per year. Thus, in most areas, land in America has kept pace with inflation, and perhaps slightly exceeded its annual average percent increase. This is a good record but certainly not one that should engender feverish speculation or even induce a strong belief that any land anywhere is now a prime investment.

6

NATIONAL LAND VALUES, 1967–1975
(IN BILLIONS OF DOLLARS)

TYPE OF LAND	CURRENT DOLLARS[a]			CONSTANT (1958) DOLLARS[b]			PERCENTAGE OF INCREASE PER ANNUM 1967–1975	
	1967	1970	1975	1967	1970	1975	CURRENT DOLLARS	CONSTANT DOLLARS
All land	591	758	1,285	387	411	472	7.7	2.6
Private farm	153	171	336	88	87	87	7.8	—
Private nonfarm[c]	302	405	706	201	220	258	8.2	3.2
Public	136	182	243	97	103	127	6.2	3.4

a. Current dollars reflect prices prevailing during the specified period.

b. Constant dollars are computed values that eliminate the effects of price changes and are derived from a specified base period. Constant dollar values are obtained by dividing current dollar values for a given period by the price indexes for the same period.

c. Private nonfarm land estimates are derived by application of rough ratios of land to structure value. Excludes subsoil assets.

Land vs. Other Investments During the 1970s. The single-family house became a notorious "hedge against inflation" during the 1970s, rising in value in many parts of the country at rates of 10–15 percent per year, and even more dramatically in such hot spots as Orange County, California, Washington, D.C., parts of Chicago, and the Houston and Dallas areas.

Land prices in strong market areas escalated during the last decade even more rapidly than buildings that were constructed on that land. Land that can be developed increased in price so noticeably during the decade that whereas the normal ratio of land value to total new housing costs was once 15 to 25 percent, land now is likely to account for up to 40 percent of the total price of a new house. In the well-researched *Harper's* article "Land Rush: A Survey of America's Land," Peter Meyer postulates that by the end of 1978, "the average price of residential land was rising two to four times faster than the price of the house that would sit atop it. . . ."

Between 1969 and 1979, land in America turned in a superior performance compared to the most widely held investment asset: common stocks. While farmland was escalating an average 10–20 percent per year

ROWS OF COTTON AROUND TENANT HOUSES ON A PLANTATION, THE DELTA AREA OF MISSISSIPPI, MAY 1940

Prime farmland is still a good investment, as mechanization has increased per-acre yields and reduced the cost of production.

and, by my estimate, well-located land of all types was increasing at a rate of some 8–12 percent per year, common stocks in America, as measured by the performance of the Dow Jones industrial average, were essentially flat. If all distributions and dividends were reinvested in Standard and Poor's 500 stocks, then an average value increase of approximately 76 percent would have been registered during the 1970s as compared to

100–200 percent for farmland, 80–120 percent for the average parcel of land, and over 100 percent for inflation.

When compared to the most spectacular forms of investment during the last inflationary decade, land did not lag by very much. Between 1968 and 1978, for instance, the Swiss franc appreciated about 12 percent per year, as did the average single-family house. Diamonds gained in value about 13 percent per year. Gold and other precious metals rose much more dramatically.

The mystique of land—all land—as a superior investment is reinforced by specific, individual success stories. In every town and city there is knowledge of the prescient buyer who purchased land and waited for the right moment to sell. In most towns near large cities, there are land

9

developers living at the best addresses. They have made land profits of 100 percent, 500 percent, perhaps even more during the course of a few years by successfully converting raw land into housing subdivisions, industrial parks, and shopping centers.

Getting caught up in the mystique of land as a superior investment is exhilarating and easy to do. There are real-estate brokers everywhere with land to sell. The willing and enthusiastic private investor who is disenchanted with stocks, who is wary of fixed-income investments such as bonds, who is nervous about the fickleness of taste that gives paintings and antiques their ultimate value, will find it easy to purchase a piece of undeveloped, raw land almost anywhere. It comes in all sizes and prices. It is certainly visible. You can walk on it. You can go visit it. The predilection is surely there. For as Kenneth R. Harney correctly notes in *Beating Inflation with Real Estate:*

From George Washington, who speculated unabashedly in home building lots on Capitol hill, to John Jacob Astor, who wowed Manhattan with his bold land grabs in the early 1800s, to the corporate developers who turned Florida's mangrove swamps into Miami, no investment has been quite so appealing to Americans as land.

The Key Question. But when it comes to land, and land as a prime investment, is the past decade a reliable guide to the future? *This is the key question,* one which this book examines. The remainder of this chapter embarks upon a discussion of certain assumptions and, I believe, misconceptions which are widely held today by many people who think that almost any land anywhere is now and will continue to be a superior investment. These misconceptions fuel the present-day mystique of land as a prime investment.

FIRST AND SECOND HOMES FUEL THE MYSTIQUE OF LAND AS A PRIME INVESTMENT

Anyone who owned a house over the past decade watched its value soar, while the value of many other assets diminished. Those who waited to buy found themselves paying much more for a house, and much more for the money needed to finance its purchase. As Arthur M. Okun, a senior fellow at the Brookings Institution, commented in the summer of 1978, "There's a love for the single-family home. It's the only good investment that most people have made in the past ten years." Indeed, a house purchased for $10,000 in 1968 is likely to be worth over twice that amount today, almost anywhere in the country. In many places, houses have doubled in value

10

in the past five years alone. The desire to own a home on a small piece of land—as a possible inflationary hedge and, above all, as an investment —remains strong despite the costs. In the minds of many, a house has become both a family center *and* a fine investment.

The story is much the same with second homes. These retreats along lakeshores, mountain ridges, and sylvan valleys have attracted, since World War II, greater numbers of Americans whose incomes and leisure time have grown. The value of second homes has risen rapidly—in 1977, on a national average, second homes were costing $30,000, up from half that price five years previously. Since 1977, second homes have continued to increase in value on average annually somewhere between 10 and 20 percent, depending on the year, the location, and the economy of the region.

By the end of 1979, the staggering and, I must point out, unprecedented performance of the house as a profitable investment had propelled many in America into a house-buying frenzy. Buyers were lining up overnight for the privilege to purchase in certain especially strong market areas, such as parts of California and Florida. Cooperative and condominium conversions were frequently snapped up two or three to a buyer: one to be lived in, the other(s) to be rented out or sold.

Rumors about spectacular prices obtained by others, knowledge that new building is likely to be even more expensive in the future, and an awareness that new development must encounter ever more expensive and exacting environmental controls, as well as increasingly costly building codes and subdivision regulations, all prop up the demand—and the prices—for housing.

In the thinking of amateur investors and speculators, the house, like other forms of improved or usable real estate, such as an office building, industrial park, or shopping center, becomes confused with raw, undeveloped land. (I will discuss this misconception later in the chapter.) This causes many to equate a parcel of raw land with "improved" real estate, that is, land with buildings on it. This most profound mistake and blurring of a critical distinction leads to the wrong purchase of the wrong asset at the wrong time for the wrong reason.

INFLATION FUELS THE MYSTIQUE OF LAND AS A PRIME INVESTMENT

Two seemingly related trends run rampant in America and in much of the world: very sharp rates of inflation and very sharp escalations in the price of raw land. Does it then also follow, as many believe without question, that so long as inflation continues, so too will land prices continue to appreciate at equivalent or even greater rates? An unequivocal "yes" means that land is a sure hedge against the financial ravages of inflation. But I doubt that an unequivocal "yes" is the right answer. A second related question must also be asked. Can an investor count on national inflation to continue, and to continue at the sharp rates of over 10 percent per year encountered in recent years?

A Brief Perspective on Inflation. To place inflation into a historic perspective, John W. English and Gray E. Cardiff charted its course in England over the last 1,020 years. They find that 820 of these years show relatively stable prices. In that time there were only four episodes of severe and protracted inflation, including our current period. Each lasted from twenty to eighty years. At the end of these periods, roughly in the years 1200, 1600, and 1800, extended times of relative price stability followed.

In America, a rather similar course of events has occurred. Even though the national population has been rising at substantial intervals during most of our history, periods of rapid inflation are rare and rarely sustained. Since the Consumer Price Index was initiated during World

ENGLAND:
A THOUSAND YEARS OF INFLATION

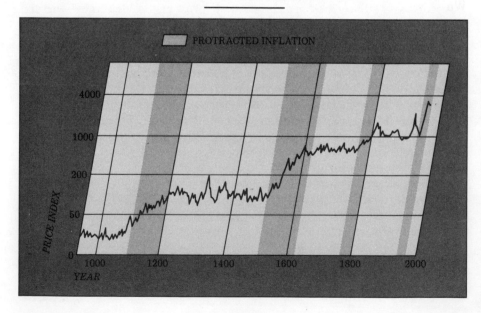

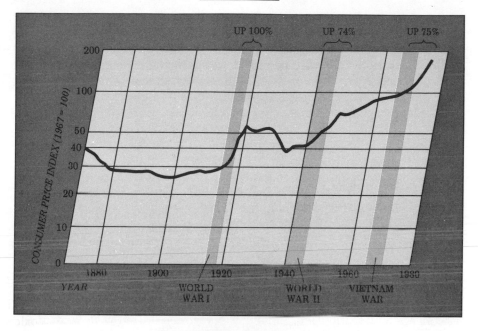

UNITED STATES:
A HUNDRED YEARS OF INFLATION

War I, when rapid changes in living costs made such an index essential in wage negotiations, America has sustained long intervals of price declines, but only moments of severe inflation, and these periods have been generally related to war and its aftereffects. The current period of inflation began about 1949, first at modest rates of approximately 2 percent per year. Since 1965, in the aftermath of Vietnam and as a consequence of a modern form of warfare—oil cartel diplomacy—the inflation rate has escalated and, in late 1979, stands between 12 and 13 percent.

We are now obviously in an unprecedented epoch, one which began forty years ago and took hold in earnest some fifteen years ago. During this time, prices have quadrupled. After four decades, it is small wonder that most people in the United States find it increasingly difficult to conceive of life without severe inflation. But what is to blame for modern inflation? When all of the possible causes are listed, and all of the mechanisms of inflation are analyzed—such as wage increases, government regulations, falling productivity, farm price supports, higher minimum wages, import restrictions, increased money supply, labor wage settlements, and increased price of fuel and energy—no decisive single causal thread can be found. Or as Robert L. Heilbroner put it not long ago in a

13

perceptive *New Yorker* article, "The blame can be fixed in turn on the Arabs, the farmers, the government, the consumer, big business, or, in some vague way on 'us.' "

What everyone does know with absolute certainty is that a long bout with high rates of inflation changes our individual psychology and attitude toward asset management. We begin to assume that inflation will continue, and at high rates. We begin to believe that tomorrow's prices will be higher than today's. We begin to feel that wages will rise steadily. And we begin to search for safe depositories for assets that will be secure in this new world of inflationary capitalism.

The high rates of sustained inflation experienced during the late 1970s have especially changed the mental attitude of many Americans toward savings and spending. Now, for the first time ever, saving in a bank or buying fixed-income bonds is thought to be both risky and unwise. The money saved, and the comparatively low interest earned, is understood to be eroded in actual purchasing value by the impact of inflation. On the other hand, buying tangible goods and buying on credit, as is possible with land, is thought to be safe and wise. The purchased item, it is reasoned, will only be more expensive next year. As wages and incomes continue to rise as a result of inflation, indebtedness will be repaid with "devalued" currency. Provided the investment escalates in value along with, or at rates greater than, the rate of inflation, the asset is protected or enhanced while the debt is repaid in "cheap" dollars.

Thus, inflation has induced "buy now, pay later" thinking among individuals, corporations, and government at all levels. This psychological response to inflation has driven up the cost of money to levels never before experienced in America, reaching 12–15 percent for the government itself late in 1979, a rate that was not matched even during the Civil War, when the future of the United States was uncertain. When private individuals, business, and government reach the same conclusion simultaneously, inflation itself is heightened. There is no clearer instance of the self-fulfilling prophecy.

High rates of inflation, however, have never survived anywhere for very long. And when the trend is reversed, it often surges the other way, as in the panics and depressions of 1873 and 1883, to say nothing of the Great Depression. All of our history indicates that the cycles of capitalism are unstable, with inflation one of its cyclical components. Inflation does not, of course, have a life of its own. It is only symptomatic of basic economic and psychological conditions and expectations.

In my view, the stage is set in America for basic changes both economically and psychologically. We now stand at the beginning of an epoch of diminished national economic potential, reduced levels of population growth, diminishing demand for many products, lower levels of productivity, reduced economic growth and less mobility, diminished control over captive markets and even less control over once-captive natural resources around the world. These new occurrences in the social, economic, and political realities of America coincide as never before. Together they challenge many former trends in this country, which will include, I believe, the rate and course of inflation, as well as the rate and course of land values.

Is the Value of Land Related to Inflation? As I argue implicitly throughout this book, there is little economic rationale for the belief that the value of land is linked directly to inflation. While it is true that land values in America have been rising over the last several inflationary decades, the value increases in land are not a simple, *direct* consequence of national inflation.

When inflation occurs, the price of products tends to increase because of "too much money chasing too few goods," or because of general cost increases at all stages of the production, transportation, and financing of that product. But the price for land is not a direct consequence of the economic forces which occur during periods of inflation. Land is not in short supply, except in the most unusual locations and under special circumstances. In fact, it is abundantly available in America almost everywhere and for almost every purpose.

There are, of course, certain types of land that do increase in economic value during periods of inflation. Such land is generally used as a *commodity,* or *ingredient,* toward the production of a product that will itself increase in *value* and *profitability.* For example, farmland able to produce a commodity whose price is rising, or a factory or office building site becomes more valuable in a strong real-estate-development market. In the case of farmland, so long as, say, a bale of cotton is being produced at increasing rates of profitability, we can realistically expect an acre of land necessary to the production of that bale of cotton to rise in value as well. The same may be said for an acre of land slated for a housing subdivision, office, park, or shopping center in a rising market for improved real estate. However, in America we are already at a point in the cycle of land values where the price of a good farm acre or prime acre for development in most parts of the country far exceeds its logical value as an economically sound component of the anticipated finished product.

Why, then, and under what circumstances, do general raw land prices tend to rise during inflationary cycles? They go up, most of all, because of emotionally grounded beliefs. People believe that all land will increase in price as inflation marches on. People believe that demand for land will mount as others seek a haven for their cash and savings. People believe that land is, in fact, a hedge against inflation.

15

The Direction of Inflation Is What Counts. The naïve statement "So long as inflation continues, land benefits as an investment" fails to take into account both the rate and the direction of inflation. To correct that statement, one would have to say, "So long as inflation continues at an increasing rate, land and real estate tend to benefit as investments."

The use of "tend to" qualifies the statement in two ways. First, it is really ownership of the *financial arrangements* related to the real estate that benefits an owner during periods of inflation; that is, older mortgages at lower rates turn out to be money borrowed for very little. If these funds are invested in any commodity whose value increases at a rate equivalent to or greater than the rate of inflation, the debt is profitable. However, anyone who owns land debt-free does not benefit from this aspect of inflation. Second, as I will discuss in detail in Chapter Twelve, unless the property in question rises in value faster than or at a rate equivalent to that of inflation, the cash invested is actually being depreciated.

This relationship between value and the direction of inflation is all the more important to ponder as I write this book at the close of 1979. The current rate of inflation is approximately 13 percent. Interest rates on a thirty-year residential mortgage (if it can be obtained at all) range anywhere from 12 to 14 percent. Interest rates on land mortgages, generally payable over a shorter period of time, are somewhat lower. Now is also a time when inflation has been declared "public enemy number one," and when business is beginning to slow down. Thus, one must wonder about the wisdom of buying land as a hedge against inflation, at least at this point in the economic cycle. The level of inflation is very high, and the trend in the direction of inflation is very much in question.

Indeed, at a certain point, and for several reasons, a high level of inflation, and therefore high rates of interest, tend to *devalue* land. Competing investments with secure and high rates of return become more attractive. When interest rates become very high—say, on the order of 10–15 percent per year, as they have in recent years—potential investors are able to lend their reserve funds to financial institutions and to the federal government at these very high rates free of risk. These safe, liquid sources of income become attractive competing investments, whether the alternative is common stocks, gold, rare coins, or land. Indeed, it is by raising interest rates to very high levels that the federal government endeavors to stop inflation. Thus, when interest paid on U.S. Treasury bills reaches, let us say, 12 percent per annum, a would-be investor in land must believe that the land will appreciate at such a fast rate that he can do the following: (1) annually pay out money for a purchase money mortgage at rates which may equal or exceed the rate he would receive for funds invested in the treasury bills; and (2) invest the cash portion of the funds used to buy land while accepting no return whatsoever, as opposed to earning the 12 percent paid on the treasury bill investment; and (3) find a buyer for the land who will take over his ownership position when the time comes to sell.

Taken together, and for the moment leaving aside questions of leverage and after-tax return (which are discussed in Chapter Twelve), one point should become clear: in a strongly inflationary period, land must perform at extraordinary rates of return to be a truly sound investment. On the other hand, if inflation is running at a more modest rate—say 4–6 percent per annum—for all the reasons outlined previously, a land investment has a better chance to turn in a superior investment performance.

Could Our Beliefs Change?   Not so many years ago the stock market was thought to be a hedge against inflation. Today, this huge capital market shudders before inflationary forces. Investors on a massive scale have shifted their attitude, their beliefs.

A similar change, I suspect, could occur with respect to land as a valid and stable hedge against inflation. Trends are at work in America today, contrary to those of any time in our past, which indicate that raw, undeveloped, and especially currently inaccessible land is likely to be less in demand in years to come. If, as a result, land values stabilize or decline, and inflation does not, this long-standing association between the two will come into question.

It is entirely possible that general land-value increases experienced during years of high inflation result in large part from a market supported by anxiety, fueled by fear, and sustained primarily by our belief that assets and purchasing power can be protected and enhanced through the intermediary vehicle of land. With this in mind, two points need to be remembered: one, inflation by itself does not cause the value of land to rise; and two, as the level of inflation escalates, it takes a more and more perfect land investment to stay even, or to make a profit. Knowledge, circumspection, and an awareness of new trends will raise your odds in favor of making a good land investment. Don't count on inflation to do it for you.

OTHER MISCONCEPTIONS ABOUT LAND AS AN INVESTMENT

A number of other misconceptions about land are widely held today by millions of landowners and would-be land buyers. These shore up the belief that land in America—almost any parcel of it—will continue to increase in value in years to come, at least at the rate of inflation. Briefly outlined, four leading misconceptions are as follows.

Misconception 1: Land, like improved real estate, has innate value.
One of the most dangerous assumptions anyone can make is to equate the qualities and characteristics of raw land with those of a parcel of improved real estate, such as a house or office building. What are some of the crucial distinctions between raw land and improved real estate that make a linking of the two so treacherous?

First: Raw land has little innate value. It even generally requires the expenditure of money, often considerable amounts of it, to convert the presumed asset into a productive one, with roads and a house, building, or working farm upon it.

Second: Holding raw land creates a definite and predictable cash drain on the owner. Financing costs and taxes mount up, with generally little or no offsetting return. These days, land values must double in four to six years if the cash tied up and the annual required expenditures are to be worthwhile. In improved commercial real estate, by contrast, besides an annual cash return, the investor enjoys a variety of tax and refinancing benefits.

Third: Most lending institutions will not commit long-term mortgage funds to a land purchase. Very often, in fact, it is the seller who must finance the transaction. Upon the sale of raw land, the former owner often obtains much less cash than the full price of the property. Typically, because of federal income-tax laws, the seller receives less than 30 percent of the sale price in cash. The balance is paid out over the years of the so-called purchase money mortgage. The typical seller of land, then, becomes a mortgage holder, the traditional posture of a financial institution. During years of increasing levels of inflation, it is the holder of the fixed-return mortgage or bond who suffers most from the ravages of inflation. By way of contrast, when a parcel of improved real estate is sold, there is usually a commercial mortgage, and the seller obtains all proceeds in cash.

Fourth: The correct market value of raw land is much more difficult to determine than the market value of improved real estate. Developed real estate generally may be reliably appraised. Land, on the other hand, is much more difficult to appraise in many situations.

The usual available guideline to the present market value of raw land is the sale price of comparable parcels nearby. This measurement is the bench mark that is commonly used. But if those comparable sales are based on wishful thinking about the future or a system of optimistic beliefs that never materializes, the price paid will be much too high.

Fifth: Unlike the future value of developed real estate, that of raw land is almost entirely dependent on social, political, and environmental trends in the community where the land is located. This means that it is both a risky investment and one that may contain a high level of speculative

18

potential. After all, a change in zoning can double the value of a parcel of raw land in one evening, or cut it in half. The future value of any parcel of raw land involves future social, legal, political, and demographic factors, which will have a much more profound impact on its eventual value than on a parcel of improved property.

Sixth: There are many fewer buyers for raw land than for improved real estate. When people invest or speculate in anything, they make one basic (sometimes unconscious) assumption: when ready to sell, there will be a buyer waiting.

Whether it is vegetables and fruits in the medieval square, or stocks, bonds, commodities, and precious-metal futures on the national exchanges, the centralized marketplace has proven benefit to buyer and seller. There is no central marketplace in real estate. The object of the transaction cannot be moved. Its value is so dependent on location that a distant marketplace is irrelevant. Real estate is thus by nature more dependent on local people, local knowledge, and local deals than most other types of investment. The lack of a centralized market vastly reduces the potential pool of purchasers for both raw land and for improved buildings.

However, improved real estate does not suffer as much as raw land. The number of people in any community or in any region willing to take the risk and willing to earn no immediate return, as required in a land purchase, is small compared to the number willing to buy a house or a reliably appraised income-producing asset such as improved real estate. Buyers of raw land, typically, are limited to experienced and sophisticated land developers, experienced and sophisticated land speculators, and inexperienced and usually unsophisticated investor/speculators who want to "get into real estate." When the inexperienced land investor finds it is time to sell, he is likely to encounter a much more experienced buyer, if any buyer can be found. When that happens, hoped for profits may melt away like a mound of snow on a warm winter day.

Misconception 2: As in the past, continued demand for land can be expected almost everywhere from a rapidly growing and restless population. People require land on which to live, to work, to shop, to recreate. More people adds up to greater land demand. But in the United States there now is a definite slowdown of overall population growth. Slower growth translates directly into less demand for land. This slowing in overall population growth is a result of both a decrease in the immigration rate and the birth rate.

In the last decades, because of various quotas and restrictions, legal immigration has declined significantly. As recently as 1920, annual immi-

19

gration to America accounted for some 4 percent of the entire population; between 1905 and 1915, years of extremely active and open immigration, this source alone accounted for approximately 62 percent of the nation's growth. In 1979, fewer than 400,000 immigrants were admitted—less than .002 percent of the nation population.

Although illegal entry continues from Mexica, Canada, and the Caribbean, and is a significant factor in booming land demand and real-estate prices in certain locations such as Miami, this flow of new people into America does not contribute substantially to national population growth. Total illegal immigration remains statistically nominal.

The dramatic decline in the birth rate has been much publicized. It is no longer considered fashionable to have more than two children; for some, it is no longer considered fashionable to have children at all. For others, it is economically indefensible, a cost burden in terms of housing, food, medical care, and education, which seems to rise beyond a manageable point. If present trends continue, this country will probably reach a point of zero population growth in just forty years, by the year 2020. Yet the value of raw land today in most areas is still stimulated in part by the *belief* that an ever-increasing demand is pressing hard against a limited supply.

Will the birth rate pick up soon? I doubt it. The course of national history and the causes of the most recent decline in the birth rate both suggest that a boom in births is unlikely. Indeed, the birth rate in America has been declining at a fairly even rate ever since 1800. A 20-year spurt in the birth rate began in about 1940 and ended in the late 1950s. This so-called baby boom is a statistical blip in the national downward trend.

Two Population Growth Sectors: Smaller Households and More Older People.   Even though population increases may end, the demand for land won't—at least not everywhere. New households and more older people will create a viable but selective demand for land in years to come. Many households will continue to be conventional groupings of people who seek a place to live and some land upon which to do it. But fewer households than ever before will be the traditional family that seeks a house and a yard—a sizable piece of terrain.

THE TEMPORARY BOOM IN HOUSEHOLDS: HERE TODAY, GONE BY 1990.   The tidal wave of children born between 1940 and 1960 hit maturity in the 1960s, 1970s, and early 1980s. Consequently, the formation of new households has been soaring. Between 1970 and 1978, for instance, while the total population of the country increased by about 6 percent, the total number of U.S. households increased almost 20 percent. This group cre-

20

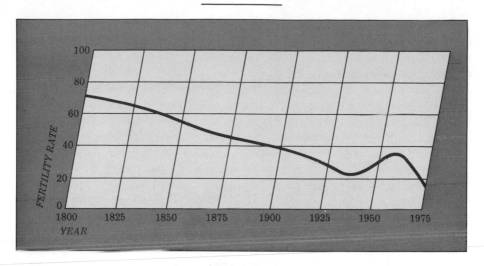

U.S. FERTILITY RATE,
1800–1975

ates a strong demand for land. At birth no land is needed; at maturity, when a household is formed, land and real estate are involved. The growth rate in households is expected to exceed population increases until at least the year 1990.

In 1980, there were approximately 66 million young adults between the ages of 18 and 25, up over 30 percent from the number in that age group in 1970. This group assures a continuing boom in new households for the next five to ten years. Typically, these new households, of which half or more will consist of only one or two people, will seek a small existing house or a relatively small apartment. They will want good recreation facilities, either at their primary dwelling or in the nearby countryside. The picture this group presents, then, is one of considerable demand per household for shelter but not very great demand for land. However, the many new, smaller households coming into maturity do present a specialized growth market that will influence land demand in certain areas.

THE CONTINUING BOOM IN OLDER PEOPLE. We are becoming a nation of increasingly high proportions of older people and older households. This undeniable fact influences the locations where land will either be in demand or where it will lose favor.

In 1910, a profile of the United States population formed a neat triangle: a few older folks at the top and lots of young newcomers at the bottom. By 1975, with increased life expectancies and decreased fertility rates, the

21

proportion of middle aged and older people had increased significantly. Within forty years the pyramid is likely to be the reverse of what it was in 1910, with a wide band of older people at the top and relatively few younger people at the bottom.

Older people tend to abandon larger houses in search of less space and a better living environment. No longer tied down to a family or job, they are able to move around, to reshape their lives. They look for smaller houses, apartments, recreation-dominated clusters, and convenient medical facilities, whether in cities, suburbs, or the countryside. As people age, the amount of land given up is greater than the amount of land required. On the other hand, increased mobility points to special recreation or natural environments, as well as city centers, where land will be increasingly in demand.

Less Land Will Be Sought by the Average Citizen.   It is not just new small households and older people who are finding less space and less land more desirable. The large house on large grounds is expensive to heat and costly to maintain. For most, just getting help from the plumber or carpenter is trying and inordinately expensive. Smaller grounds and yards are seen increasingly as desirable because of their relatively lower maintenance cost and taxes. To more and more people the attached garden apartment, linked townhouse, or cluster unit is a desirable housing solution, even in suburbs and small outlying towns. In many communities today, in fact,

CHANGES IN AGE STRUCTURE
OF U.S. POPULATION,
1920–1975

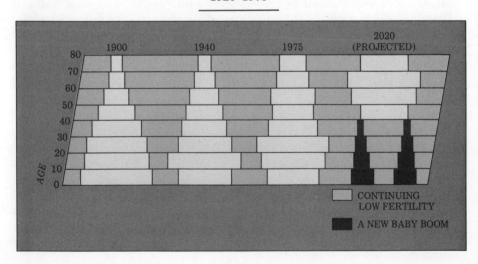

22

the large, well-located house with sprawling grounds sells for less than the smaller dwelling of equal quality in the same location. There is now often a discount for size that registers the carrying cost of utilities, maintenance, taxes, garden care, and domestic help. Both urge and necessity are causing homeowners to tighten up; and each notch tighter means less land is needed and less land is sought for each person in the country.

This trend is glaringly evident in new subdivisions. In a city like Houston, where there is no zoning regulation, lots are sized according to the market, the desire, and the ability to pay. Not many years ago, the typical new house built in Houston was placed on about one acre. However, in recent years, over half of all new residential building permits in Harris County are for townhouses, condominiums, and apartments. In adjacent suburban counties within the Houston metropolitan area, the size of the average housing lot is down as well. Within older towns and cities, as a reflection of all of these same trends, one of the most sought-after items is once again the traditional two-family house.

The Ravages of Restlessness. Moreover, many new households, especially those comprised of young people or older people, seek no new land whatsoever. Many people are moving back into the cities from the suburbs. This movement, while still not numerically significant, is having a decisive impact in many regions. As urban land is sought out, more remote areas and especially suburbs lose some residents.

In addition, migration among all age groups continues to be a pronounced characteristic of Americans. As detailed in Chapter 11, the importance of certain national migration trends to land values in the future cannot be over emphasized. Between 1950 and 1970, nearly 75 percent of the counties in this country lost net population. And only 24 percent of all the counties, mostly those along the the western, eastern, and southern shores of America and around the Great Lakes, managed to attract population at rates which exceeded average growth nationwide.

The migratory movements of the population in the next two decades will determine where new demand for land will occur and where the quest for land will diminish.

We are now entering a period in which patterns of national migration are likely to devalue more acreage than the amount of land whose value is augmented, a reversal of a trend long in evidence in America.

It is, on the other hand, also likely that national mobility will be curtailed in years to come. As moving and travel becomes more costly, as selling and buying a home becomes more expensive, as mortgage finance becomes more selective and less available, and as business finds it more difficult to relocate and less reasonable to move out of established cities and older communities, the overall mobility of the American population is likely to diminish. When and if this happens, the relative economic appeal of much land that remains undeveloped will decline.

Taken together, these factors—changes in household size, changes in age distribution of the nation's population, changes in the rate of population growth, and changes in patterns of nationwide migration—will affect the *relative* value of every parcel of land in America between today and the year 2000.

Misconception 3: There is a shortage of land in America. Except at the very best locations in the few fast-growing spots, there is no shortage of land in America. The raw land stretches out across a massive continent of 2.3 billion acres. Of this, 900 million acres are owned by one level of government or another. The federal government, as the largest landlord in the nation, owns about one third of the country's land. This land alone, if ever needed, could be released into the marketplace as a surplus commodity. Cropland covers about 400 million acres, of which a great deal is idle. Empty grasslands, idle pastures, and vast ranges claim some 600 million acres. Forest land, much of it poorly managed and relatively unproductive, consumes 400 million acres. Over 100 million acres are wilderness, federal and state parks, reservations, wildlife refuges, and defense and flood-control areas; this land is also empty and, except in rare instances, under-utilized.

Where are all the people then? A hundred years ago, in a mixed agricultural and incipient industrial economy, a much smaller American population lived on much more of the land. But in the last one hundred years, over 14 million people have moved off farms into the cities and suburbs. Most of the newcomers to America, by birth or immigration, settle in metropolitan bands in and around larger towns and city centers. Between 1950 and 1975, virtually all population growth in America occurred in urban areas. Since 1975, a new trend toward rural living has been in evidence; but this trend affects relatively few people and is not likely to change the overall picture significantly, certainly not before the end of the twentieth century.

Today, in fact, more than 70 percent of the entire national population resides on scarcely 1.5 percent of the land, on about 35 million acres. When highways and roads, railroads, airports, and state institutions are also considered, the total amount of inhabited land approaches 63 million acres, or only some 3 percent of the land in America.

Today the land-people ratio in the United States is about eleven acres for every man, woman, and child in the country. In terms of farmland alone, there are five acres per individual in the United States, while in France each person has the equivalent of 1.6 acres; in Italy, 0.9 acres; in

India, 0.5 acres. The most urbanized state in the union, New Jersey, remains 75 percent rural.

Even within the urbanized areas, there is a tremendous amount of available, under-utilized land. In 1950, each urban resident used, on the average, 0.2 acres of urban land. By 1970 the average utilization had leaped 100 percent, to 0.4 acres for each new resident. This trend of increased land utilization per person is, in large part, a consequence of metropolitan annexation of undeveloped or sparsely settled adjacent areas.

But the doubling of land utilization per person in just the last two decades has a significant and often forgotten corollary: there is now much open or under-utilized acreage throughout urban and suburban settlements across the continent. This is land that has been abandoned in the central cities, leaped over and still vacant in suburban sprawl, or simply sparsely populated. It lies there available, a potential competitor to all undeveloped acreage farther out.

In the metropolitan areas of America today there exists huge, available land reserves. According to the 1970 United States census, only 10 percent of the land contained within the metropolitan areas of the United States was fully developed. Since then new development has continued at a significant pace, but surely not rapidly enough to raise this figure by more than one or at the most two percent. Estimates vary, but without any question, as much as one half of all the so-called developed land inside the metropolitan areas is under-utilized.

There is every reason to believe that because of the national energy shortage, shortages of capital, and the high cost of new construction, there will be a new emphasis on tightening up rather than on expanding outward, as has been the trend in the past. In years to come, America is likely to settle into more compact patterns of community; to want, to need, and to use less land per capita.

Misconception 4: As in the past, new roads and highways will make today's remote land accessible and therefore more valuable. Highways work like acid upon the soft copper of the engraver's plate: wherever cast, the surface is eaten away, transformed forever. When these roadways have been carelessly splayed across the city center, all that was is changed. When they've been flung out into the open land, the scars of urbanization appear—and remain. For a very long time engineers and planners proceeded—not always thoughtfully—to cut multi-lane highways through the cities and to link one city to another, thereby altering American culture and decisively modifying national patterns of settlement and growth.

Wherever built, highways change the use and the value of land. In the countryside, acreage once remote and inaccessible generally increases in value, often dramatically. At the interchange, fields and forests give way to commercial and industrial facilities of considerable value. All along the route, open land around major cities becomes new suburbs.

Ever since the 1920s when the automobile took command of American transportation, the United States has built new roads at a rate unparalleled in the history of man. First, the Federal Highway Act of 1921 elevated road building to a national priority; then in the 1950s, the Federal-Aid Highway Act spurred construction by paying for 90 percent of the 42,000-mile interstate system. Today, most of this system is complete; in addition, over a million miles of dirt, gravel, and stone roadways have been paved over and made suitable to high-speed automobile and truck transport.

But road building in America has peaked. Between 1945 and 1955, over 40,000 miles a year of primary and secondary highways were built with federal assistance. Between 1965 and 1975, that number dwindled to 6,500 miles a year; and since 1975, it has dwindled still further.

In years to come, the pace of road building across America will slow even more markedly. To begin with, the cost of new highway construction has escalated faster than the inflation rate, with petroleum-based products needed for construction becoming increasingly expensive and scarce. Environmental guidelines now restrict gravel pit mining, cement manufacture, and new highway permits. Furthermore, in most areas, land rights-of-way are more expensive to obtain than ever before, and municipal budgets are strained. Citizens are organized, and many resist the intrusion of a new highway. As California's Proposition 13 signaled, throughout America a significant number of citizens now seek reduced taxes, not additional roads. The oil crisis in America, which began in earnest in the late 1970s, has sparked a shift in national and regional, as well as individual, priorities. When the gas crunch hit, the extension of highways was already under attack by environmentalists, slow-growth advocates, and clean-air forces. The high cost of driving accelerated people's disenchantment with spending large sums for more roads and increased their support of public transit.

In the future, the construction of fewer new roads will diminish demand for remote acreage. Indeed, as a result of the unprecedented scope of road-building activity in years past, millions of acres of land with good road access remain undeveloped. Owners of private land who expect significantly higher prices in the future when highway access is provided at public expense are going to be disappointed. We now enter a time when a more concentrated pattern of settlement will appeal and will begin to occur. Reduced driving distances will be coveted; living in proximity to jobs, shopping facilities, and institutional centers will be sought. Consequently, even land that enjoys road access but is situated far from centers of habitation is likely to lose some of its relative appeal and relative value compared to property "nearer in."

Highway building, an enormous force that has been pulling up land prices in more remote parts of America since the end of World War II, is winding down. But the country will not fall apart as a result of this; indeed, the termination of the most extensive public works program in the history of man is on balance beneficial. For decades to come, curtailed highway construction will limit the potential for the increased value of great stretches of inaccessible land.

SO, IS THE PAST A GUIDE TO THE FUTURE?

I am troubled, then, by the prevalent assumption, made with considerable assurance by so many people, that the past performance of land as an investment will protect their assets from inflation and provide for future profit. And I am troubled by a continuing belief in other concurrent underlying assumptions that have for so long fueled a passion for land as an investment. The assumptions remain while new and decisive conditions in America are ignored.

What chance is there that the individual buyer of a tiny plot among the many millions of acres of land available will chose wisely? Should the landowner today hold on to his land for the next few years, the next decade? The right land bought in the right place at the right time in America has been a premier investment, as good as any that ever was. And it surely will continue to be. But the average land investment in the 1980s is not nearly so likely to turn a profit as in the past. In years to come, those who succeed as land investors must take into account new opportunities and a network of new connections between land, power, and wealth in America.

TWO

NOTES
ON BUYING AND
SELLING
THE CONTINENT

Zalek Foster walks slowly out of the glass-front office. There is a slight smile at the edge of his eyes. The office was once Bob the barber's where, on special occasions as a child, Zalek went to have his hair cut. He squints at the parched, cracked asphalt of Second Street. His eyes sting as they adjust to the sudden glare of midday August in Oklahoma. It is hot. Second Street is nearly empty. With considerable care, Zalek folds a small oblong piece of perforated green paper and slips it into the back pocket of his overalls. Zalek Foster has just been paid $500,000 by the federal government. He earned it by agreeing not to grow cotton—or anything else—on his land this year.

Bill Mosely had dressed with care for the town planning board meeting. Of the five members on the board, two are businessmen like himself who commute to the city; one owns the supermarket in town; one teaches science at his children's school, and the fifth is a newcomer to the community. In the cramped room filled with military-surplus office equipment, these local citizens listen patiently as the chairman of the planning board reads a resolution. It approves without qualification Bill's application for a subdivision on the old Collier farm just outside of town. With this single act, agreed to by five community representatives who have had no particular experience in land law, land economics, or land planning, Bill Mosely converts 250 acres, optioned for $150,000, to a building site for two hundred 1-acre homes. Tonight that land is suddenly worth $2 million. It has been a profitable night for Bill Mosely.

Bob Wrangler loves the city; he has lived here all his life. And it has been good to him, both as a developer and an enterpreneur. The old industrial stretch of land between the river and the interstate highway looks to most people like abandoned fields of weeds and junk supporting rows of empty, collapsing brick warehouses. To Bob Wrangler, as he drives toward the city planning commission meeting, it looks like the land he has paid $50,000 to option and rezone for high-rise luxury condominum apartments. The site commands great views up and down the river, and it is a five-minute walk to the center of town.

At the hearing, members of the city planning commission staff praise the preliminary design. The director of the Department of Economic Development declares that reuse of the land will renew the downtown area and bring needed revenue into the city. Three people are in the audience. They are at the meeting to protest revised sanitation schedules in their neighborhood—the next matter on the agenda. Once his proposal is approved, Bob knows that he has just made a 500 percent profit on cash paid for the option. Tomorrow he will flip the contract to the Orion Development Corporation.

Three people. Three decisions. Three situations: open land in a rural setting; suburban land in transition; urban land in the process of redevelopment. Three contemporary examples of the buying and selling of America. Three contemporary ways that change to the landscape is precipitated by the interconnected meshing of land, power, and wealth—a link, in one way or another, that connects the history of America to the ownership and development of the continent.

EARLY HISTORY: COASTAL SETTLEMENTS

From the beginning in America, the land itself was seen and used as a source of power and wealth. Captain Giovanni da Verrazano filed the following observation in the log of his ship *Delfina* after a first visit in May 1524 to the shores of the island we now know of as Manhattan:

Therefore, we took the boat, and entering the river, we found the country on its banks well peopled, the inhabitants not differing much from the other . . . being dressed out with feathers of birds of different colors. They came toward us with evident delight, raising loud shouts of admiration, and showing us where we could most securely land with our boat. . . . All of a sudden, as is wont to happen to navigators, a violent contrary wind blew in from the sea, and forced us to return to our ship, greatly regretting to leave the region which seemed so commodious and delightful and which we supposed also must contain great riches, as the hill showed many indications of minerals.

Ultimately, of course, the Dutch were to "buy" the island from the Indians for the equivalent of $24.00 worth of trinkets.

Virginia and Maryland. By the early 1600s, the coastal plain along the Atlantic Ocean, closest to Europe, was in the first stages of white settlement. Land, recognized as the fundamental source of power and wealth in a newly developing country, was sought by everyone.

31

Consider how Virginia was colonized in the earliest stages. Virginia was basically a large estate granted by King James I of England to the Virginia Company of London. In turn, the company financed the voyage of workers from England who came to America to farm. Planters were expected to turn over their harvest to the company in exchange for a share of stock and just enough money to live on. One hundred acres would be given to the planter after seven years of labor. In time the working colonists rebelled. They were not interested in owning shares of stock but rather in profitting from their hard work by reaping the profits of direct selling. And they wanted land.

By 1616, Deputy Governor Thomas Dale of Virginia began granting 100 acres to each settler, with the promise of another 100 acres if the first were successfully improved and cultivated. Larger tracts of territory were sold to groups and organizations which purchased blocks of stock from the Virginia Company of London. These organizations recruited their own settlers to work the land. With much land available and the need to induce immigration paramount, the population in Virginia jumped from 600 to over 3,000 between 1619 and 1622, the newcomers racing to exploit the land, principally through the cultivation of tobacco.

By the mid-1600s, the governors of the colonies of Virginia and Maryland instituted new policies with respect to land as an inducement to settle their colonies. Each colonist who transported an immigrant to the New World was granted 50 acres of land. Settlers who paid their own way across the Atlantic received 50 acres outright. In 1683, Maryland legalized the sale of rights to the 50-acre parcels in the form of warrants. The going price for a 50-acre warrant was about 5 shillings.

Farmers bought these warrants, taking them to county authorities, who would then issue a certificate for land. Speculators induced ship captains and sailors disinterested in the purchase of land to obtain warrants for their rights to 50 acres and sell them immediately. Partially because of these profiteers, Maryland land prices soared upwards 135 percent between 1660 and 1700.

By 1700 it was clear that it was too difficult and expensive to defend the frontier against the native Americans. Virginia legislated land grants of up to a total of 30,000 acres to frontiersmen brave enough to build and defend a system of forts. Each venturer could secure a 200-acre tract.

New England. New England Puritans did not follow the land-tenure practices of Maryland and Virginia. The general court of the Massachusetts Bay Colony believed in dividing the land among individuals and groups "worthy" of it, that is, religious people, community leaders, or those with the financial backing to cultivate the land properly. This policy, however, translated into favored treatment of the powerful and the wealthy. In Massachusetts, half of the land granted to individuals between 1630 and 1675 was given to magistrates and governors, the other half to schoolmasters, ministers, and military heroes. Groups desiring to cultivate new towns, would first have to be considered upright and stable by the general court. If approved, they were granted a "plantation right," that is, the legal authority to stake out and settle a parcel of land about six miles square. The group was expected to determine boundaries, divide the land, build roads, and attract settlers to the area within a set number of years. The original group had the power to sell the land as it saw fit.

Town owners generally established a public village green, which contained sites for both a church and a school. The rest of the land was then distributed as private plots among the original owners: the greater their wealth, the larger their share. Wealthy individuals, it was assumed, could do more for the town, and therefore deserved more land.

PRE-REVOLUTIONARY MOVEMENT WESTWARD

The frontier was first settled by immigrants moving westward, off of the coastal plain, away from the seaboard communities, toward the nearby interior where more land was available, where more opportunity seemed to exist. The first inland migrations were short in distance. New Englanders flowed into western New York, their children farther west, their grandchildren as far as the upper Mississippi Valley.

Few, however, could endure the hardships of any move. A risk had to be assumed, and the capital needed to finance this costly venture raised in advance. The cost alone presented an initial barrier. In the mid-nineteenth century, if land and services had to be purchased, the migrant had to pay between $1.25 and $10.00 an acre for land anywhere near an established outpost of civilization; from $5.00 to $20.00 an acre to have it cleared; $100 for a split-rail fence; from $100 to $375 for tools; $150 for draft animals; $50.00 for a log cabin; $25.00 for transportation; and $100 for food to sustain his family until his own farm became productive. An 80-acre farm could hardly be established for less than $1,500, an enormous sum for the average workingman to accumulate in the East, where wages were generally less than a dollar a day.

The alternative was, of course, for the settler to do it all himself, and a choice that required the specialized skills of woodsman mingled with the talents of a farmer. And few had these pioneering skills necessary to undertake settlement in an entirely new place. Westward settlement could also be accomplished at great savings if the land were free. Through-

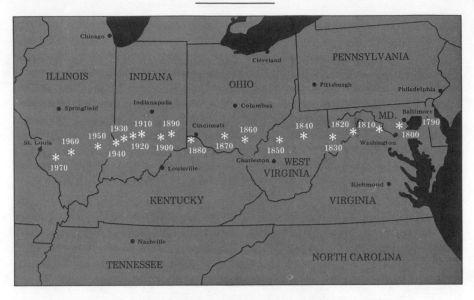

**CHANGING CENTRAL POINTS OF POPULATION
IN THE UNITED STATES**

In less than two hundred years, the westward migration of millions of
Americans pushed the central point of population from the Chesapeake
Bay to the Illinois-Missouri border. Land distribution processes during
settlement varied according to region. Most often, however, those persons
with money, positions of influence, or exceptional pioneering skills
acquired the largest and most valuable tracts.

out the history of the white settlement of America, land was, in fact, often
given away. One way or another, through a wide variety of policies and
programs designed to induce white migration into the New World, land
was made available at a very low cost or at no cost at all. Free land, say
80 acres of it, saved the mid-nineteenth-century pioneer anywhere from
$100 to $400, or up to 25 percent of his initial costs, an enormous consideration.

Allocation of the Land.   The process of land allocation before the formation of a federal government in the United States varied from area to
area. In New York, a well-connected individual had only to obtain autho-
rization from the Governor to purchase land directly from the Indians,
finance a survey, and then secure the final patent from the Governor and
his Council. In obtaining these early grants, land, power, and wealth were

34

solidly united. With funds available, and the Governor's favor at hand, vast estates could be assembled at a negligible cost. These estates were subsequently to become the lands to which enterprising townsmen and farmers would be lured.

As this process continued throughout New England, some sections of land were given away to attract settlers, as well as to enhance the value of sections retained by the land development companies, which bought the vast tracts from the colonial government. As part of this pattern of land development, absentee proprietors became commonplace. In spite of liberal ideals and agrarian slogans, the separation of user from owner was to become a typical form of American land occupancy, an established pattern from the Old World, instituted in the new. Under this system, those in positions of public authority sometimes extracted a financial interest in the patent or deed, thereby becoming a part-owner of the vast estate.

In Massachusetts the situation was somewhat different, at least in the beginning. Throughout the seventeenth century, the general court of the Massachusetts Bay Colony limited its allocation of large grants of land to nonprofit groups, generally clusters of religiously orthodox people. These grants were meant to create contiguous, church-dominated towns developed in an orderly and coherent fashion. Pressure persisted from well-entrenched businessmen from Boston and Salem, however, who demanded the sale of large domains to investors and speculators. By 1727 the pressure was so intense that the court began selling land freely to any speculative group able to have its demand heard and able to amass enough capital to pay the extremely low prices. Within the original colonies, Maine, New Hampshire, and Connecticut soon followed this policy.

During the eighteenth century, some of America's best-known patriots were in the thick of low-cost land acquisition schemes. In 1756 in Pennsylvania, for example, Benjamin Franklin petitioned the crown to create two new colonies along the upper Ohio River for the benefit of himself and some associates. Ten years later, in 1766, Franklin was in England, in part, to assert a claim of the Illinois Company (in which he had an interest) to 1,200,000 acres of land along the Mississippi.

George Washington, who kept a regular agent in the upper Ohio country staking out land claims on choice territory for himself, wrote in the 1760s: ". . . Any person who neglects the present opportunity of hunting out good land will never again regain it."

In Virginia, Lieutenant Governor Alexander Spotswood seized huge tracts of land for himself. He then made favorable arrangements for himself and other landed colonists, including a provision in 1720 that all land in the Piedmont counties of Virginia be exempt from taxes for ten years. At this point the English government insisted that Virginia land grants be limited to 1,000 acres. Speculators simply ignored the restriction, using dummy entrymen and the governor's friendship to acquire tracts of 10,000 to 40,000 acres.

THE UNITED STATES AS LAND BROKER

Land speculation in America reached its zenith soon after the establishment of a new, independent constitutional government. Throughout the nineteenth century, however, there continued a prolonged period of free-market land trades, deals, purchases, and swindles. The United States government, once established, was involved in many of these transactions. Through the central brokerage agency of various departments and acts of government, acquisition and disposition of land was conducted simultaneously on an immense scale. Inexpensive land for settlers remained a prime government objective. However, as the lands of America passed through its hands, the federal government, like an enormous trading company, generally sold at prices far above acquisition costs. After paying for acquisition, surveys, and land offices, and covering the cost of donated lands, the government used the surplus earned to help pay other public expenses.

Acquisition of the Land. In the late eighteenth and nineteenth centuries, the federal government of the United States acquired title to the vast land area between the Appalachian Mountains and the Pacific Ocean. Between 1789 and 1850, it ratified 245 treaties with various Indian tribes, thereby obtaining 450 million acres of land. The overall price of the Indian treaties was less than $90 million, or approximately 20 cents per acre. In 1803 the Louisiana Purchase negotiations were complete: France sold the United States government 529,911,680 acres of property along the Mississippi River and its tributaries for $23 million, an average cost of 4 cents per acre. Sixteen years later Spain was induced to sell the Florida territory. A land mass of 46,144,640 acres was transferred to the United States for $6 million, or about 15 cents per acre. In 1845 Texas annexed for itself without payment 170 million acres from Mexico, an event that led to the Mexican War. Five years later the state of Texas was paid $15 million for an additional 78,926,720 acres, a price of 19 cents per acre.

While Texas was operating as an independent venturer, the United States government continued its acquisition of land on the North American continent. In 1846, in negotiations with Great Britain, the Pacific Northwest was divided, thereby adding 183,386,240 acres to American

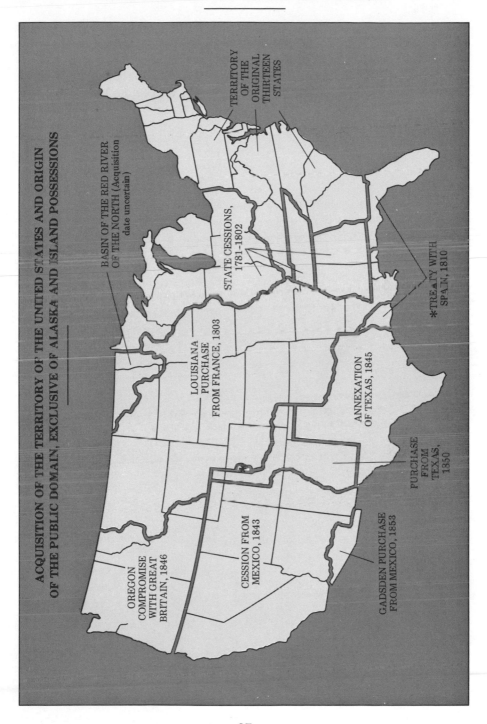

ACQUISITION OF THE TERRITORY OF THE UNITED STATES AND ORIGIN
OF THE PUBLIC DOMAIN, EXCLUSIVE OF ALASKA AND ISLAND POSSESSIONS

TERRITORY OF THE ORIGINAL THIRTEEN STATES

BASIN OF THE RED RIVER OF THE NORTH (Acquisition date uncertain)

STATE CESSIONS, 1781–1802

*TREATY WITH SPAIN, 1810

LOUISIANA PURCHASE FROM FRANCE, 1803

ANNEXATION OF TEXAS, 1845

PURCHASE FROM TEXAS, 1850

OREGON COMPROMISE WITH GREAT BRITAIN, 1846

CESSION FROM MEXICO, 1848

GADSDEN PURCHASE FROM MEXICO, 1853

territory. At the same time, as a result of the defeat of Mexico in the Mexican War of 1846–1848, the Pacific Southwest, a vast terrain of 338,681,960 acres, was acquired for only $16 million, a cost of about 5 cents per acre. In 1854 the Gadsden Purchase was negotiated with Mexico. Land that now makes up the southern part of Arizona, some 18,988,800 acres, was purchased for $10 million, or about 53 cents per acre.

U.S. LAND ACQUISITIONS[a] AND COSTS, 1781–1867

DATE	ACQUISITION
1781–1802	State cessions
1789–1850	Indian treaties
1803	Louisiana Purchase[d]
1819	Cession from Spain (Florida) Red River Basin[f]
1846	Oregon Compromise (with Great Britain; Pacific Northwest)
1848	Mexican Cession[d] (after Mexican War; Pacific Southwest)
1850	Purchase from Texas
1853	Gadsden Purchase (from Mexico; southern Arizona)
1867	Alaska Purchase (from Russia)
Aggregate	

Total area of U.S. today

a. All areas except Alaska are as computed in 1912 and have not been adjusted for subsequen recomputation.
b. Percent refers to proportion of U.S. total.
c. Georgia alone was paid for its cession.
d. Data for Louisiana Purchase exclude areas e

The last enormous acquisition was from Russia in 1867. The purchase of the 375,303,680 acres now known as Alaska was negotiated for $7,-200,000, or less than 2 cents an acre. This "land deal" was one of the most sensational and economic of all United States purchases, considering it occurred some sixty-four years after the Louisiana Purchase for about half the price per acre.

AREA (IN THOUSANDS OF ACRES)			COST (IN THOUSANDS OF DOLLARS)	PRICE PER ACRE
TOTAL	LAND ONLY[b]	INLAND WATER		
36,826	233,416 (10%)	3,410	$ 6,200	$0 & .11[c]
50,000	— (19%)	—	90,000	.20
29,912	523,446 (23%)	6,465	23,214	.04
46,145	43,343 (2%)	2,802[c]	6,674	.14
29,602	29,067 (1%)	535	—	
83,386	180,644 (8%)	2,742	0	0
38,681	334,479 (15%)	4,202	16,295	.05
78,927	78,843 (3%)	84	15,496	.20
18,989	18,962 (1%)	27	10,000	.53
75,304	362,516 (16%)	12,787	7,200	.02
87,772	1,804,716	33,054	$175,079	
13,678			Average cost per acre:	$.13

ed by Treaty of 1819 with Spain. Such areas are included in figures for Mexican Cession.

ncludes 33,920 acres subsequently recognized as part of State of Texas, which is not ublic-domain state.

epresents drainage basin of Red River of the North, south of 49th parallel. Authorities r as to the method and exact date of its acquisition. Some see it as part of Louisiana chase; others maintain it was acquired from Great Britain.

Disposition of the Land. While the left hand of the government was acquiring land from foreign powers and from native Americans, the right hand was disposing of acreage—and in big chunks. Through all of its purchases, the federal government acquired nearly 2,288,000,000 acres of land. With so much land to move, it only made sense to move it wholesale. That meant dealing with organizations and groups, and devising methods which could dispose of large quantities of land.

In the 150 years between the founding of the nation and 1930s, the United States government sold and otherwise distributed approximately 80 percent of all of its holdings. Homesteaders, states, railroad combines, mining interests, and cash purchasers were among the prime beneficiaries. As the distinguished historian Frederick Merk points out, this divestiture "was the greatest real estate transaction in modern history, with

respect to the extent of the land distributed and, even more, the value of the distribution."

About 20 percent of the land distributed by the government was sold. This land was bought primarily by individuals, and purchased in enormous bulk. Because the federal government was selling land at auction at a minimum price that ranged from $1.25 to $2.00 per acre, purchase was feasible only for those who had accumulated capital, who could arrange financing, or who understood how to take advantage of various financing programs offered by the federal government. Through these sales, which began late in the eighteenth century under the aegis of the Ordinance of 1785, and subsequently under various versions of the Preemption Act and other laws, the federal government sold increasing amounts of land to private interests. In 1836 alone, the year of the largest

FIRST SALE OF LOTS, IMPERIAL VALLEY, CALIFORNIA, APRIL 12, 1904

Once the land had been acquired by the federal government, it was distributed in a number of ways. In some areas, the government chose the auction system and sold parcels at a minimum of $1.25 to $2.00 an acre.

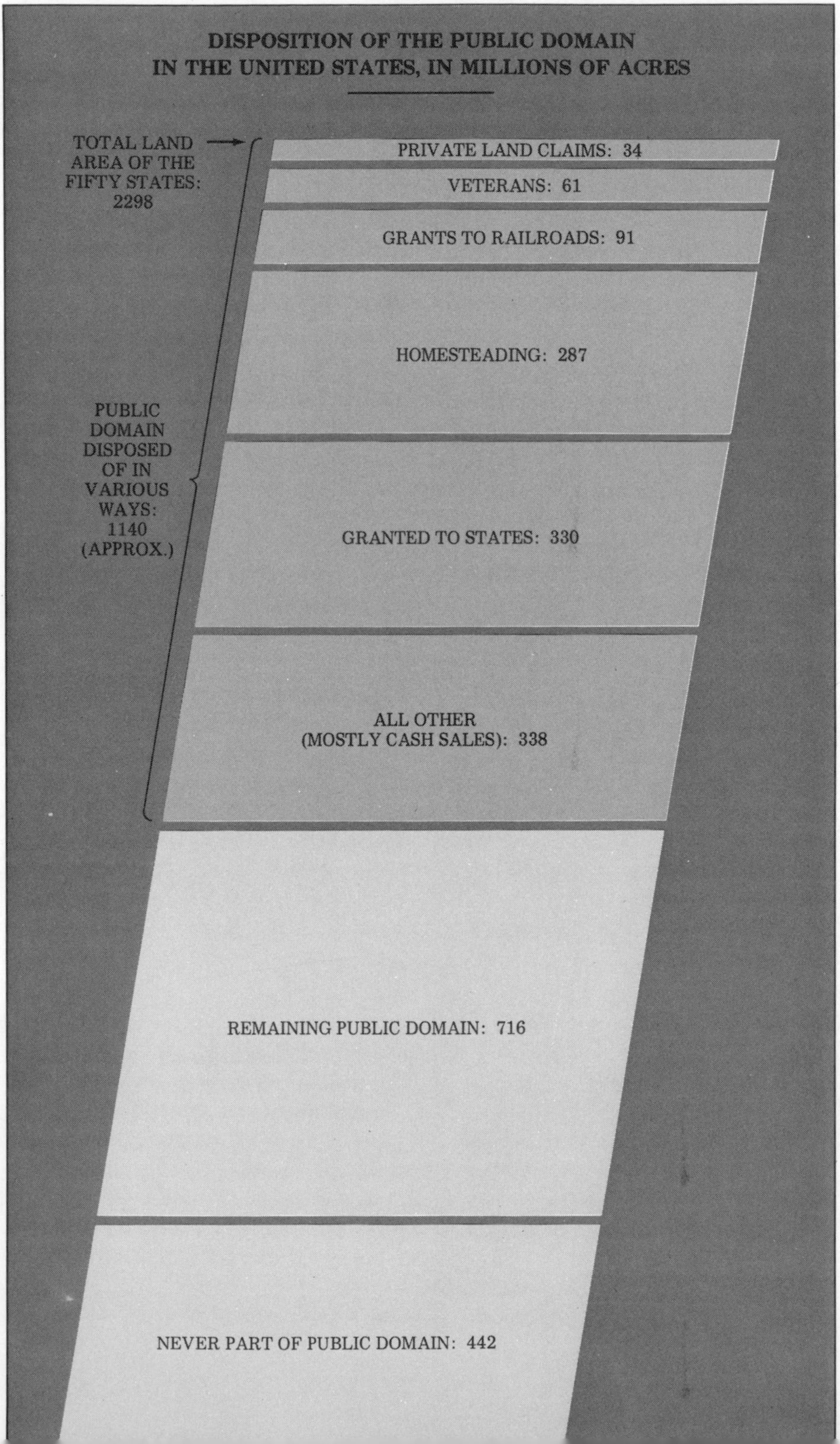

DISPOSITION OF THE PUBLIC DOMAIN
IN THE UNITED STATES, IN MILLIONS OF ACRES

TOTAL LAND AREA OF THE FIFTY STATES: 2298

PRIVATE LAND CLAIMS: 34

VETERANS: 61

GRANTS TO RAILROADS: 91

HOMESTEADING: 287

PUBLIC DOMAIN DISPOSED OF IN VARIOUS WAYS: 1140 (APPROX.)

GRANTED TO STATES: 330

ALL OTHER (MOSTLY CASH SALES): 338

REMAINING PUBLIC DOMAIN: 716

NEVER PART OF PUBLIC DOMAIN: 442

transfer of federal land to private ownership, during the nineteenth century, and the year that preceded the panic of 1837, approximately 20 million acres of land were sold at an average price of $1.25 per acre.

That year, as a result of financial trends in America, including rampant inflation, Daniel Webster advised the Senate to reconsider the national policy of fixed-price land sales:

In everything else, prices have run up; but here [i.e., public land], price is chained down by statute. Goods, products of all kinds, and indeed all other lands may rise, and many of them have risen, some forty and fifty percent; vast portions of this land are equal, in natural fertility, to any part of the globe. . . . The Government land, therefore, at the present prices, and at the present moment, is the cheapest safe object of investment. The sagacity of capital has found this out, and it grasps the opportunity. Purchase, it is true, has gone ahead of emigration; but emigration follows it, in near pursuit, and spreads its thousands and its tens of thousands close on the heels of the surveyer and the land-hunter. . . .

The very next year, the federal government, rather than raise land prices, clamped down on credit financing of land sales. It issued the Specie Circular, which made only gold and silver acceptable currency to settle public land sales. Speculators pulled out of the market, unable to come up with hard currency. After 100–200 percent increases in land prices between 1830 and 1836, there was a crash and widespread distress sale of land or reversion back to public ownership when land mortgage installments could not be met.

The Survey: Your Ticket to Terrain.   In an effort to quantify, define, register, and make available for sale or use the vast amount of land being acquired and sold, the federal government undertook to survey the new territory west of the Alleghenies. This immense enterprise, though clouded by corruption at times and marred by serious inaccuracies at others, was sound in purpose: the establishment of a uniform system of property description.

The system adopted is known as the rectangular survey and is the method of property description that today underlies ownership deeds in thirty states west of the Alleghenies, including Florida and Alaska. It does not apply to land in West Virginia, Kentucky, Tennessee, Texas, or to parts of sixteen other states whose titles originated under foreign nations.

The system is based on surveying lines, known as meridians or range lines, which run north and south. Intersecting lines which cross east and west are called base lines. Both the meridians and base lines were established as the original federal surveyors progressed across the land, and

**THE DEADWOOD
CENTRAL RAILROAD ENGINEER
CORPORATION, CA. 1880**

Public and private surveyors were poorly paid and worked with crude tools. Errors were unavoidable, and persist even today, often resulting in land disputes.

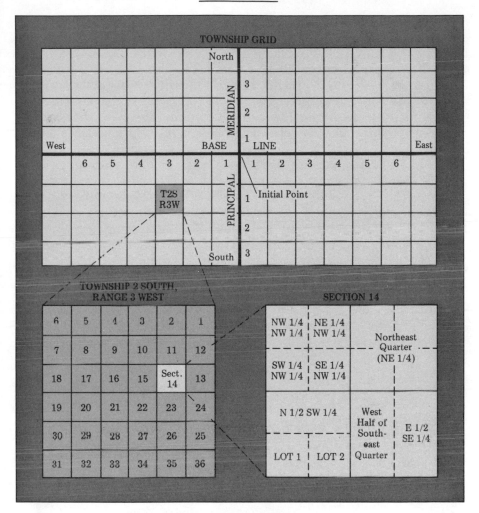

GENERALIZED DIAGRAM
OF THE RECTANGULAR SYSTEM OF SURVEYS

A basic feature of the rectangular system of land surveys is an "initial point." Through this is run a "base line," from east to west, and a "principal meridian," from north to south. Ranges are measured east and west, and townships north and south. Thus the shaded block in the upper diagram in Township 2 South, Range 3 West—or T2S, R3W, for short. This township is six miles on a side, or contains 36 square miles. It is subdivided into 36 "sections" containing one square mile or 640 acres each, as shown in the lower left diagram. The section may be further subdivided as shown in the lower right diagram.

each surveying line was given a name or number by the General Land Office in the Capitol.

The terrain of America was then further subdivided, using the meridian and base line as reference points, into immense squares, or quadrangles, twenty-four miles on each side. The quadrangle was further divided geometrically into sixteen separate areas, each measuring six miles on each side. These 6-mile squares, or townships, each contained an area of thirty-six square miles, which was further divided into sections of one mile on each side.

A system of language was subsequently invented to pinpoint the precise location of any given piece of property in America. Townships were sequentially numbered by reference to the base and meridian lines of their respective quadrangles. Within the townships, sections were numbered from 1 to 36 in a uniform fashion. The numbering begins at the northeast corner, then continues westward in the first row, west to east in the second, and so forth down through the township. A section within the central four, usually number 16, was reserved as a school site. Four sections—usually numbers 8, 11, 26, and 29—were temporarily retained by the federal government for ultimate disposition.

The grid pattern that results from this massive land platting campaign continues to be imprinted on the rural network, township bounda-

U.S. GEOLOGICAL SURVEY WITH PACK TRAIN ON THE TRAIL BETWEEN YELLOWSTONE AND THE EAST FORK, ROCKY MOUNTAINS OF THE YELLOWSTONE AREA, CA. 1871

Although the Geological Survey did not survey the public lands, it did endeavor to chart the topography and water resources of special areas. The public lands were surveyed through individual contracts let by the Surveyor General in each public land state. The Ordinance of 1785 provided that "quadrangles" twenty-four miles square be formed by intersecting north-south lines (range lines) and east-west lines (base lines). Surveying was slow, however, and often lagged behind land sale and settlement.

ries, county lines, and city streets across America today. Even the platting of hills, swamps, and waterways of the northern extension of New York City, which occurred in 1811, reflects the national commitment at the time to the rectangular survey. These plats also reflect the appeal of the urban street grid to land speculators, as will be discussed later.

HOMESTEADING AND OTHER FEDERAL PROGRAMS: THE WAY TO SPECULATIVE PROFITS ON THE FRONTIER

From the turn of the nineteenth century until 1862, when the Homestead Act was passed, land was available to settlers in one of four ways. It could be bought in a private transaction between the settler and a previous private owner, an individual speculator, or large corporate holder, such as a railroad holding company. Land acquired in this way usually cost more than the federal minimum price, often as much as $2.50 per acre, as the speculative private holder took his cut of a dollar or more on an acre.

Land could also be purchased from the federal government at auction. Especially during the first half of the nineteenth century, vast tracts of

J.F. HART'S
HOMESTEAD CLAIM,
BURNT RIDGE, MONTANA,
1906

The Homestead Act of 1862 established that each citizen could be deeded 160 acres of free land if he built a 5-by-7 foot house upon the property and tilled the soil for five years. A settler also had the option of buying the land at $1.25 an acre after a year's residence.

HOMESTEADER
TURNS THE SOD
FOR THE FIRST TIME,
MONTANA, 1908

Although homesteaders were required to improve their 160-acre claim by farming it continuously for five years, any adult in the family could claim a 160-acre tract in his own name. This meant that an assemblage of considerable size was possible, especially when dummy entrymen would claim acreage and transfer it to one owner.

the public domain were sold at or near the federal minimum of $1.25 per acre.

The third way land could be acquired was through the purchase of government land after the auction was over. At that time, all unsold land was available in unlimited amounts at $1.25 per acre.

The fourth method of land acquisition was through "preemption." As a consequence of the first Preemption Act of 1830, passed by Congress to encourage settlement of the westward frontier, and subsequent continuations of it up to 1891, when the act was repealed, any settler who lived on and cultivated or improved a tract of surveyed public land was accorded the right to purchase up to 160 acres at the minimum federal price of $1.25 per acre, cash.

The Preemption Act, however, did not result in the rapid settlement of western lands as Congress had expected. Most settlers either could not afford $1.25 per acre or found it easier to trespass on the land without payment until a land title was needed to mortgage or sell. Congress was anxious to have western lands settled, reasoning that commerce and defense would be fostered and populist sentiment satisfied. By the mid-1800s, it became apparent to some leaders of the country that the only way to populate the West rapidly was to give the land away. Thus, the Homestead Act of 1862 was adopted.

Under the Homestead Act, if conditions were met, land was given away to settlers or so-called settlers. A settler qualified for a 160-acre tract of land if he was at least twenty-one years old, did not otherwise own over 320 acres of land, and agreed to remain on his homestead and modestly improve it for a period of five years. However, any adult in the family could claim a 160-acre tract in his own name. This meant that an assemblage of a tract of considerable size was possible, especially if dummy entrymen would claim acreage and transfer it to a single owner.

By 1873 there were two additional federal programs in existence whereby free claim to public land could be obtained. The Mining Law of 1872 provides that a miner may claim 20 acres of land for $2.50 to $5.00 per acre, so long as he makes a minimum of $100 worth of improvements to the property. Provided the improvements are made annually, the claim is valid, and the title need not be purchased. In addition, multiple mining claims were permissible by any individual. The Timber Culture Act of 1873 grants title to a quarter-section (40 acres) to any individual who plants trees not more than twelve feet apart and keeps them in healthy growing condition for ten years.

Thus, by 1873, the enterprising land dealer on the frontier could legally put together a combination of a homestead claim, a preemption claim, and a timber-culture claim, thereby qualifying for over 480 acres of land virtually free of purchase cost, except for the delayed payment required for the preemption claim of $200. No mining claims were placed on land suitable for agriculture, however. Through the use of phony claimants and dummy entries, the unscrupulous operator could, of course, qualify for a much larger spread.

Nor did all settlers confine their activities to stalwart working of land originally acquired. Many original claimants to free land sold so-called relinquishments to the next wave of settlers, whereby the original claim was relinquished to a new owner for a fee. They established their initial claims through improvements, then sold out to get some capital with which to begin a new enterprise. The capital was sometimes used to buy livestock, mules, plows, and other necessary tools for homesteading on presumably more profitable land. At times claims were simply abandoned because of crop failure, drought, and high interest rates.

Preemption and homestead rights to the land were supplemented even further by the Desert Land Act of 1877, which allows a settler to claim 640 acres at 25 cents an acre by agreeing to irrigate the land. The homesteader obtains title to the land after three years' upon payment of an additional dollar per acre. By 1893, nearly 1 million acres had been acquired in this manner.

Timber and grazing lands were often acquired and then used illegally, as it was impossible for the government to supervise the vast areas being claimed. For instance, ranchers would use their employed cowboys to enter additional 640-acre allotments under the Desert Land Act, and thereby deceptively acquire large expanses of grasslands. Herds were then moved onto the territory, which in many cases was systematically abused by overgrazing.

Abuse of the Homestead Act was perhaps the most widespread. A report by the Alabama land commissioner in 1880 declared:

A vast proportion of homestead entries have been fraudulently made by men of wealth and prominence. Several owners of iron works and lumber mills have furnished money to their employees, many of them ignorant and lawless men, to enter the lands in the vicinity of the furnaces and mills, for the sole purpose of acquiring timber thereon. In one instance nearly ten sections of public land were thus entered by an iron company. From lands so entered mill owners in both this state (Alabama) and Florida have cut individually from five thousand to ten thousand logs every season.

Thus, while the pioneer is portrayed in film and lore as a courageous adventurer, more often flamboyant and carefree than conservative and circumspect, there were other types on the frontier as well. Many of the westward-moving pioneers became land speculators or their agents. It took capital to become a speculator, however, and most settlers hoped to profit in one way or another by controlling an extra quarter-section, which they would sell when demand was high.

In theory, the homesteading program and the other federal land acts enabled the legitimate pioneer to speculate with his guts, his energy. He was able to put up his life and his work as his capital in place of money, a procedure now called sweat equity. And so the land was taken, claimed, protected. For many, or for their families, the speculation has paid off. The foundations of great American private family wealth may be traced to early homestead allotments, mining claims, and other free or nearly free grants of land.

TOWN BOOMERS AND RAILROADS

Throughout the nineteenth century, private land companies and individual speculators who received or bought land from the federal government continued to offer their lands for sale in competition with the United States. To meet the competition of the government land offices, which usually priced land between $1.25 and $2.50 per acre, and still make a profit, the private sector had to offer liberal terms of credit or some other special incentive to attract settlers. Town-site building and the construction of community improvements provided such an inducement. As one Illinois pioneer, Morris Birkbeck, observed during his journeys through the Northwest in 1817: "Gain is the beginning, the middle, and the end, the alpha and the omega of the founders of American towns."

The homestead settler and the land-company owner were not the only frontiersmen with an avid interest in land speculation. Others came west to set up a small business, to develop a professional practice, to build up a society on the familiar lines of stable community and family. However, once installed in a new place, the townsman generally sought to do his part to make the community grow—and the more rapidly, the better. They also purchased additional land nearby and in town.

Growth was, of course, good for all local businesses, for all local professions. Most of all, though, it encouraged people to settle upon the land, to compete for land, to bid up the prices of real estate in the community.

As population growth proceeded, the settled townsman on the frontier prepared for the payoff. He worked hard and invested most of his savings in additional land. He also participated in land-claim schemes before government survey teams arrived and later bought property at land auctions. Most often he acquired land through the preemption regulations and the Homestead Act of 1862. It is estimated by Leslie E. Decker, an authority on American frontier speculation, that "at least half, perhaps more, of the early comers to any town—from lawyers to doctors to merchants, to just plain town developers—usually diversified in this fashion."

**SOUTH DAKOTA
SALES BROADSIDE,
FORBES, 1890**

This 1890 *Forbes* lithograph promises "free homes, government lands, and cheap deeded lands" to second-wave homesteaders willing to settle in South Dakota on former Sioux lands. As the lithograph illustrates, the earliest settlers were quick to make promises of state universities, schools, and hospitals in the hope that demand would increase the value of their own holdings.

53

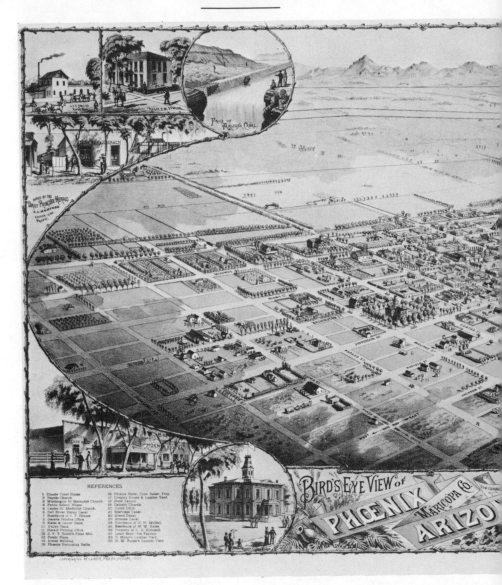

REFERENCES

The role of road builders, canal builders, new town promoters, and railroad companies in town booming is better known than the very definite role played by resident individuals as they hopefully awaited the later settlers. One of the most widespread means that local townspeople used to attract new settlers to the community in order to force up land values was to quickly establish special amenities in town which would distinguish the community. For this reason schools were built, often much

BIRD'S-EYE VIEW
OF PHOENIX, MARICOPA
COUNTY, ARIZONA, 1885

The practice of selling newly subdivided land with inflated rhetoric and embellished illustrations is an old one. From the first days of American settlement, land speculators have used an artist's pen and a surveyor's map to imaginatively transform raw land into an appealing community. In this lithograph sales piece by C. J. Dyer, the public schoolhouse, county courthouse, hotel, billiard hall, newspaper office, and general store are each shown to establish the settled quality of Phoenix. In the written description, potential buyers are assured that Phoenix is twenty-eight miles north of Maricopa station on the Southern Pacific Railroad, and that a branch line will be completed by January 1886. The town has "streams of living water through every street.... The Methodists, Baptists and Catholics have tasteful places of worship ... the territorial Insane Asylum near the town...."

larger than warranted, and indeed much larger than any foreseeable demand could justify. Elaborate courthouses were erected. Roads were extended and improved. Bridges were built across streams to link the town center to open land nearby.

Most public works and lavish town publicity campaigns were financed by the borrowing power of the precinct or county government. Local public debt, of considerable consequence, was accrued by those early resi-

VIEW OF SUMNER, KANSAS, 1857

This view of Sumner in 1857 is completely fictitious. It was commissioned
by a townsite company soley to promote real-estate sales. Many naïve settlers purchased lots based on such promotional devices only to be bitterly
disappointed upon arriving at their new "home town." As Bostonian John
Ingalls wrote when he visited Sumner in 1858, there existed
nothing but a "few log huts and miserable cabins."

dents in hope that private profit would occur—and that others would soon
arrive to share the tax burden of the newly incurred debt. Not unlike his
counterpart in the mid-twentieth century who first moved to the suburbs,
the frontier townsman was willing to risk a shared public debt in order
to obtain the enormous personal profits available from the second and
third waves of new immigration into the area.

After the 1840s, a town's principal means of ensuring its growth was
for it to become a railroad center. This could be accomplished if the town
attracted a major institution, such as a penitentiary, secondary school,

agricultural college or university; and the surest means of doing so was to become the county seat or state capitol. These designations were thus sought and fought for. In the case of main rail lines and even rail spurs, rail access was bid for by townsfolk with cash inducements sometimes paid to the railroad company.

On the open plains, where nothing but the rail line stood between town growth and inevitable stagnation, the sums paid to regional railroad builders reached fantastic proportions. In Adams County, Nebraska, for instance, an area of only twenty-four square miles, nine separate towns bid for a junction by applying to the federal land-grant railroads in the area: the Burlington, the Union Pacific, and the Missouri Pacific. The towns with any chance at all, in terms of sufficient clout and capital were Juniata, Ayr, Kenesaw, and Hastings. Hastings won out and was awarded the rail link lines; but in so doing, it stacked up a municipal debt in financial improvements of over a quarter of a million dollars and an additional county debt of half that amount. However, the people there, the settlers who had been ahead of the booming period, had claims, deeds, and land available—at a price—for the newcomers.

Public-relations campaigns and advertising for settlers sometimes reached unscrupulous levels. For example, by the year 1857, along the Missouri River in a 125-mile stretch within the state of Kansas, fourteen different cities were platted. One of them, Sumner, was widely advertised in the East. A plat map and description gave a bird's-eye view of the city as it supposedly looked in 1857. Complete with an active commercial waterfront, four churches, a university, fully developed roads, and numerous settlers, the widely circulated lithograph promised much. John William Reps, in *The Making of Urban America: A History of City Planning in the United States*, his wonderfully useful book of old maps and physical United States history, quotes a letter home written by John James Ingalls of Boston, a hopeful early settler who arrived at Sumner in 1858 to find only one rough street:

The others being merely footpaths leading up and down the wild ravines to the few log huts and miserable cabins which compose the city. . . .

There are no churches in the place—instead of four, as was represented to me. No respectable residences; no society; no women except a few woebegone, desolate-looking old creatures; no mechanical activity . . . no schools, no children; nothing but the total reverse of the picture which was presented to me. On the engraved romance a "college" was imagined, of which no person here . . . has even so much as heard of the idea advanced.

As a result of an intensive sales campaign, the promotors of Sumner managed to attract around five hundred people before 1860. By 1866, a visitor found a depleted, desolate wasteland of about twenty-five remaining residents. "All the buildings," it was observed, "save five or six have been torn down and taken away. Young oaks and cottonwoods choke its deserted streets."

The Railroads as Town Boomers.   Beginning in 1850, the federal government was induced to grant over 130 million acres of free land to the various chartered railroad companies. These grants included rights-of-way and alternate even-numbered or odd-numbered sections for a distance of six to forty miles in either direction perpendicular to the track. Each section was 640 acres. The federal government maintained title to the alternate sections not granted to the railroad companies.

Such extensive grants to the railroads were a result of strong lobbying pressure on Congress, the impact of which is evident throughout business and legislative annals of the mid-nineteenth century. Representative Thomas A. Fitch of Nevada, responding in 1870 to Representative William S. Holman of Indiana, defended railroad grants against the charge that they created monopolies detrimental to settlers:

A settler who objects to railroads! Sir, there is no such settler in reality.

Hence, horrible shadows! Unreal mockery, hence!

Sir, there are millions upon millions of acres of rich lands all over the United States . . . through which no railroad passes or is projected. If there be those in Ohio or New York or New England or Indiana who contemplate immigration to some place where they cannot market the fruits of their industry; if there be those who prefer to toil over the sandy desert or the muddy prairie in stage or wagon rather than be whirled along by a monopoly on an iron road . . . they can obtain the amplest opportunity for the gratification of their fancies. I do not believe there are a hundred such men in the country. I do not think there are five.

MAP OF NEBRASKA,
SHOWING THE UNION PACIFIC RAILROAD LAND GRANT, 1880
(Opposite)

Like most early railroad companies, the Union Pacific Railroad was granted free strips of land by the government to help finance its construction. Each railroad was granted half of all the land within six to forty miles of the rail right-of-way. The railroad owned sections of land, 640 acres each, in a checkerboard pattern, with the federal government holding the alternating parcels. If land immediately adjacent to the rail line was otherwise owned, however, the company was allowed to choose another parcel within "indemnity limits."

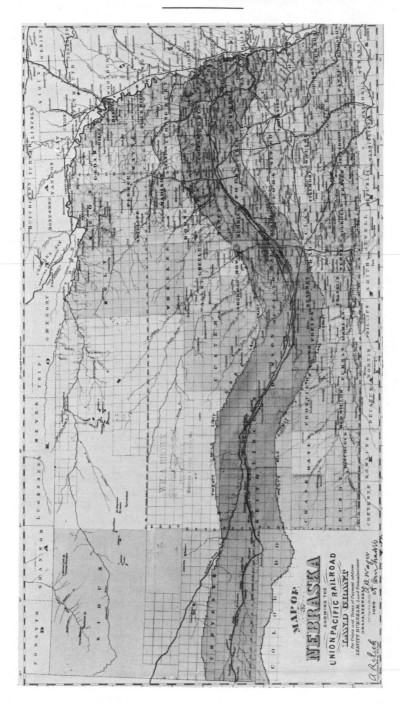

As a consequence of such sentiment, the railroads became one of the prime beneficiaries of free land in America, along with individuals. From the point of view of the federal government in the mid-nineteenth century, free land grants to railroad companies were justified in much the same way as free allocation of land was to homesteaders: without the land contribution as an incentive, settlement and development, as well as the capital required for both, would not be forthcoming.

Once their land was in hand, their route secured, and the steel laid down, the railroads became the greatest town boomers of them all. As a result of extensive construction programs, these companies often had accumulated considerable debt. One way out of this financial predicament was to persuade people to use the rail, to settle along the route, and to buy the land. In a sense, the railroads, competing with one another first for land grants, subsequently became competitors for settlers.

The railroad enterprises, then, were recognized by the federal government as the most logical and expeditious way of spreading the growing national population out upon the land, and of ensuring safety, commerce, and communication across an immense continent. As an inducement to the railroads, and as a favor to the powerful and influential men who organized the largest rail-operating companies, a national policy evolved whereby the railroads were given land grants throughout the area they promised to serve. The first such grant was made to the Illinois Central Railroad in 1850. By 1871, when the spree was over, marking the end of congressional land grants to the railroads, the United States had granted free title to some sixteen companies to 130 million acres of land. Only about 8 percent of the land granted was used for railroad-building purposes. Most of it was intended for sale by the railroads to settlers and to developers, through much was ultimately retained by the companies.

The terms of the original grants were so generous, and later so flagrantly expanded by practice, that historians still marvel. As one condition for obtaining a land grant, most railroads were required to haul government freight and personnel at reduced rates averaging 50 percent, while federal mail was hauled at a 20 percent reduction. Today, railroad interests claim that these reduced rate benefits, repealed in 1946 after the huge tonnage carried as part of the war effort, qualifies as a contribution by the railroads of $1.25 billion to the enterprise of federal government in America, or about ten times the value of the land received using nineteenth-century land prices. By comparing the value of mid-twentieth-century credits for service to mid-nineteenth-century land prices, the Association of American Railroads claims that "railroad land grants [were] one of the sharpest business deals Uncle Sam ever made." However, if one were to calculate the value of land received on the basis of twentieth-century prices, as the railroads do their claim of contributions, then the bonanza in land value of the more than 130 million acres would clearly exceed all benefits returned many times over.

The primary responsibility of the companies was to build the railroads within ten years. To further assist, permission was given to cut timber from public lands for railroad ties and fuel. Once announced, and certainly once built, a working rail line added substantial value to the immense acreage in rights-of-way granted along the route.

Congressmen supporting railroad land grants passed federal legislation requiring that reserved, federally owned alternate sections associated with railroad land grants were to be sold at a $2.50 per acre minimum at a time when most federally owned land was available at half that price. This provision defused charges of a giveaway. If twice the per-acre revenue was to be obtained on the half reserved in public ownership, then the net result was no loss of federal income. Pushed further, this line of reasoning permitted members of Congress to assert that the nation was obtaining a national network of rail lines at no public cost.

By holding alternate sections of land along the rail lines, as it did, the federal government became a coventurer with the railroad companies in terms of land-speculation possibilities. Land not occupied by settlers under the Preemption Act or after 1862 under the Homestead Act could be sold at auction. By giving up half of the land along the rail, the federal government anticipated that its retained half of the land would be served by transportation of the newest sort, and would be accessible at little or no cost to people, goods, and services at the expense of all other public and private land. Of course, it was incorrectly assumed that all of the rail lines would be built and that the land along the routes would bring at least the full $2.50-per-acre minimum.

During the mid-nineteenth century, homestead interests in Congress pressed for legislation that required forced sales by the railroads of their excess lands. The railroads resisted. Some even went another route— toward the mortgage market. By mortgaging their land grants to banks, the railroad companies could realize instant capital in vast amounts. They also could proclaim, as they did successfully in court and in Congress, that sale of their land holdings was then legally impossible, as the land was encumbered as security for debt.

In 1878, Secretary of the Interior Carl Schurz tried to force the Union Pacific Railroad, and by extension all other railroads, to throw open their unsold lands for purchase by preemption at the government price prescribed by charter of $1.25 in the case of the Union Pacific, and $2.50 for some of the lines which received later grants. This law was challenged in the Supreme Court when a speculative purchaser bid for Nebraska lands owned by the Union Pacific. In a ruling that protected the railroad companies and affirmed the basic sanctity of the land mortgage, the court ruled

AN ILLINOIS CENTRAL RAILROAD
COMPANY ADVERTISEMENT,
1860–1861

Once a railroad secured its land grant and route, it was able to sell land.
Some lines sold tracks to settlers; others held and mortgaged property for
working capital. Some railroads, however, were required by provisions
in their land grants to sell their land to settlers at $2.50 an acre.

ACROSS THE CONTINENT,
CURRIER AND IVES COLORED LITHOGRAPH
DRAWN BY F.F. PALMER, 1868
(Opposite)

By promoting new towns equipped with such "urban amenities" as schools
and roads, the railroads encouraged a westward-moving population to settle along their routes and use their lines. For the railroads, a flow
of population was equivalent to success and wealth.

that the lien of the mortgage holder superceded that of any other prospective purchaser.

It was not until the first two decades of the twentieth century that the railroads were actually forced to divest themselves by sale of certain retained and originally freely granted acreage. Although the era of acquisition and holding for speculative sale is surely over for the railroads, they remain in possession of vast holdings throughout the countryside and within the cities, as a result of both their favored treatment and the success of their profoundly significant business enterprise: the establishment of a railroad network through and across America.

Non-Planning as National History.   In the laying out and building of regional and transcontinental railroads, there was no attempt to plan the overall scheme of the rail lines themselves, their points of link, interchange, or territory of coverage. The railroads were considered independent operations under the control of independent operators. Nor was any national philosophy adopted (once the Massachusetts colonists in the eighteenth century lost interest in promoting the birth and growth of contiguous towns) regarding the orderly development of communities in relationship to one another, or even in the orderly development of individual communities. From the very outset, the motivation for development of the access network through the railroads, and later through roadways, and for individual settlement itself, was steeped in the obsession that land, and its use by individuals, is a business enterprise, pure and simple. Thus, the first lands to be opened and exploited were always those of apparent richness, those that were fertile or suitable for easy clearing. Afterwards, the migratory, land-wise early settlers moved on down the line, often to the edge of the frontier, to prepare for another round of settlement.

This approach to the land, and pattern of development, can be seen in the placement of communities across America today. Moreover, it continues to be the way in which land is exploited in each region, around each metropolitan area, indeed in each community. The specter of suburban sprawl in the major metropolitan zones of the country shows a continuation of this leaping outward to the best land, ignoring poorer lands along the way, as the highways of the mid-twentieth century, like the railroads before them, moved out into the countryside often ahead of all settlement, and almost always without a well-conceived plan that linked the most desirable patterns of settlement to the provision of access.

In 1840, Daniel Webster proclaimed in the United States Senate:

What can we do with the Western Coast, a coast of 3,000 miles, rock bound, sheerless, uninviting and not a harbor on it? What use have we of such a country? I will never vote one cent from the public treasury to place the Pacific Ocean one inch nearer Boston than it is now.

By 1869, however, the Union Pacific and Central Pacific Railroads met to form the first transcontinental rail system.

By the 1880s, immigrants were crowding the East Coast, strikes had multiplied, railroads and cattle barons were battling squatters. Suddenly land in America was perceived as scarce—and all the more valuable because of this shared perception. As Congressman Poindexter Dunn of

EAST AND WEST SHAKING HANDS

In 1869, the United States finally became "one nation . . . indivisible" when the Union Pacific and Central Pacific railroads met to form the first transcontinental rail system.

Arkansas declared in June of 1884, the vast land mass of the United States, once easily acquired by most Americans, seemed suddenly to be held in the hands of relatively few wealthy and powerful individuals and business groups:

Already these huge associations of wealth have possessed the whole vast volume of our transportation and commerce . . . the banking and currency of the country. . . . In the form of manufacturing associations they have possessed themselves of a dangerous power of insensible and stealthy taxation. . . . They have possessed themselves of vast tracts of the public domain, sufficient in extent for an empire, which they hold for speculation or sell slowly on hard and oppressive terms which practically exclude the poor from it. They have possessed themselves of nearly all the precious-metal and other mineral and coal lands in the country, and hold them as in the grip of a giant. They have possessed themselves of nearly all the valuable timber lands of the country, and now comes the last act in the drama in this effort to seize without right or law the vast arid plains of the West. . . . Their all-grasping hands are laid upon the whole earth and all the "riches thereof."

As will be discussed in Chapter Fourteen it is not until the late nineteenth century that the federal government began to adopt a policy of conservation or to reserve a portion of the remaining public domain for use by the American people. These policies emerge as liberal members of Congress look back upon the history of land disposition, development, and ownership, and perceive the inextricable tie of the land to the power and wealth of relatively few visionary landowners and enterprises. By the beginning of the twentieth century, the frontier has disappeared.

THE STATES CASH IN

While the railroads received land in great quantities, and the national government, through the Homestead Act, made it possible for individuals to claim at least 160 acres free of cost, the states themselves began to clamor for land donations for public purposes. Their efforts culminated in a number of policies. After 1841, each new state was allotted 500,000 acres, a sort of dowry from the federal government. In addition, land grants were made to the states for building public institutions.

As a result of the Morrill Act of 1862, each state not in rebellion during the Civil War was granted 30,000 acres for each senator and each representative it elected to Congress. The land was intended to endow at least one college in each state for agriculture and mechanical arts. Any state lacking federal lands within its own borders received script, or certificates, which entitled it to public lands in the West.

Through the Morrill Act approximately 13 million acres were given to the states. Today, in every state except Hawaii, there is an agricultural college supported at least initially through federal land grants.

But the grant itself was of land, not money; and it is cold cash that is needed to establish an educational enterprise, to erect its buildings, to pay the salaries of its employees. The states devised ways to build an educational institution from the resources of a land grant in many ways, some of them profligate, some of them wise. In most cases, land dealings and land transactions, often with speculator intermediaries, were involved.

For example, as an original state having no public land, New York received script. Thereafter, New York State sold the bulk of its script to Ezra Cornell, a man of considerable means with an interest in education. As a result of the sale, New York obtained the cash necessary to establish a new university in Ithaca. Cornell, a more generous intermediary than most, proposed to donate to the university any net profits above costs, plus a 7 percent profit obtained from the ultimate sale of western lands. In the late 1860s, Cornell invested the scrip in a half-million acres of pineland in Chippewa Valley, Wisconsin. By 1890, when the bulk of the land had been sold to lumbering interests, Cornell University received an additional $5 million.

INDIANS AND INDIAN GIVERS

At the beginning of America's white settlement, only the English crown could buy out Native Americans and resell tribal land to speculators or donate it to favored friends at court. Any local initiative by new settlers to intrude directly upon this enterprise was forbidden. Patents, or deeds, were then given by the crown to the various colonies. It was left up to the local administrative group within each colony, led by the governor as agent of the crown, to determine how best to dispose of the lands within the patent. The crown, then, was the grantor of deeds to lands which had for all time before been the source of food, shelter, and settlement for the native American.

Most often in New England, the settled Indians were compensated when forced to move elsewhere. While compensation was usually nominal, the Native Americans were sometimes by agreement allowed to retain hunting, fishing, and trapping rights.

After the American Revolutionary War, a different situation prevailed. By terms of the Articles of the Confederation, Congress was empowered on behalf of the federal government to set policy and administer all sales and transactions of Indian lands. The basic policy formulated was to use federal power and resources to clear the land of Indian domination, moving the Indians steadily westward as settlers proceeded across the continent.

At the same time, the policy encouraged rounding up the "unpredictable and temperamental" natives into manageable clusters and settling them on reservations. There it was possible not only to contain and supervise them, but most of all to limit absolutely the terrain upon which they would be encountered, the terrain they might indeed claim and attempt to defend. The process was effected through so-called "treaties," which were in fact descriptions of a deal often accepted by force, though at times entered into voluntarily by the Indian leader, or sachem.

Very often, special allotments of land were reserved for the tribal

INDIAN CHIEFS
AND U.S. OFFICIALS, 1891

Western Indians were nomadic, often moving from the North to the South, or from the South to the North, depending upon the season. This lifestyle was intolerable to the U.S. government, which hoped to limit the lands where the Indians might be encountered —terrain they might, in fact, attempt to claim and defend. Through so-called treaties, the federal troops confined the Native Americans to reservations.

chiefs and headmen. As might be expected, since peaceful concurrence of an influential and privileged individual was preferable to a protracted military engagement, these reserved lands were generally of some value. More often than not, however, they were entrapped either by claiming creditors who held tribal trading or purchase debts, or by speculators who had induced the chief to presell his land. In this way, hundreds of thousands of acres passed quietly into the hands of shrewd speculators and traders without ever having entered the public domain.

Indian "Treaties." Between 1789 and 1850, the United States Congress ratified 245 "treaties" covering over 450 million acres of Indian land. The

cost of this property, a vast expanse of territory equivalent to approximately 23 percent of the entire national land mass excluding Alaska, was $90 million, or an average of 20 cents per acre.

By treaty, typically four distinct categories of land were established:

1. Allotments to individual Indians. These allotments, limited in size, went to individuals in each tribe, generally those in positions of power.
2. Lands ceded in trust by the Indians. These lands were to be surveyed by the federal government and sold by the Office of Indian Affairs, with proceeds going to the Indian tribes. The sales were to be at auction, with a starting price no less than $1.25 per acre.
3. Land unconditionally ceded by the Indians, which was then put under the control of the General Land Office. These lands, in fact appropriated by the federal government, were to be disposed of under the general land laws. Whether or not the lands were sold, the United States government was to be the beneficiary, not the Indian tribes.
4. Diminished reserves. After the above dispositions had been made, whatever land remained belonged to the Indian tribe as a whole.

It was not long before all the land, with the exception of the diminished reserves, passed into the hands of the white man. Allotments were often claimed by individuals or municipalities by reason of alleged Indian debts or tax delinquences, though later taxes on these lands were held to be illegal. Trust lands were usually sold to speculators and settlers, with the proceeds rarely returned to the tribe as promised. And unconditionally ceded lands, available under the general land laws, were dispersed among white settlers and entrepreneurs.

Before 1871, at which time individual congressional treaties with Indian tribes were outlawed, there was also systematic removal of the Native Americans from lands previously granted to them. By the 1850s and 1860s, white men with influence and capital sought to open up the vast diminished reserves to land speculation, settlement, and development. Thus reservations, such as those in Oklahoma and Kansas, became the focus of intense land speculation. Before long the federal government violated prior treaty agreements made with Indian tribes.

As might be expected, one of the groups most avidly interested in the disposition of Indian lands was the railroad companies. Indian property, they recognized, was considerably more attractive than land offered through congressional land grants—and for one particular reason: it was not burdened by the alternate-section provision of federal land grants, which created an unpredictable and somewhat uncontrollable public agency that held large amounts of adjacent and potentially competitive acreage. Nor was there federal control over the eventual use and schedule of sale of Indian lands. Thus, once obtained, this property was free both of the federal government as an implicit partner and of governmental restraints.

To gain title to diminished reserves, some of the railroads secured sufficient congressional influence to become incorporated into certain Indian treaties. At such times they would be designated the rightful purchaser of certain lands, at favorable prices and on advantageous conditions. This practice became most widespread during the 1860s, when a railroad dominated by Detroit promoter James F. Joy was designated to acquire an enormous stretch of magnificent land from the Osage at 20 cents per acre. The going per-acre price for the sale of lands from the federal government in the same area was $1.25. This particular arrangement was so far below the market price, and so clearly a product of alliances between influential private forces and federal administrative authorities, who might also benefit, that Congress balked. In fact, the proposed treaty produced an outcry of reform sentiment in the Congress and, as a result, was withdrawn by President Grant. Joy and his railroad eventually acquired the land nonetheless.

Three years later, Congress passed a bill eliminating the office of Indian Affairs as the intermediary agency in Indian land dealings, and thereby terminated the system of Indian cessions through it. Nevertheless, Congress retained the right and authority to oversee continued acquisition of Indian lands and their subsequent disposition as part of the public domain.

In Oklahoma, as in Kansas, and in other areas where reservations of land had once been allotted in perpetuity to Indian tribes and guaranteed as Indian land by treaty, the Native Americans found, even after 1871, that the white man's understanding of "in perpetuity" carried its own unique definition. Toward the end of the nineteenth century, Indian tribes continued to exert a logical claim to vast stretches of land granted by treaty and clearly not in the possession of the United States government. At the same time, America was experiencing sharp increases in the number of immigrants moving westward into the interior of the continent. Between 1870 and 1890, the growing population of Texas increased nearly 300 percent, from 818,579 to 2,235,527. Population increases of nearly equal magnitude occurred in Kansas, where the number of newcomers climbed from about 356,000 to over 1,400,000. This ever-increasing population, ignorant of previous treaties or indifferent to them, settled upon Indian lands. Consequently, the United States government coerced the Indian tribes to agree to new treaties, which in one way or another—especially through the procedure of the 1887 Daives Allotment Act—drove them off their own territory.

The area presently in and around Oklahoma City is a case in point. In

**GENERAL MILES AND STAFF
VIEWING THE LARGEST
HOSTILE INDIAN CAMP
IN THE U.S., NEAR PINE RIDGE,
SOUTH DAKOTA,
JANUARY 16, 1891**

By the end of the nineteenth century, vast stretches of Indian land granted by treaty were still clearly not in the possession of the federal government.

**CHEYENNE-ARAPAHO
GHOST DANCE
NEAR FORT RENO,
CALIFORNIA, CA. 1890–1891**

Even into the twentieth century, the U.S. government continued to force new agreements upon the Indians, thereby increasingly restricting their lands. Cheyenne and Arapaho Indians believed that the Spirit they worshipped would restore their lands to them. In this photograph, they are doing the Ghost Dance, calling for the disappearance of the white man.

1889, the Creek tribe, in rightful possession of much land in the Oklahoma territory, protested illegal white entry on the land and proposed to negotiate a sale. Secretary of the Interior William Vilas agreed to pay the Creeks $1.25 per acre for 1,392,704 acres. Additional land in the Cheyenne and Arapaho Reservation was purchased for $1.05 per acre. From these two purchases, $2 million was held in trust for the Indians by the United States government, which made a cash payment of only $280,000. Furthermore, Secretary Vilas agreed to pay the Seminoles $1,912,942 for more than 2.1 million acres of additional territory. With the signing of these agreements, the federal government had acquired title to all the so-called unassigned lands of the Oklahoma territory.

An area of 1,887,796 acres, or about 4 percent of present-day Oklahoma, was thus opened to homesteaders at noon on April 22, 1889. Approximately 20,000 people flocked by foot, wagon, and horseback to the borders of the unassigned lands or traveled on one of the fifteen Santa Fe railroads which were to cross the territory slowly enough so that settlers could disembark. Settlers were allowed to cross Indian lands of the Chick-

POCATELLO LAND RUSH,
IDAHO, CA. 1903

After a parcel of land was purchased from the government from the Indians and surveyed, a day was chosen when any citizen could race for the free land. The policy was first come, first served.

GRAND RUSH
FOR THE INDIAN TERRITORY,
1879

This advertisement for a land rush near Kansas is typical of the many advertisements for the homesteading of land acquired by the federal government from Indian tribes.

asaw and Cherokee nations three days in advance in order to be at the borders by noon of April 22.

As the soldiers posted around the perimeter fired their pistols, young men and women who did not already own 160 acres of land raced into the territory. The Oklahoma "runs" were on.

Entire town sites of 320 acres, including Guthrie, Oklahoma City, Kingfisher, Norman, and Stillwater, were staked out at this time.

At times, the Indians decided to fight rather than to yield. For instance, when in 1861 federal officials demanded that the Colorado Indians confine themselves to a small reservation, they resisted, and battled sporadically for three years until, in 1864, their strongest forces were destroyed in the Chivington Massacre.

In 1867, Cheyenne, Arapaho, Kiowa, and Comanche contingents numbering 2,000 also refused to be restricted to their reservations and once more took up their nomadic existence. As punishment for violating the treaties, Colonel George A. Custer executed Chief Black Kettle and one hundred fellow tribesmen on November 26, 1868. Several months later, the bands had no choice but to return to their life on the reservations.

Indian Lands Today. The atrocities committed against the Indians are now well known. At first the land was theirs, all 2.3 billion acres of it. Between 1887 and 1935, their land holdings fell from 138 million acres to below 50 million acres. Today, including some 40 million acres in Alaska, Indians remain in possession of less than 100 million acres of land in America. This considerably diminished land reserve, however, contains great mineral wealth: one third of the West's strippable coal—more than 70 billion tons, worth over $1 trillion—one-half of the nation's uranium deposits, and vast deposits of oil.

Because of this potential wealth, Indian lands and people continue to be exploited by the white man—particularly by big business. For example, the Navajo Reservation, the largest Indian reservation in the country, covers 14 million acres in Utah, New Mexico, and Arizona. It is home to 150,000 Native Americans, or almost 20 percent of the nation's Indian population. The Utah International Mining Company, a subsidiary of General Electric, as of 1979 paid a royalty far below the going free-market rate to the Navajo tribe for their coal. As reported by *New York Times* correspondent Howell Raines: "Utah International and General Electric owe this windfall to the Bureau of Indian Affairs. For years, the BIA negotiated all reservation coal leases for the Indians to assure that the tribal leaders wouldn't make any naïve or stupid deals." Not surprisingly, then, the bureau is widely despised by the Native Americans, although 70 percent of its 13,000 employees are Indian. Assistant Secretary of the

Interior Forrest J. Gerard, who is in charge of the BIA, estimates that in 1979 at least eighty members of the House of Representatives would still vote in favor of laws that ignore treaty rights, that strip tribal governments of their powers, and that permit selling off the reservations.

Indians increasingly assert their right to decide how their lands are used. In 1975, the courts upheld tribal claims to the northern two thirds of Maine. The case was finally settled between 1978 and 1979 when the Passamaquoddy and Penobscot tribes relinquished their claim to 12.5 million acres in exchange for a relatively modest $27 million trust fund

STRIP-MINING OPERATION AT THE NAVAJO MINE, JUNE 1972

Native Americans today remain in possession of less than 100 million acres of land in America. This diminished land reserve, however, contains one third of the West's strippable coal.

and $54.4 million for the purchase of 300,000 acres on which to expand the reservation, and from which timber sales are expected to bring in several million dollars a year. However, as only federal funds are committed, Congress must still approve and allocate the money. Most importantly, the settlement left standing the ruling that Indians have an aboriginal title to lands occupied by whites who never obtained congressional sanctions required by the long-ignored Indian Nonintercourse Act of 1790, an act that requires congressional approval of any sale of Indian lands.

In South Dakota, the Sioux have been seeking $150 million for land confiscated by the federal government since 1877, and the return of the western half of South Dakota. They also claim mineral rights, including those of the Homestake Mining Company in Lead, South Dakota, the largest gold mine in the Western Hemisphere. In 1868 the Sioux signed a treaty with the federal government granting them rights to the Black Hills and other areas in South Dakota perpetually. Unauthorized persons could not settle on the Indians' land. The federal government also agreed to supply food to those Indians who decided to settle permanently in the barren area. In 1874, however, gold was discovered by an expedition commanded by Lieutenant Colonel George Armstrong Custer. Under the tacit protection of the army, large numbers of miners and settlers soon swamped the area without the Indians' consent. In the late 1870s, under threat of starvation and military reprisals, the Sioux chiefs and headmen relinquished title to much of their property to the federal government. It was in a battle to drive the Sioux from this territory that General Custer was killed in June 1876 at Little Bighorn. Not until 1979, and after fifty years of litigation, did the federal government offer to settle the Sioux's claims, and for about $100 million.

Lawsuits and appeals on land claims by Indian tribes against the federal government, public corporations, and private landowners are likely to increase. Cases are currently under review in New York, Rhode Island, South Dakota, Arizona, New Mexico, and elsewhere. In many places, the final recipients of land, power, and wealth in the struggle between Indians and Indian givers in America remain to be determined.

THREE

PRIVATE RIGHTS VS. PUBLIC POWER

Had the New World been smaller, land in America might be managed and owned differently from the way it is today. The land, whether purchased or stolen, won in war or through negotiation, could have been controlled by the government. But the continent is of enormous size; and its terrain of mountain ranges, wide rivers, open prairie, vast deserts, and extensive forests defies central administration.

In the first hundred years, a most urgent task faced by the national administration was the rapid transfer of land in America from public to private ownership. In the second hundred years, the focus shifted to the limitation of private rights associated with the ownership of this private property.

The balance between public control and private rights over the land is delicate and ever-changing. At any one time the balance that is struck reveals how much power a private owner in fact possesses over his own land.

HISTORIC BACKGROUND

The first private landowners in America were expected to be the arbiters of the administration and improvement of the land. Liberals and conservatives alike within the government fashioned land-distribution policy toward one objective: to maximize private wealth via the distribution and use of land and, through it, the public well-being in the form of income from land sales and collectible taxes, and a content population. Representative Orlando B. Ficklin from Illinois outlined this basic premise before Congress in 1846:

It is a cardinal and sound principle of political economy, that in a republican government, the people, the masses, should, as far as possible, be encouraged in their laudable desires to become owners of the soil. The relation of landlord and tenant is not favorable to the growth or maintenance of free principles. The constant aim of monarchies is to build up a landed and moneyed aristocracy; to accumulate wealth and power in the hands of the few. . . . Lands . . . should pass at an early day into the hands of the actual settler. . . . The moment the citizen becomes a freeholder, his ties to his country and its institutions is increased. He has his home, his fireside, and his personal liberty and security, to protect and defend.

80

Throughout congressional debates held during the first three quarters of the nineteenth century, it was argued by even the most ardent land reformers that the landholder must be given the absolute right to sell, mortgage, or lease his land for any purpose whatsoever, and to anyone. Fewer rights would constitute a sham, a commitment of a republican government to unfree tenure and the notions of feudalism. Until around 1880, most private owners and public officials concurred that unfettered, unlimited rights associated with the private ownership of land would bring political stability and national prosperity. Through the use of the land—broadly distributed and owned without restriction and control—the country was expected to realize its democratic purpose and promise, in contrast to the class-dominated nations of Europe. Total freedom in the private use of the land was thus equated with individualism and liberty.

Land ownership was also generally equated with access to private wealth. Big business, small farmers, and speculators sought wealth through private ownership and absolute control over the disposition and use of land. The new settler and the established legislator alike favored national policies which augmented the individual's access to private land and to the wealth it would bring.

The Tide Turns. As the country became more settled, the intent of legislation slowly shifted from a guarantee of absolute private rights to increasing public control over private property. Evolving land law in America has thus become a source of tumultuous legal battles. Many private owners still ingrained with the frontier ethic have rebelled; and individuals, outraged that the government dared assert unprecedented power over their private land, have sued.

While law in many fields is established through the quiet machinery of the legislative process, land law in America is generally hammered out amid the noise and acrimony of the courtroom. Where else would anyone expect a conflict over power and wealth to be waged? The alternative, as seen all over the world, is war or revolution.

A "quiet revolution," however, as described by such legal specialists as Fred P. Bosselman and David Callies, has indeed been waged in American courtrooms over the last twenty years. The air, the land, the energy reserves, land and water conservation, noise control, coastal zones, as well as other issues, have all found themselves increasingly within the government's sphere of influence. In 1975, for example, the Office of Land Use and Water Planning estimated that the federal government spent $40 billion on loan and grant programs which affected private land use. That same year the government acquired 558,920 acres of private land by condemnation; four years before the figure was about 60,000 acres less. In

1976, the American Society of Planning Officials detailed nearly two hundred *new* state laws which governed land use. And in 1977, Congressman Morris Udall estimated that nearly 140 separate federal programs had a significant impact on state and local level land-use decision making.

A Few Major Decisions Along the Way. Between a laissez-faire nation of the first hundred years and a nation in which it is increasingly cumbersome for the private owner to use his property, there were many cases, many decisions, many appeals, which led to current legal constraints over the private control of private land. A few major decisions along the way include:

New York City, 1826—A church buried its dead in a cemetery for sixty years but, once homes and businesses were built around the church, a law was passed prohibiting further burial in the cemetery. The church sued; and the court, citing protection of community health, upheld the law.

Chelsea, Massachusetts, 1846—A man who owned beach property defended himself when a public statute was passed stipulating that neither sand nor stones could be removed from the beach. He argued that the $20.00 fine imposed constituted a taking of his property by the state without due compensation. The court ruled that the law intended to preserve a natural embankment to a public port and that the owner deserved no compensation.

Boston, Massachusetts, 1853—When a man built a wharf beyond the boundary line for wharfs in Boston Harbor, the state of Massachusetts brought suit. The court ruled that the action was injurious to the general public, as the wharf intruded on a navigable estuary. "We think it is a settled principle, growing out of the nature of well-ordered civil society," the court determined, "that every holder of property, however absolute and unqualified may be his title, holds it under the implied liability that his use of it shall not be injurious to the equal enjoyment of others having an equal right to the enjoyment of their property, nor injurious to the rights of the community. . . ."

Los Angeles, California, 1915—As Los Angeles expanded into the countryside, new residents who moved near a brickyard owned by Mr. Hadachek argued that the industrial plant posed a health hazard. When the police closed down the long-established business, Hadachek sued and demanded the right to operate or be granted compensation for his business property, claiming that the property itself had depreciated as a result of the police order, from an approximate value of some $800,000 to about $60,000.

The case ultimately reached the U.S. Supreme Court, which ruled: "There must be progress, and if in its march private interests are in the way, they must yield to the good of the community." No monetary recompense was thus due Hadachek.

Euclid, Ohio, 1922—The Ambler Realty Company was denied permission to develop its land for commercial use. The U.S. Supreme Court ruled in 1926, after years of litigation, that the new zoning, which restricted the land to residential use, was indeed constitutional.*

Manhattan Beach, California, 1953—The owner of beach property was denied the right to develop his land for residential housing. The California Supreme Court upheld the town's right to restrict the land to recreational uses, and granted no compensation, stating that the owner could utilize the land for commercial recreational uses if he so desired.

Marinette County, Wisconsin, 1972—A middle-income couple was denied the right to fill in and develop a portion of their waterfront land because of wetland regulations. The Wisconsin Supreme Court ruled: "An owner of land has no absolute and unlimited right to change the essential natural character of his land so as to use it for a purpose for which it was unsuited in its natural state and which injures the rights of others. . . . It is not an unreasonable exercise [police power in zoning] to prevent harm to public rights by limiting the use of private property to its natural uses."

Ramapo, New York, 1972—The suburban town of Ramapo instituted a timed development program that severely restricts the rate at which certain parcels of land can be developed. When an irate property owner sued, the New York Court of Appeals upheld the growth-control measure, stating, "The undisputed effect of these integrated efforts in land-use planning and development is to provide an overall program of orderly growth and adequate facilities. . . . The landowner might be compelled to chafe under the temporary restriction, without the benefit of . . . compensation, when the burden serves to promote the public good."

New York City, 1978—Penn Central Transportation Company leased the air space above Grand Central Station to a corporation that wanted

*As will be discussed in more detail later, *Euclid* is the first Supreme Court zoning case, and represents a landmark decision of continuing importance today.

to build an office tower above the historic structure. The New York City Landmarks Commission denied permission for the development, as a large new building above the terminal would modify or destroy the appearance of the Beaux-Arts façade of the landmark building. Penn Central, claiming it would lose $3 million a year because of the decision, sued. The case reached the U.S. Supreme Court, which upheld the landmark designation and ruled that historic preservation was a declared form of community welfare, and construction that destroyed the façade would not be tolerated.

San Francisco Bay, California, 1980—Donald Agins purchased 5 acres of land in Tiburon overlooking San Francisco Bay, which is zoned for five potential house lots. In 1973, five years after the purchase, the city of Tiburon enacted an open-space zoning ordinance, which limits a site to one dwelling, with construction of four more houses possible with approval contingent on acceptance by the town of the environmental impact report of the particular plan. Agins claimed a $2 million loss in property value, though he had made no previous application or effort to use his property for one or more building sites. In its recent ruling, sure to be important in the 1980s, the U.S. Supreme Court unanimously declared that Agins had not sustained an unconstitutional taking of his property, which would require compensation. Limits placed on the development and preservation of open space in this case, the Court ruled, "are exercises of the city's police power to protect the residents of Tiburon from the ill-effects of urbanization." The Court, in its narrowly worded opinion, said, in effect, that ordinances limiting development in *specific* areas do not automatically deprive property owners of their private rights.

The Law of the Land. American land law is founded upon the Magna Charta, the thirteenth-century proclamation written after English noblemen rebelled against the constant encroachment and confiscation of their lands by King John. Signed and sealed by the king himself, the Magna Charta guaranteed the country's subjects that "no freeman shall be arrested, or detained in prison, or deprived of his freehold [private property] ... unless by the lawful judgment of his peers and by the law of the land."

By the eighteenth century, English scholars were shaping philosophical and legal thought based on the concept of private ownership of land; these doctrines would be instituted and enforced for centuries. The eminent Oxford professor of law Sir William Blackstone proclaimed in *Commentaries on the Laws of England,* his 1760s treatise on the doctrines of English law: "The third absolute right, inherent in every Englishman, is that of property: which consists in the free use, enjoyment and disposal of all his acquisitions, without any control or diminution, save only by the laws of the land." Based in part upon this hallowed tradition of English law, the fundamental sources of American jurisprudence, the Bill of Rights and the Constitution of the United States, were drafted.

The Bill of Rights proclaims: "No person shall . . . be deprived of life, liberty, or property, without due process of law; nor shall private property be taken for public use, without a just compensation." This dictum, which in 1791 became the Fifth Amendment to the Constitution, has from the very beginning been a founding tenant of land law and land regulation in America. But, as we shall see, *when* compensation is actually due and *what* is "just compensation" become major issues that affect the value of huge amounts of private property today.

The Fourteenth Amendment, passed in 1868, protects private property from legislation promulgated by one of the states: "No State shall make or enforce any law which shall abridge the privileges or immunities of citizens of the United States; nor shall any State deprive any person of life, liberty, or property, without due process of law. . . ."As we shall see, every word of the crucial Fifth Amendment continues to raise the most profound questions today concerning the rights connected to the private ownership of land.

POLICE POWER: WHAT IS IT?

When the Constitution was framed in 1787, representatives from each newly created state gathered to make a decision: What powers should be relinquished by the pre-existing colonies and vested in the new federal government. Control of interstate and foreign commerce, of defense, and of the treasury, among other powers, were delegated to the federal government.

Constitutional clauses were then drafted, specifying each power granted to the federal government by the states. Among these was the Tenth Amendment:

The powers not delegated to the United States by the Constitution, nor prohibited by it to the States, are reserved to the States respectively, or to the people.

The right of the states to self-govern eventually became known as the police power, a misleading term which, in fact, refers to government's obligation to act in the public interest, for wide public benefit. Some state constitutions specifically granted police power to local government; others assumed that localities within each state would naturally adopt this right, thereby rendering a specific clause unnecessary.

By the late nineteenth century, the concept of the police power was used in one case after another to justify the regulation of private property. It is out of this stream of legal history that a fundamental legal tenet was established: *Exercise of the police power does not obligate government to compensate a private owner of land.* This concept is completely at variance with the absolute private right of a landowner to use, control, and benefit from private property at will. It is grounded in the fundamental legal tenet that an overriding public interest of general, widespread benefit asserts a superior claim over private property. Zoning, as we shall see, becomes the outstanding example of this principle in land-use regulation. When the police power holds, because it is applied to all citizens (and all landowners) in like manner and for broad public benefit, no monetary compensation is due.

It took over a hundred years of sequential legal decisions for the full impact of the police-power concept to be fully felt. In 1831, a lower court in Boston decided that the collective rights of citizens were more important than the individual right of one property owner:

Police regulations to direct the use of private property so as to prevent it proving pernicious to the citizens at large are not void although they may in some measure interfere with private rights without providing for compensation.

The U. S. Supreme Court ruled on the police-power principle in 1887. Judge John Marshall Harlan, in the landmark case of *Mugler* v. *Kansas,* emphasized that

the exercise of the police power by the destruction of property which is itself a public nuisance, or the prohibition of its use in a particular way, whereby its value becomes depreciated, is very different from taking property for public use, or from depriving a person of his property without due process of law. In the one case, a nuisance is abated; in the other, unoffending property is taken away from the innocent owner.

As a result of this ruling, the property owner was denied his petition. The police power was invoked, the owner's interest was subordinated to an assumed greater public good, and no compensation was awarded.

As years went by, the courts broadened the potential for land-use controls through constant reinterpretation and general expansion of the definition of police power, as in the case of *Hadachek* v. *Sebastian* (see pp. 82–83), which marks the beginning of environmental regulation as a police-power matter in America.

Zoning as Police Power. The police power establishes the basis for most land regulation, including zoning. District zoning, now a widely accepted form of land-use regulation, was first implemented in 1909 in Los Angeles. (The first comprehensive zoning ordinance was enacted in New York City in 1916.) In 1924, under the direction of then Secretary of Commerce Herbert Hoover, the Standard State Zoning Enabling Act was prepared as a guideline for states and local communities. Sections 1 and 3, which follow, became the basis of every subsequent zoning ordinance:

Section 1, GRANT OF POWER—For the purpose of promoting health, safety, morals, or the general welfare of the community, the legislative body of cities and incorporated villages is hereby empowered to regulate and restrict the height, number of stories, and size of buildings and other structures, the percentage of lot that may be occupied, the size of yards, courts, and other open spaces, the density of population, and the location and use of buildings, structures and land for trade, industry, residence, or other purposes. . . .

Section 3, PURPOSES IN VIEW—Such regulations shall be made in accordance with a comprehensive plan and designed to lessen congestion in the streets; to secure safety from fire, panic, and other dangers; to promote health and general welfare; to provide adequate light and air; to prevent the overcrowding of land; to avoid undue concentration of population; to facilitate the adequate provision of transportation, water, sewerage, schools, parks, and other public requirements. Such regulations shall be made with reasonable consideration, among other things, to the character of the district and its peculiar suitability for particular uses, and with a view to conserving the value of buildings and encouraging the most appropriate use of land throughout such municipality.

By 1930, thirty-five states had modeled enabling legislation after the Standard State Zoning Enabling Act. Today, all states have done so, though many smaller communities and some cities do not have a local zoning ordinance. Nevertheless, 98 percent of all cities in America with populations in excess of 10,000, and many smaller towns which do have a zoning ordinance, now depend upon zoning as their fundamental method of land-use control. Zoning as an extension of the police power is clearly the most significant, consequential, and pervasive form of land law in America.

The constitutionality of comprehensive zoning was challenged early on and upheld in 1926 by the U. S. Supreme Court in the landmark case of *Village of Euclid* v. *Ambler Realty Company.* Euclid, situated on the rail line near Cleveland, was incorporated as a town in 1880. By 1911, the Ambler Realty Company, based in Cleveland, had begun to buy up property along the rail line in Euclid on the assumption that this would become valuable industrial property. However, in 1922, the first Euclid zoning ordinance was passed, designating part of the Ambler Realty Company holding for two-family houses, part for apartments, and part for industrial use. Ambler Realty sued, claiming that the new zoning ordinance diminished the value of most of the property, from the $10,000 an acre for industrial use to $2,500 an acre for residential use. The lower courts sided with Ambler, ruling, "There can be no conception of property aside from its control and use, and upon its use depends its value." However, the Supreme Court firmly supported the zoning ordinance on the premise that zoning regulations were a legal extension of a municipality's police-power right to govern. The Supreme Court was persuaded by the argument mounted by the village that zoning would enhance property values in general, although certain tracts would be adversely affected. "Under these circumstances," the Court declared in 1926, echoing the 1924 Standard State Zoning Enabling Act, "it must be said before the [zoning] ordinance can be declared unconstitutional, that such provisions are clearly arbitrary and unreasonable, having no substantial relation to the public health, safety, morals, or general welfare."

Two years later, the Court clarified its position on zoning in *Nectow* v. *City of Cambridge*. The plaintiff had requested a zoning change from residential to industrial use for land situated in a predominantly industrially zoned neighborhood. The town denied the request, and the property owner sued, all the way to the Supreme Court. The Court declared that the parcel had little value as residential property, given the character of the neighborhood, and that it would not harm the health and welfare of the community to rezone the land as the plaintiff had requested.

In these landmark cases, two basic principles were established. First, *zoning is legal and enforceable* as a police-power responsibility, even when private property value is lost. Communities must protect the health, safety, morals, or general welfare, and may have to encroach upon private interest to do so. Second, *zoning may be changed* if it is found that such a change does not endanger the health, safety, morals, or general welfare of the community. Between these two principles there is much room in which to maneuver, much room for controversy.

The general state of the art, then, is this. When broad general benefit can be claimed and regulation applies equally to all citizens of all types and all classes (as in a community-wide zoning ordinance), then a police-power situation exists. When there is presumption of such benefit relating to matters of health, safety, morals, or general welfare, it has been established through modern American judicial history that communities are not required to purchase these benefits for the citizen at large; rather, these are benefits to which all citizens are entitled and which government is obliged to attempt to provide. Of course, as a matter of practical reality, no community has now or ever has had sufficiently large capital assets to purchase any and all land that might in some way obstruct such general benefits. Thus, under the police-power authority, state and local governments may act in a way to promote the general public good without compensating private landowners. If, as a consequence, private property is adversely affected and devalued, the private owner is not entitled to compensation. As will be discussed in Chapter Five, nor is the individual owner required to relinquish a value benefit if one is created by zoning or other police-power regulation.

Private citizens and businesses go to court regularly when they believe that a public regulation, such as a new form of zoning or a new type of historic preservation ordinance or a more restrictive form of environmental regulation, goes beyond a reasonable interpretation of the police-power authority. And they go to court with one of two objectives: either to have the ordinance voided or to force the encroaching government to buy their land at a fair market price under the so-called rules of eminent domain.

EMINENT DOMAIN

When a specific individual situation or related situations occur in which private property is to be physically possessed and used "for the public good," but no general *broad* public benefit is necessarily demonstrable, then the government is required to buy the needed property through the exercise of its eminent-domain power. However, unlike the police power, which permits regulation of private land without compensation, eminent domain procedures require acquisition of private property by government through payment of full market value to the owner. The common legal term to describe the public purchase of private land is a "taking."

The right to exercise the power of eminent domain is limited by two constitutional restrictions, as outlined in the Fifth Amendment. First, the forcible taking of the property must be for "public use." Second, the government must compensate the owner for the taken land. The private owner's power is, nevertheless, severely restricted: he *must* sell.

Police Power vs. Eminent Domain. In deciding questions of equity when private ownership rights are abridged by public power, the fundamental question that must always be addressed is: Does the regulation of private rights constitute a permitted exercise of *police power*—in which case no compensation is due—or does it constitute a *taking* of private property—for which the owner is entitled to be fully compensated? This is not an abstract question debated solely in moot court at law schools around America. It is, rather, an issue that drives to the foundation of American society and that affects the value of much contested land in America.

Over the years, those who own private property have tried vigorously to expand the definition of "public use" so that a broader range of government regulation would entitle the owner to secure market-value payment. Public agencies and legislators, on the other hand, faced with the desire to regulate and control land, presumably in the public interest but with always limited financial means, endeavor to invoke regulation in ways which do not require monetary compensation to private owners—in other words, through the exercise of police power. In 1977 alone, $500 million worth of taking claims were pending against the federal government.

Nowhere is this conflict more dramatic or more decisive in law making than in the 1920–1922 litigation between the Pennsylvania Coal Company and Mr. and Mrs. H. J. Mahon. In the 1870s, the Pennsylvania Coal Company owned property on which the Mahons' house was eventually built. The Mahons' deed expressly stated that Pennsylvania Coal retained the mineral rights to the land and that it could, therefore, return to mine the land in the future.

By the 1920s, the expanding coal mining industry in Pennsylvania began to undermine sewer and water mains, and even some buildings. To remedy this problem, the Pennsylvania legislature passed the Kohler Act in 1921 outlawing any mining that would cause the collapse or subsidence of public buildings, public-service structures, homes, and cemeteries.

Three months after passage of the Kohler Act, the Mahons received the following letter from Pennsylvania Coal:

Dear Sir and Madam:

You are hereby notified that the mining operations beneath your premises will by September 15th have reached a point which will then or shortly thereafter cause subsidence and disturbance to the surface of your lot.

Mahon, an attorney, filed a lawsuit with the Court of Common Pleas to have Pennsylvania Coal enjoined from mining his property. He acknowledged that the coal company had the right to mine by deed but that the Kohler Act forbade the resulting destruction of his property. Pennsylvania Coal, on the other hand, contended that the Kohler Act was unconstitutional, as it deprived the company of its rights and took property without due process.

The case reached the U. S. Supreme Court in 1922. Justice Oliver Wendell Holmes delivered the Court's opinion. In so doing, he defined the still applicable distinction between police-power actions and taking of private property:

Government hardly could go on if to some extent values incident to property could not be diminished without paying for every such change in the general law. As long recognized, some values are enjoyed under an implied limitation and must yield to the police power. But obviously the implied limitation must have its limits or the contract and due process clauses are gone. One fact for consideration in determining such limits is the extent of diminution. When it reaches a certain magnitude, in most if not in all cases there must be an exercise of eminent domain and compensation to sustain the act. So the question depends upon the particular facts.

The Supreme Court concluded in effect that the Kohler Act constituted a taking, which required the government to pay compensation. "We are in danger of forgetting," Holmes went on, "that a strong public desire to improve the public condition is not enough to warrant achieving the desire by a shorter cut than the constitutional way of paying for the change." But Holmes also stated, ". . . the general rule at least is, that while property may be regulated to a certain extent, if regulation goes too far it will be recognized as a taking." This statement from the bench remains the source of untold controversy whenever private land is severely regulated. At stake, of course, is owning property controlled by police-power limitations on the one hand, or being paid a fair price as eminent-domain compensation on the other.

The Balancing Test.   The stakes could not be higher. What hangs in the balance between a police-power action and a taking is whether or not the private owner is to be compensated. The line between these two alternatives is a fine one, and one the courts are constantly asked to draw. This obligation is referred to as "the balancing test." The *Mahon* decision offers a vague guideline but hardly a firm basis for a clear distinction between just regulation and unjust confiscation.

The question remains: How far can the government go? Private owners, lawyers, civic groups, environmental organizations, among others, have their own opinion of each separate case. Almost any position can be backed by precedent from a hundred contradictory rulings which vary from state to state. The Supreme Court has done little in recent years to clarify the controversy. What should be done when a community seeks access across private land to a beach? Should an owner be compensated for monetary loss when a historic building is preserved by regulation? What should be done when land, formerly zoned commercially, is rezoned for residential use? In each case, and in thousands of others, the rights of private owners are limited, and the value of their property is reduced. But are these valid police-power actions, or do they in fact qualify as takings?

As the interpretation of the police-power authority becomes increasingly broad, private rights are effectively diminished. "Public purpose" and "public benefit," as defined and understood by the courts, now encompass a wide range of social, historic, conservation, and environmental criteria which extend public power over land beyond earlier limits. Note, for instance, the significant 1980 Supreme Court ruling in *Agins* v. *City of Tiburon*. This is a most serious general trend of which owners of private land in America should be aware. Its implications testify to an erosion of private power over land and foretell the ever-present potential for the substantial erosion of value due to public regulation.

Mixed in with the issue these days is the added consideration of whether value loss due to regulation be judged on the basis of the most profitable or most valuable use of land—the so-called highest and best use —or, alternatively, whether an owner is simply entitled to any use which offers a "reasonable return" on investment. In other words, is the fair measure of value lost because of public regulation to be the discount from the highest possible value or simply the discount from a reasonable return on the investment?

Recent restrictive zoning, environmental legislation, and historic-district regulation, for instance, force owners to limit intended uses; oftentimes these regulations prohibit intensive development. Thus, the highest possible value cannot be realized. More often than not, court rulings on environmental regulation and historic preservation proclaim that so long as a private owner is able to garner a reasonable return from his property asset, no taking has occurred and no compensation is due.

Owners of private land in America are mistaken if they ignore this trend in legal rulings. The police-power authority of local and state government has been increasing for several decades. There is little indication this will change. At the heart of the issue is an ever-growing interest in land-use regulation and control of the land by increasing numbers of citizens. Simultaneously, public funds available to purchase affected private property are extremely limited and unlikely to expand significantly in years to come. The result is a nibbling away of private rights. When the nibble turns into a big bite, the case goes to court. But more often than not, the owner of private land will be required to comply, and to comply without being compensated.

JUST COMPENSATION . . .
OR JUST COMPENSATION?

Even when a taking is ruled and just compensation is due the private landowner, there is tremendous opportunity for conflict and disappointment. Some private owners feel they are justly compensated; others proclaim in agony that they were just barely compensated, and certainly not paid by the government anywhere near the value of their taken property.

Unless a previously negotiated agreement is reached, the level of compensation paid is usually determined in court. The basis for any decision is an appraisal. The owner is entitled to have one appraisal made; the government another. These figures are compared and may form a common ground for settlement. If no agreement is reached, the courts are required to decide upon the amount of the award. As prescribed in the Fifth Amendment, the procedure of a land taking is protected by the due process rights of citizens, that is, the right to a fair hearing or trial. The basis of judgment is supposed to be the value of the land taken. Market value is generally defined as the highest price which a buyer, willing but not compelled to buy, would pay, and the lowest a seller, willing but not compelled to sell, would accept.

In most litigated disputes over land, the value of land is based by the owner on the highest and best use of the land, a euphemism for that legally permitted use of the property which renders it the most valuable. For example, land zoned for either apartments or single-family residences will be evaluated generally as an apartment site when appraised by the owner to attain its value based on highest and best use.

Notice, however, that settlement in court is related only to market value. If apartment construction in the area at the time of litigation is unlikely, then the landowner is likely to be paid for a house lot, not the higher figure accorded a multifamily apartment site.

Other legal considerations taken into account also often devalue the compensation paid for the taking of private property. In determining market value, for instance, any reduction in value created by a valid exercise of the police power such as zoning—must be considered. Thus, raw land proposed for development as a shopping center but subject to a new zoning regulation that limits its use to single-family residential homes on one acre each would, if condemned, be valued as homesites, not retail business property.

Interim Depreciation. A potentially more devastating threat to private land values arises when public intervention is planned and announced far in advance of actual condemnation. For instance, a state or federal highway authority might plan to gouge a future highway corridor through the center of a city, as was decided in Baltimore, Boston, San Francisco, New York, and numerous other major cities across America during the 1950s and early 1960s. After the announcement is made, residential land values decline throughout the immediate "impact area," where the noise of cars and trucks, the fumes from exhaust, and the chaos and confusion of construction in years to come begin to impair the desirability of the area. As owners seek to move, sale after sale is made at ever-decreasing values. But condemnation hearings and appraisals may not begin for many months or even years after the project is announced, by which time the house or the apartment block is barely salable. Consequently, when the appraisal is finally made, very low market values in the area can be reported. That appraisal becomes the public sector's base for proposed settlement.

This problem of interim depreciation has been met with a variety of solutions. Some reform in this area has been apparent lately—for example, the establishment of earlier settlement dates and thereby higher levels of value. Pressure for even more equitable means of settlement continues to be exerted.

The person whose house happens to be adjacent to the proposed highway rather than directly within its right-of-way has a much more severe problem. As ruled by various courts, because his land is not physically taken, his damage by proximity is not compensable. A 1968 ruling summed up this situation when an established resident found that his house was not quite within the proposed highway right-of-way but rather would be located next to a newly constructed freeway: "The conditions of which appellants complain are obnoxious to all persons who live in close proximity to the state's freeway, but they must be endured without redress."

Other Problems of Eminent Domain.   In many instances when a taking occurs, just compensation or anything near to a just settlement may be difficult to obtain.

Item: A business is taken, wiped out, so that a highway may be built. Is only the value of the land and improvements lost, or is an anticipated stream of business profits also taken into account? The property can be appraised and its value haggled over. But when it comes to paying for extraneous value associated with location, good will, and business value, how is their worth to the private owner determined?

Item: A state government condemns wetlands owned by an oyster company as a bird sanctuary. How is this fertile wetland valued? Is it a nearly worthless swamp or a precious incubator of shellfish, wildlife, and a glorious adjunct to upland property? Is it worth $100 an acre, or perhaps $10,000?

Item: A forest products company owns precious redwood acreage condemned to become a state park. How valuable is that redwood? A well-managed, selectively cut and seeded forest is an eternal money machine. Should the land be assessed, then, in terms of the present value of a land acre or in terms of its presumed value as a continually productive resource?

When compensation is due as a result of eminent domain condemnation, the balancing test must first be passed. But for the private owner, that may be only the beginning of trying to obtain fair or just compensation for a public taking of private property.

Less-than-Fee Acquisition. A further refinement of government land acquisition with far-reaching implications is the very recent and growing practice of condemnation of only a partial interest in property. Because the acquisition is partial, public costs are reduced. What does this mean? And how is "partial interest" defined?

Traditional condemnation entails acquisition of the landowner's *total* ownership interest, known as the fee or fee simple. Title to the property passes from the private owner to the public purchaser. However, ownership of land includes holding not just a title but also a so-called bundle of rights: the right to develop raw land within legal limits; the implied right, if a building exists on the land, to maintain and modify the structure; the implied right to utilize space above the land, so-called air rights or development rights; and the right to excavate the surface and mine below the surface of the land.

There is, then, this bundle of rights associated with the ownership of land. Private owners have long separated these rights in commercial transactions among themselves. Farmers are regularly leased the right to enter and farm the topsoil of another owner's property. Mining companies are often leased the right to probe beneath another's land in exchange for a share of any valuable product that may be extracted. Most of the buildings in London are still constructed by developers upon land leased to them by owners of ancient estates.

Owners have always had the right to voluntarily sell or lease a partial interest in their property, as they do in the sale of subsurface mineral rights. Today, this approach in conjunction with a public agency can be effectively exercised to forward any number of important objectives, such as farmland preservation, historic building preservation, environmental conservation, and so forth, if the owner is willing.

But the right of public agencies to acquire a partial interest in property via condemnation is a very new twist to an older concept. *Kamrowski* v. *State of Wisconsin,* the leading case upholding the constitutionality of condemnation of a partial right of property, was decided in 1966. Private landowners were forced by the Wisconsin State Highway Commission to sell a scenic easement to their agricultural land between a highway, known as the Great River Road, and the Wisconsin shore of the Mississippi River. The scenic easement would guarantee no development of the private property it covers. The highway commission wanted to guarantee that the parkway would exist in a natural corridor, insulated from uncontrolled development. Mr. Kamrowski, an outraged landowner, claimed that the condemnation action violated the Fourteenth Amendment's prohibition against deprivation of property without due process of law. He argued that the enjoyment of the land's beauty was not a justifiable public use. But the Wisconsin district court disagreed, finding that the protection of scenic resources along highways was indeed a valid public use:

The concept of the scenic easement springs from the idea that there is enjoyment and recreation for the traveling public in viewing a relatively unspoiled natural landscape, and involves the judgment that in preserving existing scenic beauty *as inexpensively as possible* [emphasis added] a line can reasonably be drawn between existing, or agricultural . . . uses, and uses which have not yet commenced but involve more jarring human interferences with a state of nature. . . .

In this landmark ruling, the court went on to affirm that public use did not require public occupancy—indeed, that public use was valid by holding that the occupancy was visual. The outraged landowners were then advised:

Once it has been determined that the use for which property rights are taken is a public use, and that the taking is necessary for such use, neither a property owner whose property is taken in return for just compensation nor a property owner whose property is not so taken is in a position to claim that he is denied equal protection of the law.

Thus, the Wisconsin State Highway Commission gained effective visual control over a portion of private property for the assessed value of the easement rather than for the higher fee-acquisition cost.

In certain special instances when a reasonable statute exists, when reasonable compensation is offered, and when the matter is handled skillfully, the public may effectively benefit while the private owner continues to use his property at least for a reasonable purpose. In the best of instances, through public condemnation or acquisition of a portion of the bundle of ownership rights, the public environment may be protected or enhanced at minimal cost; fair compensation is paid to the owner; private owners retain title to real property and may use their property effectively, and continue to pay local real-estate taxes on it, though at a reduced level, as a reflection of the loss of certain rights or value. The community tax base is not seriously eroded. The acquisition is effective but comparatively inexpensive and, therefore, more public money is available over the years to purchase additional partial interests in properties that are of undeniable public value. This innovative and often sensible solution leaves underlying land use in private hands while assuring a continuing public benefit.

WHOSE PUBLIC INTEREST?
THE PRIVATE SECTOR WAKES UP

Regulation in the name of the public interest is always presumptuous. It presumes that someone knows what the public interest is, or even that someone knows *who* the public is.

Over the years, the definition of public interest with respect to the regulation of land has come to rest on a sequence of court decisions which generally restrain private action and activity. "Public interest" is commonly defined, particularly in environmental regulation, as protection of the natural environment, the water, the air, and the land, when that land is of significance for the health and welfare of of the general public.

Quite recently, private industry and determined individuals have begun to suggest that there may indeed be a wider definition of "public interest." A new balancing test is suggested, a test which invokes *overall community welfare*. This suggested new definition asks that, along with environmental impact, other significant aspects of life be considered, such as jobs, tax revenues, and local wages. Under such a definition, a much broader interpretation of public "health, safety, morals, or the general welfare of the community" is proposed.

There are signs that such a change is under way. Early in 1978, the Los Angeles City Council passed an ordinance to encourage energy conservation and to lessen pollution. The approach: mandate a doubling of the cost of electricity used by industry during peak hours. Over seven hundred companies went to court to argue that higher peak hour power costs would force work shifts to night operations and would thereby disrupt workers' lives. This change in turn, they pointed out, would harm the *work* environment. The court agreed. It granted the companies an injunction and ordered the city to study the potential *impact on workers*. Even if the case should ultimately go against the private manufacturing companies, the grounds of the debate reveal a new horizon, at least when it comes to the specialized arena of environmental regulation through police power.

As early as 1975, courts began to broaden their interpretation of the "environment" beyond that of air, water, and wildlife. By claiming that environmentalists were causing a negative social and economic impact, private business interests began winning cases. As Ronald Zumbrun, a Sacramento, California, lawyer who argues cases for companies told *Wall Street Journal* reporter G. Christian Hill, "We have no trouble convincing the courts that the environment includes human beings and social and economic impacts." Other lawyers, however, such as John Phillips, a leading environmental lawyer who protested the stay of the Los Angeles ordinance, found the decision "one of the most outrageous I've ever seen. It's clear abuse of environmental law by industry. Their claim borders on the absurd."

PUBLIC POWER AND LAND VALUE

Vast stretches of land on the North American continent were initially sold or given away to private interests, in part so that government could divest itself of land-management responsibility. In two centuries America has turned from a country of unquestioned private rights over private land to one of very questionable private rights over private land.

Today, at all levels of government and at every turn, there is increased regulation and litigation. As this trend consolidates, the most profound changes occur to the value of land itself. In some situations, the private owner becomes the beneficiary of an indirect or even direct bonanza; more often, regulation brings land devaluation unaccompanied by compensation.

In the chapters which follow, especially those concerned with zoning, regulation of natural lands, farmland, the preservation of buildings and historic districts, and environmental regulation itself, the intricate interconnection between private rights and land values is a continuing theme. Along with local demographic and market trends, the public regulation of private rights will have more to do with land values in the future than any other factor. At no other juncture is the intersection of land, power, and wealth so clear, and so decisive.

PART TWO

CHANGING LAND VALUES
IN A CHANGING COUNTRY

FOUR

LAND

AND TAXES

Taxes are a force of immense power over the spirit of men. Tax policy can induce men to work hard, to risk fortunes, to take chances on the expectation of success and profit. It can also encourage men to be devious, even dishonest. Taxes have started revolutions, caused war and death.

Almost every form of tax that is encountered by each of us during the span of a lifetime affects the land. The use, appearance, cost, value, and owner are all influenced by them. Taxes determine whether a working farm continues to produce crops or whether it is forced into sale and conversion as a housing development. They influence the quality of commercial buildings erected all over America. More than any other single force in our society, taxes control the appearance of our communities.

Instructions given planners, architects, and designers are motivated by tax considerations. Landowners, building owners, land developers, land speculators, and land investors act in response to the dictates of tax policy. All listen to them intently, for they speak with the voice of authority and the power to control through local land-assessment practices, state regulation, federal income-tax codes, and federal inheritance-tax practices.

SPECIAL CHARACTERISTICS OF THE PROPERTY TAX

Real-estate tax, and especially the tax on open land—unlike any other tax with the exception of the inheritance tax—is a direct tax on wealth. When your house and yard are assessed and taxed, the basis of the tax is the value of your property and a measure of your wealth. The tax on property wealth is the largest income-producing tax for local government. In New York State, for example, local property taxes generated $8.5 billion in revenue in 1977. In contrast, all state and local sales taxes in New York, which has one of the highest rates in the United States, amounted to only $4 billion; and all states and local income taxes there, the second most populous state in the nation, generated about $5 billion.

The differences between the property tax and all other forms of taxation illuminate a set of fundamental, contemporary connections and controversies involving land, power, and wealth. First is the rationale behind the property tax. Consider for a moment the other daily and annual taxes which are commonly levied. The sales tax, one of the most pervasive in daily life, adds to the price of items we purchase. Part of the cost of consuming, it reduces effective buying power. It is levied on all who purchase, regardless of any other attribute of their income or wealth. And it is avoided if purchases are avoided.

Personal and corporate income taxes extract money from the private sector in another way. The earnings of individuals and companies are subject to a "progressive tax"; that is, the rate of taxation escalates as income increases, as opposed to the fixed percentage rate charged in sales tax. However, like the sales tax, the income tax is a levy on disposable income.

The tax on capital gains is very much the same and represents the government's cut siphoned off profits. When a capital transaction occurs at a loss, the government extracts no revenue. Indeed, it joins in sharing that loss. Each year it allows the individual or corporation to offset capital profits against capital losses. If no profit is realized, the capital loss deduction may even be carried forward and used in subsequent tax years.

The real-estate tax, however, is *not* related to income, profit, expenditures, or the ability to pay; and its level is absolutely controlled by a local public taxing authority. These unique features of the real-estate tax tend to ignite serious controversy. Taken together, they provide the foundation for the recent citizens' property-tax revolt movement, sparked by passage in California of Proposition 13.

Indeed, it is not possible to find an aspect of American life that touches more people in more ways than the local property tax. Its rate determines a cost that is borne by landowners, building owners, and tenants of every kind. The enormous impact of the local property tax on the cost of life is made all too clear when we realize that, excluding financing cost, as much as 25 percent of the money paid to rent a house or apartment, or to operate a house or building, goes to local property tax.

REAL-ESTATE TAX: ITS INFLUENCE ON VALUE

All else being equal, when property taxes go up, land values go down.

This simple statement appears to be a contradiction. But is it? Shouldn't real-estate taxes rise as land values increase? As pointed out earlier, taxes on real estate are not exclusively related to value. They also rise and fall according to need—need to finance the local public treasury.

Often ignored, indeed far from clear to most people, is the significant impact that tax *expense* has on the *value* of land and property. It is this relationship that is proclaimed in the apparently contradictory but, in fact, accurate statement that *the higher the taxes, the lower the property value.*

Some people understand this phrase from bitter experience. These are people who find they cannot sell their homes in Boston or Fall River, Massachusetts, or Nassau County, New York, because real-estate taxes have climbed so high; these are people who cannot sell their loft buildings in downtown Newark for the same reason. These are people whose vacant land is in the highest-cost tax district in town. The profound influence that tax levels have on the value of all real estate in America is so important and so subtle that one must pay close attention to this relationship. It is a relationship not easily discovered and difficult to measure. And it is a relationship that public officials charged with imposing taxes prefer to ignore and refuse to discuss openly.

The annual property tax is a basic cost of private ownership of real estate that must be paid and generally cannot be trimmed by sound management or individual frugality. Moreover, in many places around the country, the property tax can climb upwards of 25 percent of all annual costs for operating urban commercial property. In rural residential areas, real-estate taxes are likely to represent no more than 10 percent of all annual operating costs, while on open land, property tax is generally 0.5 to 2.0 percent of the market value of the property.

As an example of how property tax reduces the market value of real estate, let us compare two identical buildings which have exactly the same location, income, and operating expenses; the only variable is the annual real-estate tax as shown in the table below.

VALUE OF TWO IDENTICAL BUILDINGS AT TWO DIFFERENT TAX RATES

ITEM	BUILDING 1	BUILDING 2
Gross income	$15,000	$15,000
Annual operating expenses (excluding real estate taxes)	(4,000)	(4,000)
Property taxes	(1,000)	(1,500)
Net income	10,000	9,500
Property value[a]	125,000[a]	118,750[a]
Additional value	**6,250**	—

a. Based on an assumed capitalization rate of 8.

The tax on building #1 is $1,000; the tax on building #2 is $1,500. In all other respects—gross income and annual operating expenses—financial characteristics are similar. As a result of this single variable of $500 in the property tax, and assuming a capitalization rate of 8, building #1 is likely to be appraised at $6,250 more than building #2.

With a parcel of undeveloped land, the relationship between the property value and the tax bill is somewhat more subtle, more difficult to quantify. But any prospective purchaser should ask what the tax assessment and potential tax expense are on any parcel of land. All else being equal, a prospective purchaser will buy the land that carries the lowest tax cost. This likelihood creates a "softer" market for equivalent property with a higher tax; thus, the value of the property is reduced because of the underlying tax expense.

The vivid impact of this subtle relationship between property value and taxes can be seen on certain streets which, at their centerline, define a tax boundary between school districts. On one side of the street, houses are located in a school district that is able to operate with only modest assessments to residential property owners. Perhaps this particular school district is predominantly rural, or perhaps within it there is a valuable commercial or industrial center, which pays most of the taxes. Across the street, houses are located in a school district of equivalent quality; but here the district depends entirely on a fully developed residential area for its local tax revenue. The tax bill on this side of the street could be twice that of the other. School costs usually claim close to half the total local property tax. In this situation, a house of equal size and quality in the lower tax school district will sell for more—perhaps considerably more.

What establishes value, then, is not only the quality and location of real estate. People also compare expenses to own and to operate. This basic fact is crucial to any understanding of the social, economic, and political interlinks which motivate people in relation to any proposition of public policy (such as subsidized housing development or public works projects), which affect real-estate taxes.

HOW THE LOCAL PROPERTY TAX IS ESTABLISHED

Each year, it works like this. Local government leaders project a budget for the coming fiscal year. They then analyze the special external sources of operating income they can expect, such as significant funds from the federal and state governments. A few other sources—rents, licenses, use fees, county fees, and the like—also contribute revenue. When these sources of income are added up, they generally account for 30–50 percent of the projected budget. The rest—all of it—comes from one source: tax on local real estate.

Real-Estate Assessment and Taxes: How They Are Calculated. In almost every community in America, all land and property improvements are reviewed and valued by an assessor, an elected or appointed local government official. He is the person who checks the condition of the roof and fences and barnsiding, and the quality of the materials used to construct the building, whether it be a split-level two-family suburban house in Kansas City or the Sears Tower in Chicago. On the basis of his personal, and usually individual, inspection, he estimates the current full market value of the property.

Next, a very mysterious thing happens to the appraised market value for that property. This market value estimate, as if it were a private matter too delicate to bandy about, is converted to a sort of code, the "assessed value," which is usually arrived at by subjecting the market value to a simple arithmetic manipulation. For instance, the full market value may be reduced by a standard factor, say, 25 percent of itself. In many communities, the assessed value is the only figure shown on public records. (Obviously, since an arithmetic manipulation is involved, and since this practice has been going on over many years but at different ratios, at different times, it is inevitable that communities which do not frequently update market values and assessed values are communities in which there will be inequitable assessment.)

But the tax bill still cannot be printed out and mailed. One more significant massaging of the figures goes on first at the town hall. A "tax rate" must be determined. The tax rate is that percent of the assessed value figure which must be charged to meet projected budget needs. The tax rate is usually publicized in the newspapers, to the loud cries of anguish from the captive population, as a rate per $100 of assessed value. Reducing the rate to an expression per $100 is a device that makes the number look innocuous. It is only when that rate per $100 is multiplied out by the full assessed value of property that the real cost becomes clear.

For instance, if all local property has an assessed value of $20 million, and $500,000 is needed, then the tax rate becomes $2.50 per $100 of assessed value. If a house carries an assessed value of $20,000, then the annual property tax is $500 ($20,000 ÷ 100 × $2.50).

Assessment Methods: A Quick Review of How Value Is Established. If you understand how the assessor makes his judgment, it is possible to determine whether he has made a mistake. Every community sets aside a time each year when the property owner may examine the assessment rolls and contest a change in property assessment. There is no reason to accept the tax bill if you think there has been a mistake in the assessor's judgment. The day the assessors are available for discussion is still called, in most places and quite appropriately, grievance day.

There are three ways in which property may be assessed. The most common is the *comparative method*, described earlier. In this approach, the property to be assessed is compared to one or several of like qualities, in a similar location, that has recently been sold. Differences are noted, and factors assigned to these differences will either add to or reduce value. A determination is then made by comparing the two. The comparative method is used for assessing almost all undeveloped land and most residential property.

For buildings, but obviously not for land, a second basic assessment method can be applied, the so-called *replacement cost method*. Present replacement costs are estimated and deductions of value assigned for physical depreciation, then the presumed value of the land is added.

Numerous individual judgments are involved in this approach. How are special details, fine wood paneling, carved moldings, indeed any unusual detailing or design element, to be assessed? These features, which may have great value to the owner or a potential buyer, may be of little value to the assessor. His indifference to these elements may be acceptable if a relatively low assessment is sought—say, for tax purposes—or because you are interested in buying the building. On the other hand, if a high assessed value is desired, perhaps in order to qualify for a larger mortgage, the assessor's indifference is likely to be unfortunate. (Valuing historic buildings—a field of growing significance to buyers, sellers, and financial institutions—is becoming something of a specialized art which offers great opportunity for interesting and sophisticated work in assessing, an important professional specialty.)

The assessor must also assign a rate of physical depreciation to the structure. No doubt, with an older house there is some, perhaps even considerable, depreciation. This factor becomes a most crucial judgment, one which can greatly affect assessed value. An interested individual should question and thoroughly examine the assessor's assumption with respect to depreciation. A significant increase or decrease in assessed value can sometimes result from a well-presented and supported discussion on this point.

The *income method*, the third means of assessment, is used primarily for business property and rental housing. The underlying premise is that land and buildings may be valued as a commodity that produces a stream of income. Buildings assessed in this way are valued on assumptions related both to the likely future net earnings from the real estate and to judgment about the future desirability of the location as a place to own property in coming years.

Land Assessment: Current Use vs. Highest and Best Use.   Open land cannot be appraised by the replacement cost approach, for there is no way to replace it. Nor can land usually be appraised by the income approach, unless it happens to be a very productive farm. But its current value can still be assessed in one of two ways. The land can be appraised on the basis of either "current use" or an assessor's judgment as to its so-called highest and best use. Between these two determinants there is often a world of difference.

"Current use" is self-explanatory. A farm is a farm. If an acre brings in a free and clear net income of $500, that income can be used to deter-

mine the farmland's value through the income method, or by comparison of the property to the recent sale value of other similar farmland nearby. The same approach can be used to assess land that is being mined or cut for timber. No value is added for a possible change in future use.

The alternative is to look to the future, to establish a value based on highest and best use, a phrase that is, at best, misleading. "Highest" refers to the use that will render the greatest value to the underlying land, the highest value that can be foreseen given such determinants as location, zoning, and the way the community is evolving. "Best use" is a meaningless phrase. "Best" in whose view? For whom? For what purpose? None of these questions are asked or dealt with, though they should be. So the phrase "highest and best use" is a euphemism for appraising a piece of land at the highest market value, and therefore at the highest tax level, that can possibly be justified.

The assessment policy selected by each individual community may

SUBURBANIZATION, PENNSYLVANIA, 1972

Taxing open land at its "highest and best use"—in other words, at its most valuable use—may force agricultural land into development. Higher taxes based on speculative future uses levied as a result of public policy often become an unbearable financial burden to the farmer who attempts to preserve his land from encroaching suburbanization.

have far-reaching repercussions on the land. For instance, it can force conversion of farm field into housing development. Let us assume that there stands a field of corn adjacent to a residential subdivision, and a town is expanding toward the field. If that cornfield is appraised at highest and best use, it is valued and subsequently taxed not as agricultural land but as a residential development site. While farmland nearby may be worth $500 an acre, as subdivision land the farm is appraised at, let us say, $5,000 an acre. In this case, the farmer receives a tax bill ten times the amount it would be were the land classified as a working farm. Eventually, the farmer may be forced to sell a portion of his property to pay the annual real-estate tax, or he may decide to sell it all rather than be taxed for value he is not in fact enjoying. The assessor's shimmering vision between the rows of ripe corn becomes a self-fulfilling prophecy, as the Glen family farm is sold and gives way to Glen Acre Farms, a planned suburban community.

Because of the eventual impact of assessment policy on land development, public officials in every community are armed with a potent and volatile authority. A determination to assess at highest and best use creates a self-fulfilling prophecy, which will obliterate in time the open lands near a growing community. If highest and best use is to be maintained as a land-appraisal concept at all, I suggest a refined definition of "best." The promise of "best," a worthy concept to say the least, should be accorded a more contemporary meaning. As part of the appraiser's charge, the character of the land itself should be taken into consideration; the impact of change on the immediate surroundings should be considered; the longer-term goals and interests of the affected community, and even region, should be given weight. When the reasonable claims of terrain and environment, neighborhood and community, have been truly considered, it may be possible to arrive at a sustainable and supportable definition of "best use."

The public-policy decision of what method to use to assess and tax the land is a crucial determinant of all subsequent aspects of community growth and change. It affects population growth rates; it deeply influences when property will in fact come into development; its influence over land use is profound. This is dynamite, unlabeled. And too often it is in the hands of amateur arsenists rather than respectful demolition experts.

The local real-estate tax on land can be used with decisive authority to control community development. For example, if a community wishes to limit its growth, preserve open space, and maintain productive farms, it can assess land on a current-use basis. This permits a present owner to "carry his land," that is, to pay taxes at a level that assumes vacant or agricultural values. In this instance, the farmer or landowner is encouraged to hold on, to leave the property in its current use. On the other hand, perhaps to stimulate dense development downtown—which conserves energy, reduces sprawl, and reduces the potential length of needed roads and utilities—a community might want to force an intense use of land that remains empty in the town center. In this case, the community can assess such property at a highest-and-best-use level. The owner of undeveloped lots there is then likely to be anxious to sell or develop his property in order to help offset the higher costs.

LEGALIZED TAX FAVORITISM: WISE INEQUITY OR OUTDATED ABUSE?

When it comes to property-tax policy, the line between wise inequity and outdated abuse needs to be looked at anew. After all, privileged treatment to any one group raises the tax costs to everyone else in town. Older justifications for special treatment and lower taxes through preferential assessment, real-estate tax-abatement programs, and tax exemptions are worth considering. Each lowers the tax on favored categories and raises, by necessity, the tax on all others.

Preferential Assessment. Preferential assessment—the unequal assessment of properties of theoretically comparable value—is the most common form of tax favoritism. The old-fashioned way to obtain a preferential assessment was to send the assessor a bottle of Scotch at Christmas. Today, that may still be effective in a rural hamlet, but more subtle political and economic muscle is usually involved. Generally, a property is accorded a preferential (lower) assessment as a consequence of a particular policy or as a result of a sustained claim of economic hardship.

In some communities, however, preferential assessment is a commonplace practice, and not always justified by economic hardship. In Washington, D.C., it was discovered in 1977 that the twenty most valuable commercial properties in the city, including that of the *Washington Post* (then the sixth most-valuable property in town), were grossly underassessed. After considerable public embarrassment among certain blue-chip owners, and in the office of the assessor, a court ordered that properties throughout the city be reassessed. Millions of dollars of additional revenue are now being obtained from these commercial properties.

Most often, preferential assessment occurs quite naturally in communities where property reassessment is infrequent. Such a system generally permits older assessments to remain fixed, based on market values of years gone by, which may have absolutely no relation to current property values.

111

For instance, let us assume a house carried an assessed valuation of $20,000 when it was built in 1960. The tax on that property, let us say, is $500, calculated at $2.50 per $100 assessed value. Twenty years later, assuming no reassessment, the house still carries an assessed valuation of $20,000. However, because of annual municipal budget increases, the tax rate is up to $5.00 per $100 of assessed value, yielding a tax bill of $1,000.

In 1980, a house of comparable size and quality is constructed across the street. It is appraised at 1980 market values for the land and construction costs, which in twenty years have increased, let us say, by 100 percent. Thus, the assessed valuation of the new house is $40,000, and the tax bill will be $2,000. The newcomer, an "outsider" in effect, pays 100 percent higher taxes than the established resident.

It is thus evident that the infrequent reappraisal of local property discriminates against new residents. The social and political reality is that people who vote do not wish to change the system. This practice of infrequent reassessment, which is, in effect, a system of widespread preferential assessment, pervades America. It is defended by local government on grounds that reassessment would be an extremely expensive undertaking. At the same time, it is important to note that local government is generally composed of homeowners, citizens who have lived in town long enough to get elected and to benefit from the system.

Another form of preferential assessment is underassessment of real property, a practice that is widespread. One of the most prominent arenas in which underassessment prevails is large, economically productive land holdings in remote rural areas, such as coal lands, timberlands, and oil and gas properties. Very often these properties are assessed and taxed at a fraction of their economic value based on current use. Throughout Texas, Louisiana, Tennessee, Kentucky, and elsewhere, rural communities which could enjoy substantial local property-tax revenue fail to because of flagrant underassessment of resource-rich property, a clear preferential benefit to large business interests.

Real-Estate Tax Abatement. "To abate" means "to decrease," "to deduct," "to reduce." And this is just what is done by municipal decree to the property tax for special purposes, such as to attract certain desirable industries or to assist certain favored types of construction within a community. Real-estate tax abatement is also frequently used to attract a larger share of new commerce, industry, and construction in the competitive economic war waged by some towns and even states against other communities.

The abatement is usually a partial exemption from property tax over a specified time, often for as long as ten to twenty years. In some instances, the tax abatement diminishes each year; in others, it remains constant. There is no reliable estimate of how much real-estate tax has been exempted from commercial and industrial establishments through abatement over the years. But every dollar that is not collected as a consequence is levied proportionately against other property owners.

In New York City, as an example, between 1968 and 1972 some $200 to $300 million in property-tax abatements were received by private developers. In the busy years of active new construction between 1976 and 1979, almost $60 million of tax abatement was granted to blue-chip companies, profitable leisure-time operations, and new hotels in midtown Manhattan, one of the few parts of the city that was stable and on the upswing even without the abatement inducement. Among the beneficiaries were IBM, granted a $7.2 million abatement for a $79 million new office building; American Telephone and Telegraph, granted a $5.5 million abatement for a new office building on a prime corner, at Madison Avenue and Fifty-second Street; and influential real-estate operators and investors, granted a $6.2 million for a new hotel built, at a time when hotel occupancy rates were at their highest level in years. During the same time period, exceedingly generous tax-abatement programs were often granted to residential property redevelopers and rehabilitation specialists.

New industry and construction sustain jobs, increase the economic base of a community, and eventually lead to a full-fledged property-tax–paying enterprise. But abatement is also a practice that encourages the wielding of influence and is fraught with opportunity for corruption. The stakes are high. The game is played by skilled politicians, lawyers, and businessmen who set up their own rules. The benefits received by the private sector require no exchange of visible, tangible, or traceable funds or property; yet they are directly connected to the accumulation of wealth through the use of land. Power is the broker along with, very often, a knowledgeable attorney.

Real-Estate Tax Exemptions. Not all real estate in any given locale is taxed. Not by a long shot. In most states, religious, charitable, and educational institutions are completely exempt from property tax. In addition, all property owned by a government—town, county, city, state, federal, or foreign—is exempt, as are properties held by public authorities. Justification for tax exemption in the first case is predicated on the argument that these institutions serve the public interest. Government property is not taxed because, in some respects, such a tax would be self-defeating: inasmuch as the tax expenditure would have to be covered by higher property taxes assessed on the private sector, a meaningless cycle of payment and receipt would be induced.

However, when closely examined, both of these theoretical justifications for property-tax exemption contain remarkable inconsistencies and inherent aspects of inequity. Religious, charitable, and educational institutions, which do serve the public interest, do not earn a stream of income and so certainly require support. Yet, over the years, many have accumulated vast amounts of urban and suburban real estate, as well as undeveloped land. Much of the property is not used directly for public-interest activities, and some of it is even leased to private profit-oriented operations. Nonetheless, in many instances, these properties remain sheltered from local property tax.

Government property-tax exemption raises questions of equity of another sort. Consider the largest cities and state capitals, where extensive government buildings are maintained. Here, local citizens pay a disproportionate real-estate tax because of the cities' large percentage of tax-exempt property. One such example is New York City, where the United Nations headquarters location services many foreign governments. Expensive properties are bought and maintained by these governments; and their staffs live in the city and enjoy the privileges of school, fire, police, and other city services. Yet the properties are tax-exempt. In effect, it can be argued, New York City private property owners subsidize the local, state, and federal government, as well as a host of foreign governments.

When all categories of tax-exempt property are totaled, the quantity of land involved, especially in cities, is considerable. In some of the largest and older cities, such as New York and Boston, as much as 40 percent of all property is entirely tax-exempt, whereas in some state capitals, such as Hartford and Albany, the percentage climbs even higher. By comparison, in suburban and rural counties, even those with the highest proportion of tax-exempt property, this figure is generally below 20 percent; and for most communities, the percentage is much lower.

Over the last decade, as operating costs escalated and property taxes soared, more and more institutions and organizations sought tax-exempt status. In many older cities, the amount of tax-exempt property has grown about three times as fast as taxable property. Obviously, this trend is a harbinger of disaster, and in part it explains the considerably high tax burden placed upon the shrinking proportion of urban real estate that remains without benefit of tax exemption.

Low-income and moderate-income public housing is also generally accorded total tax exemption or partial tax abatement. Few recognize that the more than one million units of public housing in America have a market value of at least $25 billion, all of which, since 1949, has been exempt from local real-estate taxes. Excluding the costs of any special programs run in conjunction with such housing, the local real-estate tax subsidy soars well over $1 billion a year.

An evolutionary patchwork of real-estate tax abatement and tax exemption has grown up in each state and in each community over the years, generally unnoticed and rarely thought about by individuals even when the next semi-annual tax bill is paid. But it is a part of the problem for those who do pay high levies and wonder why. It results not so often from direct abuse, though abuse does occur, as from ingrained inequities which are all but forgotten today.

TAX REFORM: IMPACT AND POTENTIAL

Whether as a result of new statewide mandates or as a consequence of local need for increased revenue, there is likely to be extensive reform of property-tax policies in America during the 1980s. I doubt that the older, traditional practice of haphazard, antiquated, and, at times, corrupt real-estate tax practices will be nearly so widespread in 1990 as they are today.

Assessment Reform. The impetus for assessment reform will not come directly from the federal government, which tried unsuccessfully in 1973 to set up a uniform standard for property-tax assessment. Politically wise senators and representatives shied away from any involvement in this extraordinarily sensitive issue. The Senate Subcommittee on Intergovernmental Relations, headed by Senator Edmund Muskie of Maine, simply reported:

For too long, the average taxpayer in most states has been at the mercy of inexpert local officials, arbitrary bureaucracies, and privileged interests. Antiquated administrative practices and insufficient commitment of resources have prevented even responsible officials from protecting the public interest.

At the local and state levels, inequality in assessment rates between types of property (residential, commercial, industrial) and inequality in assessment practices within each type have become more clearly recognizable. And as they have, the strength and breadth of the call for assessment reform mounts all over America.

Studies of or revisions to property-assessment practices are currently under way in more than twenty states, including Texas, California, Washington, New Jersey, and New York. In New York State, as elsewhere, the basic approach is to establish a single, uniform base for all assessment. This requires two enormous changes: the old, entrenched use of a percent of market value, the "assessed valuation," must be eliminated; and all property within each community must be reassessed at current full market value.

For many who own houses or land that has not been reassessed for years, the new figures will be a shocking jolt. Rising real-estate values over the last two decades are not fully reflected in most assessments. While it is clear that a formula based on current full market value could be more equitable, it is not as easy to accomplish a total reassessment program as it is to write about one. Assessment requires judgment, which must be exercised by people. Computers can store the data, but they cannot evaluate it. The cost of a community-wide reassessment program in terms of salaries, administration, data processing, and new records is considerable. Because most local governments cannot afford the operation, they will require state aid.

Furthermore, there is understandable, politically motivated reluctance on the part of many local public officials to undertake assessment reform. Rather, local government, by and large, prefers to bemoan its fate, even to decry the misguided bureaucrats in the state capital who advocate assessment reform. In turn, most property owners, although they do complain about taxes, are secretly beset with private suspicions that their own property taxes are lower than they might otherwise be; and they fear that any change will be a significant increase.

Then there is the considerably more explosive and controversial question: Will relative proportions of the levy be shifted as a result of full value assessment? What policies will be established to decide what types of property (such as residential, commercial, industrial) will pay how much tax? After all, and at least theoretically, the reform in tax-assessment practices is not expected to raise more money annually for any given municipality; it is expected only to raise it more justly or equitably.

When it comes to the property tax, every owner of land has his own territory to worry about, and his own brand of concern and even fear to cope with. The established resident with an older home wonders if the ax is going to fall on him. The man with a business property tries to find out and even influence policy related to the use of full market assessment data. The corporation exploiting subterranen mineral resources fears that the real economic value of its lands will be recognized. The new homeowner paying much higher annual property tax than his neighbor across the street looks forward to some relief.

Proponents of the new system try to soothe all owners with statements such as this comment made by a state legislator not long ago:

Obviously, any tax system worth instituting must be structured to prevent one class or type of taxpayer from having to bear an overly burdensome tax liability. The property tax system thus cannot be permitted to cause excessive economic hardship to any class of property owner, whether that class be residential, commercial, utility, or otherwise.

This kind of statement may be useful to the local politician who is concerned about the political ramifications of his position on the issue, or to the fair-minded advocate of tax reform, but it does not alleviate the deep fear in the hearts of taxpayers.

There is no doubt that in the years to come, assessment reform will come to property owners in most communities. In my estimation, politicians are likely to try to ease the burden on the majority—the voters who own or rent a house in town. This is a politically sensible approach, advocated quite clearly by most politicians, including Senator Charles H. Percy of Illinois, whose opening remarks before Senator Muskie's Subcommittee on Intergovernmental Relations pointed a finger at some of the most flagrant inequities and abuses in the levy and administration of property-tax policy:

By reforming the administration of the [property] tax and broadening the base, hopefully we can lower taxes for many homeowners. The need for reform is demonstrated by such entrenched practices as gross underassessment of large mineral, commercial, and industrial properties; unnecessary and unfair exemptions for certain groups; indiscriminate creation of special taxing districts in which all properties are free from tax or taxed at low rates; Federal and State property including land or buildings leased to private industrial and commercial users, but which is not taxable by local jurisdictions; property owned by local jurisdictions which is leased by commercial and industrial use but which is tax-free because it is still owned by jurisdictions; . . . exemptions for classes of homeowners regardless of income or assets of such persons; administration of the tax by unprofessional, part-time assessors; fragmentation of states into hundreds of taxing jurisdictions.

In any future reform, a uniform policy must be established. It is essential that communities in the process of reassessment not turn to open, undeveloped agricultural or idle land as a primary source of increased property-tax revenue. Doing so will drive open spaces into a cycle of sale and development, which is usually unnecessary and uneconomical for the community. The increased revenue obtained from new residential housing derived from the land's conversion into residential subdivisions will in most cases not cover the additional public costs which must be expended in order to support and service the expanded population. And, thrown into the bargain of tax-induced new development is the loss of open spaces. The privately owned open space in each community is not just an aesthetic pleasure and ecological reservoir. It is, in economic terms, taxed terrain that earns a measure of revenue for the town without demanding any service expenditure by the community.

117

Reform in Preferential Programs. In the wake of growing tax protest across America, patchwork reform is taking place in local governments which permit property-tax inequity. In some communities, religious, educational, and other tax-exempt institutions have begun annual payments to local government "in lieu of taxes." In others, intergovernmental programs of reimbursement are being considered. In many states today, income earned on tax-exempt property may jeopardize the exempt status of the real estate and may even be used as a basis for a new property tax assessment. Elsewhere, the possibility of levying a municipal service charge on tax-exempt property to cover the public cost of maintaining, protecting, and servicing the property is being studied.

Many who support the cause of abatement and exemption reform now endeavor to bring current practices into the light of public scrutiny. They argue correctly that both are forms of subsidy paid by private landowners, though unrecognized by most residents as such. Reform advocates further suggest that real-estate taxes should be collected in full from all types and classes of property; once the revenue is in, a budgeted subsidy could then be accorded institutions, hospitals, etc. The subsidy, and its magnitude, would constitute a replacement of the hidden, indirect subsidy now paid in effect by higher taxes on other real estate.

Mandated statewide assessment reform is evident, as mentioned earlier, in a number of states. While the mandates take various forms, those being considered in New York State illustrate the sensitive political nature of this new tax policy. One faction in the legislature, the appointed and therefore politically insulated Temporary State Commission on the Real Property Tax, recommended that all classes of property be taxed at the same rate. This approach would replace the existing ad hoc practice in most communities of taxing homeowners at a rate lower than that placed on commercial and industrial property. The result would be to shift hundreds of millions of dollars in tax costs to homeowners and to relieve the owners of commercial and industrial property of this burden. In the legislature, Assembly Speaker Stanley Fink issued an immediate and politically based reaction: the chance of the commission's proposals ever becoming law, he asserted, was "remote."

Instead, the legislature, beholden as it is to the voting majority, is expected to recommend the continued classification of rates by property type. Once all property is assessed at current full market value, a higher tax rate will be applied to commercial and industrial property than to residential property. Supporters of classification point out that a shift to equal assessment, and the simultaneous elimination of the classification system, would be especially burdensome to homeowners in urban areas where there are large amounts of business property. A rough calculation suggests that such a shift in New York City would raise the average residential property-tax bill more than 100 percent.

But by far the largest and most effectively organized approach to reform is the nationwide movement to limit the amount of tax that can be charged to a fixed percent of the value of those properties that do pay tax. This is the crux of California's Proposition 13 and the various offshoots of it that are springing up across the country. This approach, however, does not address the need for specific local reform of long-entrenched privileges of preferential assessments, tax abatement, and tax exemption, which demand reevaluation as well.

How the real-estate tax is handled, and who suffers the least and who benefits the most, is a reflection of the interconnection between land, power, and wealth. In the final analysis, land in America remains the source not only of an enormous share of personal wealth but, through the property tax, of a considerable share of the annual income of almost all communities.

Education Budgets and Property Tax Unhinged: Toward a New Arrangement. In most communities, more than half of all the money paid in real-estate property tax each year is spent on education. As a result, towns with much valuable real estate tend to have schools with considerable funds to spend, whereas towns with less valuable real estate do not.

For instance, in New York State in 1978, the richest 10 percent of the school districts had over $86,000 in property value behind each pupil; the poorest 10 percent had about one fourth that amount, or roughly $20,000 per student. In the same year, in the high-property-value school districts, between $2,000 and $4,000 was spent by the school per year per pupil, while only half that amount was available in the poorer districts. In this instance, to raise only half the funds utilized per pupil in the well-off area, the tax rate would have to be twice as steep in the poorer neighborhood. Obviously, to raise the minimum funds necessary, property tax must be a higher percentage of market value in poorer districts than in high-property-value areas. In California, the situation is even more dramatic. There, forty-two elementary districts in the state have a tax base of more than $200,000 per pupil, while nineteen have a tax base of less than $10,000 per pupil. Thus, wide disparities in available funds per pupil occur across each state, even in adjacent communities, and the real-estate tax burden falls hardest on those least able to pay.

But there are distinct signs of change in the air. In years to come, the tax on land may no longer be used to finance education. In 1971, the

119

long-entrenched correlation between local property-tax revenue and the local school budget was challenged decisively in the California State Supreme Court landmark ruling in *Serrano* v. *Priest*. Ideally, the court ruled, every school district in the state should have and should spend the same amount of money per pupil per year. School financing based on local property tax "invidiously discriminates against the poor because it makes the quality of a child's education a function of the wealth of his parents and neighbors." This proclamation shakes one of the supporting pillars of the centuries-old link in the United States between land, power, and wealth.

This ruling is clearly the most significant to affect education in America since the U.S. Supreme Court's 1954 *Brown* v. *Board of Education of Topeka, Kansas* decision, which outlawed racial segregation in public schools. In moving toward unhinging the property tax from the school budget, the *Serrano* ruling throws the American way of financing public education into turmoil. Simultaneously, it eases the way for those who advocate limits and reductions on the property tax itself. Thus, while the California court sought a means to assure an equitable educational opportunity for all, it also may have inadvertently made the passage of Proposition 13 six years later politically feasible.

The *Serrano* case started a national avalanche of lawsuits and sparked a profound shake-up of primordial beliefs and assumptions. Within forty-eight hours of the *Serrano* decision, a similar legal action was filed in New York State. Not long after, additional cases were filed in New Jersey and Connecticut. Then, in 1973, the U.S. Supreme Court heard *San Antonio Independent School District* v. *Rodriguez*. Demetrio P. Rodriguez and fourteen other Mexican-Americans claimed denial of equal protection under the Fourteenth Amendment on the grounds that better educational facilities were available to children in wealthier school districts. In a 5–4 decision, the Court ruled that the suit was not a federal issue. Justice Lewis F. Powell, Jr., who wrote the majority opinion, argued that the Constitution does not require "absolute equality or precisely equal advantages" to all. When it came to tinkering with the property tax, and with the very foundations of the old connections between land, power, and wealth, a rather conservative Supreme Court backed away from these explosive issues and, in so doing, cast doubt on the *Serrano* decision.

The 1973 ruling in *Rodriquez* leaves the definition of the relationship between educational finance and property tax to the states and local communities. Consequently, there has been much state action on the issue. In New Jersey, Connecticut, and New York, high courts have ruled out excessive or predominant reliance on property taxes as a means of financing public education. In at least fifteen other states, including Arkansas, Colorado, Kansas, Maine, Mississippi, Ohio, and South Dakota, litigation focusing on the subject of public-school finance has been heard or is pending. Allen Odden, director of the Education Finance Center of the Education Commission of the State of Colorado, estimated in 1978 that legal battles and legislative skirmishes over school finance were under way in as many as forty states.

The present link between school finance and property tax continues to motivate a wide range of policies and attitudes, especially in smaller towns. Summer residents are cherished in resort areas, for they pay property taxes but do not draw on the school budget. People who move into town and use the school without directly contributing property-tax income, on the other hand, tend to be resented. This includes mobile-home dwellers, renters with families, and especially families who may live in tax-exempt or partially tax-exempt housing, as most public housing tends to be. Some towns seek to attract new real-estate tax "ratables," like shopping centers, offices, and even factories, particularly if there is a chance to do so without having to house, educate, and protect the people who might use and work in such places.

How states will revise the traditional relationship between property tax and school budgets is uncertain. The solutions which are likely to be diverse, will be hammered out across America over the next few years. States such as New Jersey advocate a basic shift from property tax to new or increased state income tax and business tax to finance education. Others support establishing a basic level of state support, with property-tax income available as a local supplement. Whatever the formula, it is probable that more affluent districts will endeavor to retain the right to vote additional funds or to sequester a portion of property-tax revenue for school budgets. It is also certain that the formulas devised for the allocation of public funds to local communities will be subject to intense lobbying and political pressure. Considering all of the social and environmental factors which actually make learning more effective, it is uncertain whether or not more equitable relationship between school quality and district wealth will create better-educated children.

What is clear is that the property tax is now entering a new stage of life. As the most resented tax of all, it is under attack, and even under control, in a growing number of states. It may not be for much longer the tax that can assure a fine foundation education for children who grow up in a wealthy community. If dependence upon property-tax income for local school budgets is severed, it is conceivable that resentment of the tax will mount significantly. Those who believe that the Proposition 13–style tax revolt is widespread now may be surprised in the future unless careful reassessment is made of the link between the property tax and school budgets.

121

PROPOSITION 13: THE ROOTS OF REVOLT

Through its right to tax property, local government possesses a source of power and a private fiefdom. In theory, tax-generated funds are to be used for programs of interest and importance to the local population. This is clearly illustrated in the local schools, where roughly half of all local property-tax money is spent. The balance traditionally has been devoted to the basic services a community requires, such as police, fire, sanitation, and road construction and maintenance.

These services obviously sustain and enhance the value of property that is being taxed, a correlation clearly perceived by residential and commercial property owners. Even the owner of undeveloped land in the taxing jurisdiction generally recognizes that basic community services, and even the existence of a school system, impute value to his property. Therefore, a reasonable level of taxation is felt to be just, even if the taxation is a tax on wealth, for it is wealth created in part by the services and programs and public works underwritten by property-tax–generated funds.

So long as property owners are able to perceive some link between property-tax payments and personally beneficial local public services, they may complain but offer little active resistance. However, since the 1950s, property-tax revenue has been used increasingly for a broader range of social and public services—such as the local funding of welfare, medical payments, and housing subsidies to the poor—which offer no discernible link to benefits received by those paying the tax. Critics of such expenditures from property-tax revenue argue that what amounts to a wealth tax is being used, in fact, to redistribute wealth on the broadest scale imaginable.

When locally levied property tax and beneficial services directly or indirectly received by the taxpayer are no longer perceived to be highly correlated, the seed of discontent blossoms. Some taxpayers leave the community. While the flight from the cities that occurred in the 1950s and 1960s cannot be exclusively characterized as disgruntled property taxpayers voting with their feet, this certainly was a significant contributing factor. As Martin Mayer, author of *The Builders: Houses, People, Neighborhoods, Governments, Money,* put it not long ago: "Among the reasons for the departure of the middle class [from the cities] was their observation that they got a much better buy for their tax money in the suburbs."

The property taxpayer, in effect, retains a measure of control in two ways. He is free to leave the taxing jurisdiction, thereby voting with his purchasing power and his disinvestment in the place he leaves. He may also vote to approve or oppose local public programs and bond issues which require expenditure of property-tax–based revenue.

In theory at least, there is a partial link between the revenue source and the revenue expenditure. I say "partial" because there is no direct connection between the vote and the payment of property taxes: citizens who do not own property obviously may vote; and, somewhat more problematical, citizens who own property in several places and are taxed locally in each may vote only in one locale. But in reality, property owners no longer live in a society in which local government is significantly bound by their interests and visions. And, what is even more certain, local government is often unable to control many of its expenditures. For instance, neither taxpayers nor local officials have much say over the increased costs of materials and operations, which reflect an inflationary economy.

In addition, when local government officials want to authorize a controversial long-term program, a commitment can generally be made without revealing its complete financial implication. A recent vivid example is the Southwest Sewer District project in Nassau and Suffolk counties, New York. There, taxpayers were told that the project cost would not exceed $291 million. A referendum authorizing the expenditure was approved. Ten years later, with the project still incomplete and now embroiled in numerous financial audits and a massive political scandal, it appears that costs to complete are likely to exceed $1.2 billion. County residents must foot the bill for approximately 12 percent of this much increased total. The revenue will come from higher property tax. The result has been a massive devaluation of real estate in the affected area. Property owners are now paying up to $500 each year for a system that has not even started operating, and an additional charge of $1,000 may come later for individual hookups. Taxes of $5,000 a year on a single-family house in the project area are not uncommon. By 1979, Suffolk County Executive John Klein had been voted out of office, principally because of the Southwest Sewer District cost overruns and consequent runaway property-tax increases accompanied by relative property devaluations.

The Revolt Itself. When the tax on property escalates to a level that is found to be intolerable—as the tax on tea did over two hundred years ago—there is a revolt among the people. This occurred for the first time on a large scale in 1978, when the Jarvis-Gann Initiative was ratified as an amendment to the California State Constitution, by a margin of 65 percent to 35 percent.

Proposition 13, as the amendment is widely known, defines and limits the amount of annual tax that can be levied against land and improved property in California. By law, it restricts the maximum amount of real-estate tax to no more than 1 percent of the market value established in the 1975–1976 fiscal year. Even more important, and generally unrecognized by most, is the additional limitation of permitted increase in subsequent years of no more than 2 percent per year in the amount of additional tax charged. This limitation on annual increases remains in effect until the property is sold. At that time, the property is to be reassessed and tax levied again based on no more than 1 percent of the new sales price.

Thus, today, two simultaneous and opposing efforts are under way. Property owners seek ways to hold the property-tax line where it is now and to limit its future upward spiral. To do so they support new statewide legislation such as Proposition 13. They are also wary of most forms of new public debt, whose cost must be paid over the years at current high rates of interest. And they are critical and more analytic than ever before about inflated municipal budgets for schools and public services.

At the same time, local government seeks ways to effectively raise more money. Like any sensible business, it turns first to conventional and reliable sources. For local government, the most obvious source, the easiest to collect, and the most inexpensive to administer is the property tax.

We are a nation of a growing number of property owners, though the average holding has decreased in size. Some own high-rise cooperative or condominium apartments in New York or Chicago; others own no more than a share of a vacation house used one or two weeks a year. With each new subdivision of a farm, the number of people who own land increases. This process has so ripened in America that the property tax is becoming subject to a new and growing form of political pressure. The great irony of the process is not to be missed. After several hundred years, the interests of the large-property owner and that of an enormous number of other citizens begin to coincide. This coincidence occurs as the result of the loss of large land holdings and incremental redistribution of America, sometimes forced by higher taxes. What has happened on the land will not explain the new, emerging conservatism in America, but it is part of the picture.

As more and more people own land in America, it becomes less politically expedient for local government to tax real estate at higher and higher levels. The democratic desire to serve all of those in the community with social benefits runs headlong into the newest political alliance: increasingly numerous property owners.

Proposition 13: The Immediate Impact. When voters in California approved Proposition 13, their vote signaled a surge of support for property-tax cuts and for a shift in the way local government is financed. Richard

P. Nathan, a senior fellow at the Brookings Institution, summed up the significance of this legislation when he remarked, "There is no doubt that it is a landmark in American Federalism."

Throughout California, the new legislation reduced total property tax by about 60 percent, with revenues from this source falling from $12 billion to about $5 billion. This savings in real-estate tax of about $7 billion annually is realized by those who own private property in the state. This sweeping statewide limitation of the property tax to 1 percent of current value slashed the total income of local government in California for the fiscal year beginning July 1, 1979 by more than 22 percent. For communities and school districts which relied most heavily upon the property tax, income in certain instances was cut by as much as 70 percent. Much of the anticipated adverse impact on public expenditures, however, was deferred by pre-existing state surplus funds of more than $7 billion and, since the late 1970s, by dramatic escalations in the value of California real estate. In 1978, the total assessed value of property in the state was $106 billion; in 1980, it has exceeded $155 billion. Statewide, rather than a deficit of some $12 million as initially projected for 1980–1981, William Hamm, the state's legislative analyst, projects a $60 million surplus.

While Proposition 13 is generally discussed as tax relief to the beleaguered, tax-bound homeowner, it is big business that definitely has been the big winner. Of the $7 billion reduction in revenue, business and agriculture qualified for $4.6 billion, or over 65 percent, of the savings. For instance, Southern Pacific Company, California's biggest private landowner, realized a tax savings of some $20 million. Oil and gas companies, such as Standard Oil Company of California, Getty Oil Company, Atlantic Richfield Company, Exxon Corporation, and Occidental Petroleum, all with large California holdings, enjoy costs savings which range from some $47 million in the case of Standard Oil down to $2.7 million for Occidental Petroleum.

All homeowners, on the other hand, realized a total tax reduction of about $2.4 billion. To the average homeowner, this translates into a substantial savings of about $50.00 per month, or $600 per year, a welcomed reduction in the annual cost of owning and operating a house. It also enables people who previously might have been able to purchase and afford to maintain their own home to do so again.

The windfall reduction in property taxes on large commercial and industrial enterprises caused a degree of corporate embarrassment and a flurry of public-relations questions. As a result, some of the companies, especially those such as banks and oil companies under political pressure and pressure from such citizens' groups as the California Campaign for Economic Democracy, have contributed substantial sums from the windfall savings to charities, cultural organizations, and other local enterprises that needed assistance.

Enlightened executives should realize that Proposition 13 tax reductions could lead to a backlash. If local government grows truly desperate for essential funds, taxes on commercial and industrial real estate may be raised through a repeal of that section of the amendment that addresses income-producing property. An alternative source of state and local revenue is likely to be increased personal income tax, a measure that would particularly affect corporate executives. Take as an example the Southern Pacific Company, which, as a corporate entity, has no vote in a state referendum. When the individual executive of the company must assess where he would rather have a tax levied, he is likely to prefer one against the corporation's property and profits than against his personal income.

Landlords, those owners of commercially operated residential property, share in the large $4.6 billion saved by commercial and agricultural enterprises; indeed, their portion is a handsome $1.2 billion, or over 2.5 percent of the total. But since tenants in states like California, which have a large number of apartment units, assert considerable political influence, landlords are required to pass along savings to tenants, as stipulated under Proposition 13. The alternative, California Governor Edmund G. Brown, Jr., warned, was mandatory state and local rent control. Many landlords, especially those who are members of such trade associations as the California Apartment Housing Association and the California Housing Council, complied with rent rollbacks or freezes. How long this will last, and what the state government will in fact do if it does not, remains to be seen.

Another, and often forgotten, beneficiary of Proposition 13 is the federal government. Local property-tax payments are deducted from personal and corporate federal income-tax levies. Thus, as the amount of local property tax is reduced, so is the value of tax deductions; and, as a consequence, federal income-tax revenues mount. When this often forgotten shift in tax payments is taken into account, private after-tax savings from reduced property tax is diminished, while income to the federal government from California property owners increases some $1.6 billion. Given this federal windfall, a strong case can be made for increased federal support to those California communities which especially suffer from the loss of property-tax revenue.

Longer-Term Consequences of Proposition 13. The overall goal of Proposition 13 is to reduce and then limit the tax cost of holding land and improved real estate. One direct consequence of this goal is to increase the

126

value of the affected property. Lower holding costs create greater market value. In addition, the assurance of a limitation on future taxes raises the desirability of all affected real estate. Immediate increases in property value were scored after the passage of Proposition 13. During 1980, property valuations in the state jumped 18 percent, a high rate compared to others around the country. Owners stand to benefit, then, not just from reduced operating costs but from the relatively higher market value accorded their land and buildings.

The least noticed aspect of Proposition 13, a limitation of future tax increases to 2 percent per year until the property is sold, will have other important long-range consequences. The amendment provides, for example, that if the tax based on 1975–1976 full market value was $1,000, it can only be increased to $1,020 the following year, and so on. The 2 percent is a compound rate, but it is nevertheless a very low rate of increase in an economy where inflation progresses between 10 and 15 percent a year, and higher. This provision, then, creates a systematic, statewide codified protection for insiders. As long as the owner does not sell, his property tax will not increase dramatically. An added consequence of Proposition 13, I suspect, will thus be a decline in the turnover of residential property. If values of real estate continue to escalate anywhere near the annual rates they have in past years, homeowners will soon be finding their property grossly undertaxed, just as it is across the country where no reassessment has occurred for years. It will become financially hazardous to move, to shift out of the old tax haven into a new house or a newly purchased older one that must be reassessed and may be taxed at up to 1 percent or a new and much higher market value. The provisions of Proposition 13 could even lead to a substantial increase in the number of residential houses that are rented out, a device whereby the owner does not relinquish a favorable property-tax protection under Proposition 13 and is yet able to earn rental income at a level that reflects the current market.

Tax Revolt: The National Arena. Taxes are not popular. In some countries such as France, many people just do not pay them. In the United States, we tend to pay . . . and complain. But the complaints heard these days are louder, angrier, and much more organized than they have been since the outbreak of the War of Independence, over two hundred years ago. A measure of the nation's discontent regarding taxes was established in a scientifically conducted poll undertaken by the Columbia Broadcasting System in conjunction with *The New York Times* shortly after Proposition 13 became law in California. The poll, in theory, was so carefully conceived that it represents, with only a 3 percent margin of error, the equivalent information that would have been obtained by interviewing all adult Americans. In the main, the results reveal a population both angry and disgusted with large federal, state, and local expenditures of public funds. Three quarters of this country believe that "people in government waste a lot of tax money," and that the "national government should be required by law to have a balanced budget—that is, not to spend more money that it collects."

When asked which tax is the least equitable, 27 percent of the people polled replied property taxes. When asked which expenditures should be reduced if property-tax income was reduced, 42 percent of Californians and 41 percent of all others wanted welfare and social services cut "a lot." Parks and library expenditures were also strong candidates. However, more than 60 percent of the people surveyed nationwide were unwilling

SUBJECT	PERCENT AGREEING
Think people in Government waste a lot of tax money	78[a]
Prefer smaller Government over more services	52
Think property tax cut will lead to reduced services	57
Oppose large tax reduction if it means a lot of public employees would lose their jobs	60
Willing to cut welfare and social services a lot	41
Unwilling to cut fire protection at all	78
Would vote FOR a Proposition 13 type measure in their area today	51
Would vote AGAINST a Proposition 13 type measure in their area today	24

NATIONAL POLL ON TAX ISSUES, JUNE 1978

a. While in 1958 only 42% of those polled by the Institute for Social Research, University of Michigan, believed the government wastes a lot of tax money, this number increased to 78% by 1978.

to see cuts, large or small, in police, fire, or school services. Most basic of all, over 50 percent favored and would vote for a Proposition 13–type limitation on the property tax in their own community. Clearly, given the chance, people will mount a decisive assault on the present scale and administration of the property tax in America, even though certain jobs, programs, and services may have to be eliminated as a consequence.

This arousal of public resentment follows a 10-year period in which property taxes increased nationally to some $60 billion, up from just under $25 billion in 1966. Although this increase closely mirrors the rise in personal income over the same period of time and the course of rising property values, higher property taxes and escalating local government expenditures have driven the owners of land and improved property to a point of serious reconsideration of the financing structure of local government.

By the end of 1979, an estimated thirty-six states had acted, or were considering constitutional amendments and other measures, to reduce government spending and to restructure the tax system. Of these, Idaho and Nevada passed measures similar to Proposition 13; Alabama residents voted to lower property assessments; in Massachusetts (sometimes referred to as *Taxachusetts*) residents voted out tax increases on homes; and Missouri residents authorized the state legislature to lower property taxes.

States without generous cash surpluses, yet pressured in a similar manner to reduce spending, are worried. National surveys in 1979 indicate a sharp nationwide shrinkage in state surpluses. According to the National Governors' Association and the National Association of State Budget Officers, state-generated reserve funds of approximately $4.3 billion, less than half the $8.9 billion in 1978, were expected at the end of fiscal 1979. The Commerce Department's Bureau of Economic Analysis concluded that state governments would show a deficit for 1979 as a whole, compared with a $6.5 billion surplus in 1978.

Many states are counting on federal aid to balance their budgets. But the federal government, in a major reversal from the pattern of the last twenty years, is also attempting to cut back on domestic spending in response to public pressure; as a result, federal aid to states and localities is not increasing. The federal budget in 1980 is likely to reduce federal grants to states to below 25 percent of the total budget for all state and local spending, a reduction from the previous year and a significant trend reversal from the pattern of the previous two decades, during which federal aid to states and local government increased at an annual rate of almost 15 percent.

What's coming is a "squeeze"—between income and expenditures— at all levels of government but especially at the local level. Because of property-tax reform, income to local government may stop increasing at past rates. Should this happen, cries will be heard across the land, from politicians and municipal workers alike. The squeeze has, in fact, already taken root in a number of communities.

A broad revision of property-tax policy does not mean that real-estate taxes will decrease for everyone or be limited at uniform levels. There have long been inequities in assessment levels and tax rates within communities and among the states. As revision occurs, many benefiaries of low, outdated assessments or preferential assessments are likely to find their status altered.

It is also doubtful, I believe, that owners of residential and business

PER CAPITA PROPERTY-TAX
COLLECTIONS, 1966–1976

STATE	AMOUNT 1966	AMOUNT 1976	PERCENT INCREASE	STATE	AMOUNT 1966	AMOUNT 1976	PERCENT INCREASE
U.S. AVGE.	$126	$266	111	Montana	162	350	116
Alabama	33	57	73	Nebraska	178	319	79
Alaska	169	1048	419	Nevada	137	272	99
Arizona	138	282	104	New Hamp.	152	348	129
Arkansas	149	101	106	New Jersey	186	446	140
California	198	415	110	New Mexico	60	103	72
Colorado	156	271	74	New York	167	412	147
Connecticut	161	369	129	North Car.	54	130	141
Delaware	65	130	100	North Dak.	130	212	63
Florida	98	191	95	Ohio	126	224	78
Georgia	62	178	187	Oklahoma	78	124	59
Hawaii	79	174	120	Oregon	142	333	135
Idaho	113	190	68	Penn.	88	176	100
Illinois	150	284	89	Rhode Is.	128	294	130
Indiana	140	226	61	So. Carolina	40	116	190
Iowa	163	278	71	So. Dakota	153	288	88
Kansas	148	274	85	Tennessee	57	129	126
Kentucky	52	105	102	Texas	100	213	113
Louisiana	53	90	70	Utah	117	172	47
Maine	125	297	138	Vermont	116	308	166
Maryland	121	239	98	Virginia	75	173	131
Mass.	190	431	127	Washington	104	236	127
Michigan	135	324	140	West Va.	55	106	93
Minnesota	165	254	54	Wisconsin	153	289	89
Mississippi	50	110	120	Wyoming	170	352	107
Missouri	97	195	101	Dist. of Col.	109	210	93

U.S. AVGE.	$45	Texas	39
Alaska	$120	Washington	38
Massachusetts	70	Ohio	38
New Jersey	67	Maryland	37
New Hampshire	66	North Dakota	37
Montana	65	Idaho	37
California	64	Utah	36
Vermont	63	Missouri	35
Maine	63	Georgia	35
New York	63	Florida	34
Wyoming	60	Virginia	30
Oregon	59	Pennsylvania	30
South Dakota	59	Mississippi	27
Arizona	54	Hawaii	27
Connecticut	53	Tennessee	27
Nebraska	53	District of Columbia	27
Michigan	52	North Carolina	26
Wisconsin	51	South Carolina	25
Rhode Island	50	Oklahoma	24
Kansas	46	New Mexico	22
Colorado	46	Arkansas	22
Iowa	46	West Virginia	22
Minnesota	44	Kentucky	22
Nevada	42	Delaware	19
Illinois	42	Louisiana	19
Indiana	40	Alabama	13

**ANNUAL PROPERTY TAX PER $1,000
OF PERSONAL INCOME, 1976**

properties will be assessed and taxed in precisely the same way, even though they were under Proposition 13 legislation. Residential owners have an advantage. As the squeeze on local finances intensifies, it is altogether likely that communities will re-examine with great care their own captive tax source: the land and improvements upon it. In doing so, local politicians will take into account the fact that residential property is owned by a powerful alliance of voting homeowners. Business property, on the other hand, is not. Much of it is owned by companies which have no direct vote; some is owned by large national and international corporations, which may not even have a resident representative in town. At the bottom line, in addition, the property tax on a medium-size to large-size business is not such a substantial financial factor as it is to the homeowner. The corporate executive considers the property tax a business expense, which fractionally reduces net income, a reduction suffered in a large corporation by thousands of shareholders who do not necessarily vote where the property tax is levied.

THE MISGUIDED ARGUMENT FAVORING HIGHER TAX ON UNDEVELOPED LAND

The private ownership of idle land, and profit gained from it, has provoked for thousands of years some of the most vituperative criticism ever leveled against any form of commercial endeavor. Profit earned from the passive ownership of land, or value increases in land due to external events, such as inflation, public improvements, and nearby local development, is called unearned increments by critics of a capitalist system that condones such profits. Social utopians have long charged that such a form of profit is one of the fundamental roots of social injustice. For instance, Winston Churchill, as articulate a promoter as ever existed for any cause in which he believed, proclaimed in the 1920s:

. . . unearned increments in land are not the only form of unearned or undeserved profit, but they are the principal form of unearned increment, and they are derived from processes which are not merely not beneficial, but positively detrimental to the general public. . . . Land, which is a necessity of human existence, which is the original source of all wealth, which is strictly limited in extent, which is fixed in geographic position—land, I say, differs from all other forms of property, and the immemorial customs of nearly every modern state have placed the tenure, transfer, and obligations of land in a wholly different category from other classes of property. . . .

In the United States, social reformers and utopian economists from the first settlements to the present day have either sought the elimination of private property or have advocated the imposition of a very high tax upon it. Utopian settlements such as those established by the Shakers and Quakers observed no rights of private property. Other somewhat less orthodox communities condoned private ownership of land but believed a very high tax should be levied upon it.

In the mainstream of the single-tax and high land-tax arguments in the United States we find ideological followers of Henry George. His influential 1879 treatise, *Progress and Poverty,* became a runaway best-seller. Over 2 million copies were sold in America alone. George and his followers advocate going far beyond the present practice of taxing both land and the improvements on it, asserting that a single high tax on land should be the focus of national taxation policy.

The English philosopher John Stuart Mill was Henry George's somewhat older contemporary. His complaint, still aired by many social economists, is that "landlords grow richer in their sleep without working, risking, or economizing. The increase in the value of land, arising as it does from the efforts of an entire community, should belong to the community and not to the individual who might hold title." This famous statement, and other similar arguments which imply an invidious link between land ownership and the unearned accumulation of wealth, provide the modern ideological basis for the stand taken by proponents of a very high tax rate on land.

However, George and his school of social economists did not go so far as to advocate the confiscation of private land. Karl Marx, a stricter socialist, while interested in George's writings as a thoughtful attempt to reform the political and economic system of private land ownership, ultimately viewed *Progress and Poverty* as an effort to salvage the basis of capitalism: the private ownership of land.

Contemporary advocates of the high land tax continue to follow in the footsteps of Mill and George and Churchill, though in America, times and circumstances and needs have changed significantly. These advocates believe that the ownership of idle land carried at low assessment and low tax is an inequitable and misguided benefit accorded those who own it. To remedy this situation, it is often proposed that the two parts of the real-estate tax—a tax on improvements and a separate tax on land—be consolidated into a single tax on *land*. The idea is to obtain the same amount of total municipal income from the new land tax as was obtained formerly from a tax on land *and* improvements. The benefits envisioned include a new emphasis on the maintenance of developed property, which is now sometimes allowed to deteriorate because physical improvements to buildings are met with increased assessment and higher taxes. It is also argued quite logically that untaxing improvements would induce a higher quality of new construction and reduce the effective cost of owning or renting housing.

Proponents of a high tax on land also argue that taxing land heavily would reduce sprawl, both in suburban and urban communities. For instance, Professor C. Lowell Harriss of Columbia University argued not long ago in the *American Journal of Economics and Sociology* that the "heavier taxation of land coupled with lower taxes on improvements would reduce 'urban sprawl.' New possibilities of, and incentive for, compactness would appear over an urban area. The new tax relations would weaken the power of some landowners to 'force' people in a growing community to settle farther out than otherwise. . . ."

High Land Tax as Misguided Policy.   Harriss and other social economists fail in such statements to take into account the impact that an elevated tax on land would have on open land everywhere. Were it determined that tax on idle land should be increased very significantly, many who hold property without immediate plans to use or develop or sell would rush to the opposite position. There would be a deluge of selling, or at least of offering. Land would be available everywhere at lower prices. There is no reason to believe that such a condition would reduce sprawl or promote better planning. New construction would, on the contrary, occur just as it does today: where the land is *comparatively* inexpensive and where there is a projected market demand. On a comparative basis, undeveloped land all over the continent would deflate. But the new tax on land, while it might lead to lower costs for open land and very much reduced demand among those who would hold it idle, might also produce considerably less revenue than anticipated, for once the tax on improved property is removed, that source of revenue is extinguished. The land itself then becomes the sole source of property tax. And, as the tax is increased, the relative value of most of the land will almost surely decline and remain deflated. This formula, extended over any reasonable amount of time, is a proscription for shrinking municipal revenue, for deflated land values, and for public acrimony of a very substantial sort. It would also lead to runaway windfall profits for the owners of improved real estate, the very individuals who benefit directly and most extensively from federal tax regulations today, as well as from locally financed public improvements and public services paid for by the tax on real estate.

The issue of how to tax land has substantial theoretical roots and specific social implications. It is a question that could not be more alive today, as demand for assessment reform abounds, as property-tax revolts appear across the nation. The right of private property ownership remains an entrenched presumption within the American social and political mainstream. However, these rights are being redefined and abridged. As private power over land diminishes, owners everywhere seek ways to limit the tax cost of holding land and property, not ways to shift a greater tax burden upon it.

ESTATE TAXES: THEIR IMPACT ON THE LAND

In long discussions over the years with people who own great spreads of open land, I've come across a pervasive obsession with the future. Stocks and bonds cause less concern: they can be easily sold; and they generally represent a share in a complex business or civic undertaking, not a personal asset that may be controlled.

With the ownership of land—unlike the possession of most other assets, such as paintings, gems, or securities—there is the constant option to intervene and transform the basic form of the asset forever: to convert open fields into a housing subdivision, to convert dense woods into a high-rise skyscraper. This potential to transform a part of the natural environment is heady stuff—and to those in possession of large tracts of land, a possibility that is never remote from conscious evaluation.

Far too often, decisions about the future are forced because of another ever-present obsessive consideration that the larger landowner rarely ignores: the impact of Internal Revenue Service regulations, especially estate-tax and inheritance-tax rules. In any forthright discussion of land and its future, a deep preoccupation with estate taxes surfaces. And it is an altogether reasonable concern, considering the way death is penalized. Death in America is many things, among them, the moment that public policy seizes to redistribute wealth.

Until very recently, at death all of one's assets were assessed by the Internal Revenue Service at current market value. Land was valued at its highest and best use in most cases, not at its current use. Thus, the soybean farm could be valued and taxed as if it were an industrial park.

Although gift and estate taxes in any given year account for only 1–2 percent of all federal revenue, these estate-tax procedures and policies cause irreparable harm and hardship to owners of farms and other undeveloped property. Very often, only to satisfy estate-tax levies, raw land is sold to those who can pay the highest-and-best-use price, those intent upon development of the property.

Today, as a result of the 1976 Tax Reform Act and the Revenue Act of 1978, some land-related improvement of estate-tax practices is evident. Estates that consist of family farms can now pay their tax liability over fifteen years at 4 percent interest instead of the former ten years at 7 percent interest; however, the low interest rate applies only to the first $1 million of the estate. Most significant of these policies is that a family farm in an estate may now be valued as a farm rather than on the basis of its highest and best use, so long as certain conditions are met: the value of the farm must represent at least 50 percent of the gross estate, and the real property must have been used in the business for five of the last eight years. Any future change in the use of the family farm during a 15-year period will trigger a recapture by the federal government of the tax saved. To limit these benefits, the special valuation of farm property cannot reduce the estate by more than $500,000.

These various, quite new provisions are of some benefit. But they apply only to a family farm or land associated with a closely held business, that is, a business owned by very few people. And while the benefits are quite real, they do not cover very much of the enormous value contained in much of the privately owned undeveloped land in America.

As a result more often than not, upon death large land holdings must be broken down and sold as smaller holdings, house lots, factory sites, or other forms of developed real estate in order to pay off estate taxes.

135

It is the specter of this often inevitable future that haunts the present for many large landowners. What will happen to the land? Will the estate actually be able to sell it? Should the appropriate stewardship of the land today include dividing it up now, even selling it before death, when there is no distress, no urgent need of cash? The way death is handled with respect to the land induces a persistent psychology of ownership that tends toward active subdivision, sale, and economic exploitation of land in America.

Engendered by this process, whose inevitable conclusion is a confrontation with estate taxes, there is sometimes calculated abuse. The list of tax-dodge methods employed includes the standard roster of tax evasion and tax avoidance maneuvers through trusts, difficult-to-trace donations, thinly held corporate shells, and fraudulent sales to others. Some are legal, just; others are not. No one has any idea just how much inheritance tax due on land is avoided through questionable, so-called estate-planning practices.

If abuses are widespread among those who possess a private militia of intelligent accountants and aggressive lawyers, scenes of pain and terror at estate land auctions are more frequent among those who do not. Forced land sales to pay death taxes at knocked-down prices are advertised daily. When the estate tax must be paid, buyers are especially ruthless. Often the heirs must leave the farm or property altogether. "Land poor" is an old phrase. It has ever-renewed meaning in our age.

At the very least there should be a federal regulation that requires *valuation of land for estate-tax purposes at current use, without limitation.* The federal apparatus should be less instrumental in forcing the sale and development of land to pay inheritance taxes, no matter how fervent its theoretical commitment to redistributing wealth. The American way of handling land at death goes deep down into the grain of why our country is poorly planned and badly designed. In place after place, at the edge of towns and cities, the farms and the fields and the woodlands are sold cheap to speculators and developers because they must be sold to pay federal government inheritance-tax claims. They are sold into a future where quick development and profit is the exclusive goal. So often the pattern of growth and change throughout a region has no connection to appropriateness of planning; rather, it bears the imprint of death.

Undeveloped Land and Tax Reform: New Options. Ever so slowly, new ideas are beginning to emerge, in part to counter the pervasive destructive impact of inheritance-tax regulation on land use and community development. The most common of these is the option now available in some states to some owners of farm properties and other open spaces to place their land voluntarily in a "special district," most of which are "agricultural districts." The owner agrees, in so doing, that he will bind himself to using the property for no purpose other than, let us say, farming. In return, he gains the right to have the government assess the land, even at his death, at its agricultural value. The farm is a farm!

Another new option that reduces inheritance tax on open land is the sale, during the owner's lifetime, of the "development rights," legal rights to develop a parcel of land as described by a zoning ordinance or master plan. For a farmer who wants to farm or a forester who wants to grow trees, the right to develop his property is not needed, though it is of recognizable economic value. In such a situation, it is sometimes possible for the owner to keep the land but to sell, transfer, or donate its development rights. Such action, however, is difficult to arrange, as will be discussed in some detail in Chapter Five. When and if accomplished, the private owner may or may not obtain a fair market value for the loss of the privilege of land development. But he surely obtains, so long as the loss of development rights is binding and perpetual, the right to claim that his land possesses no value over and above its use and value as woodland, agricultural property or open, raw acreage, shorn as it is of its conventional development potential.

What To Do. If the preservation of open space, or even certain kinds of open space, were accorded a national priority, it would be possible to improve upon our present estate-tax and property-tax practices. Any number of approaches might be followed. One suggestion is to permit the donation of development rights to a national development rights bank, or a state or country development rights bank, to qualify as a charitable gift.

Another and much less radical stroke would be, obviously, to modify the instructions given assessors, especially federal assessors who appraise estates. All land during life and at death should be assessed on the basis of *current use*. This simple national policy would transform the process, pace, and motivation for land development in America. It could do a great deal to make possible deliberate and sensible private efforts to conserve land.

The simple fact is that the power to tax and modify present tax practices is one of the most fundamental determinants of how the land will be used, maintained, and valued. It is a power that determines the relationship between property and wealth. Perhaps more than any other, and certainly more than architecture or planning, it is a power that will guide the appearance and use of vast stretches of existing metropolitan areas and much of the still-open land.

FIVE

ZONING
AND VALUE

To anyone who owns land in America, the word "zoning" conjures up strong feelings. Zoning provokes bitter and protracted arguments. It sets off complex, ingenious legal challenges. It creates sudden and decisive changes in the value of land. Zoning specifies how the land is to be *used*.

Zoning ordinances are the most prevasive and powerful part of the lexicon of land law in America. Ninety-eight percent of all cities with populations over 10,000 have a zoning ordinance, as does nearly every suburban municipality with more than 5,000 residents; about half of the suburban municipalities with fewer than 5,000 residents function under a zoning ordinance as well.

Through the forces of zoning, planning, and public expenditure allocation, a new element enters the domain of American capitalism. Pure laissez-faire dogma is diverted. The landowner loses mastery of his property. Neither the double-gauge shotgun nor the picket fence protects his borders any longer.

THE ZONING ORDINANCE

The zoning ordinance is a most fundamental determinant of the future appearance of each community. It predicts the number of people who will be allowed to live and work on a given stretch of land, and sets the density (the number of houses per acre) in each part of town. In so doing, it establishes the character and look of every neighborhood far in advance of the construction of a single building.

The zoning ordinance is a slim document available to the public at the town hall. Most zoning ordinances are composed of three parts. First of all, there is the zoning map, the blueprint of community development. At its best, the zoning map is a guideline based on "rational" decisions about a desirable future; at its worst, it is a stacked deck, held by local authorities, from which aces or deuces are dealt, depending on who is in the game. By a simple procedure, any line on that map can be changed, and doing so can convert the $500 farm acre to a $50,000 commercial site.

The map is usually an outline of the town, showing its most important streets. Superimposed over the streets are zoning district boundary lines. Within the bounded district there is usually a letter or a combination of letters and numbers, which indicates how the land may be used and what it may be used for. For instance, a district referred to as "RA-2" is limited to single-family residential houses, each surrounded by at least two acres of land.

Both the second and third components of the zoning ordinance are written texts: one describes the zoning regulation and administration of the zoning ordinance itself; the other, what can be done on the land in each zoning category. In certain retail business areas, for instance, land may be used for a wide variety of retail shops and stores but not for automobile leasing agencies or gas stations.

When these three elements are combined in that one slim document, they constitute more information in one place about the future of your town than you will find anywhere else.

The Impact of Zoning on the Cost of Land.   There is no greater influence over the cost and value of land than its zoning designation. And the impact occurs in several different ways, all simultaneously.

The most obvious control over value is control over the ultimate *use* of the land. If an acre can be used to build a shopping center, its value is very different and very much higher than it would be if use is restricted to one single-family house. The zoning designation alone can change land value 100 or even 1,000 percent.

But there is also a less obvious way that the zoning ordinance influences land value, and that is by creating shortages and surpluses. Any type of land in demand and restricted in amount by the zoning ordinance tends to appreciate. One such example is the increasingly typical and unfortunate case of the small residential lot. Theoretically, a small lot of, say, one-quarter acre ought to sell for a modest sum. But if the zoning ordinance severely limits the number of quarter-acre lots in town, their value soars to just under that of the next larger-size lot in a comparable location, despite the size of that lot. Or imagine an underdeveloped stretch of river valley land. Before any zoning ordinance is passed, the entire valley is open for housing development. Let us assume that a combined zoning and conservation ordinance is promulgated and that only one tenth of the valley remains available for development. Suddenly, the fortunate owner of that 10 percent is in possession of a most precious entity, a regulated commodity in tight supply. Zoning's ability to limit and restrict supply makes it among the most powerful determinants of land value in America.

The Impact of Zoning on the Cost of Housing.   Numerous aspects of the zoning ordinance also significantly influence the final cost of new

141

housing. While these aspects may not seem to directly affect the value of land, they in fact do, and their impact on housing costs can be substantial. One of the easiest impacts to evaluate is that related to required minimum floor area. The larger the minimum required house, the greater the cost to build it. Another impact on housing cost is lot size itself. In general, if large lots are required, the cost of the completed house plus lot will be higher.

Zoning controls and subdivision regulations demanding high expenditures for land development also cause housing costs to increase. While it is not easy to quantify the impact of stringent zoning on housing prices, careful studies of thirteen metropolitan areas in the northern and eastern sections of the United States, completed in 1978 by Bruce Hamilton of the Department of Political Economy, Johns Hopkins University, suggest that rigorous zoning controls may add 50 percent or more to the cost of housing.

Owner-occupants of housing in most communities seek to keep values high, as their homes are likely to be their largest single asset. Nothing is condoned that might threaten the value of their property. Thus, homeowners tend to pressure zoning boards to become ever more restrictive in their policies.

What has all of this to do with land and land values? Just this. *All else being equal* with regard to two identical parcels of land, the land that is most costly to subdivide and the most costly to build upon will have the lower value as raw acreage. Thus, the zoning ordinance creates an underlying value gradient for raw land.

Zoning and the Transfer of Land Wealth. As residential land generally accounts for over 75 percent of all property in town, residential zoning reveals how a growing community elects to transfer the bulk of its land wealth. In the subdivision of large parcels of raw land into many more building parcels, there is a potential shift of land assets from the original owner of raw land to a number of homeowners. How many more people will be entitled to hold land in town, and who they are to be, is unmistakably revealed in the zoning ordinance. Where residential zoning requires a single-family house on each lot, there is a single-building right per given quantity of land. In communities without apartments and with few rental units, an aspiring resident must buy a building lot or a house; and any new house he builds must conform in all respects to zoning and building code requirements. Together, these obligations of entry, a sort of rite of passage, detail what it costs to enter the community. Zoning thus distributes potential buyers (newcomers, outsiders) according to their economic capacities, and redistributes the land in town—the property wealth of the community.

The Zoning Variance.   The zoning ordinance and map profile the community as it is today and provide the best available guide to its future. But it is not carved in stone. Upon appeal, if hardship can be proven, a "variance" may be obtained. For instance, let us say that each lot in a given zone is required to be at least 40,000 square feet, and an individual who owns 78,000 square feet wishes to form two lots. He can apply for a variance, claiming hardship—that is, denial by the zoning ordinance of the full "economic" use of his property.

The request for a variance is heard on a case-by-case basis, one at a time, by the zoning board of appeals. The outcome of the request depends upon who is making the appeal and who is ruling on it. Since human and practical considerations are involved, the success of the request will also depend upon how well the argument is formulated and how convincingly it is presented.

If relief from some aspect of zoning is requested and not granted, the applicant may appeal to the courts. However, unless the local board can be proven to be arbitrary, capricious, or unreasonable, the courts, ever reluctant to enter the complex and highly fragmented realm of land-control law, generally will back the local planning board or zoning board of appeals.

Zoning Sets a Standard: Rezoning Makes a Million.   While individual exceptions to the zoning ordinance may be granted as a variance on a case-by-case basis, a change in the zoning map may be effected only by a duly constituted local legislative body, such as the town board or city council. Before any final change is considered, public comment is solicited through a public hearing or, in exceptional circumstances, through a public referendum. However, the final decision rests with the board itself, no matter what the public says or how diverse its arguments are. This means, once again, that the success of the rezoning request depends on where you are, who is on the board, and what local practices have evolved.

Zoning, then, can be flexible. It changes with ease or with difficulty depending upon the town, the applicant, and the mood of the times. Each year zoning is my personal leading candidate for the annual greatest-abuse-of-political-power award. It is, after all, subject to local law, which is administered by a small group of elected and appointed public officials. Hovering near this coterie is usually a cluster of influential political party cronies and business associates whose interests are viewed sympathetically. And the discretion available to the legislative board is enormous. Though public comment is generally required before a rezoning occurs, it may not be sought actively; nor is public opinion necessarily accorded great weight.

How to evaluate public opinion is, in fact, a thorny question for even

143

the most responsible official. At any rezoning hearing, both dissidents and advocates may appear. Where is the predominant weight of *community* opinion? What is the *public interest?* Who, in fact, is the *public?* Even in small towns, wise men do not claim to be able to answer such questions. Yet the town board, or its equivalent, must decide whether or not to grant requests for all zoning changes.

CONVERSION OF OPEN LAND TO RESIDENTIAL USE, MAY 1975

Zoning is the single most decisive arbiter of land value in America. In this photograph, an open space has been rezoned to single-family housing in the Irvine Ranch area near Newport Beach, California.

ex (Index table)

the major research journals in agricul-
he major soil science journals. Prior
ltural Index and included indexing to
al experiment station publications.

stract S 1 B52)

all aspects of agriculture

See liability for condition and use of land.

In some communities, the zoning map each year undergoes numerous revisions, revisions that respond quite often to requests from developers, investors, and speculators. This is known as spot zoning. In other communities, it is difficult to revise the zoning ordinance unless a truly comprehensive study on a community-wide basis is presented as justification of the rezoning request. Few developers, speculators, or investors are likely to undertake such a piece of work. Rather, they will be inclined to move their project over to the next town where zoning practices are less stringent.

Rezoning connected with favoritism is much more pervasive than is commonly realized. Mark Gottdiener, a New York sociologist, recently studied a large, rapidly growing town on Long Island to which he gave the pseudonym Privatown. He found that in rezoning cases between 1968 and 1971, the town board ignored the recommendations of its own planning board 30 percent of the time. In thirty-two cases where requests by citizens' groups were denied, nineteen decisions favored supporters or business associates of the Republican party leader. A local paper reported in 1968 that this same town leader had garnered $1 million in profits through rezonings. "The political machine has thus promoted construction of commercial buildings in residential areas and multifamily housing along highways to the detriment of a community that had established a plan to control such uses," Gottdiener concluded.

It is most often through rezoning that the manipulation of value is engineered by experienced politicians and land investors. Consider a 5-acre parcel of land zoned for four single-family houses. As four lots for four middle-income families, the land may be worth $50,000. But rezoned as five acres for a forty-unit multifamily housing development, it is worth at least $150,000. All it costs in some places to make the extra $100,000 is the price of a cheap option on the land and the fee paid a skillful lawyer.

When there is a market demand, a change in zoning has a most dramatic and most immediate impact on land values. A rough comparative table of relative values for the 5-acre tract mentioned above is as follows:

ZONED FOR	HYPOTHETICAL VALUE, FIVE ACRES
Agricultural only	$2,500
Two acres per house	30,000
One acre per house	50,000
Forty apartments	150,000
Retail business	250,000
Commercial	300,000
Industrial	300,000

Zoning may also significantly reduce the value of land. Consider this situation: As an investor admires a beautiful 35-acre meadow with high mountains beyond, the real-estate broker whispers in his ear, "Look at that site for thirty-five houses. What land! And, as Will Rogers said, they aren't making any more of the stuff. How could you miss? I think you can pick it up on good terms." Well, they aren't making any more of it; that's true. However, with a change in zoning, that meadow can be rendered nearly without economic value in traditional terms. A change in zoning designation from 1-acre residential to open-space residential, which requires 35 acres for a single building site, would decisively lower the land's value. In parts of Aspen, Colorado, and throughout Colorado's Pitkin County, that is, in fact, how much land you'd need in that rolling meadow to be allowed to put up one house.

OTHER LOCAL REGULATIONS
THAT CONTROL LAND WEALTH

There are several other local laws and documents which, along with the zoning ordinance, have a great deal to do with the control of land value in each town. These include the comprehensive plan, the capital-improvement plan, building and housing code, and the subdivision regulations.

Each is devised and administered by local government. A perfunctory understanding of this handful of local ordinances tells the rest of the story about the link between local law—or local regulatory power—land, and wealth. Together, they constitute an arsenal of regulations which influence every aspect of community growth and change—and control land fortunes in each town.

In general, these documents foretell how a town will develop and where it will spend federal funds, as well as its own. For example, if parks are built in one part of town, there may be no additional funds for schools. Local officials must inevitably spend public funds in ways which favor one area or group, while ignoring or even harming another.

There is also the more subtle matter of where community services are to be given priority. In which district is the school budget highest? Where is fire protection, police surveillance, and street repair given the highest and lowest priorities? Each of these matters has a direct impact on land values. But where resources are allocated may or may not be where values are enhanced. When drug addiction centers are located in a neighborhood, property values are not likely to soar. On the other hand, in neighborhoods where the surface of the streets are well maintained, where garbage is frequently collected, and where the street right-of-way is nicely landscaped and mowed, land appreciates.

146

What follows is a brief outline of the purpose and impact of each of the most important local ordinances. Anyone interested in buying, selling, owning, or planning land in America should become familiar with these documents.

The Comprehensive Plan.   The comprehensive plan, sometimes called the master plan or the development plan, considers much more than how the land is to be used. It reviews present and projects future neighborhood organization, highway and road improvements, the location of utility services, and all other physical components of town development. Zoning, as mentioned earlier, determines how each parcel of land in town may be used. It then allocates building rights to each parcel consistent with a comprehensive plan.

The basic idea is the creation of a pleasant, livable, desirable community. The federally sanctioned Standard State Zoning Enabling Act directs that land-use regulation, and especially zoning, be "in accordance with a comprehensive plan" designed to "prevent haphazard or piecemeal zoning."

The plan is fine in theory. Some who believe that planning consultants and other related experts perform miracles cling to the hope (more often expressed in the 1950s and 1960s than today) that a comprehensive plan has eternal meaning. For example, in 1955 Harvard Professor Charles Haar wrote:

The master plan, a comprehensive, long-term general plan for the physical development of the community, embodies information, judgments, and objectives collected and formulated by experts to serve as both a guiding and predictive force. Based on comprehensive surveys and an analysis of existing social, economic, and physical conditions in the community and of the factors which generate them, the plan directs attention to the goals selected by the community from the various alternatives propounded and clarified by planning experts, and delimits the means [within available resources] for arriving at these objectives.

This confident, optimistic description tells much of what a comprehensive plan was expected to accomplish, but it does not help formulate one that works. How does the community at large define its goals? Whose goals are to be adopted? Are the goals to be obvious and short-term, or subtle and long-term? How closely are the goals to be explored in terms of community-growth policies, property-tax consequences, etc.? How often is the comprehensive plan to be revised? When is it to be considered obsolete? And, perhaps as vexing as any issue, what in fact constitutes a revision of the comprehensive plan?

There may be a comprehensive plan for your community. If there is, look it over. For all its potential shortcomings, it does illustrate assumptions used as the basis of policy decisions. It is also, by mere virtue of its existence, a document that private citizens concerned with land use and development must know intimately. Within it are basic community goals which will effect land-use changes or which may be used as the justification for zoning changes.

As the comprehensive plan is the most acceptable and legally supportable basis for a rezoning request, it is sometimes scrutinized as if it were a register of old mining claims. Land speculators seek to find out if current zoning overlooks a potential and profitable zoning change supported by the comprehensive plan. However, the comprehensive plan is only a declaration of policy and a reflection of intention. It does not contain in and of itself any legal, regulatory power. That is left to the zoning ordinance.

Thus, the comprehensive plan is a critical element when zoning is challenged or rezoning is attempted. If zoning is not in accordance with goals, objectives, and projections contained in a comprehensive plan, it may more easily be declared capricious or arbitrary. On the other hand, rezoning efforts that comply with the comprehensive plan have a sound basis for support.

In the preparation of a comprehensive plan, planners rely on statistics and theory mixed with instinct. They are likely to understand less about precise economic consequences than many land owners and speculators who have less data. Audrey Moore, supervisor of Fairfax County, Virginia, pinpointed one basic source of the layman's interest in the comprehensive plan when he stated at a 1973 national conference on managed growth:

How many times have you seen the planner with his beautiful plan on the wall, all colors of the rainbow? Red is where our high-intensity uses go, yellow is where people live in their single-family homes, and green is the land that is going to be left open. What the planner doesn't tell you is that when he paints that plan red (commercial-industrial) in Annandale where I live, he paints it at least $90,000 an acre; and when he paints it yellow (residential), it decreases to about $18,000 an acre; and when he paints it green (open space), you've just gotten the booby prize. As anybody in real estate can tell you, the name of the game is to maximize the profits on land. You get a little green or you get a little yellow, and you turn it into red. If you don't believe it happens, just come to Annandale and look at the old master plan and see what took place.

Subdivision Regulations. The local subdivision regulation is second only to zoning in importance as a determinant of community appearance, the rate at which change will occur, and the value of the land. It has the force of law and affects the division of all undeveloped land.

The subdivision regulation pamphlet is sold at the town hall. It tells how undeveloped land can be subdivided into smaller pieces of property or lots, the requirements for which vary tremendously from place to place. Each step entails a cost. To a developer, the subdivision regulation is like a toll ferry ride across a river. It prescribes the boat, the location of the landing pier, and the fee for the trip. To gain the right to transform open land into developed property, the developer must cross the river according to the directions he has received.

The most important element of the subdivision regulation is the design and engineering standard for public "improvements," such as streets, drainage, sewage, water, electricity, telephone, and street landscaping. The subdivision regulation also sets up an application and review process, which the prospective subdivider or developer must follow. This is where the planning board comes in and how it spends most of its time in most communities, for it is the planning board that reviews proposals for the subdivision of land.

The planning board, elected in some communities and appointed in others, comprises citizens who may or may not be qualified to judge any submission other than the most routine requests. The board operates according to guidelines found in either the subdivision regulation itself or in another pamphlet generally entitled *Rules and Regulations of the Planning Board.* It is within this publication that the process of submission of plans and the requirements for review, fees, bonds, soil and water tests, maps, and the like are outlined. These, and other considerations as well, are the technical underpinnings that constitute the process by which land is subdivided.

In most cases, the subdivision regulation is copied from other ordinances or established by a firm of consulting engineers hired to assist the town. It may be changed, and often is, gradually over the years, by the town board or its equivalent. The way a town will look in years to come is more likely to be ordained by the provisions of the subdivision regulation than by the efforts of architects and land planners combined.

Street Design: Concrete Takes Over the Land.   The appearance of all new streets, the most visible element in any town, is determined by the subdivision regulation, which addresses such issues as whether all streets in town must have curbs or sidewalks, or whether a more rural appearance will prevail. In effect, street design controls the look of each community, inasmuch as roads constitute 30–40 percent of the land surface of most built-up places. While the width, surface, and landscaping of streets are the predominant visual elements in the public domain, these specific standards, which are so deeply connected to the look and character of the

149

A RESIDENTIAL LANE
SHARED BY FIVE HOUSE SITES, 1979

Some towns require that all new residential streets be broad enough to accommodate two moving wide-load trucks at full speed. In such towns, residential neighborhoods end up looking like grassy fringes at the edge of a superhighway; and the costs of development, housing, and municipal maintenance skyrocket. Here, a sensible alternative is depicted. Five house lots are served by a common lane. Such access is safe, inexpensive to build and maintain, and may be either cooperatively managed by its users or maintained by the municipality.

community, are ignored by most citizens. Yet, the possibility to intervene and to change street design standards clearly exists. Public works engineering and the bureaucratic administration of it, which so many feel to be incomprehensible and uncontrollable, are in fact subject to public pressure. Informed advice and organized resistance to this bureaucracy can go a long way toward changing senseless design standards and criteria.

Some towns specify residential streets of gigantic width, which create concrete runways wide enough to accommodate two moving vans passing at full speed. The result is that traffic is invited and encouraged to speed. The bias in America toward very wide roads, even on residential streets, is promoted by the automobile and concrete industries, and the big-time construction and engineering establishments. Less concrete means more open land, safer roads (drivers are discouraged from speeding), a gentler landscape, reduced artificial drainage requirements, lower costs for subdivision development, and hence lower costs of home ownership. Every town should demand a citizen's review of this incredibly significant design and planning standard, one too long ignored by the American public.

The Impact of Subdivision Regulations on the Cost of Land. Subdivision regulations have an enormous impact on the cost of land both as raw acreage sold in bulk and as individual lots sold to consumers of housing.

If it is very expensive for a developer to comply with the subdivision regulation, he will pass along those costs, thereby raising the final lot price. At the same time, there is generally a relative reduction of the value of undeveloped acreage, which must undergo costly subdivision requirements unless the land is in a highly desirable location where the market is able to absorb the high cost required for compliance.

As mentioned earlier, the subdivision regulation also determines the type of water, sewage disposal, and drainage systems which will be supplied, and how all of the utilities will be made available to new lots. Each of these has a significant impact on the cost to the developer, a cost that is passed along to the lot buyer. If a private sewage system has to be built and if a complete water system, as well as underground electricity, has to be provided, considerable costs are likely to be added to the final lot.

Thus, subdivision regulations in towns across America pose a dilemma. If they are rigorous and costly, then lot prices soar. If they are neither, then potential consumers may find inadequate water supplies, poor road drainage, shoddily constructed new streets, and a sewage disposal problem. In most locations, subdivision regulations—with the exception of required street widths—are *not* very rigorous. Consequently, the greatest degree of caution should be exercised when the purchase of a subdivision lot is being considered.

There are excellent lots, and there are unbuildable ones. At times, they may be quoted at the same price, and may even be located near one another in town. Any buyer should begin by checking the reputation of the developer. When water and sewer systems are not provided, the availability of water, as well as the ability of the soil under the lot to accept on-site sewage disposal safely and at reasonable cost, should be double-checked. Also, if electric power is not supplied by the developer, it should be determined whether it is, in fact, available and at what cost. The availability of underground gas lines, a desirable source of heat these days, should also be looked into.

Whenever a subdivision regulation exists, a developer must obtain final approval of all details before the regulatory planning board approves the final land division map or plat. Then the developer files the plat with the county clerk. If no map is filed, land development is extremely difficult and financing is generally hard to obtain. Purchasers of such land should be most wary.

The Building Code and Land Values. The building code sets construction standards for each structure in the community. The theoretical purpose of this code is to ensure that all new buildings are safe and sanitary for occupancy.

Each municipality may adopt its own building code, and compliance with it in most communities is mandatory. Each new and renovated building is inspected and certified for its conformance with the code before habitation is permitted. The building code requirements foretell the quality of local construction. They reveal whether or not new housing is likely to deteriorate within one decade or last for many. The code itself dictates minimum structural requirements and may even establish minimum room size. It may allow for inexpensive construction, or its stringent requirements may force up construction costs.

One of the reasons why building in America is a fragmented, localized industry is that each town adopts its own building code. Building standards that are required in one town may not be acceptable just across the town line. This makes industrialized mass-produced housing a most difficult enterprise.

Building codes influence the value of the land. In general, lower building costs translate into higher land values. For instance, if relatively inexpensive construction is permitted in one town, building costs there are moderate compared to those in the adjacent community that has an "expensive" code. If market values for completed houses are equivalent in both places, builders and developers will gravitate toward the town in which construction costs less. This reality creates demand for land. In the community where building costs are lower, land values will rise until the costs of the finished product—building plus land—are equivalent in both communities. Thus, savings in construction costs become profits to land sellers. If a town board wishes to stimulate development or to raise undeveloped land values, one way to realize this goal in most places is to relax building code requirements.

Capital Improvement Programs and Land Values. The last important document to anyone who wants to know what is going on in town and how land values are likely to change is the capital improvement plan (CIP), which describes capital improvement projects that the local government intends to carry out over a specified period of time. The plan generally consists of a project description, a schedule of priorities, cost estimates, and the methods of finance. If the money source is local property taxes, the project is under local control; if it is federal or state revenue, then eventual completion is less certain.

The capital improvement plan offers another glimpse into the future. It indicates which unpaved public roads are likely to be improved or widened, where a bridge is to be built or rebuilt, where park acquisition is expected, where sidewalks may be constructed, where sewers may be established or extended.

Each of these improvements, as public investment in the local physical environment, effects change and can be translated, with considerable directness, into shifting land values. For example, let us assume that a sewer is projected. The town requires sewer hookups for industrial building, and there is an industrially zoned area in the path of the proposed sewer line. Land value in the industrial zone is certain to rise in anticipation of the sewer extension. Likewise, a planned park acquisition or school site will begin to stimulate interest in residential property near the proposed park or school. Just the potential for either as projected in the capital improvement plan is apt to increase land values nearby. The capture of value in private land through public investment is the unearned increment sought by land speculators. Reform economists who focus on land note that this profitable increment represents selective private gain, often of significant magnitude, at public expense.

If one wants to be located near or far from proposed parks, sewers, schools, or widened roads, it is imperative to examine the capital improvement plan and to find out how that project is to be financed. Few homebuyers or land investors ever think of consulting the capital improvement plan. Indeed, most real-estate brokers in town do not even know what it is, and even fewer will have any specific knowledge of what it says.

A word of advice to the outsider: Armed with the zoning map, copies of the comprehensive plan and subdivision regulations, a rudimentary understanding of the building code, and a print of the capital improvement plan, the prospective purchaser of land can become more informed over a weekend than are most real-estate brokers and citizens who have lived in town all of their lives.

A word of advice to the insider: In many places, change of the physical environment is the most important activity going on in town day by day.

The fortunes of many are bound up in change. And so is the future well-being of the community's residents. Yet the subdivision of land is monitored and controlled, in most communities, by relatively few people. Though conducted in public halls at announced meetings, usually on regular evenings each month, the operation of planning boards and other local government agencies tends to be ignored by most townspeople. What goes on is hard to follow, and rarely explained. Unless special care is taken by attentive citizens, the public is, in fact, excluded. Residents feel that they have no control over what is happening, of what "they" are doing. This is only partially true. While it may be difficult to keep abreast of changes in community regulations on a day-to-day basis, it is precisely on this basis that the existing zoning ordinance and subdivision regulation are molding the future quality of the physical surroundings and the value of land. If you want to affect the future, this is where to begin.

ZONING AS SOCIAL CONTROVERSY: DATELINE U.S.A.

Riverside County, California—By law, cities may ban children from housing and require each family to include one resident over the age of 50.

Los Angeles, California—When Stephen and Lois Wolfson have their first baby, they are told that they must leave Marina Del Rey. With only 25 percent of Los Angeles apartments renting to families, and only a 3 percent vacancy rate, City Councilwoman Peggy Stevenson observes: "This is not only a problem for families with children. . . . It is a problem for any of us who believe that for any city to remain viable, it must offer hospitality to children and their parents."

Arizona—Cities and neighborhoods are allowed to evict families with children, limit the number of days a child can visit a relative, and evict grandparents who might care for them.

Miami, Florida—More and more, apartment buildings display signs that read: NO CHILDREN. In the opinion of Barry Dean, executive director of the South Florida Apartment Owners Association: "It was simply because of economic reasons [that children are excluded]. . . . These buildings had had a high incidence of vandalism by young people, and maintenance costs became prohibitive."

Leonia, New Jersey—After a 7-year battle, citizens accept a proposal for a 77-unit brick apartment complex for the aged. "I still get complaints, but the complex is going up," says Edward Chave of the Leonia Retirement Housing Corporation.

New Castle, New York—Mitchell Berenson sues the city when it refuses to allow rezoning of fifty acres and construction of two hundred condominium apartments, primarily for elderly people. The court orders the town to change its zoning to permit construction of 3,500 additional units of moderate-income housing over the next ten years.

Easttown, Pennsylvania—The town zones large lots of a minimum of four acres, presumably to protect the ecology of the area. The National Land and Investment Company sues on the grounds that the zoning ordinance denies an individual's constitutional "right to travel," that is, to settle wherever one pleases in the United States. The court rules:

The question posed is whether the township can stand in the way of the natural forces which send our growing population into hitherto undeveloped areas in search of a comfortable place to live. We have concluded not. A zoning ordinance whose primary purpose is to prevent the entrance of newcomers in order to avoid future burdens, economic or otherwise, upon the administration of public services and facilities cannot be held valid. . . .

Zoning and Discrimination. People with children, people who are not over 50, people who cannot afford a single-family house, people with low incomes, people who are black: each of these groups and others may feel discriminated against by their community's zoning ordinance. Some feel they have a *social* problem with zoning and land-use regulations. Others characterize the problem as *financial* discrimination. Still others maintain that *racism* is behind it all. Truth to tell, I believe there are elements of all three.

Large-lot zoning, together with building codes which mandate expensive forms of housing construction, and subdivision regulations which drive up lot prices, are seen by many as a systematic set of publicly enforced regulations aimed at excluding poorer people. When the sale of smaller lots and the option of apartment housing are forbidden, the cost of each dwelling goes up, and the amount of land that must be purchased to gain the right to live in town escalates. As the National Commission on Urban Problems (the Douglas Commission) reported quite accurately in 1968:

155

Zoning . . . very effectively keeps the poor and those with low incomes out of suburban areas by stipulating lot sizes way beyond their economic reach. Many suburbs prohibit or severely limit the construction of apartments, townhouses, or planned unit developments, which could accommodate more people in less space at potential savings in house costs. . . .

Several recent significant lawsuits reveal a changing situation in America with respect to social manipulation through exclusionary or discriminating zoning. Recent events in Mount Laurel, New Jersey, and Arlington Heights, Illinois, are prime examples.

Mount Laurel, New Jersey—The town of Mount Laurel is an easy commute by highway to nearby Philadelphia. In the mid-1960s, Mount Laurel zoned much of its vacant land, allocating about 30 percent of it to industrial use, obviously to help its tax base. The balance of the land was divided between what would have been expensive planned unit developments and large lots for single-family housing. This zoning, then, effectively eliminated space in Mount Laurel where new low-income families could settle.

With the assistance of open-housing organizations and residents in town, the Southern Burlington County National Association for the Advancement of Colored People (NAACP) sued Mount Laurel township in 1972, claiming exclusionary and discriminatory zoning practices. The New Jersey Supreme Court ruled in favor of the NAACP and issued a series of statements in its 1975 judgment which have been continuously subjected to close scrutiny by land planners and community administrators. In its ruling, the court observed:

. . . it has to follow that, broadly speaking, the presumptive obligation arises for each such municipality affirmatively to plan and provide, by its land-use regulations, the reasonable opportunity for an appropriate variety and choice of housing, including, of course, low- and moderate-cost housing, to meet the needs, desires, and resources of all categories of people who may desire to live within its boundaries.

Apart from this general statement of policy, as well as other references to the solid American rights of general welfare and adequate housing, one point stands out as decisive, and is spelled out in the premise upon which the court based its decision: "Certainly when a municipality zones for industry and commerce for local tax-benefit purposes, it without question must zone to permit adequate housing within the means of the employees involved in such uses."

The case was judged on the basis of fair housing and economics, without specific reference to racial segregation. One of those most offended by the court's ruling was José Alvarez, the Puerto Rican mayor of Mount Laurel, who supported restrictive zoning as a way to upgrade his community. In an interview concerning the case, Alvarez was adamant that his town had never intended to use zoning as a device of racial discrimination. "The word 'nigger' is not in my vocabulary," he argued. "The issue really is economics. We'll let anybody live here, but if they move in and throw up a shack and dig a slit trench for their waste, do you think that will be okay with the health department?"

Some weeks after the New Jersey Supreme Court handed down its decision, Mount Laurel Town Council members met to decide what action to take.

As reported by Ed McCahill in *ASPO Magazine,* a heated exchange occurred. Comments included the following:

"You can't end all of the social problems of the entire country with zoning law."

"The court suggested we could provide our 'fair share' of housing by forming a local housing authority or starting a 'regional' housing authority. What the hell is a regional authority but a bunch of honky bureaucrats responsive to no one and responsible to no one?"

"If they're going to have to be subsidized, then I want to be subsidized. Why doesn't someone subsidize me? If you want to get right down to it, I don't believe in welfare."

When the town finally did act, it planned 515 units for low-income and moderate-income housing. Unimpressed, the court ordered Mount Laurel to plan for 3,000 to 5,000 units of subsidized public housing. Because resistance to such court-mandated low-income housing has been so strong, little actual construction has taken place in Mount Laurel or in any other rural or suburban area in New Jersey as a result of the ruling.

The impact of the *Mount Laurel* decision has been further vitiated by the court's inclusion of such terms as "developing" communities and "fair share" of "least-cost" housing, in its decision. Several New Jersey towns have worked hastily to exploit the vagueness of these terms, to maneuver for exemptions from the *Mount Laurel* decision.

At the same time, legal pressure continues to mount for towns to fall into line. Stanley C. Van Ness, the New Jersey Public Advocate, filed suit in mid-1979 against twenty-six towns in Morris County, New Jersey, on the grounds that they failed to relax zoning rules in the wake of the *Mount Laurel* decision. Developers who want to build and profit from low-cost housing developments cite the ruling. Many towns, in response, seek to prove that they are "not yet developing." Harvey S. Moskowitz, a planning consultant to over a dozen suburban towns and developers in New Jersey, asserts that the main culprit is the state of New Jersey itself. As reported by Richard Higgins in *The New York Times,* Moskowitz points out that "the state of New Jersey still owns substantial amounts of surplus land in many communities . . . and it has the financial resources to make these tracts available for low-cost housing. . . . The developers ought to be suing the state."

Arlington Heights, Illinois—Arlington Heights, a suburb of Chicago with a median family income of just over $17,000, received a request from the Metropolitan Housing Development Corporation and several black individuals to rezone a 15-acre parcel of land, originally zoned for single-family houses, to accommodate 190 townhouses for low- and moderate-income residents. After three public meetings, the Arlington Heights Planning Commission determined that the residents in the area opposed rezoning for multifamily dwellings. In response, Metropolitan Housing sued, claiming that the zoning laws were unconstitutional and in violation of the 1968 Fair Housing Act, which prohibits racial discrimination.

Following a long sequence of contradictory lower court judgments, in 1977 the U.S. Supreme Court handed down a 5–3 decision in favor of Arlington Heights. The Court reasoned that although the zoning had a "racially disproportionate impact," the intent of the community was not segregation, and the refusal to rezone was not unconstitutional. The village's zoning practices were further upheld as being consistent, since the property in question had been zoned for single-family residences since 1959. As the Court observed in its majority opinion: ". . . the Village is undeniably committed to single-family homes as its dominant residential land use."

This 1977 decision is one of the most recent and important fragments available in the patchwork of American land law as related to zoning, exclusionary practices, and racial discrimination. Whether or not zoning is, in fact, used specifically to forward and enforce *racial discrimnation* in suburban and rural towns is hard to say and even harder to prove. But whether or not zoning is used specifically to forward and enforce *exclusionary practices* in suburban and rural towns is neither difficult to say nor to prove.

Once the rhetoric is stripped away, what property owners really oppose in their own neighborhoods are changes in the pattern of housing and in the composition of the population, particularly if they feel the changes will lower property values. This desire to protect property values is at the core of all exclusionary zoning practices, I believe. All the talk by planners and sociologists about the desirability of neighborhood diversity contradicts this most basic instinct. Indeed, the federal district court, in support of the Arlington Heights Planning Commission, linked the specific issue of investment protection to the citizens' opposition to the public-housing plan: ". . . The evidence shows that a multifamily development would seriously damage the value of the surrounding single-family homes. . . ." This motive is seized by the district court as a compelling and proper ground for denial of a rezoning application: "The weight of the evidence proves that the defendants were motivated with respect to the property in question by a legitimate desire to protect property values and the integrity of the Village's zoning plan."

This link between the protection of property values and a conventional local zoning ordinance, observed in the district court's deliberations and judgments, drives to the heart of the success of zoning as a land-use regulatory device across America. Conventional zoning is the most widely accepted of all land-use regulations. And, why? Because, while it withdraws certain rights from the property owner regarding land-use decisions, it delivers, free of charge and year after year, the most valuable insurance policy he owns: property value insurance.

Traditional zoning is also a contract that permits land development at any time. Thus, it unlimitedly guarantees the future utility of property; foretells the size, and therefore the value, of lots; suggests their future use; and determines the size, and therefore the value, of buildings.

For these reasons, owners, bankers, insurance companies, city councils, and nearly every chamber of commerce presently support the idea and the reality of zoning. As Constance Perin, a thoughtful cultural anthropologist and planner, states in her recent book, *Everything in Its Place:*

Opposition to anything that may "lower property values" echoes in today's disputes in settled suburbs and neighborhoods over the prospect of higher density and differing forms of housing, for whenever homebuyers move and whenever they think of selling for any reason, they expect to recoup their equity in order to use it in buying the next house, they expect the sale to cover the cost of the transaction, and always, they hope to realize some profit or a fair return on their investment.

Across America, low-income and/or high-density housing, especially for use by families, is thought to lower property values, particularly in areas where such housing does not already exist. Consequently, those who focus on zoning as a device used to perpetuate exclusionary practices certainly have a point. The intention, however, goes beyond exclusion of any particular social group or race. It extends, rather, to an effort to exclude anyone or anything that might cause property values in the

159

immediate area to depreciate. Above all else, zoning is an unarticulated but deeply felt covenant among property owners for the protection of their investment. Those who attack exclusionary zoning without understanding this fact misunderstand its roots, and its toughness.

Conventional zoning is, in fact, a permissive system that ultimately is blind to both race and religion. People who depend upon zoning to create and maintain a segregated community or neighborhood do not grasp this reality. If, indeed, zoning were a successful means to assure racial or religious segregation, vandals would not resort to burning houses owned by blacks in predominantly white neighborhoods, and bigots would not feel the need to paint Stars of David on doorways of houses owned by Jews.

Ultimately, zoning is a system of discrimination that focuses on financial value. It is a veiled club whose charter requires a specific level of dues for entry, but no check is made of skin color, social credentials, school affiliations, or police record. That is left to other means. By regulating the minimum size of a lot or house, or establishing the standard for the construction of a building, zoning and other ordinances set the dues in capital costs, which must be sustained, and in annual property taxes, which must be met. The club, in exchange, offers use of a particular community's environment and services, and acts as guardian of the members' investment. How the club deals with federal law, which requires in each community adequate provision for low-income and moderate-income housing, is an ongoing spectacle.

NEW FRONTIERS IN ZONING

Garden-variety zoning has been around for some time. Its rights are legally established, its presence socially acceptable. After fifty years, zoning, once a blunt instrument, is being refined into a collection of finely honed tools. As the century progresses, zoning for the protection of the "health, safety, morals, or general welfare" of a community is being granted an ever-widening role. Each year, new types of more exotic, refined, and flexible zoning are inaugurated. A brief survey of the frontiers on which zoning is breaking ground is outlined below, with special attention paid to the subsequent impact on land value and on new opportunities for better planning of the built environment.

Planned Unit Development.   Planned unit development, or PUD, is a term heard quite often these days. Under this land-development option, the developer negotiates an alternate land-use plan with the local planning board. No longer restricted by the ordinary controls over density, road design, and land use as defined in the zoning ordinance and the subdivision regulation, the developer is free to devise a PUD scheme for the property that includes some public amenity, such as recreation facilities, or more open space.

In the best instances, all parties benefit. The developer, for instance, may be accorded a greater residential density allowance than permitted under the standard zoning ordinance; he may also be permitted to develop commercial areas on the PUD land where such areas were otherwise prohibited by the standard zoning ordinance. With a denser plan, the developer is able to reduce development costs per unit. In turn, the town ends up with shorter roads, and thus less concrete to maintain; fewer feet of pipe and conduit for utilities than stipulated by the standard subdivision regulation; and some usable public space or attractive undeveloped areas.

In the worst instances—and there are many—the community gets nothing, and the developer walks away with all the profit. This occurs whenever the developer is accorded more housing units, and/or commercial or industrial land uses, but provides little or no amenity to the public, even in the form of publicly visible open space.

In my judgment, planned unit development should be encouraged only when a land area is in excess of 100 acres, as it is not possible to design a sensible mixture of residential, business, and recreational uses for a smaller area. Provisions must be made for well-thought-out open spaces, as well as for a generously landscaped buffer zone surrounding the PUD so that neighbors are not affected by the dense, active development.

To an experienced developer, the potential for a planned unit development means that some of the land will be valued as if it were zoned for commercial uses, and some as if it were zoned for multiple dwellings. Thus, the way a parcel of land is viewed and appraised changes if the option to develop a PUD is exercised. Even the obligatory open space, if well designed, imputes added value to the residential lots which will surround the undisturbed fields or woodlands. It is, finally, because of this added value which a well-designed PUD creates that a sensible, informed and well-organized planning board and its consultants ought to be able to secure from the developer planning and financial concessions which will forward some public purpose the board has conceived.

Cluster Zoning. Cluster zoning refers exclusively to residential development, as opposed to a PUD, which encompasses commercial and recreational, as well as residential land uses. Like the PUD, cluster zoning can waive the minimum acreage of a lot on which a house is to be constructed. The objective is to preserve open space by building in more compact clusters on less of the land than the standard zoning ordinance may require. As an example, rather than establish ten 1-acre lots, a developer might be encouraged (or required) to build ten dwellings on 5 acres, leaving the other 5 acres as open space.

When compared to conventional development, in terms of public and development costs, clustering is clearly more economic. Studies conducted in 1974 by the Real Estate Research Corporation, and subsequently published as an important research report entitled "The Cost of Sprawl," calculate cost savings using a range of hypothetical examples. These studies conclude that some 50 percent of both private and government costs associated with new development can be saved if sprawl is rejected in favor of dense, planned cluster development. The significant reduction of development costs for roads, electricity, sewers, and the like per housing unit helps lower the developer's overall front-end costs of building.

Other advantages accrue from cluster development. In aesthetic terms, more open space is preserved, since the same number of dwelling units as in a conventional development can be obtained with a 40–75 percent savings of open land. Wildlife may flourish. At very dense levels, as in apartments or townhouses with common walls, energy consumption is reduced. Water consumption also declines with less lawn area and smaller gardens. Reduced automobile travel yields environmental benefits of cleaner air and less noise. These reductions all add up to a more efficient use of resources of every kind, including the land.

The cluster alternative to conventional development, then, theoretically provides the community with either visual enjoyment of the preserved open space, or perhaps use of it, as well as with a more efficient and pleasurable environment. The developer is able to reduce construction expense and costs of road and utilities; and if these savings are passed along, the final cost of a dwelling should be somewhat lower than in a conventional layout for the same quality house.

However, in many parts of America—especially in suburbs and in outlying rural communities—people continue to prefer and are willing to pay for their 1-acre lot. Consequently, in such areas, if a developer clusters without a permitted increase in the number of dwelling units, he will generally lose substantial land value, as purchasers will pay less for the smaller land parcel allocated per dwelling.

Consider the following situation. Ten acres of land zoned for ten 1-acre building sites has an aggregate market value of $100,000, or $10,000 per 1-acre building site. In most parts of America, if this same 10 acres could, say, be developed as ten cluster sites of only one-third acre each, the market value of the land would be reduced. As a consequence, normally the landowner-developer does not voluntarily choose to cluster.

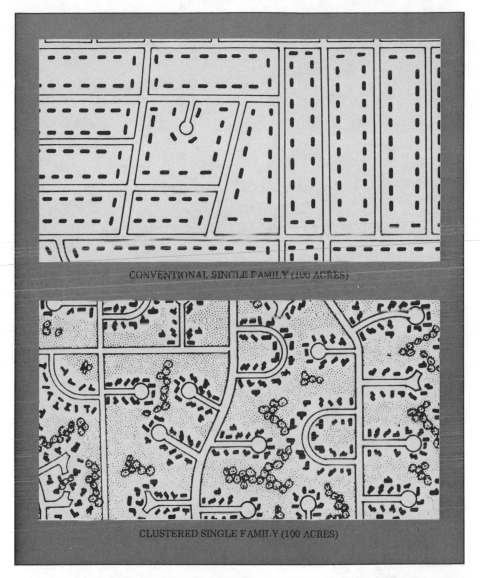

CONVENTIONAL SINGLE FAMILY (100 ACRES)

CLUSTERED SINGLE FAMILY (100 ACRES)

LAND DEVELOPED AS CONVENTIONAL SINGLE-FAMILY OR CLUSTERED SINGLE-FAMILY

This comparison of development options illustrates how a clustered development provides more open space and needs less roadway than conventional sprawl development. Clustered layouts are generally more economical to build and less expensive to maintain because sewer and water lines and street surfaces are not as extensive.

163

**CONVENTIONAL SPRAWL DEVELOPMENT,
SOUTH MIAMI HEIGHTS, NEAR MIAMI, FLORIDA**

Conventional sprawl layouts provide no visual relief,
no open-space amenity.

Planning boards and citizens must recognize that there are two viable ways to assure cluster development: (1) clustering must become mandatory (in certain circumstances); or (2) development economics and land-value realities must be sympathetically understood, and an appropriate inducement offered a developer for clustering. The only inducement that makes sense is to allow the subdivider an increase in the number of lots —or an extension of building rights—above the conventional number permitted in the zoning ordinance. To follow through with our previous example, let us assume that the ten one-third-acre building sites are worth, say, $7,000 each, or a total of $70,000, to the subdivider. If cluster development is sought by the planning board, and if the developer has an option, he must be permitted to build an additional four units, or a total of 14 (14 × $7,000 = $98,000), to approximately equal the $100,000 of land value that is obtained by creating ten conventional 1-acre lots. Otherwise, the cluster option will be ignored. With this approach, less than half of the full ten acres of land (14 × 0.33 acres = 4.6 acres) will be exploited for housing development. Such a density bonus encourages the developer to accept the cluster approach and, if correctly scaled, is an appropriate and necessary inducement if a town wants to promote cluster houses. Because the developer then truly saves the reduced cost of longer roads and longer utility lines, the option becomes a compelling economic choice.

Cluster zoning may also propel the subdivider of land into a new business: that of construction. This change is viewed negatively by many land developers. In conventional zoning and subdivision, land is broken down by the developer into individual lots, which are then sold. When very dense clustering is involved so that linked buildings such as townhouses are necessary, this traditional method of land merchandising becomes impossible. Because the units are so closely linked, or even connected, they must be built simultaneously rather than individually. A dense cluster subdivision, then, must be purchased by a builder, not by separate individuals who each intends to construct a single dwelling. This reduces the number of potential buyers dramatically, another reason that traditional land subdividers shy away from cluster development.

Today, even though many planning officials and those devoted to land conservation quite correctly favor cluster development, the option of mandatory clustering is, in my view, only justified in certain rare instances where the quality of land to be conserved is truly exceptional, as in areas of genuine environmental, archeological, historic, or ecological significance. In others—and this is in most instances—where open space obtained through clustering would be enjoyed by many people, the inducement to cluster should be made strong, and sensible, through an offered density bonus. Because this either is not being offered or is inadequate, relatively little cluster development is going on at this time.

**RESTON, VIRGINIA,
MIXED RESIDENTIAL COMMERCIAL CLUSTER DEVELOPMENT**

Allowing certain portions of a land parcel to be developed more intensively than zoning permits provides an outright inducement for the developer to leave other portions as open space. This density bonus makes cluster development a viable business proposition for the developer.

166

Mixed-Use Zoning.   Conventional zoning separates land uses once considered incompatible, such as industrial areas and residential enclaves. Zones are, in fact, named for the permitted activity: residential zones, commercial zones, industrial zones. Conventional zoning made it more difficult for people to live near their work, as they had for centuries. It also reduced commercial downtown streets to vacated wastelands after 6 P.M. each evening.

Although by the 1950s planners and builders had begun to realize the absurdity of this situation, it was not until 1971 that the first zoning law in America encouraging a mixture of offices and shops with residences within a single building in a downtown office district was ratified. Indeed, it offers a bonus in building size for more residential use above standard zoning limits if apartments and arcades are incorporated; and through additional space bonuses, it encourages the developer to create a covered public passageway, or galleria, at ground level.

This law applies to Fifth Avenue between Thirty-eighth Street and Fifty-seventh Street in New York City. While the tradeoffs offered a developer here are complex, and the results are mixed in quality and in public amenity, the concept is simple. Mixed-use zoning is encouraged through incentives to private developers to provide residential layers atop commercial buildings located in specially zoned districts. The same idea can be intelligently applied to smaller cities, towns, and even villages. There is little residential space at the center of smaller communities, mostly because town centers are zoned almost exclusively as retail business or commercial territory. Why not permit housing above the stores? This mixture of uses is surely compatible and offers desirable living accommodations to many who do not want to live farther out of town.

Mixed-use zoning, which includes residences downtown, is likely to do more than enliven the streets. It will increase land values, especially in smaller towns and villages. There, very often, the second floor above retail establishments is vacant, since most people do not like to walk upstairs to shop. But when apartments are permitted above stores, the main street is more intensively used. Conveniently located in-town housing becomes available to older people, single people, and couples. This simple and sensible shift from single-use to mixed-use zoning in retail business areas creates an appropriate stimulant to town centers and to land values within them.

Incentive Zoning.   Incentive zoning is a kind of free-wheeling deal making between public officials and private developers, centered around the issue of rentable building bulk, with the minimum building bulk set by the zoning ordinance. In an incentive-zoning arrangement, a desirable

167

public improvement or open-space objective is first established by government officials. Developers are then offered an incentive—greater usable building bulk—in exchange for providing the identified amenity. Both planned unit and voluntary cluster developments are basically forms of incentive zoning.

In the negotiations between public officials and private developers, the public is represented by a planning board, which identifies community design and land-use objectives—the sought-after amenity. This is generally an improvement to the physical environment, thought, at the time, to be a public benefit. Examples include covered arcades, open plazas, or places of public assembly. Indeed, any physical change consistent with planning for public use and implemented on private property can be promoted through incentive zoning.

The developer is represented by himself, a zoning attorney, and an accountant. Usually, the developer has a choice of either providing the amenity and building a bigger structure, or simply building according to the conventional zoning-space limits. Sometimes, if the developer declines the incentive approach, the planning board will endeavor to make the deal more appealing. However, if the additional building space offered is too appealing, and the market for this space is strong, developers throughout the region may start planning new projects that take advantage of the incentive. In this way too many empty plazas were sprinkled about in inaccessible or undesirable locations in midtown Manhattan.

While incentive zoning may be abused by developers—and sometimes it is—well-negotiated deals and well-defined requirements add up to a sensible approach, as the Citicorp Building in New York City testifies. By designing a 7,247-square-foot atrium, the architects, Hugh Stubbins and Associates and Emery Roth & Sons, were permitted to increase the tower's rental space by 114,952 square feet. In addition, Citicorp has been able to charge premium rents to retail tenants in the 60,000 square feet of predominantly interior rental space bordering the atrium. The open area of the atrium, where visitors may relax under a well-landscaped, skylighted interior, adds architectural appeal to the building and attracts the public inside to retail stores as well. Incentive zoning in this instance, and others, produces first-class results of public benefit and private profit at nominal public expense.

As any wise zoning administrator recognizes, three fundamental ingredients are essential if incentive zoning is to work. First, building bulk allowed under the conventional zoning ordinance must be restrictive compared to market demand; otherwise, a developer will not seek an alternative. Second, the bonus offered must cover, or more than cover, the amenity cost. Third, there must be a market demand strong enough to absorb

**ATRIUM, INTERIOR OF CITICORP BUILDING,
NEW YORK CITY, 1978**

Incentive zoning encourages a developer to provide a public "amenity" in exchange for added rentable space within the building. In New York City's successful Citicorp Building, a lively 7,247-square-foot atrium was exchanged for 114,952 square feet of lower rental space.

169

the additional salable or rentable spaces granted to the developer. When these three elements are present, the incentive option is sought—and works.

And when it works, land values are increased both below the building itself and in districts where similar incentive bonuses are offered. The increased economic return that may be earned from the larger building imputes greater value to the land upon which it rests.

Historic-District Zoning. Because zoning can destroy as well as protect old places, when incentives to large-scale development are offered, what exists today may very well be gone tomorrow. Zoned historic districts are thus created to protect the present appearance and scale of these areas through a form of zoning. Within these districts, owners may be deprived of their right to demolish buildings, modify exteriors, or build anew in any random architectural style.

The first historic district in America was declared in 1931 in Charleston, South Carolina; the second, established in 1937, was the Vieux Carré district of New Orleans. Today, there are over a thousand historic districts in the United States. Within a designated historic district, change to buildings is monitored by a local committee or commission, whose power is granted through the zoning ordinance. This area-wide preservation of older buildings and spaces—the *tout ensemble* of streets, alleys, façades, colors, sidewalks, and scale—is one of the fastest growing trends in specialized zoning today. As America grows up, and older, a reverence for the past sets in. This new form of zoning reveals widespread interest in history and nostalgia.

Preservation of entire districts and individual buildings is now accorded high priority even in Washington. Federal tax incentives offered in 1976 moved preservation out of the tea parlor and into the board room. As a result, preservation is now big business: values tend to rise when land and buildings are protected by historic district zoning. Once a historic district is designated and mapped, a boundary line in town of great economic significance is created. The boundary limits the supply of protected and therefore cherished properties—and up goes the price of land and buildings within it.

Historic-district zoning in cities is now a well-established practice, but it often has a much less secure standing in smaller towns, villages, and rural communities, where owners are more likely to be suspicious of it. Fearing the loss of private rights, they tend to resent the intrusion of any government-imposed restriction. This resentment blinds them to the benefits of historic-district controls. When historic-district designation is resisted, often the unspoken and, in fact, unfounded fear is that regulated land and buildings will diminish in value. Experience proves that the opposite is, in fact, the case.

As pressure for new and more extensive development mounts in smaller towns across America, these places are losing their older structures and traditional appearance. The arrangement of space, building, and landscape is more susceptible to obliteration when there is less to begin with, as is the case in smaller communities. A few demolitions, a few slick renovations—and the old place is gone. I urge property owners and administrators in smaller towns to closely examine the benefits of historic-district zoning and use it to preserve areas of the highest quality and greatest historic significance.

COVENANTS AND RESTRICTIONS: A ZONING SUBSTITUTE

Although zoning may be changed, and in some places does not even exist, the future use of land may be strictly controlled by its private owner through a legal document generally called a covenant and restriction.

The historic right of the private landowner (landlord) as lord of the manor still resides in the private right to create and to place on public record a set of "covenants and restrictions." Once certified and filed at the county seat, this legal document controls the land. So long as the covenant and restriction does not violate any existing law, it may be enforced; and it may "run with the land," that is, survive the life of the landlord.

Zoning cannot legally or sensibly attempt to control a wide range of aesthetic and development details which affect how land will be used, how it will look, and how it will be permitted to change over the years. But a private covenant and restriction can; and in so doing, it will also affect the value of the land, sometimes dramatically.

Covenants and restrictions are more commonplace, especially in residential development, than most people realize. For example, it is through the widespread use of covenants and restrictions that individuals in a large community without any zoning whatsoever, such as Houston, Texas, regulate many aspects of residential development. And where zoning does exist, owners of large tracts who subdivide are often anxious to exert a control over the future use of the land that is more rigorous and more detailed than outlined in the zoning ordinance or in the subdivision regulation. Private control may govern such matters as acceptable construction materials and style of new houses; the required type and quality of driveways, fences, and out-buildings; and a wide range of other matters.

171

Covenants and restrictions are made a part of the sales agreement between land developer and lot buyer. Most buyers do not resist. Indeed, in the view of most, covenants and restrictions add value and appeal to new lots. In addition to the other factors they define, covenants and restrictions often guarantee minimum house size and the type of construction, and thereby tell prospective buyers more about the neighborhood they might live in than the zoning ordinance could ever presume or legally hope to. The covenant and restriction is, in effect, an additional insurance policy against the future. Of course, the covenant and restriction need not be accepted by the prospective purchaser, who can opt to buy a lot somewhere else.

In the new town of Westlake Village, California, forty miles north of Los Angeles, for instance, homeowners agreed to a characteristic set of requirements that govern the planting of trees and the painting of houses, and enforce the mowing of lawns. The president of a league of nineteen homeowner associations, Larry Horner, describes the attitude of Westlake Village:

We tell people who want to exercise their freedom to the fullest extent that when they bought here they signed a contract to live up to the C.C. and R.s [covenants, conditions, and restrictions]. They shouldn't have moved into a planned community if they weren't prepared to live under the special conditions here. . . . Most of the people wouldn't have it any way else because of what it's done for their community and their property values. But there have been a few irate people—one or two that we've had to say, "We like it this way and maybe you would be happier someplace else."

The developer who establishes a covenant and restriction may be motivated by an aesthetic impulse or a positive "feeling" about the land; in either case, there is an underlying urge to guarantee that new lot buyers not compromise the value of subdivided, unsold property, or other owned adjacent land. After all, when a new subdivision is created, the initial developer possesses the largest single holding of new lots. It is the developer, during the years of new house building, who is in a prime position to benefit from incremental increases in the value of unsold lots; and it is he who will suffer most if the lots depreciate. Thus, the covenant and restriction serves a dual purpose: for the new buyer, it helps predict the appearance and quality of the new neighborhood, a neighborhood that is dependable, acceptable, and presumably capable of augmenting the resale value of his house and/or lot. For the land developer, it protects his investment against the newcomers. In general, covenants and restrictions attract buyers to the "protected" property, buyers who will pay a premium for the insurance and assurance contained in these private agreements.

172

DEVELOPMENT RIGHTS: A NEW ZONING CONCEPT

A zoning ordinance assigns and limits the right to build or develop on each particular lot; this constitutes the *development right*. Without a zoning ordinance, there is development but no development right; and the marketplace, rather than the zoning ordinance, sets the limit.

When zoned land can be built upon but is not, it contains unused development rights. If a building lot is entirely vacant, the unused development rights are the sum total of the bulk of building that the zoning ordinance permits on the parcel. Let us assume that a building exists on

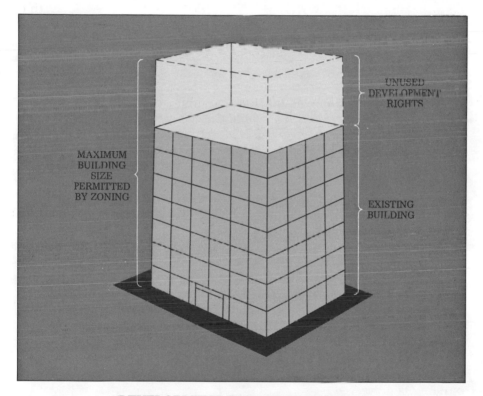

DEVELOPMENT RIGHTS PROTOTYPE

The amount of building permitted by zoning on any given parcel of land is its assigned "development right." If a building exists on a site but is smaller or lower than permitted, the unused development right is the difference between the size of the existing building and the size of the largest permitted building. This zoning concept imputes value to space, to the air above any zoned site that can be legally built upon.

173

the site and that it is smaller than permitted; the unused development right is the difference between the size of the existing building and the size of the largest permitted building.

Zoning, then, introduces a new, valuable, yet intangible dimension to the land itself. That dimension is the maximum buildable space that hovers with promise and potential above any zoned site. This is a late-twentieth-century concept, a new reality as radical in land law and land economics as was Einstein's proof to the scientific world that time is a fourth dimension in the universe. Never before has the precise value of land been so determined on the basis of how extensively the thin air above it may be invaded.

Transferable Development Rights Described. Traditional zoning further assumes that the right to develop may be utilized only on the specific site zoned. When a site is used for a low-density purpose, such as a historic building, yet the building lot is located in an area where a skyscraper is both in demand and legal according to the zoning ordinance, a classic conflict occurs. The same site cannot support both the low-scale landmark building, let us say, and a skyscraper. What can be done if the owner wishes to sell his site to realize the greater value imputed to his property by virtue of the zoning? Any conventional purchaser of the site, after all, will either build atop the lower building, or demolish it and construct the permitted skyscraper. Is there a way that the owner could be compensated for the implicit, zoned value of his site, while at the same time the landmark building is preserved?

A new concept known as "transferable development rights" (TDR) attempts to reconcile these two objectives simultaneously. Transferable development rights break the traditional link between a particular site and the *location* where its development zoned potential is implemented. The owner of the unutilized development rights above the landmark building is given the option of selling or transferring the surplus development rights to another site somewhere else. By so doing, two different, seemingly incompatible objectives are achieved: the site owner is given access to the full market value of his property, and the revered historic building is preserved.

TDR may also be used to prevent land originally zoned for conversion to urban uses from being developed at all. Assume that a farm has been zoned for thirty houses and that an ordinance exists that permits the transfer of development rights off the farmland. If the development rights to build thirty new houses can be transferred to another parcel of land, the owner may then sell the building rights to someone with another piece of land somewhere else rather than develop his farm. The sale of the

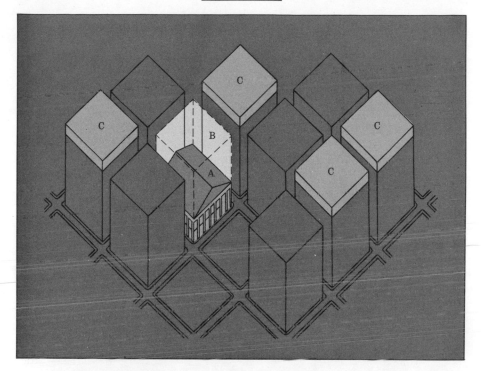

PROTOTYPE, DEVELOPMENT RIGHTS TRANSFER

A new concept known as transferable development rights (TDR) breaks the traditional link between a particular site and the location at which its development potential is implemented. In this example, presented by John Costonis in *Space Adrift,* "the landmark building (A) utilizes only a fraction of the development rights of the site. Its unused development rights (B) can be transferred to various other sites within a transfer district, and appear as additional bulk (C) on neighboring buildings."

development rights in this example, and in the best of all possible worlds, saves the farm for agricultural use, returns to the farm owner a fair market value imputed to his land as a result of the residential zoning, and allows the homes to be built in a more appropriate location. Once the rights to develop are sold, the farm cannot ever be developed.

The Benefits of TDR. Transferable development rights open up significant new planning options and opportunities, which stem from the flexibility and new conservation potentials inherent in a transferable develop-

SCHEMATIC DRAWING
OF TRANSFERABLE
DEVELOPMENT RIGHTS
IN RURAL AREA

Transferable development rights can also be used to protect land zoned for conversion to urban uses from being developed at all. If a TDR ordinance exists in a rural community, for example, an owner who wishes to preserve his undeveloped farmland could sell his building rights. The farmer is thus able to save his farm for agricultural use, while obtaining fair market value for his residentially zoned land.

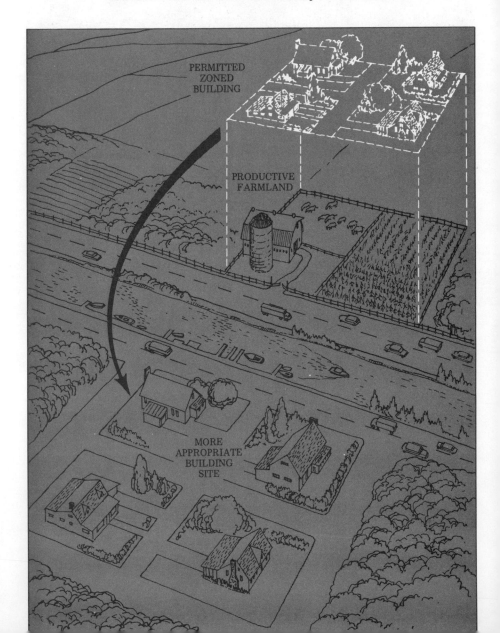

PERMITTED
ZONED
BUILDING

PRODUCTIVE
FARMLAND

MORE
APPROPRIATE
BUILDING
SITE

ment rights program. Flexibility is introduced because with TDR, zoning no longer need dictate a specific future use and appearance for a particular parcel of land. Rather, zoning simply allocates a package of development rights to the land. Conservation becomes a possibility because specific sites though zoned for building or redevelopment can be spared once the development rights are transferred elsewhere. Through an effective TDR program conservation objectives may be met without strictly limiting the rights of private owners.

Constitutional and political advantages also inhere in a TDR program. Provided there is a way to transfer the rights at a fair market value, no private property rights are denied. Neither police-power limitations nor costly eminent domain remedies need be involved. In terms of political and public benefit, transferable development rights potentially offer a means of implementing public-purpose planning actions, such as land preservation, environmental conservation, and historic-building protection, at no public expenditure. This eliminates one of the most frequent sources of citizen opposition to such programs.

TDR: The First Test Initiatives. Today, a number of cities, including Chicago and New York, have instituted limited, experimental transferable development rights programs, particularly to forward historic preservation. In New York City, a property owner may transfer or sell development rights from a landmark building to any adjacent or opposite site, or he may transfer the rights within certain limitations to another location where he owns property.

The legality both of landmark building designation and of the idea of development rights transfer was tested in a very significant case when proposed development over Grand Central Station, a designated landmark building, was introduced by its owner, the Penn Central Transportation Company. In an opinion rightfully applauded by advocates of historic-building preservation as a bench-mark victory, the U.S. Supreme Court upheld the idea that landmark buildings could be spared and that no compensation need be paid for underutilized air space so long as development rights above the landmark could be transferred. These, in effect, created a form of compensation to the private owner. Because New York City created a development rights transfer provision through its zoning ordinance, in effect, the terminal structure could be preserved in its present form without any public compensation due its owner.

In Chicago, the idea of transferable development rights was first proposed in an imaginative and thorough study by John J. Costonis, published in 1974 under the graphic and appropriate title *Space Adrift*. To

177

preserve older historic buildings in the downtown Loop of Chicago, Costonis proposed that the entire district be declared eligible for development rights transfer. Owners of landmark buildings could transfer their excess development rights to any non-landmark building or land parcel in the district. Costonis also proposed a "development rights bank" financed and operated by the city, which would purchase rights from private landmark owners who were unwilling or unable to transfer and sell them. The city could also condemn the development rights above a threatened landmark structure, were the owner unwilling to sell. Theoretically, the city could sustain the development rights bank by pooling development rights from public and private property, and selling them to owners of appropriate non-landmark sites within the transfer district.

A third initiative was pioneered in Puerto Rico. There, a TDR program was first instituted to preserve open land, the dramatic Phosphorescent Bay, whose rim was threatened by imminent development. Private owners were assigned transferable rights which could be utilized in preselected transfer districts. But in a significant departure from the New York and Chicago initiatives, the selected transfer districts were far from the protected resource, in most instances miles away in developing areas near cities or within certain city areas.

The purchase of development rights is now being used or actively considered by public agencies to preserve open land, farmland, ranches, and other undeveloped areas of special importance. In these instances, development rights are purchased by a public agency and then not resold. This is, in effect, a form of direct public subsidy to achieve a conservation or land-use preservation objective. The cost is below the full market value acquisition price for the property, inasmuch as the owner, who sells his development rights, retains title to the land and maintains a continuing right to use it for farming or ranching purposes.

In 1974, Suffolk County on Long Island led the way with the first public acquisition of development rights. A $50 million program there was promulgated to preserve thousands of acres of prime farmland by this means. Though the program has been somewhat curtailed in a fiscal and political squeeze, eventually 3,300 to 15,000 acres of the most productive farmland in America are expected to be preserved there for agricultural use. Similar initiatives are under way in Connecticut, Maryland, and Wyoming, where conservationists have waged a protracted struggle to preserve large private acreage in and near Jackson Hole, a fast-developing area of unusual beauty at the base of the Teton Range.

Unresolved Problems. The idea of TDR is superb; but because of a substantial number of still unresolved economic, political, and legal problems, the potential for transferable development rights as a conservation, preservation, and planning tool has not yet been fully realized.

Two basic concepts are at work. The first relies upon a free market transfer or sale and subsequent use of development rights, as was proposed in the New York City and Chicago plans. This I call the *reuse approach*. The second is a system of public purchase of development rights with no reuse intended; in essence, the potential right to develop is retired, or eliminated. This I call the *retirement approach*. Both methods pose unresolved issues that will, I believe, eventually be worked out in communities and in the courts, as the concept of TDR is too compelling and promising to be abandoned.

It is the reuse approach that offers the greatest potential, for it requires no public expenditure. Yet it is by far the more complex. Here are top-priority questions that need to be ironed out before widespread application of reuse TDR is possible:

1. What happens if there is no market for the rights? That is, what if no private developer wants them, in the case of reuse rights, or if no public agency is willing to buy retirement rights?

2. How is protection of private property rights, which is implicit in conventional zoning, to be maintained if TDR actions are permitted? How, for instance, is a recipient site for transferred reuse rights to be selected? What protection do residents and property owners in the recipient neighborhood potentially lose? Must they be compensated? How will transfers be rigorously controlled so that neither design abuse nor density abuse occurs in the designated recipient areas?

3. Under what conditions is the transfer of development rights to be declared mandatory, as a consequence of valid police-power authority, and under what conditions is the transfer to be voluntary? Where mandatory action is proclaimed, there must be some form of assured recipient; otherwise, just compensation is unconstitutionally denied. And there must be a legally sound basis, in the first place, to sustain a program of mandatory development rights transfer. What are the proper bases?

4. How is the program to work in terms of procedure? May only public authorities transfer rights? At which level—local, regional, county, state—is the program to be administered? How do private exchanges occur? What form of legal instrument is to be used?

5. To create a sure market for development rights, uncharacteristically restrictive conventional zoning may have to be promulgated. How is such a deliberate policy of restriction of private rights to be justified so that a selective and limited resource-protection program will work effectively?

6. Finally, is owning a development right really "just compensation"? How is the owner of a protected resource, such as a historic property, to be paid if there is no immediate cash purchaser? In effect, is the development right a sham form of compensation that leaves the private, regulated owner of property at risk? Under what circumstances might the private owner be able to uphold a claim of an uncompensated taking of private property?

Transferable Development Rights That Already Work. Given these very real and very practical problems, the most workable way to use transferable development rights at this time is through the retirement approach. The development rights are purchased by a public body or nonprofit organization, then transferred off the land or from above the building, and retired. Title to the property remains vested with the original owner, who is paid a fair value for giving up the right ever to develop further. Once the rights are transferred, the private owner's taxes decline. The land and/or buildings that remain are then more economically maintained.

When the rights do not have to be used somewhere else, or resold, the problems of establishing and maintaining a viable development rights market vanish, as do the problems of assuring no adverse impact to the physical surroundings or to individuals in the recipient area. What is accomplished is a less expensive alternative for a public authority or nonprofit group to realize specific non-development objectives than is presented by the outright purchase of property. The owner is compensated for the current value of the development right he relinquishes, a value that will always be less than the full market value of the property.

In spite of the costs involved, I believe that funds should be routinely included each year in local, regional, state, and federal government budgets as a mandatory, restricted budget line limited to the purchase of development rights on land of unusual public importance. Development itself, with all of the attendant public costs for services, schools, roads, and the like, is even more expensive for taxpayers. And the loss of unique land resources is irreversible.

When the figures are analyzed, especially for local government, open space emerges as the best buy. This is particularly true in communities where many public services are provided. Studies in Palo Alto, California, for instance, confirm that it costs resident taxpayers there less to buy and preserve 6,000 acres of open space than to permit conventional residential development of the property. In a community where few public services are required, initial development may not be so costly in terms of public expenditures; but as the population rises, so does the cost to everyone.

Reuse Rights: The Challenge of the 1980s. Reuse development rights transfer is a thrust of such importance to the equitable management of land resources in years to come that it must be accepted by innovative public officials and private owners of property as the challenge of the 1980s. Such an approach does link a more sophisticated form of public power to economic realities of the marketplace, a way to improved planning and compliance. Or as John Costonis has said: ". . . the conceit that severs physical planning from its economic consequences is slowly giving way to recognition that bold physical planning programs conceived in an economic vacuum are prime candidates for the scrap heap."

Once the notion of transferable development rights is accepted, many different, competing interests will be served. Land and building resources of public importance will be candidates for widespread preservation and conservation; questionable use of police power by local government to restrict private-property rights will no longer be so great an issue; more thoughtful long-term planning for community development will be required, and will eventually become more pervasive.

Viewed with a bit of perspective over the twentieth century, development rights transfer is recognizable as the present-day cutting edge of a consistent movement toward greater flexibility in zoning. First introduced in the 1920s, conventional zoning exerted public control over the use and therefore the value of all regulated private property. As the years have passed, more imaginative forms of public control over private rights have followed. As we have seen, cluster zoning and planned unit development options encourage planned, interrelated sequences of land uses over a total large acreage to replace lot-by-lot zoning assignments. Incentive zoning and special district zoning encourage a negotiation between public powers and private owners to induce the private developer to establish some form of public amenity.

Within this brief span of about sixty years, there is persuasive evidence that change can occur in the way land is generally regulated. Changes already on the books in most places lead right up to and stop just short of development rights transfer. All of the elements are there but unconnected. In addition, there are first initiatives that have already been tried with limited success in New York, Chicago, and elsewhere.

What is needed now is persistence and commitment. Private owners can benefit, and public policy can be advanced. The first undertakings inevitably are flawed. The promotion of TDR at this stage requires rough slogging through mires of political resistence, legal snarls, and economic tangles. In time, I believe, TDR will provide a creative new basis for more equitable and more acceptable public regulation of land in America. It may take a decade to hammer out effective strategies to implement more widespread development rights transfer, but it is a promising direction, one worth the effort.

PLANNING, ZONING, AND WEALTH: THE ISSUES

And so the interdependence of land, public power, and private wealth continues to intensify. Through zoning, land use and value can be manipulated. It is for this reason that land planning, which so often depends on a zoning solution, is itself mistrusted and even feared. As a process that increasingly seeks ways to exert public power over all aspects of private land use and community development, land planning is political and has fundamental economic implications.

Public goals, of course, are not necessarily consistent. Federal land policy is often at variance with itself, department by department. States inevitably disagree not only on what the federal direction should be but with each other's goals and policies as well. In turn, communities often oppose state policy, as well as one another's; and within every local community planning board, there is disagreement, to say nothing of inevitable conflict. Throughout this chaotic maze of regulatory conflict and disagreement, however, there is but one common direction: increased public power and control over private land.

A Few Prescriptions.   Conventional lot-by-lot zoning, as it has come to be administered, is generally archaic at worst and, at best, limited in its ability to guide sensitively and appropriately multiple aspects of community development. While no magical, instant panacea comes to mind, a few new concepts ought to be incorporated into any up-to-date community planning program:

1.   The most important ecological and historic areas in America are invaluable in their present form and should be preserved. However, for economic value lost in the realization of historic and environmental conservation, private owners of such areas should be compensated. Numerous possibilities exist: tax reductions, permitted bonus cluster development, and transferable development rights are among them.
2.   Each town should be guided by a comprehensive plan, which should

provide for long-range, orderly, and timed development related to
school sites, road capacities, and other public services. The comprehensive plan should not be a simple land-use program. Rather, it
should interconnect financial, social, and physical plans with economic forecasts, and it should be subject to systematic and periodic
revision.

3. Each community should plan for and accept a "fair share" of low-
   income housing as an integral aspect of the social, economic, and
   physical planning inherent in the comprehensive plan.
4. Especially important open spaces should be purchased each year out
   of annual budgets set aside at local, regional, state, and federal levels
   of government.
5. Zoning regulations should be re-evaluated at least every five years
   and on a community-wide basis.
6. It is imperative to plan in advance for a desired urban, suburban, or
   rural density. A decision about limits of population and rates of
   growth should be made openly and consciously in every community,
   then re-evaluated five to ten years hence.

We are now over half a century past the day when zoning was declared
legal by the Supreme Court. But few can say that most parts of most
communities are significantly better for it. People in big cities, smaller
towns, older villages, and open countryside are worried about the future
of the land. Our continued reliance on conventional zoning to perform in
a more complex capacity than it is capable of is unwise.

If effective control of land use is ever to be achieved, a new approach
is required. More than separate, innovative, or specialized regulatory
planning and legal tools are needed, as is more than a coterie of concerned
citizens and specialists. On the technical, political, and legal fronts, what
we lack most of all is clear thinking about the relationship between land
control and land value. When the interconnections between land, power,
and wealth are better understood and acknowledged, more equitable and
flexible policies for the planning and use of private land in America will
be possible.

SIX

CLOSING
THE DOOR TO
DEVELOPMENT:
NEW POWER,
NEW PURPOSES

When it comes to manipulating the relationship between land, power, and wealth, more and more people seek a new formula. They want to protect the value of their own land, and retain the life and appearance which had characterized their own community in the past. As Michael Dukakis, former governor of Massachusetts, said with clarity and accuracy not long ago, "Villages don't want to be suburbs, suburbs don't want to be cities, and cities don't want to be wastelands."

This attitude is particularly evident in the more stable suburbs and in the increasingly aware and sophisticated outlying rural towns and non-metropolitan areas. In these places, the people who live in town tend to own the land and their own houses. As their properties become more valuable than they ever dreamed, they get wise, sophisticated, political—as never before—and take a stand, to control community growth. Beyond the inner suburbs, this is happening across America.

Middle-class America no longer believes that its land investments, houses, neighborhoods, and communities can be saved or protected by scatter shot tactics or benign neglect of local social and political events. Too much time has passed. Too much has happened.

Those who bailed out of the cities or evacuated the inner suburbs now look back in anguish. They feel emancipated from a dreadful and danger-ous time. They vow never to let it happen again. And those well-off resi-dents who, from the sanctuary of farther out, have for so long watched the frightful social, economic, and environmental deterioration of so large an area of so many American cities and their connected traditional suburbs, harden the line of defense. The combination is formidable. Its strength shows up in local law, local administrative practice, local political issues, and courts of law at every level.

Out of this alliance has come a vast array of new land controls, as well as an acceptance of control over the land. Though the control mechanisms are varied and growing rapidly, the most fundamental objectives remain limited, predictable, and obvious although unstated: (1) limit the number of newcomers; (2) screen the newcomers to make sure they will not cause "problems"; (3) select newcomers—when they are welcome at all—who can pay their own way and therefore will not place a financial burden on the rest of the community; (4) do everything possible to assure the future desirable quality of land, housing, and real estate in town.

The Cost of Newcomers. The cost of newcomers to established residents is considerable. Palo Alto, California, zoned ten square miles of undeveloped land into 10-acre parcels not long ago to thwart building. It did so after thorough economic analysis indicated that each new home required (in 1974 dollars) a municipal expenditure of $17,000 over and above the annual property-tax rate. A 1972 study conducted in Denver, Colorado, established that each new residence could cost taxpayers $21,-000 for community services. Stanford University investigators determined that a 1,262-unit subdivision near San Francisco would cost the community $400,000 a year by 1982 in indirect subsidies for public services. While these very large sums relate to specific economic conditions and a high quality of service, the disclosured public cost of newcomers to any community tends to inflame the economic imagination of residents.

The central lesson of these and other similar studies is this: It is the specific demographic characteristics of new residents which fortell their impact on local community life and finances. "Immigrants" to most suburban and rural communities, particularly those who purchase new housing of two, three, and four bedrooms, tend to be young households with more preschool and school-age children than households in older communities. The cost of public education represents 50 percent or more of many local budgets. Thus, the greater the number of public school students per dwelling unit, the greater the drain on local finances.

Given this reality, unless local revenue from new households with children is substantially higher than the community average, older residents find themselves paying for the newcomers. It is, in part, for this reason that established residents in many locales are more likely to favor small condominium units, one-bedroom garden apartments, and even luxury high-rise apartments rather than conventional subdivision housing or publicly assisted family housing. And it is for this reason, in many places, that established residents prefer to abridge population growth altogether.

ZONING AND THE CONTROL OF GROWTH

In recent years, communities across America have decided to resist population growth. A few have established very new forms of zoning and associated legal control over community development. The city of Petaluma in California and the town of Ramapo in New York are two communities which push the frontiers of zoning into entirely new territory.

Conventional zoning does not include a consideration of *time*. Once the

187

zoning map is drawn, any piece of land in town can be developed, at any time. The most desirable sequence of events is not considered. The significance of both the Petaluma and Ramapo plans is that each, though in different ways, endeavors to link sequential factors in community development to an envisioned goal for the physical, social, and fiscal future. This new excursion into land-use control through control over timing of development brings with it a new and profoundly important force capable of dramatically affecting the value of land.

Petaluma, California.   Petaluma, California, became a suburb of San Francisco in 1956 when Highway 101 was redesigned and rerouted as a freeway. Between 1969 and 1970, 2,280 people moved to Petaluma, up over 100 percent from the previous year. In 1971, 891 housing units were built, a large increase from fifty-nine the year before. The next year nearly 1,000 units were proposed. During the 1970s, 90 percent of all new development took place in the eastern part of town, where zoning made it possible for developers to build inexpensive homes on 6,000-square-foot lots.

The sudden spurt of growth led to double sessions in schools, and complaints about classroom size, and inadequate parks and playgrounds. In addition, the sewage-treatment system's capacity was being sorely challenged by the population boom. As a result, Petaluma's City Planning Department grew alarmed and organized moratoriums on rezoning and land annexation. Finally in 1972 a plan was established to limit new housing construction to five hundred dwelling units a year for each of the next five years. This control over growth, and the way the units are selected, is known as the Petaluma Plan.

As a consequence of the Petaluma Plan, a large housing developer must submit complete plans, specifications, and site designs in accordance with the formulated Petaluma Residential Development Control System in order to obtain the right to build. The submitted development plan is reviewed by the Petaluma Residential Development Evaluation Board, then rated against all other submissions for the coming year. The board itself consists of one representative from the city council, the planning commission, business and professional interests, each of the four local school districts, and the public at large.

Each application must conform to the Petaluma General Plan (the city's comprehensive plan) and to the Petaluma Environmental Design Plan. Each submission is then rated with regard to specific criteria in two general categories: availability of public utilities and services; and quality of design, and contribution to public welfare and amenity.

The list of criteria in each of these two categories constitutes a potpourri of considerations which any community might easily incorporate into aspects of its own planning, zoning, and development permission procedure. The criteria are also likely to discourage all but the most determined housing developer. The list of criteria is as follows:

1. Utilities and Public Services:
   a) The capacity of the water system to provide for the needs of the proposed development without system extensions beyond those normally installed by the developer;
   b) The capacity of the sanitary sewers to dispose of the wastes of the proposed development without system extension beyond those normally installed by the developer;
   c) The capacity of the drainage facilities to adequately dispose of the surface run-off of the proposed development without system extensions beyond those normally installed by the developer;
   d) The ability of the Fire Department of the City to provide fire protection according to the established response standard of the City without the necessity of establishing a new station or requiring addition of major equipment to an existing station;
   e) The capacity of the appropriate school to absorb the children expected to inhabit a proposed development without necessitating adding double sessions or other unusual scheduling or classroom overcrowding;
   f) The capacity of major street linkage to provide for the needs of the proposed development without substantially altering existing traffic patterns or overloading the existing street system, and the availability of other public facilities (such as parks and playgrounds) to meet the additional demands for vital public services without extension of services beyond those provided by the developer.

2. Quality of Design and Contribution to Public Welfare and Amenity:
   a) Site and architectural design quality which may be indicated by the harmony of the proposed buildings in terms of size, height, color, and location with respect to existing neighboring development;
   b) Site and architectural design quality which may be indicated by the amount and character of landscaping and screening;
   c) Site and architectural design quality which may be indicated by the arrangement of the site for efficiency of circulation, on-and-off-site traffic safety, privacy, etc.;
   d) The provision of public and/or private usable open space and/or pathways along the Petaluma River or any creek;
   e) Contributions to and extensions of existing systems of foot or bicycle paths, equestrian trails and the greenbelt provided for in the Environmental Design Plans;
   f) The provision of needed public facilities, such as critical linkages in the major street system, schoolrooms, or other vital public facilities;

g) The extent to which the proposed development accomplished an orderly and contiguous extension of existing development as against "leapfrog" development;

h) The provision of units to meet the City's policy goal of 8 percent to 12 percent low- and moderate-income dwelling units annually.

To be approved, each proposed development must attain a minimum score based on compliance with these regulations. Only the top-scoring five hundred units are accepted each year, and they in turn are further selected by sub-quotas set annually by the city among the three recognized different physical sectors of the city to assure that every part of the community receives some new development. There are also quotas within each physical sector for multifamily and single-family dwellings; the city council can also require that between 8 and 12 percent of each year's quota be devoted to low-income and moderate-income housing. This system permits the kind of bureaucratic control that is understandably resented by many land sellers and housing developers. And yet its ability to time, plan, and monitor community change is undeniable.

As a consequence of the Petaluma Plan, and aided by a housing slump and the decision of some builders to work elsewhere, new development did fall off. Indeed, it subsided below the 6 percent anticipated and authorized growth levels considered desirable by municipal officials. But the goal of better planning for housing, recreation and site design, and for overall community development when new building did occur was realized.

The construction industry, as might be expected, tried to void the Petaluma Plan. There was little sympathy for public controls which force a reduction in annual housing starts—from about 1,000 a year to no more than five hundred—and which also involve a lot of red tape. The industry went to court—and came out the loser. After long hearings and one court reversal, the Petaluma Plan was upheld. The main thrust of many differing state and federal court decisions regarding the legality of controlling growth is this: The ordinance must attempt to meet anticipated problems and must not be deliberately discriminatory.

The Petaluma Plan and Land Values. The plan's impact on both housing and land values is significant. When it became difficult to obtain new building permits, many fine Victorian houses in the older central and western parts of town were rehabilitated. With the annual supply of new housing limited, the value of most existing houses tended to increase more rapidly than it otherwise would. It became easier to sell a house, and at a higher price. At the same time, bureaucratic procedures and administrative delays involved in compliance with the plan raised development costs by as much as $3,000 to $4,000 per new house.

The impact on the value of undeveloped land is more complex but equally clear. Suddenly, development of open land in town is connected to public expenditures, design analysis, and social priorities, all filtered through a review and planning procedure. Total development is cut back. A 50 percent reduction in building units each year translates roughly into a 50 percent reduction in land actually needed for development. The accelerated rate of land conversion of prior years is thus reversed. Also, scattered building activity beyond the greenbelt is curbed; and much of the vacant land there that cannot meet the utilities and public service criteria is suddenly likely to remain undeveloped for years to come.

A shift in land values results. The value of a likely development site soars, whereas the value of other parcels of land, especially beyond the greenbelt, does not keep pace, and may even decline. In the adjustments that occur, the anticipated speculative increment in land value is squeezed out of some locations and bestowed upon others. Its loss is felt deeply by those who bought unwisely or speculatively in the wrong locations.

Ramapo, New York. The town of Ramapo went about controlling community development in another way, but the objectives were the same: slow growth, control of the land, control of time as a factor related to land development.

Ramapo, a large town near New York City, more than doubled in population between 1960 and 1970. Under the direction of a conventional zoning ordinance, Ramapo was being transformed from a pleasant rural enclave into a typical, busy suburban community.

Like Petaluma, Ramapo decided in 1969 to take hold of its own future. To do so it passed a radically amended zoning ordinance. The "General Considerations" of the amended zoning ordinance state the problem of rapid growth and the way it is to be tackled:

Faced with the physical, social, and fiscal problems caused by the rapid and unprecedented growth, the Town of Ramapo had adopted a comprehensive master plan to guide its future development and has adopted an official map and a capital program so as to provide for the maximum orderly, adequate, and economical development of its future residential, commercial, industrial and public land uses and community facilities, including transportation, water, sewerage, schools, parks and recreation, drainage, and other public facilities.

In order to ensure that these comprehensive and coordinated plans are not frustrated by disorganized, unplanned, and uncoordinated development which would create an undue burden and hardship on the ability of the community to translate these plans into reality, the following objectives are established as policy determinations of zoning and planning for the Town of Ramapo:

1. To economize on the costs of municipal facilities and services to carefully phase residential development with efficient provision of public improvements;
2. To establish and maintain municipal control over the eventual character of development;
3. To establish and maintain a desirable degree of balance among the various uses of the land;
4. To establish and maintain essential quality of community services and facilities.

To implement these objectives, large-scale residential development has been put under rigorous control; and property whose development potential is delayed is granted some property-tax relief. The town issues development permits only to those proposed new developments which pass a rating test with a high score. Unlike the Petaluma approach, Ramapo's plan sets no annual limit on the number of residential units. Any proposal that can garner fifteen "development points" on the following test is issued a "Special Permit" to proceed. The standards for issuance of the permit are extremely rigorous.

No special permit shall be issued by the Town Board unless the residential development has available fifteen (15) development points on the following scale of values:

1. Sewers
   (a) Public sewers available in RR–50, R–40, R–35, R–25, R–15, and R–15S districts .... 5 points
   (b) Package Sewer Plants .... 3 points
   (c) County-approved septic system in an RR–80 district .... 3 points
   (d) All others .... 0 points
2. Drainage: Percentage of Required Drainage Capacity Available
   (a) 100% or more .... 5 points
   (b) 90% to 99.9% .... 4 points
   (c) 80% to 89.9% .... 3 points
   (d) 65% to 79.9% .... 2 points
   (e) 50% to 64.9% .... 1 point
   (f) less than 50% .... 0 points
3. Improved Public Park or Recreation Facility Including Public School Site
   (a) Within ¼ mile .... 5 points
   (b) Within ½ mile .... 3 points

    (c) Within 1 mile   1 point

    (d) Farther than 1 mile   0 points

4. State, County, or Town Major, Secondary, or Collector Roads Improved with Curbs and Sidewalks

    (a) Direct Access   5 points

    (b) Within ½ mile   3 points

    (c) Within 1 mile   1 point

    (d) Farther than 1 mile   0 points

5. Fire House

    (a) Within 1 mile   3 points

    (b) Within 2 miles   1 point

    (c) Farther than 2 miles   0 points

All distances shall be computed from the proposed location of each separate lot or plot capable of being improved with a residential dwelling and not from the boundaries of the entire parcel. The Town Board shall issue the special permit specifying the number of dwelling units that meet the standards set forth herein.

Thus, in effect, to garner enough points to qualify for the special permit, a new development must be near existing or within the path of planned sewers, parks, improved roads, and fire control facilities. The program's main objective is to restrict new development to areas of prior building, to assure optimum use of public facilities, and to guarantee that open land is not needlessly developed.

As drafted and established, Ramapo's plan is given a duration of eighteen years. Incorporating a time limit into the plan rather than relying upon implied perpetual regulation proved most important to the plan's ability to survive court challenges. Damages to landowners could be declared "temporary," and the program considered experimental.

Ramapo's plan and its implicit de-emphasis of new development on remote acreage provoked the instant ire of some large landowners, including Ruth Golden, and the contract purchaser of her land, who failed to qualify for a special permit. Golden sued the planning board, claiming that the property's value and marketability had been diminished. Round and round through the courts the argument traveled, while interested landowners, planners, and public officials across America watched attentively. Finally, in 1972, the plan was declared legal by the Court of Appeals, the highest state court in New York. In one of the most important recent cases in zoning history, the court ruled that Golden was not individually damaged, even though her land had been rendered virtually unsalable at the present time. The court declared:

The undisputed effect of these integrated efforts in land-use planning and development is to provide an overall program of orderly growth and adequate facilities through a sequential development policy commensurate with progressing availability and capacity of public facilities.

The court went on to express considerable sympathy with Golden's plight but offered no prospect of financial compensation:

The hardship of holding unproductive property for some time might be compensated for by the ultimate benefit inuring to the individual owner in the form of a substantial increase in valuation, or for that matter, the landowner might be compelled to chafe under the temporary restriction, without the benefit of such compensation, when the burden serves to promote the public good.

The court holds out the prospect to Golden that some day, some way, she may be bailed out by inflation. The court also looks upon an 18-year period as "temporary," and opines that comprehensive planning, whatever its impact on land values, serves the "public good." Thus, even if private property values are severely compromised, no monetary compensation is due.

As a result of this landmark ruling, a sequential development ordinance will most likely be sustained by the courts if it meets the following criteria, as summarized by David Robert Nelson, a real-estate development executive, in his recent article, "The Growing Problem":

There is no absolute prohibition against the the subdivision of land. (Otherwise, the ordinance may be attached as a taking.)

The controls are not exclusionary, and they permit all types of housing.

The ordinance is a reasonable solution to a community problem. (The community has limited resources.)

The ordinance is lawfully enacted.

It has a specific time limit.

It permits tax relief on properties whose development has been delayed.

Before Ramapo, never had a town dictated such specifications to landowners and developers within its jurisdiction. Never before had the potential to develop land been timed so specifically to a public-improvement plan. Never before had those in possession of private property been advised that it might be up to eighteen years—the term of the promulgated capital-improvement plan—before their land would, in fact, be marketable.

Throughout the history of land speculation and land development in America, individuals and corporations had purposefully timed land purchases and sales to public and private infrastructure undertakings of all sorts: to the development of railroads, the building of transit lines, the construction of bridges and roads, and more recently to the location of electrical power service, sewage systems, and water mains. In Ramapo, these considerations are mandatory; and as a result, public investment becomes the centerpiece of growth and control of private community development. Land speculators and developers have always wanted to capture the value of infrastructure improvements created at public cost. In Ramapo, they now have no other choice.

Losers and Winners in Growth Control. Certain landowners who want to sell or develop benefit considerably from such new regulations. The benefits may simply be fortuitous or the result of informed land selection in the first place, or perhaps even a most carefully conceived collaboration between landowners and those who exercise public power over the land-development process.

The most direct value-enhancing benefit accrues to an area earmarked for development while most other lands are restricted. This situation guarantees that significant public expenditures will be directed toward it in the form of road improvements, as well as possibly water and sewer facilities. It also means that anyone who wants to develop raw land or build a house in a new subdivision is a potential purchaser. The beneficiary is likely to raise prices to the limit that the market will bear.

In this situation, the well-positioned land seller or developer has been granted a most important premier right: the right to move forward with development plans in the present rather than sometime in an uncertain, deferred future. Consequently, land can be converted to cash, and in the near term, thereby eliminating an enormous element of risk and uncertainty. Nothing devalues land (or common stock) more than uncertainty about the future, a lack of clarity about timing, or fear of new regulations that will prevail. Therefore, the present right to develop imparts great value to land.

Those whose land cannot be used in the near future, on the other hand, cannot claim a taking so long as the ordinance is valid under the police-power definition of land regulation and other constitutional rights have been protected, such as fairness, opportunity to be heard, reasonable potential return on equity, opportunity to show hardship, and so on. The large landholder is forced into the unwanted position of uncertainty and risk, which abridges his right to act. This devalues his current equity in land.

Across the country, those persons holding large tracts of open land tremble at the implications of *Golden* v. *Planning Board of Ramapo*. Many rush their open land through a conventional subdivision process in fear of potential restrictive-growth amendments to current conventional zoning. Often these landowners seek platting approval of open land into residential lots, with no intention of building or selling. What they are doing is buying land-value insurance. If more rigorous subdivision regulations are passed, they reason, then previously subdivided lots will become all the more valuable, all the more sought after.

Ramapo's plan and its attendant court ruling should be duly noted by private landowners and public officials. In many towns with rapid growth and population pressure on land and on services, the tendency is to seek more innovative and imaginative forms of growth control, approaches which will work with low administrative costs and which do not require costly public acquisition of land.

INDIRECT CONTROL OF GROWTH: SELECTING THE NEWCOMERS

In smaller towns and suburbs, a strong, politically wise coalition of conservative citizens opposed to increased community development and higher property taxes is now forming. These people are often middle-class settlers from the cities and inner suburbs set on excluding minority groups and low-income families from their community. In a contemporary turn of events, these groups are often bolstered by the crusading vision of environmentalists and conservationists, who offer a new ideological twist to the cause.

The realization of both the explicit and implicit objectives of these groups depends upon a number of newly emerging approaches to land-use control which, directly or indirectly, limit and help in the selection of new residents. These approaches make use of a new vocabulary: upzoning; code prohibitions; large-lot frontage requirements; ecological and environmental zoning; sewer, power, and water moratorium; timed development control; neighborhood conservation; historic district ordinances; agricultural districts; open-space conservation programs. And the list goes on. Each of these terms identifies a regulatory approach that not only accomplishes its own particular stated objective but also tends to raise the cost of new development, and therefore simultaneously makes it more and more difficult for the low income and poor to settle in such communities.

The last ten years have been a decade of testing, as never before, the expanded possibilities for land-use control by middle-income and upper-income landowners for their own benefit. A brief look at the consequences of prohibiting construction of multiple dwellings, of encouraging large-lot zoning, or of establishing building code controls and of making the subdivision process more costly illustrates how certain community development controls serve to limit and select potential new residents.

The Large Building Lot. Community-wide zoning that bans apartments, mobile homes, and small housing lots reduces the overall potential number of people who can afford to move into town. These restrictions also increase the cost of a building lot. What happens these days is that the "general welfare," the original justification to zone land, is interpreted as the general welfare of those residents who have political power and already live in town. Power is being used to control community growth and to protect real estate values. As Anthony Downs, an experienced real-estate consultant and member of the Brookings Institution in Washington, has said, "No household 'must have' a 1-acre lot for healthful living, since millions of healthy Americans live on far smaller lots. In fact, there is no known, well-documented minimum lot size per household for healthful living."

A decisive increase in the size of a land parcel required before a house may be constructed significantly reduces the ultimate population limit of the community. For example, let us assume that an average-size suburban or rural family consists of approximately 3.5 people. In a town of 10,000 residential acres, where four dwellings per acre are permitted, the population potential is 140,000 people. If the density limit is reduced to one acre per dwelling, then no more than 35,000 residents might be expected, even though the same amount of land will be utilized. The procedure is simple. The difference is immense, and resident owners of land and houses recognize it.

In their article "Political Values and Population Density Control," James G. Coke and Charles S. Liebman point out, "By this simple device of large-lot zoning, suburbanites believe that a municipality can achieve its developmental goals in a single stroke. The community will be beautiful, its taxes will be low, and 'undesirables' will be kept out."

Large-lot zoning in the final analysis is not aimed at assuring a healthful, safe environment. Rather, its goal is to assure a restrictive environment in which suburban and rural residential land values and real-estate values are protected, and even positively stimulated in an upward direction.

A recent statewide study of attitudes among suburban leaders in New Jersey yielded the expected results. Of all housing types, the single-family house on the large lot was found to be "desirable" by nearly 80 percent of the people polled. The single-family house on a "small" lot was ap-

197

proved by just under 50 percent, as were garden apartments. High-rise apartments and mobile homes were considered "undesirable" by very large majorities. Of course, apartments are viewed in suburban and non-metropolitan America as a dangerously permissive housing form. Rental housing, many believe, encourages and facilitates transient, lower-income people to become residents. Without an ownership interest, such residents are assumed to be irresponsible. Apartments thus become synonomous, in the minds of many established residents, with blight, crime, decay, and high taxes.

As construction and land costs mount, increasing numbers of suburban towns, and even some nonmetropolitan communities, do permit apartment developments. But where these developments are permitted, and what kind of apartments are tolerated is extremely revealing of an ingrained bias. Quite often, the apartment zone is in a commercial area, where land costs make apartment development unlikely or even unfeasible. Or development in an apartment zone may be laced with many other restrictions which guarantee that the only tenants will be residents with high incomes. In other places, some apartments are acceptable, but not those large enough to house a family. This restriction precludes the family with school-age children. Another way to ensure that the "right" newcomers move into available apartments is to approve only those developments which guarantee age restrictions, a stipulation by no means limited to so-called retirement communities.

Restrictions with a bias toward older people, whether in free-market projects or in subsidized housing, assure that most new community residents will be beyond the age of high-crime incidence and safely beyond the child-rearing age. These residents come with dependable incomes, medical insurance, normal consumer tastes, and no resident children. At the same time, if the project is a subsidized unit, by accepting it at all, the community scores points for compliance with federal regulations and qualifies for money that can be used, let us say (as it is in some places) to reduce property taxes or to buy open space—both of which further reduce the number of sites in town where newcomers can settle, and tend to raise the value of local real estate.

By far, however, the most common regulatory approach is to prohibit apartment construction altogether, mobile homes as well. As recently as 1973, 8 million Americans, or about 4 percent of the population, lived in mobile homes. In 1971, over 30 percent of all single-family housing units started were mobile homes. In 1979, the average purchase price for a mobile home was under $30,000, less than half that for a conventional single-family home. Also, operating costs for mobile homes are low, a consequence of their efficient design, small interior space, and minuscule land occupancy. While mobile homes do offer affordable, mass-produced housing, they are generally barred from, or severely restricted in, most middle-income– and upper-income–dominated suburbs and towns.

When the zoning ordinance designates available mobile-home park space at all, it is apt to be in an unpopular commercial or industrial zone, "across the tracks," tucked away. This reduces the likelihood that upwardly mobile visitors and prospective home buyers will see the development, and increases the likelihood that most residents will forget its presence.

The High-Cost Building Code.   There are other regulatory measures, though more indirect, which help a community select its residents. One is to adopt a very rigorous building code, the blueprint for local construction quality that must be satisfied before the developer can obtain a "certificate of occupancy," the right to use a new building.

In many communities, a building permit is required before construction can begin. All local building regulations and standards must be adhered to in projected plans and specifications before the permit is granted. If these standards add extra costs, fewer people will elect to build, and the houses which are constructed will be more expensive.

Hidden in the building code is a message, then, of how anxious a community is to attract new development. It is hidden in specifications for drainage pipe, electrical wiring, the thickness of fireproof sheetrock; in the requirement for the spacing of wall studs and roof beams; in the depth to which the foundation block must be laid or the concrete for the cellar floor poured.

The building code dictates a basic level of construction expense per square foot of building. An average-size house of 1,200 square feet might cost $50,000 to build in one town and $72,000 across the town line. This difference affects many construction decisions and many prospective purchasers as well. It slows community growth in one community and stimulates it in the next, where a lenient building code permits relatively inexpensive construction. Thus, building codes are one of the most subtle of all growth-management tools. They quietly proclaim the ante required to get into the club. Towns which opt for top-quality construction in their codes generally opt for top-income residents in their communities.

Inflating the Cost and Limiting the Availability of Utility Service.
While some people relish domestic existence without running water, electrical service, and subsurface sewage disposal, they usually envision this independent way of life in an isolated cabin amid a sylvan glade. Most people, however, prefer to live with modern conveniences; and to do so,

these three fundamental services are needed. Each comes at a price and, in most instances, is controlled by town regulation and/or utility monopoly. If any of these three is either terribly difficult or expensive to obtain, an immediate incentive *not* to build is created. Locally written and promulgated ordinances may be responsible.

For instance, the stipulation that all new electrical lines run belowground, while improving the appearance of an area immeasurably, also more than doubles the cost of electrical services to the prospective home buyer. The provision that any new house must obtain water from an organized water company or water authority requires the laying of water lines, perhaps miles down a public road and then throughout the new subdivision and beneath each lot, a costly enterprise. And the requirement that all sewage disposal be handled by a treatment system, perhaps thereby preserving underground and visible streams from pollutants, all but eliminates the possible use of most land for development that is not located near an existing treatment plant and adds very substantial cost even to property that is nearby. These subtle controls over essential services dictate where new land is developed, where outsiders may gain entry —and at what price.

Expensive Subdivision Regulations.   Zoning defines the minimum lot size in each zoning area; the subdivision regulation defines its shape and what improvements the developer must provide. Here is another area in which very subtle control can be exercised to maintain high construction costs, as well as high existing lot prices.

The largest improvement cost the developer usually encounters is that of new road construction. In most places, even residential roads must be sufficiently large and substantial to become public rights-of-way. This requirement generally requires the paving of a hard surface road of anywhere from 18 to 35 feet wide, and means a cost from $25.00 to $100 per lineal foot. If each lot must have only 20 feet of road frontage, as in city lots, and if the road costs $40.00 per foot, the developer's cost that is added to the land value for the road is $800. However, in more and more communities which mandate large lots and which want to "preserve their rural character," road frontage requirements of 120 to 140 feet are commonplace. Assuming the same road development costs per lineal foot, this single requirement adds $4,800 to $5,600 to the cost of the lot. These are costly expenditures, especially when added on top of the costs of house construction, financing, and all the rest.

Indeed, as can be seen from the figures above, a town can exert enormous control over the cost of new lots not just through lot frontage requirements but also through the engineering standards, which must be met in the development of a new subdivision road. If a town demands that a residential road be built more like an interstate highway, a foot of road may not cost $40.00, as in the previous illustration, but more likely twice that amount, as it does today in many elite towns, such as Greenwich, Connecticut, and Southampton, New York. On the same lot of 120 to 140 front feet, the road cost alone escalates to between $9,600 to $11,200, more than most people in America can afford to pay for the entire building lot. The type of road and the amount of road frontage, both which fall under the absolute control of local government, assume an importance that is rarely recognized.

In all, large lots, expensive building standards, large frontages on new streets, costly utility services, and high-cost road requirements contribute substantially to the cost of new housing. When added to these regulations is a prohibition against multiple dwellings of any sort and against mobile homes, the door for new development may be open, but you had better be thin, fast, and well-off to get through.

The Environmental Approach.   Very often, the enthusiastic reception accorded no-growth and limited-growth land-development regulations is expressed as a new interest in "the quality of life" or in the environmental quality of the town. It is sometimes explained as a new understanding of the limited water resources available, or as a special sudden interest in open space or forest preservation. But these explanations, true as they may be, might not receive the great public support they have attained lately if they stood alone.

Unlike most other reasons used by communities which want to restrict entry of newcomers, environmental considerations are increasingly founded on a realistic assessment of specialized and localized resource limitations. If it is discovered, for example, that local subsurface water required for all aspects of domestic and commercial life is in limited supply, why should a community endorse unregulated growth in new population? Such a policy surely commits the community to predictable problems in future years and to potentially high costs to obtain needed water from afar. In the West, where limited water supply can be proven, and in coastal areas, where fresh water availability is always critical, the environmental path is often an altogether sound and forthright justification for limited growth policies.

Communities may also reasonably restrict certain areas from intense development because of soil and and subsurface land characteristics. Precious, nutrient wetlands need not be filled and converted to housing lots

201

to permit greater population growth. Nor should clay soils, which will not absorb waste and are likely to cause building foundation problems for homeowners, be willingly and knowingly subjected to dense development. Nor should the air be carelessly polluted by a new industrial installation.

Land, water, and air are the earth's most precious resources. If any one of them is abused by man, the quality of the living environment is diminished. While some environments can tolerate drastic change and intrusion, others cannot. In such places, human beings impose themselves in greater numbers at their own peril. Thus, in certain communities such environmental considerations as limited water availability or soil and wetland limitations become an appropriate basis for restrictive-growth policies.

While it is true that environmental information in the hands of a knowledgeable group can be manipulated to make a particular point, much like year-end financial statistics assembled by a skillful corporate accountant, it is also true that this information is basic, critical data that should be taken into account. Communities will not thrive long if massive, remedial public works are necessary because the dictates of the land, and the water below it, have been violated. Nor will the value of land in these communities be upheld for very long once the local environment is strained beyond the point of dutiful and free service.

For these reasons, the quite new requirement of an Environmental Impact Statement (EIS) is appropriate whenever a land development proposal contains the potential of significant adverse impact on the water, air, subsurface, and wetlands of a community. In an increasing number of towns, an EIS is required as part of any application for a zoning change, large subdivision or major commercial development. The information called for usually includes a detailed description of present conditions and the anticipated scale of modification to soils, surface water, ground water, ground cover, topography, water supply, sewage disposal, solid waste disposal, air quality, noise levels, and the foreseeable impact of the action on plants, animals, marine life, birds, drainage, and so on.

This grab bag of considerations invariably angers would-be developers, and enriches consulting engineers and environmental scientists. At times the EIS is invoked by local agencies as a punitive measure to cause delay and added expense to unwanted but perfectly legal development proposals.

The EIS is still, indeed, a roughly hewn tool: not well prepared in so many cases and often not well understood by many who must use it to evaluate a particular case. Yet it is a much-needed beginning of the codification of environmental aspects and restrictions to land development. What is still needed, of course, is a more candid disclosure of secondary and tertiary impacts of the proposed intrusion as time goes by.

THE CONTROL OF GROWTH:
POWER IN THE SERVICE OF WEALTH

Enlightened residents now realize that it is in their own self-interest to protect and enhance the environment of their community, maintain its social stability and atmosphere, preserve older buildings and existing downtown areas, and retain surrounding open fields and woodlands. With this realization has come greater support of public control of the land.

Controlled Growth as Sound Business. The control of land in a particular community would seem, at first, a way to discourage unfounded land speculation, uncontrolled land development, unnecessary expenses for large and scattered utility systems, and unwanted extension of older roads and construction of new highways. These meritorious objectives are more likely to be achieved than not if well-conceived land-development and growth-control systems indeed exist. At the same time, there is probably no better way to assure the increased long-term increments both in the value of existing homes throughout the community and, because limited-growth policies restrict the amount of new land that may be developed, in the cost of land available for development as well. Residents of smaller cities, well-preserved suburbs, and smaller towns know intuitively that the value of their property rests, finally, in the property's being especially desirable and, at the same time, rationed.

Limited-growth policies particularly benefit those who already own a house in town. This group constitutes a voting majority. In Boulder, Colorado, for example, after restrictive-growth policies were promulgated, home prices soared over 13 percent during the first three months of 1978, and another 4 percent in the following two months.

In all of this there is a special minority that is apt to suffer adverse economic impacts. This group consists of holders of large parcels of raw acreage which are beyond the path of logical growth. Slow development translates into less demand for the conversion of raw land, the process that adds the greatest value to remote acreage. When the anticipated time of conversion is deferred, the value of the affected property may be significantly reduced.

In years gone by, all but the most exclusive communities sought ways to attract more people, more development. In most places, those who owned land and houses went along with the popular assumption that growth at the fastest rate possible benefitted the community and was likely to lead to a high rate of increase in land and property values. But this and other long-held assumptions are being re-examined. Few believe any longer that the economic bonanza once thought to be associated with rapid community growth and change stands up to a realistic appraisal of the facts. In our own time, and for years to come, community residents of small towns, older suburbs, and even many cities will begin to seek growth and development controls as a way to assure the continually increasing value of real property.

Supply and Demand. No-growth, slow-growth, and selective-growth policies do, indeed, add value and security to most of the property owned by most of the people already living in an affected community. Consider these supply-and-demand realities in a popular, regulated slow-growth town:

1. If fewer new building lots become available—and/or are very expensive—existing vacant building lots become more valuable.
2. If fewer new building lots become available, existing houses become more valuable.
3. If new housing is made expensive to build as a consequence of local ordinances, such as costly building codes and costly subdivision regulations, then existing older housing become more valuable.
4. If the amount of new housing is severely restricted through a prohibition against apartments, a building or or utility moratorium, or annual residential development quotas, then existing older housing becomes more valuable.
5. If few or no new commercial or industrial areas are permitted, land already zoned for such uses becomes more valuable.

Taxes. In addition to supply and demand, a basic principle of real-estate economics—that land and houses attain a greater value as their expense of annual operation and maintenance is reduced—can be observed in the recent stand taken by desirable communities against rapid growth.

One of the most important annual expenses that every buyer of property is concerned about is the cost of local real-estate taxes. As these rise, to pay for sewers, schools, police, social services, and so on, an additional operating cost burdens the taxed property. Over the years it has become apparent that a larger population generally means higher community taxes, especially if many of the people have children.

This correlation becomes particularly evident when new residents have both children and low incomes, a deadly combination to entrenched owners. The children require expanded schools, recreation areas, municipal medical services, and so on. In addition, a low-income family often incurs greater expenditures for a host of social services at community expense and subsidy. Under the present prevailing system of municipal finance, this all adds up to higher local property tax. Thus, many residents who own property, and who therefore pay a visible real-estate tax (as opposed to a hidden property tax, which forms a component of rent cost), have recently come to the following economic observations:

1. Any population growth that requires an increase in real-estate taxes tends to lower property values.
2. Low-income residents are more likely than high-income residents to effect an increase in real-estate taxes.
3. Residents with children are more likely than residents without children to effect an increase in real-estate taxes.
4. All residential development that becomes sufficiently dense and pervasive to require municipal water systems, sewer systems, and a large administrative governmental staff of planners, lawyers, and engineers raises property taxes.

Anticipatory Value. Built into the value of any piece of land, and especially any house, is the obvious present, perceivable quality of the neighborhood, of the broader community environment, and of life in the community. But many landowners and homeowners have also come to understand that there is another major increment in present value, which only can be ascribed to *anticipation,* to a vision of the future of the community. If the town has a decisive record of strong control over development and competent environmental management, the future of that town is likely to be assessed by property owners and would-be purchasers as a positive one. Or if the town has established and appears intent upon maintaining a "desirable quality of life," its future is once again likely to be assessed favorably.

The anticipated future has a most profound and stunning impact on the present value of land and residential real estate. The future imagined is there all the time, working in the realm of private awareness, a part of the feeling of security and satisfaction, or a part of the feeling of distress and uneasiness. When the future feels "right," property owners hold on to their investments and others want to buy in. The more secure the future of the community appears, the more secure the residents feel. These assessments of the social, economic, and environmental quality of the future affect land and housing values significantly: a positive assessment raises present real-estate values, whereas anticipated deterioration of the physical or natural environment lowers present values.

Some critics of controlled growth emphasize that new residents in a fine community want to "close the gate behind them"; other critics focus on the ways in which exclusionary practices contribute to social and economic segregation; and still others charge that the correlation between environmental quality control and slower community growth is a camouflage for exclusionary practices.

Each of these observations is indeed at times and in some instances valid. The trends cited require a great degree of public, regulatory intervention, generally on the level of local government. Why, it might be asked, in a country so dedicated to free enterprise, unfettered capitalism, and the sanctity of private property rights, is all of this tolerated? I think it is naïve to reply simply that the "country is going that way and no one can stop it; we are victims of creeping socialism." While this may be a valid answer for regulations imposed by the federal government upon business, industry, and law, it is inappropriate when applied to land regulation, which is almost exclusively governed by local government, a political body voted in and out by private, resident citizens.

Large landholders in remote areas may experience economic loss. They become a disadvantaged political minority, much like the poor who, at the other end of the economic spectrum, own no land whatsoever. But it is clear that the millions of middle-income and upper-income people, who in increasing numbers own real estate, are using political power and land-use regulations to protect and enhance their wealth in land. By taking the slower, more conservative route, more and more people with land assets have come to recognize new and unconventional ways to achieve these goals. This realization, I believe, goes far to explain the strength of the growing alliance found at the heart of the restrictive-growth and environmental movements now so powerful for the first time in the history of the United States.

SEVEN

ACCESS
AS VALUE:
PUBLIC
PRIORITIES
AND PRIVATE
PROFIT

When it comes to land, *access is value.* Inaccessible wilderness may inspire reverie, and inaccessible plains may permit wildlife to flourish. But in the lexicon by which men in all social and economic systems throughout time have assigned value to land, value is a function of access. From the beginning, along the rivers and oceans, the natural and first access arteries, land values increased far above those elsewhere.

Throughout all cultures, and in all places, one of man's obsessions has been to extend access to more and more land, to push forward out of curiosity, to move farther out to utilize new resources. Man has carved trails across continents, canals through lowlands, networks of roads and

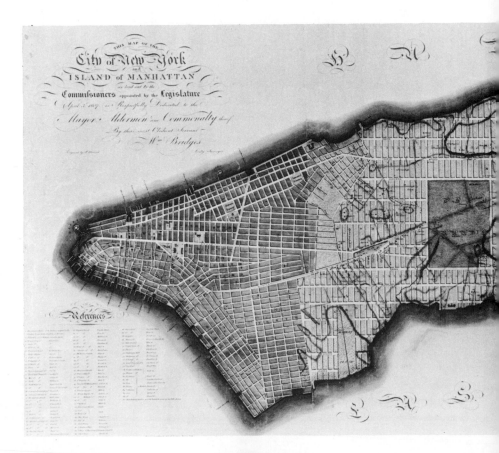

rail lines across the mountains and plains, he has exploited remote islands as resorts through air access; and he has ventured forth to probe
other planets.

THE GRID STREET SYSTEM

With few exceptions, the cities of America are gigantic grid subdivisions.
They reveal streets laid out by surveyors in advance of intense settlement.
More often than not, these are streets delineated so that a large landowner or group of landowners could sell subdivided land with a minimum
of effort at maximum prices. They are subdivisions of terrain which ignore
the picturesque, which ignore the character and quality of the land. They
are subdivisions intended to foster profit from the land itself.

Even in the open countryside, way beyond the cities, nineteenth- and
early-twentieth-century speculators divided the continent up into grid

**CITY OF NEW YORK
COMMISSIONERS' MAP OF 1811,
BASED ON RANDEL SURVEY
OF 1807 (DETAIL)**

Cities all across America bear the
stamp of the expedient and profitable grid subdivision. As the commissioners of New York City reasoned in 1811, the "strait-sided and
right-angled houses are the most
cheap to build and the most convenient to live in"—not to mention the
most profitable parcels to sell. All
forms of irregularity, as well as
European circles, ovals, stars, and
other urban street patterns, along
with natural hills, valleys, and
streams, fell prey to the earliest engineers' and planners' more pragmatic considerations in laying
out America's cities.

209

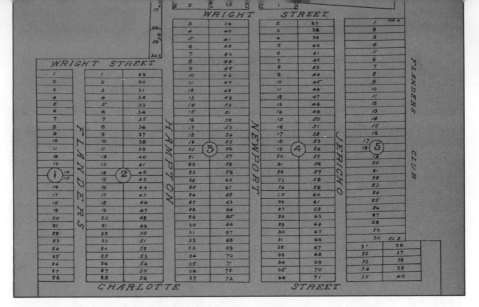

AN OLD FILED MAP, LONG ISLAND, 1926

Grid maps were once routinely filed across the open land of America. This one—typical of thousands of others—is for remote rolling oak woodland almost a hundred miles from New York City. These maps were investors' town plans for America, drawn up by the rote rules of surveying under the knowledgeable instructions of land speculators. Only now is there a growing interest in communities far outside the city, and even beyond the suburban fringe, to require some modification of these old filed maps before development is permitted.

lots. On virgin terrain one hundred or more miles from principal regional cities, it is still possible to find such subdivision maps, or "plats," filed long ago with the county clerk for proposed development of hundreds, and even thousands, of exactly similar house lots. The plots, which back up upon one another, generally measure 20 feet across the front, at the street, and run 100 feet deep, as they did in the city. In this way a block of salable lots, just wide enough for a single house, or more likely a row of attached houses, is defined.

What is this basic grid design, after all? A glance tells us. When the parcels are backed up to one another, and front with their narrow dimension upon the street, road access is made available to the maximum number of individual pieces of land for a given length of road. In addition, the rectangle is easily described by a surveyor and, repeated at the scale of the block, constitutes the basis for a most efficient and simply designed town plan.

Thus, the street grid, with its rectilinear lots and narrow street frontage accomplishes three objectives with perfection. First, the larger property is broken down into the maximum number of smaller parcels that can be individually sold. This almost always adds to the overall market

210

value of the original property. Second, the length of the road system per lot is minimized. Third, it is possible to justify the interconnected road system as a public expense, for roads all line up, link up. One of the most desired goals of land subdividers is to obtain access to private land at public expense.

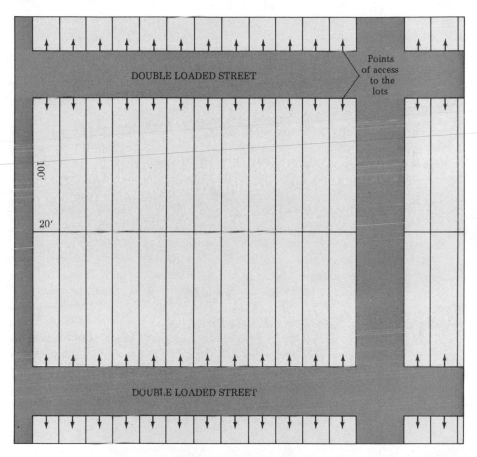

DOUBLE LOADED STREET

Points of access to the lots

100'

20'

DOUBLE LOADED STREET

SCHEMATIC DIAGRAM
OF THE BASIC GRID SYSTEM

The basic grid system is designed to make road access available to the maximum number of individual parcels with the minimum amount of road surface. A double-loaded street with narrow frontage of each lot on the street creates the greatest number of salable lots for a given amount of road improvements. In addition, the rectangular grid stacks up conveniently like square milk cartons, a reproduceable, uniform element from which whole cities can be easily laid out.

EARLY SPECULATORS BRING ACCESS
TO AMERICA'S INTERIORS

The critical significance of access and its stunning impact on land value have been understood from the very beginning by the American land speculator. Remote from oceans, generally untouched by contiguous navigable rivers, and most often isolated from an existing or potential canal system, the vast interior of America remained untapped of its economic value for decades.

With the advent of the railroad, a new situation prevailed. Even in advance of its arrival, the land along the proposed rail route came alive with value, attracting both imagination and investment.

The Railroad Companies as Speculators.   Though many failed along the way, the largest and most successful speculators in land were the railroad companies. Between 1850 and 1871, these private corporations obtained over 90 million acres of land grants from the federal government, and another 50 million acres from the states. These powerful combines controlled access to the interior and across its vast expanse. They exerted enormous influence over relevant agencies and offices of the federal government. They were, in effect, a basic instrument of federal land-settlement and land-development policy in America. Private railroads companies brought settlers to the West, commerce to the interior, armies and militia to protect the vast reaches of newly acquired or recently expropriated America.

While it is generally believed that railroads were given all their land by federal grants, this is not the case. In fact, over 90 percent of all initial railroad construction was undertaken with no federal land grant whatsoever. Only about 8 percent of the more than 260,000 miles of track laid down went through federally granted lands. Railroad builders, land speculators, and settlers all bought land in advance of the railroad to profit from use and resale once access was available.

Railroad Stops and Towns.   At specific points where railroads or large land combines held substantial acreage along a rail line, the owners sought station stops. The railroad companies had a tremendous advantage: they could determine where the station stop would be. The station stop is not only the point of primary access for land along the line; it is also where the town could most easily be promoted. And promote the railroads did. The familiar grid was drawn up by a staff surveyor who may never have seen the town site. The station was put in. And the surrounding land went up for sale, all laid out, with perfect grid access.

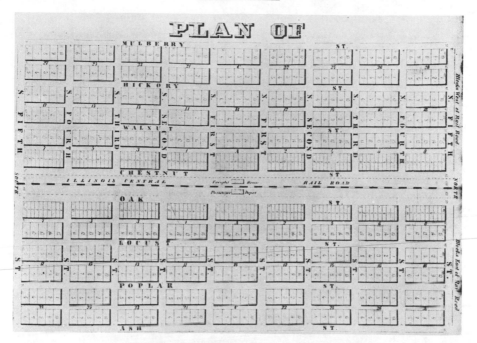

**THE ILLINOIS CENTRAL ASSOCIATES
STANDARD TOWN PLAT, UNDATED**

During the 1850s, insiders at the Illinois Central Railroad organized themselves into the "Associates." The group employed an agent, who was in-
structed to buy certain alternate sections of government land that broke
up the railroad's own federally granted holdings. These specific sections,
however, were not only valuable because they divided the railroad's property. More importantly, the Associates bought and consolidated holdings
where they planned station stops. Under the guise of the Associates,
officials of the Illinois Central developed thirty-three different
towns using an identical plan.

The railroad was in business, two times over. It charged to bring you
and your goods to a potential settlement; and then it sold you land, by the
foot, that had been obtained free or bought in 1,000-acre chunks.

Railroad Holdings Today. Today, railroad holdings stretch out across
the breadth of America, way beyond the edge of the track. On this land
are apartment houses, high-rise office buildings, major hotels, shopping
centers, warehouses, resorts, mines, or simply fields of grain. For instance,
the Union Pacific Railroad not only maintains some 9,700 miles of road

213

but owns, through the Union Pacific Corporation, some 1.2 million acres of land, and holds mineral rights on an additional 7 million acres in thirteen western states. In 1978, the Southern Pacific earned $50 million from real estate and natural resources as a result of its ownership of 3.7 million acres, together with mineral rights held on an additional 1.4 million acres.

Valuable central-city developments sit upon other railroad land holdings in such cities as New York, Washington, D.C., New Orleans, and San Francisco. In New York City, for example, Grand Central Station and all of the buildings on Park Avenue are built on railroad land.

SALE OF
RAILROAD RIGHTS-OF-WAY,
OCTOBER 1979

Penn Central today endeavors to sell rights-of-way long ago obtained by the New York Central throughout the Northeast and into the Midwest. Land obtained free or bought cheaply in thousand-acre chunks is sold as fee property or for air rights and subsurface exploitation.

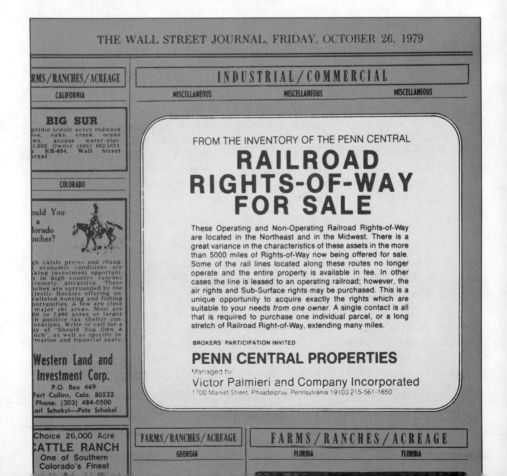

THE WALL STREET JOURNAL, FRIDAY, OCTOBER 26, 1979

FROM THE INVENTORY OF THE PENN CENTRAL

RAILROAD RIGHTS-OF-WAY FOR SALE

These Operating and Non-Operating Railroad Rights-of-Way are located in the Northeast and in the Midwest. There is a great variance in the characteristics of these assets in the more than 5000 miles of Rights-of-Way now being offered for sale. Some of the rail lines located along these routes no longer operate and the entire property is available in fee. In other cases the line is leased to an operating railroad; however, the air rights and Sub-Surface rights may be purchased. This is a unique opportunity to acquire exactly the rights which are suitable to your needs *from one owner*. A single contact is all that is required to purchase one individual parcel, or a long stretch of Railroad Right-of-Way, extending many miles.

BROKERS' PARTICIPATION INVITED

PENN CENTRAL PROPERTIES
Managed by
Victor Palmieri and Company Incorporated
1700 Market Street, Philadelphia, Pennsylvania 19103 215-561-1650

PARK AVENUE, NEW YORK CITY,
CA. 1902–1923

Railroad land holdings today still course across the breadth of America.
They stretch right through many U.S. cities. In New York City, for example,
Grand Central Station and Park Avenue's buildings sit upon railroad land.
By 1923, the deck over the railroad yards was complete and formed a
pedestrian enclave amid a parklike setting. Buildings are anchored
below in land leased from the railroad.

Transit Investors as Land Speculators. Nearly all of the trolleys, elevated rail lines, and subway systems in America were initially financed, built, operated, and owned by private investment groups. Those who financed, designed, and built these access systems were often looking for value and profit in land. Their overt activity may have been transportation service to people, but the hidden agenda was often profitable land speculation and development.

Urban transit systems were seized upon from the outset as a way to increase nearby land values. They also made settlement beyond the center of town convenient and desirable. As a consequence, the possibility for a transit business mixed with a land-development scheme appealed to alert entrepreneurs.

In Boston, for example, street railways helped to promote the expansion of the city from a tiny seaport town of 200,000 in 1850 to a sprawling metropolitan area containing thirty-one smaller towns by 1910 of over 1 million inhabitants within a 10-mile radius. The first street railway in 1852 triggered an immediate and large-scale real-estate boom. As service expanded to 2.5 miles from City Hall, new construction along the line accelerated. In a sterling display of capitalistic genius, one Brookline real-estate speculator, Henry M. Whitney, owner of the West End Street Railway, bought up the stock of the other five existing railway companies and forced a merger. Between 1887 and 1897, Whitney was king of the railway. His belief that rapid suburbanization of cities would keep the railway profitable, and that the railway would stimulate land development, prompted him to maintain the 5-cent fare and expand the line six miles beyond downtown Boston. Whitney strongly advocated that workers buy tracts of land in the suburbs and build their homes there.

Between 1850 and 1920, across America land values along the new transit lines soared. Access from the nearby open land to the town center increased; and as regional links to adjacent areas were established, remote farms and isolated villages came alive with new development, new settlement. By 1935, more than 7 billion passengers were carried annually on surface transit lines, and another 2 billion used subways and elevated service. Today, both combined amount to only around 1 billion passengers per year.

By the onset of World War II, transit patronage began to diminish as the automobile took command. In addition, development of the most easily accessible land along the lines had already been completed. Transit builders began to phase out of business. The land-speculation rewards were over. Profits from the sale of land in and around the expanding towns of America were safely in the bank. The cost of operating a mass-transit system is not matched, generally, by revenue. As private entrepreneurs threatened to abandon service or shut down the lines, city after

**THIRD AVENUE ELEVATED RAILWAY
AT 18TH STREET,
NEW YORK CITY, SEPTEMBER 1942**

The earliest trolleys, elevated rail lines, and subway systems were originally financed, built, operated, and owned by private investment groups.
These groups were not solely interested in providing transportation services, however. By extending access to undeveloped areas, alert
entrepreneurs combined the transit business with
land speculation and development.

217

TROLLEY ROUTES
IN NEW ENGLAND,
NEW ENGLAND
STREET RAILWAY CLUB,
BOSTON, 1904 (DETAIL)

Trolley and electric railway lines ran through the American countryside, opening up increasing amounts of land to settlement and raising land values all along the route. By 1904 Boston was linked, for instance, to Lewiston, Maine, to the north; Worcester, Massachusetts, to the west; and Providence and Newport, Rhode Island, to the south. Land speculator and railway operator Henry M. Whitney consolidated the system, kept fares low, and urged workers to buy tracts of land and homes in the suburbs.

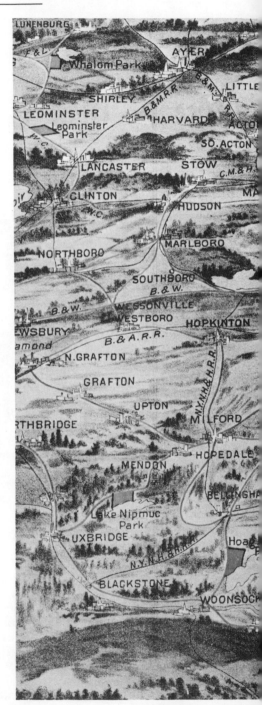

city was forced to step in and acquire the transit system, its poorly maintained operating equipment, its substantial operating costs, and often its heavy debts. The network of private transit systems was abandoned by private owners for whatever value could be salvaged. Consequently, though nearly all urban transit lines were initially private operations, almost none remain so today.

Commuter Interurban Rail Lines.   The story is much the same for the commuter interurban rail lines, which opened up land farther out beyond the cities. By the 1930s, there were 20,000 trains in passenger service in the United States, more than ten times the amount of railway track that remains in use today. Yet most of the opportunity for town booming and easy land-sale profits from rail access had already been realized. As the automobile became the new force in real-estate development, the rail lines stopped maintaining their equipment and their rights-of-way, employee moral diminished, and dynamic managers departed. The big years were over. By 1970, those few private companies which remained in the passenger rail industry were bailed out by the the National Rail Passenger Corporation (Amtrak), funded by the federal government.

Energy shortages and the high cost of gasoline are likely to stir renewed public and government interest in what remains of the national system of passenger rail lines. The availability of rail service is already having a positive impact on land values. Commuter towns, resort areas, and outlying communities with rail service will experience higher land prices than unserved areas in the same region.

In years to come, I believe, rail travel will indeed gain a new level of appeal, especially for short trips. Then, the area around the station, once so seedy and socially unacceptable, is likely to take on new prominence. This has already happened along the commuter lines in the Northeast in such cities as White Plains, Stamford, and New London. Indeed, down by the depot is likely to become the new spot to hang your corporate shield or professional shingle.

THE HIGHWAY TAKES OVER

While stagecoach trails and private toll roads once flourished, they were rendered obsolete by more efficient and less expensive transportation provided by rail and inland waterways. The role of railroads and canals in the life of America was soon challenged by the coming of the automobile and the birth of the modern highway. Designed to stretch across the country, and between and through the big cities, the modern highway—

and the federal interstate highway system in particular—is the twentieth-century analogue to the vision and practice of the railroad builders
of the nineteenth century.

The stated purpose for the building of interstate expressways across
America was, as General Dwight D. Eisenhower put it, "for the personal
safety, the general prosperity [and] the national security of the American
people." The enabling legislation that initiated the highway program in
America was the national-defense-oriented Federal-Aid Highway Act of
1944, which was conceived with the idea of connecting the nation's principal metropolitan and industrial areas via an interstate highway system.
However, it was the Federal-Aid Highway Act of 1956 that actually
created a financing mechanism for the program—the so-called Highway
Trust Fund—and thereby committed the nation to 42,500 miles of new
national highways, the largest public works project ever undertaken.

A Dowry for the Interstate Highway System. The Federal-Aid Highway Act of 1956 was conceived of and promoted by an alliance of powerful
industry executives and federal bureaucrats. The big roads, it was recognized, could earn their own way. They could be built without seeming to
ask the public for special funds, without appearing to siphon off resources
from other projects. In fact, the interstate system could be so cleverly
financed that the unpopular alternative—a national toll-road system—
was not seriously considered.

The keystone of the massive public-works financing was the creation
of the Highway Trust Fund, in which monies would be continuously
replenished from earnings generated by all roads and highways in America. Prior to the Federal-Aid Highway Act of 1956, funds for federal
highway construction came from the General Fund of the Treasury. In
effect, highways had to compete with other national demands for financial
backing.

The source of money for the exclusive use of the interstate highway
program was established as a 4-cent tax on every gallon of gasoline sold
in the United States. As America spread out along the new highways, and
as people and industry relocated out of town, use of the big roads would
increase, it was accurately forecast; and the new settlement pattern,
combined with the subsequent depletion of human and business resources
from the city, would induce ever greater use of automobiles and trucks,
and therefore a greater reliance on gasoline. Every stop at the pump,
every new suburb that wiped out a farm or a forest, every new factory
constructed in a remote industrial park along the highway and no longer
at the edge of the railroad, refurbished the fund with added revenue.

Today, the system approaches completion, with only 3,000 miles left

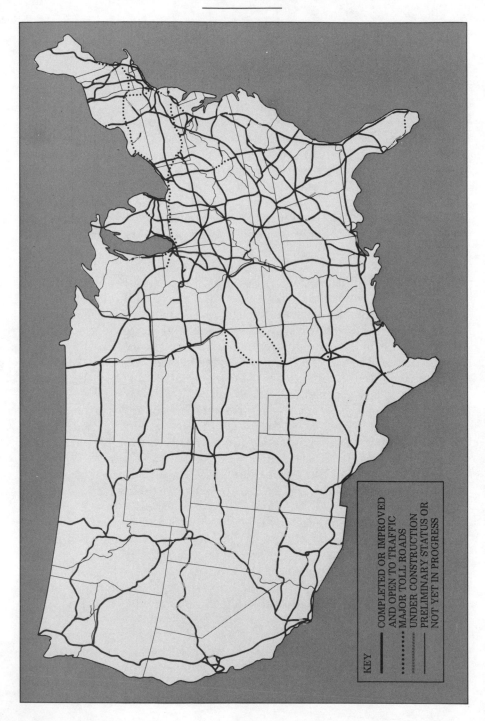

KEY

COMPLETED OR IMPROVED
AND OPEN TO TRAFFIC
MAJOR TOLL ROADS

UNDER CONSTRUCTION

PRELIMINARY STATUS OR
NOT YET IN PROGRESS

unbuilt, and much of that still in dispute. As stipulated by the Federal-Aid Highway Act of 1956, 90 percent of this vast enterprise continues to be financed by federal trust funds generated from the 4-cent-per-gallon gasoline tax. The original cost estimate of the interstate system had been $27 billion, based on a $600,000 mile. At this time, total costs exceed $65 billion, with a projected final figure of more than $100 billion, almost four times the original estimate; and the cost per mile now runs in excess of $2 million. The interlinked combine of oil companies, big-time construction outfits, automobile manufacturers, and land developers became a beneficiary of specialized public policy and public finance of enormous proportion.

Impact of the Interstate Highway System. The interstate highway program is, in fact, a national policy of immense consequence for the opening up of millions of acres of undeveloped land in America. And as it turned out, and must have been recognized in advance, the program initiated a policy that would cripple the growth and financial power of the cities as well. The bias of America to move on, to settle the westward frontier, to develop lands that remain untouched, to forego the familiar, the settled, the used, is nowhere more vividly evident than in the promulgation of the National System of Interstate and Defense Highways. The strategy was so well-conceived, so inevitable in its consequences once under way, that it changed the pattern of life in America. And it opened vast reaches of terrain, bringing staggering increases in value to millions of once relatively inaccessible acres of land. In the process, restaurants, motel chains, and gasoline stations sprung up amidst interchanges. Whole financial empires, in fact, now flourish because of the new roads. For instance, Holiday Inn, a major hotel-industry power, is an offspring of the interstate.

Once the new interstate roads were complete, all over the country, small towns along older two-lane highways shriveled. As one small-town

THE NATIONAL SYSTEM OF INTERSTATE AND DEFENSE HIGHWAYS IN THE CONTIGUOUS U.S., STATUS OF IMPROVEMENTS AS OF JUNE 30, 1979
(Opposite)

After only twenty years, the National System of Interstate and Defense Highways approaches completion. Only 3,000 miles remain to be finished of the total 42,500-mile enterprise. The system has radically affected the use and value of land—and the pattern of living—across the entire country.

**INTERSTATE 25,
NEAR LAS CRUCES, NEW MEXICO**

The interstate roads consume forty-two acres of land for each mile built.
Almost 40,000 miles of four-lane highways with median strips, large shoul-
ders of about 30 feet on each side, feeder roads, and interchanges have
directly utilized over 1.5 million acres of land. This acreage is but a small
amount that must be added to millions of acres of new development
induced by the interstate system before its full impact on the land
can be assessed.

resident commented to *The New York Times* reporter William K. Stevens, the smaller, isolated communities "didn't dry up and blow away, but they are much like towns left off the railroads a hundred years ago."

Central cities suffered, too. Interstate spurs in many cities slashed indiscriminately through neighborhood after neighborhood, destroying the city's social fabric. In addition, every interstate is an escape route out of the city, a funnel down which money and people flow away from urban concentrations.

Out in the countryside, the superhighways disturb or destroy streams, hills, woodlands, marshlands, and rock formations as they move across the land. People, businesses, and industry which follow transform rural settings into suburbs and into new cities.

The highways use a lot of land. Four lanes, a mediam strip, and a large shoulder of about thirty feet on each side require a width of some 150 feet. Feeder roads and interchanges must also be constructed. In all, each mile of interstate highway requires over forty acres of land. The almost 40,000 miles of interstate open to traffic have consumed over 1.5 million acres. But land consumed by the highway itself is nominal compared to the enormous amount of new development it has spawned.

In the wake of a publicly financed interstate highway system come all forms of state and local feeder roads, as well as privately financed subdivision roads. These open up vast stretches of terrain, bringing staggering increased value to millions of acres of once relatively inaccessible and undeveloped land. Because of the basic laws of geometry, as highway access radiates each mile out from the regional center, it lays bare increasingly large amounts of land to potential development; and with each mile farther out, the amount of new land development potential expands exponentially. If, for instance, four highways were extended for nine miles east, west, north, and south from a 3-square-mile central area, they would bring potential access to over 250 square miles of land, or some 160,000 acres, enough space at the low density of two families per acre to house over 1 million people. If the this same area were developed at a more traditional suburban density of four families per acre, it could house more than 2 million people.

When a single highway segment pushes outward in a straight line, its feeder access and connected local and private subdivision roads stimulate more land development than is generally recognized. Change occurs as far away as two miles from the highway route, on either side. Thus, for each mile of extended new road, 2,500 acres of land are opened to new development. At a low density of two families per acre, and assuming that as much as half the land is consumed by roads, parks, public sites, and so on, each mile of interstate in a developing region could conceivably contain some 2,400 new houses and a population of some 8,500 people.

HIGHWAY PLANNING AND LAND VALUES:
THE CITY

Where the highway rips up the city, land values decline, especially in residential neighborhoods. No one with a choice wants to live with the noise and air pollution highways generate. The office, business, or restaurant also will languish if it is suddenly severed from the rest of town by the highway. Ironically, the wall of the highway produces an impediment to access within the city, just as it encourages the flow of people and value away from it.

Rights-of-Way at Discount Prices. Builders of the big roads capitalized on the land devaluation produced by highways. They recognized, in advance, that acquiring rights-of-way through cities would be both time-consuming and costly. After all, buying rights-of-way across vacant farms and forests held in hundreds or thousands of acres by a single owner is one thing. Compared to urban property, the land is relatively inexpensive, the owners few; and no human dislocation need occur. But it is an altogether different matter to acquire rights-of-way through residential areas, where families live, often in individually owned houses on lots 20 feet wide.

So the highway builders traded on their knowledge and calculated judgment. Long before urban landowners were individually contacted, long before any need for the real estate was expressed, the highway corridor was selected, designed, and its location publicized. Panic. Cold fear. A hollow, empty uneasiness penetrates deep into the being of private owners, residents, and small businessmen all along the city route, as they suddenly hold land that will be beset by noise and fumes, land that will become inconvenient to reach, land that no one but the highway builders want. This panic took root in cities all across the land.

Corridors were indeed selected by highway planners where the land appeared to have low initial value. Once selected, the land was allowed to plummet in value. The most common corridor route, consequently, passed through "poor neighborhoods," where land was cheap and where, inevitably, inner-city neighborhoods, whose residents had little political power, would be destroyed.

Local politicians often had little special interest in these areas; taxes were low, and "upgrading" was thought to be needed. Consequently, land values plummeted to give-away levels.

Typically, once designated, the proposed highway corridor was allowed to remain untouched for years, sometimes for decades, while incremental disinvestment and abandonment within it occurred. Consultants who analyzed the impact of a proposed interstate corridor through various selected inner-city neighborhoods in central Baltimore, for example, made the following accurate set of observations relative to one of these neighborhoods, known as Rosemont:

Description of the Area: Rosemont presently is a relatively stable, middle-class, predominantly Negro community. . . . However, despite the present indication of stability, any major public action could substantially change the character of Rosemont. . . . In view of this we must examine the consequences that a highway might have if superimposed upon the Rosemont residential area. Indications are that losses imposed upon the Rosemont community as a result of a large-scale highway project could indeed force it into precipitous decline. Certain signs of decline have already begun to show. Many of these obviously are a result of the uncertainty associated with the highway. . . .

In many cases, land acquisition for the planned urban highway corridor was purposefully delayed so that land could eventually be picked up at minimum cost when voluntarily sold or when obtained through condemnation. Because of this delay, owners of private property earmarked for highway use were often inadequately compensated. Of course, the land had to be purchased at fair market value, but this determination was made often times when the appraisals were actually undertaken, which could be years after the corridor had been designated for highway uses.

By the early 1960s, however, city dwellers in San Francisco, New Orleans, Boston and elsewhere began to resist urban freeway construction. This resistance was stimulated by the patent injustice of a national public works program that not only severely damaged local urban neighborhoods but also inadequately and unfairly compensated owners for the land it took so recklessly.

The anti-urban highway revolution continued throughout the 1960s and 1970s. Communities which successfully resisted urban highways benefitted decisively; urban parks, street-level boulevards, and pedestrian walks along the waterfront, appeared in the corridors that narrowly escaped being transformed into highways.

Public resistance to the urban links of interstate highways spawned an effort on the part of highway program administrators to promote "joint development." The notion was to see the corridor in a new way, as new real estate that could be devoted to multiple uses. This was to be accomplished by decking over the new highway itself. Once a deck was in place, it would form a platform to accommodate offices, schools, housing, and other institutions, as well as parks. But the cost of such ambitious efforts to conceal the highway in urban areas was almost always prohibitive.

During the 1970s, some perceptive city politicians began to observe a shift in the mood of their own constituents. In some places, they joined

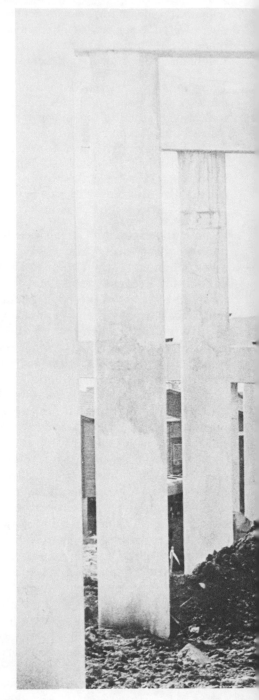

URBAN RENEWAL PROJECT, INCLUDING MASSIVE SUPER HIGHWAY CONSTRUCTION, BIRMINGHAM, ALABAMA, NOVEMBER 1969

The highway corridor is selected and publicized long before actual construction begins. Routes are established through low-income neighborhoods where land is cheap; values plummet further with the highway's promise of noise and pollution. At the expense of these areas, then, the federal government purchases or condemns the cheapest possible urban land.

THE MOON WALK,
NEW ORLEANS, LOUISIANA

Beginning in the 1960s, city dwellers protested the urban freeway's encroachment upon their neighborhoods. Highway construction not only fouled the environment but lowered property values as well. In some areas, these protests produced decisive gains. In New Orleans, for example, a popular waterfront pedestrian boardwalk now exists where a freeway had been slated.

in denouncing the highway building program, as it traversed the cities; occasionally, they even worked to have a long-established corridor "demapped," wiped off the face of all official plans.

Once a highway was successfully stalled and demapped, the spared neighborhoods underwent a stunning metamorphosis. For example, while Broome Street in lower Manhattan was marked as the designated corridor for the Lower Manhattan Expressway, land along the route could be bought for little, and the neighborhood became a ghost town. Yet once the expressway was demapped, the land began to appreciate, rising in value upwards of several hundred percent. Today, that corridor flourishes as a central part of Soho, a fashionable district of converted loft buildings, artists residences, and light industry. People returned to the neighborhood. Stores reopened. Shops were restocked with inventory. And life resumed.

In my view, the development of an interstate highway—or any form of a high-speed, massive highway—through an urban center today is an antiquated and misguided policy. Highways require too much space and interfere too dramatically with the interchange of people and goods within the city itself. They also compete with every form of public transit, while promoting noise and air pollution. The car and the highway will surely be essential in the foreseeable future out in the countryside of this immense continent, but both should be more effectively and progressively curbed at the portal to the city center.

HIGHWAY PLANNING AND LAND VALUES: THE COUNTRYSIDE

Out in the countryside, the coming of the highway used to be greeted by almost everyone with cheers reminiscent of a lonely settler's response when he heard that the railroad was coming through. Today, that is still how many large landholders feel, and respond, especially those who want to make a profit on their land assets. To them, the interstate means a new dawn, a new life for the land they have held for so long—land that may be a working farm, or land that may not be productive at all; land on which taxes have been paid, or land on which taxes are due. In any case, news that the highway is a possibility always brings instant change.

Speculators in the Countryside. Speculative purchasers often turn up even before the news of an imminent highway is widely known. They have this news from reliable sources: the district engineer's office, the planning department within the state highway department, friends in the state capital. They know that the highway will mean accessibility that was never there before—accessibility to other towns along the route, to the big cities in the region. And with access, particularly near urban centers, will come housing, industry, and finally large-scale retail business and offices. It will take time. But the value of the future is reflected in advance in the land.

Out in the countryside, advance news of a possible highway is greeted with such excitement on the part of sophisticated holders of large tracts of land that they do rather odd things. Often, they will travel to the district engineer's office and offer to donate a strip of their holding for the highway right-of-way. This assures that the highway will pass directly through their property. They are even more anxious to give it away in the right spot—at a location that will guarantee a cloverleaf intersection on the property—for the intersection creates the highest new land value along the route.

The highway engineers know that intersections of the interstate with state or county roads must be built. Why not build it precisely where the land can be obtained free? As a result, the private inaccessible land suddenly becomes prime commercial real estate at the intersection and accessible residential property elsewhere. Its value may multiply 100 or even 1,000 percent. The landholder cashes in. And the highway, traveling along as it does on partially donated land, is constructed at reduced public cost. In effect, the sequence seen in railroad speculating is reversed. Now private land is given to a public agency to be built at public expense, thereby enhancing the value of retained private land nearby. During the railroad era, public land was given to a private agency to achieve the same results.

The Cycle of Land-Value Changes. There is, in fact, a predictable rhythm to the changes in the value of land both along a proposed highway corridor and in its immediate area of development. This cycle, once thought to be a mysterious series of ad hoc occurrences, is now better understood in a market governed by time, distance, and expectation. It is a cycle that affects the value of an immense amount of land.

There is a distinct land-value shift that accompanies the sequence of events from the first quiet and often secret planning stages of a new highway, through its period of completion, and finally into the later stages of its use. This sequence usually spans a period of between fifteen and twenty-five years.

In general, strong increases in the value of land within a half-mile of a new highway right-of-way begin as soon as the route is definitely established and continue for approximately ten years. These increases tend to raise land values between 200 and 500 percent, a most significant increase, and one that has made many a poor farmer or alert speculator a rich landowner.

Land values within approximately one mile of a new right-of-way begin to increase somewhat later. After the highway route is established, the principal increase in value of land approximately one mile from the right-of-way takes place between the fifth and tenth years. Value increments continue to occur in lands up to approximately two miles of a new freeway, but principally within one mile of the right-of-way, for approximately fifteen years after the route has been established. Land values as far away as two miles from the right-of-way are generally not specifically affected by the development of a new highway.

Houston, Texas: The Gulf Freeway   Specific examples of this land-value change sequence can be seen along most highways near urban centers. A land-value impact study of the Gulf Freeway in Houston, Texas, serves as a case in point. The highway route was first designated in 1940. Five years later it was definitely established and publicized. In 1948, the first sections of the road were opened. By 1950, value changes were experienced along the total length of the facility, though much of it was still under construction. In 1952, the Gulf Freeway was opened to through traffic to Galveston. By 1955, the facility was an integrated artery strongly affecting land changes in its corridor—no longer a novelty of any sort—but still influencing property values. By 1960, no value changes were occurring as a direct result of the development of the highway.

The timing and location of these value changes are summarized in the table on page 234. Within a half-mile of the right-of-way of the Gulf Freeway, the price per square foot of land increased approximately 140 percent between 1940 and 1945. This increase is of approximately the same magnitude as value increases experienced in land unrelated to the highway corridor of the Gulf Freeway. On the other hand, between 1945 and 1950, the period after which the route of the freeway had been specifically determined and the first sections of the roadway opened, land within a half-mile of it increased an additional 122 percent in value, or about 20 percent annually, while land unaffected by freeway location in the same quadrant of Houston increased only 26 percent. Land within one mile of the right-of-way during this same interval increased in value approximately 75 percent, or nearly 13 percent annually. Between 1950 and 1955, ten years after the route was selected, land within a half-mile of the right-of-way of the freeway continued to increase strongly, registering value increments of approximately 9 percent annually, while land within one mile of the right-of-way increased in value at a 4.5 percent annual rate. Land unaffected by freeway location increased approximately 1 per-

233

PERIOD	WITHIN 0.5 MILES OF RIGHT-OF-WAY		WITHIN 1.0 MILES OF RIGHT-OF-WAY	
	PRICE PER SQUARE FOOT	PERCENT CHANGE	PRICE PER SQUARE FOOT	PERCENT CHANGE
1940	0.27	—	0.67	—
1945	0.65	141	0.89	33
1950	1.44	122	1.58	78
1955	2.23	55	2.00	27
AVERAGE ANNUAL PERCENT CHANGE				
1940–45	—	+22.1	—	+11.3
1945–50	—	+20.2	—	+12.9
1950–55	—	+9.1	—	+4.5

LAND-VALUE CHANGES AT VARYING DISTANCES
FROM GULF FREEWAY RIGHT-OF-WAY,
1940–1955

cent annually. By 1960, twenty years after designation of the route and twelve years after the first sections were open to vehicles, the effect of the freeway on land values had become relatively unimportant. It is also relevant to note that land within two miles of the right-of-way, and with good access to it, did not increase in value between 1945 and 1955 as much as land completely unrelated to the right-of-way but within the same quadrant of the city.

Too Close for Comfort. Over the years, as traffic intensifies, residential land in close proximity to or abutting the highway itself tends to depreciate. Noise and air pollution increase, events incompatible with maximum residential value. Their impact on land value is especially evident within a zone of 1,000 feet of the highway right-of-way; the effect tapers off to a negligible negative impact on land values between a quarter-mile and a half-mile from the highway. Beyond the half-mile mark, there is generally no devaluation to residential land as a consequence of the in-use, active highway corridor.

The Highway Interchange in Operation: Land Values Shift Again. Once the highway is complete and in full service, land located near highway interchanges generally continues to increase in value, especially if the site is suitable as an industrial or commercial location. Holiday Inns, Howard Johnsons, regional shopping malls, and other road-side enterprises are the offspring of the interstate system. The values they bring to land, the development they symbolize, and the pervasive influence of the system and its points of interchange on the appearance of our continent make one wonder, along with Senator Lee Metcalf of Montana, who for years has been interested in preserving the environment from highway development, whether or not "the cloverleaf is becoming our national flower."

The beltway around Raleigh, North Carolina, serves as an illustration of the specific impact the highway has on commercial and industrial development, particularly at the interchanges. The beltway was planned in 1950, and construction began six years later. Thirteen miles and eight interchanges were completed by 1961, the balance by 1974. A focus on the eight initially completed interchanges reveals the following sequence of commercial and industrial development taken in aggregate:

— 1960: little development
— 1964: 5 service stations, 1 moderate-size industry, 1 apartment complex with 60 units
— 1964–1970: 1 service station, 1 major-chain hotel, 17 industries, 1 regional shopping center, 7 office and institutional developments
— 1972: 1 chain hotel, 2 new industries, 1 moderate-size shopping center, 2 large shopping centers, 38 office and institutional developments, 3 apartment complexes with 200 units

During this same 12-year period, as reported in studies undertaken by the Department of Civil Engineering at North Carolina State University, over a hundred rezoning cases were filed along the beltway corridor. Ninety-five percent of these requests sought changes from lower-value residential categories to multifamily, commercial, and industrial zoning. In general, single-family residential areas were rezoned for apartment development, and areas already zoned for dense residential use were rezoned for office, institutional, and commercial development. Consequently, during the years 1961–1972, the following concentration of development occurred as a result of new access provided by the beltway: more than 50 percent of all apartments built in the entire Raleigh Standard Metropolitan Statistical area were within 1.5 miles of the beltway; more than 50 percent of all industrial development was located within less than one mile of the beltway; and more than 50 percent of all private offices and institutional development was located within one mile of the beltway, and 80 percent was located within two miles of it.

During these same years, as other parts of the metropolitan area were being drained of activity, traffic on the beltway escalated from approximately 5,000 vehicles per day in 1963 to 20,000 vehicles per day by 1971.

INTERCHANGE
OF INTERSTATE 635
AT DALLAS, TEXAS

Land values around proposed interstate interchanges rise dramatically
if the site is suitable as an industrial or commercial location.

237

Between 1960 and 1970, census tracts on either side of the beltway were deluged with 90 percent of the total increase in population in the area.

The Larger Picture: The Highway and Community Development. The role of the highway as a powerful catalyst to future community development tends to be insufficiently understood. In towns across the country, the question of whether or not a new highway, bypass, or interstate spur is desirable is fervently debated, often over months or even years. Residents and officials alike line up on either side of the issue, often staking out an inflexible and sometimes uninformed position. The focus is usually on the immediate consequence to local *traffic* patterns, with too little consideration given the all but inevitable longer-range impacts to land all over town.

Once a commitment to a new highway is made, there is little mystery about the ways in which land values, future commercial development patterns, the environment, and the future direction of community growth will be affected. It takes time, but the changes are predictable. Some landowners will benefit enormously as their land values soar. In the center of town, commercial areas are likely to suffer initially as business moves out nearer the highway or interchange. Contrary to some expectations, traffic probably will eventually increase as the highway brings with it more development. And the physical complexion of town will change.

Many who support highway development are aware of these possibilities and stand to benefit from them. Others who seek only the immediate, short-term objective of "cleaning up the traffic jams in town," and therefore endorse development of a new highway, are more naïve.

The Highway Trust Fund Challenged. The interstate system is 92 percent complete. Parts of it are even beginning to fall apart. But more important, the physical organization of America has changed, and the highways have been the prime instigators of the change. Almost 50 percent of the people in this country now live in suburbs; over 42 percent of the jobs in America are outside cities; there were about 26 million registered motor vehicles in 1930 as compared to nearly 144 million by 1975; also in 1975, there were 1.6 people for every car as compared to 3.1 people for every car in 1950.Today, three decades later, some begin to wonder. What happened? And how did it all happen so fast?

The sanctity of the Highway Trust Fund has come under attack recently. Many reckon, with accurate hindsight, that the interstate highway system allowed the suburbs to exist and sprawl, thereby cutting up farms and draining the cities of people, financial resources, and real-

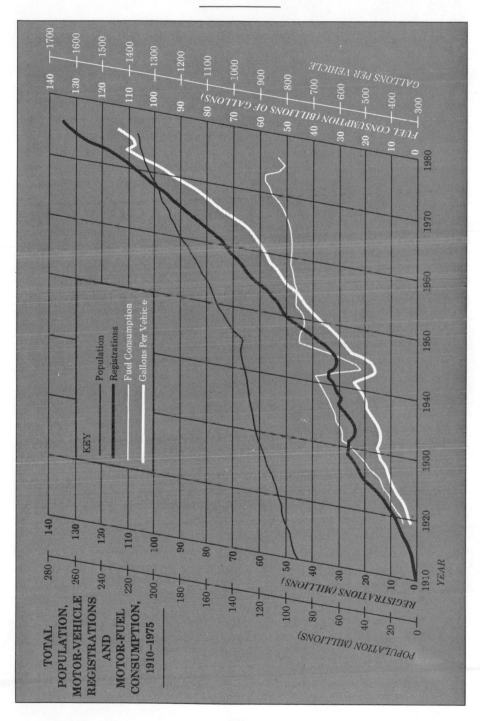

TOTAL POPULATION, MOTOR-VEHICLE REGISTRATIONS AND MOTOR-FUEL CONSUMPTION, 1910–1975

estate value. The system fostered the development of vast amounts of land for commuter suburbs, out as far as twenty to fifty miles from the central city, and even farther. It allowed once-remote areas in all regions of the country to thrive as resorts, and many to become year-round communities, whether they wanted to or not. Towns, once independent entities with their own ways, customs, and leaders, twenty-five to seventy-five miles away from larger cities, were homogenized into expansive suburban domains; others along big highway intersections blossomed into new suburban development centers with hotels, enclosed shopping malls, and expanding manufacturing industry. More and more cities are now choked with traffic and reel from air pollution brought in on the ebb and flow tide of the daily commute to work.

Those who attack the Highway Trust Fund, the financial source of this transformation of the social, economic, legal, and political balance of power in America, say it has gone too far. They say this very late in the game, when the system is nearly complete and when the transformation of America is already visible.

The beginning of the end of the interstate highway program is indeed in sight. A few essential links remain incomplete in urban areas. Some will be built; others will be successfully resisted amid bitter disputes. But most of this program's impact on land use and new development in suburbs and in the countryside beyond has already occurred. The impact is reflected in land-value adjustments, which have been made throughout urban, suburban, and rural America. Those who are wise will see that the end of the immediate impact of this program is less than a decade away.

Reduced State and Local Highway Construction. At the same time, the construction of new roads financed by state and local governments has slowed dramatically. These roads account for 99 percent of the nation's total road and street mileage. In community after community, funds for new road construction are no longer available. Priorities are changing. The need for new roads diminishes as population growth slows, as the future is questioned. In all of America, an average of 47,000 miles of state and local surfaced roads were laid each year between 1945 and 1960. In the 1960s, this figure dropped to 36,000 miles; since 1970, the pace has slowed even more significantly to an annual average of 23,000 miles—50 percent of the average production of the 1950s and just over 60 percent of that of the 1960s. And the trend continues.

The same problems and issues which beset the interstate highways now impede the construction of roads by state and local governments. In addition, the nation is in the midst of a burgeoning tax revolt; and trapped by the reality of unprecedented inflation, it finds its local public funds strained as never before. There is also an avalanche of criticism concerning the condition of the older interstate segments as well as the existing local and state systems.

From this criticism comes a message. It is a message not unlike the one so often communicated about public parks: If you're going to create it, maintain it. And maintain it before building any more. As people drive less, as gasoline revenue from the interstate decreases, and as public budgets contract relative to purchasing power, even proper maintanance of the existing American highway system will be a struggle to finance.

MASS TRANSIT STEPS AHEAD

Today, few people go out and lie down in front of the bulldozer to stop the physical invasion of the highways as they did in the 1960s. Rather, a more subtle and ultimately more profound counterattack is now under way against the Highway Trust Fund. Highway advocates argue, even though the interstate system nears completion, that the trust fund must remain intact, reserved for road-related construction and maintonance, to improve arterial roads and bridgoo. Thuse who support public transit, urban America, fuel conservation, and environmental protection question these priorities. They insist that a shift to federal support of mass transit is essential now. And their voices are being heard.

In 1970, the first federally approved mass-transit subsidy bill became law. Although only a small sum—$3.1 billion over a 5-year period, or roughly $620 million per year—was allocated, the revival of mass transit had begun. Three years later, the Highway Act of 1973 earmarked for the first time a portion of the heretofore sacrosanct Highway Trust Fund for urban transit, thereby heralding a shift of enormous importance in public priorities and in the political strength of mass-transit advocates. Under this bill, approximately $1 billion over a 3-year period was made available for transit of all sorts—buses, rail systems, and subways—and another $3 billion was allocated from general revenue to mass-transit grants for urban areas. The act also inaugurated "interstate transfer," whereby cities and states may waive their rights to interstate highway money from the federal Highway Trust Fund, and in its place obtain general funds from the United States Treasury for transit.

A glaring inequity exists in this 1973 bill, however. Whereas federal support of 90 percent of costs is offered for highway construction, only 80 percent is paid for transit projects. Since passage of the bill, the federal share has been raised to 85 percent, but this remains 5 percent below the level allocated if a highway is built. An equitable public policy consistent with the needs of today and tomorrow does not yet exist.

The interstate transfer provision is proving popular, especially in urban areas. By 1978, over $2.1 billion of trade-in money had been committed to specific projects, including construction of the expanding rapid-rail metro system in the Washington area, as well as urban and suburban bus, rail, and other transit-related projects in and around Boston, Hartford, Philadelphia, Chicago, Denver, and Portland. In 1979, New York City, for the first time, used the trade-in privilege, thereby receiving $200 million of the $241 million originally earmarked for rehabilitation of the Long Island Expressway, to improve subways and renovate bridges and perimeter roads.

There are increasingly strong signals that the political clout of transit advocates is gaining rapidly. The Surface Transportation Act of 1978 allocates $13.6 billion to transit over a 4-year period. This sum, along with

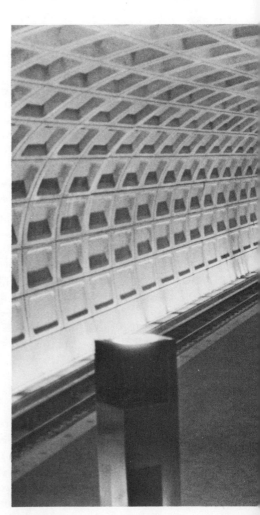

REGIONAL RAPID TRANSIT SYSTEM, WASHINGTON, D.C.

In 1970, the first federally approved mass transit subsidy bill signaled the beginning of an effort aimed at revival of transit in America. The Federal-Aid Highway Act of 1973 inaugurated the interstate transfer, whereby cities and states may substitute interstate funds for mass transit. By 1978, over $2.1 billion in trade-offs had been committed to specific projects, among them the rapid-rail metro system in Washington, D.C.

approximately $2.8 billion anticipated from interstate trade-ins, raises the total to about $16.4 billion, or over $4 billion per year—a significant increase from the $620 million of just eight years before and twice the approximately $2 billion total per year authorized in 1973. The sums still remain pitifully small as measured by need. But the trend is just beginning.

The so-called windfall profits tax on decontrolled oil, the largest single tax ever imposed on an American industry, is likely to yield huge new resources for transit. Estimates vary, but many indicate that this source will help increase the nation's capital investment in transit from $15 billion in the 1970s to $50 billion in the 1980s.

Transit Stops as People Places: Joint Development. One of the most promising consequences of the new emphasis on transit is the likelihood of well-planned development centers around transit stops in city centers, as well as along commuter rail lines. Those points of maximum access will attain great economic value, as they attract the combined attention of public officials anxious to promote use of publicly financed transit systems and, simultaneously, the interest of land investors, speculators, and building contractors.

This collaborative mutual financing and development between the public and private sectors, known as joint development, has worked with great success in Toronto, Montreal, and to a limited extent along the new metro system in Washington, D. C., and Philadelphia. New buildings are erected which combine offices, residences, entertainment centers, and even hotels within a structure that also incorporates the transit station. At station stops and points of interchange where design, zoning, and development work together, land values soar, and the establishment of retail and commercial facilities has been successful. One upshot of all this is to increase the appeal of the transit system to its riders. Access creates convenience; convenience induces use; and so the cycle goes.

Today in America, as transit construction and the transit riding tempo accelerate, land around station stops is in demand. Portland, Oregon, for example, has embarked upon a $16 million project—the Portland Transit Mall—that is a reconstruction of twenty-two blocks of the city's central business district, which integrates urban design with mass-transit needs.

A recent report by the Urban Land Institute, quite appropriately entitled "Joint Development: Making the Real Estate-Transit Connection," estimates that planned and projected transit improvements to the various systems being developed or upgraded could involve approximately four hundred new stations, each with an immediate impact area of approximately one square mile. In the cities where fixed rail transit is again coming alive, or just being introduced, these are the spots to watch, the locations where new joint development opportunities will incorporate both public power and private finance to create higher land values and real-estate wealth.

The Unearned Increment. Increased value in land resulting from publicly financed improvement is referred to as unearned increment. The concept of unearned increment, which had always been a factor in speculation in the past, has raised new issues: Are private owners who benefit from mass transit entitled to this unearned increment or, alternatively, should it be recaptured for public benefit? Should owners along the new regional rapid-transit rail lines in Washington, D.C., for example, be specially assessed to help finance the transit stytem? Should they be placed within a special transit-improvement district, like a sewer district, and assessed a special tax, or alternatively, should the beneficiaries pay higher real-estate taxes? Additional funds collected from transit-related assessments might be funneled back to the transit authority or segregated to repay its bonded indebtedness.

Numerous ways do exist to assure some public recapture of this value added to land and buildings by massive public expenditures for a transit system. The expectation of recapture of funds leads forward-thinking transit experts to posit a number of different ways that public transit might become self-supporting.

Toward a Recapture of Transit Values. While the direct impact of mass transit systems on real-estate values is extraordinary, as yet no attempt has been made to measure the income they bring into the public treasuries. In addition, the money transit systems generate from indirect sources such as sales tax and real-estate tax is considerable; fare box revenues pale by comparison. These funds are quietly and skillfully merged into the general treasury of revenues collected from all other sources and are not credited to the transit systems. Ultimately, the subway or transit system is permitted to languish. It is declared uneconomic, its fares deemed too low. As a result, service is cut back, fares are raised, maintenance falls by the wayside, and the passenger suffers.

The fact may be that the city, not the private landowner along the route, is ripping off the transit system. Surely some radical twist is needed to help assure the long-term quality and financial stability of both existing transit systems and those now being constructed. Such a policy should require local and state governments to reserve income earned by the transit system from indirect sources for the exclusive use of operating, maintaining, and expanding the transit system. While enacting and administering such a policy would admittedly be complex, were it worked out, transit systems would be infinitely better operated and maintained than they are today.

WHERE WE ARE HEADED

After decades of decline, transit is definitely on the upswing. The gas crisis helps. So does—decisively—the provision of modern, attractive, comfortable, reasonably priced, and dependable bus and rail service. Transit ridership during 1978–1979, while gas prices steadily increased, rose an average of 4.4 percent a month. In several cities where there are new transit systems, notably Denver, Seattle, and Portland, mass transport now carries nearly 50 percent of all commuters, and demand is growing.

245

**PROPOSED
"PEOPLE MOVER" SYSTEM
DRAWN OVER A PHOTOGRAPH
OF LOS ANGELES,
CALIFORNIA,
1979**

One of the most dramatic urban transit proposals in the past decade is an elevated "people mover" slated for Los Angeles' business district. The $44 million-a-mile system will attempt to unclog the central city's traffic. Elevated lines, long ago abandoned, continue to intrigue some transit planners because of the availability of the right-of-way and the potential to leave the street surface intact.

For the first time in many years, subways and surface transit lines are being built again. In the past decade, new urban transit lines have been planned and/or built in Buffalo, New York City, Washington, D.C., Atlanta, Miami, Los Angeles, and San Francisco.

Land Without Roads Today: Devaluation Tomorrow. If automobile access to land in America is to be limited, for the most part, to the current

road network, as I believe it will be in the decades ahead, then attention must be paid to the meaning of that situation for land values everywhere in the country. Over time, land that has no chance of obtaining new publicly financed road access may well depreciate. On the other hand, land that already enjoys well-developed, well-maintained, and connected highway access, and that is located close to cities, thriving towns, and resorts, will be increasingly in demand—and will become increasingly scarce and valuable.

It will take time, years or even decades, for some to recognize that America is at the end of its 50-year splurge of nationwide road building. The assumption that road access will be available in the future continues to inflate prices asked—and often paid—for inaccessible land. In time, awareness of our limited resources, of changed national priorities, of ever higher costs of road building and of automobile travel, will bring these culturally ingrained expectations into line with reality. When that happens, as it did at the end of the railroad-building era, significant adjustments will occur in the value of remote, undeveloped, and inaccessible private land.

Mass Transit and Land Values. Between 1945 and 1970, the nation's investment in highways amounted to more than $150 billion. During the same period, less than twenty miles of subway were built, thousands of miles of rail were abandoned, and bus companies all over the country stopped service. However, we now face a future of diminishing fuel supplies and increasing costs for those that are available, a future in which dramatic population expansion is not likely, and thus a time in which much new community expansion on the land is unwarranted. We also appear to be destined to exist either within the frightening economic uncertainties of inflation or the equally frightening uncertainties of recession.

Today, in a most stunning turnaround, less than a decade old and gaining momentum, new transit systems are being built across the country. Ridership on transit now shows signs of turning upward on a sustained basis for the first time in over thirty years. In years to come, buses most of all will be recognized and cherished as a dependable, flexible, and relatively economical form of public transit. No costly right-of-way construction or acquisition is involved, given the existing intricate network of streets and highways all across the country. Cities and towns that have operating bus companies and authorities will pay more attention to them and will begin to allocate more money to their maintenance, operation, and extension. And I suspect many new types of bus service will be implemented by federal, state, and local government: large buses for long trips, mini-buses for urban and brief regional trips, commuter buses, and so on.

All efforts at reorienting America to mass transit will reinforce present land-use patterns. Transit systems must service points of existing concentrations of people and jobs; no other approach is economical or rational. Thus, in years to come, neighborhoods and communities serviced by buses and rail will attract more people and command higher real-estate values because of the transit service. In years past, when an upwardly mobile family could afford an automobile, it moved away from the bus line. In years to come, the family may move closer to it. The poor, in turn, may be forced further away from the bus and and rail lines. If the going really gets rough, they may even be pushed out into the suburbs.

As we enter a new era of emphasis on transit, the unearned increment available from new and growing public expenditures for access will not be so much on open, undeveloped, remote acreage, as it was throughout the highway era; rather it will be found on land where people are already densely settled.

EIGHT

ENVIRONMENTAL REGULATION: PUBLIC POWER CONFRONTS AND CREATES WEALTH

By 1970, the degradation of the physical environment in America could no longer be ignored. It was impinging in some form on everyone's life. The first massive environmental regulation programs started in the early 1970s; and by the end of the decade, they were firmly entrenched as an intimate part of the economic, cultural, political, and social life of America.

The environmental protection and regulation surge is also, in part, an extension of broader political and social struggles which surfaced in the turbulence of the 1960s. Women, homosexuals, blacks, Native Americans, and other politically neglected groups began to seek a fair share in all that is best in America, to assert a claim to power and wealth, and thereby to broaden the bases of privilege. These are ideological soundings into the soul of America, and each is fueled by the most primordial source of energy: the quest for economic parity with those at the top. So too, in my view, is the relatively sudden political and social emphasis on the quality of land, water, and air.

Across America today, rivers and lakes are polluted by industrial waste, outboard motors, yacht toilets, and inadequate sewage-treatment systems. The air is no different. Along the freeways, auto exhaust spoils the environment. Near factories and plants, gas and particle-laden exhaust billow into the air. From apartment houses, ash and carbon monoxide are continually released into the ambient air.

And the environmental impact is widespread. The water and air flow restlessly onward, downward or downwind, to carry their waste and poison beyond the source, to degrade the environment along their path. Pollution in a lake two hundred miles from your house is not necessarily remote and inconsequential. It may affect what you eat and where you are permitted to swim. It will certainly reduce the value of all land that depends upon that lake for drinking water, recreation, and visual enjoyment. The waterways, used as a discharge sewer hundreds of miles upstream, poison animals and plants down the watershed and force people to find a new source of clean water to drink. The air, poisoned elsewhere, brings a health risk to all who breathe it, corrosion to one's property, and possible ruin to gardens, trees, and crops far away. And noise, a less prevalent but nonetheless significant type of pollutant, affects us all. Like the airport, the highway can be heard in the distance, throbbing as trucks pass in the night. Each of these environmental disturbances, and all the others you might think of, reduce the relative value of hundreds of thousands of affected acres of land.

Conservation vs. Preservation. An aside is in order here to clarify two historic streams of thought and action that came together in the 1970s: the mainstream concerns of those long interested in "conservation," and those concerns of groups committed to "preservation." Throughout the twentieth century, conservation advocates have remained dedicated to public and private land management as an exercise in the scientific and economically sound utilization of the American resource base. Economic development is embraced, provided it is conducted wisely with respect to effective and long-range "management."

Preservation, on the other hand, has a historic tradition of opposition to industrialism, to materialistic striving, to rapid change. While the national forests, for example, are seen by traditional conservationists as a resource properly made available for the continuous cutting of timber, most preservationists would prefer the forests to be designated as unexploited, forever-wild preserves. To the mainline preservationist, environmental protection is a moral crusade, while to the centrist conservationist, it is a means of sound economic resource management. What is now called the environmental movement is an often uneasy alliance between these two strains in American culture.

THE 1970s: AGE OF THE ENVIRONMENT

The environmental decade begins when Americans have the time, leisure, and economic latitude necessary to invest in improving the quality of physical and natural surroundings. It could not have begun at the end of the decade, a time of national recession, high inflation, and unsure energy supplies.

After decades of debate, compromise, and skillful maneuvering on the part of many interest groups, and despite the opposition of various federal agencies, as well as of an alliance of major industrial interests—holders of significantly large tracts of land along rivers, lakes, and oceans—President Richard Nixon signed the National Environmental Policy Act of 1969 (NEPA) into law on January 1, 1970.

The National Environmental Policy Act was promulgated "to declare a national policy which will encourage productive and enjoyable harmony between man and his environment; to promote efforts which will prevent or eliminate damage to the environment and biosphere, and stimulate the health and welfare of man; to enrich the understanding of the ecological systems and natural resources important to the nation." This preamble has the ring of a declaration of independence, asserting, as it does, the freedom of the environment to be heard, to function, to survive. It is also a sort of bill of rights, declaring the inalienable right for "enjoyable harmony between man and his environment."

The cornerstone of NEPA is its requirement that the federal government complete a document, now known as an Environmental Impact Statement, or EIS, before undertaking a major project, such as a dam, highway, or military installation, which has potentially harmful effects to the environment. The impact statement is expected to include an analysis of both the positive and negative environment effects of the project, possible remedies to adverse affects, a review of resource use, and project alternatives.

Interpretations of NEPA have extended this requirement to include a review of private projects which use federal funding or are governed by federal regulation. Numerous states and local communities have adopted environmental review policies which require impact statements when state money is used, when large-scale private development is proposed, or when private development in certain environmentally sensitive areas such as wetlands is planned.

It is thus through citizen and government review of the Environmental Impact Statement that large-scale private development is now routinely challenged. Though the EIS is still far from a completely satisfactory instrument in most cases, it does contain a wealth of information. In addition, the EIS review process generally allows that a challenge to proposed development may be asserted by anyone, even groups or individuals who will not sustain any direct impact. In this way preservation, conservation, and environmental advocacy groups have made themselves heard.

Soon after the promulgation of NEPA, an avalanche of environmental regulation over land, air, and water poured out of federal, state, and local governments. These have a substantial impact on the ways in which a landowner can use his land. The federal Clean Air Act of 1970, and as amended in 1977, requires states to review the location of all possible pollutant sources. In many cases, it is requisite that a special permit be acquired to discharge exhaust and residue into the air. The Federal Water Pollution Control Act of 1972 finances the cleanup of polluted rivers and the building of sewage plants, and regulates pollutant discharge into navigable rivers. The Coastal Zone Management Act of 1972, the first and only nationwide land-planning measure to receive congressional approval, provides federal control over virtually any large-scale development along the shorelines of the thirty coastal and Great Lakes states, even on private residential property. The Federal Land Policy and Management Act of 1976 (FLPM) attempts to coordinate and reorganize the manner in which the nation's public land resources are administered and utilized. Under FLPM, over $4 million is being spent to prepare a land-use plan for the 37,000 square miles of public desert land in California. According to Frank Gregg, director of the Federal Bureau of Land Management, the desert's surface—"a national storehouse of minerals, flora, fauna, historic artifacts, and energy potential"—has been scarred by recreational vehicles; vegetation and rocks have been pilfered; deposits of Indian relics have been vandalized; and ancient wall paintings have been defaced.

Fear and Conflict. The parent prevails over the child; the lieutenant over the sergeant. Regulation of any sort is the exercise of power. Environmental legislation is the control of land and wealth through the exercise of public power. It causes predictable conflict, and it produces land-value windfalls and land-value wipeouts.

The owner of land resents being reduced to a subordinate or dependent position, like a child or a sergeant, by a bureaucrat who, through the existence of new environmental regulations, has been elevated to a position of power over the land. The mere existence of this power, lodged in the drab corridors of government, is considered personally offensive, to say nothing of misguided, by many who may not so much oppose protection of the environment as a general concept as they oppose regulation of the land they personally own.

In addition, behind the rage that private owners feel toward public officials who shuffle the papers, there runs a dark undercurrent of profound and unspoken conflict of world view, of class, and of wealth. It is the "haves" against the "have nots." It is a confrontation of old-style power, derived from wealth, property, and success, against a new type of power: bureaucratic, regulatory power for the "common good." There is also fear of economic loss or of unreasonably limited gain. And there is ideological opposition by theorists who see the environmental movement as the beginning of the end of private property in America. For instance, John McClaughry, president of the Institute for Liberty and Community, a nonprofit group studying private property, had the following to say about the increased role of federal and state governments effected by the environmental protection movement:

The supreme irony of this movement is its determination to move forward by moving backward—backward to feudalism. . . . For the advocates of new land use control theories . . . the ideal society is one in which all property in land is not held in fee simple . . . but "of a superior." That superior is no longer the King, since in a moment of possible irrationality our forefathers scuttled the idea of monarchy in 1776, but the State, a less personal but more permanent institution.

The control of land, water, and air to protect the environment brings with it massive new issues and deep conflicts. When examined closely, this movement reveals a kaleidoscope made of quicksilver. The formations of public vs. private interest, with the slightest turn, give way to a pattern of insiders vs. outsiders, only to be changed with another slight twist into a design of big industry vs. the hapless worker, which then dissolves into a momentary image of national productivity vs. radical obstructionism. And so the cylinder may turn, each slight shift of position able to expose a convincing new pattern of conflict and apposition.

All of the effort, regulation, expense and care is aimed at one national objective: "to improve the quality of life." Yet, "quality of life" is an

expression that raises as many questions as it answers. One must ask: "Whose quality of life?" and, especially, "What is 'quality'?" To ask a factory production worker or a taxi driver about the meaning of this expression, is to hear that higher wages are the way to raise the quality of his life. To others, fortunate enough to enjoy greater economic security, quality of life has to do more particularly with a cleaner physical environment.

BUSINESS AND INDUSTRY: A NEW MONKEY WRENCH IN THE CLOGGED MACHINE

American industry, once the most productive and flamboyant in the world, is becoming a clogged machine. Environmental control and regulation is part of the reason. Big steel, big oil, and big shots find themselves

BURNING DISCARDED
AUTOMOBILE BATTERIES
NEAR HOUSTON, TEXAS,
JULY 1972

American industry and environmental legislation often battle each other head-on. New industrial development is subject to regulation; old plants and machinery must now be equipped with expensive devices that protect the environment. The Environmental Protection Agency, for example, was empowered to shut down this plant after the photograph was taken.

less efficient, less independent, and less exuberant. Every new expansion that industry wants to make is subject to environmental regulation: permits to obtain, standards which require compliance, and legal papers to file. And, simultaneously, the old plant and its machinery must be retrofitted with expensive devices that protect air and water from former pollutants. Ultimately, it is the consumer who pays; the cost to buy or use or occupy goes up as the cost of compliance is tacked on.

Many industrialists assert that the environmental protection movement signals the end of their industries and the end of the well-being of America. Henry Ford II, surely one of the most articulate spokesmen for the struggling and sagging giants of American industry, wrote recently in an article entitled "Corporate Environmentalism: The Bottom Line": "... *balanced growth* is a euphemism often employed by those who argue that economic expansion must be sacrificed to *environmental quality*. I realize that this means different things to people, but to me it suggests government regulation, industrial disruption, and wholesale abandonment of our marketplace economy. If the term [balanced growth] hasn't any other meaning, it is an invitation to disaster."

Ford's is a strong and representative statement, one that expresses his fear of the end of traditional capitalism in terms of cost-saving initiatives, conventional competition, and management allocation of capital resources to further exclusively the goals of production, expansion, and profit.

And, indeed, when any new large-scale land-development project becomes subject to environmental regulation, it may be forced through extensive delays and exposed to greater scrutiny and ultimately to much higher costs than it would otherwise have been. There is also the frustration and aggravation of additional submissions, presentations, and public meetings. These reduce the entrepreneur's independence, as does all regulation when it becomes complex on its way to becoming effective.

There is no doubt that cleaning up America is expensive, and will continue to be so. There is also no doubt that environmental regulation of land development adds cost. In fact, over the last eight years, environmental regulation is responsible for an estimated 1 percent reduction in national productivity. However, progressive leaders in industry and government are finding ways to incorporate the costs involved. As resistance to regulation ebbs, it is replaced, in the most enlightened instances, by a new understanding of national well-being. "Better access to clean air ... does not show up as an increase in GNP," Charles L. Schultze, chairman of the Council of Economic Advisers, told a blue-ribbon audience in 1978. "What we do when we make environmental improvements is to accept lower economic growth, as conventionally measured, in return for an increment in unmeasured output, or welfare. And if we choose wisely,

258

**SUBURBAN ACRES HOUSING PROJECT,
EVERGLADES NATIONAL PARK, FLORIDA, JULY 1972**

The southern half of Florida is actually a huge river that includes the Everglades. Developing land in this area involves dredge and fill operations, which are now generally prohibited by strict state environmental laws.

the national welfare is improved, even if the measured growth in national income is reduced."

ENVIRONMENTAL REGULATION AS ITS OWN GROWTH INDUSTRY: COSTS AND CONSEQUENCES

The environment and its control is now big business—in fact, one of the fastest-growing businesses in America. It is a growth industry in law, in government budgets, and by commonplace economic standards.

The lawyers have certainly noticed. It is a prime area for litigation and an ideal field for a young, inquisitive lawyer to gain experience, attention, and respect. It is also a field in which the public good, the social well-being, is loudly asserted, if not always exerted.

At every level, the number of jobs and the size of budgets in government and industry have expanded because of the environmental protection movement. There are environmental administrators and staffs on the public payroll in most cities, towns, and practically all regional and county government offices, as well as in state and federal agencies. The EPA projects that over 300,000 people are now directly engaged in environmental protection endeavors, with perhaps twice that many employed in related fields. The Labor Department estimates that over 65,000 jobs are created with each billion-dollar expenditure for pollution control alone.

Annual expenditures also reveal the growth spurt stimulated by environmental regulation. Consider the area of pollution control. In 1965, before the environmental movement had a firm foothold in the national consciousness, American industry spent approximately $840 million annually on water pollution controls, while municipalities were spending over $1 billion per year. Federal expenditures were nominal. By the mid-1970s, American industry was spending about $10 billion every year, while state and local costs approached $1.5 billion. And the federal government, as a result of myriad new programs established to forward water pollution control, was spending $4.2 billion in 1975. By 1977, the Council on Environmental Quality estimated that some $40.6 billion was being spent on pollution control by industry and government combined.

While the growth in pollution control expenditure is awesome and clear, its impact on the overall economy is less well understood. Today, pollution control expenditures account for approximately 2 percent of the entire GNP. This compares to defense expenditures of 5.3 percent, education expenditures of 7.3 percent, and national health expenditures of 8.8 percent.

On the other hand, in a country in which inflation appears to be inexorable, this new growth industry is making a very substantial contribution to the increased cost of living. Remember, government and industry do not pay for environmental control; consumers do. The Consumer Price Index, basically an inflation gauge, goes up each year that inflation occurs. In 1978, according to the House of Representatives Committee on Banking, Finance and Urban Affairs, it was agreed that environmental regulation contributed as much as .75 percent to the increase in the Consumer Price Index, which rose about 10 percent that year. Based on these figures, environmental regulation accounts for between 7 and 8 percent of the total increase in the annual cost of living.

On the local level, environmental regulation adds extra cost to all products associated with land development, including housing itself. For example, three years after the New Jersey Coastal Area Facilities Review Act (CAFRA), which implemented stringent land subdivision regulations, was in operation, the New Jersey Office of Coastal Zone Management studied its impact on low-income housing costs. The conclusion: All regulatory costs, including CAFRA permits and requirements, added about one-third to total site costs. After a review and analysis of twenty-one residential developments along the New Jersey coast, it was estimated that the environmental protection process added some $1,000 to the cost of a house that sells for $35,000 to $40,000.

In the years to come, it is unlikely that this high level of expenditure for environmental regulation, and the subsequent costs passed along to consumers, will abate. For the period 1976–1985, the Council on Environmental Quality estimates that some $300 billion will be spent on pollution control alone. This compares, for instance, with $140 billion urged by President Carter in July 1979 as a decade expenditure to "secure the nation's energy future." At the same time, the $300 billion figure seems minimal when compared to the estimated $1 trillion taxpayers will pay for defense in the same decade. The trade-off is likely to be a rejuvenation of the rivers, lakes, streams, and ocean boundaries of America, and the air we breathe. It is a long-term proposition. Success is not assured. But the benefit is widely spread out and, so finally, is the cost.

ENVIRONMENTAL REGULATION: LAND-VALUE WINDFALL OR WIPEOUT?

No group of Americans holds a more divergent view of the meaning of "the quality of life" than those who own and often disturb the natural environment. Landholder, farmer, speculator, planner, architect, builder, and space consumer hear the words differently and react to them accordingly. To each, environmental control and regulation possess the specter of interference. But for each, the interference may produce either an economic bonanza or a financial disaster.

Environmental regulations, and the procedures they entail, are sometimes effective in keeping potential buyers, users, and speculators away from certain terrain. Elsewhere, in the very same area, the same regulations may add value to land far beyond its owner's wildest expectation. What generally happens is this: After new environmental regulations become effective, land that can be easily and quickly used for building and development soars in value. Land subject to complex and expensive permit processes, or of questionable future use, generally declines in value.

The first case is exemplified by almost any well-located residential subdivision approved for development before new environmental regulations become law. Once the new regulation is promulgated, the added expense and red tape discourage competing subdividers. Demand for building sites, on the other hand, is likely to increase. The new regulations raise expectations of a better living environment, intended as they are to protect the water and the air. Less supply and increased demand work to raise the value of all land that can be sold and used expeditiously. Available residential lots, approved shopping center sites, office building locations, and industrial zones dramatically appreciate in value.

And it all happens very fast. There is a jolting upward reaction in the value of usable land following the onset of environmental regulation. For instance, shortly after California passed its first coastal zone legislation (Proposition 20), Harold Miossi, a land appraiser in Southern California, remarked:

Since Proposition 20 has been in effect, there has been a marked escalation in the values—selling prices—of improved coastal properties and of subdivided lots where exemption [from regulation] is in effect or probable. . . . Lots in Combria Pines—for years a dog—are undergoing a veritable boom; building there is rampant. The same goes for all these coastal subdivisions, Cayucos, Paso Robles Beach, Morro Bay, Baywood, and Cuesta-by-the-Sea.

When sweeping environmental regulation becomes law, however, most land is on middle ground: it is neither easily slated for development nor rendered completely undevelopable. On this land the new regulations are tested, fought over, often litigated. Very often, government permits or specific exemptions are required for sewage treatment, water use, exhaust purification, endangered lands protection, wetlands conservation, and so on. Approvals which may have once taken sixty days to obtain may now drag on for one, two, or even five years. Planning and design for all forms of energy, water, and air use, which once required little more than reproducing a plan out of a recent trade magazine, must now be individually prepared and carefully engineered. Planners, lawyers, scientists, environmental engineers, wetlands experts may all have to be hired. The consequence is measured by the traditionally impatient private developer in the two words which hurt the most: time and money. Time, when you come down to it, also means money. So the consequence to the private developer is higher cost. And, very often, to adjust and compensate for the higher costs to develop, the higher interest expense, and the higher professional fees which must be paid, a developer must pay less for land. The initial value of land may be diminished, then, by the imposition of environmental regulation.

At times, though in rare instances, environmental regulation does not just add cost to development and reduce the value of affected property; it may also appear to wipe out all land value. This could happen, for instance, if you own a swamp or tidal marsh that could have been filled and developed before it was legally designated a mapped wetland. After the designation, however, the wetland may not be disturbed. This can happen if you own a piece of property that is found to be populated by the last surviving members of a particular species of plant or insect. But it is exceedingly rare for the regulatory process to produce such a virtual decimation of land value.

When all value is wiped out, oddly enough, some owners find themselves atop a bonanza. The state or county or local government may be obligated to purchase the property. The land may even be appraised with value added for its rare fauna stands or for its unique estuarine value. In addition, within certain limitations, sales made as a result of public condemnation offer favorable tax options to the owner. For instance, no tax need be paid if the funds are reinvested in land.

All over America there is another, and very often unaware, landowner beneficiary of environmental regulation—the owner of usable, developed, private land that has been devalued over the years by one form of pollution or another. A 1967 study in the St. Louis metropolitan area concluded that if sulfation level per family unit dropped by 0.25 mg/100cm^2 per day, property values could rise between $100 and $250. On the other hand, a 1970 study in Washington, D.C., Kansas City, and St. Louis found that a 10 percent increase in pollution yields a 1–2 percent decrease in housing price or a marginal reduction of $2.00 to $4.00 per month for rented housing, and a capitalized loss ranging from $300 to $700 per owned property. In the town of Toledo, Oregon, which has a population of 2,818 and a pulp mill that employs 1,000 persons, a 1972 study found that a unit of pollution caused a $29.00 drop in property value. The Council on Environmental Quality predicted in 1971, in fact, that the annual level of existing pollution lowered property values by $5.2 billion.

Viewed in this manner, the huge national cost paid by everyone in the form of a higher Consumer Price Index goes, in part, to benefit and repay a limited group: those who own usable land and real property formerly devalued by unfettered environmental despoilation.

On the other hand, there is an ironic analogy between the highway-building program of years past and the current environmental movement. Just as the former added enormous value to particular parcels of remote land which suddenly became more accessible, so the environmental movement, as it becomes effective, causes most affected properties to appreciate. Indeed, the renaissance now evident along the water edge of many American cities is inconceivable without the concommitant national commitment to cleaning up the water itself. Usable open land along lakeshores, canals, and rivers, which had been abused during the industral decades, will become more appealing, and more valuable.

BACKLASH POTENTIAL

Questions, of course, remain: Will we ever have really clean air again? Will the waters across the land realize the objectives of the Federal Water Pollution Control Act, set for the mid-1980s, of zero discharge of pollutants and a condition that is "fishable and swimmable"?

For the first time in the history of the country, there is potential to realize these objectives. However, fear for the economic future of America is becoming a useful wedge against timely compliance with clean-air and clean-water deadlines. By the end of the 1970s, this fear had indeed made political and economic inroads toward undermining the foundation of the environomental movement. In August 1979, the EPA announced that it was relaxing water pollution controls for companies that discharged non-toxic substances, a move the agency estimated would save business $200 million. As Barbara Blum, the EPA's deputy administrator, explained,

DEVELOPMENT OF ARTIFICIAL REEFS AT MARCO ISLAND, FLORIDA, 1973

It is very rare for environmental regulation to drastically reduce land value. In the case of flagrant dredge and fill operations in fragile wetlands such as this one, however, all development is halted. Wetland regulations today quite appropriately protect coastal land more rigorously than ever before.

some controls are "tougher and more expensive than needed. . . . Most of the affected industries are already removing up to 98 percent of the conventional pollutants in their discharges. Additional requirements to clean up the last few percent could cost them as much or more than they have spent so far."

In December 1979, the EPA put into effect a new air pollution policy —the "bubble concept"—which allows a business to increase pollution from some sources if it reduces pollution at others, provided that the total amount of pollution remained within clean-air requirements. State authorities have the right to forbid companies to use the bubble concept, and only pollutants of the same type can be so interchanged. Business, not surprisingly, welcomed this innovative policy, while environmental groups were less supportive. Not only is the new system difficult to monitor, but it allows for new construction in areas that do not meet air-quality standards if builders reduce pollution elsewhere in the vicinity.

The federal government itself is now considering relaxing fuel economy and environmental standards, which could save the ailing automobile industry billions of dollars. Secretary of Transportation Neil E. Goldschmidt was quoted in December 1979 as saying, "Energy-efficient automobiles are important, but we don't want to end up with less competition in the business and less employment as the end-product. In all the shifts that we make, we want to make sure that people are working." Meanwhile, the oil industry has been pressing the EPA to halt its phase-out of lead in gasoline in order to stretch out its supplies of crude oil; electric utilities have joined oil companies in urging a general easing of sulfur limits on the burning of oil; and coal producers have advocated a relaxation of clean-air rules and strip-mining controls to permit more coal use. At the same time, environmentalists view the development of most alternative energy sources—synthetic fuels, coal and oil shale, nuclear power—as equally, if not potentially, more damaging to the environment. "We will protect the environment," President Carter assured the nation. "But when this nation critically needs a refinery or a pipeline, we will build it."

By the end of the 1970s, a crisis in energy supply and in confidence about the nation's economic strength had emerged. We were routinely described as a hostage to OPEC, and inflation made us all feel poorer and less powerful. Yet national opinion surveys indicated sustained public support of environmental improvement. Despite public pressure for governmental belt tightening, there has not been a significant cutback in public expenditures to improve the environment. In a sampling of seventeen states surveyed recently by *The New York Times,* eleven showed increases in annual appropriations for pollution abatement, national resource management, and other environmental controls. In six states, expenditures remained about the same. Among those polled, only New York showed a pronounced reduction.

Environmental regulation will survive the budget stringencies of the 1980s, in part because it addresses a much broader issue than most are willing to admit. At its base, it touches a strong and profound aspect of general welfare, as well as the future health of millions of people. Consider for a moment the medical consequences of chemical waste on all who live near the Love Canal; the impact of poisoned cattle feed found in Michigan; the air pollution generated in Los Angeles that drifts slowly eastward; the poisoning of shrimp in the Gulf of Mexico, and of fish and crabs in Chesapeake Bay; and most of all, the endangered water supplies all over the continent.

With certain justification, officials of the EPA point out that that agency operates, in part, as a public health organization. Indeed, justifiable efforts are being made by groups such as the Corporate Accountability Research Group, which surveys federal health and safety regulations, to justify EPA expenditures partially on the basis of preventive medicine benefits. Using its own form of cost-benefit analysis, this group has found that EPA regulation in 1978 cost $22.7 billion, while benefits—many of them connected to savings in health costs and the creation of new jobs— were estimated at $22.2 billion. This type of comprehensive cost-benefit analysis indicates a very low real cost to the nation for environmental protection, some $500 million, or about half of the funds spent by the federal legislative branch of government in the same year.

In terms of environmental protection legislation and achievement, the 1970s will emerge as an unprecedented and unique decade. The legislative gains of the seventies will not be repeated. In the decade ahead, on the other hand, I doubt that environmental regulation will be severely compromised; but this movement will never again assert the quantum leap in power over policy, and over the use of land, water, and air, that it did during its stunning and unprecedented performance of the 1970s.

Much remains to be done. "Acid rain" is a key word for environmental legislation in the 1980s. Perhaps the most serious worldwide environmental problem, acid rain occurs when pollutants trapped in the earth's atmosphere inevitably return as a component of rain or snowfall. This precipitation, spread far and wide from its original pollutant source, causes fatal chemical reactions to fish and animals; decreases soil fertility and damages crops; and causes the deterioration of numerous building materials exposed to it. As a start, acid rain can be reduced through more stringent regulation of the exhaust from coal-burning power plants, from other industry smokestacks, and from car exhaust.

**SMELTER AND CEMETERY,
SOUTH EL PASO, TEXAS,
APRIL 1972**

Acid rain promises to be one of the major challenges of the 1980s. The
smelter in this photograph, a contributor to acid rain, also reportedly
pollutes the air for three miles around.

268

ENVIRONMENTAL RIGHTS AND
LAND VALUES IN THE FUTURE

If ever there was a clear case of an inalienable right that should be made part of any revision of the original Bill of Rights, it is the right to experience and enjoy pure air and clean water. If ever there was an abuse of the vital resources of this land by a small segment of the population, it is surely the degradation of the land, water, and air by a handful of enormously powerful industries, municipalities, and government agencies.

Until the last decade, the air and the water and the land had no rights. Until very recently there was no basis from which a charge of unethical, to say nothing of illegal, behavior could be asserted against the sources of environmental pollution. In a little over ten years' time, all that has changed. Today, environmental considerations go way beyond the discrete task of regulating industry, government, and regional developments. They go, in part, to the heart of a changing set of priorities in America. Environmental regulation reveals a shift in power, from the domination of business and industry over the land toward public power, toward the ordinary citizen as the beneficiary of a cleaner environment.

As land developers and industrialists become accustomed to environmental controls, I suspect the process will become less frustrating and less distasteful. As government agencies begin to know more about what they are doing, procedures will become less personal, less chancy, and probably more efficient. Yet how quickly environmental regulation will proceed as years go by is an open question that involves the mood of the nation, the balance of legislative power, and probably the stability of the national economy.

What is also on the horizon, I believe, is growing support for environmental control from almost every landowner, though this is not yet the case. Just as zoning was so virulently resented and resisted by private property owners fifty years ago, only now to be approved and even cherished by so many, so too, in time, I suspect, will environmental regulation eventually be accepted. The landowner, especially of residential property, will find that such legislation safeguards the future quality of the land, as well as its desirability and value. Activity permitted on adjacent land is regulated as well. In the long run, the value of land in environmentally regulated areas will increase significantly in comparison with land that has unprotected borders, unregulated water, and unguarded air. As buyers of land grow accustomed to environmental regulation, they are apt to feel safer and more confident dealing with environmentally regulated land than with property that may be subject to extremely adverse impacts. In time, the ordinary citizen and consumer of housing is likely to demand the benefits of environmental protection, and wonder how things were ever allowed to get so bad.

Some day, when fish can again be caught down at the lake and children can again swim in the streams nearby and sailboats again appear on warm Saturday afternoons all over the riverfront downtown, the cost that was paid, the blip in the Consumer Price Index, and the years of anguish will all be quietly forgotten.

NINE

THE
CONSERVATION OF
PRIVATE LAND:
HIDDEN VALUE
IN OPEN SPACE

For the first time in America, private wealth and power are being devoted to the conservation of land in its natural state. The motives behind this new trend are as mixed as the quality of the lands preserved. Nevertheless, there is a thoroughly innovative and pragmatic interweaving of special regulations which permit private owners to conserve land, especially valuable and particularly important land, at modest or no cost. There are various ways that the private owner, while preserving his own most desirable land, is able to benefit financially from the altruistic endeavor.

The Appeal of the Land.   Throughout time, the long vista, the view across the water, the imposing presence of a snow-capped mountain in a distant view, has inspired a human reverence for nature. Beautiful and especially unusual land stirs men's souls. It also enhances the life of everyone who lives nearby or who encounters the land. Poets, painters, and troubadours know this but can do nothing to conserve the land itself. Instead, they invoke it in verse, replicate it in paintings, and celebrate it in song. In America this tradition runs deep. The nineteenth-century portrait painter Thomas Cole felt the majesty of the Hudson River Valley, but he was powerless to conserve it. His paintings remain lyrical depictions of the lost wild and solemn beauty of the American wilderness. John Marin, in the early twentieth century, captures in his heroic visual imagery the rocks and sun and sea along the Maine coast, which now gives way to housing developments.

In 1845 Henry David Thoreau went out to live a utopian coexistence with nature at Walden Pond. Thirteen years later he advocated what is only recently taking hold within the American consciousness—"preserves, in which the bear and the panther and some even of the hunter race may still exist, and not be civilized off the face of the earth—not for idle sport or food, but for inspiration and our own true recreation."

The natural land is alive in our imaginations—as well as in reality. Upon it, change occurs constantly: animal and plant life thrive, even in the seemingly barren desert. Any of it, with familiarity and time, seems to become as precious and special as the deserts to Georgia O'Keeffe and the swamps to William Faulkner.

THE PRIVATE CONSERVATION MOVEMENT
AND NONPROFIT POWER

In recent years, as destruction of the natural land continues before the onslaught of highways, settlement, and sprawl, private conservation efforts are taking hold. While individual owners are involved in this movement, there has emerged as a critical intermediary a unique type of nonprofit organization devoted to the protection and stewardship of land that will be conserved in its natural state.

Such an idea, of course, goes against the traditional grain of the American frontier ethic, which propelled patriots to sequester the land from its initial inhabitants in order to use it for profit. Indeed, it was used with a lascivious viciousness that left great stretches of the national lands ravished of its original grasses, forests, and majesty.

Nonprofit Power. The oldest of the nonprofit land conservation organizations is the Appalachian Mountain Club, founded in 1876 and still operating today. The Sierra Club, founded in 1892 and established in order "to explore, enjoy and preserve the nation's forests, waters, wildlife and wilderness," is probably the most renowned, however. In eighty-seven years the organization has grown from a membership roster of 200 to 183,000; from very little funding to an $8 million yearly budget; and from one office in one state to a network encompassing all fifty states and several foreign countries. The special prominence this national organization now enjoys is largely a result of its openly entering the political arena. Through its legal battles against despoilation of the natural environment, it has received publicity and notoriety. Indeed, the Sierra Club Legal Defense Fund, with an annual budget of $550,000, employs seven practicing attorneys and several legal assistants. Michael McCloskey, executive director of the Sierra Club, regrets the continuing high legal expenses. He recently observed to Bill Barich in *Outside,* an environmental magazine, "It's not normal for a relationship to be entirely adversarial, and our relationship with industry has been entirely that way." While the Sierra Club stands as a legal watch group over the destiny of special quality natural land, it does not actually acquire and manage any of it.

When it comes to the acquisition and administration of open space, it is The Nature Conservancy (TNC) that is the primary national force. The Nature Conservancy's objective is to receive and/or acquire natural lands of special quality, after which it attempts to assure the continuation of the land in its natural state. It may, however, turn the property over

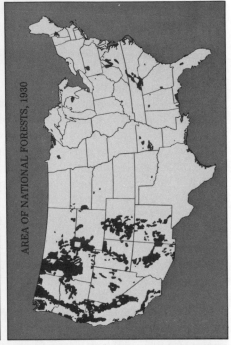

AREA OF VIRGIN FOREST, 1850

Each dot represents 25,000 acres

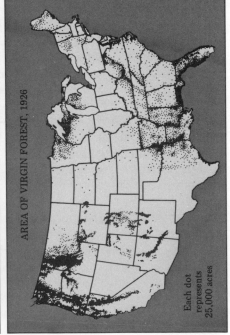

AREA OF NATIONAL FORESTS, 1930

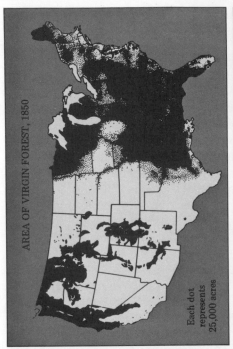

AREA OF VIRGIN FOREST, 1620

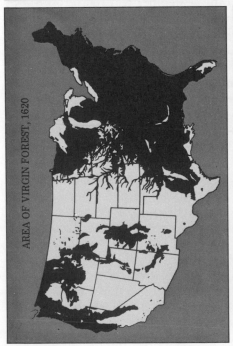

AREA OF VIRGIN FOREST, 1926

Each dot represents 25,000 acres

to a government agency, such as the Department of the Interior—occasionally for a substantial sum—or maintain the land as an administered preserve.

The Nature Conservancy begain in 1917, when the Sociological Society of America formed the Committee for the Preservation of Natural Conditions. In 1946 this committee became a separate entity, the Ecologist Union. Since the first year of operation in 1950, The Nature Conservancy has been involved in over two thousand preservation projects involving about 1.3 million acres of land. This land is spread across forty-seven states, the Caribbean, and Canada. Holdings range in size from under 10 acres to its huge 49,000-acre tract in the Great Dismal Swamp of Virginia, donated by the Union Camp Company, a forestry products corporation that owns large tracts of land.

Today, nearly two hundred businesses are corporate dues-paying members of The Nature Conservancy. Many private landowners and business giants, such as International Paper, Union Camp, Georgia Pacific, Anaconda Copper, Gulf Oil, and Metromedia, have all given or sold, below market value, thousands of acres of choice wilderness land. Other corporations, including IBM, Ford Motor Company, and Atlantic Richfield, have provided timely loans and cash donations to make an acquisition possible. Large corporations with a sense of public responsibility—and perhaps some with an environmental image problem—find the tax-deductible donation or gift to TNC a suitable and sensible outlet for corporate largesse. The publicity is always good, and favorable tax laws lessen the actual cost of the donation.

Another national organization dedicated to the acquisition and preservation of land in America is the Trust for Public Land (TPL), established in 1973. TPL is one of the few nonprofit, charitable organizations interested in the open-space needs of urban people, as well as the preservation of wilderness. Unlike many other charitable organizations, TPL is almost completely self-sustaining, with 80 percent of its yearly income coming from land transactions and the remainder obtained from foundations and contracts. When TPL is given property or acquires it by purchase below

**VIRGIN FORESTS IN THE UNITED STATES, 1620, 1850, 1926,
AND NATIONAL FORESTS, 1930**
(Opposite)

Only recently have efforts involving the private sector been directed toward conservation of land in America. This movement goes against the traditional "frontier ethic," which encouraged citizens to exploit the land for profit. Consequently, much of America's wilderness has already been depleted.

the market price, the difference between the land's fair market value and TPL's cost becomes a charitable donation from the landowner. TPL then sells the acquired property to public agencies, though generally still at costs below those on the open market, and retains a margin of "profit" on each transaction to fund its nonprofit conservation activities.

In addition to providing the public with over 30,000 acres of land between 1974 and 1980, two thirds of which are located in cities or metropolitan areas, TPL has also saved public agencies an average of about 30 percent of the cost of acquiring those lands, while funding its own operations. For example, TPL persuaded The Southern Pacific Land Company to sell over 1,900 acres near Palm Desert, California, at 50 percent below appraised value. This particular tract includes Eisenhower Mountain, a local landmark, as well as specialized living habitats for the endangered kit fox and the desert bighorn sheep. The property also links up to a network of hiking and riding trails. The company obtained a tax deduction for the difference between sale proceeds and appraised value. In turn, TPL, with the help of local community funds and a federal matching grant, was able to transfer the property to California's Wildlife Conservation Board for public use and conservation protection.

In its well-prepared and persuasive literature, the Trust for Public Land encourages corporate participation with the following skillfully pitched appeal:

More and more corporations are accepting the responsibility of good citizenship, and are trying to benefit the community as well as their shareholders. The Trust for Public Land offers a practical and highly visible way of doing this. Using its specialized skills to acquire excess or problem lands, TPL can guide them into the public domain as parks or open space. TPL's program can offer corporations such benefits as: tax savings from the charitable donation of land value and from reduced capital gains taxes; increased liquidity from conversion of excess land into productive assets; optimum timing through expediting transactions or effecting them during advantageous accounting periods; flexibility in structuring terms; positive public relations from favorable publicity; and saving management energy by providing skilled partnership in complex land problems.

The Nature Conservancy and the Trust for Public Land, however, are not the only organizations which acquire open space for conservation purposes. There are numerous regional and local nonprofit groups which work toward the same goals. The Vineyard Open Land Foundation on Martha's Vineyard, The Nantucket Conservation Foundation on Nantucket Island, and the South Fork Land Trust in Eastern Long Island are but a few examples in one area of the country. Other local and even more specialized nonprofit land trusts, such as the Mohonk Trust in New York's Shawangunk Mountains and Wye Institute on the eastern shore of Maryland, are established to hold a particular large tract of land but do not acquire or deal with new land conservation projects.

Many of the local and regional groups endeavor to guarantee their own survival by mixing land conservation objectives with income-producing activities. The Vineyard Open Land Foundation acquires, plans, and sells some land in order to generate funds with which to hold and preserve the most significant portion of lands donated to it. For example, in 1973 the Vineyard Open Land Foundation arranged for the removal of certain development rights on sixty-seven acres of farmland near Edgartown, a piece of property known as Sweetened Water. The property had been zoned for half-acre lots. One hundred and ten houses could have been constructed there. The foundation bought the property, and arranged for the preservation of thirty acres. It also developed a plan for fifteen large home sites and five low-cost sites. The sale of the sites helped cover the foundation's operating costs.

Wye Institute, an innovative educational organization that owns 610 acres in Queen Annes County, Maryland, has adopted a different approach. Portions of its property are leased to a regional university for agricultural experimentation; other portions are leased to local farmers for crop production. In addition, some of the land serves as a summer camp for exceptionally gifted children.

Thus, there are private nonprofit organizations at both the local and national levels whose objective is the conservation of undeveloped land. A few, including the Sierra Club or the Natural Resources Defense Council, function primarily to marshall public awareness and to mount legal challenges on behalf of endangered lands. Others, such as The Nature Conservancy and Trust for Public Land, get into the land business itself. They become involved protagonists on the scene of land dealing and land transactions. How and why they work tells much of how some of the most important and most cherished land in America can and will be conserved through the sophisticated and informed coincidence of nonprofit power and private wealth.

How and Why It Works.   While some wealthy American families and corporations are celebrated for their philanthropy, the recent success of land conservation trusts depends on more than pure generosity. Once a parcel of undeveloped land is transferred to a nonprofit land conservation agency, a number of ways in which the donor can benefit financially emerge. First, however, the value of the land must be determined.

The Appraisal: Key to Valuing the Donation.   Before a land donation or below-market-value sale occurs, the value of the land is determined by appraisal. But this is a very unusual appraisal situation. Consider the case of land that is to be donated. No check will be written. The signed-over deed will arrive with proper fanfare and publicity, laced with the language of magnanimity, environmental responsiveness, and appreciation. The recipient organization does not pay for the property that is given; thus, the appraised market value is of little concern to it. However, the appraised market value of the gift is of enormous interest and importance to the donor, for while he expects no check from the recipient organization, the declared market value of his property will be the precise amount of other income he is able to shelter from tax.

Thus, unlike most purchase-and-sale transactions, while there is a "seller" anxious to receive the highest sustainable appraisal, there is not a vigilant buyer anxious to obtain the lowest accurate judgment of market value. The "buyer" in this instance takes no adversary stance in the transaction. Indeed, though recipient organizations do not intervene in the appraisal process, in order to assure that the gift is actually donated, they are likely to favor the highest possible appraisal of the property. As the benefits increase for the donor, his interest in making the donation increases.

There is unusual latitude in appraising open land of particular beauty or having special environmental characteristics. By its very definition, there is little land like it around. This scarcity makes it difficult to compare the to-be-donated parcel to similar property that has been sold in the same area, which is how most appraising of open land is done. Land appreciated for its awesome scenic beauty cannot be valued based on the income it produces or on the cost to replace it. The appraiser, then, is often left with the donor as the major factor to consider in appraising the value of the land. The Internal Revenue Service does require an independent appraisal from an established appraiser, such as a member of the Appraisal Institute.

Private Land Donations: Conservation and Profit.   What are the consequences to the value of your house if you happen to live next to that beautiful field or wetland that will remain forever undisturbed? Or perhaps you own thousands of acres surrounding that forever-protected open space for which you have just been paid. Possibilities glimmer. The increased value that an adjacent preserve may impute to privately held nearby land may make the below-market sale, or even a land donation to a nonprofit organization, a very attractive proposition to the private owner. Like additional insight that is possible if one studies the edges of

278

a complex Bellini painting, so looking around the physical edge of a land donation often turns up some interesting artistry.

As intimated above, there is sometimes more to the gift of land to a nonprofit conservation organization than meets the eye. The possibilities break down, roughly, into two ways to give something away—in this case, an important piece of land—and then to get as much value—if not more —as was given away. These two ways are through tax advantages or through value added to adjacent land. Nor are these mutually exclusive. When they are combined, a pyramid of profitability is constructed from the societally praiseworthy act of donating land. The alchemists' dream of turning base metal into gold is realized at last.

First of all, there is the tax advantage. Within limits, the appraised value of the land to be donated will offset ordinary income before federal taxes are calculated. Thus, the land donation saves the private donor a predictable expense: a portion of year-end federal income tax.

Second, and less often recognized, is the potential to earn large sums of money as a consequence of the land donation. Consider the impact on the value of a private land holding when at its edge there is a newly donated Nature Conservancy preserve that guarantees forever-undisturbed a stunning wetland. The donor of the wetland in this case also owns the surrounding land which is not donated but rather is slated for subdivision and development as residential housing. Certain restrictions, however, are placed on such donations. In instances when land is already legally precluded from development, as in a subdivision "reserved area" or planned-unit development open space, no donation and charitible deduction claim is possible.

But where donation of a centrally located wetland is possible, what are the multiple consequences and advantages of this arrangement? First, the donor might have been restricted by local, state, or federal environmental regulation from using the wetland for development in the first place. If this is so, any value obtained via an off-setting tax savings is "profit" beyond normal market expectations. Second, the value of land surrounding the donated preserve appreciates. People seek and will pay for guaranteed privacy, guaranteed common property lines with land that will remain forever undeveloped and not accessible to the public for intense recreation use. Thus, new and often significantly higher value is added to the surrounding land. Higher prices will be paid because the best possible future—a future of privacy, security, and beauty—is guaranteed.

A study of Boulder undertaken by economists at the University of Colorado in 1978 attempts to quantify the value added to land adjacent to preserved open space. In 1967, Boulder voters supported a 0.4 percent city sales tax to raise revenue for the purchase of open space. By 1978, 8,000 acres had been purchased. Mark Correll, Jan Lillydalh, and Larry

Singell examined three residential areas incorporating greenbelts and discovered that property adjacent to open space was 32 percent more valuable than land three thousand feet away. In one neighborhood during 1975, a greenbelt added $5.4 million to property value. From the viewpoint of public benefit, the researchers estimated that such an increase would warrant increased property taxes of $500,000 a year, with the $1.5 million cost of the greenbelt being recovered over three years.

The conservation of land once privately held can be thus accomplished without the private owner incurring a devastating loss. And the public

AERIAL VIEW OF
MOHONK MOUNTAIN HOUSE
AND SURROUNDING LAND,
NEW PALTZ, NEW YORK

Mohonk Mountain House, a resort in upstate New York, is surrounded by 5,000 acres of land owned by the Mohonk Trust. Smiley Brothers, Inc., owns the resort; the two brothers founded the nonprofit trust when pressures from real-estate subdividers and land developers increased the value of, and consequently the taxes upon, their large wilderness holding. The trust holds an open-space covenant on the land and therefore pays 10 percent of the tax levied on similar land categorized as commercially developable. Meanwhile, Mohonk Mountain House profits from its more attractive setting.

interest may be served if the land is appropriately located, or of genuine quality, unusual character, or even of great significance to the local drainage shed, underground hydrology, or cherished scenic vistas. That a private donor may, in fact, realize a tax benefit or even a substantial profit from the sale of the property itself, or from value added to adjacent property, should be no cause for alarm. Without such directly linked benefits, some of the most important and precious land resources in America would not be conserved today, and placed in trust for all to see and quietly enjoy down through the ages.

Tax Exemption Stimulates Turbulence. When privately owned land is conserved by a nonprofit group, the cry goes up all over town, "You mean it's coming off the tax rolls?" Many will complain that conservation is a fine idea, but not affordable by the community, which needs tax revenue.

In fact, when land is sold or donated to a nonprofit organization, it does generally come off the tax rolls. Its donor is not only relieved of the property, but as a private citizen he is relieved of paying property tax on the land. Nor does the recipient nonprofit organization generally assume responsibility for the tax. Because nonprofit land trusts seem to, and may indeed, reduce local public-tax revenue, resident citizens often resent them, much as they do a hometown university that occupies prime real estate but pays no real-estate tax.

It is such local resentment, for instance, that has brought the Mohonk Trust into court. Founded in 1963 to protect an important expanse of natural lands in the Shawangunk Mountains, the Mohonk Trust possesses a vast holding of some 5,000 contiguous acres in the rural New York state towns of New Paltz, Rochester, Marbletown, and Gardiner. It was created out of a larger holding of 7,500 acres, which in addition to the open land contains the picturesque, rambling Mohonk Mountain House, a resort perched at the edge of Lake Mohonk. The trust preserve is open to the public for hiking and hunting. And on it the trust conducts periodic programs in environmental education and ecological research. However, as development pressure mounted around the property, the towns that contain the land preserve claimed that tax should be paid on the very considerable speculative value of the land for residential and commercial development. In 1974 the town of Gardiner, site of 1,800 acres of trust lands, began assessing the property at its full development value. Gardiner's real-estate tax levy would have forced incremental sale to developers in order to meet the tax bill. The trust consequently filed suit, arguing that its purposes and activities met the requirements for tax exemption under New York State law. In 1979, the New York Court of Appeals, ruling that the Mohonk Trust is entitled to exemption from property taxes, stated that all "lands used for environmental and conservation purposes which are necessary to the public good and which are open to and enjoyed by the public" on a nonprofit basis are entitled to relief from property taxes.

This ruling enhances the possibility for tax exemption on all land held by the Mohonk Trust and, indeed, on land sheltered from tax held for legitimate conservation and educational purposes by nonprofit organizations throughout New York State. The court's decision is a positive step toward encouraging an expansion of private land conservation efforts. At the same time, of course, the preservation of this magnificent spread of open woodland, hills, and valleys enhances the commercial appeal of the adjacent Mohonk Mountain Resort, owned by the very same family that originally established the Mohonk Trust. While in this case the prime purpose of establishing the trust was not to insulate a resort business from adverse surrounding impact, the use of a nonprofit land trust to forward a resort business enterprise is nevertheless achieved. Since conflict of interest is often inherent in the option, judgment of each action can only be made, I believe, on the legitimacy of the conservation effort itself.

IMPACTS OF THE PRIVATE LAND CONSERVATION MOVEMENT

There are divergent sources from which the private conservation movement originated. It is aligned, in part, with a historical concern for the perpetuation of land as a natural resource; this concern first surfaces on a large scale through the conservation efforts initiated under Theodore Roosevelt's administration. A strain of environmentalist and preservationist elitism, the desire to maintain the status quo against an unfamiliar and uncertain future, also characterizes the movement. And, more often than not, a logical component of enlightened self-interest is also at work. Because of its various sources, when private conservation efforts do take place, a number of positive as well as less desirable consequences occur.

Science and Conservation.   Most of the preserves donated to nonprofit trusts are said to be sources of scientific or educational research and investigation. They may not be developed or exploited in any conventional way, and they may not be used for a wide range of recreational activity; but they can become areas in which animal and plant life are studied, in which the cycles of nature are charted, and in which the impact of eternal environmental forces affecting the land, its growth, and wildlife are observed.

Slowly, the preserves which have been accepted, at least by The Nature Conservancy, are being investigated by the organization itself. Each summer teams of young people are at work observing, identifying, and preparing plans and inventories for certain holdings. Some of the preserves are visited by students as study sanctuaries; others remain relatively unknown and unexplored, even for study purposes. The extent to which social objectives of study and research are, in fact, realized in this kind of situation depends entirely on local school or college programs and personalities, and on regional activities that may relate to the sanctuary.

In time, particularly when conserved land is located in an area that becomes highly developed, these preserves will be recognized for their

283

incalculable value as open space. People will come to wonder at the providence and foresight involved in preserving such places. Elsewhere, where sparse settlement and little actual development remain predominant, these preserved areas will play a less significant role.

Effect on Land Values.   When a large parcel of land is withdrawn from development potential and designated a forever-wild area, the amount of land left in town for conventional development may diminish significantly. If demand for this land is intense, a land donation can raise the cost and value of the remaining developable land nearby. As mentioned earlier, higher market value and presumably higher sales value accrue, particularly to land adjacent to the preserve.

As a potential social impact, the donation of large tracts of land into conservation areas may also raise the cost of housing in a given community. Bernard J. Frieden, professor of Urban Studies and Planning at MIT, in *The Environmental Protection Hustle* (1979), suggests that in some suburban communities efforts to preserve open lands are in fact veiled and effective means of housing discrimination:

In political controversies the new concept of the environment has been able to absorb an earlier and more selfish agenda concerned with preserving the status quo against newcomers. During the suburban build-up of the 1950s, suburbs were already using their land development controls to keep out undesirables. The main fiscal undesirables then were families living in modest homes with young children whose education would use up property tax dollars. Other undesirables were people whose arrival in a community would lower its social tone—that is, people whose occupation, income level, lifestyle, religion, or skin color might threaten the prestige levels established by earlier residents. Concern for the environment, as such, was not an important political factor in the 1950s. When this concern emerged later, it reinforced and provided cover for the local groups more concerned with fiscal and social undesirables than with protection of wildlife.

While Frieden's caustic view of the motives which fuel environmental regulations are, in certain instances, accurate, this unfortunate conflict of interest should not cloud the generally positive accomplishments achieved when a significant stretch of unusual land is preserved. The amount of conserved land is always minuscule in proportion to land available for development.

Effect on Community Development.   Land withdrawn from ordinary use may cause a greater—and undesirable—dispersal of community development than might otherwise be the case. This scarcely matters when ten, fifty, or several hundred acres lie in the path of development; but the situation changes if several thousand acres are involved. Then, the pattern of dispersal or sprawl forced by the preserve may require additional and/or longer roads, extended utility and sewer lines, and perhaps even a second primary school. Since the community must absorb these costs, they translate into higher tax rates for all residents. Such dispersal, however, is rare and can be prevented through more rigorous land preservation programs developed in concert with local and regional government planning programs.

On the other hand, if a preserve is well located, it may very well contribute to a tightening up of the community development pattern. This constriction happens when, because of its location, the tax-exempt land produces a natural border or boundary. In this case, the community will evolve in a more economic and concentrated pattern rather than extend itself—as it might otherwise naturally do—into the preserved area.

Potential for Abuse. Given the inherent potential for abuse by property owners in search of tax relief, certain large reaches of land should not be entirely devoted to conservation purposes. Land with neither surface quality nor subsurface value, with no visual appeal, and with no importance in terms of location should not be purchased, and probably not even be accepted for donation, by a nonprofit land conservation organization.

Most of these organizations are aware of the potential for abuse. As a result of responsible leadership, as well as limited powers to manage and purchase, most nonprofit land organizations have rigid criteria which condition and limit lands they will accept. And this is as it ought to be. The private land conservation movement is achieving important long-term benefits. To continue to do so, it must not be coopted by property owners as merely a convenient instrument of tax relief, estate planning, or investment.

COVENANTS AND RESTRICTIONS: DO-IT-YOURSELF LAND CONSERVATION

At times, a private owner of land may want to control future development of his land rather strictly and specificly. Or he may want to preserve his property in a forever-wild state or as a nature preserve for study and educational purposes, without the use of any intermediary nonprofit organization. In such a case, the owner does not have the advantage of a transfer of title, with the resultant sale income and/or income-tax donation deduction.

Through the use of covenants and restrictions,* a private owner may exercise control over the use of his property long after he has sold it and long after his death. Such covenants may be created to "run with the land," that is, to survive the present ownership and all subsequent ownership. The legal provisions become a part of the land itself, so to speak. When this happens, the covenants and restrictions are likely to have a great deal to do with the way the land is valued, for they specify its future use. If the covenants and restrictions do, in fact, restrict the land—for instance, for open acreage or agricultural uses—then property taxes assessed by the host community should reflect both this low-intensity use and the elimination of future speculative value. In this way, an owner may benefit from a lower property tax, and the community may benefit from open space.

Covenants and restrictions are commonly employed when the owner of private farmland decides to restrict the future use of his land from any kind of development or, conversely, when he decides to develop his property and wants to control the development very precisely. What follows are excerpts from a set of covenants and restrictions that apply to a new subdivision created out of farmland. The "declarant," the private owner of farmland undergoing subdivision, states that "these restrictions, covenants and conditions shall be deemed covenants running with the land and the Declarant, its successors, and assigns shall have the right at any time or times to proceed at law or in equity against any person violating or attempting to violate any provisions contained herein. . . . "

No part of said property shall be sold for any purpose other than residential. No trade or business of any kind shall be conducted upon said property or any part thereof. No structure shall be erected, placed, altered, used or permitted to remain on any residential building lot other than one detached single-family private dwelling not to exceed two stories, and one private garage for not less than two (2) automobiles. . . . Under no circumstances will a house trailer or camper be used as a dwelling house.

No building or structure shall be erected on any lot nor shall the exterior of any building or any structure be altered, except in accordance with plans and specifications therefore which have received prior written approval from the Declarant.

No residence shall be erected or used which has a livable floor space of less than twenty-five hundred (2,500) square feet exclusive of garage, carport,

*See Chapter Five, pages 171–172, for a discussion of covenants and restrictions.

porch, breezeway, balcony or terrace; in a two-story residence, said livable space shall not be less than three thousand (3,000) square feet.

No fences shall be erected or maintained other than wood fences except in areas surrounding gardens and swimming pools; all such fences shall be subject to specific written approval of Declarant.

Covenants and restrictions, then, allow for personal prescription. They are, in effect, an extension of feudal power over the landed domain. Like the proclamations of a lord of the realm, they are challenged only with the greatest difficulty, even after death. More often than not, in fact, covenants and restrictions, once placed upon the land, remain sovereign controls unless they are proved to contradict public law.

Anyone who owns land, of course, can make a private, unspoken, covenant with himself that his land will be preserved as open space. The owner fulfills this covenant by neither selling nor developing the land. This approach to the stewardship of property is the most beneficial to the neighboring community, as the owner continues to pay real property tax at the full rate. Likewise, this approach is the most costly to the owner, who derives no financial benefit from his resolve to conserve his land. And, because the land will survive and the owner will not, this private covenant is the most fragile, the most risky, and a course of action more likely to be reversed than not. Heirs or future buyers may feel differently about the land or may be unable to afford to maintain the property in its natural state. Indeed, the inexorable assurance of the owner's eventual death places the future of such property in absolute jeopardy. At death, estate taxes will have to be paid on the assessed value of the land based on its full market value. To raise cash, time and again estate administrators and heirs look, as they reasonably must, to the "unproductive" land asset in order to pay the federal government. In fact, estate taxes cause more land sales each year in America than any other single force.

CONSERVATION RESTRICTIONS: NEW RIGHTS, NEW BENEFITS

It is possible for a private landowner who wants to retain title to land but is willing to restrict its use to some form of open-space or conservation purpose to do so through a formal conservation restriction. The private owner, in most instances, initiates whatever restrictions are to be imposed. For this legal document to be effective, the restriction must either span a very long period or, even more certain, be declared to run with the land.

The conservation restriction enables the private property owner to obtain direct financial benefit, though of a lesser magnitude, of the same types available through a land donation or sale to a nonprofit organization. To realize this benefit, he must find a government agency or a nonprofit organization willing either to accept a donation of or to purchase the conservation restriction.

Appraisal of the Conservation Restriction. Whether the conservation restriction is donated or sold, it has value. Its value can be established by determining the difference, through appraisal, between the market value of the property before it is burdened with the restriction and the value of the property after the restriction is placed on it. The value of the land burdened with the restriction represents the new and reduced value of the property itself.

Appraising conservation restrictions is a new and clouded area of land appraisal. Numerous factors have to be considered, including the nature and duration of the restriction, the location of the property, and market trends in the region.

The conservation restriction, when it is perpetual, eliminates the development potential of the restricted land and, in a sense, the property's development rights as well. These rights might contribute as much as 90 or 95 percent of the value of well-located prime land in or near a robust city or thriving suburb. Farther out, where farms and forests prevail but where new development is under way, development rights may contribute between 50 and 75 percent of the total land value.

Amenity Value. Amenity value, on the other hand, is the value retained by the landowner after development has been restricted and after the value of any land-related business, such as farming or foresting, has been taken into account. Amenity value may be prized above all else by the landowner. Created by privacy, scenic beauty, quiet, hunting or fishing rights, and waterfront access, the amenity value of the land contributes the largest single increment to market value in remote resorts, areas of spectacular natural beauty and serenity, in which the land has little or no capacity for agricultural development or conventional urban development.

The conservation restriction cannot diminish amenity value, nor does it generally diminish agricultural value. Its prime purpose, on the contrary, is to enhance and ensure both of these aspects while extinguishing the right to use the property for conventional residential, commercial, or industrial development. If a landowner seeks to possess only amenity value and is willing to give up value attributed to development rights, he

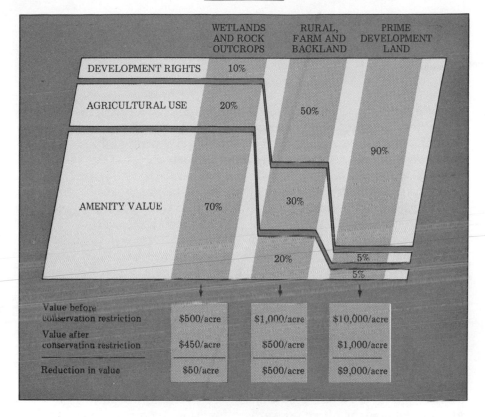

	WETLANDS AND ROCK OUTCROPS	RURAL, FARM AND BACKLAND	PRIME DEVELOPMENT LAND
DEVELOPMENT RIGHTS	10%	50%	90%
AGRICULTURAL USE	20%		
AMENITY VALUE	70%	30%	
		20%	5%
			5%
Value before conservation restriction	$500/acre	$1,000/acre	$10,000/acre
Value after conservation restriction	$450/acre	$500/acre	$1,000/acre
Reduction in value	$50/acre	$500/acre	$9,000/acre

VALUATION OF LAND UNDER A PERMANENT CONSERVATION RESTRICTION

Illustrated here is the hypothetical impact of a permanent conservation restriction on valuation of three kinds of land that are frequent subjects of restrictions: wetlands and rock outcrops; rural, farm, and backland not under development pressure; and prime development land. Not only is the value of each type different, but the portion of value representing development rights is very different. In most cases, it is only this portion of the value that is affected by a conservation restriction. Wetlands and rock outcrops have little or no development value but may have substantial amenity value. A conservation restriction should have little impact on their value. Rural and backland might be perfectly suited for development, but under little development pressure. Its value under a conservation restriction might be its potential value for agricultural use, plus a factor for amenity value. Prime development land near a growing population center, with access, good drainage, and no special problems obviously has the highest value, and the highest portion of its value represents development rights.

289

may be able to enjoy land ownership at reduced personal cost and simultaneously guarantee no future development of the property by selling or donating a conservation easement. This has numerous financial benefits to both the owner and his heirs.

The Value of the Conservation Restriction.   This restriction, if it can be valued, is useful to the private owner. It may significantly reduce federal income tax, annual real-estate tax, and ultimately the tax imposed upon his estate. The precise value of each aspect of the tax benefit depends, among other factors, upon the cost base of the property itself, the tax bracket of the private owner, local real-estate assessment, and taxation policies in the community of jurisdiction. But the general benefits are as follow:

Real-Estate Tax   Once a property is burdened with a conservation restriction guaranteed to remain in force, the land's use for development is restricted. Because, in most instances, its market value is thus reduced, the lower adjusted value of the property becomes the basis for a reduced municipal property assessment and taxation. This lower tax presents an annual cash savings to the landowner.

Federal Income Tax   When the restriction is donated to a public agency or nonprofit organization, the donor reduces his federal income taxes in two ways. First, if the assessed value of the restriction contains a profit over the original cost, the donor escapes capital gains tax on the amount donated, as he would were he donating a common stock that had appreciated in value over its original cost. Second, and within limitations, the current fair market value of the restriction donation is deductible from gross income, as would be a cash donation to a nonprofit organization. To avoid losing the benefit of a portion of this deduction in any given year, the donor is entitled to spread the value of the donation over a total of six years. He may even choose the years; they need not be sequential. In this way, he is able to use the charitable donation incrementally in special target high-income years.

Federal Estate Tax   Estate taxes are based on the full market value of property at the owner's death, though certain exemptions do exist. If during his lifetime an owner donates or sells a conservation restriction that is valued at, say, 50 percent of the full market value of the land, then the value of his estate is reduced. Upon his death, the estate is then spared taxation on the previously disposed of increment in value. The estate remains in possession of the land and is, in fact, more likely to be able to hold on to it intact at the owner's death, as taxes will be lower.

Gift Taxes   Under federal statutes, when a perpetual conservation restriction is granted to a public or nonprofit agency, no gift tax is charged. Indeed, the value of the gift is deductible, as outlined above. However, a gift made directly to a private individual, in excess of $3,000, is taxable. In the long run, the conservation restriction is a gift to heirs, as it reduces the estate taxes which they must pay. At the same time, of course, the restriction does limit, and often greatly reduces, the market value of the land itself, which is what is actually inherited.

When these factors are considered, it is unlikely that any profit will be made on the tax aspects of the conservation restriction in comparison to the potential profit of a full value sale of the land. But tax savings do help reduce the difference, sometimes quite substantially.

There are also times when a full value sale in the commercial marketplace is not desired by the owner, or not all that easy to make. Perhaps there are few buyers; perhaps the land is more suited to conservation than to development. In such instances, which certainly abound, the donation of a conservation restriction, particularly if it is favorably appraised, may provide a higher return than the owner could otherwise obtain. When the owner's primary objectives are continued existence of the land as open space, as well as his continued use and enjoyment of the amenity value of the land, no other approach is as sensible or effective as the conservation restriction.

Controversy Over Conservation: The Sale of Conservation Restrictions or Development Rights on Private Land to Public Agencies. Once a conservation restriction becomes perpetual and runs with the land, it is, in effect, a restriction of all development rights. Consequently, the sale of this conservation restriction differs little from the sale of development rights; conversely, the sale of development rights is very much like the sale of a perpetual conservation restriction.

For the first time, counties and municipalities in a few selected areas are buying development rights from private landowners in order to assure the continuation of agriculture, forestry, and/or other productive uses of undeveloped land in the path of community development. The clear leader in this field is Suffolk County on eastern Long Island, an area that contains some of the best agricultural soils anywhere in the nation. There, since 1977, a limited amount of development rights has been purchased to assure the continuation of agriculture on prime land. After the sale of these rights, private landowners continue to own the land: they may farm it or even sell it, but only as farmland or fallow fields. As Suffolk County Executive John Klein, the man most responsible for initiating the program, explained to the *East Hampton Star* in 1978, once the rights are

291

bought, "that land may never be used for anything except agriculture. What you are selling to us is all of your rights and title of everything except raw ownership, the right of possession, and the right to use your land for agriculture for all time. . . . We have bought the future in that property. . . . " By 1979, a considerably reduced program, caught in political controversy, was being implemented; in effect, it would preserve only about 8,000 acres of prime agricultural land at a cost of some $21 million.

In Suffolk County, top-quality farmland most sought for development is valued at between $2,000 and $4,000 per acre on the basis of agricultural yields, although it is worth $10,000 per acre or more as a potential house site. Yet, in order to purchase the maximum number of acres of development rights on prime agricultural land with limited funds, the Suffolk County program has been able to pay much less than the value of development rights on farms located in the prime development areas. Thus, these areas will not be preserved, even in part, by the program.

This public policy of limiting the value paid for an acre of development rights illustrates a central dilemma of such a program: how to best stretch the funds available. If prime agricultural lands are to be preserved, can they be preserved in the path of active development, where land costs are high? Without almost unlimited financial resources, the answer is clearly no. But as an ironic result, development rights may be purchased on more remote land that would, infact, continue to be farmed at no public expense.

A development right purchase program will certainly be unable to guide or substantially retard private development of most open land. Because of inevitable financial limitations of public agencies, it is likely to preserve only very limited amounts of acreage.

Critics of public purchase of development rights—those who are either social activists or fiscal conservatives—contend that the use of public funds for the purchase of open space is a recklessly misguided policy. Social activists argue that land conservation raises housing prices, preserves the status quo socially, and creates private amenity at public cost. Fiscal conservatives, on the other hand, argue from a narrow and strictly economic viewpoint. William E. Lesher and Doyle A. Eiler in their 1977 report "Farmland Preservation in an Urban Fringe Area: An Analysis of Suffolk County's Development Rights Purchase Program," conclude that the program will result in substantial cost savings in public services "only under unrealistic assumptions." It is their belief that the cost of development rights in this rural area will be greater than cost savings obtained by eliminating new residential development, and thereby eliminating the public service, costs that are avoided if land is not developed.

Development Rights Purchase: Justified but Limited in Scope.   In my judgment, where there is a compelling purpose served by the public acquisition of development rights, the approach has absolute merit. Examples of appropriate objectives, to name a few, are protection of the highest-quality agricultural soils, if contiguous and in large acreage; conservation and management of scarce varieties of woodland; and the preservation of unusual historic or natural land. The purchase of development rights enables the effective control of special land resources without payment in full. And it allows the land to continue accruing tax income for the community.

However, I do not believe that the acquisition of development rights is a way to safeguard large amounts of land against encroaching development. Not only is it too expensive, but the political parity involved almost guarantees public resistance if any program becomes too extensive. In the final analysis, it is an approach that should be reserved for the most environmentally and ecologically significant terrain.

But to realize even this limited scope of achievement, a program must be funded in every county throughout America. In most rural counties, though budgets are relatively low, development rights are relatively inexpensive, since most of the land value inheres in its agricultural or amenity value. On the other hand, counties on the developing fringe between suburban towns and rural communities face higher costs for development rights; however, they do have higher annual budgets as well as a larger number of tax ratables. It is in the fast-growing resort areas, however, where development rights may be most costly. But the land is often held by private owners for its amenity value alone. In such instances, negotiations with a private owner may yield the sale of development rights far below market value—a coup for the community in years to come.

PREFERENTIAL ASSESSMENT:
ENLIGHTENED PUBLIC POLICY
AIDS LAND CONSERVATION

If public officials in any community want to help preserve privately owned open space in town, there are policies they can implement which are available at much lower costs than the purchase of development rights or the purchase of land itself. The most direct, least expensive, and most effective of these is a system of preferential assessment. This entails an owner's commitment not to develop his land for a period of time in exchange for reduced land assessment, and thus reduced real-estate taxes on the property.

293

A system of preferential assessment can be established to further a wide variety of land-related public objectives, including the maintenance of lands in forest areas or in forever-wild states. It is also a useful approach to the preservation of certain types of buildings.

More than forty states now have some form of preferential-tax assessment. In California alone, participation in a farmland preferential-assessment program has risen from 200,000 acres a decade ago to over 14 million acres registered by 1976. Under the provisions of the 1965 California Land Conservation Act (also known as the Williamson Act) and its various amendments, which set the stage for this massive program, cities and counties were authorized to designate preserve areas in order to conserve farmland and open land throughout the state. Within these areas a landowner may agree to continue agricultural or open-space use of the land for ten years in exchange for a preferential-tax assessment. In addition, California agreed to partially compensate cities and counties for lost property-tax revenue. By 1976, California was spending about $16 million annually to reimburse locales. Total property-tax reductions on Williamson Act lands were estimated that year at about $60 million.

Preferential Assessment: Pros and Cons.   As with any public policy of such large scope, there are definite inequities in the system. Taxpayers throughout the state foot the bill for a limited number of communities, businesses, and residents. But is the inequity any greater than the school-tax portion of property tax paid by local residents who have no children? Certain public objectives are important enough to be shared by all; and conservation of the most productive farmland or land of special ecological or environmental quality, in my opinion, happens to be one of them.

In California (as elsewhere in America), about 60 percent of all farmland is owned by speculators, corporations, and non-farmers. At the end of each year, they consult their profit and loss statements, and review the costs to hold land. While loyalty to the land will not convince them to continue farming or holding the open space, lower taxes very well may.

Preferential assessment works. It reduces the amount of land that is developed, especially by independent private owners. A surprising number of decisions to develop rather than not to develop occur as a result of ever-increasing real-estate taxes on land assets. Many private owners are content to leave their land in its natural state—at least for the time being, which may even stretch into decades—if property taxes remain low.

Preferential assessment, then, is a hidden public subsidy to private landowners. For the local authorities who implement the program, this fact constitutes a much safer approach politically than any form of cash payment, such as the purchase of development rights. No public funds are actually spent, although incoming revenue may be reduced, and taxes elsewhere may be raised.

Critics of this program point out that individual farmers are not the only beneficiaries. Agribusiness combines and speculators with lands located far from the development frontier may also qualify for preferential-tax reductions. And there is really no way to easily, inexpensively, or conclusively determine the motive of the person or concern that benefits from a preferential-assessment system. He may be a speculator holding land at low cost as he watches the pattern of development move directly toward his farm. At the right time, he will pull out of the program, pay the modest tax penalty, if there is one, and sell.

The most serious shortcoming of preferential assessment—sometimes called differential assessment—is that it is always time-limited; it is never perpetual. Indeed, the 1976 study "Untaxing Open Space: An Evaluation of the Effectiveness of Differential Assessment of Farms and Open Space," prepared by the Regional Science Research Institute for the Council on Environmental Quality, concluded: "With respect to the goal of retarding the conversion of farm and other open land, differential assessment is marginally effective and its cost in terms of tax expenditures is high, in most cases so high as to render it an undesirable tool for achieving this goal." The study found that differential assessment will prevent the sale of open land in no more than 10 percent of all potential instances. This is primarily because, except in rural areas, urban uses can almost always outbid agricultural uses, no matter how efficient and productive the farm. Economic obsolescence of the farm, imminent retirement, and the encroachment of suburbia so as to hamper farming practices also can override the "benefits" of preferential assessment. Therefore, as the study points out, "preferential assessment is likely to make a difference in the rate of conversion to urban use primarily for land that is in the hands of owners who either want to maintain a country home, or those relatively young farmers who want to continue to farm and are in a location where farming is not impeded by urban neighbors."

A Suggested Policy. Some degree of preferential assessment for all agricultural or vacant land is, in fact, equitable and constitutes an enlightened public policy. Real-estate assessment and tax in America, as argued elsewhere in this book, should be based solely on current use rather than on speculative value or highest and best use. Because undeveloped land requires no direct public service, taxes on it should be lower than on subdivision building lots or other fully utilized land. If, in addition, its eventual use is legally restricted, taxes should be reduced even further.

Such a program that will retard conversion of open land into urbanized property should be incorporated into all local community planning. There are no direct cash expenditures to budget, no direct financing costs, no administrative expenses needed for implementing and administering the program.

In my judgment, the intention or the profession of the landowner who benefits is inconsequential. It is the land use that counts, and the guidance of that use. After all, can you really differentiate between the motives of a private land speculator, dressed in a suit in his city office, who leases his property to a farmer, and those of a farmer-owner, dressed in his overalls, seated on his tractor? The city man may want to farm that land forever. And the farmer out there in the sun may be dreaming of the day when he can sell out to a developer.

The Land Swap. There are other forms of private/public cooperation that can be used to forward conservation objectives. The most effective and least expensive is the land swap. All that is required is knowledge, patience, and just the right ingredients of skill and attitude.

Privately owned land in America may be exchanged without the owner having to pay any income tax, so long as the lands involved are of equivalent type and value. If an owner possesses a special parcel of land needed by a community, he may be willing to swap it for land owned elsewhere by the town. Through a land-swap program with private owners, communities are able to forward such public objectives as greenbelts or park and land preserve assemblages, often at no cost for the land.

In recent years, exchanges between regional agencies of government and public corporations have ranged from thousands of acres, down to fractions of an acre, to complete greenbelt planning along streams and creeks, and to ensure continuous paths for hikers, cyclists, and horseback riders. Not infrequently, such programs involve drawn-out negotiations concerning the swap of hundreds of parcels of land, as in the creation of the 900-acre greenbelt in the South Richmond Special Zoning District of Staten Island.

Abuse by private owners and their friends in government, once rampant in the land-swap arena, is now infrequent. More often today, it is the public objective of a land swap that arouses consternation among citizens. Creation of a fully developed public park, for instance, may be applauded by those in the region who will benefit and violently opposed by those living adjacent to its projected boundary.

RURAL CONSERVATION:
A NEW MOVEMENT IN AMERICA

Rural conservation, an important movement that began about a decade ago, is concerned with the protection of the countryside in terms of settlements rather than the protection of land resources alone. As defined by the National Trust for Historic Preservation, rural conservation includes "the preservation of buildings and villages of cultural significance, the protection of the surrounding open space, and the enhancement of the local economy and social institutions." The trust, in extending its more traditional domain beyond architectural conservation and preservation to the land itself, signals a new concern for an aspect of community preservation that has been ignored far too long:

A functional and harmonious relationship exists between a rural area's buildings and villages and their surrounding open space because traditionally the setting, types and design of rural developments were heavily influenced by topography, climate and indigenous building materials. To preserve this relationship, rural conservationists must concern themselves with the protection of such open-space resources as farmland, forests, wetlands and wilderness. The interdisciplianry nature of rural conservation requires careful attention to local agricultural, economic, environmental, historical, political and social factors as well.

As the trust has come to recognize, preserving the countryside is in many ways more difficult to justify and as difficult to accomplish as urban preservation. Acquisition of land is often involved, as are the more traditional historic preservation issues of landmark preservation and adaptive use of older structures. Local ordinances must be modified; all forms of conservation easements must be introduced; National Register designations must be explained; and cooperation must be gained from land conservationists, agricultural agencies, and those who fear that rural conservation and local economic development are incompatible—which they are not.

Economic development in rural areas is, in fact, often stimulated by wise use of rural conservation tactics, just as it is in cities when district-wide historic preservation programs succeed. Yet political leaders and private property owners in many rural communities continue to look upon rural conservation as an impediment to economic development. All that is needed, when the rhetoric is stripped away, is controls which protect special lands and the limited number of rural historic enclaves. Most of the land and settlement upon it in most places could not possibly qualify.

Some Methods That Succeed. In rural areas, as in towns and cities, one of the most effective ways to protect and enhance structures, sites, and land within districts of historic or environmental significance is to enact a district preservation ordinance, which defines the boundaries of the protected area. The ordinance also may require a special level of review before alteration to existing features and new development can be initiated.

Nearly six hundred communities throughout the nation have enacted such a rural conservation ordinance. In Loudoun County, Virginia, for instance, a countywide amendment to the zoning ordinance now protects the area's agricultural, architectural, cultural, and scenic resources. "Historic and cultural conservation districts" can be superimposed on existing zoning districts when a district is established, such as the 10,000-acre Goose Creek Historic and Cultural Conservation District in Virginia. Also, a historic-district review committee is empowered to consider "the relationship of the size, design, and siting of any new or reconstructed structure to the landscape of the district."

Vermont in 1970 pioneered such legislation at the state level by enacting the Vermont Environmental Control Act. As directed by the act, proposed development in urban and rural areas must first be reviewed by a district environmental commission appointed by the governor. Among its other functions, the commission must establish that any proposed project "will not have an undue adverse effect on the scenic or natural beauty of the area, aesthetics, historic sites or rare and irreplaceable natural areas."

Enforced rural conservation by blanket public law of the types promulgated in Loudoun County and in Vermont produce mixed results, and sometimes too much red tape. But the required review of the impact of proposed changes on the resources protected by rural conservation is, on balance, positive.

I believe land values will rise in areas protected by rural conservation codes—and, in the long run, better planned and more efficient new development of the land is likely to be mingled with well-maintained and recognized vestiges of the past.

Living Historical Farms, Villages, and Agricultural Museums. Living historical farms, villages, and agricultural museums are another growing trend and a new idea in America that promotes the preservation of rural land settlements—in this instance, by private nonprofit organizations. These so-called living historical farms and agricultural museums are located throughout the country and vary in size from 10 acres to over 1,000 acres.

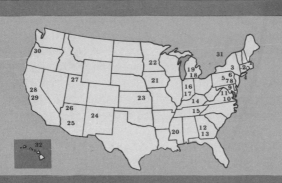

LOCATION OF LIVING HISTORIC FARMS
AND AGRICULTURAL MUSEUMS, 1978

Living historic farms and agricultural museums are located across
America. Many provide an unusual opportunity for visitors to view
the rural past and to gain insight into the country's land resources,
together with vernacular buildings, and social
and economic organization

1. Plymouth Plantation:
   Plymouth, Massachusetts
2. Old Sturbridge Village:
   Sturbridge, Massachusetts
3. Farmers Museum: Cooperstown,
   New York
4. Old Bethpage: Old Bethpage,
   New York
5. Colonial Pennsylvania
   Plantation: Edgemont,
   Pennsylvania
6. Quiet Valley Living Historical
   Farm: Stroudsburg,
   Pennsylvania
7. Amish Farm and House:
   Lancaster, Pennsylvania
8. Pennsylvania Farm and
   Museum of Landis Valley:
   Lancaster, Pennsylvania
9. Oxon Hill Children's Farm:
   Oxon Hill, Maryland
10. George Washington Birthplace:
    Washington Birthplace, Virginia
11. Turkey Run Farm: McLean,
    Virginia
12. Westville: Lumpkin, Georgia
13. Agrirama: Tifton, Georgia
14. Shakertown: Pleasant Hill,
    Kentucky
15. Pioneer Farmstead, Great
    Smoky Mountains National
    Park: Gatlinburg, Tennessee
16. Conner Prairie Pioneer
    Settlement: Noblesville, Indiana
17. Lincoln Living Historical Farm:
    Lincoln City, Indiana
18. Greenfield Village and Henry

Ford Museum: Dearborn,
Michigan
19. The Museum, Michigan State
    University: East Lansing,
    Michigan
20. Mississippi Agricultural
    Museum: Jacksonville,
    Mississippi
21. Living History Farms: Des
    Moines, Iowa
22. Gibbs Farm Museum: St. Paul,
    Minnesota
23. Agricultural Hall of Fame and
    National Center: Bonner
    Springs, Kansas
24. Old Cienega Village Museum:
    Santa Fe, New Mexico
25. Pioneer Arizona: Phoenix,
    Arizona
26. Pipe Spring National
    Monument: Moccasin, Arizona
27. Ronald V. Jensen Living
    Historical Farm and Bread
    Museum: Logan, Utah
28. Camillus Nelson State
    Historical Farm: Sacramento,
    California
29. Pioneer Museum and Haggin
    Galleries: Stockton, California
30. Bybee-Howell House and
    Pioneer Orchard: Portland,
    Oregon
31. The Loyalist Farm at Upper
    Canada Village: Morrisburg,
    Ontario, Canada
32. Kipahula Living Farm: Hana,
    Maui, Hawaii

On most living historical farms, people farm or work as they did during some specific time in the past. The farms utilize tools and equipment, and raise livestock and produce representative of the period. Their immediate purpose, then, is to demonstrate to visitors what community life was like and how the land was used at that time. In the process, living historical farms hold the land in its past use and form. Old Sturbridge Village, a re-created New England farm community of the early nineteenth century, located in Massachusetts, is probably the best known of these innovative enclaves.

The idea of a national network of such places grew out of a proposal published by agricultural economist Marion Clawson in 1965, followed the next year by a grant from Resources for the Future to the Smithsonian Institution to study the feasibility of the idea. By 1967, the first

living historical farm, and still one of the most adventurous, was established in Iowa; by 1970, there were enough farms in existence or in prospect to foster the formation of an Association for Living Historical Farms and Agricultural Museums; today they number over sixty-five.

These "museums" offer a special and splendid form of vacation, as over 600,000 people found out in 1978. While these "museums" may not pay property taxes, they do contribute substantial revenue to the communities in which they are situated. Retail sales and other spinoffs from tourism contribute to the financial influx. At the same time, most of the museums manage at least a hundred acres of land, and quite a number possess holdings of well over 1,000 acres. These sometimes eccentric places, many of them off the beaten tourist track, present an imaginative

OLD STURBRIDGE VILLAGE, MASSACHUSETTS

Living historical farms, villages, and agricultural museums are a growing trend in America, promoting the preservation of rural land settlements. One of the best known is Old Sturbridge Village, a re-created early-nineteenth-century New England farm community.

and unique resource for the enjoyment of land in America, presented in a historical and cultural context of time past.*

The Individual Rural Preservationist. Private owners of certain types of acreage can play a crucial role in rural conservation. For example, most of the nation's forest land, or about 300 million acres, is privately owned by only 4 million individuals. In New York State there are about 300,000 private owners of forest land, 50,000 of them living in New York City.

Every state offers land-management programs, which help individuals set up their own personal rural preservation program. The most accessible resource and first source of advice is the U.S. Department of Agriculture's county cooperative extension office. Experts there will visit your land and offer advice on its best use and management.

Landowners can also obtain free technical assistance from private industry. The International Paper Company, a major manufacturer of forest products, has a private landowners' assistance program under which company foresters will draw up management programs for property within reasonable access of the company's holdings.

Under certain conditions, financial assistance is available from the federal government. Under the 1973 Forestry Incentive Program, up to $10,000 per year per individual is granted for tree planting and timberland improvement. The program is administered by the Soil Conservation Service, a branch of the Department of Agriculture.

Interest in rural conservation is accelerating as local, regional, and nationwide legal and financial resources become better known and more effective. For anyone inventive enough to look around, there are interesting opportunities. Some require the sacrifice of potential profit from the land; some require deferral; and others require neither.

THE NATURAL ENVIRONMENT:
NEW ECONOMICS, NEW PERSPECTIVES

Innovative work is being done today that sheds a new perspective on the economic value of the undisturbed, natural environment. When Dr. George Woodwell, director of the Ecosystems Center at the Marine Biological Laboratory in Woods Hole, Massachusetts, speaks of the natural environment as having a capacity "to produce services," he makes a radical statement. How, after all, can a presumably passive natural envi-

*A selected list of living historical farms and agricultural museums across the country, along with their approximate location, can be found on page 299.

ronment produce anything that might be even loosely classified as a "service"?

Here is how. In conventional economic analysis, when cost and benefit of a new development are projected, no economic value is assigned to the service contribution of the natural environment. For instance, when the cost and profit impact and economic value created by a construction project are commonly analyzed for a "go" or "no-go" decision based on the "figures," the pre-existing service contribution of the land and water, which will be disturbed, does not enter into the calculations—or into the decision. The only way land is taken into account is in terms of the economic cost to acquire the land that is to be severely disturbed by being developed. Not until recently has there been any consideration of the alternative value of the same land if left alone as an undisturbed natural environment with its own capacity for productivity.

Today, a new trend is gathering support. As Dr. Eugene P. Odum, director of the Institute of Ecology at the University of Georgia, observes, "As the country gets more populous and more industries come along, we're going to have to assign monetary values to things that we haven't considered before." Odum has developed a new method of assessment. For instance, in a conventional economic feasibility study, Odum indicates, a salt marsh would be valued somewhat below local farmland, say, between $100 and $200 per acre. If it is seen as a site for commercial and sports fishing, its value could marginally rise. Higher up on the scale, as a resource for the commercial cultivation of oysters, the marsh land might obtain an appraised value of $600–$700 per acre. That is the conventional limit.

But what about the natural services being performed in the salt marsh for the benefit of men, to support life? Odum asks. That service has never before been valued. Appraisers still have no idea of how to assign numbers to such vague but significant functions. In the case of a salt marsh, Dr. Odum estimates that the value of its natural ability as a system able to clean water of phosphorus, nitrogen, and sulphur, as compared to the cost of an equivalent waste-treatment plant, to be $2,500 per acre; on top of that he adds another $4,000 per acre for life-support value, including a marsh's ability to absorb carbon dioxide, produce oxygen, support water fowl and other animals, and protect cities and beaches from the damaging effects of storms. Suddenly an acre of marsh, once a giveaway almost without cost, is valued at over $6,500. Other environmental economists value functioning wetland at an even higher level, between $50,000 and $80,000 an acre. When that value is inserted in alternative feasibility studies, it may turn out that a flat *inland* site is more economical to acquire and transform.

Progressive, innovative economists such as John V. Krutilla, director of the natural environment program at Resources for the Future, and

303

Anthony C. Fisher, professor of economics at the University of Maryland, go even further. Based on a recently published analysis of such projects as a hydroelectric construction project in Hells Canyon, Idaho, mining in the White Cloud Peaks Mountains of Idaho, resort development in the Mineral King Valley of the Sierra Nevada Mountains, and construction of the Trans-Alaska Pipeline, they urge that dollar amounts be assigned to the long-term value of the "service flows" that the public will enjoy from land left in its natural state. They argue, for instance, that wildlands as natural environments are irreplaceable. Whatever is irreplaceable is scarce and valuable. Thus, the irreplaceability of the wildlands should be given value. At the same time, interventions which change these wildlands that are irreversible and that have irreversible consequences should be saddled with a cost when assessment of the feasibility of a project is calculated.

Krutilla and Fisher also maintain that like oil wells and silver mines, natural lands are depleted when used up; a limited resource is involved, not an unlimited one. The consumption of this resource, they suggest, should be assigned a depletion value in feasibility calculations which is charged as a cost when the natural area is destroyed. If economic recognition of depletion were costed out and charged, they argue, the feasibility of disturbing the most important natural environments—those with the highest value, as undisturbed land and water—would be altered. In certain instances, it might even be reversed. At the very least, the public and the project sponsor would be made aware of the real cost of moving ahead, which includes assignment of a meaningful value to the natural environment.

Lester R. Brown, president of Worldwatch Institute, a nonprofit organization that analyses global problems, presents an almost apocalyptic vision of the future if we do not begin to let the real value of the natural environment work toward its own preservation. The biological underpinnings of our economic system are ignored at our own peril, he points out in his 1978 article "A Biology Lesson for Economists" (1978). Brown asserts that our economic system depends heavily on four biological systems: croplands, fisheries, forests, and grasslands. "These four systems provide not only all our food but, with the important exceptions of minerals and petrochemicals, all the raw materials for industry as well. In short, they are the foundation of our global economic system. Their health and that of the economy cannot be separated."

With the increased scarcity and abuse of these natural resources, commodities such as seafood, lumber, leather, firewood, and soybeans have indeed soared in price. The most immediate symptoms of ecological stress, as Brown indicates, are "physical" and are visible now—the deterioration of grasslands, the shrinkage of forests, and soil erosion. The next level of stress, which Brown defines as "economic," embraces such primary national concerns as scarcity of natural resources, inflation, unemployment, and economic stagnation or decline. In later stages, he predicts, a nation that does not recognize the economic necessity of conservation will experience forms of stress that " . . . assume a social and political character—hunger, forced migration to the cities, deteriorating living standards and political unrest."

Concepts such as these, and others now being postulated, shed new light on the economic value of the natural environment. If they were refined and accepted in feasibility accounting and tax law, a creative foundation would come into being by which the real costs and benefits of new construction in environmentally sensitive areas could be evaluated, as could the cost and value of leases, sales, mining permits, and exploration agreements on such lands. While these ideas are still a part of "far-out" economics, their direction is valid. The salt marsh is doing a job that cannot be done by anyone else, anywhere else, possibly at any cost. We must figure out how to turn biological and ecological facts into sound economic statistics. In such new environmental economics there is an urgency and potential of immeasurable importance to the conservation of natural environments and, by extension, to the conservation of amenities, health, and safety, which affect all of human life.

New Perspective: The Natural Environment as a Life Force. In prehistoric times, one species became extinct every 10,000 years. Scientists estimate that by the year 1600 one species vanished every thousand years. Today, between one and twenty individual forms of life are killed off each year. The purpose of the Endangered Species Act of 1973 is to retard—indeed, to reverse—this trend.

Man has not become a more avid hunter, and he probably is no more cruel than ever before. In most instances, the culprit is not the hunter, the growing numbers of sports fishermen, or even modern, effective commercial fishing techniques. Rather, it is the destruction of natural plant and animal habitat by the ordinary, conventional, and inexorable activities of man as he uses the land.

To the destructive use, and often misuse, of specialized breeding grounds, wetlands, and natural ecosystems must be added the seemingly systematic poisoning of the earth by all aspects of our society: industry's waste, cities' refuse, humans' inadequately treated sewage, farmers' pesticides. Poison is injected daily in massive quantities into the earth, air, and water. The land in many places is dying, along with the water below it, and the rivers and lakes and even oceans that surround it.

The picture is bleak. The impact of environmental abuse on treasured forms of life is just beginning to raise impassioned, literary outcries, as

305

in *Beautiful Swimmers,* William W. Warner's moving Pulitzer Prize–winning account of the life and plight of watermen, blue crabs, and the Chesapeake Bay; or John N. Cole's *Striper,* a lucid plea for the survival of the striped bass, once a most plentiful fish in American coastal waters. Environmentalists everywhere are deeply disturbed, and with good reason. Odd as it may sound, when this century is reviewed, it may turn out that the bulldozer was more permanently destructive to the planet Earth than all the weapons of war, including the atomic bomb.

Endangered species of one sort or another, such as the whooping crane, the snail darter, and the Furbish lousewort plant, are now famous near-victims. As species of life, three among a million on earth, they may be of nominal significance; but as signals of a threat to the earth and to man's ability to remain on earth in safety and in health, each is a sacrificial litmus. Dr. Woodwell puts the issue of endangered species into accurate perspective. As he told Philip Shabecoff of *The New York Times* not long ago, loss of species " . . . has a direct bearing on and cannot be separated

**BULLDOZER
DIGGING A FOUNDATION
IN OCEAN DUNE**

The destruction of America's natural plant and animal habitat is not the result of man as hunter, but of man as settler and developer.

from a larger problem—the biotic impoverishment of the earth, which is reducing the capacity of the environment to produce services. It is one of the great issues of our time, right up there with nuclear proliferation, the stability of government, and health care. The ultimate resource is biota [earth environment]—there is no other. And we are destroying it."

THE PROMISE OF
PRIVATE LAND CONSERVATION

We are at a remarkable juncture, a new turning point. Only in the last several decades have the economic forces, the legal competence, the scientific ingenuity and the literary power of the private sector been devoted in some measure toward the preservation of the best natural lands and resources in America. Private individuals, nonprofit associations, and large national corporations are involved.

In recent years a new awareness has come into being. With so many waters polluted, with so many millions of acres of woodland now cut down, with erosion washing away fertile valleys, and with second homes spreading out upon the mountain ridges and coastal dunes, a new terror has emerged, provoked by the recognition that, in fact, the land is not renewable, not endless. This awareness signals the beginning of a reversal in attitude and social conscience among private citizens and private business which, I suspect, will have a lasting impact on the future of land in America.

Heretofore, only public programs—and principally federal ones—made any effort to conserve permanently the most important natural land and water.* During this century, through the system of national parks, wilderness areas, wildlife refuges, national monuments, and lands purchased through the Open Space Program and the Land and Water Conservation Fund, the federal government has been at work to set aside open spaces. While these efforts are often marred by management policies that permit partial destruction of so-called wilderness areas or include vast tracts of land that most citizens will never be able to see, they are substantial and basically credible efforts toward natural land conservation.

Today the private land conservation movement moves forward. As it proceeds, a fundamental question continues to raise a fundamental issue: How is privately owned land to be perpetually conserved and, at the same time, how is the private owner to be equitably compensated for the loss of his historic right to use and to exploit at will his land holding? To be effective on a large scale, and across the country, ways must be devised to at least partially compensate private owners.

Various solutions to this dilemma are now being developed with increasing skill. Innovative private, nonprofit agencies are at work; new forms of easements are being invented; rules governing local property tax are being amended; federal tax regulations are being adjusted; and new types of economic analyses are being forged. It is a multifaceted, sometimes unconnected set of endeavors which together, I believe, add new impetus. A major, if incremental, effort within the private sector—and directed toward it—is now beginning to use legal and economic systems, for the first time, to protect and enhance some of the most precious natural environments in America.

Within the notion of private conservation there is a core element of tremendous land value adjustment and the exchange of one form of equity for another. The results, in the long run, will be of the widest imaginable public benefit.

*See Chapter Fourteen.

TEN

PRESERVATION
AND PROFIT

I store up old objects in the attic. I want to remember. I define myself through the past I have created. "The past is not only what we spring from but what we return to for our daily nourishment," Brendan Gill, president of the New York Landmarks Conservancy, reminds us. And so it is, and always has been. Every society, by design or not, defines its values and its view of the universe through its culture; and part of this definition is expressed through the architecture and physical configuration of a community. To those who learn the language and understand the gestures, major structures built long ago provide a commentary on the past.

Through the course of America's short history, the preservation of specific buildings or entire neighborhoods has not been a high priority in very many communities. The past, to this ambitious, optimistic, and mobile society, has not been revered, much less appreciated. Rather, it has been a frontier to move beyond: as communities grow, people choose to move uptown; as the suburbs become an option, they choose to move out of town, to leave entirely what has been, to embrace the newer style of living.

But priorities are changing. More and more people are beginning to perceive the past as a bountiful source of nourishment. Many also have a need, even a quite personal longing, to live in a society that is slowly producing a visible culture rather than slowly exterminating its vestiges. A growing number of people in increasingly organized groups also now have the leisure, insight, and discretionary capital which make it possible to preserve buildings and neighborhoods. In every town across the country, this is happening.

There are now more than six thousand preservation organizations in America. The largest, the National Trust for Historic Preservation, a nonprofit, independent service organization chartered by Congress in 1949, has jumped in membership from 165 to more than 140,000. When James Biddle was president of the trust, he characterized the historic-preservation movement with undeniable accuracy as a "growth industry."

Growth is evident not only in the private sector. More than six hundred American cities now have preservation ordinances which seek to save the remaining legacy of America's past. Also, federal, state, and local laws now provide financial incentives to corporations and individuals who

310

appropriately adapt older buildings to present use rather than tear down and build anew. Through congressional appropriation, the U. S. Department of the Interior contributed $60 million in 1979 to this end, up over $59 million from its $300,000 allocation in 1968. And the National Register of Historic Places, the official listing of the nation's historic and cultural resources officially considered worthy of preservation as defined by the National Historic Preservation Act of 1966, now exceeds 19,000 designated properties, and is growing by some four thousand new listings each year.

This accelerating interest in historic preservation in both the private and public sectors, at the local, state, and and national levels, represents more than an increased appreciation of America's visible past. In part, it reflects the maturing of a nation. Few people living today remember settlement as a struggle against the environment. Rather, remains of the past are only signs and symbols, those buildings which prevail over time. Most people living in America today, especially in the cities, witnessed the expanded demolition programs of urban renewal—federally financed takings through condemnation of enormous stretches of urban centers. The presumed public purpose that justified this obliteration of the past was slum clearance and the subsequent redevelopment of the land for more modern residential, commercial, and industrial accommodations.

And, in part, the recent gains of the preservation movement reflects new conditions of American society. At a time when Americans are facing inflation, recession, and a future of severe energy shortages, we gravitate —even if intuitively—toward programs which stress conservation, whether they be of the natural or man-made environment. One recent federal report concludes that an existing building can operate sixteen years on the amount of energy it takes to build the structure from scratch. Conservation is, for the first time, clearly economically justified and socially responsible.

The formal historic preservation movement—as opposed to the less formal marketplace trend of conserving and recycling buildings—calls for increased legal control over individual structures and over entire neighborhoods of historic and cultural significance. As it does so, conflict naturally arises. Owners of historic buildings or sites often are not anxious to have private rights over their property restricted. Many believe that these restrictions decrease property value as buildings and neighborhoods become confined, controlled, unable to be altered, not permitted to grow. So there is often a struggle between private owner and public power.

The dynamics of a neighborhood slotted for historic preservation intensify another pervasive struggle: that between tenant and owner. Despite building owners' fears, as discussed in some detail below, preservation policies generally create new and higher value, especially to residential land and structures. As this occurs, tenants find themselves in a changing, upwardly spiraling neighborhood in which the cost to occupy space rises. In this way, tenants of older structures may become victims of the preservation process. As with any other movement that seeks to restructure the control of land, historic preservation is often an impetus to struggles over power and wealth.

THE HISTORIC DISTRICT

It is not my intention to discuss the preservation of individual landmark buildings, as there has been much written on this popular subject. Nor will I discuss at length the inherent and understandable nationwide trend to conserve and reuse more and more older buildings. While I believe this to be socially constructive and one of the great growth opportunities in both real-estate investment and architectural practice, it has little to do with land—which is what this book is all about. Rather, it is the larger aggregates of neighborhoods and districts which I focus upon in the discussion that follows.

The first interest in district-wide preservation in America goes back to the Depression. Economic crisis always brings opportunity for preservation, since it is during periods of slow development and little new building that conventional developers lose interest in demolishing old buildings to make way for the new. In 1931, citizens groups in Charleston, South Carolina, including the Society for the Preservation of Old Dwellings, backed the establishment of the first historic district in the United States. After public hearings prompted no opposition, the city council approved the designation, and the local zoning ordinance was amended to incorporate new rules that would govern the Charleston Historic District.

Five years later, Louisiana amended its constitution, allowing New Orleans to create the Vieux Carré Commission; and the City Planning and Zoning Commission legislated the designation of the Vieux Carré Historic District the following year.

It was in controversy over governance of the Vieux Carré that a new standard of uniform control over all structures within a designated district, regardless of age or quality, was decided. And it was decided in court, as are so many issues connected with preservation. Five years after the Vieux Carré came into being as a historic district, owners of neither particularly old nor unusual buildings within the Vieux Carré sought exception from control by the Vieux Carré Commission. The state court ruled that all buildings in the designated district were subject to all of the

312

controls. Through this ruling, the concept of *tout ensemble* was established and defined: "The purpose of the ordinance is not only to preserve the old buildings themselves but to preserve the antiquity of the whole French and Spanish Quarter, the *tout ensemble,* so to speak."

Only in the last decade has the idea of historic-district preservation caught on and become a significant national trend, whose pace is accelerating. In 1950 there were a dozen historic districts, in communities such as Savannah, Nantucket, Santa Fe, and Boston, where some civic leaders had a strong cultural instinct, broad ties to the past, manifest personal nostalgia, political power, and some money to devote to the cause. As recently as 1965, only a hundred historic-district ordinances were extant. By 1974, however, the figure had doubled. Today, close to two thousand historic districts exist in cities and towns across America. New York City's thirty-eight historic districts alone comprise at least ten thousand properties. And the number of places being surveyed, proposed, and considered for district designation is rapidly growing. Designated historic districts now contain approximately 10 percent of the buildings listed in the National Register.

Preservation of entire neighborhoods is gaining in acceptance and backing. Maintenance of the general ambiance of an active, functioning district demands changing the focus, from the individual building to the existing, organic, physical environment as a whole. This approach to preservation incorporates a concern for the streets, sidewalks, and public spaces surrounding the architecture. It recognizes that the relationship between buildings and spaces creates a special kind of place.

Involved is much more than either a cultivated aesthetic appreciation of older architecture or an abstract interest in historicity. Amid the complexities of contemporary urban life is a renewed appreciation by many people of the special "livability" and "neighborhoodness" of older, generally lower-scaled residential areas. A pleasing "texture," or mixture of dwellings, materials, streets, spaces, and land uses, all in less massive agglomerations than conventional high-rise apartments, characterize these areas; they are also generally in closer proximity to work, cultural centers, and important institutions than are the dispersed, homogeneous suburbs. Moreover, there is a return to values of convenience without total dependence on the automobile, to familiarity with neighbors and shopkeepers as part of a comforting quality of neighborhood living, to a simplification of daily routine. As will be discussed more fully in Chapter Eleven, in-town neighborhoods are becoming more frequently chosen as desirable places to live. This preference of a living alternative was all but inconceivable to a large majority of people a decade or two ago. The appeal of historic districts is part of this new trend in America.

313

VIEUX CARRÉ
HISTORIC DISTRICT,
NEW ORLEANS, LOUISIANA,
1977

In 1941, a Louisiana court ruled that private property rights of *all* buildings and open spaces within the Vieux Carré district could be abridged for its protection. Through this ruling, the concept of *tout ensemble*—the protection of the entire area—was defined and established.

A Historic District Isn't Just Any Place. Considerable time, work, money, and persistent advocacy on the part of interested individuals are requisite if a historic district is to be established. Three sequential steps —identification and documentation, nomination, and official designation —must be taken in order for historic district status to be granted.

The most fundamental decision of all preservation activity is the selection, or identification, of a potential historic district. The underlying assumption is that the district is of sufficient quality or individuality or "historic significance" to be preserved.

There are two quite distinct types of historic districts: the district that, because of its national prominence, ultimately is included in the National Register; and the district that is only locally recognized and legislated. Local government may designate a historic district through local ordinance, provided appropriate state-enabling legislation exists. Most historic districts are, in fact, of local rather than national prominence.

The local ordinance, which spells out rules for controls within the historic district, is of paramount importance. Its admonitions, prohibitions, and processes are the muscle in historic district legislation. Most often, the historic district ordinance or landmark statutes set up a special commission of local government to oversee implementation of the approved legislation. By way of contrast, inclusion in the National Register, while prestigious, carries with it only nominal protection and does not even protect against arbitrary demolition by private owners or by agencies of local and state governments; nor does it insure that any height or bulk guidelines for new buildings will be observed. Thus, an emphasis on the local level and on the local ordinance is practical and most meaningful, as it is here that legal protection resides.

In terms of legal protection for a cherished area, in fact, inclusion in the National Register provides only one major benefit: Before a federal action that would adversely affect the area is allowed to occur, such as a highway cut-through, there is a 6-month review and appeal procedure that may be invoked. The Advisory Council on Historic Preservation, a group of high-ranking federal officials, may be called upon to review initiatives of federal agencies which other persons consider detrimental to the historic district. Because this council, however, is endowed with no more than an advisory power, its practical benefit is merely to gain valuable time to publicize, politicize, and find acceptable alternatives. Other than prestige, it is economic benefit, as will be outlined later, that inclusion in the National Register really provides.

There is a third—and hybrid—type of historic district. This is one in which local documentation and the local historic district ordinance are submitted for approval through state channels to the office of the Secretary of the Interior and approved in Washington, although the historic district itself is not considered significant enough to be placed in the

National Register. But federal approval of the local ordinance and documentation is itself sufficient for obtaining certain federal tax benefits for commercial properties. Qualified properties within such historic districts are accorded the same economic and tax benefits as those that are listed in the National Register.

Preservation and Protagonists.   In the process of identification, nomination, designation, and finally governance of a historic district, a new layer of governmental control is created. A historic district ordinance is new local legislation. It establishes the rules of the preservation game in town.

Preservation legislation—whether for the governance of an individual landmark building or of a historic district—is occasionally resisted by local residents who resent the restraint it imposes on their control of certain aspects of private property. Such was the case not long ago in the Steinway section of Astoria, Queens. There, the New York City Landmarks Commission, arguing that designation would promote "stability," sought control over exterior alterations and painting. As Benjamin Barbere, president of the Astoria Heights Homeowners Association, told the commission, "We don't need stability. This is one of the most stable areas in the state." Another resident was more direct in his testimony: "Nobody told my father how to keep this house, and nobody is going to tell me."

Recently, the legality of landmark preservation and historic ordinance controls has been openly challenged in court. What has emerged is legal precedent linking preservation to "general welfare," that is, an appropriate exercise of the police power of government. This was the rationale behind the U.S. Supreme Court ruling in 1978 when it denied the Penn Central Transportation Company the right to destroy the architectural quality of Grand Central Station, a designated landmark in the center of Manhattan. Because of Grand Central Station's landmark status, because the air rights above it could be transferred to other sites, and because the terminal itself forms part of a comprehensive planning scheme, the Court declared that "the restrictions imposed are substantially related to the promotion of the general welfare and not only permit reasonable beneficial use of the landmark site but afford appellants opportunities further to enhance not only the terminal site proper but also other properties."

Focusing on "general welfare" as the legal cornerstone of historic-preservation enforcement may at first seem farfetched. Indeed, some owners of controlled landmarks and property in historic districts find it so. But I do not. In the longer scheme of culture and history, public benefit and well-being are promoted by the maintenance and preservation of our most important buildings and most interesting older districts.

A more exact legal connection between preservation and general wel-

THE STEINWAY SECTION OF ASTORIA, QUEENS

In 1974, the New York City Landmarks Commission endeavored to designate the Steinway section of Astoria, Queens, a historic district. Twenty-two out of twenty-nine homeowners in the area objected because they would have to apply to the commission to make certain exterior changes. At their request, the Board of Estimates revoked the designation. The thirty or so two-story brick houses were originally part of a "company town" built by Steinway and Sons, the piano manufacturer, in the nineteenth century.

GRAND CENTRAL STATION, NEW YORK CITY

In a historic decision by the U.S. Supreme Court in 1978, the lessor of the Grand Central site was not allowed to build an office tower above the terminal because of its landmark status. The Court declared that private property rights had not been taken without compensation, especially since under New York law the air rights could be transferred to another site. Most importantly, however, the Court linked the benefits and purposes of historic preservation "to the promotion of the general welfare."

fare is defined by Tersh Boasberg, one of the founders the National Center for Preservation Law: "The elements of general welfare which the courts find to support historic preservation zoning and districting are: an increase in property values, an encouragement for tourism, insurance of orderly growth, and the preservation of a community's heritage, pride and aesthetic quality."

Consider two of the justifications: " . . . increase in property values, an encouragement of tourism. . . . " Both are valid, and both cut to the core of historic preservation land-use controls as profitable and as business stimulants. Also, " . . . orderly growth, and the preservation of a community's heritage, pride and aesthetic quality" are, in part, thinly veiled code words for assurance of present value and the likelihood of a strong increase in future values of preserved and controlled real estate. These notions operate quite clearly within designated historic districts.

The Evolution of a Historic District.   Once subject to historic-district controls, more often than not land and property values increase within the district. Even before historic-district designation is formally declared, property slowly begins to be improved and property values begin to rise. People interested in fine, older, neglected neighborhoods move in.

The first to move in are the "urban pioneers," people with limited financial means and unlimited handy skills who take possession of run-down properties in chancy neighborhoods in their quest of a place to live that is both affordable and potentially desirable. Quite often, these newcomers risk all they have. In this way they resemble frontier pioneers: they substitute "sweat equity"—hard work—for the money they lack. At times, these first resettlers intend to improve their properties and then move on, or they buy two buildings, one to live in and the other for speculative resale, a procedure known as flipping real estate.

These first buyers often learn early on that research to support a historic district application is under way or that an application for designation has already been filed. They will pay more for a property, partly because of new recognition of the special architectural character of the place. But they are primarily interested in a sought living ambiance, a residential neighborhood in which the right of others to build perhaps discordant edifices or to destroy what exists is abridged. And they seek living space—sometimes a lot of it—at very reasonable prices.

The next stage in the evolution of a historic district generally involves outright speculation and speculators. Savvy real-estate dealers recognize the up-value situation. They buy properties with no intention other than profitable resale. These speculators know what is going on. They realize what impact the creation of a historic district in a well-located area is likely to have on available properties there. Speculators also know the consequences of upgraded social ambiance, in terms of economic payoff. Frequently, to render a structure more attractive for resale, they make modifications to the physical character of the building. Unfortunately, this may forever damage the building's basic historic quality.

In the process of property speculation, older established tenants are often evicted en masse to make room for the more affluent residents sought to increase the annual rent roll and improve the character of the neighborhood.

In the third stage, which generally occurs after local designation of a historic district has been officially granted, middle-class and upper-middle class people with cultural interests begin to purchase property and move in. These are people with an interest in the past; people who wish to become a part of its continuity through the use, possession, and habitation of older places and spaces which are to be preserved. In this third wave, the remaining poorer original tenants are forced out. The inner-city resident, who years ago could not figure a way out to the suburbs, is forced to move on. As the safety of the neighborhood and the quality of the investment become clearer, "blue chip" and many who aspire to blue blood push out the remaining vestiges of "blue collar."

This three-stage process does not occur in clearly delineated phases. The shifting of people, the renewal of properties, the rising of neighborhood and district awareness, goes on for years before and after designation. There is a mingling of pioneers, speculators, and middle-class residents whose roles and intentions are as varied as their personalities and financial resources. Through it all, though, there is an infusion of capital, a general uplifting of neighborhood appearance, and a dispersal of residents who had occupied the area for so long. This process, which has come to be known as gentrification—the replacement of the urban poor by a so-called urban gentry—has brought with it some of the most vexing social implications, as I will discuss later in this chapter.

The Historic District as a Profitable Commodity.   To aware residential property owners, historic district designation provides an impressive list of economic benefits. The overriding reasons are fundamentally connected to supply and demand. Suddenly, once a historic district is established from among the vast undifferentiated neighborhoods in town, a definite boundary is declared, which limits supply. Once it becomes a fact, a legal boundary as meaningful as a mountain range comes into being: on one side is the limited historic district; on the other side is the rest of town.

Even the initial process toward historic designation brings significant increases in property values. Studies of historic districts around the country—such as Beacon Hill and Back Bay (Boston, Massachusetts), Cobble Hill (Brooklyn, New York), Lafayette Square (St. Louis, Missouri), and Swiss Avenue (Dallas, Texas)—prove that considerable value increases accompany the process of neighborhood revitalization and rehabilitation, which normally *precedes* historic-district designation. Due to demand for properties, at the peak of activity, housing prices soar as much as 25 percent per year. Over a sustained period of transition, on the basis of the anticipated future appeal of the area alone, values are likely to increase annually from 10 percent to 25 percent above changes elsewhere in the community. Of course, another large increment in value is added to each property once renovation and rehabilitation expenses are added into a resale price.

Studies published by the National Trust for Historic Preservation, released under the banner of "information," suggest the specific economic benefit of historic-district designation. In the Olde Towne district of Portsmouth, Virginia, for example, property values are 2.5 to 4.0 times those of comparable properties located elsewhere in the same community. The trust observes that "the related phenomenon of well-above-average to extraordinary residential property value increases and higher-than-average residential property value levels were noted in all urban historic districts canvassed."

Instances of increased property value within designated historic districts proliferate. In the Beacon Hill and Back Bay areas of Boston between 1955 and 1972, property values rose by 200 percent compared to 126 percent in the city as a whole. During this period, both areas were first placed under local historic district controls and then on the National Register. Between 1946 and 1955, prior to the establishment of the districts, residential property values had increased by only 61 percent in the Beacon Hill and Back Bay areas compared to 66 percent in the city as a whole. Likewise, on the other side of the country, in the Pioneer Square-Skid Road District of Seattle, Washington, property values rose by 114 percent in six years compared to 79 percent for the city as a whole after approval of a local historic district ordinance and National Register listing in 1970. And a 1977 study of historic districts in Washington, D. C., Winston-Salem, North Carolina, St. John's, Richmond, Virginia, and Portsmouth, Virginia, prepared by property-tax expert John B. Rackham for the National Trust for Historic Preservation, concluded that:

a related phenomena of well-above-average to extraordinary residential property value increases and higher-than-average residential property value levels were noted. . . . Further, reports on value trends and levels show that market confidence was achieved or strengthened with the institution of local architectural controls in such diverse districts as Society Hill in Philadelphia;

Brooklyn Heights in New York; Savannah Historic District; Colonial Annapolis, Maryland; Vieux Carré in New Orleans; and the Old and Historic District in Charleston, South Carolina.

Nor must a building within a historic district have a particularly distinguished appearance or history to be highly valued. People are buying the neighborhood even more than the house itself. They are buying the *tout ensemble*. In Newport, Rhode Island, "the real estate dollar doesn't have much value today," according to Kenneth Stein, the former tax assessor. "Take the house on Church Street. It's a nothing house, not a colonial, not a Victorian, not a federal. But it is on Historic Hill in Newport. The house sold not long ago for $12,000. It was just auctioned off for $73,000."

The total ambiance of a historic district contributes so pervasively and directly to value that specialized assessment manuals are now being written to help appraisers understand and justify prices. No longer are the traditional guidelines for assessing a building's value—cost, income, and sales—valid. Instead, as appraisers Anthony Reynolds and William D. Weldron observe in their article "Historical Significance: How Much Is It Worth?" four entirely new factors must be weighed: (1) the degree of historical significance; (2) the physical integrity of the structure; (3) the cost of needed repair, restoration, or reconstruction; and (4) the environment of the property.

This last factor is the one that makes historic districts so economically attractive. The environment of each individual property and district is being preserved by law and enhanced by private capital investment. In historic districts across America, the purchaser values and pays for a setting that cannot be duplicated. As Rackham points out in his study for the National Trust, the purchaser buys, in part, "the aesthetic and historical identification that they embody."

Once the historic district is declared, there is no longer any speculation as to possible designation. Buyers are now dealing with a fact. At this juncture, a second wave of property purchases and capital improvements begins. Property owners inside the new district begin to receive unsolicited offers to buy, something that has never happened before. Purchasers who learn of the designation inquire from other parts of town; buyers from out of town drive up and down the streets of the new historic district, looking for property.

As a part of this process, more than just real-estate values change. The perception of the neighborhood is transformed. Some who move in opt for a new residential alternative, one that substitutes a townhouse in the city, near work and cultural resources, in place of their suburban lifestyle. Others, already city dwellers, attracted by the special location, ambiance, and neighborhood quality, move in from less distinctive and often more remote areas within the same community.

More often than not, neighborhoods surrounding the designated historic district also benefit. Brokers selling property on the fringe and just beyond do not work excessively hard to disclose the precise boundary. They want to expand the impact of the district to incorporate as much real estate as possible. And so the loose rubric of "historic-district area" begins to spring up. A study of Park Slope in Brooklyn, for example, reveals that 30–60 percent of the residents outside but near the historic-district boundary believe they live within the Park Slope Historic District itself.

In each district and along its fringes, considerable sums of private funds are spent on rehabilitation and upgrading of property, as people attracted by the human scale and beauty of the area endeavor to assure its future stability. All this promotes jobs and creates other local economic stimulants, including retail sales.

Sooner or later, real-estate classified advertisements offer houses with *views* into the historic district, views which cannot be disturbed by new building. The restricted domain is capitalized upon even from beyond its walls. In this way, historic district legal restrictions produce many types of value which eventually are recognized and captured by private entrepreneurs.

TAX BENEFITS: PUBLIC HELP
FOR PRIVATE COMMERCIAL VENTURES

Special federal tax benefits credited by the 1976 Tax Reform Act are now extended to individual historic properties used for commercial ventures. The most significant benefit is the right to depreciate "certified improvements" in as short a time as five years—faster than most other permiteed schedules. This opportunity to deduct capital costs from earned income in commercial real-estate ventures is one of the most attractive tax incentives available. In this most important way, preservation and rehabilitation are being stimulated by federal policy: they becomes good tax deals.

To qualify for these tax advantages, the income-producing structure may be either (1) listed in the National Register itself; or (2) designated a "certified historic structure," that is, a building in a registered district that contributes to the historic significance of the district; or (3) located in a historic district designated as such by a state or local statute that has been certified by the Secretary of the Interior. (A property owner within a historic district—whether the district is listed in the National Register or only locally designated under a historic district ordinance approved by the Secretary of the Interior—therefore must apply to have his *individual building* declared a "certified historic structure.")

Once the quality of the structure has been determined, the Department of the Interior must certify that the proposed renovation is consistent with the historic character of the building and/or the district in which the property is located. Department of the Interior guidelines which must be followed faithfully include the following:

Every reasonable effort shall be made to provide a compatible use for a property which requires minimal alteration of the building structure or site and its environment, or to use a property for its originally intended purpose.

The distinguishing original qualities or character of a building, structure or site and its environment shall not be destroyed. The removal or alteration of any historic material or distinctive architectural features should be avoided when possible.

All buildings, structures and sites shall be recognized as products of their own time. Alterations that have no historical basis and which seek to create an earlier appearance shall be discouraged. . . .

Deteriorated architectural features shall be repaired rather than replaced, wherever possible. . . .

The surface cleaning of structures shall be undertaken with the gentlest means possible. . . .

Every reasonable effort shall be made to protect and preserve archeological resources affected by, or adjacent to, any rehabilitation project. . . .

The guidelines are crucial to assuring that restoration of the most important buildings is faithfully undertaken. By September 1979, over a thousand applicants from forty-three states had applied to the Department of the Interior for the tax-incentive program; this includes private investments of more than $500 million. To date, about 90 percent of all applicants have been accepted.

Approval means important tax savings, and tax savings means money in the owner's pocket. It also means that it may be more profitable to invest in a business property in a historic district than in any other part of town. Investors and speculators have been quick to recognize the special appeal of these tax incentives. The Office of Archaeology and Historic Preservation of the Department of the Interior estimates that by 1981, between 100,000 and 125,000 properties may be rehabilitated under the provisions of the 1976 Tax Reform Act.* At the same time, it is estimated

*This estimate assumes an extension of various provisions due to expire in June 1981. See pages 326–327 for a more detailed discussion.

that there will be approximately 700,000 nonresidential historic structures in the United States which could qualify for these tax advantages. Melvin A. Gamzon, writing in the *National Real Estate Investor,* told his professional audience recently that these tax provisions " . . . offer the developer an opportunity to leverage public funding and investment incentives for rehabilitation." Not long ago, a specialist in preservation confided in me that his once-struggling architectural practice was booming out of control. "The place," he said, "is full of lawyers, accountants, and other clients doing 1976 Tax Act historic rehabs." Indeed, the 1976 Tax Reform Act elevates private rehabilitation of certain commercial properties into that ever-shrinking celebrity circle: the tax shelter.

Some of the most notable projects involved in the first round of 1976 Tax Reform Act historic "rehab deals" include the conversion of the Old Public Safety Building, in Seattle, into offices; restoration of the Biltmore Hotel, in Providence; and conversion of the Hart Block cast-iron warehouse, in Louisville's West Main Street Historic District, into an office building.

All commercial historic rehabilitation projects are assumed by their developers to be commercially viable. All involve major expenditures of private funds, sometimes with special grant or loan assistance. Investment capital is attracted by the hope of a good business proposition, which is strongly encouraged by the rapid depreciation write-off accorded the initial owner of a certified historic structure devoted to commercial uses. I doubt, for instance, if the Rouse Company, one of the most prominent and perceptive developers in America, would have been so attracted to the prospect of commercial development of the South Street Seaport in Lower Manhattan if the area had not been within a historic district.

A note of caution is in order here—or, if you will, a personal observation related to taste: Commercial redevelopment can be overdone, as it is at times. In some places, such as Boston's Faneuil Hall, the historic ambiance is overwhelmed by feverish commercial vitality. The same problem is now evident in New Orleans' Vieux Carré. Frequently, redevelopment *within* individual commercial structures and the accompanying decoration are in questionable taste. In restaurants, cafés, and other retail establishments within historic buildings, the clutter of banal furniture and decoration, obtrusive signs and quaint lighting, go a long way toward demolishing or obscuring what was presumably saved of a building's historic, structural, and decorative character. Once the interior is decorated and furnished, it often requires a vivid imagination, and even some considerable training, to find what it is "of significance in American history, architecture, archaeology, and culture" that enabled the building to qualify for its elevated status in the first place.

Under the original provisions of the 1976 Tax Reform Act, the opportunity to realize substantial tax write-offs through certified renovation of historic properties is slated to expire in June 1981. Whether this program is, in fact, extended or modified or replaced or simply allowed to end will depend upon political circumstances and the results of an evaluation of it during late 1980 and early 1981. Because of its clear overall effectiveness in turning investment toward preservation and maintenance of older buildings of high quality, and because of the undeniable conservation benefits of recycling and reusing older structures, the broad objectives of the program merit continuation.

At this juncture, as the law is evaluated, new details of how that continuation ought to be carried out should be considered. A number of questions should be asked—and dealt with—if the operative policies are to be enriched. Among the important questions raised as a consequence of past success are these: Does historic preservation sufficiently elevate the general welfare to merit such favorable treatment in federal tax law, which is, of course, an indirect form of national public policy? Should the benefits available be extended to residential properties, and if so, how? How could a wider base of the population benefit from historic preservation? How might some planned restraint on the total volume of commercial activity in each historic district be introduced so that a vital mix of uses, people, and traffic is established without allowing excessive commercial attractions and centers of development to overwhelm the district? Should not the integrity and quality of buildings sufficiently important to be certified for generous tax benefits be protected both inside and out?

Preservation and Scenic Easements. The 1976 Tax Reform Act provides a second and entirely different type of tax-related benefit to owners of property in a historic district or a building with landmark status. This is the permitted donation of a so-called preservation (or scenic) easement, to a qualified private nonprofit organization or public agency. The easement is nothing more than a properly executed legal document that conveys the right to use or control a portion of the property without conveyance of ownership itself. Most often the easement restricts the facade or private open spaces surrounding the buildings from change. It thereby transfers control away from the owner and vests is with a recipient agency, such as a historic-district commission, much as a conservation restriction conveys control of development rights.*

This right-of-easement donation is not restricted to commercial real estate. Anyone may donate such an easement, or restriction, even one to your own house, provided an approved recipient agency can be found to

*See Chapter nine, pages 285–293 for a discussion of conservation restrictions.

accept the gift. The benefit to the private property owner is twofold: the donation of such an easement creates the potential for a reduced annual property tax, and it is considered a charitable donation of a part of the value of the property.

Demolition Disadvantaged.   Prior to passage of the 1976 Tax Reform Act, demolition often made economic sense to a developer. The cost of demolition could be either deducted immediately as a building expense or added to the capital cost of the new building and thereafter depreciated. However, two new significant accounting rules contained in the 1976 Tax Reform Act are calculated to disadvantage and discourage demolition of certified historic structures or any other structure in a registered historic district unless the structure is specifically certified by the Secretary of the Interior *not* to be of historic significance. First, if such a building is, in fact, demolished, no deduction may be taken for the expense incurred, nor may any deduction be claimed for the value of the remaining undepreciated cost basis of the building. Second, an owner who demolishes or substantially alters a certified historic structure may not use any accelerated depreciation with respect to the replacement building or substantially altered improvement.

OTHER PUBLIC STIMULANTS
TO HISTORIC PRESERVATION

The 1976 Tax Reform Act is the first time that an Internal Revenue Service regulation has contained provisions specifically intended to encourage a national movement toward the preservation of historic structures. In addition, these provisions are virtually the only recent examples of a liberalization of the tax laws relative to all real estate.

Important as it is, the 1976 Tax Reform Act is but one of numerous new federal aids dedicated to the cause of historic preservation. There currently exists a substantial array of policies and public programs which may be used, directly in some cases and indirectly in others, by the knowledgeable, creative owner or community to forward preservation objectives. A digest of the more than fifty applicable federal programs, entitled *A Guide to Federal Programs,* may be obtained from the National Trust for Historic Preservation Bookstore, Washington, D.C. A useful summary of many of these programs is issued by the Department of the Interior as *Sources of Preservation Funding.*

A recent poll taken by the Department of the Interior reveals that 50 percent of those taking advantage of preservation tax incentives would not have undertaken rehabilitation otherwise. Fourteen percent of the 1976 Tax Reform Act participants, furthermore, have combined those tax write-offs with other public funding to make seemingly impossible ventures feasible development projects.

The increasing economic and political power of the preservation movement is demonstrated by the amount of monies recently invested in it directly by federal agencies with grant programs. For example, in fiscal 1978, the Department of the Interior disbursed $41.5 million to the states and to the National Trust for Historic Preservation for the identification, acquisition, and protection of National Register properties. These matching funds generated a minimum of 50 percent additional non-federal money. Under the Local Public Works program of the Department of Commerce, $300 million went into restoration projects. The National Endowment for the Arts reported that it gave $1.3 million in grants that benefitted historic preservation. These were dollars matched by the non-federal sector at a rate of three to one. Between 1975 and 1977, cities used $71.5 million from the Community Development Block Grant program of the Department of Housing and Urban Development for projects designed to restore historic structures. In addition, the Historic Preservation Loan program within the FHA Title I Home Improvement Loan program and the Public Buildings Cooperative Use Act of 1976 offer major impetus.

Two additional programs, while not restricted exclusively to historic preservation activities, are of great significance as federal incentives to both rehabilitation and historic preservation. The 1978 Revenue Act offers an investment credit of 10 percent of a taxpayer's "qualified investment" to rehabilitate industrial and commercial (but not apartment) buildings which have been in use for at least twenty years and have not been previously rehabilitated. The investment credit is, of course, especially valuable, as it is (within certain limitations) a direct credit against tax liability. The second program, and one which dwarfs all others now in terms of committed funds, is the Urban Development Action Grant, or UDAG, program. Initially established by the Housing and Community Development Act of 1977, the program is intended to provide grants to severely distressed cities and urban counties so as to alleviate physical and economic deterioration. Committed funds are also expected to stimulate increased private and public investment. Commercial, residential, and industrial projects are eligible, as are projects which involve preservation. Through this program in fiscal 1979, some $675 million of federal funds was committed all across America to a wide array of targeted projects.

State Government Assistance. State governments have climbed aboard the preservation bandwagon as well. Many states currently support preservation through enabling legislation, which permits local governments to indirectly aid preservation efforts. Oregon, Texas, North Carolina, Maryland, and Connecticut now allow, in certain instances, direct real-estate tax reductions or abatements on improvements made to rehabilitate historic buildings. More specifically: in Texas a 1977 amendment to the state constitution allows municipalities to exempt from property tax all or part of a designated historic structure and the land necessary for its access and use. Maryland supplemented its tax code in 1977 to allow an owner of property located in a historic district to take a tax credit of up to 10 percent for maintenance and restoration expenses; owners constructing new buildings which are architecturally compatible with the district are allowed a credit of 5 percent of construction costs. And cities in North Carolina must tax designated historic properties at 50 percent of the property's value if owners apply for this reduced assessment.

Lower taxes mean lower operating costs, which makes it more likely that commercial property will operate at a satisfactory profit. Lower taxes also reduce the cost of owning, rehabilitating, and occupying residential property. At the same time, tax reductions or abatements increase the market value of commercial real estate.

Local Government Assistance. Just recently, a predominance of local government officials have begun to support preservation, and with more than the relatively simple and relatively invisible property-tax benefits. Across the country, positive economic and physical results are noticed and being better understood by public officials, especially those responsible for older, struggling districts and city centers. They are persuaded by facts, figures, grant programs which come down from Washington, and widespread benefits which accrue locally.

Preservation and rehabilitation, many local politicians now realize, also means new jobs. The Department of the Interior points out that rehabilitation work is often 25 percent more labor-intensive than new construction. In its own testimony to Congress in support of the Public Buildings Cooperative Use Act of 1976, which encourages the use of historic buildings as federal offices, the General Services Administration estimated that for a given expenditure of money, rehabilitation creates two to five times as many jobs as new construction. Some of these construction jobs, which are partially supported by federal funding, include job-training provisions not only to assist unemployed people who seek a new career but to augment the limited number of skilled craftsmen available across the country as well. This dearth of experienced, capable artisans is a seldom mentioned but nevertheless critical impediment to top-quality results in restoration work.

Wise local politicians also recognize that the effective use of historic preservation, especially throughout a district, is likely to bring other community benefits, particularly in older towns where a needy population is matched by a shrinking tax base. From the perspective of the government, then, private investment, private redevelopment, and private speculation eventually add up to higher property taxes and thus a higher municipal income. Even if rehabilitation expenses receive a tax abatement initially, the abatement is not perpetual. Often, it is reduced annually and generally expires after ten to fifteen years. At that time, full tax benefits are received annually by the community.

Beyond the Historic District: Benefits of Rehabilitation. The legal and economic magnet provided by the 1976 Tax Reform Act and other federal programs with historic-preservation stimulant components draw monies toward historic district areas. These monies might have otherwise been spent on new or rehabilitated commercial real-estate projects in other areas or even on the demolition of the very same buildings that were ultimately preserved, simply to obtain the land for the construction of modern structures. Certainly, the 1976 Tax Reform Act created preservation incentives of its own and eliminated previous ones, created by tax and accounting policies, to demolish older areas.

But market trends and public policy of the last several years have worked independently to stimulate the preservation movement far beyond the narrow confines of historic buildings and districts. Preservation of older buildings everywhere is now a growth industry of its own. It is fueled by the high cost of well-located vacant land, as well as by the increasingly high cost of new buildings.

Today, rehabilitation of an older commercial building generally costs 20–40 percent less per square foot than demolition and new construction. While rehabilitation work is considerably more labor-intensive than new construction, and experienced redevelopment architects, engineers, and contractors charge fees often higher than those for ordinary construction, there is still a savings. Demolition expenses, including site clearance, are eliminated; and a good deal of the inflationary impact of new material costs is avoided. Also, rehabilitation, unlike new construction, can proceed year-round; in most cases, it progresses at a faster pace than does new work; and often it may proceed while portions of the building are being used productively. All these factors save money in the end. And each of these particular financial advantages helps reduce construction costs, thereby so often tipping the economic balance in favor of rehabilitation. Not long ago, new construction was always less expensive than reuse of an older building. Today, economic feasibility of one versus the other is an open question.

As a result of economic benefits in recent years, rehabilitation work has grown from a small fraction of all construction industry sales in 1960 to over 30 percent in 1978. The Department of the Interior estimates that well over $50 billion is now spent annually in rehabilitation work. Much of this effort, known as recycling, is devoted to using old buildings for new uses. Cost-saving examples abound. In downtown San Antonio, not long ago, the Alamo National Bank recycled its 23-story 1930s landmark building at a cost of $38.00 per square foot; similar new construction would have cost $70.00 per square foot. In Seattle, the Pioneer Building was rehabilitated at less than $19.00 per square foot, versus a cost at that time of more than $30.00 per square foot for new construction work of similar quality.

GENTRIFICATION:
ANOTHER SIDE OF THE STORY

What can happen to a single local area when it becomes popular? Consider the Haight-Ashbury district of San Francisco. In 1970 it was the dilapidated, drug-obsessed center of hippie culture in America; just a few years later, its location and architecture attracted middle-class residents. Between 1971 and 1975, the sale price of real property in the district jumped 75 percent, and crime dropped 20 percent. Between 1970 and 1977, the number of residents who earned more than $15,000 per year increased from 15 percent to 24 percent. During the same years, commercial vacancies declined from 40 percent to 10 percent. Houses on some blocks in the speculative upward spiral changed hands every year; consequently, many residences over the last decade more than tripled in value.

Calvin Welch, a long-time resident of Haight-Ashbury, witnessed the process of gentrification from the other side of the fence. "On my block alone, since 1973," he told Marilyn Chase, a *Wall Street Journal* reporter, "I know of fifteen families with children who have had to move when their buildings were sold."

The federal government, through the Department of Housing and Urban Development (HUD), has recently awarded more than two hundred grants totaling $3 million for studies of gentrification. One preliminary finding in 1979 concludes that the displacement of poor people by private revitalization is statistically minimal. Only 3.8 percent of all household moves between 1974 and 1976 were found to be involuntary.

In its own research into the impact of the 1976 Tax Reform Act (and of the Revenue Act of 1978), the Heritage Conservation and Recreation Service of the Department of the Interior concludes that 80 percent of the residential units created by utilizing tax incentives were either previously vacant or inserted into nonresidential buildings.

But stubborn problems—the dilemmas of human displacement and social justice—persist. The first efforts at their resolution are just emerging, for the most part, from joint private and public efforts. These tend to be focused on areas where historic district rejuvenation is under way. The Savannah Landmark Rehabilitation Project and the Neighborhood Housing Services Program in Baltimore, for example, are using funds from HUD to provide low-cost rehabilitation loans and subsidies to enable poorer people to remain in neighborhoods where preservation and conservation activity is occurring.

Concerned planning and legal specialists are devising other initiatives which would mitigate the negative effects of gentrification. Some of the most constructive ideas currently being considered include federal assistance in the form of low-interest loans and mortgage insurance; bank assistance to low-income owner-residents through specially tailored mortgages; to discourage speculation, a capital transaction tax that contains a graduated payment on profit, which begins at a very high level and declines the longer the property is held; and a preferential property tax, which is lower for residents who have been longest in possession.

Gentrification, a new word for an old process, presents vexing questions. In earlier decades, the urban poor were displaced by other widespread national development and redevelopment programs, most notably by urban renewal and interstate highway projects. Now it is preservation. While solutions are sought, the widespread benefits to entire communities should not be halted. And the benefits are indeed crucial ones: preservation of older buildings and the upgrading of neighborhoods; the creation of jobs; increased municipal revenue from sales and property tax; and a way that cities can begin to partially compete with suburbs for valued middle-class and upper-middle-class families by creating a special ambiance, an environment pleasing in its own right.

The historic preservation movement revives the hope and future of certain limited areas within small towns and older cities in America. Positive economic forces and political realizations, so recently set in motion, must not be victimized by a constellation of much older and broader negative local, state, and federal policies, and social and economic trends that have seized urban America since World War II.

In years past, federal housing, welfare, medical care, and legal service subsidies enticed the poor into the cities. At the same time, federal highway programs, economic development policies, and middle-income housing subsidies lured jobs and middle-income workers to the suburbs. For most of the post–World War II period, cities, to qualify for their share of federal money, were forced to compete for the poor.

Today, it is not displacement through gentrification that creates the most serious problems of residential dislocation. Rather, it is the abandonment of buildings, the opposite of neighborhood vitality. This generally occurs when owners find it no longer economic to maintain basic services. This happens when income earned by a property cannot pay for repairs, taxes, and other expenses; and when the prospect of continued financial loss appears to outweigh any advantage of holding on to a property.

Preoccupation with history and with the past now leads to promise in the future. The long-term objective of "saving the cities" is, in part, forwarded by the narrower objectives of historic preservation and those wider impacts associated with gentrification. Within historic areas, a successful combination of private finance and public incentives is stimulating conservation and preservation, a new priority in America. With this success comes unprecedented district-wide rehabilitation and revitalization. Large amounts of land and the structure of community life are affected. There is now a new future for special-quality older areas, in small towns and large cities alike—a future made possible by a specialized link, formed in the past decade, between land, power, and wealth.

ELEVEN

MIGRATION: THE CITY STRENGTHENS; SUBURBS IN TRANSITION; RURAL AMERICA AWAKENS

Where people want to live—and where they in fact move—has the widest imaginable impact on the demand for and value of land. During the next several decades, most of the new demand for undeveloped land in America will depend on whether people remain where they are or move elsewhere.

New migration trends that break with the past are now evident in cities, suburbs, and the rural countryside. These changing patterns are going to affect the relative value of land across the country.

A pronounced preference for the South and West has been clear for some time, where between 1970 and 1977, almost 90 percent of the nation's population growth occurred. Between 1975 and the year 2000, the U.S. Census Bureau projects that the population of these two regions may grow at three times the rate of that of the Northeast and Midwest.

Within this larger context, this chapter examines population trends and their impact on land within the three basic types of residential communities: the city, the older suburbs, and nonmetropolitan America.

A Few Terms. To discuss likely future settlement patterns with precision, definition of a few statistical terms is necessary. The most basic term is "Standard Metropolitan Statistical Area," or SMSA. This is a county or group of contiguous counties which exhibit an integrated economic and social system and which contain at least one central city (or twin cities) with a population of at least 50,000. Minneapolis-St. Paul is an example of a twin-city SMSA; the St. Louis SMSA is a single-city SMSA. Counties within SMSAs are referred to as metropolitan counties. In the United States in 1975, there were 272 SMSAs. These metropolitan counties contained only 15 percent of the nation's land but housed 73 percent of its population.

STANDARD METROPOLITAN STATISTICAL AREAS
IN CONTIGUOUS U.S. AS OF OCTOBER 1975
(Pages 338–39)

The basic statistical term used to describe demographic trends in the United States is the Standard Metropolitan Statistical Area, or SMSA. An SMSA is a county or group of contiguous counties which exhibit an integrated economic and social system and which contain at least one central city (or twin cities) with a population of at least 50,000.

336

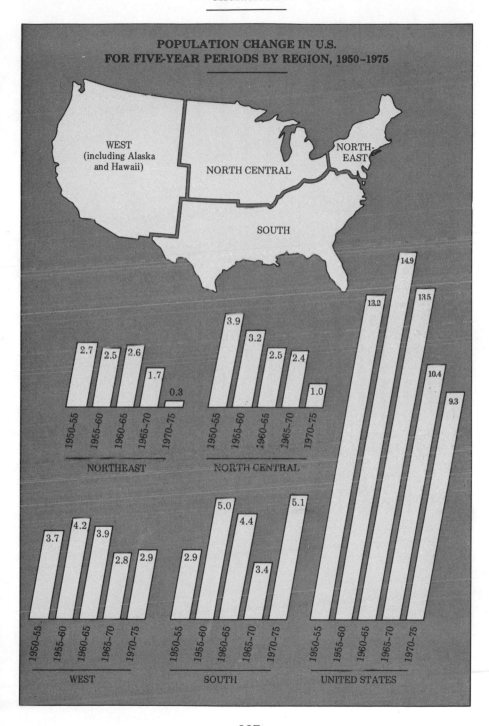

POPULATION CHANGE IN U.S.
FOR FIVE-YEAR PERIODS BY REGION, 1950–1975

WEST
(including Alaska
and Hawaii)

NORTH CENTRAL

NORTH-
EAST

SOUTH

NORTHEAST

| 1950-55 | 1955-60 | 1960-65 | 1965-70 | 1970-75 |
| 2.7 | 2.5 | 2.6 | 1.7 | 0.3 |

NORTH CENTRAL

| 1950-55 | 1955-60 | 1960-65 | 1965-70 | 1970-75 |
| 3.9 | 3.2 | 2.5 | 2.4 | 1.0 |

WEST

| 1950-55 | 1955-60 | 1960-65 | 1965-70 | 1970-75 |
| 3.7 | 4.2 | 3.9 | 2.8 | 2.9 |

SOUTH

| 1950-55 | 1955-60 | 1960-65 | 1965-70 | 1970-75 |
| 2.9 | 5.0 | 4.4 | 3.4 | 5.1 |

UNITED STATES

| 1950-55 | 1955-60 | 1960-65 | 1965-70 | 1970-75 |
| 13.2 | 14.9 | 13.5 | 10.4 | 9.3 |

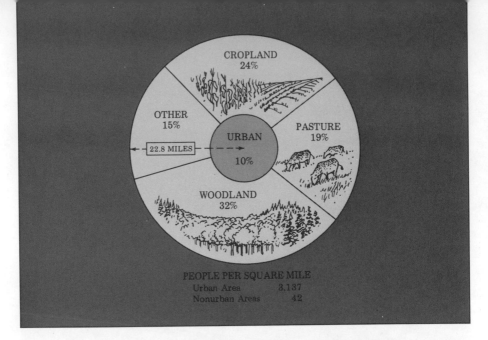

**AVERAGE DISTRIBUTION OF LAND USE
WITHIN A STANDARD METROPOLITAN STATISTICAL AREA, 1970**

Nonmetropolitan counties, on the other hand, are all those which exist outside of SMSAs. This includes most of the land in America but excludes the residential location of most of the people in America.

The word "metropolitan," however, implies that SMSAs are comprised entirely of densely populated counties and cities. This is not the case. Most of the area within so-called metropolitan counties (those within SMSAs) is not intensively developed. Indeed, in the average SMSA, only 10 percent of the land is classified as "urban." Most people within each SMSA live within the proportionately small central urban areas, where population density averages more than 3,000 persons per square mile.

"Suburb," for the most part, refers to a residential area within an SMSA but outside the "central city." The central city is the core of the SMSA.

As would be expected, land use within SMSAs varies by region. In the Appalachian, southeastern, and Delta states, more than half of the non-

**DISTRIBUTION OF LAND USE
WITHIN THE AVERAGE SMSA, BY REGION, 1970**
(Opposite)

Land use within the SMSAs varies across the country. In the Appalachian, southeastern, and Delta states, more than half of the nonurban SMSA land is woodland; in the northern plains and the Corn Belt, in contrast, over half of the nonurban SMSA land is cropland.

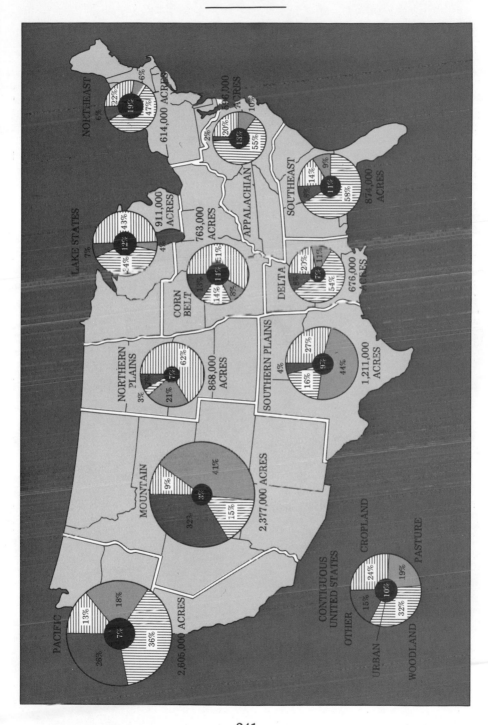

urban SMSA land is undeveloped woodland. In the SMSAs of the northern plains, and the Corn Belt, over half is cropland. More than 80 percent of the population residing in the Northeast, the most populous region of the country, lives in SMSAs, yet more than 15 million acres, or almost half of that region's SMSA acreage, is woodland.

Two sets of sometimes misleading paired terms must also be clarified: rural/urban and metropolitan/nonmetropolitan. These terms don't always mean what they seem to imply. All places with a population greater than just 2,500 people are classified by the census as "urban." Thus, everyone who resides in an isolated village of 3,000 persons would be classified as "urban" but not "metropolitan." Conversely, people living in sparsely populated areas within metropolitan counties are classified as "rural" *and* "metropolitan."

SCHEMATIC DIAGRAM OF METROPOLITAN/NONMETROPOLITAN AND RURAL/URBAN AREAS

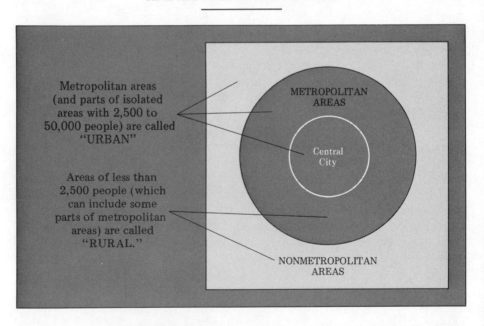

Now, with these terms in mind, let us see where people have been moving and living in America, and what new trends are underway. This consideration is the all important people factor. The shifts in population bring new demand for land to some areas, while elsewhere, the demand and need for land subsides.

THE CITY STRENGTHENS

Over the past decades, in many parts of America, city centers have been through the ringer in every way imaginable—financially, socially, legally. Like a once-powerful business family, some are on the brink of bankruptcy; and others may be soon. And yet in many, the potential for revitalization and increased land values in the future is stronger than it has been for years.

There are many factors other than new demands from migrating citizens which are effecting this change. For some people, the high cost of new construction is avoided by moving into an established residential district. For others, more speculative in motivation, there is a sense that the cities have hit bottom in terms of services, and that land values are on the rise. With this set of assumptions comes the accompanying assumption in our inflationary time that values are likely to rise, that an investment in the city, in a place to live there, is perhaps now a good investment. There is, of course, the associated awareness of the savings made possible in operating costs by living in more densely constructed quarters, which are less costly to heat, and of holding a job that can be reached by city transit.

Stories about real-estate turnabout situations in the cities abound. The press is full of them. And a lot of people have friends who remained in town or who have moved back in the first wave who "couldn't afford to buy in our neighborhood now."

In the most desirable parts of the largest older cities, housing prices have escalated dramatically in the last several years. In some of the best areas, the value of urban houses and cooperative apartments doubled and more between 1974 and 1979, while the stock market stood still, the dollar fell off the cliff, and living in the suburbs became increasingly expensive.

The turnabout in values and in the new perception of the city has roots that go back a decade and more. Social, political, and economic changes in the way life is lived in America, the way government is financed, and the way our increasingly limited natural resources are deployed all contribute to this shift. These and other factors continue to garner support for the value and appeal of land and real estate in American cities.

The New Household: Matched to the City. Although the overall population is no longer growing rapidly, America is in the midst of a rapid formation of numerous smaller households. Between 1970 and 1976, the United States population grew by slightly more than 5 percent; during the same period, the number of households grew by 15 percent. Because of the disproportionately large number of young adults and older people in the

343

country, the formation of new households will exceed population growth during the 1980s.

The word "household" today describes every kind of adult living arrangement: married adults with or without children; single-parent families headed by a male or female; households which consist of a lone adult; and the fastest growing group of all, households which consist of unrelated individuals living together. The Census Bureau finds that as of March 1979, one of every five American households consists of just one person, up a dramatic 42 percent since 1970. One of every four households in America now consists of a person living alone or with an unrelated person. Cohabitation, defined by the Census Bureau as "households which contain two unrelated adults of opposite sexes," has increased by over 100 percent since 1970. Today, as longevity increases and baby-boom children form first households, more than half of all households in the United States comprise no more than two people.

The cities will continue to attract more than their share of these generally smaller households. Many have no children, so the yard and big house become unnecessary. Women are more likely to hold a job; for them employment opportunities in the city are more diverse. In households with two jobs and fewer children, higher discretionary income accumu-

AVERAGE ANNUAL GROWTH RATES
IN POPULATION AND NUMBER OF HOUSEHOLDS,
1940–1970, AND PROJECTIONS TO 1990

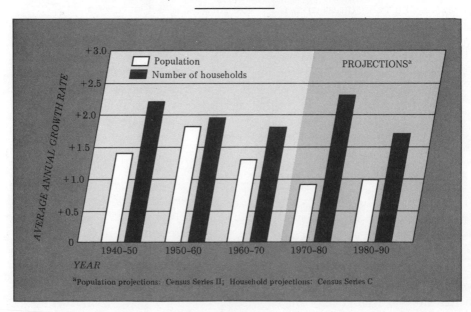

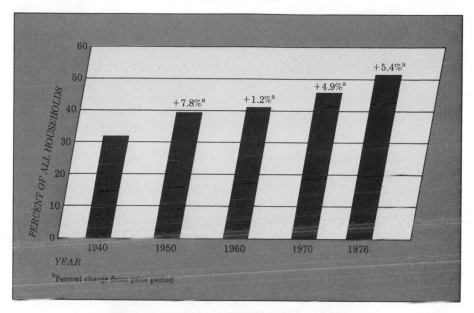

**ONE- AND TWO-PERSON HOUSEHOLDS
AS PERCENTAGES OF ALL HOUSEHOLDS,
1940–1976**

lates. Money can be used on amenities and pleasures best found in cities
—top entertainment, more interesting shops, and the best cultural presentations. As urban economist Anthony Downs pointed out in 1974:

The impact of more adult-oriented households has already been felt in our
major metropolitan areas. In the main, adult couples seek small housing
units, place no emphasis on school quality, are willing and able to pay relatively high rents, and are content with multifamily and high-rise units. They
also have a taste for theaters, museums, and restaurants. In short, the adult-
oriented household is made to order for city life.

Jobs in the City. Many industries which should not be housed in contemporary central cities because of space, labor and access constraints,
and accompanying higher operational costs have already moved out. Most
have found a suitable location somewhere else—along the interstate or a
rail siding in a rural area. Manufacturing enterprises, for instance, once
attracted blue-collar workers off the farm and into the city. Today they
draw production-line workers, who originally lived in the city, out to the
suburbs.

What remains are nonindustrial and nonmanufacturing jobs. The city
has held and nurtured offices and businesses which depend on direct

interpersonal exchange; smaller, growing service businesses; cultural institutions; service institutions, such as hospitals and libraries; and specialized professional services of all sorts. Job types found in the cities are the fastest growing of all in our post-industrial economy. They also tend to require less space per person and per net dollar of profit. The city is thus the center for intangibles, for the interaction of ideas, for negotiations, for imagination and innovation.

The Energy Crunch. The continuing shortage and high cost of energy affect all land in America. These new realities are sure to assist the stabilization and rejuvenation of urban centers. By 1979, real-estate values along and near well-established public transportation lines were going up, whereas in the 1960s and early 1970s relatively few people cared to be located near them. Also, by 1979, city retail trade had picked up, while suburban stores in distant shopping malls did less well. In New York City in the summer of 1979, as an example, major retailers reported increases of 5–10 percent above 1978 summer levels, while New York suburban store sales were down 5–10 percent.

The high cost of energy also affects the cost of all travel. The Worldwatch Institute, an independent research group in Washington, D. C., estimates that within the next five years, it may cost U.S. motorists $50.00 to fill the tank of a standard American car. Because high fuel costs raise the ante to move around, people begin to think twice before driving fifty miles to a good restaurant or twenty miles to the movies. As time goes by, they are likely to realize that it is in the cities that jobs, entertainment, cultural enrichment, superior medical facilities, and high-quality education are most readily at hand. The culture of high-density building and close-proximity living, which for so long troubled Americans who value privacy and open spaces, is apt to become a desirable lifestyle.

Transit Resurgence. For the first time since World War II, transit ridership around America is on the upswing. In all urban areas during 1978 and 1979, passenger loads on subways, elevated lines, buses, and trolleys increased 4–8 percent.

Most transit systems, quite naturally, are found in the larger, older cities. Aware that transit is a sure way to save fuel nationwide, the federal government is stepping up its assistance. Major transit construction projects are either under way or in planning stages in many cities across the country, including Atlanta, Boston, Detroit, Honolulu, and Los Angeles. While federal assistance is still inadequate, transit projects are likely to garner increasing support in the decades ahead.

The Costs of Construction. Rising costs of new construction reflect the persistent upward spiraling of our inflationary economy. In 1979, these costs were increasing at an annual rate of 9–12 percent, as they have been for the past several years. Cities, however, are benefitting from this situation, since much urban real estate is already built up and habitable. A good deal of this property is for sale below replacement cost, at prices knocked down over the past decades of urban decline. As new construction becomes ever more costly, the real-estate value of urban properties becomes all the more alluring.

The market appeal of all well-located urban housing has already increased significantly in the past several years. A study of housing in America conducted by the Harvard-MIT Joint Center for Urban Studies finds that in the target year of 1965–1966, the great majority of middle-income and lower-income families purchased new rather than "used" houses. A comparable study one decade later, however, reveals that new-home purchases declined from 70 percent in the mid-1960s to about 40 percent in the mid-1970s.

This shift in patterns of real estate buying is not mysterious. As recently as 1970, the relative costs of a new house and of a well-maintained, renovated, older house in most places were equivalent. By 1976, the median price for a new house had escalated 16 percent over that for a remodeled older house.

Cooperatives and condominiums, forms of housing which require relatively little land per dwelling, have become the most sought-after properties in residential real estate. They offer tax and investment advantages equivalent to home ownership but are more economical to maintain, more secure from theft and other crime, and often benefit from large-scale institutional financing. Whereas an insurance company might not be interested in handling a mortgage on one $60,000 single-family house, it is apt to be more interested in initiating a transaction that combines fifty or even five hundred units.

While money to buy cooperatives and condominiums, like new single-family housing, may be harder to find during certain periods, in the long run demand and prices for them, I suspect, will be greater than for detached, conventional housing. In addition, several public subsidy programs such as HUD's Section 8 rent-subsidy program and the Federal Housing Administration's (FHA) 221(d)4 insured-loan program, work to effectively increase investors', developers', and financial institutions' interest in creating and owning multifamily housing, most of which is in the cities.

Once a new development or rehabilitation project is approved, the Section 8 rent-subsidy program provides federal funds to the owner of rental multifamily units to compensate for the difference between the rent a lower-income household can afford and the fair-market rent an adequate housing unit in the area would command. This program has made feasible numerous housing projects which would otherwise not have been undertaken by private developers and investors. The 221(d)4 program can be used independently or in tandem with a Section 8 project to assist ordinary commercial development of apartments, whether they are rental units or cooperatives and condominiums. In essence, the program grants a form of federal insurance to mortgage lenders, which lessens the lender's potential risk. This in turn ordinarily lowers the interest rate charged on loans for construction and financing. Such a reduction should ultimately be reflected in relatively lower per unit rent or purchase cost to the housing consumer.

The City as Land Bank, and the Role of Annexation. Inside most city limits, a storehouse of developable land exists. And all utilities are there, available. In a 1971 study, Ray M. Northam of Oregon State University estimated that in cities with populations of 100,000 or more, as much as 24 percent of land is vacant, of which 75 percent is considered buildable. Very recently the U.S. House of Representatives' Subcommittee on the City reported that "in the nation's largest cities the amount of vacant land is more than twice as extensive as the land occupied by all their commercial and industrial activities combined." In smaller cities and contiguous suburban areas, the proportion of vacant land to population is much higher. Though this land may not be situated in the most desirable locations, it is often for sale at prices far lower than those of comparable lots on the rural-suburban fringe.

This storehouse of developable urban land exists, in large part, because of favorable tax treatment most cities accord vacant land and because of annexation. Between the end of World War II and the early 1970s, cities—except those in the Northeast—sought to ingest more land, more people, a wider tax base, and thus greater political power through consolidation of adjacent territory into the city. Since 1945, most cities with a population of 10,000 or more have extended their boundaries significantly, as have many smaller communities. Between 1950 and 1970, of the 177 cities of 50,000 or more population in the South and West, where annexation has been most popular, only six failed to make significant annexations.

Partly because of annexation, which disproportionately increases a city's land holdings relative to its population, and partly because of migration away from the cities in prior decades, the average population density in central cities has declined over the last twenty-five years by about 40 percent. Because Northeastern cities did not generally annex new territory during this period, the decline in density in that region—approximately 9 percent—was the lowest. The result: plenty of room to build more, and plenty of land upon which to do it in the cities.

Federal Boosts to the Cities.   There are new indications of federal aid to the cities, above and beyond a higher level of funding for mass transit systems and for historic preservation. "Neighborhood revitalization" is being promoted in older city centers by funds and programs sponsored by the National Endowment for the Arts, the Internal Revenue Service, and other federal agencies. A much higher level of funding is also being made available for urban recreation by federal and state governments. And the Economic Development Administration (EDA) is seeking $3.6 billion through fiscal 1983 to bring new business into needy areas. This figure represents an 800 percent increase over the last three fiscal years.

The $1.2 billion UDAG program is attempting to revitalize cities by using public funds to attract private development. The aim is to persuade private business to move into, remain in, and expand within distressed areas. Results have been visible and immediate: an $11.4 million grant to Akron, Ohio, for land acquisition and improvement, for example, helped convince the Goodyear Tire Company to stay in the city; a $10 million grant to Baltimore will help finance the construction of a Hyatt Corporation Hotel, which is to be part of a convention center; and a $1.7 million grant to Troy, New York, will subsidize the construction of a shopping complex. Each dollar of UDAG funds, in fact, has generated $6.00 in private capital.

As discussed in greater detail in the previous chapter, federal historic-preservation programs and tax-credit programs of 1976 and 1978 have prompted a resurgence of interest in urban redevelopment of historic areas and older properties. Under the 1976 Tax Reform Act, owners of certified historic structures used for commercial purposes can amortize costs of certified rehabilitation work over a 5-year period, even though the real "life" of the improvements is likely to be much longer. The Revenue Act of 1978 significantly increases the investment tax credit applicable to all nonresidential commercial real estate, with special emphasis on the rehabilitation of older industrial and commercial buildings.

In a dramatic turnaround for the federal government, the cities are also now being protected. In 1979, President Carter announced a new policy intended to guarantee that federal programs would no longer contribute to the economic deterioration of cities. The policy, to be enumerated in "urban conservation guidelines," is expected to create a means to weigh in advance the advantages and disadvantages to cities of various federal loans and grants. The Department of Transportation's highway

349

program, HUD's urban action grants, and the Commerce Department's economic development loans and grants, among others, would fall under such scrutiny. Not surprisingly, the National Retail Merchants Association and the Congressional Suburban Caucus have already raised objections, claiming that the new urban conservation approach will aid cities at the expense of suburbs.

Municipal Tactics. Cities everywhere are actively seeking a better and brighter future. For the first time since the end of World War II, in one way or another, they have clearly defined goals: to attract more people who can pay their own way as residents, to encourage the owners of underutilized or idle but sound real estate, to stimulate development and redevelopment of urban land. In Baltimore, for example, public subsidy to the Coldspring townhouses attracted private investment and helped create a subsidized mortgage rate of 7.5 percent interest. As a result, middle-income purchasers realized an annual savings of between $1,000 and $1,500 in pretax dollars. St. Louis has finely honed Missouri's Urban Redevelopment Incentive program into a major redevelopment tool. The program grants various forms of tax abatement for twenty-five years; it also accords the developer of a certified private project the power of eminent domain. This unusual tactic allows the developer to condemn private land for his development once the project is approved by municipal officials. By 1979, as a result, there were thirty newly implemented city projects using more than $800 million in private funds.

Radical Twist: Aid to the Urban Middle Class. The use of public funds by a city to attract and subsidize middle-income residents is both a wise and creative approach. It is also controversial. Supporters applaud the Coldspring development in Baltimore, and other projects like it, as a boost to the city's shrinking tax base and an aid to encouraging citywide redevelopment. Critics, however, charge that such projects ignore the more pressing housing problems of the poor. When challenged about the propriety of using public power and wealth to assist the middle-class would-be urban resident, Baltimore City Council President Walter Orlinsky replied, "What else can we do? The major ill of urban areas is that we've got a rotten socioeconomic balance. We monopolize poverty. For years the country subsidized the middle class to move out. It was national policy to move them into the suburbs. . . . "

Increasingly, other cities, corporations, and banks are arriving at the same conclusion. In Detroit, General Motors has inaugurated a $20 million program of residential renovation and subsidy in the neighborhood surrounding its world headquarters. In Salt Lake City, banks now band together to provide a shared pool of mortgage funds for homeowners who have been rejected by lenders.

In New York City, the J–51 rehabilitation tax-abatement program has been extremely successful. Developers who recycle underutilized business and manufacturing buildings into residential projects are granted a generous abatement of property tax for up to twenty years, as well as twelve years' protection against any increase in assessed value as a result of rehabilitation. These provisions provided so strong an inducement to investors in the late 1970s that projects, not capital, became scarce. Critics began to wonder if the city was giving away too much in a strengthening real-estate market. Beginning in 1977, New York City also instituted a generous property-tax abatement incentive program aimed specifically at assisting commercial and industrial projects. Under it, more than 270 projects received tax exemptions on the order of $180 million. Both this program and the J–51 program, as a consequence of their own success, are now being cut back.

As cities enhance their own appeal, private investors increasingly seek them out. Generous stimulants, needed to encourage investment during most of the 1970s, are no longer so imperative. In this new situation, better public control over planning and wiser use of urban space are called for.

Slowly, (assuming that mortgage money is available at all), as urban residential real estate proves itself, and as local and state governments, private corporations, and financial institutions come to realize how valuable, how increasingly stable, and how potentially profitable much city property really is, larger mortgages become available at standard market rates. Red-lining, the practice by banks and other financial institutions of discriminating in their mortgage loans against high-risk urban areas, diminishes. And so a broader urban real-estate market comes alive.

The impact of these various revitalization programs can be measured in part through expenditures for residential rebuilding and renovation. The figures are way up, and the share garnered by the cities is skyrocketing. In 1971, some $9.5 billion was spent on renovation, repair, and maintenance of houses. By 1975, that figure had climbed to $15.4 billion, an increase of over 60 percent. During the same period, the amount spent in cities increased 100 percent, rising from $2 billion to $4 billion.

Developers Move In: The Path of Least Resistance. Developers are being encouraged—and sometimes even compelled—to reinvestigate urban opportunities. No longer is cheap land readily available on most urban fringes, as slow-growth and no-growth legislation in suburbs and rural areas has erected subtle barriers to new building. Environmental regulation fosters increasingly expensive construction projects, and in some instances completely inhibits them altogether. The path of least resistance, for the first time ever, is a return to previously developed areas: the cities. Thomas J. Kutznick, president of Aetna Life Insurance Company's Urban Investment and Development Corporation, marked this trend several years ago. "For future development," he told Isadore Barmash of *The New York Times,* "it is quite possible that cities are the best place for major building projects. The infrastructure is there—transportation, utilities, sewage, and so on. The environmental problem is no more complex than elsewhere. The zoning is there. And most important, the market is there."

Leading the way in most downtown revitalization today is not the often publicized rehabilitation of stunning middle-class townhouses. Rather, it is the sustained growth in office and commercial expansion, which has been under way in downtown areas across America for a good part of the 1970s, and some even earlier. With these projects has come growth of employment and increasing retail sales. Think of Chicago's Water Tower Place, which, in a single downtown complex houses a Marshall Field & Company, a Lord & Taylor, and the first Ritz-Carlton Hotel to be built in the United States in the last fifty years. Or of Boston's Prudential Center, L.A.'s Century City, Washington's L'Enfant Plaza, and Detroit's Renaissance Center. These and other major commercial urban projects may be architecturally undistinguished or socially questionable. Nevertheless, their positive economic impact is undeniable. Successful major investment and development spurs confidence and attracts other projects to the same market areas. Thus, the demand for and value of nearby urban land rise as each project succeeds. It was, we recognize in retrospect, adventurous office and commercial construction in the downtown areas during the late 1960s and 1970s that so improved the status and image of urban America. With these high-risk ventures came significant increases in assessed valuation, new capital investment, and employment opportunity.

In contrast, residential return by a selective middle class is just beginning. As it does, new and renovated housing in the established city will create higher land values over relatively large areas. If the "back-to-the-city movement" becomes a significant residential trend, as I believe it will over the next decade, part of its impact will be to raise the value of accessible and desirable urban land.

It is in the cities, then, for the first time in many decades, that speculators, packagers, and developers seek land for their projects. Compared to the suburbs, smaller towns, and rural areas, opportunity in the cities seems bright. Environmental advocacy is still less intense, as is public and political resistence to new construction and high-density building.

In time, however, I suspect new urban development will become more difficult as well. As land prices rise, as new middle-class residents want to shield their neighborhoods from increased development or change, as greater pressure for more development restriction is placed on city, state, and federal governments by an environmentally aware electorate, the going will get tougher for urban developers.

Prices Are Up. For several years now, because of the simultaneous trends of inflation, high energy costs, relative job stabilization, growth in service industries, smaller families, increased urban development, and the influx of greater numbers of higher-income residents into the cities, the price and value of the best urban real estate is way up. In the Queens Village neighborhood of Philadelphia, for example, residential property that was assessed at $2,500 in 1974 was reassessed at $8,300 in 1977. In 1978, 250 units, mostly townhouses, were added to the area: in 1973, they would not have cost more than $45,000; in 1978, however, they were selling for $100,000. Likewise, in the downtown section of Savannah, homes bought within the past fifteen years for $6,000 to $8,000 are now selling from $35,000 to $70,000. And in San Francisco's Western Addition neighborhood, competition for housing has increased costs since 1971 by as much as 200 percent. These statistics are much the same for selected areas of other major cities throughout the country.

CITY PERILS:
THE OTHER SIDE OF THE COIN

None of the new vigor found in the central cities of America should lead anyone to the conclusion that investment in land anywhere in any city is a surefire way to capitalize on this turnaround situation. There is another side of the coin.

It is prudent for the wary investor in urban land to recognize several deep-rooted, fundamental issues that continue to adversely affect the value and promise of much land in urban America:

(1) *Real population growth is marginal.* Had no annexation occured during the 1970s, there would have been no growth in the combined populations of all the central cities of the eighty-five largest SMSAs. Even in the South and West, where central cities are reported statistically to be growing in population, a significant part of that growth is due to annexation.

(2) *Employment growth is slow; unemployment remains high.* Between 1960 and 1970, while employment outside the eighty-five largest central

cities grew by 46 percent, employment within these cities increased by only 16 percent.

Since 1970, unemployment within the cities increased from about 5 percent to nearly 9 percent. High unemployment rates in the central cities reflect a relatively higher black unemployment rate. For instance, in 1976 black male unemployment stood at more than double the rate for white males.

It is also relevant to note, in terms of the emerging problems in suburbs (discussed later in this chapter), that during the same interval, unemployment in the suburbs jumped from under 4 percent to over 7 percent.

(3) *Poverty in the cities is increasing.* During the 1970s, the central cities experienced an increase in concentration of people at poverty levels. About 250,000 more families in poverty status lived in central cities in 1976 than in 1970, a 16 percent rise. Poverty areas in central cities housed almost 13 million people by 1976.

(4) *Gentrification breeds distress and public cost.* Gentrification means dislocation, rather than revitalization, for the poor. It brings more than shifts in the age, race, income, lifestyle, and political preference to a neighborhood. With it comes demand for additional municipal expenditures for relocation and/or income supplements for the poor. New middle-income residents, as a collective political force, also seek increased expenditures from city governments for such amenities as street improvements, education, and recreational facilities. Increased tax revenues provided by higher real-estate values are swallowed up by this costly upgrading demanded by an aware and politically active professional class, as well as by additional costs needed to assist the dislocated poor.

A 1979 HUD report indicates that neighborhood revitalization is sweeping through selected spots across the country. Renovation projects are reported in 60 percent of the major cities in the South, 53 percent in the Northeast, 43 percent in the north-central areas, and 25 percent in the West. Activity is strongest in Boston, New York, Philadelphia, Washington, New Orleans, Detroit, Chicago, and Denver.

(5) *The dependent poor remain concentrated in the cities.* Poor people remain concentrated in the inner city, where they experience severe economic hardship. While some are able to migrate out into suburbs, and perhaps nearer jobs suited to their skills, others are trapped, shoved around from one part of the city to another, often unable to survive without substantial public assistance. These urban residents are economically dependent on the cities for the public funds they receive. At the same time, increasing social welfare service costs diminish the attraction of the city for many who do manage to pay their own way.

Public assistance trends and figures tell a story that cannot be ignored.

Approximately 34 percent of all central-city families now depend on some form of public assistance. Between 1969 and 1976, the increase in public assistance in all metropolitan areas was a staggering 70 percent, an increase from about 4 percent to over 7 percent of all central-city income. During the same period, public assistance in the suburbs escalated from 2.5 percent to 4.4 percent of total income. In terms of the poor's dependence on public assistance, this means that the suburbs in 1976 look a lot like the central cities did in 1969.

(6) *Sociocultural problems abound.* The sociocultural problems of the cities (and suburbs) play their part in reducing the appeal of land in urban America. Crime tops a great many lists as to what is wrong in the cities. High taxes, poor schools, and a polluted environment further aggravate the situation. These same problems, in somewhat diminished form, are now appearing in the suburbs, especially around the largest cities, as I will discuss later in this chapter.

Locations with Symptoms of Distress. Several recent studies identify the cities in America with the greatest number of problems. While the ranking of cities differs somewhat, depending on the criteria used in each study, general conclusions correspond. The Northeast remains a troubled area, the Midwest has its problems, and elsewhere it all depends.

To be more specific, a recent study by the Brookings Institution indicates that of 123 cities on their distressed list, eighty-three are in the Northeast. Likewise, in a report by the Urban Institute, twenty-six of its twenty-nine "distressed cities"—defined by population loss, slow growth in per capita income, and rapid growth in unemployment—are in the north-central or northeast regions. *Sales & Marketing Management* magazine predicts that between 1978 and 1983, of the thirty cities expected to suffer population losses, twelve are in the Northeast and sixteen are in the Midwest. The Steubenville-Weirton, Ohio; Elkhart, Indiana; Charleston, West Virginia; and Utica-Rome, New York, market areas head the troubled list.

The President's National Urban Policy Report for 1978 includes a synopsis of characteristics which tend to create urban distress: a very large number have been manufacturing centers; the city is old in terms of age of its residential and commercial construction; the city is landlocked by surrounding incorporated municipalities and cannot grow through annexation; the city is fully developed; the city contains a substantial minority population.

Cities with a combination of these characteristics should be approached with the utmost caution by land investors. Imagination and large redevelopment efforts are prerequisites to success in these instances. On the other hand, older cities in difficult straits which impose enlightened redevelopment practices to attract new service industries and middle-class residents will be the communities in which the turnaround in demand for land, and consequently price, will be the greatest.

What Lies Ahead.   As recently as the early 1970s, a majority of Americans sought a more rural environment in which to live. The President's Commission on Population Growth found, in 1972, that although two thirds of all Americans lived in metropolitan areas, only 14 percent actually liked the city or the suburb in which they were located. Even more significant, about 35 percent of the people who then lived in metropolitan areas said they would like to move out into "open country," while another 30 percent preferred a small town or small city.

While I doubt that national inclinations and proclivities for more space and a less dense residential environment will totally change in just a few years, there will be, I believe, a shift in emphasis among a significant number of people. And enough of a shift, caused primarily by massive economic changes—dramatically higher costs for energy, new construction materials, and financing—to bring new vitality and higher land prices to many parts of many cities.

I do not see the cities of America on the brink of a new era of overall dynamic growth in population, jobs, or territorial size. Rather, I see a strengthening of price and increase in land value within those selected urban areas which, by virtue of physical location, existing building quality, transit access to the central core, and other desirable traits, will be sought out increasingly in years to come.

Urban growth and development is most likely to occur in the South and West. *Sales & Marketing Management* magazine projects, for instance, in a continuation of already evident trends, that between 1978 and 1983 seventeen of the twenty-six fastest-growing cities will be in the South —eleven of which are in Florida—and another eight in the West. The top five locations for future growth, according to this market report, are Fort Myers-Cape Coral, Florida; Richland-Kennewick-Pasco, Washington; Brownsville-Harlingen-San Benito, Texas; Rapid City, South Dakota; and West Palm Beach-Boca Raton, Florida.

During the 1980s, as cities come to grips with their own survival, I see increasing difficultiy for the significant numbers of relatively helpless elderly on fixed incomes, as well as for the poor and the poorly educated of all ages. More enlightened and humane state and national social service and housing programs must fulfill a function the cities have assumed for too long. Within the cities, though, in the immediate years to come, increasingly sophisticated political power, so long directed otherwise, is likely to be exerted in favor of increasing the desirability and value of urban land.

SUBURBS IN TRANSITION

In years past, particularly between 1940 and 1970, older cities dramatically lost people, jobs, and investment, particularly to the nearby developing suburbs. As *The President's National Urban Policy Report for 1978* states, with a clarity that is both accurate and shameless: "The most powerful direct action that has contributed to metropolitan decentralization and central-city decline, the opening up of nonmetropolitan America, and the regional dispersal of population and economic activity has been the construction of the interstate highway system."

The big highways let people out of the cities, linking one place to another, suburban center to suburban center, suburban center to city. Residential builders sought the advantages of cheaper land, and buyers sought the lure of open space, trees, and a peaceful community. Industry became as footloose as residents, as it too moved out to highway locations. The growing suburbs offered acres for inexpensive storage, manufacturing, and parking.

But today, many suburbs are showing signs of decline. Over a decade ago, in a letter dated December 1, 1968, Charles M. Haar, then Louis D. Brandeis Professor of Law at Harvard University and chairman of the President's Task Force on Suburban Problems, wrote to former President Lyndon B. Johnson: "Our findings and proposals . . . make clear that beneath the popular image of the suburbs as middle class, happy and affluent, there is a quiet crisis that threatens the quality of life to be enjoyed by millions of Americans." In his 1974 introduction to the published report of the President's Task Force, Haar stated more specifically: "Growing crime, pollution, inadequate transportation, industrial ugliness, and rising costs of municipal services confront the suburbanite all over again with the very problems that motivated his migration from the urban core."

Indeed, much has changed in the forty years since the suburbs first began to develop. Perhaps most important, as a result of over three decades of rapid development, suburban land is now relatively scarce and thus relatively expensive. In fact, it is often more expensive than land within a nearby city. And there are other changes as well in the ways people are moving, job locations are shifting, and land is being used and reused in the metropolitan suburbs which signal a new situation.

Population Stagnation. One of the most fundamental indications of recent suburban faltering is a slowdown of population growth. No longer are the suburbs garnering new residents predominantly from the ailing cities and the emptying countryside, as they traditionally have. Instead, the "bulk of new immigrants to the suburbs are coming from equivalent suburbs," Dr. George Sternlieb, director of the Center for Urban Policy at Rutgers University, points out. This is supported by data from the Bureau of the Census, which indicates that 40–60 percent of all people moving into a suburban residence now come from suburbs nearby.

For the first time, the suburbs, for the most part, are generating their own settlers, people who move from one suburb to another in search of a job, in the wake of a corporate shift, in the forming and reforming of the family unit. This pattern of settlement and resettlement means that demand for a house in one suburb is created by someone with a house to sell in another.

Traffic and Commuters. In recent years, the number of suburban jobs has increased at a faster rate than resident population. Many of these jobs no longer result from an urban exodus but from expanding suburban businesses. As a result, suburbs have begun to sprout regional centers of business and industry and, in the process, have begun to look more like central cities.

New roads and highways, which first spurred suburban growth, now undermine the quality of suburban life. With the relocation of employment centers and retail stores to the suburb comes inevitable traffic congestion and air pollution. Today, over 60 percent of working suburban residents hold jobs in their own or in nearby suburbs. The result has been an increased volume of local traffic. Also, sharply increasing numbers of city residents now commute to work in the suburbs. In 1960, 10 percent of central-city residents worked in the suburbs; by 1970, this figure had increased by more than 50 percent. Today, in medium-sized cities, about 20 percent of all city residents commute to suburban jobs.

This tremendous growth of the metropolitan suburbs as employment centers rather than as exclusive residential enclaves marks a change that affects all aspects of social, environmental, and political life of the suburb.

Social Changes. In the wake of job relocations and new work opportunities, there has been an ever-increasing number of minorities who seek and have gained suburban residential status. In 1960, 2.4 million blacks lived in suburbs; in 1977, this number had grown to 4.6 million. In fact, between 1970 and 1975, black migration accounted for 7 percent of suburban population growth; in the following two years, black migration alone accounted for 14 percent of the net increase in the number of suburban residents. Geographically, the gains were widespread for these same five years. In the Atlanta suburbs, for example, black households increased by 132 percent; in the Washington suburbs, by 90 percent; in the Philadelphia suburbs, by 25 percent; in the surrounding Los Angeles-Long Beach suburban area, by 48 percent; in Chicago, by 46 percent; and in Boston, by 25 percent.

Most new black suburbanites, like their white predecessors, are young, educated, middle-class, and upwardly mobile. However, as housing patterns change and as a more diverse population gains entry into the suburbs, many observers, including David L. Birch, senior research scientist at the School of Architecture and Urban Planning, MIT, anticipate that:

[suburban] . . . communities will face demands for services which never surfaced during their existence as bedroom communities. Welfare case loads will rise. Bilingual teachers will be needed for schools. Crime prevention will become a far more serious matter. Providing utilities and roads and traffic control for specialized facilities and business complexes will strain local planning departments, as will the pressure for high-density residential contruction to keep housing costs down.

A Change in the Pattern of Development.   In many older suburbs, as a result of growing industry, changing socioeconomic population status, and increased retail shopping demand, pressure has intensified to rezone more and more property with good highway access to accommodate multifamily housing development, manufacturing endeavors, business offices, and shopping centers.

Residential developers find themselves faced with high land costs and land shortages, mounting construction costs, and fewer potential buyers with enough discretionary income. As they do so, requests for multiple-unit construction increase. Developers thus find themselves more frequently requesting permission to build multiple dwellings in neighborhoods once restricted to single-family houses. Between 1960 and 1970, multiple-family housing units in the suburban parts of metropolitan areas increased by more than 96 percent, whereas the number of single-family suburban houses built increased by only 17 percent. Since then, the tide has not changed.

The Result: Suburbs in Transition.   Some older, well-managed suburban communities are clear in their commitment to physical, economic, and social planning designed to resist haphazard change. Consequently, they are likely to retain sought-after qualities of a semi-rural environment, such as clean air, open space, high-quality public services, and good schools, benefits so long associated with a well-financed, well-managed suburb.

But other older metropolitan suburbs are in the first throes of drastic change, on the way to becoming nearly indistinguishable from nearby cities. This situation, according to many observers, including Louis Masotti, director of the Center for Urban Affairs at Northwestern University, makes " . . . the notion of moving to the suburbs . . . less appealing because suburbs today are a lot like the city without the advantages of the city."

A 1977 HUD survey of suburban residents supports Masotti's comment. Of the five "quality of life" indicators tested—schools, shopping, police protection, outdoor recreation, and medical care—suburbs enjoyed a lead over central cities and nonmetropolitan areas in only police protection and outdoor recreation.

A 1978 survey of the New York metropolitan area, furthermore, found that nearly 40 percent of the people who lived as far as away forty-five minutes from the city center said their own suburban area is becoming "more like a big city"; yet almost 50 percent of all Americans now live in suburbs.

Suburbs in the 1980s. In the next decade, most older suburbs will experience conflict and pressure for change, accompanied by a slowdown in their rate of growth. There will be dramatic changes in the way that much of the land is used, what kinds of land use will be in demand and, with these changes, a realignment of land values. Many suburban areas will become a setting where emphasis will be on rezoning, multifamily residences, retail business, and commercial development. These areas will be an arena for experienced, large-scale, well-financed real-estate developers who have the expertise, financial resources, and the commercial contacts necessary to carry out such large-scale land-development and building-construction projects. Conversely, most older metropolitan suburbs will be tricky waters for the amateur land speculator.

RURAL AMERICA AWAKENS

During the 1970s, the population growth rate in nonmetropolitan America surged. The latest available statistics, which chart the period 1970–1975, indicate that nearly 40 percent of all people who move now settle in nonmetropolitan areas. Calvin Beale of the U. S. Department of Agri-

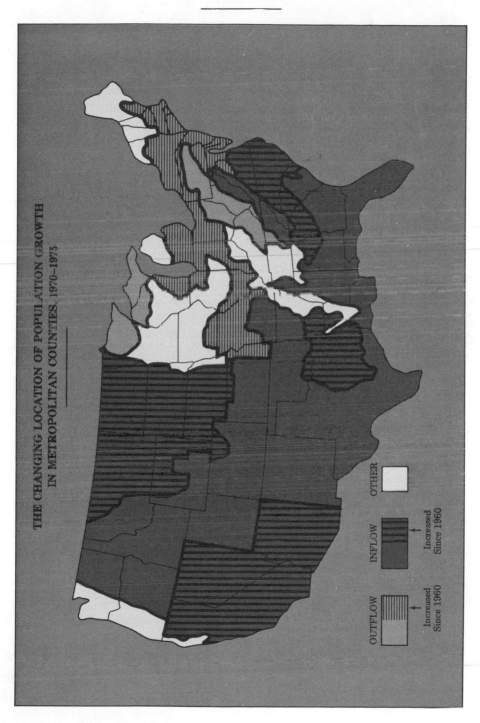

THE CHANGING LOCATION OF POPULATION GROWTH
IN METROPOLITAN COUNTIES 1970–1975

OUTFLOW   INFLOW   OTHER

Increased   Increased
Since 1960   Since 1960

culture, and one of the most perceptive and experienced demographers in America, points out with absolute justification: "The renewed growth of population in nonmetropolitan communities vies with the continued low level of the birth rate as the most significant demographic fact in the United States today." Gordon F. DeJong, former director of the Population Issues Research Office of Pennsylvania State University, and his colleague Ralph R. Sell noted recently: "Clearly an increasing number of Americans are choosing to move beyond the daily influence of metropolitan living toward those areas which have historically provided the population of our cities." This new migratory trend toward open land beyond the suburban fringe must be examined by anyone wishing to understand a most basic and generally unrecognized force in our society, one that will affect many aspects of land, power, and wealth in selected regions of the country for years to come.

The very new nature of nonmetropolitan population resurgence can be best understood by way of contrast. During the latter half of the nineteenth century, the great pull of people was toward the large metropolitan centers. Then between 1940 and 1970, people began moving out of the central cities and rural enclaves to adjacent suburbs within metropolitan counties.

As they moved, and as new households formed, people clustered mainly in metropolitan counties along the oceans, lakes, and the Gulf of Mexico. Between 1950 and 1970, an average of 75 percent of all counties in America sustained net out-migration. Of these, only 6 percent were either metropolitan core or suburban counties; the vast majority were rural counties, with the largest losses in the Great Plains, the Deep South, and Appalachia. Of the 24 percent of counties that gained at all from migration, the vast majority were suburban counties.

In stunning contrast to this is the impressive resurgence of nonmetropolitan population growth in America since 1970. During the 1970–1975 period, while population growth in all metropolitan areas, which includes the metropolitan suburbs, scored a 3.6 percent increase, the population growth rate of the nonmetropolitan areas soared at nearly double that figure, a rate of 6.3 percent.

How Did It Happen?   As the suburbs became more congested, some people left for farther out. Many who tire of urban life now envision nonmetropolitan America in much the same way that urbanites a decade or two ago envisioned the nearby metropolitan suburb. In addition, because of interstate highways and improved communication systems, huge areas of formerly inaccessible land have been opened up to development. Once-remote spots have become suitable for job centers, residential

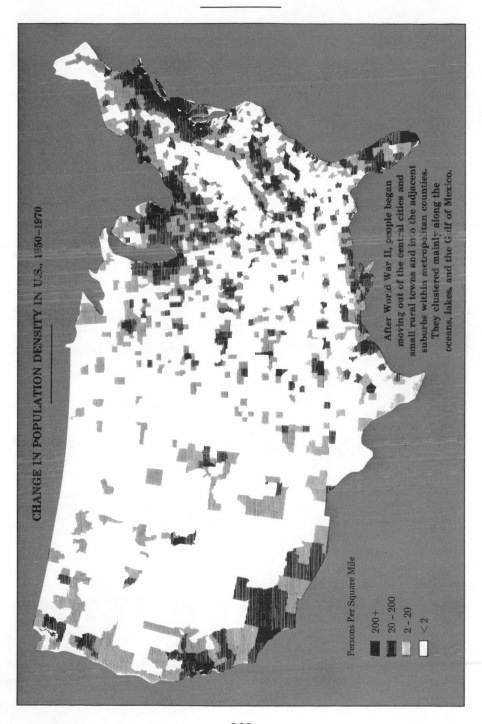

CHANGE IN POPULATION DENSITY IN U.S., 1850–1970

After World War II, people began
moving out of the central cities and
small rural towns and into the adjacent
suburbs within metropolitan counties.
They clustered mainly along the
oceans, lakes, and the Gulf of Mexico.

Persons Per Square Mile

200+
20 – 200
2 – 20
< 2

NET OUT-MIGRATION IN U.S., 1950-1970

Between 1950 and 1970, almost 75 percent of all counties in America sustained net out-migration. The vast majority were rural counties, with the largest losses in the Great Plains, the Deep South and Appalachia.

Migrants Per 1,000 Population

> -200

-200 - -100

-100 - -0

0+

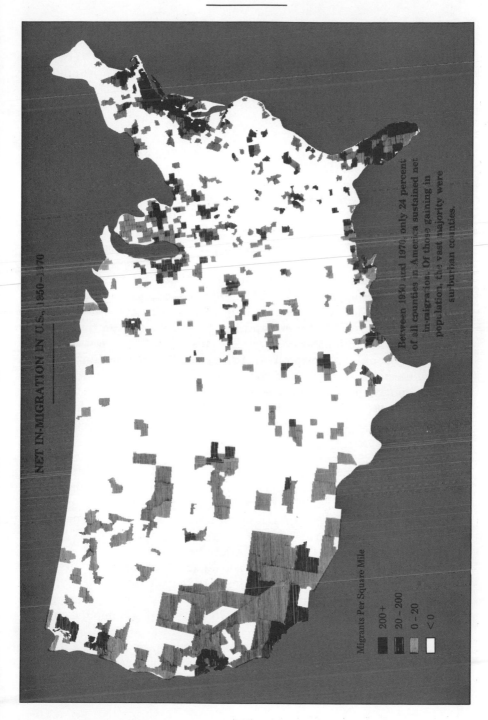

NET IN-MIGRATION IN U.S., 1950–1970

Between 1960 and 1970, only 24 percent of all counties in America sustained net in-migration. Of those gaining in population, the vast majority were suburban counties.

Migrants Per Square Mile

200+
20 – 200
0 – 20
< 0

buildings, and recreational development. Many industries, too, especially those involved in manufacturing, have moved farther out along the highways into nonmetropolitan areas. Countless institutions, such as research centers, corporate headquarters, and colleges and universities, have expanded into cheaper land in environmentally desirable locations beyond the city and its suburbs.

What Are the Attractions?   These days, people focus increasingly on "the quality of life." Housing is sought wherever it is perceived to be the best possible. Job location and easy access to work are no longer necessarily the dominant influence over residential location. As DeJong and Sell correctly point out in their 1977 study *Population Redistribution, Migration, and Residential Preferences,* people are increasingly willing to give up urban and suburban conveniences for the better physical living environment generally found in a rural community.

A larger proportion of the nation's population than ever before has now reached or is approaching retirement age. To this group, quieter, less expensive, and more convenient living arrangements available in nonmetropolitan areas hold strong appeal. Older people often move within the same region to a smaller town—for instance, to the less congested towns in Arizona and Florida, two of the nation's most popular Sun Belt retirement states, rather than to the more densely populated cities of Phoenix and Miami. Others are settling in such rural places as the Upper Great Lakes region, the Ozarks, the hill country of central Texas, the Sierra Nevada foothills in California, and coastal New England.

The Location of Nonmetropolitan Resurgence.   The nonmetropolitan areas, so long ignored, comprise an enormous portion of this country —over 85 percent of the country's total land area. This encompasses 85 percent of all counties, 30 percent of all townships, and 70 percent of all municipalities. Within this vast terrain there are over 2,000 cities or towns with more than 10,000 population.

As would be expected, most new settlement on nonmetropolitan land is located primarily in counties adjacent to metropolitan areas. Remote and sparsely settled counties, however, are also attracting more people than ever before. Between 1970 and 1975, the so-called nonadjacent nonmetropolitan counties (which typically have fewer than 10 people per square mile and no town larger than 2,500 residents) attracted four out of ten people moving to nonmetropolitan areas and were accumulating new population at an annual net rate of 8.9 people per thousand—a rate approximately 1.5 times the overall growth rate for the United States.

POPULATION AND NET MIGRATION
FOR U.S. METROPOLITAN AND NONMETROPOLITAN COUNTIES:[a]
1950–1960, 1960–1970, AND 1970–1975

	METROPOLITAN (1)	NONMETROPOLITAN TOTAL (2) =	ADJACENT (3) +	NOT ADJACENT (4)	TOTAL (1) + (2)
Population[b]					
1950	100,720	50,606	24,727	25,879	151,326
1960	127,185	52,126	26,107	26,019	179,311
1970	148,882	54,419	28,025	26,394	203,301
1975	155,044	58,008	30,064	27,944	213,051
Percent distribution of population					
1950	66.6	33.4	16.3	17.1	100.0
1960	70.9	29.1	14.6	14.5	100.0
1970	73.2	26.8	13.8	13.0	100.0
1975	72.8	27.2	14.1	13.1	100.0
Population change[b]					
1950–60	26,465	1,520	1,380	140	27,985
1960–70	21,697	2,293	1,918	379	23,990
1970–75	6,162	3,589	2,039	1,550	9,750
Percent distribution of population change					
1950–60	94.6	5.4	4.9	0.5	100.0
1960–70	90.4	9.6	8.0	1.6	100.0
1970–75	63.2	36.8	20.9	15.9	100.0
Net migration[b]					
1950–60	8,950	−6,302	−2,337	−3,965	2,648
1960–70	6,015	−2,850	−635	−2,215	3,165
1970–75	627	1,841	1,139	702	2,468
Number of counties	629	2,471	969	1,502	3,100

a. Counties are categorized according to their metropolitan status as of 1974. Alaska is represented by 24 Election Districts for which comparable census data could be obtained over the time period. The Independent Cities of Virginia were combined with adjacent counties.

b. Number in thousands.

367

| | METRO-POLITAN | NONMETROPOLITAN | | | |
		AVERAGE	ADJACENT	NOT ADJACENT	TOTAL
Annualized Population Change					
1950–60	23.2	3.0	5.4	0.5	16.9
1960–70	15.7	4.3	7.1	1.4	12.5
1970–75	7.7	12.2	13.4	10.9	8.9
Annualized Net Migration Rates					
1950–60	7.9	−12.3	−9.2	−15.3	1.6
1960–70	4.4	−5.3	−2.3	−8.5	1.7
1970–75	0.8	6.2	7.5	4.9	2.3

**ANNUALIZED U.S. POPULATION CHANGE
AND NET MIGRATION RATES (PER 1,000)
BY METROPOLITAN STATUS AND ADJACENCY STATUS:
1950–1960, 1960–1970, AND 1970–1975**

Nonmetropolitan growth is a nationwide phenomenon. In every region except the South, 1970–1975 net migration and population increases were greater for nonmetropolitan areas than for metropolitan areas. In the South, where metropolitan areas are booming, there is nevertheless selective, strong nonmetropolitan growth.

Calvin Beale has defined and mapped twenty-six contiguous U.S. subregions by grouping together areas reasonably similar in economy, history, physical setting, and settlement patterns. (See pages 370–71.) This organization of the continent according to economic subregions highlights the specific location and relative strength of nonmetropolitan growth between 1950 and 1975. While the western regions and the Florida peninsula reveal the highest growth rates, other subregions—the Southern Interior Uplands (region 10) and East Texas and Adjoining Coastal Plain areas (region 19)—present a very dramatic picture of nonmetropolitan resurgence within the past decade as well. The Ozark-Ouachita Uplands (region 20) witnessed extensive development of its recreational and retirement facilities between 1970 and 1975, as did the Upper Great Lakes area (region 6) of the north-central region. In the Northeast, the Northern New England-St. Lawrence area (region 1) has likewise experienced development of recreational facilities, increased resort-related activities, and second-home development—and consequently an upward surge in nonmetropolitan population.

All in all, it is estimated that during the 1970s, rural counties in the United States gained more than 2 million more people by migration than were lost by emigration to the cities and suburbs. This strong, positive pull of rural America, still not widely recognized, is based on a number of important new trends which are drawing people toward the less populated countryside. Increased leisure time and demand for recreational facilities are contributing factors, as is the ability of increasing numbers of retired people to seek out locales relatively free of crime, where the air is cleaner, where leisure time is shared collectively by others in the same age bracket, and where living costs are lower. Mining for precious minerals and metals, for coal and, above all, for oil and gas has resumed in long-abandoned areas and fans out into new rural locales. At the same time, the decline in agricultural employment has nearly stopped, mechanization of the American farm has slowed, and world demand for America's agricultural products has increased.

Another stimulant to population increases in rural areas has been the growth of service, construction, and retail-trade jobs in the booming suburbs during the 1960s and 1970s. By leapfrogging into nonmetropolitan towns, residents live in rural America and commute to work in the metropolitan suburbs. Recently, there has been noticeable growth in jobs in these same fields in nonmetropolitan areas as well.

The search for a better "quality of life" has increasingly prompted relocation decisions. Some people are willing to sacrifice a higher city salary to live in a simpler place, having decided that cuts in their income are more than compensated for by the pleasures of existence in a remote, less costly, nonmetropolitan community.

Nonmetropolitan Land Values in the Future: Caution Ahead for Most Areas. There is a lot of land out there; and while a shifting trend of migration onto that land is of substantial interest, it will hardly move the United States back into a pattern of scattered settlement, as in an agrarian society.

In fact, because of the already tremendous concentration of people in metropolitan areas, a continuation of the trend of migration to nonmetropolitan areas over the next twenty-five years would have very little impact on the relative distribution of the United States population. Such a continuation might lower the population of metropolitan areas by the year 2000 from a current level of 73 percent of the population to perhaps 70 percent. Because the actual number of people involved in nonmet-

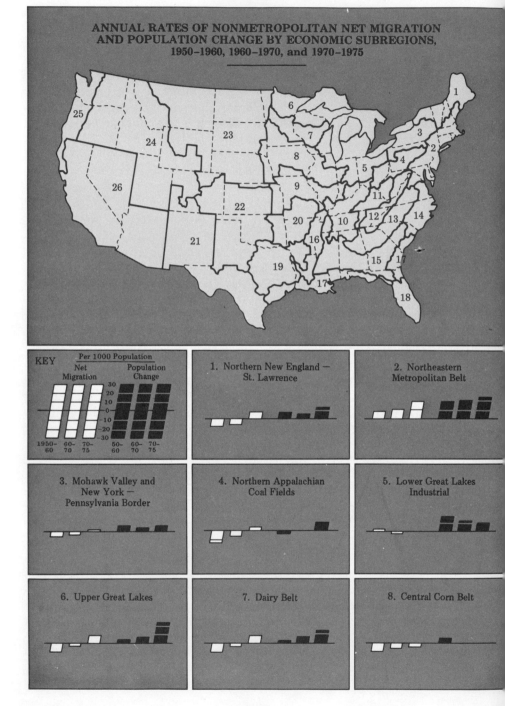

ANNUAL RATES OF NONMETROPOLITAN NET MIGRATION
AND POPULATION CHANGE BY ECONOMIC SUBREGIONS,
1950–1960, 1960–1970, and 1970–1975

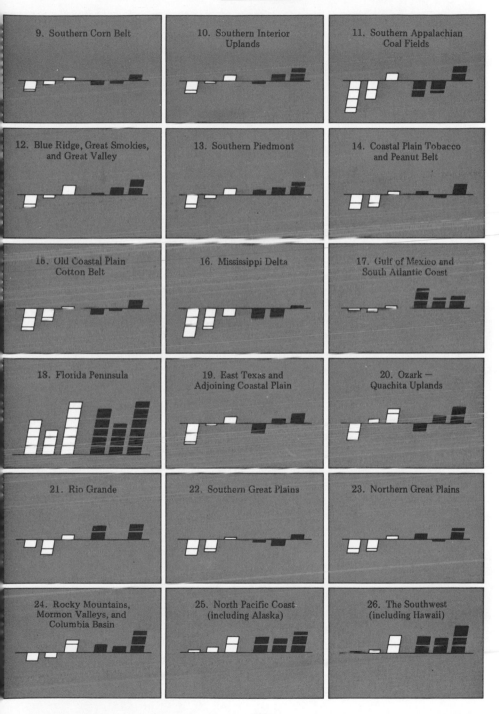

ropolitan migration is relatively small, the location of land value changes promoted by this phenomenon will be highly selective.

The life line of nonmetropolitan America remains the interstate highway. This means that future availability and price of fuel are crucial to further rural development. Settlement is already too dispersed in most nonmetropolitan areas for transit to satisfy work, recreational, and commercial requirements. If we become a country in which energy is so costly and so scarce that living patterns are dramatically influenced, the growth of many nonmetropolitan areas will be curtailed. Furthermore, if because of poor growth management nonmetropolitan areas lose those qualities that draw people to them in the first place—attractive open space, freedom from pollution, negligible crime—their appeal will markedly decrease.

Nonetheless, it is likely that in the decade to come, certain parts of nonmetropolitan America may turn out to be the only areas of the country to experience substantial population growth. Demand for well-located and especially attractive land in numerous nonmetropolitan counties has already surged. Geographical areas with scenic qualities or fine recreational resources will continue to experience dramatic increases in land demand and price. Nonmetropolitan places where older people may retire comfortably will also continue to attract attention. Small towns in temperate climates not far from top-quality cultural and medical facilities will find a surging demand for land and housing.

Most people who move to nonmetropolitan locations are neither able nor inclined to live in a remote valley or on an isolated farm. Rather, they wish to settle near or within small cities and towns within rural counties. Public-opinion polls and relocation statistics alike clearly indicate that when people retire, change their lifestyle, or begin a new job, new residents in nonmetropolitan areas tend to prefer to live within communities not out on the open land. In resort locations near congested cities, of course, more remote areas will remain in demand and be accorded a premium by those who seek certain amenities from the land, from vistas, from isolation. This distinction between the residential location the permanent resident seeks and that of the seasonal resident or visitor is of great importance. It determines the location of optimum demand for land and real estate in different types of nonmetropolitan communities, and the demand from different types of residents within the same community.

Assuming that we avoid political and economic chaos in the next decade, the opportunity for sharply increasing land values in selected spots in nonmetropolitan America could not be better. There will likely be continuing out migration from the metropolitan suburbs, the present residential base of almost half the American population. Many who leave, young and old alike, will seek a location outside the cities; they will move farther out into the countryside, most probably into small towns in non-metropolitan areas.

Nonmetropolitan areas where land values are likely to rise most significantly in years to come are the limited number of places in America which possess all or at least several of the following characteristics: outstanding scenic or natural land quality; a functional rail or bus service; a completed highway system linked to regional cities; a location that is not remote from institutional centers, especially hospitals, centers of higher education and cultural facilities; and a local political system in which growth and land development are not allowed to occur in such a way as to destroy physical and environmental qualities, which attract newcomers in the first place.

What is required to sustain the appeal of such areas is a vision of what is sought, as well as sympathetic and sophisticated link between political power, public awareness, and the efforts of private citizens who control local resources and wealth. This takes strong public and private leadership and sound land-use planning. Together, these constitute primordial forces in American culture which will determine how the land is used and the future of each community.

THE PEOPLE FACTOR:
CHANGE BRINGS OPPORTUNITY

In the years ahead, then, I believe the stage is set for significant change in all three predominant physical locales of American life —the cities, metropolitan suburbs, and nonmetropolitan areas. Migration trends caused by new and evolving economic, social, and demographic currents, as well as by shifting personal preferences, all flow together. These constitute a reorganization—hardly perceptible day by day—but nevertheless of fundamental significance when added up at the end of a decade. This reorganization brings with it selected changes in demand for both raw land and for redevelopment of land already in use. There is neither mystery nor magic in any of this. The most basic realities of human behavior are involved. The most reasonable responses by large groups of people to changing conditions in America are involved. It is all, finally, imprinted on the land.

TWELVE

LAND
SPECULATION

Speculation at its most elevated level has to do with man testing his own insight and judgment, testing his capacity as a thinker. Speculation is man testing his vision against the ultimate nature of reality. For the land speculator, the ultimate nature of reality is a profit or loss.

Speculative scientists and intellectuals, such as Kepler, Newton, Einstein, and Fuller, in the act of speculation, subject their most precious and personal resource to public scrutiny. This resource, in the case of the inquisitive mind, is intellect and imagination. The land speculator also commits his most precious resource: his money backed by his judgment.

The word "speculation" has its own curious and perhaps revelatory life in English usage. Until the late eighteenth century, its meaning related to the faculty or power of seeing, of insight, of vision, especially a vision determined by inquiry and intelligence, as opposed to mystical insight. It was not until the late eighteenth century, and specifically the 1770s, as America gained independence, that the term "speculation" began to describe the act of engaging in any business enterprise or transaction of a venturesome or risky nature that offered the chance of great or unusual gain.

It cannot be surprising that the very presence of America, a land of 2.3 billion acres, fired an insistent drive in men possessed with speculative energy and vision. The American continent of 3.6 million square miles is almost as large as all of Europe, which totals 3.7 million square miles. Its variety of terrain, forests and mineral wealth, abundance of water, and generally hospitable climate, increasingly described and reported beginning in the 1500s, indicated a vastness, a richness, and an opportunity for land speculation that stirred the imagination of many all over the world. As the distinguished historian Frederick Jackson Turner wrote in 1893:

Since the days when the fleet of Columbus sailed into the waters of the New World, America has been another name for opportunity, and the people of the United States have taken their tone from the incessant expansion which has not only been open but has even been forced upon them. . . .

It was a land with no dominating and adequately armed possessor; a land not burdened by a long history of government, regulation, feudalism, protected zones, or established private rights. A land, it is no wonder, that quickly became subject to so many levels of speculative endeavor that they may be said to characterize the foundation of this country. It was a land and a promise so tempting, so new, that it may, in fact, have given the older meaning of the term "speculation" a brand-new connotation.

The history of America is inextricably tied to the fact, the concept, the privilege and the protected right of speculation. The vast reaches of the original forty-eight states were settled through publicly condoned programs which encouraged all manner and form of speculation: homesteading, railroad land grants, conveyed water rights, tax-exemption programs.

Some of America's most revered leaders were among its earliest big-time land speculators, including Thomas Jefferson, architect-philosopher-planner; and George Washington, a hard-driving surveyor. Together, with the assistance of Andrew Ellicott, a professional surveyor of high reputation, and Major Pierre Charles L'Enfant, architect, surveyor, and engineer, the precise site of Washington, D. C., as the nation's capital was selected by them in relative secrecy so as to keep land prices down. By early 1791, word of the exact site got around; and soon afterwards, the owners of the land at the confluence of the Potomac and Anacostia rivers began to evidence a reluctance to sell—they were holding out for higher prices. President Washington, a most practical and experienced man, came down to Georgetown and called together all the owners of land upon which he expected to establish the federal capital, a domain of between 3,000 and 5,000 acres. In one evening, he devised a plan that would limit the costs to the federal government and still allow the proprietors an enormous speculative benefit.

Afterward, Washington reported enthusiastically to Jefferson:

The terms . . . are that all the land from Rockcreek along the river to the eastern-branch and so upwards to or above the ferry including a breadth of about a mile and a half, the whole containing from three to five thousand acres, is ceded to the public, on condition that, when the whole shall be surveyed and laid off as a city (which Major L'Enfant is now directed to do), the present Proprietors shall retain every other lot, and for such part of the land as may be taken for public use . . . they shall be allowed at the rate of twenty-five pounds per acre. . . . No compensation is to be made for the ground that may be occupied as streets or alleys.

Then, to finance the purchase of the public lands from the proprietors, and the subsequent development of Washington, the federal government got into the business of selling lots—some 15,000 of them—in competition with the original landowners, who owned the other half of the new capital

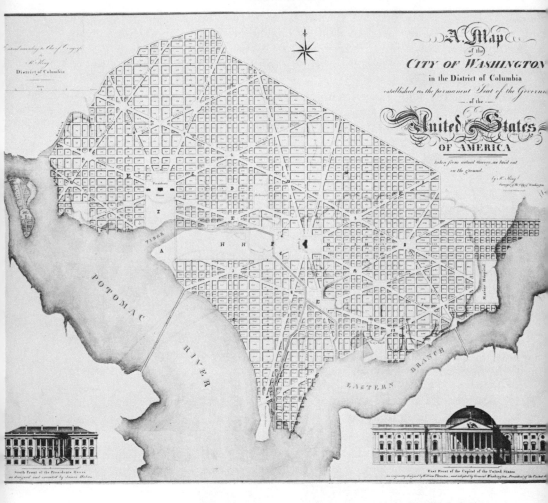

**SURVEY AND PROPOSED LAYOUT OF WASHINGTON, D.C.,
BY ROBERT KING, BASED ON PLANS
BY L'ENFANT AND ELLICOTT, 1818**

The history of America is inextricably tied to the fact, the concept, the
privilege, and the protected right of land speculation. Some of America's
founding fathers in fact were among the earliest big-time speculators.
Thomas Jefferson and George Washington selected the site of the nation's
new capital, working out a plan to hold down the cost of land acquisition
to the federal government. Landowners were induced to give up half the
land, maintaining title to every other lot as compensation based on future
speculative gain. This survey of Washington, D.C., is in effect a
promotional broadside with lots numbered for sale.

378

city. The Ellicott Plan for Washington of 1792 and its subsequent refinements, which maintain L'Enfant's basic design as revised by Thomas Jefferson, are, among other things, each a sales broadside, lots numbered for identification and sale. As the Duke de La Rochefoucauld observed eight years later when he visited Washington:

In America, where, more than in any other country in the world, a desire for wealth is the prevailing passion, there are few schemes which are not made the means of extensive speculations; and that of erecting the Federal City presented irresistible temptations which were not in fact neglected.

Today, the memory and speculative aspirations which forwarded settlements and fortunes across the continent a hundred years ago and more re-emerge in the ongoing deliberations about the future of the land in Alaska. The land mass of Alaska is 375 million acres, one-fifth the size of the continental United States. Over half of that land is now owned by the federal government and may be permanently regulated by federal legislation. The battle over the use and control of these 170 million acres is fierce.* The game is for high stakes. Those who seek the right to commercial and economic development of the government-owned land envision a scenario little changed from the notorious exploitation of the land by vested commercial interests that occurred throughout most of the history of federal management of land in America. Those who seek conservation of the land, wilderness, wildlife, and recreational areas envision what they consider to be the only route to a better future.

The vision of the preservationist and the conservationist is new to this nation; it is also contrary to the collective memory of the people, for it seeks to protect vast domains of land from economic exploitation and therefore from speculation. Indeed, as Tom Snapp, editor of the prominent Fairbanks *All-Alaska Weekly,* has bitterly remarked, "We were supposed to be taken in as a state on an equal basis. . . . But we're not going to be allowed to develop the way other states develop their resources. We're going to be nipped in the bud. . . . It's reneging on the promises of statehood, and I don't believe the people would have voted statehood if they had known this was going to happen."

So there it is, the American Dream. Not just the right to earn a living, to travel freely, to enjoy our cherished freedoms. No. A large part of the reason to become a part of the nation is, on the one hand, to be granted the privileges and protection offered by American legal codes and massive defense apparatus, and, on the other, to enter into a social and economic sphere of influence which, through law and custom, encourages land speculation.

*See pages 455–457 for additional information.

LAND SPECULATION
VS. SPECULATION IN STOCKS
AND COMMODITIES

Speculation in land has always been singled out by economic and political egalitarians, by labor advocates, and by social utopians as a venal, even sinful, activity. Some years ago, Professor John Henry Denton, head of real-estate studies at the University of Arizona, echoed a source of particular disdain for land speculation:

Unlike speculation in commodity futures or common stocks, land speculation does not support a market or provide a stimulus to production. In fact, it has just the opposite effect. It destroys the marketability of large areas of land by pricing them out of reach of immediate users. It deprives our communities of many facilities needed for good living (such as parks and playgrounds) by driving the price of land beyond what communities can afford. It limits competition by holding a large part of the land supply off the current market. It channels capital funds away from productive investment into sterile adventures and may be responsible for the present-day dearth of private risk capital.

And, indeed, in a number of ways, the activity of land speculation is unlike more traditional speculation in commodity futures or common stocks, activities sometimes described as "investing." Land speculation, for instance, does not occur within the confines of a regulated market. Nor does even the initial transaction of sale generally occur for a purpose other than to turn a profit. By way of contrast, the initial transaction in either the commodities or securities markets is often unrelated to earning speculative profit. For example, the market in commodity futures enables a corn or cotton grower to hedge his crop production against cataclysmic price changes; that is, he may sell the corn for future delivery on the commodity futures market to a buyer who will use the corn. He is not, in a sense, speculating; he is merely selling corn that is growing in his field. Securities markets, as another example, enable large corporations to issue and sell common stock or bonds to raise capital that is needed for business operations or expansion. The corporation is not speculating; it is selling a share of ownership in exchange for working capital. The farmer and the corporation, then, benefit from a centralized market in the orderly pursuit of their individual businesses. After the first sale by the farmer or the corporation, however, most transactions which follow are generally speculative exhcanges. Buyers and sellers hope to profit on the change in value of the commodity contract or on the rise in the price of the stock share.

There are, nevertheless, several positive contributions made through a market for land based on speculation. The speculative purchaser enables a market to exist. Demand for land enables a seller to dispose of real property, and thereby to stop paying taxes on it and to convert the land into liquid funds. Just as in the commodities business or the securities market, without the speculative purchaser very often there would be no buyer at all.

Indeed, after the initial commodity, stock, or bond transaction, the land speculator is engaged in an activity not so very different from that of any other speculator, although he still stands alone, accused of profitting from unearned increments, that is, values not created by his own labor or effort. Is his objective really any different from that of millions of individuals, pension funds, trusts, and nonprofit organizations which hold common stocks? There is no need to belabor the parallels between the passive role and profit expectation of the land speculator and those of the investor in securities. In neither case are the increments earned as a consequence of the labor or additional investment of the beneficiary; and in both cases, they remain untaxed prior to sale.

There are, nevertheless, substantial differences between the average common-stock holding and the average land holding. To begin with, the common-stock investor is often paid an annual share of profits. This income offsets the overall cost of carrying the investment. The landholder, on the other hand, must pay annual taxes and other expenses. Through the mechanism of a centralized securities market, the common-stock investor is generally able to find a ready buyer for his securities. This means that his investment is liquid and marketable—a very significant difference from land, which may be offered for sale at a reasonable price for months or years before a buyer is found.

The common-stock certificate, like the deed to land, may be pledged as collateral to secure a loan. However, in most instances, it is easier to obtain the loan with securities than with land because of the certain value and the ease of liquidation of stocks and bonds. And a higher percent of the total value will be loaned against good-quality listed common stock than against good-quality land. Thus, in a sense, securities have a greater inherent value as a capital asset. With stock ownership, you know what you have: a piece of paper that guarantees your proportionate interest in a specific business. With raw land, however, you may hold an unproductive asset whose future usefulness is uncertain.

There are basic differences, as well, imparted by the fixed location of land and its limited alternative uses. External events will surely influence the destiny of a business, as they will the destiny of the land holding. However, prudent and inventive management of a business is likely to overcome most adverse events, such as new competition or shift in types of market demand. With land, flexibility in management is drastically reduced. No matter how prudent or inventive the management of inert land, it is sometimes exceedingly difficult to counter adverse local regulation or unfortunate local, regional, or national social, political, and economic trends. In these respécts, ownership of a share in an on-going business is not at all like owning a parcel of land.

Wherever speculation occurs—in land, stocks, or commodities—prices tend to rise, values tend to inflate, as each successive owner seeks to profit. However, it is possible to sell short in securities and commodities transactions; that is, speculators can sell shares of corporations or commodities contracts which they in fact do not own. Their expectation is that prices will decline before a purchase is made, which will produce a profit in their speculative short sale. There is no such mechanism in land speculation, for there is no centralized marketplace or regulated land contract. The owner must possess the land to sell it, or risk a jail sentence when convicted of fraud.

An even more decisive distinction between land speculation and other forms of speculation exists. Commodity prices, stock prices, prices of art, and even the price of gold, diamonds, and furniture may be forced upward by speculation. But the activity of speculation in these valued assets does not generally change the inherent appearance or use of the valued object. Indeed, works or art, jewelry, and furniture are particularly cherished in their original and unaltered condition so as to assure maximum value.

Speculation in land, however, eventually *changes* for all time the basic appearance, character, and use of the land itself. As it is bid up in price, it is also eventually forced into some form of development. As its value is pushed upward through speculative exchanges, it goes through inexorable stages of economically feasible uses. This cycle begins with natural land, which may have no inherent economic value. Cultivated and forest lands, on the other hand, do have an economic value, one based on the annual earning potential of the product they produce. Even higher values may be assigned to land that can be used for residential housing, and then on upward for commercial and industrial property. At some point on this ascending scale, the land will be profitable only if developed. At that point it is converted, transformed in use, appearance, and purpose.

Speculation may be said to send property through a predictable cycle of life. Once it begins, the force is both relentless and powerful. Speculation, like the seasons, works constantly to modify the land. But unlike the inexorable changes brought about by the seasons, those effected by speculation are at first invisible and later not easily or commonly or naturally reversed.

LAND SPECULATION AND DEVELOPMENT: A THREE-STAGE CYCLE

Land, on its way to being developed, goes through three stages, each conducted as part of a different type of business. The first stage is carried out by the land speculator, whose intention is to purchase land and hold it for profit. He does not expect to add value through his own initiative, labor, or additional investment. Nor does he intend to hold the land perpetually or to use it indefinitely as a productive agricultural resource or forest or open space. Very often, he prefers to be "invisible," an unknown participant hidden behind a joint venture or a protective corporate shield. Land speculation has a bad name. Yet executives, doctors, lawyers, statesmen, even presidents of the United States participate.

The unflattering term "land processor" or "land packager" refers to the individual or organization that handles the second stage of the land business. The land processor buys raw land, often from a land speculator, and then "packages" it for development. He obtains a development plan, its approval, and perhaps even permission for rezoning. He then holds the land for sale, ready to develop. This operation takes skill and financial resources. In recent years, the increasing level of legal and environmental sophistication needed to obtain planning and development approval complicates this operation. Ever larger funds are necessary to hold and carry land through the lengthy process. Oil companies with large cash flows, public corporations not otherwise in the real-estate business, utility companies, insurance companies and pension funds are becoming the big land processors and speculators. They have the financial clout and management strength to earn a good return from holding land and packaging it for development. Notice that the land packager, like the speculator, does not touch the land itself.

Finally comes the land developer, the most publicized of the three. His intention is to increase property value as quickly as possible through land development, and to derive profits from the sale of developed land and perhaps from buildings constructed upon it. The developer is anxious to minimize the inactive period, when the land is not being transformed. Of the three, only the land developer makes a profit by building and by selling improved real estate.

While all three roles are different, they often merge in a single person or organization, or in a sequence of interrelated people or organizations. Some of the largest corporations in America—including Gulf Oil, Exxon, and International Telephone and Telegraph—are now active in one, two, or all three of these roles. Joining speculators in open-land or large-scale development schemes are the managers of pension funds, investment trusts, banks and brokerage houses, and even the largest foundation in America, the Ford Foundation. Indeed, between 1970 and 1977, in its role as land speculator and investor in land packaging and development schemes, the Ford Foundation lost over $40 million. During the 1970s, many corporations were big losers as well: American Standard lost over $30 million, and Boise Cascade more than $200 million. As Clayton Pritchette, vice president of Landauer Associates, a major real-estate

A GHOST GOLD-MINING TOWN,
EUREKA, COLORADO, SEPTEMBER 1940

Since World War II, land speculation has created more *individual* millionaires than any other form of business or investment in America. Just as people once flocked to the mountains to pan for gold, today many scatter to the countryside to buy land.

consulting firm, suggested recently to Paul Sturm of *Forbes,* "Land development simply doesn't fit the corporate framework. . . . Important decisions must be made on a day-to-day basis at a local level, and that just isn't compatible with the accountability that public companies require."

Each of these aspects of the land business, from speculation to packaging to development, has its own pitfalls. At every step along the way increasing amounts of invested capital, specialized knowledge, and active involvement and management are essential. Consequently, it is land speculation at the first stage that attracts most individuals. The hope is to profit from a minimum of specialized knowledge and invested capital, with the exertion of a minimum of management time devoted to the enterprise.

And, indeed, over the years speculating in land has created more individual millionaires than any other form of business or investment in America. Marshall Field, the celebrated retail merchant, made most of his first $100 million outside the store by speculating in land. Inexperienced people in increasing numbers seem to believe with unwavering vehemence in Field's famous dictum that "land is not just a good way to make money; it is the only way to make money." People scatter to the countryside to speculate in land, as they once did to pan gold. Second-home buyers are often land speculators in disguise, as are many farmers, concerned environmentalists, managed-forest owners, golf-course operators, and so many others who use land as an interim holding device with a speculative eye toward the future.

LAND VS. IMPROVED REAL ESTATE: THE MISUNDERSTOOD DISTINCTIONS

"What kind of real-estate investment are you looking for?" the broker asks the young couple. Far too often their reply is, "Oh, either a piece of attractive land that we could later resell at a profit or where we might build a house someday, or a little house that we can rent out and maybe use off-season." These amateur speculators fail to make the crucial distinction between land on the one hand and improved property on the other. They lump the two together; both become real estate, a good investment. But this is a fatal connection to make, and a critically incorrect one.

Consider some of the major distinctions between the two. Unlike a building, land may not be served by available utilities, such as electric service and water, and it may have no road access. Its current zoning designation may be changed by local law, and environmental regulations may even forbid building in the future. What's more, in most instances, there is no way to use the land economically so that it produces a stream of positive income, and it is often difficult to borrow money against it.

Unlike a building, land does not even possess salvage value. In fact, many who buy land discover that when it comes time to sell, the deed they own is of little value, particularly when buyers are scarce. What happens when you do want to dispose of your land but cannot? The hapless speculator then encounters a reverse twist. What once appeared to be an asset is no longer. Indeed, it becomes a most insistent liability. The money paid for the land is tied up or lost. The income that cash committed to the land could have been generating for its owner is lost as well. Moreover, there are the continuing costs of perhaps a land mortgage, and certainly property taxes.

Annual carrying costs associated with a valueless land holding actually impute a potential negative value to it. The capital investment is wiped out and the land becomes worth less than nothing. In fact, its owner would be better off without it. In such a situation, the owner may abandon the land entirely by not paying taxes. The property is then seized for unpaid taxes and either reverts to the government or is purchased for a bargain price at auction by another speculator who is willing to settle up back taxes and begin to pay present ones. The new buyer has new expectations; he may also have ideas how to use the land, and he has brought it at a knockdown low price.

This specter of valueless real estate may sound farfetched to some, but it shouldn't. One need only remember, in very recent times, the great land busts of Florida and the Southwest.

LAND IS A SPECULATION, AND SOMETIMES A VERY PROFITABLE ONE

Buying land and dealing in raw land, then, is a highly speculative enterprise. I like the definition of "speculation" Howard J. Ruff offers in *How To Prosper During the Coming Bad Years:*

You need to understand the difference between speculation and investment. There are elements of both in most real-estate purchases, but basically, you can draw the line between them by defining an investment as something that returns sufficient income to meet all of the expenses and give you a spendable return. A speculation generally does not produce income and you are betting solely on the rise in price. . . .

Land speculation offers all the possibilities for a thrilling ride up the roller coaster to fast wealth accumulation—if in your purchase you are right and maybe even a bit lucky. Like commodity options, natural gas exploration, and currency speculation, land purchased can be highly leveraged with relatively little cash needed to put you in possession of a large amount of valuable terrain. When things break just right, these committed funds can indeed produce lifetime windfall profits. Land outside of Miami or Los Angeles or Chicago, for instance, bought at the right time in, say, 1950 for less than $2,000 cash could have been resold less than fifteen years later for over $500,000, and a decade after that for over $1.5 million. But timing has to be right, location right on the mark, and financing arrangements carefully tailored.

One immense category of American land—farmland—of which there is over 400 million acres, some located in nearly every state of the union, has itself proven to be a superior speculation, surely one that has kept its owner ahead of inflation. The average acre of farmland during the last several years increased in value at an annual rate of 15–20 percent. When these rates are compounded, increase upon former increase, values double every four to five years. And this is only the average. Some areas, such as Illinois, Iowa, and Indiana, have sustained farmland land-value increases during the 1970s as high as 25–35 percent in given years, especially when commodity prices have risen. Should these rates of increase continue, the $1,000 acre of American farmland today will be worth over $30,000 by the year 2000.

Another highly profitable type of land speculation has been undeveloped or agricultural acreage positioned for conversion to urbanized uses. When land is successfully converted—or even planned and approved for conversion, its value soars, so long as there is demand. Conversion to residential status is the most common change in land use. Wherever there is a market for new housing, it has proven a speculative bonanza.

In a typical conversion of farmland into house sites, who profits and by approximately how much? Let us say that a farmer sells his property to a speculator, who packages the land; he then sells it to a housing developer. As illustrated in the diagram on the next page, today the agricultural land might have a value as tilled farmland of $600 per acre. Induced to give up his farm, the farmer sells out to the speculator at, let us assume, $2,600 per acre. The speculator then spends a little money on planning and market studies, after which he finds a housing developer willing to pay $6,000 per acre. Costs of roads and utilities and permits and financing add up to another $12,000 per acre; the housing developer then sells the 1-acre lot for $20,000.

In this generalized example of costs and transactions associated with the conversion of undeveloped land into a residential lot, it is the farmer who realizes the largest absolute gain above the active farm value of the land. His profit is more than 300 percent. But then, of course, he has given up a part of his business as well. Furthermore, he may have owned that land for many years and worked hard to earn a living from it. On the

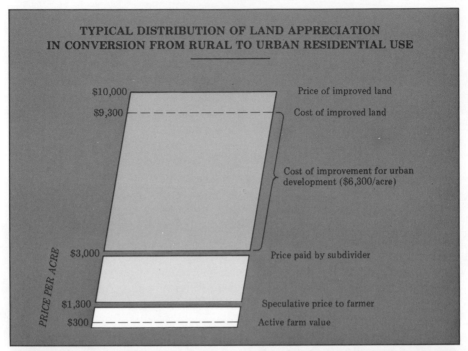

TYPICAL DISTRIBUTION OF LAND APPRECIATION IN CONVERSION FROM RURAL TO URBAN RESIDENTIAL USE

PRICE PER ACRE

$10,000 — Price of improved land

$9,300 — Cost of improved land

Cost of improvement for urban development ($6,300/acre)

$3,000 — Price paid by subdivider

$1,300 — Speculative price to farmer

$300 — Active farm value

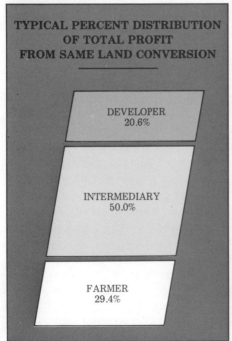

TYPICAL PERCENT DISTRIBUTION OF TOTAL PROFIT FROM SAME LAND CONVERSION

DEVELOPER 20.6%

INTERMEDIARY 50.0%

FARMER 29.4%

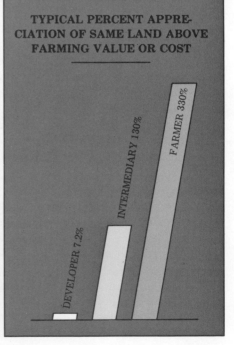

TYPICAL PERCENT APPRECIATION OF SAME LAND ABOVE FARMING VALUE OR COST

DEVELOPER 7.2%

INTERMEDIARY 130%

FARMER 330%

other hand, the speculator, the intermediary in the transaction, may hold the property for only a short while, yet his profit exceeds 100 percent. The land developer—that fellow accused by many in the community of destroying the natural environment for his own selfish ends—may also earn a tidy profit from building houses, but his profit margin on the land is by far the lowest—in our model, just over 10 percent. In addition, he has had to spend $12,000 per lot, in cash or in borrowed funds, to convert the land from raw acreage into an approved housing subdivision.

Advantages of Land as a Speculation.   Land has certain advantages, then, for a speculator. Quite often, it can be bought with little cash, so long as the buyer is willing to assume a relatively large proportion of debt. This feature of seller financing, as will be discussed in some detail later on, provides leverage for the speculator. It is leverage, when all is said and done, that yields a high return of dollar invested for dollar received (cash on cash) at the end of the speculation, if it is successful. Leverage, of course, works both ways. If the investment is unsuccessful, losses will also be magnified.

Second, the land speculator, like the supermarket patron, has a variety of land types to choose from. There is land out there to fit every dream and every budget. Land can be bought in almost any metropolitan area or nonmetropolitan county for less than $600 an acre and up—about the cost of one small gold Kugeraand.

Another advantage is that land, once purchased, is among the easiest speculations of all to manage. Little is required of the owner except paying annual property tax and paying off the mortgage. No business need exist. No patrons need be involved. Maintenance and repair tend to be nominal, certainly as compared to any other form of real estate.

Land also provides a tax advantage, though a limited one compared to most real estate. Like other capital transactions, once sold, the speculative investment is likely to be accorded favorable capital-gains treatment by the Internal Revenue Service, provided the owner is not a "dealer" and has remained a passive possessor for more than one year. With today's tax regulations, this means that some 60 percent of the profits survive untaxed. Losses, if they occur, can be used to offset other types of profit, and mortgage interest and real-estate taxes are both deductible expenses.

But none of these general advantages to land speculation should be misunderstood as elements that, if combined, create an easy, guaranteed, trail of profit. Indeed, in my view, land speculation is one of the most specialized and potentially treacherous ways to deploy venture capital. I suggest, at this point, that if you are considering speculating in land, you review Chapter One, "The Mystique of Land as a Prime Investment." Pay

389

particular attention to the four commonly held misconceptions which I discuss. To refresh your memory, these *misconceptions* are:

1. Land, like improved real estate, has innate value.
2. As in the past, continued demand for land can be expected almost everywhere from a rapidly growing and restless population.
3. There is a shortage of land in America.
4. As in the past, new roads and highways will make today's remote land accessible and therefore valuable.

I want now to examine in detail five special land-speculation pitfalls which present especially hazardous traps to the amateur land speculator. Then, with these in mind, I will outline at the end of this chapter what the experienced land speculator looks for.

LAND SPECULATION PITFALLS

Speculation in land is a two-way street: money can be made, and it can be lost. There are traps everywhere. Some are so insidious that the amateur land speculator is unaware of being wiped out until it is too late.

The Residential Subdivision Lot. More people have spent more money speculating in building lots in undeveloped residential subdivisions than in any other type of land. Often, the lots are offered on financing terms which attract amateur speculators who have a limited budget. It is presumed that roads and utilities, if not already in place, will soon be provided by the land subdivider, the developer.

A 1976 study by the American Society of Planning Officials estimates that 2.3 million families in America own a recreational lot, and that at least 10 million recreational lots have been subdivided in America. In addition, in almost every town a large tract of land is being subdivided into lots intended for new residents. In most cases, over half of the buyers of the lots hope to resell later at a profit. This practice has been going on since the railroads platted towns along the tracks.

Yet, as many people have come to realize, the subdivision lot is the one type of land speculation with the greatest potential for disappointment. Since 1969, a number of facts about the large-scale residential land subdivision business have been openly publicized. That year, through the Interstate Land Sales Full Disclosure Act, the Office of Interstate Land Sales Registration (OILSR) within HUD began to require developers who

UNDEVELOPED SUBDIVISION OF 1948,
MOHAVE DESERT, CALIFORNIA, 1972

More people have spent more money speculating in building lots in undeveloped residential subdivisions than in any other type of land. This particular type of investment, however, has the greatest potential for disappointment. Thousands of acres in the United States have been divided and platted to be sold to amateur land speculators.

make interstate sales involving more than a hundred lots in a single subdivision to provide prospective buyers with a detailed statement of information about the subdivision, including type and schedule of utility service to be installed, precise form of road access to be provided, and the real costs of mortgage financing. In addition, as a result of new amendments over the years, the developer must now provide OILSR with numerous other detailed facts and statistics, including a property report and information about the environmental impact of the subdivision.

Under this act, in 1976 alone, there were nine hundred separate administrative decisions by HUD which forced developers to refund money to buyers. Fraud was discovered in a number of different forms. Lots advertised as amenable to building, for instance, were found to be inaccessible or to have no available water. Some lots were located in swamps, others on the sides of mesas too steep to ever accommodate any form of construction. People bought lots through the mail with the same trust with which they bought clothes out of the Sears Roebuck catalog. In 1977, a Federal Trade Commission ruling forced one company to refund some $4 million to 14,000 buyers of lots in land-development projects in California, Colorado, and New Mexico.

In 1976, INFORM, a private research organization based in New York, investigated reports and operations of ten land-development projects in Florida, Arizona, California, New Mexico, and Colorado. In sixteen of the nineteen projects, lots had no resale value or had to be resold at a loss as a result of inaccessibility, unbuildable land, or unfeasible utility services. And in two of these projects where lots could be resold for some gain, the gain was minimal and was experienced only in the older, more developed sections of the subdivision.

Such statistics cover only the largest subdivisions filed in recent years, and it is only in these that a measure of consumer protection is enforceable through the Interstate Land Sales Full Disclosure Act. There are thousands of smaller residential lot subdivisions which are never registered with HUD, and thousands more which were platted and filed before federal or state controls were imposed. The latter are often known as old filed maps, that is, maps filled with platted subdivision lots filed years ago with the local county clerk. Most of these lots are much smaller than would be permitted today; and most of the layouts, even on open land a hundred miles from the city center, are in a grid pattern. Today, America is full of disappointed amateur land speculators who bought subdivision lots from one of these sources.

The amateur speculator believes a subdivided lot is a safe investment, one sure to appreciate over the years. But too often he fails to understand enough about residential land speculation. Where is the water, the utilities, the access? How many thousands of other lots are there being sold and resold nearby? Is there any demand for building? How much does it really cost to hold on to the property over the years, compared to a reasonable expectation of eventual return? These are but a few of the questions that should be asked . . . first.

No Established Market. There is, in effect, little liquidity and little certainty as to what a parcel of land is worth. There is no stock exchange; there is generally no auction house. There are not even many real-estate brokers who know very much about raw land: its potential uses; the ability of the soil and subsurface character of the land for drainage, for the support of a building, for available well water; its likely future in terms of zoning and building controls and environmental restrictions, which may limit its use. Yet buyers and sellers alike must generally depend on a limited market, one created and promoted by local real-estate brokers.

Most real-estate brokers do not specialize in land but rather in commercial or residential properties, with the latter by far the largest group. Except for jobs in government and the retail trades, more people are employed in the various sections of real property development, management, and sales than in any other area of endeavor. Few realize that this fragmented industry supports more than 1 million workers full time— about 1 percent of the total labor force—and thousands of part-time workers. Of the 1.5 million people who are now licensed to sell real estate, about one third actively practices full time. The real-estate brokerage business is protected from the ravages of inflation. As housing prices rise, for instance, so do commissions, which are a fixed percentage of the selling price. When the price of a house bought for $25,000 a decade ago rises to $50,000, the broker's commission doubles. Residential real-estate brokers alone during 1978 earned gross commissions of some $15 billion—more than all earnings by lawyers in America, and five times the earnings of the approximately 40,000 stock brokers, who grossed $3 billion in commissions.

The residential real-estate business is so good that companies such as Merrill Lynch & Company, the nation's largest Wall Street brokerage firm, and Sears Roebuck and Company, the nation's largest retail firm, are now investing in it. The industry is also being infiltrated by nationwide franchising, just as the corner grocery store gave way years ago to the A & P. Today, there are at least five major national franchisers: Gallery of Homes, Red Carpet Corporation of America, Century 21, Electronic Realty Associates, and Realty World Corporation. The smallest has more than seven hundred affiliated offices; the largest, over 7,000. Each operates in at least thirty states. More than thirty franchise chains have

sold well over 10,000 franchises annually, accounting for over $800 million in gross commissions. While this figure is smaller than the fast-food industry's 60,000-odd franchises, real-estate franchises are growing at an annual rate of 30 percent and more, compared to 11 percent for the maturing fast-food business.

Despite their coverage of America, their prosperity, and their existence in nearly every hamlet in the country, real-estate brokers tend to be much less well-informed about land than about improved real estate. In part, this is because with raw land different types of information are essential. Land-development regulation; sewage, water, and drainage standards; and local land-development, environmental, and zoning policies change constantly. Compared to reselling a house or an office building, the most informed land brokerage requires command of an entirely different field of knowledge.

OL' MAC DONALD HAS A FARM.

It's a sound investment. Tax shelter. Dream come true. He used a little leverage to get the most out of his investment dollars. Pretty soon he'll be able to invest in an apartment complex. And an office building. Then Mac Donald won't have a farm. He'll have an estate!

But he won't have built it alone. He has CENTURY 21. 51,000 strong. Offices all over North America. Mac Donald can invest across the street. Or across the country. CENTURY 21 investment brokers know how to turn investment dreams into down-to-earth realities. Find out more by calling today. Then maybe someday you'll have a farm.

We're the Investment Real Estate Professionals.
Each office is independently owned and operated. ©1978 Century 21 Real Estate Corporation

REAL-ESTATE OFFICE,
POTEET, TEXAS,
MARCH 1939 AND
REAL-ESTATE CORPORATION
ADVERTISEMENT,
JUNE 1978

The era of the independent real-estate broker in America is virtually over. Today, the real-estate brokerage industry is controlled by nationwide franchises growing at 30 percent and more annually.

Political Risks. Now consider the political situation. The land speculator has a partner—everyone else in town, as represented by the local government and myriad local, county, and state regulatory agencies. Sometimes public policy helps the land speculator, as when the town, at its own expense, builds a road out to the speculator's property. He then becomes the beneficiary of "unearned increment." At other times, a change in the law, such as new zoning restrictions or new environmental control or a new master plan, can sap potential value from the land. This may not be temporary. Ask anyone whose land has been "down-zoned" in a public referendum, that is, whose permitted use of the land is changed by public regulation from a use such as commercial, which attributes a high value to the land, to residential, which generally accords the land a lower monetary value.

As a consequence of court cases and common practice, (as discussed in

Chapter Three) when the landowner's undeveloped property is devalued by regulation, he has little recourse unless a taking of nearly all value can be proven. No one is guaranteed a profit; the loss of value in the land as a result of changes in law does not necessarily entitle an owner to compensation.

Costs To Hold Land. The most prevalent land mine that explodes in the face of an amateur speculator is the real cost of holding, or "carrying," vacant land. This is because he forgets to take into account two often unrecognized costs: the cost of inflation and the impact of compounding costs, year after year. The cost to carry land, it turns out, is more than just the obvious cost of annual property tax and mortgage payments. Let's look at these two "hidden" costs, one at a time.

Inflation is so well known that many politicians, including former President Carter, declare it public enemy number one. It raises the price of everything, from handkerchiefs to houses. The conventional land speculator thinks he is fully protecting his assets by buying land. Compared to leaving the invested funds in ordinary currency or in a fixed investment such as a bond or annuity, he is indeed acquiring a tangible asset that may serve as a hedge against inflation. On the other hand, the speculator must not ignore the rate of inflation as a holding cost. And this is what most of us do. We take the benefits of inflationary increases on the sales side of the transaction to total up profit and fail to include the annual impact of inflation as part of the holding cost. But inflation impacts must be computed as part of the holding cost. Over the years of cash commitment, the value of invested funds is influenced by the rate of inflation itself. Consider the outcome if you invested $35,000 cash in land ten years ago instead of buying the average American house for the same amount. Assume that today, ten years later, that house sells for $70,000, due entirely to inflation. Unless the land has increased in value 100 percent to around $70,000, which is the current cost of the house, you've "lost" value as a result of the impact of inflation. Yet on paper, your calculations indicate a "profit" of $35,000. Thus, the cash invested in land must increase in value at a rate greater than the rate of inflation if the speculation is to be truly profitable. This in turn means that the real cost to carry land rises with the rate of inflation.

In terms of the cash invested several more obvious costs which are part of the overall cost of holding a parcel of unimproved land must be accounted for. These include the loss of income that could have been earned from invested cash, the cash value of property taxes, mortgage interest, and insurance. These costs must then be compounded annually. Amateurs forget to compound costs. Experienced professionals never do. The result of compounding large sums over considerable lengths of time can make an enormous difference, as any banker will tell you. One example that dramatically points out the power of compounding is the following riddle, proposed by Mark Haroldsen, president of Marko Enterprises: Which would you choose: to work for $1,000 a day for thirty-five days; or to work one day for one cent, which would then be compounded 100 percent per day for the next thirty-five days? The first alternative grosses an obvious $35,000 at the end of the thirty-five days of work. With the second alternative, you'd end up with over $340,000,000! Since the cash invested in a land deal is not earning interest at compound rates, this "loss" of revenue must also be considered.

When all of these quite real costs are taken into account, the annual cost of holding a piece of land can be realistically portrayed, in most situations in recent years as follows:

COST TO CARRY LAND AS A PERCENTAGE OF TOTAL VALUE

ITEM	MINIMUM	AVERAGE	MAXIMUM
Return on alternate investment	8.0%	10.0%	12.0%
Real estate taxes and insurance	0.5	1.0	1.5
Inflation	6.0	8.0	10.0
Annual holding cost	14.5%	19.0%	23.5%

Note that the inflation rates are those more generally experienced during the 1970s, not the very high rates in effect as this book is written. This simple table reveals that for the owner just to break even, the cash invested in land must appreciate anywhere from 14 percent to 24 percent annually *before* the impact of compounding is considered.

If these percentage holding costs are then projected on a more sophisticated *compounded* basis, it can be determined how much the cash investment in a parcel of land must actually appreciate over a period of years for the owner to simply break even. Were cash not tied up in land, it could presumably be earning a return at compounded rates. A careful look at those figures reveals a truth suppressed by land boomers and ignored by most amateur speculators. They tell you, for instance, that if a parcel of land you think a good speculative investment has a real economic holding cost (inflation plus annual cash expenditures) of, say, 20 percent per year

397

PERCENTAGE OF TOTAL APPRECIATION NEEDED TO BREAK EVEN IN FIVE YEARS AND IN TEN YEARS AT VARIOUS HOLDING COST RATES COMPOUNDED ANNUALLY	ANNUAL HOLDING COST (AS PERCENT OF TOTAL VALUE)	TOTAL COMPOUNDED APPRECIATION (PERCENT)	
		5 YEARS	10 YEARS
	8	46	116
	10	61	159
	15	101	304
	20	149	519

of its current value, it must appreciate about 150 percent in five years and over 500 percent in ten years if you are to break even.

When value jumps of this magnitude do occur, there is usually an external stimulating force, such as a new zoning designation, improved access to the property, or an unexpected and nearby good-quality development of some sort. Such events tend to change the perception of a parcel of land and its immediate development potential. But such changes occur rarely, and only on a minuscule fraction of the enormous acreage of undeveloped land.

If these value increases do occur, the speculator breaks even with or exceeds the impact of holding cost and inflation—something very few investors in commodities, stocks, or bonds, have accomplished in the last decade. Certain land in the path of development, near emerging communities and elsewhere, as discussed earlier in this chapter, has escalated in price far beyond meeting compounded holding costs. At today's very high rates of inflation of 12–18 percent, it works out that land values must roughly double every three to five years if a speculation is to be genuinely profitable.

The Cost to Buy and to Sell.   Another set of costs too often ignored by the amateur speculator are the one-time charges entailed in buying and selling land. As buyer, the speculator must have a budget for legal and other closing costs; and as seller, the speculator must budget for a brokerage sales commission. The combined costs of buying and selling typically add up to 6–12 percent of the gross value of the property.

Finally, it is important to calculate the capital-gains tax you must pay (if you make a profit) to see what really happens to your initial speculative plunge.

These words of caution lead to another major error made by the garden-variety land speculator. With no idea how much appreciation is needed to break even, the amateur has neither a sales-price objective nor a purchase-price requirement. This missing set of controls causes many to pay too much; it allows others to hold on to the land too long. Time marches forward meaningfully. As the table on page 398 shows, ten years may be only twice as long as five years, but the appreciation in the value of the land required to stay even must do much more than double.

WHAT THE EXPERIENCED
LAND SPECULATOR LOOKS FOR

In almost any town or any undeveloped part of America, you can buy all the land you can pay for. This being the case, finding the right land is like looking for the most beautiful shell on the beach. It takes care, a lot of searching, and a preconceived idea of what you are searching for. Some of the basics that experienced land speculators keep in mind include the following.

The Right Spot.   If the location is wrong, it is doubtful that the speculation will be profitable. The right parcel of land is one that is going to be desirable to others in the future. Ideally, it is one that is not especially desirable to its present owner or to other current buyers, one that has a possible future which the land speculator understands while others may not. The future of this parcel of land can be figured out, more often than not, from thoughtful research and analysis of community and regional trends, among others. The successful speculator has his eyes focused ahead; he peers into another time; he is speculative.

The Right Kind of Land.   All too often, amateur speculators forget that land is real. It is not a deed or a mortgage note. Neither is it a surveyor's drawing on a piece of bluish paper. Rather, it is earth, and each piece has its own topographic surface and subsurface characteristics. Below some, there is good water to drink; elsewhere, there may be none for miles around. Some land drains well, which would leave the potential building and cellar dry; other land is clay and provides poor drainage. Some land accepts on-site septic disposal; other land offers no effective and sanitary way to remove human waste belowground.

In the old days, the right kind of land made little difference. The bulldozer could fix anything that was "wrong." There was no county or state health department to certify that sewage and septic systems would

399

work. There were no environmental regulations which forbid filling and development of marsh, wetlands, watercourses, and adjacent areas. But now there are, and America is better for it. As a result, the most adept land speculators try to learn what the earth itself is about and what its best uses are.

The Right Community Jurisdiction. The right spot has to be situated in a community whose legal and political structures can accommodate the speculator's goals. This requirement means more than concurrence with the current zoning ordinance, master plan, or local government. It means that the speculator approves of the way things are going—and appear to be going in the future—in terms of taxation policies and land regulation.

Absolute private control over the land in America no longer exists. In many ways, the use of land involves participation with local, state, and even federal regulations. Land-use controls and environmental controls, and the way they are interpreted locally, are observed and studied. The wise speculator knows that these controls can work for him.

He watches plans for community-based institutions as well, particularly the school system, whose quality in years to come will influence land value enormously. A very good school system will attract more people, and thereby increase demand for land. But taxes to support the system, if excessive, will make it too expensive to hold the land and to live in town.

The Right Price and the Right Financing. When negotiating, amateur land buyers and sellers focus almost exclusively on per-acre price. This is a serious mistake. The price of the land means little by itself. The price per acre is only one part of a two-part value consideration. The second part, and in many instances the most significant, is the financing terms of the purchase.

The amateur seller likes to "get his price." He then agrees to finance the sale at his price with a purchase money mortgage, which permits the buyer to pay for the land over a long period of time. In effect, the seller accepts from the new buyer a mortgage for a portion of the value of the transaction. If the seller calculates the future value of this transaction, combining the mortgage and the cash received, and if he accounts for a reasonable inflationary deterioration of the value of the dollar and delayed receipt of his cash, he might find that his "price" was obtained but that his real return was considerably less than it appeared.

To understand this point clearly, look at the table on page 401 derived from Howard J. Ruff's *How To Prosper During the Coming Bad Years.*

YEAR	INFLATION RATE					
	10%	15%	20%	25%	30%	50%
1	$1,600	$1,800	$2,000	$2,200	$2,400	$3,200
2	1,960	2,310	2,640	2,950	3,240	4,200
3	2,284	2,743	3,152	3,512	3,828	4,700
4	2,576	3,112	3,562	3,934	4,240	4,950
5	2,838	3,425	3,889	4,251	4,528	5,075
6	3,074	3,691	4,151[a]	4,488[a]	4,729[a]	5,137[a]
7	3,287	3,917	4,361[a]	4,666[a]	4,871[a]	5,169[a]
Total of inflation loss & tax cost to lender on $28,000 interest	$17,619	$20,998	$23,755	$26,001	$27,836	$32,431
% of interest income lost to taxes & inflation	63%	75%	85%	93%	99%	115%

a. Cost greater than income due to fixed nature of tax cost.

INTEREST ON A $40,000 MORTGAGE:
YEARLY TAX AND INFLATION LOSS OF INTEREST
TO LENDER AT VARIOUS INFLATION RATES

This table outlines the real financial return to the lender, that is, the seller who takes back a mortgage for a part of the purchase price at various rates of inflation. Let us assume that the mortgage is for $40,-000, that it is to run for seven years, and that the interest rate is 10 percent, or $4,000 per year, with no amortization of the principal. In addition, the lender is in the 30 percent tax bracket. As shown in the table, when rates of inflation are taken into account at varying levels of intensity from 10 to 50 percent per annum, the actual percent of income lost to taxes and inflation by the lender is a minimum of 60 percent up to 100 percent!

In addition, as outlined in the table on page 402, during the seven years while the lender is waiting for the repayment of the $40,000 principal, at these same rates of inflation, the cash value of the $40,000 mortgage is reduced by at least one half. If the rate of inflation were 15 percent per year, at the end of seven years the $40,000 mortgage would be worth less than $13,000. These should be sobering figures for anyone negotiating

	RATE OF INFLATION					
	10%	15%	20%	25%	30%	50%
Purchasing power loss	$20,868	$27,177	$31,611	$34,661	$36,706	$39,687
Percentage of purchasing power lost	52%	68%	79%	87%	92%	99%
Future value of mortgage remaining after 7 years	$19,132	$12,823	$8,389	5,339	$3,294	$313

**$40,000 MORTGAGE: LOSS OF PRINCIPAL OVER 7 YEARS
AT VARIOUS RATES OF INFLATION**

a sale or a purchase. The one overwhelming lesson that experienced speculators have learned is not to let price alone be the focal point. The terms of the sale count, sometimes more than anything else.

Land deals are an area of free-wheeling creative negotiations, so no two land-acquisition agreements are alike. In general, the seasoned land speculator seeks to invest as little cash as possible at the outset. He endeavors to have the seller take a "purchase money mortgage," with a long permitted period of principal repayment at the lowest possible rate of interest. However, the interest cost, as a deductible expense, is much less critical than the permitted period of repayment of the principal.

An indication of how the real effective cost of interest payment is blunted by tax deductibility and by the impact of inflation is outlined in the table on page 403. Still examining our 7-year $40,000 mortgage at 10 percent interest, held during varying rates of inflation, it turns out that when inflation is at 10 percent per year, the 10 percent interest for someone in the 30 percent tax bracket carries a true cost of less than 4 percent. At higher rates of inflation, the cost is even less.

Or consider another example, one based on the actual experience of the insurance industry in recent years. Not long ago, S. Michael Giliberto of the Real Estate Investment Department of Aetna Life & Casualty Company and Anthony Downs of the Brookings Institution computed the average real interest rate earned by anyone holding a typical mortgage during the period 1968–1973. In their test case, a traditional 25-year mortgage term was assumed, and it was further assumed that the mortgage would be paid off in ten years. Its rate of interest was the average contract interest rate attained by major life insurance lenders for loans made in 1968, which was 7.66 percent. Then, interest and amortization

402

income from the mortgage for the ten years was discounted for the actual declining value of the dollar and rate of inflation experienced during the test period. Their important conclusion, announced to the real-estate industry in *National Real Estate Investor* magazine in 1980 under the banner headline " 'Real' Interest Rates Short-Change Lenders" is that the contract rate of 7.66 percent "produced a true *real* interest rate on the loan of only 1.28 percent." (Italics theirs.)

The experienced buyer also generally seeks certain rights or conditions as part of the land-acquisition agreement, depending on his plans and expectations for the future. For instance, he usually wants the right to pay off the mortgage sooner than required, without penalty. And few sellers will object, except those already in high tax brackets.

$40,000 MORTGAGE: TRUE COST AT 10 PERCENT INTEREST TO BORROWER IN THE 30 PERCENT TAX BRACKET AFTER INFLATION AND TAX BENEFIT

| YEAR | INFLATION RATE | | | | | |
	10%	15%	20%	25%	30%	50%
1	$2,400	$2,200	$2,000	$1,800	$1,600	$800
2	2,040	1,690	1,360	1,050	760	(200)[a]
3	1,716	1,257	848	488	172	(700)[a]
4	1,424	888	438	66	(240)[a]	(950)[a]
5	1,162	575	(111)[a]	(251)[a]	(528)[a]	(1,075)[a]
6	926	309	(151)[a]	(488)[a]	(729)[a]	(1,137)[a]
7	713	82	(361)[a]	(666)[a]	(871)[a]	(1,169)[a]
Net interest cost to borrower after inflation & tax benefit	$10,381	$7,001	$4,023	$1,999	$164	($4,431)[a]
Average true interest rate paid per year by borrower	3.7%	2.5%	1.4%	.7%	—	—

a. Represents negative expense—or income—due to tax benefit of interest expense.

The land speculator who acquires a large parcel will certainly want the right to release part of the land from the mortgage upon proper payment. This right permits the buyer to pay off in full a selected portion of the property without paying off the mortgage on the entire purchase. Once this portion of land has been released, the speculator is able to sell part of his acquisition before he pays for the total purchase. Through this phased approach, the experienced speculator can generate income and cash flow from land which is, in part, still being paid for.

One IRS regulation that all experienced buyers and sellers of land know about and often use concerns the installment sale. While regulations may soon be modified, currently if the seller accepts less than 30 percent of the value of his property in cash in the year of the sale, the sale qualifies as an "installment sale." Staying below this 30 percent cash cutoff permits the seller to declare and pay capital-gains tax in the first year only on the value of that percentage of his profit represented by the percentage of the total transaction for which cash is paid in the first year. For this reason, many land deals are negotiated for 29 percent cash (or less) in the first year. In subsequent years, as the seller is paid (and in this example, is presumed to profit), he pays the capital-gains tax for the annual proportion received. This particular IRS law thus allows a seller to extend and defer reported profit. By so doing, the seller may effectively reduce capital-gains tax. If profit is deferred to years in which the speculator finds himself in lower tax brackets, or to years in which there are off-setting capital losses, the tax on the profit is diminished. An amateur seller may not be aware of this important tax regulation. But an informed buyer will be, and may be able to reduce the initial cash sought by the seller if the consequences of this regulation are understood.

The Right Amount of Leverage. Buying land with a low initial cash investment is known as leverage. With a little weight (the cash equity), a land purchaser controls, as with a lever, big value (the entire parcel of land). The use of leverage is the key to profitable land speculation. At the bottom line, the only real profit is the profit on the cash invested.

Take the following comparative illustration of leverage regarding the purchase and sale of fifty acres of land at $1,000 per acre, or a total value of $50,000. One purchaser pays 100 percent cash. The second pays only $20,000 cash and leverages 60 percent, thereby carrying a $30,000 purchase money mortgage. The mortgage the leveraged buyer obtains is payable over ten years at a 10 percent rate of interest. In both cases, the land is sold after three years for about $110,000; its value has increased 30 percent per year.

As outlined in the balance sheet at the bottom of page 405 (and omitting a number of more refined but not central financial considerations), the 60 percent leveraged speculator emerges from the transaction with a total after-tax return on cash of over 150 percent profit. The buyer who has paid cash ends up with a return of about 70 percent, or about 80 percent less than the leveraged investment!

COMPARATIVE PURCHASE AND SALES CHARACTERISTICS
WITH ZERO LEVERAGE AND 60 PERCENT LEVERAGE

ASSUMPTIONS	ZERO LEVERAGE	60% LEVERAGE
Price (50 acres @ $1,000)	$50,000	$50,000
Loan (mortgage) (10 yr., 10% level-annual payments)	0	$30,000
Down payment	$50,000	$20,000
Holding period	3 yrs.	3 yrs.
Assumed selling price (value increase: 30%/year)	$109,850	$109,850
Assumed selling expenses (10% of selling price)	$10,985	$10,985
Net selling price	$98,865	$98,865
Income tax rate	50%	50%
Capital gains tax rate	30%	30%
Interest expense	0	$8,417
Mortgage amortization	0	$6,229
Tax saving on mortgate interest	0	$4,808

BALANCE SHEET AT TIME OF SALE
WITH ZERO LEVERAGE AND 60 PERCENT LEVERAGE

	ZERO LEVERAGE	60% LEVERAGE
Net selling price (net of selling expenses)	$98,865	$98,865
Less unpaid mortgage	0	(23,771)
Less effective interest expense	0	(8,417)
Plus tax savings on interest paid	0	4,808
Less amortization expenses	0	(6,229)
Net sales proceeds	$98,865	$65,256
Less tax on profit @ 30%	(14,660)	(14,660)
Sales proceeds	$84,205	$50,596
Profit on cash invested	68%	153%

Keep Your Eye on the Cash. There is one unrealistic component of this example: to illustrate the impact of leverage, in both cases a cash sale is assumed. In reality, a cash sale is rare. To forget this fact is a serious mistake many amateur speculators make when they get into a land deal.

Why is this such a serious mistake? As a buyer, the speculator correctly seeks leverage. He then pays the principal and interest on the mortgage, and taxes over the years. All this time, the inexperienced speculator is assuming that the sale of his land will be for cash. The new buyer, however, is also likely to want to minimize his cash investment, that is, benefit from leverage. This means that the initial buyer will be asked to finance a land sale, too, by taking back a purchase money mortgage. If too much money is invested, and not enough appreciation of land value occurs, it may be quite a while before the amateur speculator realizes any profit.

When the land is sold for $109,850 in our previous example, let us assume that instead of a cash sale, the terms are again 29 percent cash. After brokerage fees and other closing costs, which total about 10 percent, are paid out of the first cash received on the full $109,850 of value, the following occurs:

Selling Price	$109,850	
Gross cash received	$31,860	(29% of $109,850)
Closing cost and brokerage expense	$10,985	(10% of $109,850)
Actual cash received by seller	**$20,875**	

Remember, the leveraged speculator bought the land three years previously for $50,000, with a cash down payment of $20,000. Over the three years since the purchase, his out-of-pocket cash carrying costs amounted to about $11,000. Thus, the leveraged speculator's cash account at the end of the transaction in which his land has more than doubled in value in three years reflects a deficit. (See table on page 407.)

The unleveraged speculator emerges with an even larger cash deficit, as he has invested an additional $30,000 in cash at the time of purchase. In either case, the cash deficit is substantial, and income taxes must still be paid in cash in the year of sale on 29 percent of the profit.

What the leveraged speculator is left with from the new buyer is a mortgage of about $54,000. He does not end up with a mortgage of over $77,000, that is, 71 percent of the $109,850 sales price, since he sold without fully paying off the original $30,000 mortgage, on which he owes nearly $24,000 at the time of the sale. If we assume the new buyer takes

CASH ACCOUNT AT TIME OF SALE AFTER 3 YEARS
(Brought at $50,000, 40% Cash, Sold at $109,850,
Receiving 29% Cash)

Cash Expense

(Cash to purchase (40% of $50,000)	$20,000
Cash to carry (3 years)	11,00
Total cash investment	$31,000

Cash Receipts

Gross cash from buyer (29% of $109,850)	$31,860
Cash Expense of sale	10,985
Net cash receipts	$20,875
Total Cash Deficit at End	**$10,125**

over that old mortgage, then the speculator ends up with a "second" mortgage for the balance, or roughly $54,000. Here is where the sizable profit comes in—down through the years, as the mortgage principle and interest are paid out to the seller. But to benefit, the speculator must have access to a lot of discretionary cash along the way. Without the cash to hold on, the speculator has but one alternative: a distress sale, and often a wipe-out of money invested. Land speculating sounds daring; but its profits, when they come, often require patience.

The Right Timing. Timing makes all the difference in life. And in speculation. The objective is to hold the land (or the contract or the option) as long as it appreciates in value at a rate that far exceeds all the various costs to hold the property. The market value for land tends to rise dramatically in anticipation of certain legal or economic changes, such as a new regulation, a new access road, a new zoning possibility. At some point, the value stops rising rapidly, but the cost to hold and carry continues. When the percentage-value increase per year that can be realized from a sale dips below the percentage cost to hold and carry, the speculator is taking a loss whether or not he realizes it. At sale time, if too many years like that go by, a net loss on the whole transaction results.

"Perfect timing" necessitates buying when a seller is anxious to sell, when other buyers are not interested in the property, and when the speculator's own research and analysis indicate that some imminent change will soon increase the inherent value of the property. The prescient speculator then sells while the price is still rising, while buyers are around and interested. Land values generally move in spurts, not in a slow and orderly progression. External events may cause values to suddenly increase 100 or even 500 percent. Then a plateau may set in for years. The idea is to capitalize on a surge in value. The experienced speculator never tries to obtain the last 10 percent of a value rise. That last increment takes a long time to occur. Or as J. P. Morgan advised when asked how to get rich, "Sell too soon."

Reduce Property Tax. The property tax is the second-largest element in cash-carrying costs, after the cost of financing. It is a wild card—a factor that cannot easily be controlled by the owner. The cost of paying off the mortgage is known once the deal is finalized. The lost opportunity on cash invested can be assigned a value that will not fluctuate, as it is based on the opportunity value of the money in the year it is invested, though of course the inherent rate of inflation or deflation, prime interest rates, and so forth control and may change this value assignment.

But the property tax is an externally manipulated expense, one that must be paid out in cash every year. It is also, of course, a deductible expense for federal income tax purposes. When the property tax rises rapidly, as it does often in developing areas, it imposes an additional cash burden on the cost of holding land. As the tax escalates, it increases the final sales value that must be obtained if a profit is to be made. The future of the property tax rate in any given place is thus one of the elements that astute speculators research most carefully.

The thoughtful land speculator seeks ways to reduce the cash expense of property tax. If the land seems incorrectly assessed, he can make an appeal. There are other more innovative ways to reduce tax expense. Often, the most promising direction is to seek out special (and reduced) taxing districts offered to further land conservation and environmental objectives. For instance, to forward conservation over a period of time for farmland and forest uses, many states and some local communities now have instituted special reduced property-tax programs, as outlined in Chapter Nine. These include the creation of forestry, agricultural, and conservation districts. A landowner who agrees to place his property in such a district is generally accorded, in return, a reduction in property tax. The owner must commit his land to that particular use for a number of years, often five or ten. But property taxes, and therefore this element in holding costs, can be reduced by as much as 50 to 90 percent. Furthermore, it is usually possible to extract the land from the conservation district, though sometimes at a tax penalty.

Interim Land Uses.   While holding it, the experienced speculator may choose not to leave his land idle. It can be farmed, forested, or leased to be used as an equestrian center, a drive-in theater, a golf driving range, a tennis court, even a country club. Mobile-home parks, rental apartments, warehouses, children's day camps are sometimes projected by land speculators as interim land-holding operations. They exist until the land becomes ripe for other uses. In the interim, improvements are being depreciated and operations may help to finance the underlying land. This is "land banking" at a reduced or even no-cash cost over long periods of time.

Interim land-use operations, however, may present major pitfalls for the unwary amateur speculator. With the exception of net lease arrangements, almost all operations require management; and some, in fact, demand additional capital investment. Even net lease arrangements are subject to market fluctuations. Fields leased to farmers and woodland leased to foresters must be profitable to the operator. If the wholesale price of wood or potatoes goes down, so does the lease value the following year. There is an upside possibility as well, especially in years of inflating commodity prices.

Interim use of land may appear to be a viable way to help offset carrying costs. But the odds are against finding a situation that will prove profitable. Most of the time, the speculator has to count on holding idle land and paying out the carrying costs, year after year, with cash.

A Little Extra Money To Make a Lot More, Faster.   The charts and tables presented earlier in this chapter reveal why the experienced land speculator is in a hurry. He feels time like a resident of the Florida Keys feels the cold: it chills him to the bone.

Generally, he is willing to spend a little extra money to quickly change the value of his land. When this happens, he slides out of the classical stance of the passive operative waiting for external events to occur. He becomes, in effect, a land packager.

The traditional way to escalate land values was to build a railroad or a canal, and to own both sides. In this century, rezoning is king. With a flourish of a pen in the hands of the "right" person, the $1,000 acre can become the $10,000 acre. Sometimes the pen is flourished for a financial consideration or business interest in the property, a seemy practice of back-room cronyism, less prevalent today than in years past.

But new ways to speed up land-value price escalations have been discovered. Indeed, recently, sophisticated land speculators support planning of various sorts. Some speculators promote elaborate community development plans, with the expectation that their own property will receive favorable treatment. Others engage planners and engineers to design a subdivision or a planned-unit development for their own land. In most towns, a well-located, suitable parcel of open land can be approved

for subdivision with substantial work and a time interval between six and eighteen months. Once approved, if market demand exists, land value will increase significantly. The $1,000 acre can become the $15,000 acre in a short time span.

Some of the most sophisticated land speculators are now promoting restricted community growth, environmental controls, and ecological planning, as discussed in Chapter Six. If their own land is properly situ-

REAL-ESTATE OFFICE, CENTRAL VALLEY, CALIFORNIA, NOVEMBER 1940

Wise investors of all types know that spending a little extra money can produce a great deal more money, faster. Sophisticated speculators in America now employ advertising and public relations experts to inject new value into land holdings; and the promotional devices they use have come a long way since the simple sign above the roadside real-estate office of days past.

ated, these new socially and environmentally oriented controls may diminish the value and utility of competing property, while propelling upward the value of their speculative holding.

Public relations is another inexpensive device that land speculators utilize to inject new value into land holdings. The slick brochure; the shimmering description in *The Wall Street Journal;* the enthusiastic advertisement on television, radio, and in the auctioneer's catalog: promotion has come a long way since the simple sign above the roadside real-estate office of days past. All are ways to stimulate demand, just as demand is built up for soap powder. Only with soap powder, there is an endless supply. When the land speculator interests a few buyers and receives a number of offers, he has what he wants. Prices may then be increased, moved up faster than holding costs. The chill in his bones turns to a warm glow.

From Speculator to Land Developer: A Big Step.   If the land speculator becomes desperate, he may take the final step and become a land developer or the partner of a land developer. If the owner develops the land himself, a lot more cash is required for engineering, roads, utilities, and even buildings. A lot more time must also be committed. The risk magnifies accordingly. And his tax status is likely to change from investor to dealer in the eyes of the IRS. If this serious change occurs, profits can no longer be treated as capital gain.

If the landowner becomes a partner with a land developer, which often happens, an entirely new situation prevails. More often than not, the land speculator contributes the land as his share of the partnership. The experienced developer then provides the cash and expertise necessary to cover development costs. In such an arrangement, the land speculator usually waits until the property is developed and sold as "improved" real estate before he receives any return on his investment. Depending upon time, cash, and land value invested, and upon the value of the return, he either makes money or loses it. Along the way, he has lost control of his options. And he enters a new domain, the world of improved real estate, with its myriad benefits and pitfalls.

A Note of Caution.   We have now entered an era of extraordinarily high rates of inflation. These transfer directly, as shown above, into higher real costs to hold vacant land. If high inflation rates were the only issue at hand, the risk could be weighed with focus on this single variable. However, it also looks as if we face years of periodic uncertainty about the future cost and availability of credit, as well as reduced national demand

412

for new land development. There will continue to be increasing public regulation over the conversion of raw land into developed property as well. These trends add up to considerable risk for anyone buying or holding open land as a speculation.

The shortage of credit alone presents a force that can diminish the value of land rather than permit it to rise in accordance with or even at rates greater than the annual rate of inflation. When buyers cannot finance construction to build profitably, their thirst for raw land dries up. When people cannot afford interest costs to finance new homes, land developers disappear from the market.

These new factors, which I believe will periodically become part of the business environment of the 1980s, are entirely capable of reversing the post war trend in America of general annual escalating values of raw land. Unless the greatest care is exercised in undertaking new commitments to speculative purchases of raw land, the unwary buyer is more likely than at any time since the 1930s to be making a costly purchase, one expensive to hold on to and one difficult to sell profitably.

SPECIAL TAX ADVANTAGES: HELP FROM THE GOVERNMENT

In any business endeavor, what counts is the bottom line *after taxes*. I wish half as much money was spent on architecture, design, and planning as on tax advice. For the casual speculator who does not make land dealing his regular business, there are federal and local tax advantages which, in effect, help support land speculation. However, such favorable tax treatment is regularly criticized by single-tax land-reform groups, which trace back to Henry George, the notable author of *Progress and Poverty* (1879). Much of the criticism, I believe, is a consequence of inadequate insight. Consider the major tax advantages accorded land speculation and the traditional critique of them.

Property-Assessment Practices. Support of land speculation by local government comes in the form of relatively low assessment of, and therefore relatively low property tax on, undeveloped land as compared to improved real estate. The impact of this widespread assessment practice is to contain the real-estate tax component of carrying costs on undeveloped land.

In most communities, farms and undeveloped acreage are generally assessed at the lowest percent of market value of all other types of property. Typically, open land is assessed somewhere between 10 and 25 per-

413

cent of market value. By contrast, vacant lots and residential homes are generally assessed at 20–40 percent of market value, while business properties may be assessed at 35–60 percent of market value.

Uninformed critics of land speculation complain that low land assessment represents an unfair subsidy to those who hold undeveloped and unproductive land. They argue that higher taxes on undeveloped property would destroy the appeal of land speculation.

But such criticism, I believe, is misguided. A higher tax rate on vacant land would force more rapid land sales, sales to those who want to rush the property into any form of development that will produce sufficient income to pay the property tax and leave net income for profit. Alternatively, a low tax rate on land that does not and could not create a stream of income is an equitable, appropriate, and perceptive way for local government to help maintain open and undeveloped land in its natural state. After all, the idle land demands no municipal service or other public expense. By not selling and by not developing, the owner—whether he be a dutiful farmer or a calculating land speculator—provides open space. He also holds land vacant which, over time, is likely to become subject to more informed environmental and planning controls.

When, in order to earn additional revenue, a local community abandons its policy of low assessment on undeveloped land, it is generally set on a course of certain disaster. As owners find real-estate taxes insupportable, the rate of land sales increases and the quality of land development descends. In all but the rarest instances, the cost of new and/or expanded municipal services required by new residents exceeds the additional revenue obtained by raising the assessment level on vacant land and taxing the new buildings built upon it.

Deductible Property Tax and Mortgage Interest Expenses. A second tax support comes from the federal government and concerns federal tax treatment of property tax and mortgage interest costs. These significant components of carrying costs receive preferential treatment from the IRS and state government. Both interest and property tax are treated, in effect, as business expenses and are therefore tax deductible. However, as vacant land, unlike most businesses, may produce no annual income, the business being subsidized may indeed be the business of speculation.

These deductions can be charged (within certain limits) against other ordinary annual income, thus sheltering from federal income tax various unrelated earned income. For a speculator in the 50 percent tax bracket the federal and state governments are, in effect, paying 50 percent of his annual property tax and mortgage interest costs.

Critics of this system argue that interest and tax expenses should not

414

be deducted from income but rather should be added every year to the original cost of the property. This approach, which is called capitalizing the expense, recognizes the basic economic fact that the expense of carrying a nonproductive asset over a period of years is part of the investment itself.

Those who support this approach omit two critical considerations. First, under the capitalized expense system, if there is a profit at sale, the capital gains tax is reduced, as the cost basis of the property is increased each year by the amount paid in property tax and interest expense. Also, tax is paid on only 40 percent of a long-term capital gain. Thus, the amount of additional tax that would be paid to the federal government is questionable and defies calculation. Second, there is no foundation in law—and no logical reason—for treating undeveloped land held for speculation differently from a house, a factory, a farm, or any other type of real property. The homeowner is permitted to deduct mortgage interest payments as well as property tax from ordinary income, even though his home is not an income-producing business. Businesses are able to deduct similar expenses. And all businesses, as well as all individuals, are permitted to deduct interest expenses (within certain limits) for federal income tax calculations. Were it otherwise, banks and other financial institutions would shrivel along with much of the national economy. I see no reason why the activity of owning and holding undeveloped land should be singled out for punitive tax treatment.

Profits as Capital Gains, Not Ordinary Income. The third tax benefit granted land speculation—when it is not a habitual business—is the treatment of profit and loss as a capital transaction rather than as ordinary income. If the property is held for at least twelve months, it qualifies as a long-term capital transaction, and is taxed at lower rates than ordinary income. But take note: Any individual declared by the IRS to be in the *business* of dealing in land as a regular occupation loses this favorable tax treatment. When land speculation is recognized as a form of a regular business endeavor, the speculator is quite properly declared a "dealer," in which case profits and losses are treated as ordinary income. In a sense, federal tax regulations promote amateur land speculation—a curious state of affairs, considering the inherent risks.

Land as a Capital Asset. Because land is a capital asset, any increase in value is accorded the same benefit as an increase in value of a house, furniture, or common stock. The increase in value is not taxed until the property is sold or until estate tax is paid. When you think about it, this is a most important benefit. If value increases were taxed annually, it would be quite expensive–and perhaps even senseless—to hold undeveloped land that was appreciating. Its luster as an "investment" would soon dim.

Equally important, as with other capital assets such as stock, the property can be pledged as collateral to secure a mortgage or a loan, though, as outlined elsewhere, it is often difficult to do so when undeveloped, unplanned land is the only collateral. However, to the active and sophisticated speculator who holds property that has appreciated, the untaxed increase in land value can sometimes be converted to tax-free cash through the use of a mortgage or other form of loan. If a portion of the capital appreciation of the property is captured by the owner in this way, no taxable transaction occurs. The owner must then, of course, come up with additional annual cash to pay off the new mortgage or loan.

The refinancing tax breaks which accompany all transactions involving developed property are of tremendous value and significance. The use of undeveloped land to secure refinancing, and therefore tax-free capital, while much less prevalent, remains significant. And, of course, when land is a large part of the total value of a house, business plant, or office center, its contribution to refinancing proceeds cannot be ignored.

SPECULATION AND ACCOUNTABILITY

Buying land is all the rage in America these days, as we face an uncertain economic future for the dollar and an uncertain political future as a nation. The stories of profit and protection of assets abound, while those of speculators who have encountered difficulties along the way are rarely shared. Some speculators do not even realize that their assets are evaporating, in effect, due to high holding costs for land that is not moving up in value fast enough during a period of accelerating inflation.

Yet land in America can be a wise speculative investment, as many professionals know and as many casual speculators are finding out. People who regularly speculate in land and succeed realize that they must buy the right site for the right price at the right time. They must also have taken into account many other external and relevant factors. Some of these are outlined above, others are discussed elsewhere throughout this book. As Murry Seldin, professor of real estate at American University, has aptly cautioned amateur investors, because of risk, because so much information is needed, "It's best to do your investing in your own backyard."

Unlike speculation in commodities, stocks and bonds, paintings, and precious collectibles, however, land speculation, sooner or later, is likely

416

to transform the thing being speculated in—the land itself. The process of speculation and consequent land transformation is usually undertaken with only minor regard for the long-range impact on the local community and its surrounding region. It also allows a special role to emerge. This is the role of indifference: indifference to the complexities of community life and to the design of human settlements, which the speculative process so profoundly affects. Instead, the land speculator focuses on a more quantifiable concern: profit.

The speculator is a catalyst; his activity sets off multiple chain reactions. Yet the catalyst is only modestly affected by these reactions, by the impacts on the tax base, the social composition and physical and aesthetic character of a community. The impact on future real-estate taxes and on adjacent or nearby property is usually not the speculator's concern.

The precedent for indifference to the impact of land speculation on communities can be traced to the English common law rights of absentee landlordship. It goes back to the granting of deeds and charters by the crown to favored noblemen and subjects, to the American experience of selling land in Nevada from law offices in San Francisco. Most of all, it continues to reflect a national conviction that the frontier is still here, that it is always possible to move on. The assumption persists that this vast land can contain all that will be done to it by anyone who wants to try.

It is not, then, isolated tax reform that is needed. And certainly I see no reason to try to reduce the amount of land held vacant and in private ownership. Rather, the direction to strive toward is a more sensible combination of taxation policy and policy for open-space conservation, as well as planning for new development of open land as it is converted to urbanized purposes. The land speculator is an effective and often useful intermediary whose motives are well understood. What is needed is insightful and equitable handling of his profit orientation. Before that is possible, local, state, and national objectives for the huge reserves of vacant land in this country must be worked out more clearly.

THIRTEEN

RECREATIONAL LOTS AND SECOND HOMES: WHERE AMERICA PLAYS, IT BUYS AND SPECULATES

No area of land investing and speculating has soared in interest and value more dramatically than the most sought-after recreation spots in America. Increased incomes and leisure time, and an increased national emphasis on health and exercise contribute to this surge. In fact, 5–8 percent of all American households today, or about one family in twelve, own a parcel of recreational property, as either a vacant lot or a second home.

The buyer of a subdivision lot in a recreational area is more likely to be an amateur land speculator than just about anything else. A survey of buyers in several northeastern California recreation subdivisions, for instance, found that during the 1970s, over 30 percent of all buyers purchased land for speculative gain, not for personal use. Another 11 percent bought with the expectation that a capital gain would be realized, and 5 percent bought as an investment for their heirs. Much the same story prevails elsewhere: 30–60 percent of all recreational lot purchases are for investment and speculative purposes rather than for home building and use by the first buyer.

REASONS FOR PURCHASE OF RECREATIONAL LOTS AS REPORTED BY RESPONDENTS IN NORTHEASTERN CALIFORNIA SURVEY, 1972[a]

REASONS FOR PURCHASE	PERCENT OF RESPONDENTS
Speculative gain	31.0
Future recreational use	22.0
Permanent retirement use	12.0
Capital gains	11.0
Occasional retirement site	9.0
Immediate recreational use	9.0
Purchased for estate (heirs)	5.0
Other	1.0
	100.0

a. The number of respondents was 564.

Most people who intend to buy a piece of open land, in fact, end up buying a building lot. Most other parcels of vacant property are too large and therefore too expensive for the average buyer. For anyone who wants land but is unable to buy a large parcel, the recreational building lot has great allure. After all, it can be built on some day as a rural retreat, or it can be resold. This lot, in most buyers' imagination, is nestled somewhere in the bright sunlight along the seashore or secluded amid a shaded grove of trees. A tidy road runs alongside it; and below the perfect surface of the property, water lines, electric conduit, and a modern septic system await. What is more, the lot is envisioned by the buyer to be ready for construction and perfectly located for resale. In short, an ideal investment or an ideal place to erect that long-awaited second home. But such an ideal is rarely found.

LOTS VS. HOMESITES:
A MOST CRITICAL DISTINCTION

An enormous number of recreational or retirement lots cannot, in fact, be built upon—at least not in a way that is economically feasible for the buyer. In some cases, the developer does not provide promised roads; in others, there are no available utilities and little hope of being able to secure them.

Distinguishing between an unimproved lot and an improved lot is crucial. The unimproved subdivision in which a lot is sold to an unwary buyer is an arena of widespread abuse in land sales in America. The unimproved lot within that subdivision need be no more than a parcel of land indicated on a map and described by a surveyor in terms of outline boundaries. This so-called meets and bounds description of the perimeter of a land parcel is all that is needed to identify the lot for the purpose of creating a deed. And the deed—the title to a described parcel of property —is all that is needed to transact a sale. In no facet of land development and land buying is the old *caveat emptor* (let the buyer beware) admonition more justified.

The improved lot, by way of contrast, may generally be built upon without delay. It is served by an adjacent road; water is available; a source of electric power is ready at the lot boundary; and permits have been obtained for sewage disposal, and other necessities that convert a simple lot into a homesite.

Abuse of the Uninformed. Widespread abuse and business scandals have characterized many land subdivision operators, especially those who specialize in recreational subdivisions. These were chronicled in 1976 when the American Society of Planning Officials presented its report *Subdividing Rural America: Impacts of Recreational and Second-Home Development* to the Council on Environmental Quality and to HUD. In many parts of Florida, Texas, the Southwest, and other Sun Belt and resort centers, abuse was found to be particularly rampant. At the site of numerous large-scale recreational land subdivisions, it was discovered that "heavy front-end investments are poured into mass-marketing and advertising schemes rather than into the basic site improvements necessary for housing construction and occupancy." In other words, the developer lavishes money on selling campaigns and on luring buyers rather than on the more essential and costly capital expenses ("front-end costs") required to provide roads, utilities, sewage, and so forth. By improving the lots so they may be used, he incurs cost. By merely selling lots, on the other hand, he realizes cash flow, and profit. Also, since most recreational lots are sold on credit terms, the developer begins to earn additional interest income—often charged at high levels—as soon as a sale occurs.

Nor has widespread abuse of land subdivision and lot sales escaped the recent attention of regional investigative reporters and nationally oriented organizations such as INFORM, Inc., a New York–based nonprofit research and educational group that studies the impact of U. S. corporations on the environment, employees, and consumers. Yet, the public remains basically uninformed. It is as if the information about such matters as road access, utility costs, and the high interest rates charged to buy lots with minimal cash down payments conflict with the dream, with the mystique of land ownership.

INFORM's recently completed three-volume research study of recreational land development, *Promised Lands,* chronicles the pitfalls. The business practices of nineteen land-development companies, including Horizon Corporation, AMRAP, and ITT Community Development Company, are reviewed. Among other findings, Jean Halloran, the editor of the study, concludes:

1. Though buyers were led to believe that land would increase in value, eighteen out of nineteen lots were resold for less than the original price paid. In seven of the ten subdivisions, no resale market was reported.
2. Lots in some subdivisions sold for as much as $60,000 simply because the developer had designated them as "commercial" on his master plan.
3. Access to utilities was sometimes as far away as ten miles, and the cost to bring these services to the private lot owner was prohibitive.

Halloran has remarked recently, "People clung to the belief—because of what they were promised—that the developments would grow out to their lot. But based on our studies, only 5 percent of the 900,000 lots were ever built on, and at that rate of growth we calculated that the number of years it would take for a community to build up ranged from fifty years to as long as 3,600 years."

Rio Rancho Estates, located in New Mexico some eleven miles from Albuquerque, is a notorious example of abuses within the recreational land subdivision business in America. The parent company, AMREP Corporation, bought about 90,000 acres of land in the early 1960s for less than $200 per acre. After subdivision into 100,000 lots, land was sold through an aggressive marketing effort in thirty-seven states at prices which escalated from $1,500 per acre in 1961 to over $7,000 an acre in 1974.

Areas outside the central core of Rio Rancho Estates were provided with only a dirt road. If a lot owner wanted water, a well would cost another $4,000 to $15,000; a septic tank could be installed for $500 to $900; electrical lines were available at $12,000 per mile, with refunds possible as other owners hooked in; and telephone service was priced over $2,000 a mile, without a possible future refund for any part of the cost. Obviously, most of the property was thus rendered unbuildable.

Few initial buyers actually went to look at the property. Rather, after a fine dinner, followed by an enthusiastic pep talk, and sometimes capped by a professionally slick film that projects a tranquil, elegant future for Rio Rancho Estates, they signed up for installment purchases, in motel lobbies in cities like Albany and St. Paul, all across America. They went home with a new financial obligation for years to come. But, unlike buying a car or refrigerator "on time," because of the financing system employed, they received no deed—and thus had no title to the land—until it was fully paid for. And even more unlike the refrigerator or car, the lots could not be used without enormous additional cost.

Lots of Lots. As a result of these and other related issues, including speculative purchases, there persists a low ratio of homes constructed in new recreational subdivisions compared to the large number of lots subdivided. This ratio is extremely dramatic in states such as California (1:33), Arizona (1:60), Pennsylvania (1:120), and Florida (1:73,268). In California alone, statistics present a market so flooded with platted second-home lots that it would take, at current rates of construction, over a hundred years to fill half of them.

The impulse to purchase unimproved mountain, desert, and other recreational lots is so pervasive that it has prompted Eugene Kaplan, a senior trial lawyer who handles land-fraud cases for the Federal Trade Commission, to comment, "They agree to purchase land with no water,

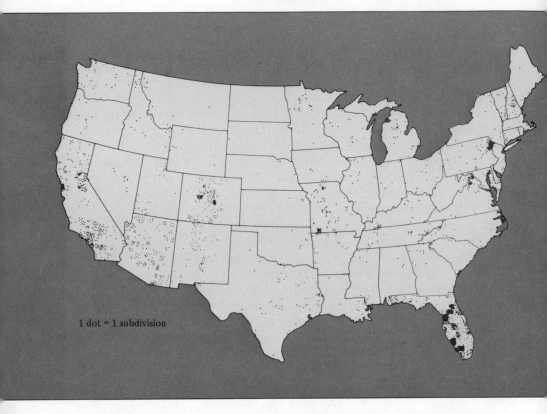

1 dot = 1 subdivision

RECREATIONAL LAND DEVELOPMENTS IN CONTIGUOUS U.S. REGISTERED WITH OILSR, JUNE 1973

There are now over 10 million subdivided recreational lots registered with HUD's Office of Interstate Land Sales (OILSR). In most states, however, if fewer than a hundred lots are involved or interstate sales are not contemplated, registration is not required.

no utilities, and no future. My explanation can only be that the myth and the ego trip of owning land drowns out reality."

Abuse by subdividers and misinformation among purchasers were so extensive in the recreational lots subdivision business by 1976 that the conservative American Society of Planning Officials, after considerable investigation, was forced to observe:

Consumer victimization in recreational land sales has been a serious national issue for over 10 years. . . . Thousands of consumers have been the victims of high-pressure sales tactics, deceptive and fraudulent advertising practices, and broken promises."

Counting only those subdivided recreational lots registered with the Office of Interstate Land Sales at HUD, as of 1973 more than 10 million were spread across rural and suburban America. HUD tries to keep tabs on the largest commercial subdividers. But in most states, if fewer than one hundred lots are involved or interstate sales are not contemplated, HUD registration is not required. The Interstate Land Sales Full Disclosure Act, passed in 1968, omits consideration of all those myriad smaller operators found in almost any well-located, desirable community where recreational second-home or retirement-home subdivision is likely to succeed. If this smaller-scale activity were added to the known national statistics, it is likely that the number of subdivided recreational lots in America would be over 20 million rather than 10 million.

Like so many other facets of the land business, including who actually owns individual parcels of land, little information is available. But then, little is required. In the large-scale land subdivision business, an aura of privacy and secrecy is basically enhanced, or at least condoned, by very lax local, state, and federal disclosure practices.

Of all the recreational or retirement lots, it is my guess that less than 25 percent have been built upon. And yet, it is estimated that in recent years approximately 10,000 recreational land sales and development firms were conducting business in the United States. This industry has sold or still owns 35 to 40 million acres of land, or about 2 percent of the total land area—slightly less than the area of Washington, the twentieth largest state in the nation.

Self-Protection. Before buying a subdivision lot for either investment or use, the would-be purchaser should ask a lot of questions and demand definitive answers. I have included environmental and consumer checklists created by INFORM as a guide. (See pages 426–27.) Also, I have prepared a list of additional and sometimes costly items which a buyer must anticipate and investigate when installment purchase is involved and when the individual buyer must procure utility services. (See page 428.) These are too often overlooked—and always add significant costs to the purchase of a vacant lot when building takes place.

Armed with these checklists, the amateur buyer can begin to ask the right questions. He must also look at the asking price for the lot itself and at the mortgage terms. Taken together, these will reveal the quality of the subdivision and the overall cost that must be incurred to render a vacant lot buildable.

When planning and subdividing in a good location are carried out properly and thoughtfully, the subdivision lot may be worth every cent that is invested, if not more. But all too often, total cost far exceeds value obtained.

ENVIRONMENTAL CHECKLIST
FOR PURCHASE OF A SUBDIVISION LOT

Plans

Does the subdivider:
Plan for complete basic services? _____
Phase lot sales and extension of services? _____
Get 80% build-out in 10 years of each section marketed? _____
Prepare an Environmental Impact Report? _____

Land

Does the subdivider:
Use a curvilinear or cluster design? _____
Retain 25% or more open space? _____
Reserve from lot sale and development the following areas of critical concern:
 —wetlands? _____
 —dunes and beaches? _____
 —water sources? _____
 —prime agricultural lands? _____
 —habitats of endangered species? _____
 —prime historical, archaeological, cultural, aesthetic, or recreational resources? _____
Reserve from lot sale and development the following areas hazardous for building:
 —geological hazard areas (earthquake, landslide)? _____
 —flood-prone areas (100-year floodplains, arroyos)? _____
 —areas of slope exceeding 25%? _____
Blade roads only in immediate development areas? _____
Clear only for buildings and roads? _____
Preserve existing topography? _____

Water Resources

Does the subdivider:
Design the drainage system to control erosion? _____
Retain 100-foot buffer zone around water bodies? _____
Replant disturbed land immediately? _____
Limit septic systems to one-acre or larger lots with adequate: percolation rates, slope, and distance from bedrock, water table and surface waters? _____
When utilizing central sewage disposal, provide tertiary treatment (or secondary and land disposal)? _____
Avoid major stream alteration? _____
Avoid major wetland dredging and filling? _____
Use groundwater only up to the safe yield? _____

CONSUMER CHECKLIST
FOR PURCHASE OF A SUBDIVISION LOT

Sales

Does the subdivider:

Conduct a credit check on lot purchasers? ____

Limit lot sales per purchaser? ____

Sell only residential, i.e., no industrial, commercial or multi-family lots on installment contracts? ____

Require a cash down payment of 20% on all sales? ____

Limit duration of installment contracts to 5 years? ____

Charge no interest on installment contracts? ____

Encourage attorney review of sales documents? ____

Require a pre-purchase site visit? ____

Allow a 14-day rescission period in which purchaser can obtain a refund for any reason? ____

Offer a partial refund if purchaser defaults? ____

Guarantee a refund, with interest, if promised services are not made available by date specified in contract? ____

Escrow contract payments, or provide equivalent surety bonding, for refund purposes? ____

Title

Does the subdivider:

Offer only platted lots? ____

Offer a recordable contract, and record the sale? ____

Offer unmortgaged land, or land mortgaged with a release clause, only? ____

Upon contract signing, deed title to purchaser, or place title in trust? ____

Basic Services

Does the subdivider:

Guarantee, or have available, to each lot:

—central water, of adequate quantity and quality? ____

—central sewage disposal, as necessary? ____

—drainage system, adequate for 100-year storm? ____

—solid waste disposal, via adequate method? ____

—roads, paved, to county standards? ____

—electricity and telephone? ____

Guarantee completion through escrowing or surety bonding? ____

If services are financed through special service district bonds, employ them only if:

—initial governing body includes a county official? ____

—elections include all landowners on one-man, one-vote basis? ____

—sum of bonds is less than twice the developer's investment in basic services? ____

—sum of bonds is less than 15% of the assessed value of land in the district? ____

—developer co-signs all bonds? ____

427

**CHECKLIST OF
EXTRA COSTS TO
INVESTIGATE FOR LOTS
BOUGHT ON AN
INSTALLMENT PLAN,
AND BASIC
IMPROVEMENT COSTS**

Lot cost:

Cash required   ____
Interest rate   ____
Cost per year, interest and
        amortization cost, to the
        end of purchase   ____

Annual assessments:

Property owners' association   ____
Special service districts   ____
Property taxes   ____
Total, per year   ____
Estimated annual increase   (____%)

One-time costs for services and site work:

Closing costs   ____
Lot survey   ____
Water
    Well   ____
    Central extension   ____
    Central hookup   ____
Sewage
    Septic system   ____
    Central extension   ____
    Central hookup   ____
Electricity   ____
Telephone   ____
Landscaping   ____
Driveway   ____

FLORIDA: A TWENTIETH-CENTURY ARENA OF RECREATIONAL LAND SPECULATION

For over two hundred years now, Americans have willingly succumbed to the land boomer's dream machine. Nowhere is this more evident than in Florida.

The state of Florida contains almost 37 million acres of land, much of it swamps and lakes. At the beginning of the twentieth century, land boomers and developers discovered Florida. Land there was both inexpensive and available. And so the chronicle begins. In the early 1900s, the governor of Florida, Napoleon Bonaparte Broward, sold 500,000 acres of wet, low-lying land to New York land speculator Richard Bolles for $1

428

million, or $2.00 per acre. From the $1 million he received, Governor Broward agreed to spend $500,000 to properly survey and drain Bolles's land, thereby making it marketable.

Bolles quickly subdivided and mapped 180,000 acres of the land into 12,000 farms, 8,000 farm tracts and a town of 12,000 lots. Throughout the East and Midwest, Bolles's salesmen fanned out, proclaiming that Florida Fruit Lands Company offered each individual a piece of the "Promised Land," the "Poor Man's Paradise," the "Land of Destiny." Purchasers were further lured by easy land mortgage payment terms of $10.00 a month. As a result, 12,000 contracts were sold for $240 each. The initial cash take was $2,880,000, or a beginning profit of $1,880,000. Only upon completion of all payment was a deed delivered. Many purchasers bought from Bolles without even asking the precise location of the farm or town lot.

As other companies, such as the Florida Everglades Land Company of Chicago followed suit, the first residential land boom in Florida was on. The city of Miami was conceived, drained, and developed out of a mangrove swamp when in 1896, Henry M. Flagler extended the Florida East Coast Railway to Miami. Flagler also built the first major resort hotel in the area, and engineers back at his headquarters in Saint Augustine laid out downtown Miami's pattern of narrow one-way streets.

From a village of several hundred people when the first train arrived, Miami became a city of tens of thousands by 1920. Between 1920 and 1924, property values soared more than 100 percent a year. The population of Florida nearly doubled between 1920 and 1930; in the same interval, it more than tripled in Miami, growing from 29,500 in 1920 to over 110,500 in 1930. Because of prodigious advertising of lots and property, in 1925 the *Miami Herald* could boast the largest advertising lineage of any newspaper in America.

In 1925, at the height of the Florida land boom, sales of the new "developments" were enormously successful. Around Miami, platted subdivisions often sold out in a day. Receipts were in the millions. Lots without waterfrontage sold from $8,000 to $20,000 each. Seashore sites were priced from $20,000 to $75,000.

In subsequent years, as crash and boom followed, one after the other, Florida remained a center of land speculation fortunes and failures, of aspirations and schemes of land developers and would-be lot buyers alike.

By 1970, a new cycle had begun. Each month 25,000 parcels of land were being sold to out-of-state purchasers. Construction grew so intense, in fact, that in 1972 one eighth of all housing permits filed in America were filed in Florida. During this time, Real Estate Investment Trusts (REITs), an aggressive if not always prudent industry, were providing construction loans and permanent financing for amounts in excess of the total market value of the financed property. When this kind of financing is available, the builder is "leveraged out"; that is, he no longer has cash invested in the project. The developer who puts up the structure owns it, although he has no out-of-pocket cash equity investment.

Florida during the early 1970s was a boom environment in which everyone counted on continued inflation, continued immigration to Florida, and continued demand. There was tremendous overbuilding. In Fort Lauderdale alone, at the peak, sixty units a day were being completed in a market that could absorb only twenty. When sales collapsed and mortgage payments could not be met, builders with leveraged-out positions abandoned their developments. The lenders, financial institutions, the REITs and their investors, were left with unfinished projects and some finished buildings for which there was no market demand. Between 1974 and 1976, in Dade and Broward counties, more than 1,000 projects each worth in excess of $250,000 failed, and more than 30,000 new condominium units remained on the market—empty.

WATERFRONT DEVELOPMENT SOUTH OF MIAMI, FLORIDA, AUGUST 1972

Florida has always been one of the nation's most popular states for speculative development of recreational lots. The height of the Florida land boom, in 1925, was followed by another land boom in the early 1970s. Construction fever became so intense in 1972, in fact, that one eighth of all housing permits filed in America that year were in Florida. In the photograph, wetlands are filled and bulkheaded. Today's environmental controls make this practice impossible, and raise the value of houses and lots with such an amenity.

After the debacle, Thomas Bomar, former chairman of the Federal Home Loan Bank and then executive vice president of First Federal Savings and Loan Association of Miami, remarked to *U.S. News & World Report:* "People got drunk on Florida. . . . People who didn't know Fort Lauderdale from Pumpkin Corners were building or financing projects there. They produced row on row of junk. Bulldozers should go in there and tear them down."

THE SECOND-HOME SPLURGE

Second homes, those coveted dwellings, dot the rural landscape of the physically most attractive land across the country, especially within fifty to two hundred miles of the larger cities. Owning a second home is traditionally associated with wealth. But contrary to this assumption, availa-

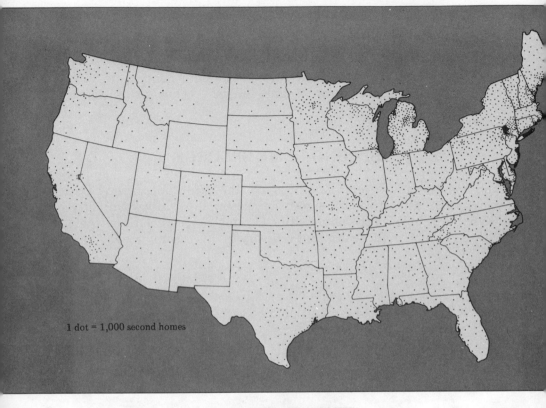

1 dot = 1,000 second homes

SECOND HOMES
IN THE CONTIGUOUS U.S., 1970

In 1970, the U.S. Census Bureau reported that over 2.1 million households owned second homes; by 1973, a similar survey indicated that approximately 3.4 million households were second-home owners. In recent years, somewhere between 75,000 and 150,000 new second homes have been built annually; these now constitute 3 percent of all the housing stock in America.

ble statistics clearly indicate that owning a second homes is no longer the exclusive province of the very wealthy. In fact, today's typical second-home owner is white, middle-class, urban, and about fifty years old. But ownership also crosses all economic boundaries. Average family income tends to be only slightly higher than the national average. In 1974, 40 percent of all second-home owners had annual family incomes of less than $11,000.

A 1967 census study indicates that almost half the second homes included in the survey were relatively small, between 500 and 1,000 square feet in size, with about one fourth smaller than and one fourth in excess of 1,000 square feet. By way of measuring scale, a 500-square-foot dwelling has two or three compact rooms plus a bathroom.

The number of second homes built in a year is anyone's guess, as a building permit is not required in many rural locales. In recent years, depending on economic conditions, somewhere between 75,000 and 150,000 new second homes are being constructed annually, a figure up dramatically from 40,000, the average number constructed during the 1950s. While this number still represents a fraction of the 1 million to 2 million homes generally started in America each year, second homes now constitute 3 percent of all housing stock in America. In certain states, second homes represent an enormous share of total housing. In sparsely settled states such as Maine, Vermont, and New Hampshire, second homes account for 15–20 percent of all housing units.

Most second homes are found near the largest metropolitan districts, at water's edge or in mountain areas. Their highest concentrations are near the industrial centers of the Great Lakes and in the Northeast near the metropolitan complex of "Boswash," the stretch of linked commercial-industrial-administrative cities and towns that extends from Boston to Washington. In addition, with the growth of the Sun Belt cities, about one third of all second homes are now located in the South. States with the most intense concentration of second homes are Michigan, New York, Wisconsin, California, Pennsylvania, Texas, Minnesota, Maine, North Carolina, and Missouri.

The Second-Home Urge.   There is such a profound commitment to the acquisition of a second home that a surprising number of city residents rent in the city and buy in the country. Many young people, especially couples who have just gotten married, actually buy a country lot or second home before their jobs are secure. It is a first-priority investment.

One of the most sustained national trends that greatly contributes to the boom in second-home investment is the increase in the amount of leisure time available to more and more people. Vacation periods from work are twice what they were twenty years ago. Also between 1940 and 1970, the average life expectancy of Americans increased from sixty-two years to about seventy years. Increased longevity, coupled with the fact that more people are enjoying paid, early retirement, creates many more years of leisure. The impact of this trend on land in America could not be more important.

Although many consider their income inadequate, retired people in America have more money to spend than ever before. The number of private pensions and deferred profit-sharing plans more than tripled between 1950 and 1970. Recent legislation, including the Keogh Bill and Individual Retirement Accounts (IRA) programs, guarantees that this number will increase significantly in future years as tax-deferred retirement income accrues. In addition, the number of people who receive Social Security doubled between 1960 and 1970; at the same time, actual disbursements from the source tripled to almost $146 billion, or about 15 percent of the Gross National Product.

Added to increased leisure time and increased income has been a dramatic growth in access to the countryside from metropolitan areas. In 1950, fewer than 60 percent of all American families owned a car. By 1970, this figure had increased to 82 percent, with car registrations up from 40 million to nearly 90 million. Between 1950 and 1970, more than 400,000 miles of municipal and rural highways were added to the road system in America.

An even greater impact on accessibility to rural areas must be credited (or debited, depending on how you see it) to the interstate highway system. This network of immense highways opened up vast amounts of previously undeveloped countryside. Whenever automobile travel time to desirable rural sites and smaller towns in metropolitan areas is cut down, second homes go up.

Second-Home Building and Investment During the 1980s. In recent years, just as millions of people have found their primary house to be a wonderful investment, so have many found the same to be true of a second home. While price fluctuations in second-home properties vary enormously, the trend has certainly been toward higher prices. Nationwide in the summer of 1977, the average existing second home sold for about $30,000, almost twice its 1973 price. In the most desirable second-home communities, such as ski resorts, beach resorts, and mountain retreats, prices have been escalating at rates of 10 to 15 percent per year.

A few examples of both the sharp price increases and nationwide range of prices were reported in 1979 by Kenneth R. Harvey in *Beating Inflation with Real Estate:*

. . . [O]cean-front cottages in Outer Banks, North Carolina, that went for $30,000 to $35,000 four years ago sell for $70,000 to $80,000 today. Condominiums in Vail, Colorado, that cost $50,000 in 1975 went for $75,000 and up in 1978. . . . Units in Killington, Vermont, that sold for $45,000 in 1974 bring $65,000 to $70,000 today.

But the past is history. Today we are faced with very expensive and very limited mortgage funds, and an energy crisis that is certainly not abating. In this new world of the 1980s, what rate of second-home building can be expected? And what are future prices likely to be? Part of the answer depends upon expected demand. Over two thirds of all Americans live in metropolitan areas today. Crime, pollution, traffic congestion, and deteriorating cityscapes do not disappear rapidly. Many city and suburban dwellers seek a place where they can escape and relax, a place where work stress and environmental distress are absent. In 1972, the President's Commission on Population Growth and the American Future found that 34 percent of a wide sample of Americans surveyed expressed a preference to live in the open countryside, whereas another 30 percent preferred to live in a small town or city. Only 14 percent preferred either a large city or a suburb. While the ratios may have shifted slightly since then, I doubt that aspirations have changed decisively. Many of these preferences are being realized. When they are, loyalty and buying power shift. In many instances, the once infrequently visited second home becomes a primary residence; or a move farther out occurs. Indeed, preliminary counts of the 1980 census track the pattern since 1970. There is dramatic evidence of the continuing substantial growth in small towns and rural areas, especially those twenty-five to a hundred miles from the largest cities.

At the same time, new restraints on mobility and higher costs are sure to impede the aspirations of many metropolitan residents in the 1980s. Recent surveys indicate that because of soaring construction and financing costs, some 30 percent of lot owners who once intended to build now find that they can no longer afford to do so. In addition, high gasoline and heating costs and the questionable availability of fuel for years to come are certainly dampening enthusiasm for new construction in remote recreational areas.

Congress has also made it more difficult for second-home owners to cover their operating costs and real-estate taxes by renting out their property on a part-time basis. The 1976 Tax Reform Act limits the deductions an owner can take if he uses a vacation home for more than either two weeks a year or 10 percent of the time it is rented.

On the other hand, a continued sharp increase in the number of new households being formed will stimulate demand for second homes for at least the next five years, and most likely through the 1980s. Because of the postwar baby boom, between 25,000 and 30,000 new households will be formed in America each week—at least until 1985. If ownership of second homes continues at present rates, this source alone will create demand for 20,000 to 50,000 second homes per year. This source, together with a somewhat reduced demand from existing metropolitan families, makes it likely, I believe, that at least 100,000 second homes will be built annually through the 1980s.

The value of *existing* second homes and developed recreational properties will be continually boosted by the rising cost of new construction and steady demand, though I doubt that prices will continue to escalate at the heady rates they did during the 1970s. Higher utility, maintenance, and refinancing costs will hold down the rate of increase in most markets.

Then, of course there is the disaster syndrome. If the economic and political stability of this country begins to crumble more decisively, many urban and suburban residents may seek a house in a smaller town in a rural area in order to be near food and supplies, and in a community felt to be safe and wholesome, and away from the dangers and disruptions of supplies and services upon which cities and suburbs so desperately depend.

While I do not personally anticipate a total breakdown of social order and disruption of goods and services, there is an element of fear that now pervades the fringes of many individual investment decisions. This leads to the deployment of some assets into land and houses in the recreational areas surrounding major population centers. So long as the social and economic stability of this country remains uncertain, I do believe that there will be a concomitant pull, in part, toward well-situated, attractive, small-town recreational areas, as well as because of the various other trends discussed above.

The Second-Home Owner as Land Speculator.   Second-home owners often become land speculators. Would-be purchasers gravitate quite naturally toward land near their second home, not only a location they enjoy but also a place where they have time to look at land nearby.

Second-home areas tend to be selected in the first place because of an appeal, a particular quality that makes them special and desirable: a good climate, scenic beauty, historic interest and charm, waterfront location, and so forth. These same qualities tend to make the land nearby attractive as well and, therefore, scarce in comparison with other land across the country. This fact whets the land buyer's appetite.

When searching for a second home or while living in one, many urban Americans discover the land for the first time. They begin a love affair with it that culminates in the purchase of a larger parcel for use, investment, preservation—often all three in a blurred "sometime in the future, somehow" frame of mind.

By spending vacations and weekends in a second home, many city dwellers become acquainted for the first time with the small town or village, and its conflicts and diversity of opinion over the appropriate future of land within its jurisdiction. This exposure builds an awareness of land-policy and land-development issues. Through a second home, then, land enters the consciousness of urban folk; and, in various ways, the second-home beachhead often becomes the first maneuver toward a land speculation.

RECREATIONAL LOTS AND LAND INVESTMENT DURING THE 1980s

Putting aside the question of a second home altogether, the purchase of a vacant recreational lot or land can be a prudent investment, as it has been for thousands of individuals and families. The success of the venture depends on the location of the land, the quality of the developer (in the case of a lot), and the financial arrangements under which the land is purchased.

In the best of instances, the first buyer of a newly subdivided recreational lot is able to double his cash within a year or two. But most available subdivision lots are neither in the most desirable locations nor in subdivisions owned by the highest-quality land developers. And, as pointed out earlier, there is currently a tremendous surplus of subdivided recreational lots all across the country.

Over half of all recreational lots are less than one acre. My guess is that the average-size lot is no larger than three fourths of an acre. Thus, if we assume a minimum of 15 million vacant lots (75 percent of the estimated 20 million) at a national average of three fourth of an acre each, a total of over 10 million acres of subdivided land is surely involved, or

DISTRIBUTION OF RECREATIONAL LOTS REGISTERED WITH OILSR, JANUARY 1974

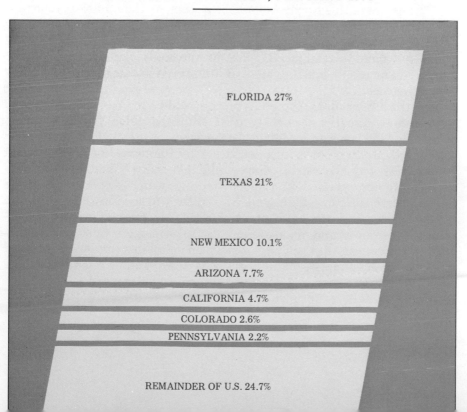

FLORIDA 27%

TEXAS 21%

NEW MEXICO 10.1%

ARIZONA 7.7%

CALIFORNIA 4.7%

COLORADO 2.6%

PENNSYLVANIA 2.2%

REMAINDER OF U.S. 24.7%

about one sixth the amount of all land now consumed for all urban purposes! This is a very considerable amount of land and subdivided lots held in relatively speculative ownership.

This market is especially significant in certain areas. By the mid-1970s, Florida, Texas, New Mexico, Arizona, California, Colorado, and Pennsylvania contained three fourths of all large-scale recreational lot development, with Texas and Florida the clear leaders. With over 30 percent of all initial lot buyers speculating to resell at a profit, it is obvious that there is no shortage of either offerings or available lots. This places a tremendous weight on the supply side of the supply-demand equation, a situation that suggests weak prices and competition for sales in many areas.

At least three fourths of all subdivided recreational lots, or more than 15 million, remain vacant today, and the actual number is probably much higher. But let us assume for the moment that there are only 15 million vacant recreational lots, that all new second homes are built on existing recreation lots (which they will not be), and that average construction of second homes occurs at a high rate of 150,000 units per year. Even in this, the maximum demand case, there are already enough vacant subdivided recreational lots to satisfy all demand for the next hundred years! Certainly it becomes apparent that the foreseeable demand for recreational lots can be accommodated on a national basis without the additional development of a single new one.

The extent of this surplus should be a sobering thought to anyone now anxious to plunge into the speculative development of a recreational subdivision or purchase of a vacant lot. In any particular location, the ratio of demand to available lots may be unusually high with demand far exceeding available lots and sites. But more often, the opposite is likely to be the case.

On the other hand, in years to come, it will be increasingly difficult to create new recreational developments and subdivision lots on the most desirable land near and abutting waterways, on steep slopes, and amid other sought-after physical amenities. Environmental regulations and community growth-control policies will increasingly restrain such endeavors. In nonmetropolitan regions that have watched open land become second-home territory, a growing awareness will lead to the shoring up of subdivision and development standards. This will add greater protection to consumers, and much greater cost to developers. Substandard dirt roads, open sewage ditches, septic tanks on small lots that leach into and pollute the groundwater, will become as they should, remnants of the past. Permitted erosion of hillsides and condoned drainage into waterways fortunately is diminishing every year.

These long-needed and too-long-neglected social, environmental, and ecological controls over the development and destiny of the land will be accorded more attention. Improved standards for the protection of air, land, and water will make it increasingly difficult and increasingly expensive to subdivide rural America into ever more second-home and recreational sites. This means, inevitably, that those land parcels and lots in inventory, where there is sustained demand, will become all the more valuable.

But in most locations, demand will not be as strong as in the past, and the surplus of recreational lots will become apparent. Locations where there is no waterfront available, where there is poor road access at present, where there is little promise of electricity and other utilities, will lose their appeal, as will undeveloped lots and raw acreage appropriate to second-home use in communities that grow too fast, and mindlessly. The environment that attracts will be destroyed; and once that happens, demand for and the value of the land will subside.

Taken together, these trends and potentialities indicate that many land speculators who seek to cash in on a recreational land boom in the 1980s are in for an unpleasant surprise. During this time, purchasers will become more selective than ever before. And I suspect, given the vast supply of such property in all but the best spots, they will have much to select from.

Continued value appreciation, in all but the most difficult years, is more than likely in waterfront areas—wherever they are—along a river, ocean, bay. Buildable land that enjoys water *views* will remain in demand, as will most buildable, accessible acreage and lots with especially fine and protected landscape views and especially beautiful topography. Good-quality recreational land and properly subdivided lots in sought-out locales will increase in value at a rate at least equivalent to annual rates of inflation. Very often, they will exceed this mark by a substantial margin.

Almost all other undeveloped recreational property is likely to be unusually vulnerable to cracks in the increasingly fragile national economy. Tight mortgage markets lead quickly to a cutback in second-home financing, which in turn dampens demand for recreational property. Oil and gas costs and supplies are crucial. Because the lot held for development of a second home is a luxury, it will be given up if sustained constriction of incomes and of the national economy take place.

There is a strong probability—stronger than at any other time since the end of World War II—that the value of average-quality and lesser-quality recreational property will stagnate, or even plummet, sometime during the 1980s.

FOURTEEN

———

THE FEDERAL LANDS: PUBLIC WEALTH AND PRIVATE PRIVILEGE

Trying to understand land in America without knowing about the public lands is a little like trying to find out who owns Italy without a list of the Vatican's properties. Both governing forces control large percentages of their nation's land. The parallel may go considerably further. Both the Vatican and the United States government obtained their immense domains through a gnarled and well-covered trail of conquest, acquisition, and gift. It is a fair guess that the Catholic Church runs the largest real-estate office in the world; and if it doesn't, then the United States government does.

Only, again like the Vatican and unlike a well-managed business, the operation is dispersed, broken into many parts. This patchwork organization makes it difficult for anyone to piece together a clear picture of the immense scale of the operation. This also makes it especially difficult for the ordinary citizen to know what the federal government is actually doing with the so-called public lands—lands which, by accepted definitions of "public" and "we, the people" and all of that, supposedly belong to everyone. The spread of land holdings is so wide, and the account books so far flung, in so many dusty corners of so many offices across America, and in the most impenetrable parts of Washington, D. C., that even well-meaning legislators and jurists find it nearly impossible to discover who controls some of the federal lands, and how they are used.

One fact alone, however, establishes the scale on which the federal government is a major land player on the American scene: about one third of all land in America is owned by Uncle Sam. About 46 million acres, little more than 2 percent more, is held in trust for the Indians by the government. The aggregate of all publicly owned lands, including all state and local government holdings, is 42 percent of all land in America. In addition, the federal government has recently expanded its territory significantly by exerting a claim to—in effect, annexing—the Outer Continental Shelf, a land covered by the sea whose subsurface wealth and water-born value are incalculable.

That leaves private ownership of the nation's total 2.3 billion acres at about 58 percent. And that percentage has been declining, slowly but steadily, for decades. Between 1959 and 1974, for instance, a total of 17 million acres was transferred from private ownership to state and local governments, for public parks, wildlife refuges, airports, public buildings, highways, and streets. State and local governments have been acquiring property at about an annual rate of one million acres and have increased the amount of their holdings in the 15-year period by about 12 percent!

Location of the Federal Lands.   Although some federally owned land is to be found in every state, it is concentrated for the most part in the eleven western states of Arizona, California, Colorado, Idaho, Montana, Nevada, New Mexico, Oregon, Utah, Washington, and Wyoming, and in the United States' latest acquisition, Alaska. Over 90 percent of the federal land outside Alaska is located in these eleven states, and averages 63.5 percent of their territory. However, nearly half of the total amount of all federal land is in Alaska; this represents over 96 percent of all land in the state. In comparison, the federal government owns only 5 percent of the land in the South, 4.1 percent in the Midwest, and 2.2 percent in the Northeast.

The large amount of federal land in the western states results from immense federal purchases from foreign governments. The two largest of these were the acquisition of 183 million acres of land covering the states

LAND OWNERSHIP IN U.S.

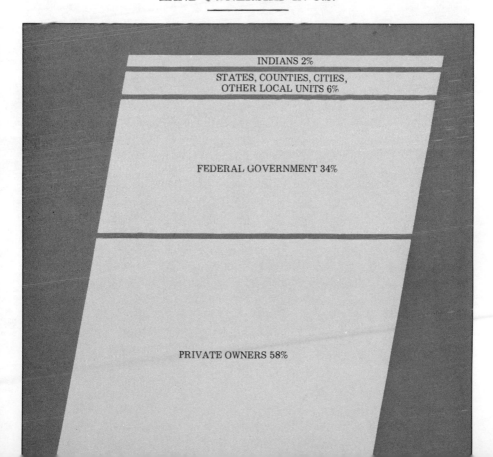

INDIANS 2%

STATES, COUNTIES, CITIES, OTHER LOCAL UNITS 6%

FEDERAL GOVERNMENT 34%

PRIVATE OWNERS 58%

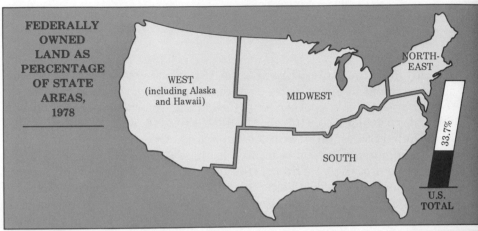

FEDERALLY OWNED LAND AS PERCENTAGE OF STATE AREAS, 1978

WEST (including Alaska and Hawaii)

MIDWEST

NORTH-EAST

SOUTH

33.7%

U.S. TOTAL

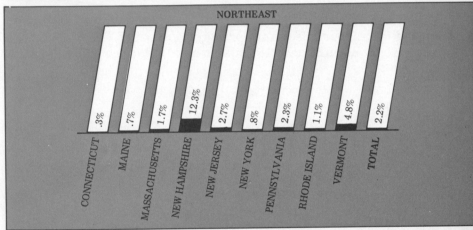

NORTHEAST

CONNECTICUT	MAINE	MASSACHUSETTS	NEW HAMPSHIRE	NEW JERSEY	NEW YORK	PENNSYLVANIA	RHODE ISLAND	VERMONT	TOTAL
.3%	.7%	1.7%	12.3%	2.7%	.8%	2.3%	1.1%	4.8%	2.2%

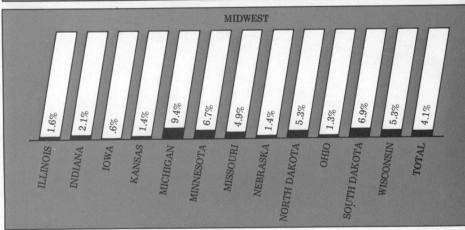

MIDWEST

ILLINOIS	INDIANA	IOWA	KANSAS	MICHIGAN	MINNESOTA	MISSOURI	NEBRASKA	NORTH DAKOTA	OHIO	SOUTH DAKOTA	WISCONSIN	TOTAL
1.6%	2.1%	.6%	1.4%	9.4%	6.7%	4.9%	1.4%	5.3%	1.3%	6.9%	5.3%	4.1%

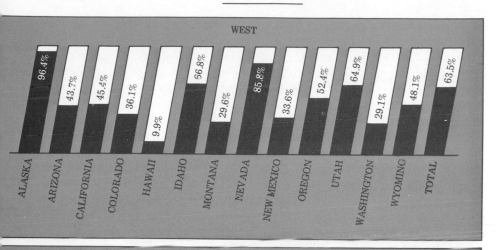

WEST

ALASKA 96.4%
ARIZONA 43.7%
CALIFORNIA 45.4%
COLORADO 36.1%
HAWAII 9.9%
IDAHO 56.8%
MONTANA 29.6%
NEVADA 85.8%
NEW MEXICO
OREGON 52.4%
UTAH 64.9%
WASHINGTON 29.1%
WYOMING 48.1%
TOTAL 63.5%

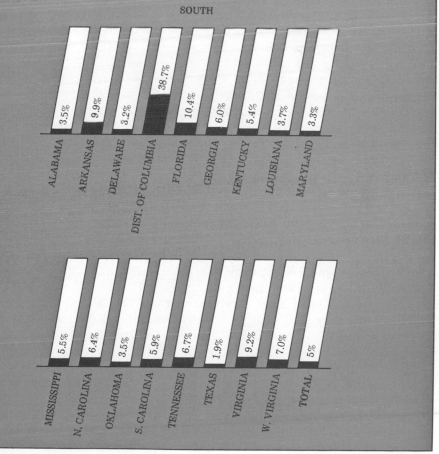

SOUTH

ALABAMA 3.5%
ARKANSAS 9.9%
DELAWARE 3.2%
DIST. OF COLUMBIA 38.7%
FLORIDA 10.4%
GEORGIA 6.0%
KENTUCKY 5.4%
LOUISIANA 3.7%
MARYLAND 3.3%

MISSISSIPPI 5.5%
N. CAROLINA 6.4%
OKLAHOMA 3.5%
S. CAROLINA 5.9%
TENNESSEE 6.7%
TEXAS 1.9%
VIRGINIA 9.2%
W. VIRGINIA 7.0%
TOTAL 5%

of Washington, Oregon, and Idaho, the outcome of the Oregon Compromise with Great Britain in 1846; and the acquisition of 340 million acres, including the territory which became the states of California, Nevada, Utah and most of New Mexico, the consequence of the Mexican Acquisition in 1848. What the government owns today remains after its buying and selling of the continent (as outlined in Chapter Two), and constitutes the current public domain.

The very low level of federal land ownership along the eastern seaboard is the result of a specific decision taken at one moment in the history of the formation of America. When between 1775 and 1776 the country was being pasted together as a relatively unified entity, the East Coast colonies, for a variety of reasons—including overlapping claims and inequitable land holdings beyond the seaboard—yielded all claims to lands beyond the Appalachian Mountains to the federal government. This single act cut the western boundary of these states at the mountain range. It also gave the new government a large domain of in-demand real estate that could be converted into working capital but left very little federal land east of the colonial boundary.

Administration of the Land. A score of federal agencies administer the federal lands on behalf of the public, more often than not as one of the less important aspects of their operation. More than 99 percent of all federal lands are administered by three cabinet-level departments: Interior, Agriculture, and Defense. Even within these three departments, however, a system of inter-agency fragmentation often results in conflicting or overlapping jurisdictions, which complicates the management of the lands.

Consider the Department of the Interior, the largest land manager in the country. Within the department, the major administering agency is the Bureau of Land Management, which has exclusive responsibility for about 60 percent of all federal lands, or some 470 million acres. More than half of this area is located in Alaska.

The Bureau of Land Management is a department of government with which the ordinary citizen rarely has any contact; in fact, most people are not even aware that it exists. Yet this agency alone, and the department of which it is a part, exerts an enormous influence over the price of food in America, and over the value of much public and private real estate. On its land, cattle and sheep graze, food is grown, and the value of adjacent lands is influenced by management policies.

Other principal land-holding and operating agencies within the Department of the Interior include the United States Fish and Wildlife Service, which oversees some 30 million acres of land; and the National Park Service, manager of over 25 million acres within its system.

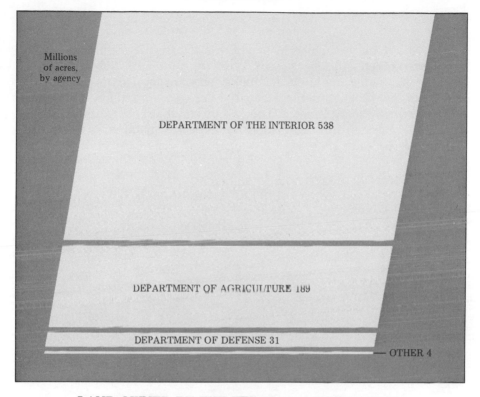

Millions
of acres,
by agency

DEPARTMENT OF THE INTERIOR 538

DEPARTMENT OF AGRICULTURE 189

DEPARTMENT OF DEFENSE 31

— OTHER 4

**LAND OWNED BY THE FEDERAL GOVERNMENT,
BY AGENCY OF JURISDICTION,
1976**

Within the Department of Agriculture, the Forest Service, another agency generally well-insulated from public contact, has jurisdiction over 24 percent of the federal domain, or approximately 187 million acres. Its policies affect almost 20 percent of all commercial forest land in America which contributes 40 percent of the supply of salable timber and 60 percent of all softwood saw timber. The prices of houses and of paper are deeply influenced by policies which given these resource holdings. The price and availability of basic commodities and natural resources, along with food, are rarely thought to be subject to government control and regulation as a consequence of federal ownership of land. More often, price controls on private industry, import regulations, and government influence upon bank interest rates and other legal regulatory interventions apart from land ownership policies are noticed as ways the federal government intervenes into the large-scale economic operations of America.

In 1957 it was estimated by one of this country's preeminent agricultural economist, Marion Clawson, that the total universe of economic activity on the federal lands, including lease income, and sales of goods, and foods and products derived from the land, accounted for 8–10 percent of the Gross National Product. This is a larger share of that fundamental index of American life and prosperity than is registered by most other single industries or sources.

SELECTED FEDERAL AGENCIES
AND THEIR LAND HOLDINGS

AGENCY	LANDHOLDINGS (IN ACRES)
Bureau of Land Management	470,174,318
Forest Service	187,536,142
Fish and Wildlife Service	30,385,232
National Park Service	25,097,463
Department of the Army	11,035,335
Department of the Air Force	8,364,296
Corps of Engineers	7,883,856
Bureau of Reclamation	7,551,589
Bureau of Indian Affairs	4,967,971
Department of the Navy	3,583,138
Energy Research and Development Administration	2,108,947
Tennessee Valley Authority	931,615
Agriculture Research Service	399,137
Panama Canal Company	365,843
National Aeronautics and Space Administration	136,178
International Boundary and Water Commission, U.S. and Mexico (Department of State)	122,062
U.S. Coast Guard	102,447
Federal Aviation Administration	60,364
National Oceanic and Atmospheric Administration	51,310
Federal Railroad Administration	30,034
Bureau of Prisons	27,896
Veterns Administration	21,946
General Services Administration	17,208
Bureau of Mines	13,082
Office of the Secretary of the Interior	11,560

Thus, the federal lands are not only immense in scale. They present a vast resource of potential economic consequence to the underlying cost of living in America. As we shall see, there is much about the use of these lands in our ever more costly and resource-restricted national system that merits considerable attention and reform. The aggregate economic scale of the federal lands, unrealized by most, and indeed remote from most of the large population centers in the country, is of inestimable significance.

A LITTLE HISTORY

At one time or another over the past two hundred years, the federal government held title to about four fifths of the land in America. Chapter Two highlights some of the ways this land was acquired, and some of the programs and policies under which much of it was disposed.

During the twentieth century, some 55 million acres have been bought back either from private individuals or the states. These so-called acquired lands represent just over 7 percent of all federal holdings, and are devoted to two principal uses: national forests and defense. Many of the forest properties were bought by President Theodore Roosevelt. The lands used for military installations have been acquired incrementally over the years as the perceived needs of the military establishment shift—and tend to increase.

The rest of the federal lands were obtained by wholesale purchase or conquest. Enormous acquisitions were negotiated with foreign powers: the Louisianna Purchase of 1803 from France, the Oregon Compromise of 1846 with Great Britain, and the Mexican Acquisition of 1848 are among the largest. The remaining land was obtained directly from native American tribes, some by so-called treaty, which included nominal compensation; some by rights of passage and conquest by invading, marauding, and dominant bands of militia.

The amount of land that has passed through federal title and out again is approximately 1.1 billion acres. This land has been given to and sold to individual citizens; it has been given to and bought by businesses; it has been transferred to other levels of government, principally to the states as a sort of dowry upon their formation and as a negotiable asset to help them finance extensive projects. This vast brokerage operation was carried out under a set of uncoordinated, often contested, and certainly controversial sequence of acts, mandates, and proclamations.

Operation: Land Disposal. In the eighteenth century, founding lawmakers gladly gave the national government the right and responsibility

449

to buy or steal and then police the land in America. After all, the government did represent the small number of white people who set up the laws, the army, and the treasury. Needed at the time was a legal method to get hold of all of that valuable real estate and then secure the borders. It was considered the obvious responsibility of the new federal government to

**A SHEPHERD WATCHING HIS FLOCKS,
MADISON COUNTY, MONTANA,
JUNE 1939**

Federal lands have historically been made available to private interest groups at nominal cost and on generous terms: to railroad combines, timber interests, mining operators, cattle and sheep ranchers, and others who seek to exploit the federal lands to commercial advantage.

function a bit like a conduit: acquire the land, have it properly surveyed and registered, and then distribute it to private citizens.

Organized business, disorganized settlers, and dazzled immigrants all concurred: when it came to land, the federal government was supposed to make it readily available to them either at no charge or at affordable prices. Along the way, it was all right for the treasury to replenish its funds and even to take a little cream off the top to run some other parts of the government.

The only land policy questions debated with fervor in the early years of Congress had to do with who got what, and how much of it, and at what price. The notion that the federal lands should be entirely disposed of continued right through the last major national purchase, the acquisition of Alaska from Russia in 1867.

Until approximately 1870, federal land ownership was not perceived

to be in conflict in any way with the dominant ideology of private enter-prise. Indeed, it was not. Rather, the federal government was viewed as a temporary land-holding operation, a sort of elaborate brokerage office, buying and selling, or buying and giving.

Federal lands were granted for many kinds of major business endeavor —most notably railroad building—often with the government as a tacit co-venturer, due to the checkerboard pattern of land disposition. Federal lands were made available at nominal cost and on generous terms to those who wanted to exploit the inherent natural resources on or below the land. Sales or leases were made to railroad combines, timber interests, mining operators, cattle and sheep ranchers, and others who could exploit the federal land to commercial advantage. The terms and prices worked out in these arrangements make Uncle Sam the great Sugar Daddy of all time.

But in the late nineteenth century, a new sentiment emerged. Flagrant abuse in the management of the federal lands and increasing concern among many that the ordinary citizen was benefiting less and less from the "public" lands elicited a call for reform. The idea began to take hold that the national government should not dispose of all of its property but rather should begin to preserve some of it. By the time this became the overriding attitude, however, much of the easily exploitable property was long gone. The most productive agricultural lands, the best grazing lands, the richest, then exploitable mining areas, and the most accessible mature forests had been sold to aggressive and knowledgeable private entrepreneurs. What remained was the less accessible terrain, as well as the rugged mountain lands, the watershed slopes, the deserts, and vast grazing lands of marginal quality.

A New Direction in Federal Land Policy. A key shift in the use and management of federal holdings was signaled by the designation of Yellowstone National Park in 1872 as the first national park. Within the next two decades, additional public lands were set aside by both federal and state governments. However, the older tradition that public lands should be a source of federal revenue led to the assumption that lands set aside at least should be self-sustaining.

The administrations of Presidents Rutherford B. Hayes (1877–1881) and S. Grover Cleveland (1885–1889) and (1893–1897) were the first to be conspicuous in their support of reform in federal land management. The report of the Public Land Commission of 1880 remains one of the great pieces of investigation into the history of management of the public domain. It focused public attention on abuses of federal land grants in such a way that the problem could no longer be ignored. As a result, in 1891, the Forest Reserve Act was adopted, empowering the president to set aside timberlands for conservation purposes. In 1905, under the dynamic leadership of President Theodore Roosevelt, and inspired by the intellectual probity of Gifford Pinchot, chief of the U.S. Forest Service, 33 million acres were added to the national forests, thereby nearly doubling the area previously set aside. Another 30 million acres were added in 1906.

In 1903 the national government set up the first waterfowl and wildlife refuges. During the 1930s, as part of an effort to bail out impoverished landowners in the depression years, the government purchased nearly 11 million acres of so-called submarginal lands, which were later added to the first wildlife refuges, national parks and monuments, national forests, and grazing districts. At the time, many of these lands were considered of little value to anyone. Crops could not be grown on them productively, buildings could not be supported on them safely, and much of the land was remote from road access and settlements. Today many of these lands have a born-again existence as precious, coveted stretches of unique wetlands, such as the Everglade estuaries in southern Florida, which became the Everglades National Park in 1947.

Nor were the prairies ignored. Most of the desirable agricultural and grazing land had long since been disposed of, sold off to private operators at per-acre costs of $1.25 and up. From these sales began the great ranching and agricultural fortunes of America. In the mid-1930s, there remained more than 180 million acres of "unreserved and unappropriated" public domain lands. In fact, in 1933 it was still possible to buy this land directly from the federal government, as it had been for over a hundred years. During that year, however, all sales totaled less than one million acres, still a staggering figure but a mere trickle compared to the average annual sale to private interests of roughly 10 million acres, which had been disposed of every year between 1850 and the late 1920s.

In 1934, following years of discussion, the Taylor Grazing Act received congressional approval and was signed into law. Heretofore, the public domain lands had been open to livestock grazing as a sort of poacher's paradise. There was no requirement to lease, and there was little effort to exclude. Policing the boundaries of 180 million acres requires riding a lot of fences. But the Taylor Grazing Act launched the first attempt to classify types of federal lands. Land was separated into property that either could be sold or would not be disposed of. Isolated tracts were identified. Land still suitable for homesteading was marked. Sites in these two categories continued to be offered for sale. The rest was placed into a sequence of vast grazing districts. Land was still leased to private owners of herds or used under a permit system, but it could no longer be bought from the federal government. The grazing districts located predominantly in the eleven western states are administered today by the Bureau of Land Management, Department of the Interior.

As a result of the Taylor Grazing Act, a total terrain of over 130 million acres now remains within grazing districts. Of this, while no published figures exist, informed observers estimate somewhere in the magnitude of 100 million acres to be within the national forests. In addition, about 17 million acres of public land outside the grazing districts are used on a lease or permit basis by cattlemen and sheep herders. Grazing lands are found in twenty-eight different states, though the great bulk of the property is also in the eleven western states. Together, this nearly 150 million acres represent an enormous asset and benefit to the private herd operators in America. During the calendar year 1975, for example, about 20,000 private operators held licenses or permits to use the range for a nominal fee. This represents an average of over 7,000 acres per operator. An estimated 14 percent of all livestock raised in this country graze on federally owned land.

Consequence of Conservation. There is, then, between 1880 and 1930 a shift of great consequence to the management of the public domain and to the control of land in America. When the largest landowner in the nation stops selling, everyone and everything is affected. Land already held in the private sphere becomes more valuable. It remains a marketable entity that may be sold to both other successive private interests and units of government, especially at the local, county, and state levels.

The value of land along the boundary of the federal holdings is also profoundly affected. If land on the boundary of private property cannot be arbitrarily sold or developed in any manner whatsoever, the private holding gains considerable value. A future can be predicted. If this future includes a forest reserve or national wilderness or some other environmentally desirable purpose, the private land on the perimeter soars in value. People seek such property. And people will tell you when selling or simply describing their good fortune that their land abuts a national forest or seashore or other type of preserve.

The same upward valuation is experienced when adjacent land is given for conservation purposes to agencies of government, newer environmental land trusts, or nonprofit associations such as The Nature Conservancy. The degree of security and the prospect of continued beauty and tranquility are instantly reflected in the market by higher prices.

Beginning in the last quarter of the nineteenth century and continuing at a more rapid pace during the first third of the twentieth century, the federal government became a major buyer of private lands—of land it once sold or gave away. This profound shift in approach signaled the time when many in the country began to realize that the frontier was not going to stretch out forever. By the early 1930s, the federal government began to treat its precious homestead more like a boardinghouse. It inaugurated policies aimed at earning income from the use of its premises rather than sell the property. The lease of federal lands to private operators for their own business use, and presumed profit, now contributes, though only minimally, to the vastly expanded federal budget.

The federal government began to grow rapidly by 1900. At the same time, its income from land sales was curtailed. Consequently, new sources of operating income had to be devised. The income tax, a profound shift in the source of federal revenue and one that now accounts for almost 60 percent of annual federal income, was inaugurated in 1913. By comparison, land-related income now accounts for less than 5 percent of all revenue.

ALASKA: THE LAST STATE AND THE LAST FRONTIER

Alaska, of course, changed the whole picture. Admitted to statehood in 1958, it is the largest state by far, with over 365 million acres. Alaska is more than three times the size of California, the third largest state, and twice the size of Texas, now the second biggest state in land area. No other state in the country contains even 100 million acres. Most have 30–60 million acres, with a few under and a few over that mark.

The acquisition of Alaska, moreover, represents a twentieth-century situation analogous to those which occurred during the early days of the formation of the nation. As in past federal purchases from foreign governments, the new owner of the land—at least over 95 percent of it—is the U.S. government.

Special-interest groups now bargain for control of the land, as they did throughout the nineteenth century. Only now it is 1980, not 1803 or 1848. The rules of the game have changed, and so in many respects has the balance of power. Commercial interests no longer assume they will either be favored with outright grants of land or benefit from nominal laws that create low cost land acquisition privileges. However, they do vie for favorable rights and terms to develop and exploit federal lands, with an intensity reminiscent of the railroad companies, the lumber combines, the mining trusts, and the livestock interests of an earlier time.

An altogether new coalition is also now evident. Preservationists and environmentalists, a rubric that covers so many types and so many inter-

ests—some of them clearly closet economic interests—are new participants on the scene. This alliance of diverse groups, which includes land
developers already in possession of private property they hope to sell at
extraordinary prices, wants *all* of Alaska protected from any change
whatsoever.

Complicating the situation is a segment of the population that has
always been pushed out before the pie was cut: the tribal groups. Native
Alaskans are perhaps the only true beneficiaries of the history of atrocities to the natives in the lower forty-eight states. On their side is a national collective memory of social injustice and guilt. The dreadful and
lurid physical abuse and economic exploitation suffered by native Americans throughout the history of America haunts those now in charge of
national land policy. The theft of America below the fiftieth parallel is
being atoned for on the new frontier.

The Pie Is Cut.   In 1971, when the Alaska Native Claims Settlement Act
(ANCSA), the most generous land-claim deal in U.S. history, was passed,
Congress began to cut the pie among the contenders. Under the act, the
United States ceded 44 million acres, or 12 percent of Alaska's 365 million
acres, to the state's 70,000 native Eskimos, Aleuts, and Indians. Unlike
the situation that prevailed on the Indian reservations, good land, placed
where the people live now, and have traditionally, is ceded. There is no
massive migratory resettlement, no forced march to ever poorer and ever
more remote terrain.

In addition, the federal government agreed to pay the native Alaskans
$932 million in reparations. The bulk of this money is to be used in setting
up a series of profit-making corporations owned by the natives themselves. The Bering Straits Native Corporation, for example, holds assets
worth $50 million and 2.2 million acres of Alaskan land.

Other claims on Alaska's 365 million acres complicate the issue,
though. As Jerry Gilliland, an Interior Department spokesman, said to
U. S. News & World Report in 1978, "The status of landownership in
Alaska is a mess right now." Congressional approval of statehood in 1958
included a grant of 104 million acres to the state, more than one fourth
of Alaska's surface, and the most generous grant to any new state in
American history. The state and the natives are still sorting out their
rival and often overlapping claims. Only about 1 million acres are privately owned. The balance, about 217 million acres, is federally owned.
Of this, some 75 million acres were designated by early 1978 principally
as national parks, forests, and wildlife refuges. Of the remaining 142
million acres, in November 1978, 110 million acres were barred from

development for up to three years. In December 1978, President Carter placed more than 56 million acres of these lands in the National Park System—the largest national park designation any president has ever made—which more than doubled the size of the system itself. By designating them as national monuments, the lands are locked away from mineral or oil development unless Congress decides otherwise.* President Carter also directed another 39 million acres of those lands to be preserved as national wildlife refuges. Thus about 95 million federally owned acres are protected by presidential action.

John B. Oakes, former senior editor of *The New York Times,* has termed Alaska the "number one land-use problem of the decade—perhaps even of the century." And well he might, for the problem of striking a balance of land use in the fiftieth state goes well beyond merely dividing the pie wisely and fairly among Alaskan natives, conservationists, developers, and an energy-conscious nation. Alaska is America's last chance to conserve vast areas of its natural terrain for public benefit. But this opportunity is available amid energy and natural resource shortages of unprecedented gravity. Surely a sound program of priorities and beneficiaries can be worked out when so very much land is available, and when its surface and subsurface attributes are of such variety and diverse potential use. No land issue in America deserves more thoughtful attention.

PUBLIC LANDS, PRIVATE DEALS

The management and administration of the federal lands today reveal significant vestiges of privileged arrangements with special-interest groups. In addition, federal land-management practices still forward private commercial objectives more than they address broad national economic and social needs. The giveaway era of outright grants and low-priced sales of valuable land to favored parties is obviously over. But exploitation of public land by private, privileged groups which work so closely with land-managing federal agencies obviously is not.

The ability to lease valuable federal property under lenient terms at low prices is a lure that draws the most serious and concerted attention of vested private interests—whether they are from the forest industry, oil

---

*The Alaska Lands Bill, signed into law while this book was on press, designates more than 97 million acres as national parks and wildlife refuges, which doubles the nation's holding of such areas. The bill also triples the country's wilderness area by classifying 56 million acres in that category. The compromise bill, a last stroke of the Carter Administration, is criticized by environmentalists and developers; both claim they will seek revision.

exploration combines, mining operations, or recreational facilities developers. Here the link of land, power, and wealth is vivid, as different interests compete for control of federal lands.

The Forest Business: Land in the Service of Wealth.   Of the almost 500 million acres of commercial timberland in the country, only 14 percent is owned by the forest industry. Most of the timberland, about 59 percent, is actually owned by private citizens, and 27 percent is owned by federal, state, and local governments. Yet, the government-owned forests contain about half of all the softwood in America. Softwood includes all forms of pine, spruce, fir, and redwood—the most important timber for building houses and making paper products. The national forests are also the repository of about half of all the available growing stock of timber, that is, sawtimber plus smaller and younger trees. In addition, extensive grazing, mining, and outdoor recreational activities are conducted within the national forests.

Because of Forest Service management policies, a tremendous proportion of the standing trees within these forests are quite old, even fully mature; in fact, they are of such old growth that there is considerable waste from tree mortality. The mortality per acre on national forests is almost *double* the loss of productive woodland found in forest industry forests. The result is low annual net growth from natural development, much waste from dead and dying timber, and inefficient and uneconomical harvest of timber. The Forest Service itself estimates that its timber yield is less than 40 percent of the potential annual capacity of an economically managed forest preserve!

If all acreage within the national forests were managed on an intensive basis ("intensive" meaning with all other outputs of the forest subordinated to the one objective of producing wood, regardless of cost), over 10 billion cubic feet of wood could be grown annually. Instead, less than 3 billion cubic feet are now produced each year. Indeed, in 1976, only 23

THE NATIONAL FOREST SYSTEM,
IN THE CONTIGUOUS U.S. 1979
(Opposite)

Approximately 27 percent of America's 500 million acres of commercial timberland are owned by federal, state, and local governments. Yet the National Forest System, administered by the Forest Service of the Department of Agriculture, contains about one half of all the softwood in America, the most important timber for building housing and making paper-products, and also about one half of all the growing stock.

percent of softwood, 4 percent of hardwood, and 19 percent of all wood in the national harvest came from the national forests.

Thus, the national forests' contribution to harvest wood is less than one fifth of the national total. Yet, about half the nation's housing timber supply and total inventory of timber originates in the national forests. This contrast points out the greatly underutilized resource of the national forests. It is a much-needed vast storehouse, but currently it is making only a limited contribution to the annual supply of lumber.

For the last twenty years, while national forests have continued to underproduce, lumber has been one of the runaway cost elements in America. In 1955, the cost of lumber was pegged at an average of $26.10 per 1,000-board feet; by 1970, this figure had escalated to $83.79 per 1,000-board feet, by 1977, the same softwood that supports your roof and walls cost $231.54 per 1,000-board feet. This increase of 787 percent in twenty-two years, or an average annual cost increase of about 28 percent, is more than double even the unprecedented 1979 inflation rate.

The Multiple-Use Policy. Although high lumber costs are in part the result of poor management of the existing national forests, less than optimum wood production, the Forest Service claims, is also a consequence of a deliberate specialized management policy within the Forest Service. This policy—the "multiple-use" management policy—is a land-management program that along with timber production, allows for grazing, recreation, watershed management, and mining on Forest Service lands. Because of a commitment on the part of the Forest Service to conduct all of these activities on their holdings, it is argued that it is impossible to concentrate exclusively on timber production. Through its multiple-use policy, the federal government in effect encourages diverse interest groups which seek preferential access to the national forests. The result is that Forest Service funds and lands are not concentrated exclusively on wood production endeavors. Furthermore, though federal lands are used, the federal government has no wood production operation itself, and control of private operations on federal lands is limited.

In my judgment, such activities as wildlife protection, recreation, watershed management, and environmentally responsible mining should not necessarily be excluded from any areas of the national forests. However, these simultaneous activities do not truly explain why so many of the public forest lands today are too dense to grow well, replete with so many fully mature trees, falling, wasting, and dying each year. By way of contrast, the average privately owned industry forest annually produces about 50 percent more sawtimber per acre and nearly 70 percent more wood of all sizes per acre than the average national forest! And, as

Marion Clawson points out, "These comparisons are for all national forests and all forest industry forests. If the comparison were with a 'well-managed' forest industry forest, it would be still sharper. . . ."

Twenty-five percent of public lease revenue from the national forests is allocated to states and counties where the forests exist, 10 percent is cycled back for use by the Forest Service, and an impressive 65 percent enters the general fund of the United States treasury. Cash income from the national forests today exceeds $500 million a year. This money, every year, operates in part as a check on taxes, which must be collected from individuals and private business. By earning less income as a result of lower production, higher federal, state, and county taxes are paid by individuals. In another way—one that is more direct than either those in the federal agencies, which manage the national forests, or those in private industry, who exert influence over this management, would care to acknowledge—inefficiency in national forest management functions as a profit stimulant to the private forest industry: it keeps the cost of lumber up.

Other Private Rights to the Public Domain: Mining the Federal Lands. The federal lands are the special preserve of other interests as well, including private mining, grazing, and exploration interests. While the management and utilization of the national forests may serve as a single example, those other enterprises which have enjoyed for so long a special and historic power over the public land in America are still exercising their clout. Two of the most obvious which benefit in substantial ways from the land that remains in federal possession include the livestock growers, through favorable grazing rights, and natural resource mining interests (including the most prominent ones these days), those who mine coal and explore for oil and gas.

Federal lands were available to mining interests and prospectors for purchase on very favorable terms for a long time. The Mining Law of 1872 legalized and codified the means by which these special interests were able to appropriate the public domain for mining purposes at nominal costs. Mineral rights, and the public land containing them, were sold between $2.50 and $5.00 per acre to the first person or corporation to find a commercially valuable deposit. This is a prime example of an older attitude in America that all land, public or private, is a commodity to be exploited for private gain.

Some provisions of that same law still pertain today to hardrock mining. The hardrock explorer and miner can go onto any public land that has not been specifically withdrawn from mining activity—about 68 percent of the almost 800 million acres of public land are open to mineral

VIEW OF AN
OPEN-PIT MINE, UTAH

Until very recently, no restrictions were placed on mining exploration techniques on public land. The relatively inexpensive process of strip mining became rampant. The Surface Mining Control Reclamation Act of 1977 sets a slow mechanism for the recovery of strip-mined lands, whereby operators pay a reclamation fee for each ton mined. Although inadequate, the fee acts as an incentive for deep mining, which is more costly but less damaging environmentally.

development—and look for mineral deposits, claim them, dig them out of the ground, and process the ore. The hardrock miner, furthermore, has the option to buy the land that contains a marketable mineral deposit, still at the bargain price between $2.50 and $5.00 per acre.

With the passage of the Mineral Leasing Act of 1920, Congress brought the operation of oil, natural gas, coal, and phosphate companies on public land under federal control. This act provides for leasing of the public domain, and has been amended to change regulations governing prospecting and multiple use. Provisions include wildcat or noncompetitive leases issued on a first-come, first-served basis, and competitive leases for lands within a known mineral area. Acreages are limited, and rental fees and royalties to the federal government are set. At this stage in the evolution of reform, however, neither the Mining Law of 1872 nor the Mineral Leasing Act placed restrictions on exploration technique. Because the cheapest route to the goodies was inevitably selected, stripmining became rampant. By 1978, over 1 million acres of federal land had become a stripmined wasteland abandoned by the coal industry, only one of several industries which exploit stripmining options.

The Surface Mining Control and Reclamation Act of 1977 set in motion a mechanism for the recovery of the ravaged land. Strip-mine operators of mined coal, for instance, are to pay 35 cents a ton, and deep-mine operators, 15 cents a ton, toward a reclamation fund, which was established by Congress at an entirely inadequate limit of $25 million for 1978. The fee differential acknowledges the major responsibility of the surface mining operators for past abuse to the land, and creates an incentive for deep-mining, which is more costly but less damaging environmentally. In its polished-up 1970s image, the Interior Department, which sanctioned the practice of stripmining in the first place, now condemns it as a practice of "rape and run."

In 1979, however, in the name of energy independence, Congress began a drive to weaken this major environmental law—which took ten years to pass. At the start of 1980, a federal district judge in Virginia ruled that portions of the 1977 act were unconstitutional. As a result, miners no longer have to rebuild mountains they strip, the Office of Surface Mining can no longer stop mining or assess penalties under the act without a hearing, and mining can no longer be halted if any party complains. In the wake of ever-increasing national energy shortages, controls are likely to loosen even more.

The New York–based Council on Economic Priorities, among others, believes that federal and state coal leasing of public lands in the West is still a "giveaway" of public resources. The council's 1978 report finds that while coal production on federal lands in the West had tripled since 1973, "attempts to correct the historical travesties of the federal leasing program have been ineffectual." Lease prices paid the federal government and Indian tribes were, in 1977, reportedly at a very low average rental fee of $1.00 per acre, while the state governments of Utah, Wyoming, Colorado, New Mexico, Montana, and North Dakota collected an average of just 41 cents per acre. More than half of the nation's coal is in the West, and about 85 percent of the western deposits are on federal, state, or Indian lands.

In 1973, only 52 of 474 federal leases, covering nearly 700,000 acres, were producing any coal. In 1977, as the availability of alternate energy sources and relative mining costs diminished, the number increased to 67. Output was more than 52 million tons, a 241 percent increase in four years. However, a majority of leases are held for speculation. Many coal deposits which might be productive are not currently being developed; mining is held off in anticipation of higher prices in the future. Only 14 percent of all federal leases and 0.7 percent of all state leases are now in production.

A few large corporations dominate the coal-leasing picture. The five largest federal leaseholders control about 31 percent of federal coal leases. Exxon Corporation is the largest holder of state, federal, and Indian leases in the West.

Toward Reform. During the 1970s, Congress endeavored once again to reform and clarify the use of all federal lands. Efforts were made through the Renewable Resources Planning Act of 1974 to create more economic and purposeful management of the national forests. The broadest reform effort, however, was the Federal Land Policy and Management Act of 1976, which attempts to coordinate and reorganize the manner whereby the nation's land resources are administered and utilized. In general, it endeavors to increase public income, promote fairness, and eliminate what Congressman Stewart Udall has called, in referring to the Mining Law of 1872, "a blatant giveaway of public lands."

The Federal Land Policy and Management Act of 1976 also calls for a major redistribution of income. In amending the Mineral Leasing Act of 1920 and the Geothermal Steam Act of 1970, for example, the new mining law provides for the payment of 50 percent of the revenues from royalties, rentals, and sales to the state in which the leased land or deposit is located. In the case of Alaska, the sole exception, 90 percent of the income is to be delegated to the state, to be used as the state determines, with no priorities or directives imposed by the federal government. These revenues have already earned each Alaska resident a cash dividend. And they promise to lower taxes and increase general prosperity vastly in oil-, gas-, and eventually coal-producing states. It is under this act as well that the Outer Continental Shelf is currently being leased for mineral, and especially for oil and gas, development. Outer Continental Shelf revenues are now as large or larger than revenues from the federal dry lands.

Today, most of our remaining energy reserves are on or under public land. It is estimated that over half our oil and natural gas reserves, 40 percent of our coal and uranium, 80 percent of our oil shale, and 60 percent of our geothermal resources lie under public lands. And the battle rages on. Giant private economic combines—the so-called oil companies—control the energy future of America. Most of the available oil and gas reserves on federal lands are leased to fewer than a dozen major corporations. These, in turn, must operate under those changing rules established as America gropes its way toward wider distribution of wealth contained within the public domain.

Today, lease rights are secured by competitive bid, with the "bonus revenue" paid directly to the federal treasury. In addition, the government derives income from all sales of mined products, usually through a 12½ percent royalty interest. Finally, at the end of the process there is private profit—and the tax upon it. The so-called windfall profits tax provision of 1979–1980 is only the most recent step in the long and very slow transition from private deals for private profit on public lands toward a policy that seeks to utilize the public domain for the benefit of the much larger population to whom it in fact belongs.

The federal government is no longer running a large-scale real-estate sales office. Instead, it is operating an immense land-leasing and management company—the biggest in the world.

And when it comes to the connections between land, power, and wealth, there is no more potent set of historic illustrations or shifting contemporary links than these which tie together private enterprise and public policy in the use and administration of the federal lands.

AH, WILDERNESS

Within the national forests, there co-exists with major logging operations a considerable amount of hunting, grazing, active mining, and sometimes intense tourism. The burden of these activities on land in many places is so substantial that a strong cadre of conservationists and environmentalists argue more of the land should be preserved in designated "wilderness" zones. Within such zones, no aircraft or other vehicle may be used, no timber may be cut, and neither mining, oil production, nor road building will be tolerated. However, hunting and fishing are allowed, cattle may be grazed, and travel by foot, horseback, or motorless boat is permitted.

The idea of maintaining "wilderness" in America does not go back very far. Settlers, congressmen, and businessmen joined together during most of the first-150-year history of white America to obliterate the wilderness. The objective of conserving federal land originated at the beginning of the twentieth century, at which time the land was still considered primarily an economic resource, whether renewable, as in timbering and grazing, or depletable, as in mining.

America's new frame of mind is marked by the reservation of the first wilderness areas in the 1920s. These first tracts of federally owned land, each at least 100,000 acres, were to remain unexploited. It was not until ratification of the Wilderness Act in 1964 that a unified set of objectives and regulations was promulgated and the National Wilderness Preservation System (NWPS) was set up.

As of 1979, the National Forest System holds over 80 percent of the land, or more than 15 million acres, incorporated into the National Wilderness Preservation System, excluding Alaska. This amounts to about 8 percent of all national forests and grasslands administered by the Forest Service. In addition, there are over 14 million acres of wilderness administered by the Bureau of Land Management. And the system is growing. Between 1964 and 1978, more than 6 million acres were added to the system from national forest lands. In 1978 alone, Congress designated a total of over 2.5 million additional acres from national forest land into the system; and another 3.3 million acres from National Forest Primitive Areas have been proposed by the Department of Agriculture since 1974 but were still awaiting congressional action at the end of 1978.

In recent years, there has emerged intense controversy over the potential to expand the wilderness area in America. This expansion, environmentalists hope, will come in part from designating a larger part of the national forests as wilderness. As a consequence of the Wilderness Act of 1964, the secretary of the Interior was directed to review all potential wilderness areas in the National Park System and the National Wildlife Refuge System which exceed 5,000 acres in size, remain roadless, and satisfy a checklist of wilderness attributes. Not until the hallmark Federal Land Policy and Management Act of 1976, however, was a review of the vast holdings of the Bureau of Land Management required for potential inclusion in the wilderness system. First comes inventory of roadless public lands of 5,000 acres or more, and all roadless islands having certain wilderness characteristics, then a study of areas determined to have wilderness characteristics, and finally, reports and recommendations, all conducted through the Bureau of Land Management.

Though the secretary of the Interior is to make recommendations to the president, he does not have to do so until 1991! And then the president has another two years before sending his recommendations to Congress.

This very substantial delay, plus the restriction that a wilderness area must be roadless, reflects the fine hand of an experienced set of lobbyists, long-accustomed to exploiting federal lands for private operators.

Although the Federal Land Policy and Management Act directs that lands under review for inclusion in the wilderness system are to be managed so as not to impair their suitability for preservation and wilderness, mining, grazing, and forest interests now have time to obtain permits and leases, and even to devise ways to cut rough roads into the potential wilderness preserves, thus forever eliminating these areas from the legal definition of "wilderness."

Conservation groups, including the Sierra Club, the Friends of the Earth, and the Wilderness Society, estimate that more than two thirds of the roadless areas of the national forests could be open to timber and mining interests under present proposals. They charge that the Forest Service has failed to protect some of the best wilderness areas, leaving instead mostly ice and rocks. Indeed, by the end of 1979 when the mandated "initial inventory" of western lands was tallied, the Bureau of Land Management reported that of the approximately 175 million acres reviewed, more than 113 million acres "appear clearly and obviously to lack wilderness characteristics." In a bit of understatement so mute as to betray considerable trepidation about the monumental conflicts that, in fact, exist, Secretary of Agriculture Bob Bergland and Secretary of the Interior Cecil D. Andrus reported to President Carter in their fifteenth annual report on the status of the National Wilderness Preservation System for calendar year 1978, "Wilderness matters are frequently controversial, and conflicts arise between individuals or groups who appear to lack a thorough understanding of the role of wilderness in American society."

Conflicts do indeed intensify and the lines of argument harden as an energy-conscious nation pits environmental groups, which want more land protected, against industry and energy concerns, which claim that development of the land's resources is essential for the well-being of the nation. A major problem in deciding where wilderness areas ought to be is the lack of information about what, in fact, so much of the federal land might best be used for, considering the conflicting claims of conservation and economic realism. With more than one third of all the land in America federally held, it seems that solutions could be worked out.

The destiny of a large portion of the irreplaceable land resources of this country remains in question. The General Accounting Office predicts that it would take a half-century for federal geologists to assess the federal lands. Said one federal bureaucrat to *Wall Street Journal* reporter William E. Blundell, "We're the biggest landowner of all, and we don't know the value of our holdings."

RECREATIONAL OPPORTUNITIES
ON FEDERAL LANDS:
ORGANIZATION AND USE

Many types of land owned and controlled by the federal government are available for recreation. Only the land held by the Department of Defense is generally restricted from all public access. By far, the largest amount of land and the largest degree of public use centers on property owned by the Department of Agriculture, which is administered by the Forest Service, and land owned by the Department of the Interior, which is administered by the National Park Service. In addition, there is growing use for recreational purposes of land within the general public domain, administered by the Bureau of Land Management on behalf of the Department of the Interior.

Bureau of Land Management Sites. While substantial hunting and camping did occur in wholly undeveloped areas, until 1960 almost no developed public recreational facilities existed on any of the approximately 470 million acres of land under control of the Bureau of Land Management (BLM). That terrain—millions of acres in public terrain—is land which, as a 1976 *New York Times* editorial noted, "Cattle and sheep raisers and mining companies and some, though not all, members of Congress from the Far West—have tended to regard as their private fief."

As late as 1953, there were only two or three developed areas in all forty-eight states and two or three in Alaska. Since then, recreational use of BLM-administered public domain has increased dramatically. As of 1976, 326 recreational sites covering approximately 23,000 acres were developed on BLM land. By 1980, this number had increased to 550 sites covering more than 130,000 acres. But even this remains a minuscule portion of the vast BLM holding.

For recreational exploration of land in America outside the more heavily traveled national parks, the network of federally maintained sites on BLM land is an attractive and relatively unknown option. These range from highly developed campgrounds to more primitive outposts in spots of majestic natural beauty such as Angel Peak, New Mexico; Pinnell Mountain, Alaska; Red Cliffs, Utah; and the Petroglyph zone near Three Rivers, New Mexico. For details, contact the Bureau of Land Management, U. S. Department of the Interior, Washington, D. C. 20240.

The National Forests and Wilderness Areas. The national forests have been open to public recreation of limited sorts and in limited areas since the outset of the program at the beginning of the century. The Forest Service recreation policy emphasizes integration of recreation with all other uses of the national forests. Minimum restrictions are placed on visitors consistent with protection of the environment, public health and safety, and the rights of others.

By 1930, there were almost 7 million visits to the national forests each year, a "visit" being like an admission to a movie: one individual might visit several times a day. Thirty years later, when outdoor recreation was just beginning on BLM property, the national forests were receiving more than 92 million visits each year. In 1970, with only an approximate 13 percent increase in the United States population since 1960, visitation to the national forests had increased about 90 percent.

Most people who visit national forest property do not venture into the wilderness areas. Yet it is within the national forests that 80 percent of the growing but controversial National Wilderness Preservation System is to be found. For anyone sufficiently experienced and hearty to manage in the wilderness (there were thirty-eight known fatalities in 1978) and willing only to walk, ride horseback, or canoe, these wilderness areas provide a little known and refreshing opportunity for vacation and recreation away from all but the majestic beauty of unspoiled, undeveloped land. There are twenty-six states which contain national wilderness lands. Information is readily obtained from the U.S. Department of Agriculture or the U.S. Department of the Interior, Office of the Secretary, Washington, D.C. 20250.

The National Park System. When it comes to recreation on federal lands, the national parks are what most people think of . . . and go to. In 1975, there were more than 16 million acres of federal land devoted to national parks and well over 200 million visits to them. This number increased to 268 million in the bicentennial year of 1976, a number that most observers at the time believed to be a peak and, perhaps, plateau . . . that is, until over 280 million visits were recorded to the park system during 1978.

In 1979, in expectation of more summer visitors than ever before, a pilot program covering 1,287 campsites at Yosemite and Sequoia-Kings Canyon National Park in California and Grand Canyon National Park in Arizona was introduced. One hundred fifty Ticketron computer terminals were used as part of a reservation system for overnight stays.

The great number of total annual visits attests to the numerous visits some U.S. residents make each year to one national park or another, as well as to the great number of foreign tourists who visit these sites. When we recall that the entire national population is only about 220 million people, spread out across the entire 2.3 billion acres of America, this onslaught of over 280 million visits to a terrain of 16 million acres becomes all the more remarkable. And the crowding, too, becomes all the more evident.

While the original purpose of the national parks, described as the provision of recreation at "its highest inspirational level," may now be difficult to realize because of the large numbers of people, which interfere with the potential for inspiration, the experience of nature and majestic beauty derived from a visit to one of the great national parks in America is one that few forget.

The National Park System is a large and diverse set of federal holdings open to public visit, of which the national parks are but the best known element. Under the direction of the National Park Service, this system comprises more than twenty distinct categories of land. By far, the largest area, encompassing 54.5 million acres, is that of the national monuments, of which there are ninety-two around the country. Next come the thirty-nine national parks which total slightly over 16 million acres of land, all but a million acres of which are owned by the federal government. The National Recreation Areas, encompassing over 3.5 million acres, are the only other National Park Service holdings which exceed a million acres.

Other categories of national lands under the control of the National Parks Service include: national battlefields, national battlefield parks, national battlefield sites, national cemeteries, national historical parks, national historic sites, national memorials, national memorial parks, national military parks, national seashores, national lakeshores, national scenic riverways, national rivers, national scenic trails, national preserves, and in and around Washington, D. C., the national parkways, the national capital parks, the White House, the National Mall, and the National Visitors' Center. This wide range of holdings includes some 320 properties, totaling over 76.5 million acres. These lands, in one way or another, touch the lives of an enormous number of people in America at least once. On the other hand, a substantial number—perhaps more than half the population—do not benefit from these lands at all. Circumstances of age, income, and residential location inevitably render access selective. Consequently, recreational sites in and near urban areas are terribly important and must be developed more extensively.

National Park vs. National Monument. The national parks may be designated only by an act of Congress. The first park, Yellowstone, was established in 1872. Since then, the system has grown slowly but regularly. In 1920, there were some 6,950,000 acres designated as national parks; by 1950, the land area had increased to 12,222,000 acres; and by

471

1979, excluding Alaska, the acreage had increased to over 16 million acres.

Establishing these national parks is no easy matter, even when no land acquisition is involved. Most of the land now designated as national parks, in fact, had been federally owned before park designation, as part of either the general public domain or the system of national forests. However, once land is designated by Congress as a national park, traditional forms of economic exploitation of it are usually required to cease. The area becomes closed to grazing, mining, and timber harvest, though in spots pre-existing oil and gas exploration and development permits continue in force.

National monuments, in contrast, can be more readily established. Though only Congress may designate a national park, national monument designation merely requires a presidential proclamation. Pressure is often easier to exert on a single individual, even if he is the president of the United States, than on the Congress, beset as it is with an instinct for horse trading and the powerful influence of special-interest lobbies. Thus, establishment and protection of the land by proclamation rather than by congressional act has been seized upon many times as an expedient way to obtain protected status for terrain that can be convincingly shown to contain sites of great historic or geologic significance. Recently, as a clear example, while political wrangling left Congress unable to act, President Carter designated some 56 million acres of Alaskan land as a national monument. This is the largest designation a president has ever made; in a single stroke, it more than doubled the size of the entire National Park System.

The National Parks: Inspiration or Claustrophobia? Big parks are like public housing: Everyone believes in them and wants them—but not next door. Parks such as the great national parks or the major state parks are big business. They are also a major national asset. Quite often, they are inherently very valuable, as a result of their spectacular scenic beauty, high-quality improved access roads, and, when present, abundant streams and lakes. As leisure time multiplies and as the population ages, more and more people are making more and more trips to the big parks each year.

Millions of visitors with their very large spending power attracts those who would provide a service and cash in on leisure. With these visitors comes an enormous number of cars, buses, and camping vehicles. To service and profit from this influx, gas station, motel and lodge operators, franchise fast-food operators, all swarm in like bees to honey.

Today, the experience of visiting a national park has little to do with that envisioned by Congress in 1872 when it set aside Yellowstone National Park as the first such national preserve. In the summer of 1870, a party of nineteen men under General Henry D. Washburn, a former Union officer in the Civil War and later surveyor-general of the territory of Montana, set out to certify questionable accounts of "a land where smoke and boiling water poured out of the earth to form a landscape of yellow rock and ghostly shapes." Lieutenant G. C. Doane, in charge of the expedition's military escort, later described the region:

The river breaks through this plateau in a winding and impassable canyon and trachyte lava over 2000 feet in depth; the middle places, and in others forming still pools of seemingly fathomless depth. At one point it dashes here and there, lashed to a white foam, upon its rocky bed; at another it subsides into a crystal mirror wherever a deep basin occurs in the channel. Numerous small cascades are seen tumbling from the lofty summits, a mere ribbon of foam in the immeasurable distance below. . . . Standing on the brink of the chasm, the heavy roaring of the imprisoned river comes to the ear only in a sort of hollow, hungry growl, scarcely audible from the depths, and strongly suggestive of demons in torment below. Lofty pines on the bank of the stream "dwindle to shrubs in dizziness of distance." Everything beneath has a weird and deceptive appearance. The water does not look like water, but like oil. Numerous fishhawks are seen busily plying their vocation, sailing high above the waters, and yet a thousand feet below the spectator. In the clefts of the rocks, hundreds of feet down, bald eagles have their eyries, from which we can see them swooping still further into the depths to rob the ospreys of their hard-earned trout. It is grand, gloomy, and terrible; a solitude peopled with fantastic ideas; an empire of shadows and turmoil.

This was the romantic West of mysterious creatures and majestic landscape that all America imagined. The group agreed that the land ought to be deeded to the people of the United States. And so a bill establishing "a pleasuring ground for the benefit and enjoyment of the people" sped through Congress in 1872.

Today a trip to Yellowstone is more like a family outing on Saturday to the regional shopping center than an inspirational visit to the wilderness. There is a lot of traffic to get through, a lot to buy once you get through it, and a lot of other folks doing the same thing at the same time —and all are competing for the same parking places. The pilgrimage to the wilderness, like the pilgrimage to salvation at Lourdes, is now overwhelmed by the car and by consumerism. Even the scenery, like a product, is consumed. People go out to, say, the Grand Canyon to confirm that it really does look like all of the pictures of it they have so often seen in the background of automobile ads. Armed with a camera, people shoot their picture, then move on. The photography validates the trip—proves to all back home, and for all time, that "we were there." As Susan Sontag has written in her probing introductory chapter to *On Photography:*

As photographs give people an imaginary possession of a past that is unreal, they also help people to take possession of space in which they are insecure. Thus, photography develops in tandem with one of the most characteristic of modern activities: tourism. For the first time in history, large numbers of people regularly travel out of their habitual environments for short periods of time. It seems positively unnatural to travel for pleasure without taking a camera along. Photographs will offer indisputable evidence that the trip was made, that the program was carried out, that fun was had. Photographs document sequences of consumption carried on outside the view of family, friends, neighbors. . . .

A way of certifying experience, taking photographs is also a way of refusing it—by limiting experience to a search for the photogenic, by converting experience into an image, a souvenir. Travel becomes a strategy for accumulating photographs. The very activity of taking pictures is soothing, and assuages general feelings of disorientation that are likely to be exacerbated by travel. Most tourists feel compelled to put the camera between themselves and whatever is remarkable that they encounter. Unsure of other responses, they take a picture. This gives shape to experience: stop, take a photograph, and move on. The method especially appeals to people handicapped by a ruthless work ethic—Germans, Japanese, and Americans. Using a camera appeases the anxiety which the work-driven feel about not working when they are on vacation and supposed to be having fun. They have something to do that is like a friendly imitation of work: they can take pictures.

Within many of the most popular national parks, neither the land nor the visitor is protected from commercialized exploitation. Indeed, private individuals and corporations have been encouraged to construct, within and at the edges of these parks, hotels, and motels, stores and restaurants, gasoline filling stations, and other facilities demanded by the millions of annual visitors. These facilities are rarely carefully planned in relationship to the landscape or governed by standards of appropriateness and taste which would do so much to mute the brutal impact of these facilities on scenic areas.

A National Park Service report in 1977 criticizes the Yellowstone National Park Company, the park's concessionaire, saying, "Management cannot respond to visitor needs because the company is not oriented to service to the public, but only to the generation of profit dollars." Reportedly the first intensive review of concessions management in a park, this study criticizes virtually every phase of the concessionaire's services, a wholly owned subsidary of General Host Corporation. Although the contract between the National Park Service and the Yellowstone Park Company will not expire until 1996, the latter has not met all terms of the contract, such as spending by the end of 1975 the required $10 million minimum on park renovations.

In Yosemite National Park, a series of hearings was conducted in 1978 seeking ways to reclaim much of its natural serenity from the automobile and from commercial development. In the limelight is the Music Corporation of America, the Los Angeles–based movie-making conglomerate which in 1973 bought out the previous concessionaire, the Yosemite Park and Curry Company, for $13.3 million. Music Corporation's program of expansion runs counter to the ideas of a group of park service planners

CLOSE-UP OF LITTER LEFT ON A BEACH IN YOSEMITE NATIONAL PARK, CALIFORNIA

Over 280 million visits now take place yearly to the 16 million acres of the national parks. Within many of the most popular parks, however, there is little apparent protection of the land or of the visitors from commercial exploitation, crowding, and litter.

and organized conservationists who envisioned a gradual reduction of auto use and commercialization.

Indeed, a generally unrecognized but intense controversy rages over proper management policy of facilities and concessions located throughout the national parks. The concessions are big business, big enough to attract conglomerates such as Trans World Airlines and Del Webb Corporation. The concessionaires seek exclusive, park-wide agreements and low franchise payments. Most of all, they cling to a practice sanctioned in the Concessions Policy Act of 1965 that gives concessionaires a "possessory interest" in park facilities. This provision requires that the government buy out a concessionaire's investment, even if the company has performed unsatisfactorily, when a concession is lost. Because of this provision, when General Host Corporation was removed in 1978 as the Yellowstone National Park concessionaire, the National Park Service had to pay the company $19 million before it could install T.W.A. as the new concessionaire.

To protect themselves in the national parks business, corporations are willing to flex political muscle. In early 1980, Secretary of the Interior Cecil D. Andrus fired William J. Whalen as head of the National Park Service. Whalen had been working hard to obtain greater control over the concessionaires throughout the park system. He believed that certain parks, especially Yellowstone, Yosemite, and the Grand Canyon, were being overdeveloped. He asserted that concessionaires were earning excessive profits from their park operations. On franchise renewals, he began to increase the fees charged. He also endeavored to have the "possessory interest" provision deleted from the Concessions Policy Act of 1965. He resisted the development of larger hotels, swimming pools, and tennis courts within the parks, and objected to the practice of inviting conventions to use national park franchise facilities. When removed from office, Whalen told Philip Shabecoff of *The New York Times,* "My firing is a clear signal that you don't mess around with those powerful concessionaires. Park directors that stand up and do the job won't last too long."

National parks are certainly not wilderness areas. With people comes traffic. With people comes litter. With the large number of people admitted to land that is not well patrolled or protected comes serious damage to the land itself. Neither the soft earth nor the rugged mountain trail can sustain its natural state in the face of incessant tramping by thousands of people a week.

The most elemental issue of numbers of visitors allowed inside the parks today vexes those who must try to administer and maintain large city, state, and federal parks. A given parcel of land can accept and accommodate people only up to a point. Beyond that point, it gives way. Its grassy surface becomes pitted, washed out. Its open meadow becomes a dusty field. Its most accessible large trees are brutally scarred by initials carved into their trunks by those wishing to memorialize the tender affection and inspiration they felt there at that moment, a selfish act of egoism that precludes that same experience from all who follow. Grafitti upon the subway door in Manhattan or on the building façade in Los Angeles finds its counterpart upon the land in the natural environment wherever people in great numbers are encouraged to congregate. Or, as National Park Service Director Gary Everhardt observed, in 1977, upon viewing his entire operation and the numbers of visitors that are now accommodated by the national parks, "We have reached the crisis point in some areas. We will simply have to find more ways of controlling visits, or else the parks will no longer be worth visiting."

Unfortunately, the Grand Canyon National Park is already witness to the consequence of success. In 1977, 250,000 people hiked through the park, another 250,000 toured the Canyon in airplanes and helicopters with their associated noise and exhaust fumes, and over 3 million people arrived by car. Tourism is so overwhelming the land there that Superintendent Merle Stitt, in an interview with W. E. Garrett of *National Geographic*, recently admonished, "As the visitors increase, so do the demands for protection. So we've had to set limits on camping, hiking, and river running. We may have to set limits on how many can enter the park." Looking at the terrain, Ranger Marvin Jensen observed, "Our trails are in poor shape. They're a safety hazard to mule trips. I've got only nine full-time people, counting myself, to manage almost a million acres." Garrett himself points out that:

At flood stage the [Colorado] river used to flush detritus and plant life downstream and deposit new beaches. Now thick stands of tamarisk, an invader, conquest the shorelines, and trash is collecting at an amazing rate on overused beaches. Also piling up on the beaches, an esthetic and health problem, is most of the 20 tons of fecal matter produced by river passengers every year.

The observed degradation of the land and the natural resources of Grand Canyon Natural Park has so infuriated some environmental advocates that now seek legal action. The Sierra Club and the Grand Canyon National Park are suing the National Park Service in the U.S. district court of Arizona. The charge: mismanagement of river trips that result in irreparable damage to the environment and to the public's ability to enjoy the park.

New efforts are also under way to improve management of tourism on the Colorado and of visitor volume at peak seasons in the park itself. There is now a National Park Service Research Study Team investigating management alternatives. A river management plan is being developed

**RUTS LEFT BY OFF-ROAD
VEHICLES IN VIOLATION
OF PARK RULES,
CANYONLANDS
NATIONAL PARK, UTAH**

The impact of millions of visitors
to the national parks presents
serious and growing man-
agement problems.

**WATER POLLUTION,
ROCK CREEK NATIONAL PARK,
WASHINGTON, D.C.**

**DEFACED TREE TRUNKS,
GRAND CANYON NATIONAL PARK, ARIZONA**

The national park lands can only accept and accommodate people up to a point. Beyond that, the lands give way. Grassy meadows become pitted, dusty surfaces; the most accessible large trees are scarred brutally by initials carved into their trunks. Graffiti on a subway door in Manhattan or on a building façade in Los Angeles finds its echo upon the land.

by the National Park Service. Successful completion of this work and forceful implementation of significant proposals to protect and conserve these unique public resources are of the utmost importance.

The Impact of Public Parks on Private Land Values. Land preserved to remain in its *natural* state, whether managed or left entirely alone, probably will increase the value of private property in its vicinity, and certainly will increase the value of private property on its immediate boundary. The same result is not necessarily achieved when a park accepts and promotes high-volume public access.

The edge of a natural preserve is a desirable edge, especially for housing. The preserve itself cannot be destroyed to accommodate a man-made structure. It also serves as a boundary, even a fortification, against noise and other forms of environmental pollution. The natural open space at the edge of the preserve also creates an attractive view. Further, though often not expressly understood by private property owners, this space, free of water wells and open to natural percolation, may function as a reservoir and recharge basin belowground to protect, amass, and store drinking water. The "protected" private land that abuts such a preserve is limited in amount, absolutely. And it is cherished. The combination is a guaranteed formula for higher value, and probably increasing value as time goes by.

The boundary, especially near the access way into a much frequented public park, is another matter. The precise success of the park as a people magnet is an inverse measure of its desirability as a neighbor to abutting owners of private property. With the attraction of people to the public park may come a loss of the natural features of the land itself. The terrain is scoured for parking lots, lodge sites, restaurants, and souvenir stands. The normal tranquility of open land is bruised by the cadence of tires, the blast of horns, and the cacaphony of voices. Groundwater resources are taxed for intense use, and sewage is flushed back into the earth.

Crime is another problem inevitably associated with public access. As a national problem, crime, like inflation, is a top-priority issue. Consequently, the specter of vandalism induces widespread anxiety in those who have a common border with a public place. Traffic, crowds, noise, possible destruction of the natural environment, and insecure borders do not add up to the right formula for hallowed space, cherished terrain, or increasing land values.

Indeed, in urban, suburban, and even rural areas, neighborhood citizen groups argue today that *no* new actively used parks are wanted. They assert that such places will not be well maintained and cannot be well policed. Thus, the park, once a joyous amenity in any community, is perceived now as a place that attracts problems and conceals undesirables of every sort, from the most innocuous drunk to the most dangerous lunatic.

Whether it is a new public parking lot at the beach-end of a quiet rural road on Martha's Vineyard or a new state park in Nebraska, whenever the public is admitted in great numbers, controversy surfaces. Our abstract social premise may be to encourage public housing, public parks, and all other forms of publicly supported amenities for the health, welfare, and enjoyment of people in America. But in the harsh light of the marketplace, most people prefer not to have this premise become a reality next door.

BIG BROTHER—RESENTED AND RESISTED

Many people in this country resent and resist the control of land by remote county, state, and federal government. Resentment is especially prevalent when the government agency dictates how the local resident will use the local land. If these dictates require any change in accepted patterns of traditional business or recreation—such as prohibiting the slaughter for profit of wolves and mustangs, or prohibiting the discharge of motorboat effluent into the lakes—some local citizens become outraged.

Not long ago, 25,000 residents who live near the Canadian border in Minnesota went to court to have their right to use motorboats on lakes around their homes and businesses upheld. They happened to live within the Boundary Waters Canoe Area, the only canoe lake area in America designated by the federal government as a wilderness. The protected zone stretches across 100 miles of the Minnesota-Canada border, contains over 1,000 lakes, and attracts annually more than 160,000 campers, canoeists, and fishermen.

A period of federal land acquisition in the Boundary Waters Canoe Area began in the early 1900s. By 1964, when the area was designated as a wilderness, the federal government held title to 94 percent of the land and water there. At the time, it allowed motorboats on 124 of the lakes, which in aggregate accounted for about 60 percent of the water surface in the wilderness. Recently, the National Audubon Society, the Sierra Club, and the Wilderness Society have urged the federal government to restrict motorboat use on all the lakes. Private residents have objected vehemently. Chet Lindskog, Cook County commissioner and chairman of the local county board, shares the view of the resisting private residents, and indeed represents it in large measure. In an interview with Lawrence Rout of *The Wall Street Journal*, Lindskog observed of federal involvement in the area: "They've taken away logging. They've taken air travel.

They've taken away mining. And now they're slowly taking away all the lakes." The dispute was finally settled in late 1978 when Congress decided that the million-acre wilderness area should remain free of logging and mining, and that motorboats and snowmobiles must be severely restricted.

The inauguration of any new public recreation area or park, if purchased from a private owner, brings cries of protest, especially from local fiscal conservatives. The land, when privately owned, pays its proportionate share of property taxes. These funds are paid out every year and, for the most part, remain in the community. Once the land becomes public property, however, it is exempt from local real-estate taxes. An additional tax burden thus falls on property owners in town, while the recreation benefits are gleaned by all.

The other side of the story, of course, is that private owners are often anxious for a government agency to purchase their personal holding. Why is this? When it comes time to sell, any buyer will do. However, if the landowner wishes the land to remain as open and undisturbed as possible, then the number of potential buyers is seriously limited. Furthermore, purchase by a government agency very often means full value as assessed at the time of the transaction. And if the government purchases the entire parcel of land, it simplifies and hastens what could otherwise be a lengthy and/or costly process of planning approvals, partial sales, etc., along with less favorable tax consequences.

The saga of the proposed expansion by the federal government of the Redwood National Park in Northern California presents the protagonists on open stage. Until recently, the 58,000-acre Redwood National Park included 30,000 acres of three California parks: Prairie Creek, Del Norte, and Jedediah Smith. Adjacent to these there were 48,000 acres of land owned by two private lumber companies, Arcata National Corporation of Menlo Park, California, and Louisiana-Pacific Corporation of Portland, Oregon.

Since the inauguration of the plan to create a consolidated Redwood National Park over ten years ago, the federal government has sought to obtain the parkland owned by the state of California. The state has been disinclined to relinquish its property in exchange for other federally owned land, the deal offered by the national government. The private companies, however, are being forced to sell their timberland for conversion to parkland through condemnation proceedings and at prices they believe to be too low.

Opponents to the loss of private logging activity in the redwood area, other than the companies themselves, include many local citizens as well as many local government officials. Citizens and government alike fear the loss of both tax revenue and jobs. In characteristic fashion, all foes of the federal acquisition and park expansion program find that the money allocated to parkland expansion could be better spent for parks somewhere else. Industry specifically has mentioned urban parks across the nation, which is the antithesis of a single large rural enclave in one place —that place being their own backyard.

In turn, the proponents of the park, who may be loosely categorized as "environmentalists," are determined to support expansion of the federal holding. They argue that traditional redwood logging is a dying industry, as it takes coastal redwoods about two hundred years to reach maturity. They point out that related jobs in the industry in the region are declining precipitously. And they assert that 125 years of logging has severely damaged the environment, including the nearby streams and regional wildlife. They also point out that the second largest local industry is tourism. And that is where a bright future is seen, one which brings diversified jobs, local income, a protected and rejuvenated natural environment.

The lumber companies, the local labor unions, and many local citizens in Humboldt, Del Norte, and Mendocino counties, where the park acquisition is to occur, are united in their opposition to encroachment by the federal government. A logging industry spokesman stated recently, as reported by Peggy Wayburn in *Cry California*, "Most residents of our county fear we will be swallowed alive in continual grabs for parklands. The environmentalists want to force us out of work, off our land, and out of the county." Even the most dedicated members of the environmental protection groups acknowledge that a very large segment of the local community has joined enthusiastically in the battle to restrain the expansion, to support what the folks out there like to call "Big Timber."

Thus, the Redwood National Park controversy contains many of the conflicts and impassioned positions that underlie the links and tensions between land, power, and wealth as they are focused on parkland and recreation. It is federal government vs. state government. It is parks vs. local residents. It is conservationists and environmentalists vs. big industry and small-time workers. It is private ownership, jobs, and property-tax payments vs. subtle and sophisticated values of environmental protection, land conservation, and the salvation of magnificent natural phenomena. It is—in one place—one scene dramatically played out by protoganists who link, in their own way, the forces connecting land, power, and wealth in America.

Nowhere is Uncle Sam more resented than in the West, where the largest percentage of land is federally owned. For example, 65 percent of the state of Utah has been in federal hands since those lands were acquired by the United States under the terms of the treaty ending the Mexican War. Because of its immense land holdings, the federal government, more than any other legislative body, has the most to say about land use, water, grazing, timber, and mineral rights in the state. As Jed Kee, state planning coordinator for Utah, said in a recent issue of *Planning*, "The Bureau of Land Management's Director has more to say about the future use of Utah's land than the governor."

Nevada, whose federal land holdings amount to 87 percent of the state (second highest after Alaska, at 96 percent), has initiated what has come to be known as the Sagebrush Rebellion. In 1979, Governor Robert List signed a bill declaring state sovereignty over 49 million acres of Nevada land which have been owned by the Bureau of Land Management for over a century. The state claims that it was blackmailed into giving the federal government the acreage as a condition of statehood in 1864. Supported by mining and ranching interests, which resent federal regulatory delays and threats of environmental restrictions, the state has accumulated $250,000 for legal fees in what could be a decade-long battle to regain the land. Nevada is also encouraging other states to join in the rebellion. Alaska's legislature passed a resolution commending Nevada's action, and Oregon and California are considering similar challenges.

Environmentalists, who fear the influence of ranchers and other special-interest groups, charge that private exploitation, not state control, is the underlying motive of the Sagebrush Rebellion. The movement, they claim, is little more than a land grab.

MORE CONSTRUCTIVE USE
OF FEDERAL LANDS

Most people in America have no idea about what is going on with and on "their" land—the federally owned domain. Many never even see a parcel of it. Others, a select minority of private businesses and individuals with large private land holdings, recognize with great sophistication the management and policy issues that the federal lands present. Their energy is devoted, in large measure, to support of the status quo. Their interests are intimately attached to the understaffed, underfunded, and often relatively inert special bureaus within the Department of Agriculture and the Department of the Interior that administer, under an accretion of outdated regulations and statutes, so much of the federally owned land.

Because many of these older regulations were written to benefit special-interest groups, at present, there is no cohesive policy for the preservation, management, development, or disposal of federal lands; no policy that copes with the competing contemporary demands of social, economic, and environmental claims upon the public land of America.

The public land is no longer being sold outright. That is one positive policy shift that emerged in the twentieth century. Yet there is little evidence that this enormous resource is being marshalled to the fullest extent possible to help overcome fundamental national problems, such as inequitable distribution of recreational areas; runaway prices for food and building materials; lack of adequate energy resources; inflation in all natural resources and commodity prices, which adversely affects everyone in America and, indeed, weakens the position of the United States in the world. Recreation is one of the fastest-growing national activities; and inflation is the most insidious, virulent domestic problem. Both can be improved by better use of the federal land.

This simple reality must be matched by reordered federal management and expenditure priorities. For instance, the still vast grazing range and impressive timber stands could be operated much more effectively to bring down the cost of meat, milk, and timber, and still protect the long-term quality and future of the land.

In addition, could not the land committed to intense recreation be more thoroughly cared for and more diligently administered? The entire annual national park operating budget is about $390 million. This is less than 0.4 percent of U.S. defense expenditures in 1978. In the ever-present tug for resource distribution, the federal agencies in charge of the public's land, backed by an aware and interested national population, must demand and receive a better deal.

Further expansion of federal and other public land holdings, when over 40 percent of the country is public property, hardly seems as important as care of the land already possessed. Nevertheless, very selective expansion of this domain when it protects an area of truly significant natural beauty is surely justified. In addition, emphasis on development of recreation resources in and near cities, as is now occurring in San Francisco, New York, and the Cleveland urban area, is of the utmost importance. This new thrust in policy, which has brought the Golden Gate, Gateway, and Cuyahoga Valley National Recreation Areas into existence, makes greater access for more people economically possible.

The general principle of a well-conceived, balanced, multiple-use management approach to each federal preserve has never been implemented with care and insight. Yet surely recreation and grazing and foresting and subsurface mining and conservation are not incompatible—and may even be carried out simultaneously on the same preserve—if each is governed by sound management and land conservation practice. But it takes effort, coordination, and allocation of more public financial resources. It also requires concensus among all those people in remote musty offices, throughout the land bureaucracy of America, where the deeds are kept.

From the beginning, federal priorities did not focus on the care, use, management, and maintenance of the public land in America for broad public benefit. Two hundred years have passed, and there is still an ingrained bias away from this objective, although during the 1970s, a decade of high environmental, consumer, and regional advocacy, Congress did slowly and falteringly endeavor to initiate more careful management and control of certain aspects of federal land policy. There is no end to what might be possible if one third of the land in America were managed otherwise. For far too long the public—the nominal owner of the federal lands—has been unwisely indifferent to use, disposition, and management of this immense resource.

FIFTEEN

FARMLAND: GEM OF THE NATION

As more and more people move into metropolitan areas, fewer and fewer will ever see a farm. Even most children who live in farming communities never go beyond the rows of new houses along their own subdivision street, carved out of the farmland beyond. As a nation, we are rapidly losing touch with the land, but we cannot shed our dependence upon it for food and for all other resources ultimately necessary for life.

Less than a hundred years ago, the United States was a country of small farms and farming families scattered across the landscape. At the beginning of the century, roughly one out of every three people was engaged in farming or in some form of agricultural enterprise. Presently, only one out of every twenty-eight Americans lives on a farm; this totals about 10 million, a number lower today than it was in 1830, when the national population was one twentieth its current level. More than 45 percent of all American farms disappeared between 1960 and 1977. As recently as 1940, there were over 6 million farms in America; today, fewer than 3 million remain.

But does the decline in the number of farms, and the number of people living on them and working the land, mean that agricultural land is a shrinking and threatened national asset? Hardly. Today, farms are bigger, more efficient, and vastly more productive than ever before. Indeed, the roughly 2.7 million farms now operating utilize about the same total acreage of cropland as has been in production throughout the century. Today, 30 percent of the largest and most productive farms take in 90 percent of all cash receipts. Since 1959 the average size of an American farm has increased about 35 percent, from 288 acres to 389 acres. Big farms have gotten bigger, while most smaller farms have not acquired more land; indeed, many have gone out of business.

Because of their scale, the biggest farms are able to acquire the most expensive modern machinery and the most effective fertilizers. With the widespread mechanization of American farms, crop output increased nearly 70 percent between 1940 and 1970, accompanied by a corresponding drop in farm labor input. These factors, along with excellent soil, make our large farms by far the most abundant and and productive in the world. The average American farmer is able to feed fifty-nine other people, whereas the farmer in Western Europe can feed only twenty; in Japan, he can feed fourteen; and in the Soviet Union, ten. The world average is five, roughly the size of an average world family.

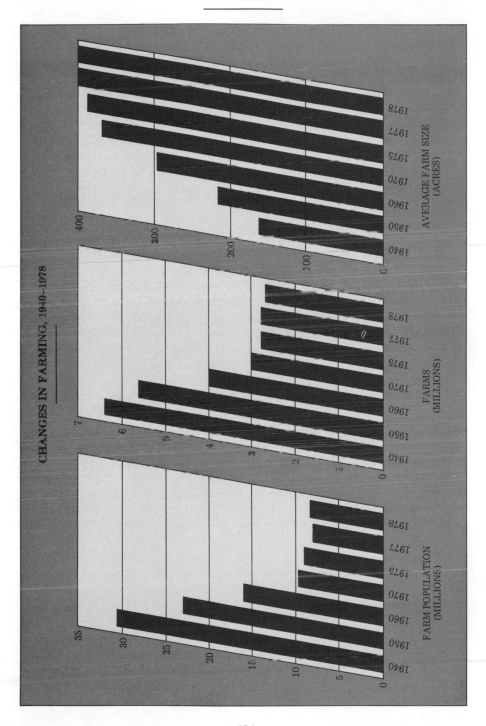

CHANGES IN FARMING, 1940–1978

AVERAGE FARM SIZE (ACRES)

FARMS (MILLIONS)

FARM POPULATION (MILLIONS)

Despite the facts of very high levels of productivity and no significant reduction in agricultural land availability, many economists and agricultural experts are troubled about the future of America's cropland. Many laymen, especially those living in agricultural areas who want to preserve nearby farmland, perceive disturbing trends. They deplore the activities of those who seek to convert existing well-located farmland into housing developments, shopping centers, and factories. Loss of farmland to urbanization, highways, reservoirs, and public recreation is much talked about and grabs headlines. Are fears now held justified? To separate the impassioned rhetoric from the real issues, it makes sense to examine the basic facts and recent trends related to American farmland, as well as the needs that can be anticipated in years to come.

HOW MUCH FARMLAND DO WE HAVE?

If we take the long view, one that scans the whole century to date, it readily becomes apparent that we are a nation of substantially larger population than a hundred years ago. We also have ample cropland to satisfy all domestic demand and much more. Presently, we grow a surplus of food, fiber, and meat. Over the last six years alone, farm produced exports have tripled. In fact, the United States exports more wheat, corn, and other coarse grains, such as barley, oats, and sorghum, than the rest of the world combined. The production from approximately three out of every ten acres is now exported for combined commercial and food-aid purposes. And exports could be even higher were it not for a variety of international controls, quotas, tariffs, and a shortage of hard currencies.

The enterprise of agriculture in America today is carried out on about 400 million acres of cropland. It is particularly concentrated on approximately 220 million acres classified by the United States Department of Agriculture (USDA) as "Class I" and "Class II." These are the best cropland soils, those that have few or moderate limitations to cropland use.

LAND CAPABILITY CLASSES
(Opposite)

The U.S. Department of Agriculture has classified American land into eight "capability classes," beginning with Class I and ending with Class VIII. Class I soils are those with few or moderate limitations to cropland use; Class VIII soils are those best suited for wildlife and recreation. Classes I through IV are considered suitable for cultivation; and classes V through VIII are considered best used as grazing lands, woodlands, and wilderness areas.

492

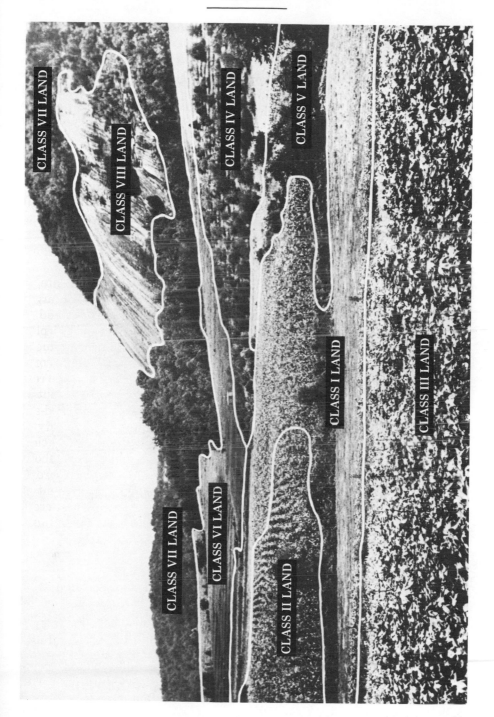

The federal government classification system spans eight classes. Class VIII soils, the least productive, are soils and landforms that "have use to recreation, wildlife habitat, water supply, or aesthetic purposes." These are, in effect, soils farmers avoid but which so many people clamor after for primary homes, second homes, and recreation sites, located as they are at the edge of hills, the top of cliffs, and upon ledges overlooking the water.

The soils of America have been tested, analyzed, and mapped in great detail for almost every region of the country. At any one place, the ground upon which you stand, the land that supports your house and yard, the soil in your garden or farm, is likely to be a complex mixture of known soil types, each with its own special characteristics. Planting on Class VII or Class VIII land—soils which have "severe limitations that make them generally unsuited to cultivation and limit their use largely to pasture or range, woodland or wildlife habitat"—is more an act of love than an act of good agricultural judgment.

LAND CAPABILITY CLASS OF THE 1975 CROPLAND ACREAGE BY FARM PRODUCTION REGION (IN MILLIONS OF ACRES)

FARM PRODUCTION REGION	CLASSES I–III	CLASS IV	CLASSES V–VIII
Northeast	14	2.0	1.3
Lake states	39	3.7	1.5
Corn Belt	80	4.7	1.6
Northern Plains	78	9.0	4.2
Appalachia	18	1.4	1.3
Southeast	13	2.7	0.6
Delta states	19	0.6	0.9
Southern Plains	36	3.4	1.5
Mountain	30	7.8	2.3
Pacific	17	4.3	1.0
Alaska, Hawaii, Puerto Rico, Virgin Islands	0.4	0.1	0.2

This classification system is more subtle and sophisticated than merely a grouping of land into eight basic classes. It catalogues special limitations which may prevail within any class in any specific location; these are called capability subclasses. Subclasses within each class are designated by a lowercase letter, either e, w, s, or c. The letter e indicates that the main limitation of the soil is a risk of erosion unless close-growing plant cover is maintained; w, that water in or on the soil interferes with plant growth or cultivation; s, that the soil is limited mainly because it is shallow, droughty, or stony; and c (used only in some parts of the United

494

States), that climate is the chief limitation, being either too cold or too dry. For Class I, the premier vintage of soils, there are no subclasses, no important limitations to high agricultural productivity. This class represents the gem of the soils, a gift of nature that deserves much more acclaim and much more protection.

Cropland Acreage in America: No Sign of Shortages Today. In all, the United States possesses about 465 million acres of arable land in all classes, or about 25 percent of its land area. Of this acreage, about 400 million acres are considered the readily usable cropland base. Though exact amounts actually planted and productive each year vary depending on prior crop success, political and economic policies, and government programs related to land banking, agricultural subsidies, and the like, between 360 million and 380 million acres are generally in productive use.

TRENDS IN MAJOR USES OF U.S. LAND
IN SELECTED YEARS (IN MILLIONS OF ACRES)

MAJOR LAND USE	1900	1920	1940	1950	1959	1969	1974
Cropland[a]	319	402	400	409	392	384	382
Available grassland pasture and range[b]	832	731	719	701	699	692	681
Forest and woodland[c]	719	721	727	721	728	723	718
Other land[d]	400	416	426	442	452	465	483
(Special use areas)	N.A.	N.A.	N.A.	*(134)*	*(146)*	*(172)*	*(182)*
(Unclassified areas)	N.A.	N.A.	N.A.	*(308)*	*(306)*	*(293)*	*(301)*
Total[e]	2,270	2,270	2,272	2,273	2,271	2,264	2,264

N.A. = Not available.

a. Excludes cropland used only for pasture.

b. Grassland pasture and other nonforested grazing land plus cropland used for pasture.

c. Exclusive of reserved forest land in parks, wildlife refuges, and other special uses of land.

d. Includes such special land uses as urban areas, highways, and roads, farmsteads, parks, and military reservations, and also land having little value for surface use (desert, rock, marshes, tundra, etc.).

e. Changes in total land area are attributable to changes in methods and materials used in occasional remeasurements and to increases in the area of artificial reservoirs.

This leaves a readily available surplus of 20–40 million acres in recent years.

Of the total 465 million acres of cropland, approximately 80 million acres now serve as pasture and more than 20 million acres are idle. To bring about 75 percent of this particular pasture or idle land into economical agricultural production would require substantial capital investment for projects such as drainage, irrigation, soil reclamation, and leveling and grading.

AGRICULTURAL AND NONAGRICULTURAL USES
OF U.S. LAND, 1974

LAND USE	MILLIONS OF ACRES	PERCENTAGE OF TOTAL
Agricultural:		
Cropland used for crops[a]	361	15.9
Idle cropland	21	.9
Cropland pasture	83	3.7
Grassland pasture and range[b]	598	26.4
Forest land grazed	179	7.9
Farmsteads, farm roads	8	.4
Total agricultural land	**1,250**	**55.2**
Nonagricultural:		
Forest land not grazed[c]	539	23.8
Urban and other built-up areas[d]	61	2.7
Recreation and wildlife areas[e]	88	3.9
Public installations and facilities[f]	25	1.1
Miscellaneous land[g]	301	13.3
Total nonagricultural land	**1,014**	**44.8**
Total land area	**2,264**	**100.0**

a. Cropland harvested, crop failure, and cultivated summer fallow.

b. Excludes cropland used only for pasture.

c. Excludes forest land duplicated in parks, and other special uses of land.

d. Urban areas; highway, road, and railroad rights-of-way; and airports.

e. National and state parks and related recreational areas, national and state wildlife refuges, and national forest wilderness and primitive areas.

f. Federal land administered by the Department of Defense and the Nuclear Regulatory Commission.

g. Includes miscellaneous uses not inventoried, and areas of little use such as marshes, open swamps, bare rock areas, deserts, and tundra.

What is especially significant to isolate, then, is the amount of economically available cropland and the amount of good-quality cropland that is being converted to other uses at any one time. Together, these trends signal whether or not any serious loss or shortage on a national scale is in the offing.

In general, over the past ten years, a relatively consistent pattern of shifting land uses has emerged. This involves the simultaneous gain and loss of cropland. In the past, during some years as much as 1 million acres of cropland were added to the national cropland base as newly cleared, irrigated, drained, or intensively fertilized land. At the same time, year after year, because of erosion, marginal fertility, inadequate drainage, or terrain unsuited to modern machinery, smaller uneconomic fields were converted by disuse or design to grasslands, pasture, range, and woodlands.

In addition, in the last decade approximately 1 million acres were lost annually to urban and rural encroachment, of which roughly 500,000 acres were cropland. Of this, approximately 55 percent, or some 275,000 acres, were composed of top-quality Class I and Class II soils.

Thus, given current conditions and past experience, it would appear that our cropland base is adequate for present need. In an average year during the past several decades, more than 1 million acres have been added to the national cropland base, while roughly 500,000 acres were irrevocably lost to urbanization. Other subtractions from the cropland base for pasture, trees and idled fields of 1–2 million acres per average year are not irrevocable and reflect basic economic decisions made by landowners.

It is well to recall at this juncture that all of the urban and built-up land in America, including all roads, railroads, and airports, consume less than 3 percent of our land, some 61 million acres.

How Much Farmland Do We Need for Coming Years?   In the world of farming, as in so many other aspects of life in America today, the rate of change accelerates. The past is not necessarily a reliable guide to the future. Can we rely, as in the past, on continued increases in productivity to boast crop yields without adding more acreage? Can we project with assurance the economically sound conversion of some 1 million acres of new cropland each year in decades to come?

Today, brand-new problems are heaped on top of older ones. Together, they signal a new era for agriculture and farmland in America. First, consider erosion, one older problem and one of the most serious problems which will lead to a reduction in farmland availability in future years. Between 100 million and 200 million acres of farmland have already been

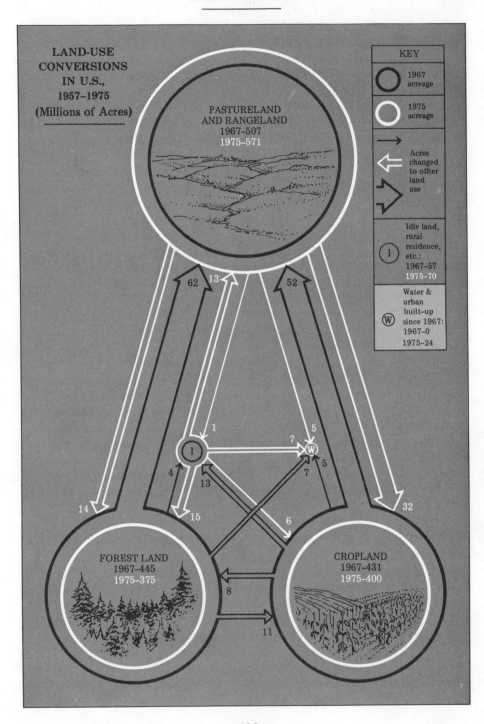

LAND-USE
CONVERSIONS
IN U.S.,
1957–1975
(Millions of Acres)

PASTURELAND
AND RANGELAND
1967–507
1975–571

KEY

1967 acreage

1975 acreage

Acres changed to other land use

Idle land, rural residence, etc.:
1967–57
1975–70

Water & urban built-up since 1967:
1967–0
1975–24

FOREST LAND
1967–445
1975–375

CROPLAND
1967–431
1975–400

either totally degraded and lost to cropland production, or so severely eroded that the land is now of only marginal quality. For example, in the 1800s, Iowa had a topsoil cover of about sixteen inches. Today, farms there have an average of eight inches of topsoil.

The rate of topsoil erosion remains extremely high throughout the country. It is estimated at about 12 tons annually per acre! As a result, it is judged that the United States has lost roughly one third of its topsoil. Where does it all go? Look at the choked and degraded reservoirs, rivers, and lakes, which receive some 3 billion tons of sediment annually. These soil deposits, with their associated fertilizers and pesticides, have an incalculable adverse ecological impact upon all animal and plant life in the waters of America.

Now, as to altogether new conditions confronting agriculture today: Reduced productivity caused by soil erosion is no longer easily offset by increased doses of fertilizer, a form of fossil energy. In the late 1970s, an estimated five gallons of fuel equivalents per acre were being used to offset the impact of soil erosion loss on cropland. As the cost of fertilizers rise in concert with the costs of other forms of energy and energy equivalents, it will become much more difficult as well as expensive to compensate for the impacts of erosion. At a certain point, this will lead to increased demand for additional farmland in order to maintain national levels of crop production.

As a result of mechanization, and fertilizer and pesticide programs, crop yields increased dramatically for many years. But there is now every indication that the rate of increase will not be sustained on balance; few experts expect more than maintenance of prior rates of increase through the use of new hybrids, crop substitution, and genetic restructuring of certain crops.

Because of increasing concern over environment and health, including the quality of sub-surface water, a number of effective chemical stimulants to growth and pesticides which protect crops have been withdrawn from permitted use. Those best known include DDT and, in certain areas, Temik. Temik was discovered recently in unacceptable concentrations in about one fourth of the more than five hundred water wells tested in the eastern portion of New York State's Suffolk County, a productive agricultural area where farming and booming residential expansion coexist in uneasy juxtaposition. By the beginning of 1980 dozens of public and private water wells in Suffolk County were ordered closed by the county's health department because of Temik contamination.

Intensive, effective, high-yield modern farming demands, then, not just an enormous amount of expensive equipment, but also the consistent application of selectively lethal insecticides, herbicides, and fungicides. Especially since 1950, U. S. farmers have boosted total food output

SPRAYING FERTILIZER
NEAR BLYTHE, CALIFORNIA,
1972

Certain trends signal a possible reduction in farmland availability in
America in future years. Reduced
productivity caused by soil erosion
is no longer easily offset by increased doses of fertilizer. As the
cost of fertilizer, which is a form of
fossil energy, rises along with other
energy costs, it will become much
more expensive and difficult
to compensate for the
impact of erosion.

through great reliance on machinery, fertilizers, and other chemical stimulants. As a result, despite increasing national and worldwide demand, land in crop production has not had to expand; and labor expended has declined. But it may very well be that yield and productivity peaks have been reached.

Water, and its availability for cropland use, is another new problem that is surfacing with an intensity never before encountered in America. Most of the land that is naturally watered and composed of good-quality soil is already in crop production. In addition, most of the easy irrigation projects are now complete. Water is crucial as a resource to growing crops. Just as human life is impossible without it, so is the cultivation of crops which yield the food to sustain that life. In the United States, in fact, it is neither people nor industry that consumes most of the water; rather, it is agriculture, which uses over 95 percent of the water consumed. Despite this astonishingly high figure, only 10 percent of all cultivated cropland in America is irrigated.

Today irrigation is increasingly difficult to extend to other areas, as large expenditures of money and energy are necessary. An acre of corn, for instance, requires about 1.3 million gallons of water per growing season. To provide that water artificially, three times the total energy needed to grow corn without irrigation is required. This reduces the cost effective economic yield of land brought under irrigation in these times of very high energy costs. In addition, since energy is now limited in supply, competition for it from both the urbanized population and industry is a limiting factor. In coming years, it is indeed possible that U. S. farmers in the West may lose some of their potential water supply for irrigation as competition increases from growing settled communities, industry, and newly active mining and exploration interests, and as these forces assert socially and economically compelling arguments and power. Consequently, it is going to be difficult to expand in a dramatic burst the amount of dependable, high-yield irrigated cropland acreage in the West.

Then, what about the anticipated demand for agricultural products? Today, world population exceeds 4 billion and may reach 7 billion by the year 2000. The domestic population of the United States will grow modestly but perhaps by as much as 20 percent by that time as well. Future worldwide demand for agricultural products is a wild card whose numbers it is impossible to predict. On the one hand, in less developed nations there is great potential for increased productivity. On the other, there is considerable evidence that productivity is not increasing. Indeed, as in the United States, productivity is leveling off worldwide, while population growth is not. The Worldwatch Institute reports that "from 1950 to 1971, per capita grain output in the world increased by 30 percent. Since 1971, per capita grain output has not increased at all."

In a twist of fate, energy shortages themselves may accelerate the demand for cropland. Ethanol and gasahol, possible automobile fuel substitutes, are distillates of agricultural products, especially corn. At today's high price of gasoline, agriculturally based substitutes become price competitive as fuel. Under current practices, it requires almost eight acres of cropland to run a typical American automobile entirely on ethanol for one year. By way of comparison, according to Worldwatch Institute calculations, providing food for people in Third World countries requires a quarter-acre of cropland a person each year, and a richer consumer needs approximately one acre. Gasahol, a mixture of 10 percent ethanol and 90 percent gasoline, if widespread in use, alone could double North America's demand on cropland. Any widespread shift of cropland use in the United States toward the production of fuel rather than foodstuffs will surely reduce our grain export capacity. Brazil, Australia, South Africa, and the United States are already embarking on national programs to divert crops from food to fuel. At a time when worldwide productivity may be straining its limits, this new potential source of international demand could boost the price of certain foodstuffs and of agricultural land quite significantly.

So —do we or do we not have an impending shortage of cropland? The answer to this much debated question tells us about not just the state of agriculture today but about the future price and value of farmland in America as well. On the domestic side, it is certain that we possess sufficient cropland to satisfy all national needs far into the next century. Beyond that, much will depend on how much of the worldwide demand we ourselves try to fill. Experts in the USDA are trying to estimate future cropland need. In doing so, they must somehow gauge the largest uncertain variable: export demand. According to the USDA, it would take a combination of increased export demand, strong environmental constraints, and unfavorable weather conditions to necessitate a very substantial increase in cropland acreage. If export demand rose to a very high level by 1985, and if we endeavored to meet the demand, some additional 80 million acres of cropland would have to be harvested. Is there any chance that even that requirement would precipitate a shortage of cropland in America?

Potential for Cropland Conversions. What few people who worry over the net loss of cropland in the past several decades realize is that there is more land available for agriculture than is generally recognized. The true supply of potentially productive cropland is masked by two factors. First, there is a considerable amount of good cropland that has been removed from agricultural production and categorized as "pasture," "range," "forest," and "other" in recent years. Second, top-quality soils which have been idled for improvement and regeneration do not appear in cropland statistics. The immediate economic availability of quality cropland from these two sources is proven in years of anticipated high export demand. At such times, substantial increased plantings occur. There is no shortage, for instance, if an additional 30 million acres are needed, as they were temporarily between 1969 and 1974.

Indeed, reliable estimates suggest that there is a reserve of about 110 million acres of now idle pasture, range, and forest lands which have high or medium potential for economic conversion to cropland. Of this land, the USDA acknowledges some 35 million acres to be available from the cropland base. However, often unmentioned but nevertheless as outlined by Linda K. Lee, of the Economics, Statistics and Cooperatives Service of the USDA, there exist an additional "78 million acres (from a total of 1 billion acres of noncropland in the United States) designated as having a high potential for cropland development." Of the more than 110 million acres with high potential, more than 35 million acres can be converted to cropland simply by turning over the soil and sowing seeds.

Over and above this more than 110 million available acres are about 76 million more acres of cropland, and 33 million acres not presently designated as cropland, which could be converted to productive agricultural use with additional expense.

Productive cropland plus the reservoir of immediately available land is probably sufficient at this time to satisfy all forseeable domestic and foreign demands for the next decade, and more. By then (though at varying levels of cost) about 80 million acres can be brought into production, enough to satisfy current levels of demand right through the middle of the next century. While expenditures for clearing, drainage, and even irrigation may be required to render the additional 80 million acres highly productive, such expenditures would certainly be justified if the demand were there. Against the backdrop of this huge reserve of more than 100 million acres, the current annual loss of less than 1 million acres to urban encroachment, pasture, forest, and all other uses should be no cause for panic. It is, nevertheless, a trend that cannot be allowed to become perpetual if this country wishes to guarantee self-sufficiency in food, fiber, and livestock, as it should.

Other Neglected Sources of Cropland. Presently, three out of every ten acres of our cropland produce foodstuffs exclusively for export. In a crunch, this food could stay at home. Furthermore, the amount of purposefully idled cropland in America is so immense, on the order of 100 million acres in a given year (classified by the USDA as "idle cropland" and "cropland pasture")—that it exceeds the total number of acres throughout the country that has ever been converted for any urbanized use. In 1978 alone, as a recent, typical example, all wheat, cotton, and livestock feed-grain farmers did not plant approximately 20 million acres of top-quality, productive cropland. Instead, because of surplus production in previous years, low anticipated prices, and available federal subsidies, loans, and disaster payments that can be collected by leaving the ground unproductive, these farmers idled more than 20 percent of their land. In turn, the USDA paid out $2.2 billion in price-propping subsidies, of which almost one third was in payments *not* to plant crops at all.

FARMLAND PRESERVATION NEAR SETTLED COMMUNITIES: A MISGUIDED BATTLE WAGED WITH THE WRONG WEAPONS

There is one more source of readily available agricultural land that is all but forgotten and that never appears in the statistics of idled pasture land and forest. This is the immense reservoir of cropland in and near built-up areas, much of which has been rezoned for urban uses but still remains undeveloped. While the amount of such land is extremely difficult to calculate, it is estimated at between 20 million and 30 million acres, of which half is considered to be of Class I and Class II quality. In most places, because the land is isolated by urbanization, zoned for development, and not economically feasible to crop with advanced methods of farming, it tends to remain idle or farmed only occasionally.

These isolated tracts also tend to be especially cherished by those who enjoy a view across it for the privacy it affords their own house site and the illusion it provides of a rural existence in close contact with nature and the seasons. This is the land that attracts environmentalists, ecological action groups, and farmland preservation advocates within towns and villages whenever development of these areas is proposed. And yet, as any farmer will tell you, this is the land that is the most difficult to farm economically. And, as any member of a responsible agricultural extension service will tell the people in a town, this is also the land upon which farming may be dangerous to the health of those who live nearby. Modern farm practices entail the percolation of highly charged chemicals into the land. Many of these are toxic to people, and there is no way to keep them out of the air or groundwater as they travel on the wind and seep through the earth.

Thus, I would suggest, the rationale for farmland preservation at the fringe of and within built-up areas is much more an argument about aesthetics and amenity than a reasonable effort to conserve a precious natural and national resource. I say this not to demean or trivialize community efforts to preserve nearby open spaces, open fields, and expan-

505

sive vistas. These areas do play a fundamental part in creating an attractive and varied environment, one that gives pleasure to and creates a sense of well-being within nearby residents. But I do feel that the argument must be made on grounds upon which there is a substantive foundation, and that foundation is not the preservation of a dwindling, threatened agricultural resource, at least not one that is in short supply nationally. Rather, the argument should be focused on how communities and individuals can preserve such terrain as open space—ideally, open space that will be maintained as fields, meadows, or woodland, and not as farm patches, which are neither economic, healthy, nor rational for the farmer, or for the community.

It is as open space, ultimately, not as farms, that these lands can be most useful as part of the settled community. It is as areas of natural beauty, as open lands which help maintain clean water, and control storm-water runoff and sediment damage; and which serve as buffers of natural landscape between highways, factories, commercial zones and residential parts of town that these spaces are profoundly significant.

Not until the argument shifts away from the insupportable and misguided basis of farmland preservation to the altogether reasonable and meaningful basis of open-space preservation will the problem be accurately defined. Once the real problem is indeed stated, progress can be made toward its solution. Land-use regulation, planning controls, and open-space acquisition programs are needed, not enforced agriculture. It will not work.

PERSPECTIVES ON FARMLAND PRESERVATION

While farmland idled in and around established communities does not warrant a major preservation effort as farmland, the same conclusion should not be drawn about Class I and Class II agricultural soils outside built-up areas within farming regions, especially within areas where these top-quality soils are relatively scarce.

Local and Regional Perspectives. From the local and state perspective, the maintenance of top-grade agricultural soils yields positive consequences which go far beyond satisfying national and international demand for food and fiber. Agriculture is a critical component of the economy of many states and of many smaller municipalities. It means jobs, retail sales, and bank loans.

In addition, when shifts of land usage in each region of the country are analyzed, one important regional issue emerges: while the total amount

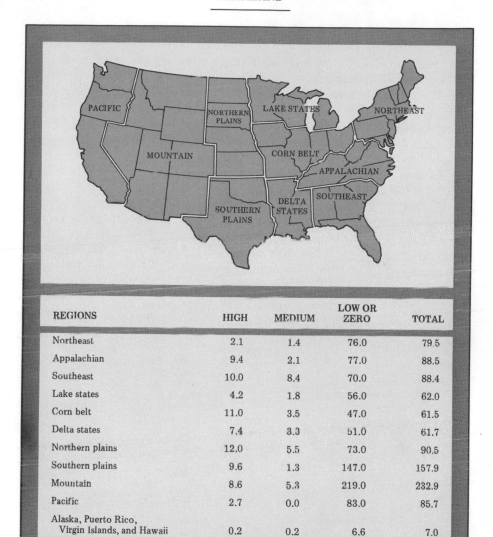

REGIONS	HIGH	MEDIUM	LOW OR ZERO	TOTAL
Northeast	2.1	1.4	76.0	79.5
Appalachian	9.4	2.1	77.0	88.5
Southeast	10.0	8.4	70.0	88.4
Lake states	4.2	1.8	56.0	62.0
Corn belt	11.0	3.5	47.0	61.5
Delta states	7.4	3.3	51.0	61.7
Northern plains	12.0	5.5	73.0	90.5
Southern plains	9.6	1.3	147.0	157.9
Mountain	8.6	5.3	219.0	232.9
Pacific	2.7	0.0	83.0	85.7
Alaska, Puerto Rico, Virgin Islands, and Hawaii	0.2	0.2	6.6	7.0

POTENTIAL CONVERSION TO CROPLAND BY FARM PRODUCTION REGION IN U.S. (MILLION ACRES)

The potential for cropland conversion varies from region to region in the United States. Cropland availability is becoming scarcer in the Northeast, the Pacific, and the Great Lakes areas, in which the overwhelming majority of the population lives. This imbalance makes the remaining top-quality soils in the most populous regions all the more important targets for new policies that will conserve these lands for agricultural production.

of good-quality cropland for present and future domestic needs nation-wide need not be questioned, such cropland is becoming scarcer in the Northeast, in the Pacific area, and around and within the Great Lakes states. There, the amount of land used for forests, pastures, or ranges, which has high potential for conversion to quality cropland, is about 3 million acres in the Northeast and Pacific, and about 4 million acres in the Great Lakes states. These low figures compare with between 7 million and 12 million acres of potentially productive cropland in each of the other farm production regions.

There is a fundamental imbalance, then, between the location of most of the nation's productive farmland, and that of most of the nation's population. In the Northeast, Southeast, Great Lakes states, and Pacific region, where the overwhelming majority of the national population now lives, there is a relative paucity of top-quality cropland soils for agricultural production. In these four regions combined, there are about 80

COMPARATIVE VALUE CHANGES
IN CONSUMER PRICE INDEX, FARM REAL-ESTATE INDEX,
AND STANDARD AND POOR'S 500 STOCKS, 1920–1979

	CONSUMER PRICE INDEX		FARM REAL ESTATE		500 S&P STOCKS	
	INDEX	AVERAGE ANNUAL CHANGE (%)	INDEX	AVERAGE ANNUAL CHANGE (%)	INDEX	AVERAGE ANNUAL CHANGE (%)
1920	60	—	48	—	8	—
1940	42	−0.9%	21	−1.4%	11	+0.2%
1950	72	+3.0	43	+2.2	18	+0.7
1960	90	+1.7	72	+2.9	56	+3.8
1967	100	+1.6	100	+4.0	92	+5.1
1970	116	+5.3	117	+5.7	83	−3.0
1977	182	+9.4	283	+23.7	98	+2.1
1978	195	+7.1	308	+9.0	96	−2.0
1979 (Nov.)	227	+12.0	351	+14.0	104	+7.3
Average annual compounded changes 1970–1979	+11%		+22%		+3%	

million acres of soils ranging in quality from Class I to Class III. This is less than 25 percent of all such soil in America. Yet within these four regions, about 55 percent of all Americans now live. It is this vivid imbalance that makes the remaining top-quality soils in the most populous regions of America all the more important targets for new policies that will conserve these particular lands for agricultural production. In years to come, it will be more important than ever before to grow food near population centers as deregulated, long-distance rail and truck distribution networks, which now handle most American produce, will add more significant cost to final consumer prices than in the past.

Existing Efforts To Preserve Farmland: Complexities and Contradictions. In most instances, prime agricultural land in America may be sold to anyone for any purpose. While some land is restricted by local zoning, most of it is not limited as to use in any way. And conventional zoning, when it occurs, usually marks the land for residential uses, thereby raising taxes and dooming the agricultural enterprise.

In recent years, local, state, and federal government efforts have shown some signs of moving more imaginatively—if all too slowly and meekly —into the arena of farmland preservation. The approach used in most areas of the country, usually as a consequence of state-level legislation, is to focus on property-tax relief for the farmer. Three distinct types of tax benefits or inducements are offered: (1) preferential (or differential) assessment; (2) deferred taxation; or (3) restrictive agreements.

Preferential-assessment laws authorize assessors to assess eligible land on the basis of farm-use value rather than on the highest possible market value. This usually creates a lower real-property-tax cost. Deferred-taxation laws add a stipulation to preferential assessment: owners of lands which are assessed below highest value are required to pay some or all back taxes from which they have been exempted in prior years if they convert their land to a noneligible use, such as a housing development.

Restrictive-agreement statutes combine the concepts of preferential assessment and deferred taxation, and add one other stipulation: the owner must sign a contract that explicitly states his rights and duties. Usually, this contract specifies the number of years during which the landowner must keep his land in farming use (or another eligible use), and a schedule of economic or tax penalties which must be paid if conversion precedes the time established in the restrictive agreement. For example, in California, a penalty of 12.5 percent of market value can be assessed if an owner converts without permission and before the contract period has expired.

Since 1957, when Maryland enacted the first statewide statutes that authorized preferential assessment of farmland, at least forty-two states have ratified some form of a preferential-taxation program aimed at the preservation of farmland and/or other types of open space. Some of the most widespread state programs include the Wisconsin Farmland Preservation Program, the Oregon State Land Conservation and Development Commission program, the Maryland State Agricultural Land Preservation Fund, and California's Williamson Act program. Each state has its own individual statutes; and within each, many counties and even local municipalities have their own regulations. In some states, eligible lands include a broad range of agricultural lands, as well as pasture land and forests. In almost all states, a minimum farm size is stipulated, and, in several, a minimum level of gross income must be earned from the land.

While these various statutes are, without question, a beginning, they are often too timid or too broad or both. The temerity is revealed in the option frequently given the farmer or speculator who holds farmland: he can simply pay back taxes and/or a penalty, and then sell. The sellout, when it comes, is generally so valuable that the tax or penalty payment is inconsequential. Or, alternatively, of course, the farmer or speculator can wait for the period of agreement to expire and then sell. Stated bluntly, there is nothing in any of these state acts that assures the continuation of prime farmland in its agricultural use. Each is a pallative to buy time, literally, through the use of an indirect subsidy.

Also, the programs are too broad. They deal with vast amounts of eligible land that is not so critical and, therefore, not so reasonably included. Vast stretches of marginal cropland, pasture, and timberlands of all sorts are included in the same legislation calculated to promote preservation of prime agricultural land. This taints and complicates the issue by making the terrain covered by specialized regulation more vast that it need be. And it makes the regulations seem more complex and, in fact, potentially more expensive. If the focus were only on those lands in each state which are classified as Class I and Class II farmland, the problem would be simplified. The legislation would have more defined limits; it would include a manageable amount of terrain; and administrative complexity and tax-reduction costs would both be minimized.

Most of the state and local farmland preservation programs which we have today, dependent as they are on voluntary admission and voluntary compliance, are patently ineffective. A recent report entitled *Untaxing Open Space: An Evaluation of the Effectiveness of Differential Assessment of Farms and Open Space,* prepared for the Council on Environmental Quality (CEQ) by the Regional Science Research Institute in Philadelphia, concluded quite correctly:

With respect to the goal of retarding the conversion of farm and other open land, differential assessment is marginally effective and its cost in terms of tax expenditures is high, in most cases so high as to render it an undesirable tool for achieving this goal. . . . It may even cause effective demand to increase, since developers will be willing to bid more for the land, realizing that as long as they keep it in approved uses, their carrying costs will be lower.

Many ordinary citizens in communities where a significant amount of the land is given preferential assessment are likely to oppose the program. After all, taxes shifted from eligible tax-sheltered land are collected from the land owned by everyone else. For this reason, passage of legislation that promotes some form of preferential-taxation program is often difficult at the local and county levels.

As might be expected, the tax shift in a rural township may be quite significant, whereas in a large county with a differentiated economy and a larger population base, the increased tax on other real estate will be less noticeable. Nevertheless, in either situation, the specter of a landowner receiving a publicly acknowledged publicized tax break at the expense of other voters in town brings risk to the politician and resistance among other citizens. In some states, such as California, New York, and Michigan, this political fact of life is remedied by state programs which assure a form of state reimbursement to counties and local municipalities that forego property-tax revenue in order to achieve land-preservation programs.

Alternatives to Preferential-Assessment Programs. There is growing recognition among politicians and preservationists alike that current preferential-assessment programs do not work well. And they do not work at all when a developer wants to buy land. At this juncture, the developer does not care if it is top-quality agricultural land or marginal pasture land. He is interested in the location—not the soil quality—and believes he can make a profit by converting it to another use. When the developer is willing to pay enough, the farmer or land speculator who participates in a land-conservation program is generally willing to pay back taxes and/or any imposed penalty in order to sell the land.

To counter the conversion of prime agricultural land, a growing number of states and counties are now testing or considering stronger measures, principally the public purchase of development rights. Elsewhere, efforts are under way to set up a private sector purchase-and-sale program to permit the transfer of development rights off prime agricultural soils to land more appropriate for development.

This quite recent approach to the problem, discussed in much detail in Chapter Five, has several decisive limitations. First, given the political realities of America today and the competition for local public funds from every conceivable source, local public acquisition of development rights on a meaningful scale over a sustained number of years is far too expensive. Moreover, there are not enough people in most communities or counties who perceive the preservation of prime farmland as a high-priority issue.

The other alternative, the private sale of development rights, is also of limited potential in most rural areas. Each community would have to legislate a "preservation zone," where development would not be allowed. A "transfer zone," where development would be encouraged, would have to be simultaneously created. Landowners in the preservation zone would receive certificates in some form which would represent the land's development rights. Developers could purchase these certificates and apply the development rights to the transfer zone, where they would be permitted to build at a higher density than normal zoning law allows. Under ideal conditions, a private transfer of development rights permits the farmland owner of the rights to receive money from a private purchaser, and the sale removes the development potential from the farmland. In turn, the private purchaser obtains the benefit of more intensive development on his nonfarmland property.

While the sale of development rights may sound relatively uncomplicated, it is, in fact, difficult to implement. It presupposes a market in which private entrepreneurs are willing to purchase these development rights; a recipient site which can be intensively developed; and community acceptance of the entire idea.

Setting up such a market and workable system requires a very sophisticated set of options, controls, and circumstances. In addition, especially in small towns and rural areas, development rights transfers are not likely to be especially popular with many people. Most citizens prefer to know that conventional zoning means what it says: they do not want development rights which may land on the lot next door floating around town. While a transferable development rights program in the private sector has a substantial basis of fairness to the farmland seller and could theoretically preserve prime farmland (or anything else) at little or no public cost, I believe it must be recognized as a very difficult concept to implement.

Other Options. In mid-1979, the USDA and the CEQ organized an interagency study to identify and assess methods which state and local governments could use to alleviate farmland losses. The study group includes representatives from the USDA, the CEQ, the departments of the Interior, Energy, Treasury, Defense, Commerce, Transportation, and

Housing and Urban Development, plus the Environmental Protection Agency and Water Resources Council. Recommendations are to be forwarded to the president. Unless the federal government is willing to commit its own legal and financial powers to the issue, I doubt that strong, long-term preservation of prime farmland will be accomplished by state and local government alone.

First, I believe that we need some form of mandatory national preservation effort for Class I and Class II agricultural soils, which can be productively and economically farmed. Second, I suggest that other open spaces, such as less critical agricultural lands, pastures, and woodlands, should not be entirely ignored or suddenly excluded from preservation consideration. But these are less critical as agricultural lands, less clearly and less surely connected to vital national interests, and therefore I find voluntary programs for these lands, such as those being formulated by states and local communities around the country, satisfactory and appropriate. Third, special mandatory open-space preservation initiatives—*not* farmland preservation programs—need to be established within and very near settled communities.

TOWARD A WORKABLE FARMLAND PRESERVATION POLICY

Precisely where should a viable national policy of farmland preservation focus? Should we try to conserve through regulation all 220 million acres of Class I and Class II soils, the best of the approximately 400 million acres upon which crops are now grown? Such a policy would endeavor to regulate the use and value of almost 10 percent of the land in America. And such a policy, I believe, is unwarranted and potentially wasteful, at least in this century. Most of this cropland is not now and probably will not be threatened by irrevocable development or conversion to urbanized use for as long as half a century, or maybe longer.

However, what about the 33 million acres of the very best of all the cropland, the Class I soils in America? And what about the other 10 million acres of Class I soils currently devoted to pasture, range, forest, and other uses? In all, we possess perhaps a total of 43 million acres of Class I soil, less than 10 percent of all cropland and less than 2 percent of the total national land mass. It is for these most precious, scarce, and productive agricultural soils that a national policy of care and conservation is warranted and should be directed.

The first expensive and most critical task toward the creation of such a policy has already been completed. Testing and mapping efforts undertaken by the USDA over many years are now complete; the location of these soils is known.

ENCROACHMENT ON AGRICULTURAL LAND, SAN MATEO, CALIFORNIA, APRIL 1956

In 1953, this entire area was producing artichokes. As housing and other forms of urbanization take hold of agricultural lands, land values escalate, developers are attracted, and farming becomes less economic. The intimate mix of farming and suburbanization, as desirable as it may seem to some, creates an uneasy and unsatisfactory alliance.

A Policy Framework. Any proposal for a policy to save prime farmland—whether it be limited to Class I or inclusive of Class II—I believe, should be premised on certain basic principles, some of which are too often overlooked, especially by organized and usually urban-based land preservationists. First and foremost, a farmer must not be denied the right to sell his property at its market value. Second, certain new ideas about the use and value of farmland, if clearly established, would in themselves help to promote a viable and equitable basis upon which policy can be developed.

What might these new ideas be? The first is that *farmland is farmland,* and not farmland-waiting-to-be-something-else. If it is prime farmland, then it deserves to be fully valued as prime farmland, and thus at a higher value than nearby agricultural land that is less productive. But it should be valued as farmland, not as land being farmed temporarily until an ambitious housing subdivider or shopping-center developer comes along to convert it to its highest and best use.

The highest and best use of prime farmland in America is as cropland. This simple sentence, if used to formulate law, could save the best soils in this country in perpetuity.

What consequences automatically follow? What if, for instance, by national law, all cropland soils classified as Class I could never be converted to any use other than crop production? First, local communities would be obliged to zone all of these lands as agricultural. Second, the local communities would have to assess and tax these lands at the agricultural rate, not at a level that anticipates urbanization and development. Third, the federal government, when appraising an estate at death, would be obliged to classify and value these lands at their agricultural value, and thus tax them at these levels of value. Fourth, many speculators, who now hold over one third of the nation's cropland, would no longer be interested in these particular agricultural lands. The hope of future windfall profits from land-use conversion would not merit tying up huge sums of speculative capital in prime farmland. Indeed, much speculative interest would shift toward marginal farmland, pasture land, and nearby woodland, located in a likely and sensible spot for eventual conversion to urban uses. These lands are not in short supply whatsoever, and form an appropriate and sensible foundation upon which new development may occur.

Such a policy, I suspect, would be resented by many of the farmers who own Class I land. After all, as stated recently by the Regional Science Research Institute in Philadelphia, everyone is aware of farmers as "producers of two entirely different classes of goods for two different markets: agricultural commodities and development sites." Selling a development site instead of cauliflower provides a once-in-a-lifetime bonanza, which some farmers understandably seek.

But my suggestion is that the farmer in possession of top-quality prime soil be treated much like the owner of property in a historic district: he should be obliged to use the land for its special purpose. Like the owner of a historic district property, he should remain free to sell the land to anyone interested in continuing its present use. And the preservation of this use is, indeed, important, for the land in question has a use basic to national well-being, national security, and the future of this country. Even more definitively than the highest-quality buildings and districts of historic America, the best agricultural soils once lost are not replaceable; once destroyed, are not reproducible.

This program would do much to halt one of the most destructive diseases that attacks prime farmland: creeping, patchwork, leapfrog conversion as rural communities expand, as the rural fringes of towns and cities continue to develop. As each large farm field is broken up, farming nearby becomes less feasible, less economic. The farmer needs a critical mass of land to utilize efficient technologies. Each agricultural region needs a high level of production to support viable produce transportation, marketing, and supply systems.

A program that halts the loss of Class I soils allows the contiguous fields of top-quality soils that exist today to remain intact. Inefficiencies of scale created by noncontiguous farmland interspersed with housing are so acute that I would exempt from the proposed development restriction any area not composed of at least fifty contiguous acres. Areas smaller than this slated for conversion should be seen as potential open space, not as viable farmland.

Is It Feasible? Would such a sweeping statement of national land-use policy be possible to implement? Are there any precedents, particularly for innovative federal legislation, to start the process? Yes, definitely. Historic district designation and preservation legislation are familiar examples, and the nationwide coastal zone program that is just emerging is a relevant precedent.

Initiating federal legislation could mandate some form of state and local zoning of Class I soils restricted exclusively to agricultural use. In addition, funds should be set aside annually, perhaps as part of the USDA budget, to purchase the development rights from Class I soils located in communities in which mandated agricultural zoning would represent a substantial taking of existing land values. Once development rights are purchased, the land would then be leased back to the selling farmer or to another farmer wishing to use it exclusively for agricultural purposes.

As a third ingredient of the program, the use of federal funds to finance most forms of development on Class I agricultural soils should be prohibited. This would restrict bank lending and federal expenditures for new project development on these particular lands, such as sewers, airports, and federally subsidized rural and suburban housing. At the same time, insured loans or favorable interest rates might be offered for financing farm-related expenditures.

As far as the possible magnitude of the expenditure involved for the development-rights-purchase portion of this three-pronged program is concerned, let us assume for a moment that the average acre of threatened Class I soil, susceptible to alternative development, is worth $5,000 to $10,000 an acre. Although this estimate is far above the average price of agricultural land in America, whose median price in 1980 was below

CROP DUSTING
IN THE IMPERIAL VALLEY,
NEAR CALIPATRIA,
CALIFORNIA, 1972

There are certain variables that could dramatically affect the price of, and demand for, farmland and food for years to come: the long-range potential population of America and the world; and an energy shortage, which could bring about a shortage of pesticides, fertilizers, and fuel, as well as increased demand for the use of cropland for energy rather than for food. To insure against future crises, we should now establish a national policy to preserve the 2 percent of American land that is the most productive cropland.

$1,000, it is within the range of prices paid by housing developers and others who want to assemble large tracts of the most strategically located cropland for conversion to urbanized uses. Of the total national resource of all cropland, approximately 15 percent is near major metropolitan centers—that is, a county or group of contiguous counties containing at least one city of 50,000 or more inhabitants. If we assume that the same percentage of prime lands is also so distributed, then the total acreage of Class I land that is the most likely to be lost to urbanization and other forms of development is roughly 15 percent of 43 million acres, or approximately 6.5 million acres. If the development rights upon all of this land had to be bought, which is entirely unlikely, and the average development rights were valued at, say $10,000 per acre, the total acquisition would amount to $65 billion dollars.

I would guess that perhaps one third of this land would be equitably covered by the above suggested restrictive zoning and not tendered for development rights sale. This assumption reduces the total potential cost to, say, $43 billion.

This money would not have to be spent all at once. On the contrary, it could be appropriated each year and spent as necessary. Remember, only 3 percent of the cropland across America comes up for sale in the average year. And 3 percent of the land targeted for development rights purchase in this suggested program amounts to an annual expenditure of $1.3 billion, about half the funds lavished by the USDA on crop subsidies in most years. I can think of no more fundamental investment in the future of America that might be made with public funds.

It takes a miraculous coincidence of climate, precipitation, chemical consistency, and molecular composition to create an exceptionally fertile morsel of land. If we are to behave like a mature country, one able to influence and protect our own future, as well as order our most essential priorities, then a national policy to preserve Class I agricultural soils must be established.

This proposal is presented as a sketch outline. It is presented in this manner as an acknowledgment of the complexity of formulating a policy, a funding source, and a method of implementation that will work effectively. Most of all, it is presented in order to give impetus, not to suggest a precise approach. But the direction could not be more important.

We will hopefully have a long and successful history of survival in this country. We are not now in a time of rapid population expansion or other type of national activity that would consume great quantities of cropland; we are, however, in a period of sharply rising prices for such land. Both factors make this the time to act. There is no national emergency, no rational basis to fear that the land will be consumed in the near future. Thus, from a prospective of broad national policy, which must be slow, deliberate, and equitable, this is the time to implement a program of permanent protection of a miraculous national resource.

Prices are likely to be higher in years to come. And there is no predicting the very long-range potential population of either America or the world. Social and economic shifts in the next century may provide the foundation for a renewed surge in the natural growth of the resident population. An energy crisis could bring about a shortage of pesticides, fertilizers, and fuel, as well as increased demand for the use of cropland for energy rather than for food. World events may even require dramatic relaxation of policies that now limit immigration into America.

All we know is this: If the world is to continue functioning even vaguely as it does today, then competition for developable lands in America will grow in centuries to come, as will the demand for top-quality cropland. There is sufficient space to accommodate both. But we do need to sort out our priorities for the 10 percent of land in America that is productive cropland, and especially for the less than 2 percent of our nation's surface which is the most productive land of all.

FARMLAND MAY NOT BE SCARCE, BUT YOU WOULDN'T KNOW IT FROM THE PRICE

In recent years, average farmland prices have been soaring in a runaway boom. Between 1970 and 1979, the average annual compounded value of farm real estate escalated over 20 percent, as indicated in the table on this page. This increase outstrips almost all other traditional forms of invest-

GRADES AND SUGGESTED VALUES PER ACRE
OF FARMLAND, PERMANENT PASTURE, AND WOODLAND.
STATE OF INDIANA, 1968

KIND OF LAND	ESTIMATED TRUE CASH VALUE		RECOMMENDED TRUE CASH VALUE	PERCENTAGE OF TOP QUALITY VALUE
	LOW	HIGH		
Farmland				
Excellent	375	565 & up	420	1.00
Good	315	375	320	0.76
Average	190	315	210	0.50
Fair	115	190	120	0.28
Poor	40	115	75	0.17
Permanent Pasture				
Excellent	90	190	150	1.00
Good	65	90	85	0.57
Average	50	65	60	0.40
Fair	25	50	45	0.30
Poor	15	25	20	0.13
Woodland				
Excellent	N.A.	150 & up	150	1.00
Good	100	150	110	0.73
Average	65	100	75	0.50
Fair	25	65	55	0.37
Poor	15	25	20	0.13

N.A. = Not available.

ment. It also exceeds by approximately 100 percent the rate of inflation as measured by the Consumer Price Index.

This escalation in the price of farmland is both astonishing and very much out of character, as illustrated in the figures on page 523. During the twentieth century, until about 1970, the value of farm real estate was influenced by and reflected quite closely the basic trends in the American economy. Between 1920 and 1950, farm real-estate values, much like the Consumer Price Index, barely increased. These were years, of course, when marginal farmers were selling out, moving off the land; when, for many reasons, people were flowing into the urban centers of the nation.

Then, between 1950 and 1970, farmland prices began to increase rather steadily at rates somewhat in excess of the rate of increase in the Consumer Price Index. During these same years, or at least until the late 1960s, the stock market performed even better than farmland, as it rose from depressed postwar prices. By 1970, the stock market faltered and sputtered, unable to keep pace with the inflationary economy.

Then, between 1970 and 1979, while inflation increased at the even greater compounded annual rate of about 11 percent, farmland prices took off. And by the end of the 1970s, they had compounded in value at twice the rate of inflation.

It is certainly true that now the migration off the less productive farms is just about over, that the distress sale of farmland is increasingly rare. At the same time, there is no shortage of cropland or pasture land in America. Under these circumstances, when land prices—or prices of anything, for that matter—are escalating on the order of 20 percent or more per year, people with any degree of circumspection have to wonder: How long can this go on? They might even step back from that question to ask: Why is this going on?

The Increase in Farmland Value: Why?   First, much of the increase in farmland value in recent years, I believe, is fueled by the expectation of even higher costs in the future, which induces farmers and speculators alike to buy now. The farmer will expand; the speculator will sell later, at anticipated higher prices.

Second, as a farmer friend of mine pointed out recently, the successful farmer "will always pay too much for land. He is looking two or three generations ahead." And, of course, to the successful farmer, land contiguous to his existing farm is especially important to obtain. Owning it permits both a logical expansion and an economical operation. It eliminates the possibility of a potential farmer competitor. And, if housing sites are the alternative, it avoids the social and environmental nuisance of non-farm neighbors. Thus, the farmer-purchaser is a most potent force in

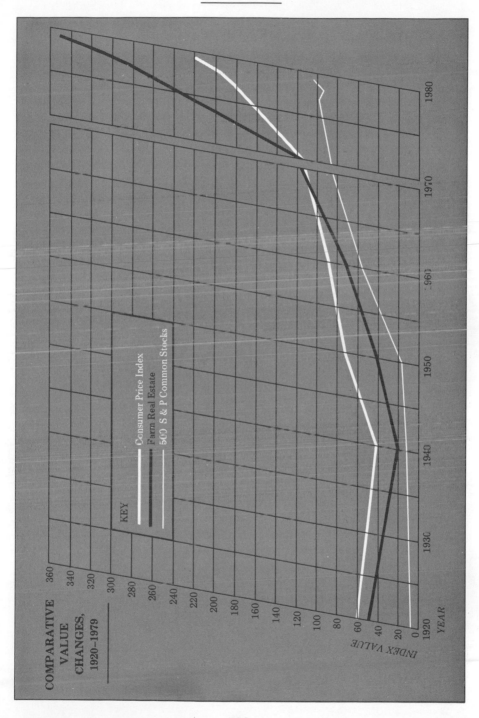

COMPARATIVE VALUE CHANGES, 1920–1979

KEY

Consumer Price Index
Farm Real Estate
500 S & P Common Stocks

INDEX VALUE

YEAR

continuing the upward surge in value of American farmland. Indeed, a very high percentage of all cropland sold each year at these higher prices is purchased by farmers.

A major factor which assists farmer-purchasers is subsidized farmland purchase financing. Various federal agencies, including the Farmers Home Administration and the Production and Credit Administration of the USDA, lend farmers large sums of money at relatively low cost for farmland purchases. Furthermore, federal lending agencies are extremely reluctant to force a farmer who is experiencing financial difficulties to sell his farm. The foreclosure sale is consequently increasingly rare, and farmland prices are propped up by the farmer's ability to buy at lower financing costs.

Third, as a result of the 1976 Tax Reform Act and the Revenue Act of 1978, new relief has been granted to farmers' estates. Those estates which consist of family farms (or closely held businesses) can now pay their tax liabilities over fifteen years at 4 percent interest rather than at the former requirement of ten years at 7 percent interest. The low interest rate, however, applies only to the first $1 million of the estate. The subsidized estate-tax support to farmers, though still quite nominal, is intended to reduce the number of forced sales of family farms and businesses to meet estate-tax obligations. At the bottom line, this special farmland estate-tax treatment, along with limited relief under certain circumstances in the way a family farm is appraised for estate-tax purposes, helps keep farmland prices up.

Realities of the Marketplace. It is estimated that presently 60–65 percent of all farmland is owned by farmers who work the land themselves, and another 5 percent is rented from other farmers. Most of the balance, or over 30 percent of all farmland in America, is owned by investors and speculators who have no intention of farming themselves; rather, they rent land to working farmers or allow it to remain idle. Contrary to scare exposés, sensational headlines, and the occasional enterprising news story about activity in a very local area, foreign investors and speculators own less than 1 percent of U. S. farmland.

Of the roughly 400 million acres of cropland that has escalated in average price in recent years, the market is established by a minuscule proportion of the property. On average about 3 percent is bought and sold annually. If much more were placed on the market in a given year or annually over a number of years, it is altogether likely that prices would fall substantially.

The reality of the situation is that news of a sale at a high price sends ripples of anticipated wealth through speculative property holders in the region. And it sends the farmer-owner to the bank with a new financial statement on which he increases the value of his land assets. It is on the basis of this financial statement, and estimated crop production and its future value, that a farmer finances his new equipment and operating expenses each year.

Land Quality = Land Value: Knowledge Is Essential. A note of caution to the amateur buyer who hears about the large profits reaped by those speculating in farmland: It pays to know the land itself.

Remember, the most likely successive buyer will be a farmer. Even if you are an amateur, do not count on finding another amateur to buy your land when it comes time to sell. The difference that land *quality* can make to value, whether it be cropland, pasture, or woods, is enormous.

The underlying productive quality of agricultural, pasture, and woodland can affect the value of the land by 100, 200, 300 percent or more. An acre of cropland in one field may be worth $500. But to an experienced agricultural buyer, an acre upon which the exact same crop is growing in the adjacent field may be worth only $250, or even less.

This difference in value results primarily from the inherent differences in the productive capacity of the soil itself. As illustrated on page 521, the uninformed buyer who pays the price of "excellent" cropland, pasture, or woodland but receives only "good" or "average" soils for those purposes is going to receive between 40 cents and 75 cents for every dollar spent. This immediate loss of value of 25 percent to 60 percent of the purchase price makes care, experience, and information much warranted. As in all other forms of dealing with land in America, it makes sense to understand the land itself, not just the papers upon which it is described. Sometimes land is not worth the paper on which it is mapped; and sometimes, it is worth a great deal more.

THE INCREASE IN FARMLAND VALUE: FOR HOW LONG?

During recent years, of course, farmers have sought and obtained higher prices for their crops and livestock, while also raising per acre productivity. But spiraling costs of raw materials, interest expense, taxes, wages, and land have kept agricultural profits well below the level of land-value escalations. What many farmers have gained in the past several years is an enormous increase in land wealth and an insignificant increase in their annual income.

In some respects, as land values increase, the inherent risk in farming,

your CROP is your INCOME

**FRAME OF A FILMSTRIP PREPARED
BY THE FARM SECURITY ADMINISTRATION
IN SEPTEMBER 1942**

During recent years, farmers have sought and obtained higher prices for
their crops and livestock, while also raising per-acre productivity. Increasing costs of raw materials, money, taxes, wages, and land, however, have
kept agricultural profits well below the level of land-value escalations.
What many farmers have gained in the past several years is an enormous
increase in land wealth and an insignificant increase
in their annual income.

a treacherous business under any circumstance, increases even more. Most purchasers of farmland are farmers themselves. As the farmer pays for ever more costly land from farm earnings plus borrowed funds, his debt and annual interest expense rise. Though land purchases are not the only cause, since 1950 the ratio of net farm income to all farm debt has seriously decreased. In 1950, net farm income (before inventory adjustments) and farm debt were nearly equal. Ten years later, as more land and equipment were purchased by large farm operators, each dollar of net income was matched by nearly $2.25 in outstanding liabilities. By 1970, there was nearly $3.75 in debt outstanding for each dollar of net income. By 1978/1979, as land costs increased dramatically and as more new equipment was purchased on credit, this measure of indebtedness in relationship to annual net income soared to over $6.00. Then, during 1979, farmers' total indebtedness escalated from $137.5 billion to $161.8 billion, an increase of nearly 18 percent. More than half of this enormous level of debt is debt on real estate.

In recent years the federal government stepped in to support this high level of debt. Lending provisions issued by the Farmers Home Administration have been liberalized. Commodity Credit Corporation low-interest loans to farmers swelled between 1976 and 1979 from about $1 billion to about $4.5 billion; and for the first time, the Small Business Administration was authorized to make loans to farmers. Government payments to farmers overall have escalated from $185 million in 1949 to over $3 billion in 1978.

Thus, in the most general terms, it is clear that farmers carrying very high debt balances are now seriously exposed to possible economic reverses. If production of crops, livestock, and farm produce were expanded without a parallel increase in export demand, prices would fall; or if the basic economy of the nation should further deteriorate in a deflationary cycle, prices might decline along with agricultural profits. Even if farm income declined significantly, debt would nonetheless remain, as would the requisite payments on it.

This situation helps explain why cropland is purposefully idled while the federal government maintains extremely expensive programs which encourage farmers not to use their cropland productively. Without an artificial control on the quantity of production, a control that forces all consumers to pay somewhat more each year for the necessities of life, a serious economic squeeze on farmers could occur. In such a situation, to satisfy debt and to reduce costs, many farmers would turn to their most valuable asset—and in many instances, only tangible one—the land. Decisions to sell off part of the farm, sparked across the farming terrain of America, would dramatically reverse recent precipitous increases in farmland prices.

Recent farmland price increases have far outstripped basic economic justification, whether on the basis of net profit obtainable from a productive acre or land-value escalations that may occur as a result of anticipated national economic inflation. I wonder how long this land-value trend can continue.

Farmers and speculators alike who now seek to acquire more farmland should look carefully at the past. And they should remember the vast amount of agricultural land available in America.

Farmland Values in the Future: Special Situations. A few special situations stand out as I contemplate the future value of farmland in America.

Class I soils will remain expensive, and keep going up. The roughly 43 million acres of top-grade Class I agricultural soils are those most likely to increase in value over the years. This land is scattered around the country, its location no secret to those who care to discover it. And in certain areas, especially in the Northeast, and Pacific and Great Lake regions, where populations are high and growing, where farmland continues to be converted to urban uses, genuine scarcities of the best soils will occur unless wise protective and conservation programs for Class I soils are implemented.

In addition, the shortage of energy, which we now face for the foreseeable future, will raise the cost of farm production (fertilizers and fuel), thereby potentially limiting incremental increases in general agricultural land values. Because Class I soils will require relatively lower investment to remain relatively more productive, the relative value of the underlying land will increase. Just as a home that is very expensive to heat may lose relative value compared to one next door that is efficient and less costly to maintain, so soils that are costly to maintain at a high level of productivity are likely to be adjusted downward in relative value.

Farmland prices will continue to rise at the crossroads of urbanization and farmland usage. The exceptional and limited amount of all classes of farmland within the path of urbanization or small-town expansion is where the farmer's opportunity to sell out and cash in is most pronounced. It is here, at the edge, that farmland prices become a wild card, that speculation is the most intense. Where there is ready road access, suitable soil for development, and a nearby growing center of urbanization (whether it be a small town or growing suburb), the adjacent farmland will be sought by those who want to convert it to urban uses. It is precisely here, at the edge of development, that sensible and informed farmland and open-space preservation policies must be inaugurated.

Top-quality irrigated farmland with an adequate and protected water

528

supply will be increasingly valuable. As the cost to irrigate skyrockets, the relative value of land that is already protected from drought increases. In addition, as competition for water intensifies, irrigated farmland with a protected water supply becomes a most sought-out resource. Such cropland, I believe, may decline in price during a time of severe deflation, but not nearly so much as other tangible assets and not nearly so much as the Consumer Price Index. In years of inflation, such farmland should more than keep up in value.

General Farmland Values in the Future: A Note of Caution. To farmers looking to expand, to speculators seeking land profits, future trends in farmland values are a subject of consuming personal and business interest. What I see across the broad spectrum of farmland acreage is cause for caution ahead. I believe it is a mistake to bet on the same astronomical rates of increase in farmland acreage values as those experienced during the 1970s. During that period, the average per-acre value of farm real estate accelerated more than 20 percent per annum. But things are changing. There are certain trends the present-day farmland buyer should consider.

First, let us review what is happening to demand for the land itself, and even more importantly, to the demand for what it can produce at a profit. The population of the United States, the source of over 70 percent of the annual demand for food and livestock products, is not expected to grow at a rapid pace. The amount of foreign demand for agricultural products that domestic sources are allowed to fulfill is politically regulated. Recently, in fact, grain exports have been limited to the Soviet Union as a politically motivated aspect of America's international policy. Overall, demand for agricultural products could level off.

The per-acre productivity of cropland in America also shows signs of leveling off. As it does, the agricultural value of the acre itself tends to stabilize. When per acre productivity stops increasing, the economic justification to pay higher prices for the acre of land is weakened.

The most uncertain question connected to demand for our agricultural and livestock products is related to demand from outside the United States. World population is still growing dramatically. It presently exceeds 4 billion and may reach 7 billion by the year 2000. The Chinese population alone, now estimated at 960 million people (including 17 million on Taiwan) is growing at an annual rate of 1.2 percent. While population growth rates have diminished substantially in all the developed nations, they exceed 2.5 percent per annum in some of the most underdeveloped countries.

The question remains: Will world agricultural production rise in concert with world population, thereby eliminating any increased pressure for exports from the United States? The answer is uncertain. But what is certain is that American domestic and foreign policy can control levels of export, and thereby the price of agricultural commodities in this country. It is doubtful that any wary national government would permit substantial and sustained increases in agricultural prices to occur as a result of competing foreign demand. Such a policy would be—or should be—political suicide at home. Thus, while agricultural and livestock produce prices may continue to rise in America due to such cyclical factors as supply and weather, and occasional foreign-purchase intervention, I doubt that competing bids from Asia, Africa, China, the Soviet Union, or the rest of the world will be allowed to bid up prices substantially for very long without the implementation of some form of government price control and export limitation.

Another question that arises is: Has productivity on the farm in recent years kept pace with the increase in land values? To answer this question, I analyzed various farm productivity and real-estate asset figures which have characterized American agriculture since 1950. When man-hours of labor, farm production, farm output, and farm real-estate debt are reviewed, stark evidence emerges that increases in productivity overall, and increases in productivity per man-hour, although present in recent years, are much less steep than they were during the years between 1950 and 1970. In those years, farm modernization, mechanization, and scientific agriculture came to the fore. The large investments in new farm equipment and modernized agricultural practices made in the aftermath of the Second World War allowed record levels of productivity to occur through the 1970s. But increases in productivity are no longer being sustained.

The picture today is one, I believe, of land prices catching up with investment and productivity gains which took place in years past. I see no current foundation being established, from the viewpoint of productivity, for a renewed spurt of general farmland real-estate values of the magnitude experienced in recent years. Whether general farmland prices will continue to increase at or near the rate of the Consumer Price Index, as was more commonplace throughout this century, is even uncertain.

Trends in land values change slowly, but they do change, and change dramatically. Once the forward momentum is no longer fueled, stasis and even regression set in. It takes considerable social, economic, political, and psychological power to keep the value of hundreds of millions of acres of land escalating at extremely high rates—much more power than I see available in the decade or two ahead.

Farmland in America represents a huge repository of national wealth, both as real estate and as a fundamental natural resource upon which this country and much of the world depends for food. It is land used as part of a cycle of production and consumption. In this respect, cropland is land used quite appropriately as a uniquely efficient commodity able to convert energy into foodstuffs needed for human and animal survival. This land is a most fundamental source of both our power and our wealth as a nation.

Some of the land—about 43 million acres—is better than all the rest at doing the job. National planning for the protection and enhancement of this particular function for this particular land is a most appropriate use of public power in the control of both a small portion of our national land and of the wealth which it embodies. At the very same time, open-space preservation and natural land conservation—important endeavors in their own right—must not be confused by advocates or in public policy with the special character and special issues associated with Class I farmland, gem of the nation.

SIXTEEN

———

LAND: POWER AND WEALTH

Each civilization imprints the land differently. And each land is a force so strong and so fundamental that it directs the course of the civilizations which depend upon it, which build upon it, which war over its possession, which come to cherish its particularities.

America can be evaluated as a nation by looking at what we have done with and to our land. So may each region, and finally each community. Indeed, an individual is revealed in diverse and profound aspects by the ways in which he uses and transforms the land. Intricate and intimate connections link land, power, and wealth in America. These connections, though misunderstood or not even considered by most people, are levers which determine how land in America is used.

Today we are an energy-short nation with a slow-growing and rapidly aging population. We are also a nation with no land shortage. Housing demand, long on the upswing, will peak during the 1980s. Many forces today contribute to tightening up and reusing rather than expanding anew: this is a dramatic shift, a new direction never before encountered in our brief history. We are a young country learning to live with unprecedented limitations on personal power, on private landownership, on energy resources, and on credit availability. We are fundamentally weakened by inflation, yet tied to its superficial euphoria.

As argued in earlier chapters, America is at a new juncture: public policy rather than unfettered market forces will dominate land-value trends in years to come. Tax legislation, environmental regulation, public improvements, controlled-growth legislation, and transit location have more to do with future land values now than ever before. Nevertheless, a limited number of situations exist in which anticipated supply-and-demand market forces present a potential for land scarcity, a foundation for future value increases. Unless checked by the exercise of public regulatory power, I believe there will be strong demand in years to come for situations in which land *remains* scarce or is *made* scarce or will *become* scarce. However, these three possibilities by no means include the great majority of undeveloped, vacant land in America.

Land will continue to be in short supply in the most desirable urban, suburban, and small-town locations within communities that are carefully managed, well-maintained, and socially stable. Class I farmland, the most economically productive in the country, is limited in availability.

534

Irrigated western farms with an assured supply of water are needed and will become more precious. Land will remain scarce in the most desirable second-home and resort locations, which enjoy climatic advantages, transit access to large regional cities, clean water, pristine environments, and sound control over the quality of planned change.

How can land be *made* scarce when in fact it cannot be made at all? Principally by new perceptions and new regulations which increase demand and, therefore, value while limiting the amount of affected land. As we have seen, older city centers where neglected housing is taken over by affluent newcomers are just one example. Property within designated historic districts is made scarce by the district boundary line and desirable as a result of multiple legal, economic, and physical attributes newly accorded or perceived. Land adjacent to conservation and forever wild areas is made scarce and desirable by the act of protecting it from encroaching development.

Where is land that today is available and plentiful but because of trends already set in motion and not yet fully understood likely to become scarce? Surely one location is along the shores of bays, canals, and waterways which are still polluted as the result of nearly a century of environmental abuse. As pollution control becomes more effective, the inherent amenity value of this land for recreation and open vistas afforded by a water edge will increase. Where major public investment is made in improved, convenient, comfortable transit, as I expect it will have to be in the decades to come, the limited amounts of land around station stops will be increasingly in demand for commercial, residential, and recreational use. Land will be sought out in the limited number of smaller communities which set a public policy of management excellence that delivers essential services without waste. Land will also become scarce within active, thriving neighborhoods that foster controlled conversion of older, underutilized, sturdy buildings to new uses, while limiting the intensity and density of new development to appropriate scale for older neighborhoods.

In those few places where the "amenity" aspects of community are accorded a strong priority, land will also be in demand. Recreation, cultural resources, tourism potential, natural and scenic attributes, the quality of air and the water—all of these, *as they are enhanced*, distinguish a place and attract people. In the most enlightened circles, such as the federation of individuals and organizations that collaborate nationwide through Partners for Livable Places, an awareness is springing up that the sensible and sensitive enhancement of natural, historic, and man-made resources in a community contribute to its distinctiveness, to its allure.

Yet public policies more often than not affect the appearance, value, and use of land as an indirect spinoff, not as a primary objective. I find this a troubling state of affairs. Why should the future of so much land in America be dependent upon the *indirect* impacts of public policy controlled by agencies such as the Internal Revenue Service, the Department of Agriculture, the Department of Transportation, and a handful of state and local departments whose primary interests lie elsewhere? The physical environment, and especially the land, deserves more focused attention. Connections between land, power and wealth need to be dragged out of the closet, carefully examined, and used to forge more direct and more effective national, state, and local policy. We should imprint the land purposefully, intentionally, by design—not by wistful indifference or frustrated negligence.

I do not suggest a new massive national planning bureaucracy in America. I do not suggest greater direct control over land use through new federal, state, and local agencies. There is already so much relevant legislation affecting the most significant trends in land use and land value that we hardly need more.

What is needed, on the contrary, is clear revelation of how so much legislation, which on the surface appears to have only minimal reference to the land, affects it so profoundly. There first needs to be elucidation, not proliferation. There first needs to be careful, forthright examination of what we are doing to land in America with existing public power and private options—not new layers of law and regulation.

In one respect this book is a very selective first effort to indicate the possibilities and the importance of a consistent commitment to such a direction. I have explored some of the secondary impacts on land of national transportation policy, of federal tax regulation, of the environmental and preservation movements. *Land In America* is a beginning, a personal interpretative tap dance around an immense issue. As I try to make explicit in the argument throughout this book, there is no reason to believe, given the record, that the public use and administration of land in America is more exemplary than its treatment by the private sector. At times, land has been systematically abused as a resource and systematically exploited as a commodity by both.

We are, I believe, a culture and a country that during the 1980s must adjust to a new set of circumstances. These will have a wide and sustained impact on the correlations between land, power, and wealth in America. So far, many trends analyzed in this book have not been at work long enough to replace formerly operative assumptions about our country, our culture, and our economy. But as these new conditions begin to affect land in America, they expose former mainstays and once-reliable beliefs as current myths.

A wide variety of outmoded myths connected to the land continue to order our lives, our decisions, and our public policies as we begin to try to accommodate to strands of new evidence. We cling to these myths, as well we might, for they were each so true and so powerfully influential for so many years.

APPENDIX

MILESTONES

1607 —Jamestown is founded and contact is made with Chief Powhatan by English explorers and settlers.

1631 —Roger Williams argues that the royal charter for the colony of Massachusetts has illegally taken Indian land.

1633 —The General Court of Massachusetts prohibits settlers from direct purchase of Indian land.

1650s—Speculators continue to purchase land illegally from the Indians.

Late 1600s—"Worthy" individuals or groups are given a "Plantation Right" of land about 6 miles square by the Massachusetts General Court. Groups owning land distribute it according to the wealth of the individual and by the lottery system, surveying the land before it is allocated.

1682 —William Penn signs a treaty with the Delaware, Susquehanna, and other Indian tribes, beginning long-standing peace in Pennsylvania.

1700s—Land companies petition the king of England for tracts of land. The king often delegates the responsibility for granting land to the Privy Council, the Board of Trade, and the Lords of Treasury.

—Governors of the colonies have the power to make land grants of up to 1,000 acres to individuals. Special deal-making is common, and favored individuals are often granted 10,000 to 40,000 acres.

—In Virginia, land grants of 10,000 to 30,000 acres are made to groups of frontiersmen who defend the forts and stockades located on the fringes of settled areas.

1727 —The Massachusetts General Court expands the practice of granting large tracts to religious groups and allocates land to speculative groups as well.

1748 —The Ohio Company is granted 200,000 acres between the Allegheny Mountains and the Ohio River with the provision that an additional 300,000 acres will be granted if 100 families settle there in 7 years. Settlement of the area is slow, however, and the quota is not achieved.

1756 —King George III appoints superintendents to purchase land from the Indians. In 1761, he decides that the British Lords of Trade will be responsible for regulating purchases.

1763 —Indian Chief Pontiac's War of Indian Independence—siege at Fort Pitt and Fort Detroit.

—A boundary line is established along the Appalachian Mountains, and settlers are ordered by the king not to settle to the west of it.

1776 —Declaration of Independence from England. Drafting of the United States Constitution and Bill of Rights, which declares that "no person . . . be deprived of any property without due process of law. . . ."

1785 —Congress passes the Ordinance of 1785, which states that the government will survey all land not designated to the 13 original states, using east-west (base) lines and north-south (range) lines. Townships of 6 square miles are divided into 36 sections of 640 acres each. These sections are sold in entirety at a public auction for a minimum price of $1 an acre. Payment is by cash or loan-office certificates of liquidated debt. Each purchaser must pay a surveying fee of $36. Congress reserves 4 sections out of the 36 in each township for the federal government for subsequent disposal, claiming rights to a third of any minerals discovered. An additional section is reserved for schools. Townships may be sold as an entire tract to organized groups. The Board of Treasury keeps records of land sales.

1787 —The Ordinance of 1787 provides that new territories may be set up on Western lands. In order to vote, a settler must own 20 acres of land. To be a legislator, an individual has to own 200 acres.

1796 —Minimum price of an acre of government land is raised to $2 an acre, to be paid on a one-year credit plan.

Late 1700s, Early 1800s—There is much confusion about the boundaries of the original 13 states, because the grants to the colonies were contradictory. Smaller states with no claims to land west of the Appalachian Mountains are fearful that larger states will become more powerful if their claims are honored. The larger states finally agree to cede their Western claims, beginning with New York in 1781 and ending with Georgia in 1802.

—States sell surplus state land for as little as 6 cents an acre.

—The federal government gives free land to military heroes, religious organizations, and governments setting up asylums.

1800 —Local land offices are established to regulate the sale of government land. Credit is allowed. Buyers may take 4 years to pay for their land.

1803 —The Louisiana Purchase—530 million acres of land are purchased by the federal government from France for $15 million.

1804 —Congress, under the Jefferson administration, authorizes moving the Indians out of Georgia.

1807 —The Intrusion Act allows settlers to live on public land until they can pay for it or until someone else buys it.

1812 —The General Land Office is created within the Treasury Department to keep track of the sale of federal land.

1819 —Approximately 46 million acres of land (now known as Florida) are purchased by the United States from Spain for $6 million.

1820 —Minimum price of federally owned land is reduced to $1.25 an acre, to be paid in full, in cash. A minimum purchase of 80 acres is required.

1830 —The Act of 1830, the first of the Preemption laws, states that any settler who has been living on and has cultivated a tract of public land may purchase it for $1.25 an acre, to be paid in cash. Congress authorizes President Andrew Jackson to set up Indian districts in the area that is now Kansas and Oklahoma, to make land exchanges with the Indians, and to assist in relocating and protecting them. $500,000 is appropriated for these measures to be carried out. This and subsequent Preemption Acts are in force until 1891.

—By 1830, a total of 50 treaties with Indians have been concluded, the terms of which grant 200 million acres of land to the federal government at a cost of approximately $70 million.

1834 —The Act of 1834 sets up the Bureau of Indian Affairs within the War Department.

1821–1836—Eleven laws are passed allowing credit and delayed payments when purchasing federal land, superceding the requirements of the Act of 1820.

1836–1837—20 million acres of land are sold at an all-time high of $54 million. The government, fearing wildcat banking, requires that land be paid for in gold or silver. Wildcat banks crash, and rampant speculation in land subsides in the "Panic of 1837."

1838 —General Winfield Scott rounds up all of the remaining Cherokees in the Southeast and moves them farther west. The exodus is named the "Trail of Tears" when 1 out of every 4 Indians dies along the way.

1840s—The beginning of free land grants (eventually totaling 100 million acres) by the federal government to the railroad companies. The companies are allowed to sell specified parcels alongside the track to help finance construction. Parcels not sold are supposed to be returned to the government (a practice often avoided).

1846 —The Oregon Compromise transfers ownership of the 183-million-acre Pacific Northwest from Britain to the United States.

1848 —Mexico gives up 338 million acres to the United States after the Mexican War.

1849 —The Department of the Interior is created and the Bureau of Indian Affairs is moved to it from the War Department.

1850 —By this date, 245 treaties with Indians have been ratified, granting a total of 450 million acres to the government at a cost of less than $90 million.

1853 —In the Gadsden Purchase, land that is now the southern part of Arizona is purchased from Mexico for $10 million, adding over 18 million acres to the public domain.

1854 —Graduation Act provides that federal land that has been on the market for 10 years will be sold for $1 an acre; if on the market for over 15 years, the price is $.75 an acre; $.25 an acre if available for 20 years; and $.125 an acre if the land has been on the market for over 30 years. Mineral and railroad lands are excluded. (Repealed in 1863.)

1855–1856—Military Bounty Act grants quarter sections (160 acres) to soldiers or their heirs who served in any war after 1790.

—In 1856, the Military Bounty Act is extended to soldiers of the Revolutionary War. Prior Military Bounty Acts had been restricted to veterans of specific wars such as the Mexican War, War of 1812, and Indian campaigns.

1862 —The Homestead Act allows settlers to claim up to 160 acres of free land if they live on and farm the land for 5 years. The act leads to widespread fraud among ranchers, farmers, and speculators.

—The Morrill Act grants a total of 13 million acres of land to the states for the establishment of agricultural and mechanical-arts colleges. States not in rebellion are each granted 30,000 acres per senator and representative in Congress.

1864 —Yosemite Valley is established by Congress as the first national park.

1867 —Congress reports that the boundaries of Indian reservations are being constantly crossed by settlers and that reservation conditions are deplorable.

—Alaska is purchased from Russia for $7 million, adding 375 million acres to the United States.

1871 —Congress outlaws the making of treaties with the Indians.

1872 —Under the Mining Law, a miner may claim 160 acres of free land if he has made $100 worth of improvements to the land.

1873 —The Timber Culture Act provides that an individual who keeps 40 acres of timber in healthy growing condition for 10 years, planting trees not more than 12 feet apart, will be granted title to that land.

1877 —The Desert Land Act provides that a settler may purchase 640 acres of desert land for $1.25 an acre if he irrigates the entire parcel for 3 years.

1878 —The Timber Cutting Act allows settlers and miners to cut timber on public land for their own use.

1879 —The United States Geological Survey is established to manage the surveying of public land. The Public Land Commission is established to assist.

1881 —The Division of Forestry is established within the Department of Agriculture.

1887 —The Dawes Severalty Act or General Allotment Act—Congress legislates a program of alloting individual parcels of land to Indians. The head of each family is alloted 160 acres and a "trust" patent to the land. The act states that after a period of 25 years, "fee" patents—actual title to the land—are to be granted. "Surplus" Indian land may be sold by Indians upon congressional approval.

1889 —Creek Indians sell 1.4 million acres and the Seminoles sell 2.1 million acres in the Oklahoma Territory to the federal government for $1.25 an acre. The land, thereby open to homesteading, is settled by 150,000 pioneers who gather in April for a race known as the Oklahoma Rush, or Runs.

1890 —The National Park Service is established. By 1916, the charter reads that its purpose is to "conserve the scenery and the natural and historic objects and the wildlife therein and to provide for the enjoyment of same in such manner and by such means as will leave them unimpaired for the enjoyment of future generations."

1891 —"Forest Reserves" are set up under the Department of the Interior.

—The U.S. Cavalry is forced to occupy parks to protect them from illegal sheep-grazing.

—The General Revision Act repeals the Preemption Acts. The Timber Culture Act is repealed. The Homestead Law is amended to require 14 months residence before title may be purchased for $1.25 an acre. The Desert Land Act is amended to require improvements of $3 per acre over 3 years time and cultivation of one eighth the area. The cash sale and auction system for sales of public land are repealed. The president of the United States is authorized to set aside timber lands as national parks.

—A rider to a general land use act provides that the president may reserve portions of the federal domain as forest preserves.

1892 —John Muir establishes the Sierra Club to preserve the nation's forests, waters, wildlife, and wilderness. By 1979, the club has a budget of $7.5 million.

1893 —By this time, President Harrison has allocated 13 million acres of public land as national forest.

1894 —The Carey Act allows the federal government to offer up to 1 million acres of land to every Western state, if that state will irrigate such land.

1897 —The authority to sell timber from federal lands is delegated to the Secretary of the Interior.

1902 —President Theodore Roosevelt pushes through the Reclamation Act, which limits the sale of water from federal water projects to farms of 160 acres or less, dedicates millions of acres of public land as forest, park, and wildlife refuges. The act is widely violated.

1905 —The administration of 63 million acres of forest reserves by the Interior Department is transferred to a new United States Forest Service, under the Department of Agriculture.

1906 —Thirty million additional acres are added to the forest preserves.
—The Burke Act states that the Secretary of the Interior may grant fee patents on land to individual Indians on reservation land regardless of the 25-year waiting period legislated in 1887. Indians are granted American citizenship if they acquire a fee patent.

1909 —The Enlarged Homestead Act provides that a rancher may claim 320 acres of free land to be used for grazing if he cultivates 160 acres of it.

1911 —The Weeks Act provides that the federal government may purchase private land to be designated as national forest.

1915 —Mr. Hadachek, a brickyard owner, sues when a Los Angeles policeman closes down his brickyard. The police claim that Mr. Hadachek is polluting the neighborhood, which has gradually become residential. Mr. Hadachek wants compensation if he will not be able to operate his business. The United States Supreme Court decides that since public health and safety are being protected, no compensation is due.

1916 —The National Park Service is established by Congress to conserve natural and historic areas and protect wildlife.
—Stock-Raising Homestead Act states that 640 acres may be homesteaded for grazing purposes. The land claimed may not be suitable for timber or farming.

1920 —Mineral Leasing Act allows the federal government to lease 640 acres per miner of government land, taking 12½ percent of the royalties as rent.

1922 —General Exchange Act states that owners of private property are allowed to exchange their land for an equally sized parcel of government land.
—Justice Oliver Wendell Holmes declares that the line between *police power* actions, not requiring monetary compensation to private owners, and *eminent domain,* where government must pay a property owner to take or use his land, depends upon the specific conditions in each case, and that a balance of rights must be maintained.

1924 —The Model Standard State Zoning Enabling Act is developed by the Hoover administration, stating that zoning is enacted to protect health, safety, morals, and general welfare.

1926 —The Supreme Court declares zoning constitutional when the Ambler Realty Company in Euclid, Ohio, sues to have the zoning of its property changed from residential to commercial.

1927 —John D. Rockefeller, Jr., begins restoring Williamsburg to make it the most extensive museum town in the United States.

1930 —By this time almost all present-day land in federal forests and parks has been designated.

1930s—The Forest Service adopts the term "primitive area" for wilderness areas.

1931 —Citizen groups in Charleston, South Carolina, succeed in establishing the first historic district in the United States.

1933 —The Tennessee Valley Authority is established by Franklin D. Roosevelt. $37 million is allocated to purchase forest land. The Civilian Conservation Corps is created to help with conservation measures such as tree planting.

1934 —The Taylor Grazing Act authorizes private interests to graze on public land for a fee. Eighty million acres are reserved by the government for leasing to ranchers. A 1936 amendment increases allowable acreage to 142 million.

—The Indian Reorganization Act, or Wheeler-Howard Act, states that land on Indian reservations withheld as surplus land will be restored to Indian ownership.

1935 —The Soil Conservation Service is established.

1936–1937—The City Planning and Zoning Commission of New Orleans sets up the Vieux Carré Commission and designates the Vieux Carré Historic District, the second in America.

1940 —The Fish and Wildlife Service of the Department of the Interior is established.

—The Supreme Court hears a suit involving the Northern Pacific Railroad concerning land granted to the railroad; the land was not sold and therefore should have been returned to the federal government. The company is forced to return land worth $100 million.

1946 —Indian Claims Commission Act provides that a tribal claims based on treaties may be brought to the courts for financial retribution.

1947 —President Harry Truman establishes the Bureau of Land Management, an offshoot of the General Land Agency, to survey public lands, administer grazing, and hold unclassified public lands.

1949 —The National Trust for Historic Preservation is chartered by Congress and grows to include 140,000 members by 1979.

1950 —The Nature Conservancy becomes independent of the Ecologists Union set up in 1946. The operating budget is $2.8 million by 1977, with $135 million being spent in 1978 for land purchases.

1956 —The Highway Revenue Act specifies that 4 cents per gallon of gas will go into a Highway Trust Fund to finance the construction of 42,500 miles of interstate highways across the country.

1958 —Alaska's statehood charter promises a grant of 104 million acres to the state, more than a quarter of Alaska's surface, and the most generous grant to any new state in American history. Lands are still in the process of being distributed.

1961 —An open-space program is set up by the federal government to help communities purchase land that will be used for parks.

1963 —The Bureau of Outdoor Recreation is set up by the federal government to coordinate outdoor recreation, give permits to those who would build on park land, develop the National Trails System, identify Wild and Scenic Rivers, and supervise new recreation lands.

1964 —The National Park Service implements the National Registry of Natural Landmarks. Regional studies are undertaken and the Secretary of the Interior may designate selected areas as Registered Natural Landmarks.

—The Wilderness Act establishes a National Wilderness Preservation System, which now includes almost 20 million acres. The Forest Service controls 87% of these lands; the Fish and Wildlife Service and Park Service administer the balance.

1965 —The Land and Water Conservation Fund is set up by Congress under the Bureau of Outdoor Recreation. It is funded through offshore oil leases, the sale of tickets to national parks, motorboat fuel taxes, and money from sale of surplus federal land. An allocation by Congress of $300 million to the fund in 1977 tripled to $900 million in 1978.

1966 —The National Historic Preservation Act is passed, directing the Secretary of the Interior to maintain and expand a National Register of districts and buildings "significant in American history, architecture, archeology, and culture, hereinafter referred to as the National Register." The National Park Service will provide 50 percent matching funds to states for the preservation and acquisition of historic properties. By 1978, $100 million was authorized by Congress for these purposes.

1969 —The National Environmental Policy Act is passed by Congress, calling for increased legislation to protect the environment.

1970 —The Federal Clean Air Act is passed; it is amended in 1977 to require states to classify land according to allowable air pollution.

1971 —The Alaska Native Settlement Act cedes 44 million acres of Alaska's 365 million acres (12 percent) to its 70,000 natives. Lands are still in the process of being distributed.

1972 —The Water Pollution Control Act mandates that all U.S. waters be "fishable and swimmable" by the mid-1980s.

—The Coastal Zone Management Act is passed, providing funds for state coastal land-use plans.

—New York State's highest court upholds a timed growth-control plan that restricts land development, after a private property owner sues the Town of Ramapo.

1976 —The Federal Land Policy and Management Act is passed, providing, among other things, that 25 million acres of federally owned desert land be protected.

—The Tax Reform Act of 1976 allows owners of commercial property listed in the National Register to make certified improvements and to depreciate them for tax purposes over a 5-year period. By 1979, 650 structures in 40 states are rehabilitated under the act. Charitable deductions of "conservation" properties are also allowed. For the first time, deductions for contributions of a *partial* interest in real estate are allowed when the property is important environmentally or historically. The investment credit for real estate is liberalized, including credits under the Energy Tax Act for energy conservation.

1978 —The Supreme Court rules that, because it has been designated a landmark, the facade of New York City's Grand Central Station may not be destroyed by a proposed office tower.

—California voters approve Proposition 13, amending the state constitution to limit property taxes to 1 percent of market value.

—Under the Bureau of Land Management's Organic Act, 110 million acres of Alaska are barred from development for up to 3 years. President Carter places more than 56 million of these acres in the National Park system—the largest National Monument designation any president has ever made.

—The Revenue Act of 1978 states that within certain limits, estates consisting of family farms or closely held businesses are allowed to pay tax liabilities over 15 years at 4 percent interest, instead of the former 10 years at 7 percent interest.

1979 —Nineteen thousand properties are listed in the National Register of Historic Places.

—By this year, 2,000 historic districts exist in cities across the country.

1980 —The Alaska Lands Bill signed into law creating 104 million acres of national parks, wildlife refuges, and wilderness areas for federal holdings in Alaska. This act doubles the size of the national park and refuge system (adding over 97 million acres) and triples the wilderness areas in the United States (adding 56 million acres).

STATISTICS

Total Land in the United States: 2.3 billion acres.

Total land owned by the federal government: about 762 million acres (34%).

Total land privately owned: about 1.3 billion acres (58%).

Total land owned by states, counties, and municipalities: about 138 million acres (6%).

Total land held in trust for Indians: about 46 million acres (2%).

Principal Federal Land Agencies in the United States:

Bureau of Land Management, U.S. Department of the Interior, administers 470 million acres of land, or 62% of federal land.

U. S. Forest Service, Department of Agriculture, controls 187.6 million acres, or 24% of federal land.

National Park Service, U.S. Department of the Interior, administers over 70 million acres. These lands include the National Parks, National Monuments, and the White House land, among others.

U.S. Fish and Wildlife Service, U.S. Department of the Interior, controls 33.9 million acres and has units in every state. Three hundred sixty-seven National Wildlife Refuges are administered by this office.

States with over 50% of Land Federally Owned:

Alaska: 96.4% (over 360 out of 365 million acres).

Nevada: 86.6% (over 60 out of 70 million acres).

Utah: 66% (35 out of 53 million acres).

Idaho: 64% (34 out of 53 million acres).

Oregon: 53% (32 out of 62 million acres).

Land as Percentage of Wealth in the United States:

Government wealth: 11.5% in land.

Personal wealth: 12% in land.

Business wealth: 18% in land.

Major Uses of the Land (approximate):

Cropland: 465 million acres (20%).

Grassland pasture and range: 598 million acres (26%).

Forest land: 718 million acres (31%).

Special uses—urban areas, highways, parks, etc.: 182 million acres (8%).

Other land—desert, swamp, water tundra, etc.: 336 million acres (15%).

SELECTED BIBLIOGRAPHY

Note: References are cited only once, even if used in several chapters. News-papers are not included.

ONE

THE MYSTIQUE OF LAND AS A PRIME INVESTMENT

Adams, John, Jr. "Analysis of Factors Influencing Value." *Appraisal Journal,* April 1969, p. 239.

Babcock, Frederick M. *The Valuation of Real Estate.* New York: McGraw-Hill, 1932.

Barnes, Peter, ed. *The People's Land: A Reader on Land Reform in the U.S.* Emmaus, Pa.: Rodale Press, 1975.

Brigham, Eugene F. *A Model of Residential Land Values.* Santa Monica, Calif.: Rand Corporation, 1964.

———. "The Determinants of Residential Land Values." *Land Economics,* November 1965, pp. 325–334.

Cardiff, Gray Emerson, and English, John Wesley. *The Coming Real Estate Crash.* New Rochelle, N.Y.: Arlington House, 1979.

Clonts, Howard A. "Influence of Urbanization on Land Values at the Urban Periphery." *Land Economics,* November 1970, pp. 489–497.

Cobb, Steven A. "More on the Interpretation of Property Value Changes." *Urban Studies,* June 1978, pp. 221–222.

Coughlin, Robert E., and Fritz, James. "Land Values and Environmental Characteristics in the Rural-Urban Fringe." Discussion Paper no. 45. Philadelphia: Regional Science Research Institute, 1971.

Craig, Robert H. "Basic Principles of Land Value." *Assessors Journal,* April 1969, pp. 35–41.

Denne, Robert C. "The Determinants of Value: An Annotated Bibliography." Bibliographic Series, Research and Technical Services Department. Chicago: International Association of Assessing Officers, June 1976.

Downing, Paul B. "Factors Affecting Commercial Land Values: An Empirical Study of Milwaukee, Wisconsin." *Land Economics,* February 1973, pp. 44–56.

———. "Computerized Urban Land Valuation." In *The Application of Multiple Regression Analysis in Assessment Administration.* Chicago: International Association of Assessing Officers, 1974.

Edwards, David. "Who's Buying America?" *New York,* 22 May 1978, pp. 45–48.

Fellmuth, Robert C. *Politics of Land: Ralph Nader's Study Group Report on Land Use in California.* New York: Grossman Publishers, 1973.

Field, Kenneth E. "Factors Affecting the Value of Development Lands." *Appraisal Institute Magazine,* April 1976, pp. 18–19.

Fullerton, Paul. "Development Analysis for the Valuation of Vacant Land." *Appraisal Journal,* April 1965, pp. 211–225.

Gunning, Walter E. "Gross Estimate of Value for Large Land Areas." *Appraisal Journal,* October 1963, pp. 489–492.

Harney, Kenneth R. *Beating Inflation with Real Estate.* New York: Random House, 1979.

Holland, Daniel M., ed. *The Assessment of Land Value.* Madison: University of Wisconsin Press, 1970.

Johnson, Warren. *Muddling Toward Frugality.* Boulder, Colo.: Shambhala Publications, 1978.

Kendrick, John W.; Lee, Kyu Sik; and Lomask, Jean. *The National Wealth of the United States: By Major Sectors and Industry.* New York: The Conference Board, 1976.

Knetsch, Jack L., and Parrott, C. Jennings. "Estimating the Influence of Large Reservoirs of Land Value." *Appraisal Journal,* October 1964, pp. 537–546.

Knos, Duane S. *Distribution of Land Values in Topeka, Kansas.* Lawrence: University of Kansas, 1962.

Meyer, Peter. "Land Rush: A Survey of America's Land." *Harper's Magazine,* January 1979, pp. 45–60.

Mills, Edwin S. "The Value of Urban Land." In *The Quality of the Urban Environment.* Edited by Harvey S. Perloff. Washington, D.C.: Resources for the Future, 1969.

"The New American Land Rush." *Time,* 1 October 1973, pp. 80–99.

Ridker, Ronald G., ed. *Population, Resources, and the Environment.* vol. 3. Washington, D.C.: U.S. Government Printing Office, 1972.

Solomon, R.J. "Property values as a structural element of urban revolution." *Economic Geography,* January 1969, pp. 1–29.

Stanford, Melvin J. "Forecasting Future Land Values with Present-Value Techniques." *Appraisal Journal,* January 1973, pp. 45–55.

Swanton, W.F. "Land Value Trends in the United States." *American Journal of Economics and Sociology,* April 1965, pp. 163–170.

Urban Land Institute. "Energy and Land Use: A Statement by ULI—the Urban Land Institute." *Environmental Comment,* September 1974, pp. 1–7.

Ways, Max. "Land: The Boom That Really Hurts." *Fortune,* July 1973, p. 104.

Weiss, Shirley F.; Donnelly, Thomas G.; and Kaiser, Edward J. "Land Value and Land Development Influence Factors: An Analytical Approach for Examining Policy Alternatives." *Land Economics,* May 1966, pp. 230–233.

Wendt, Paul F. *Real Estate Appraisal: A Critical Analysis of Theory and Practice.* New York: Henry Holt & Co., 1956.

———. "Theory of Urban Land Values." *Land Economics,* August 1957, pp. 228–240.

———. "Urban Land Value Trends." *Appraisal Journal,* April 1958, pp. 254–269.

Wendt, Paul F., and Goldner, William. "Land Values and the Dynamics of

Residential Location." In *Essays in Urban Land Economics*. Los Angeles: University of California, 1966.

Wignjowijoto, Hartojo. "Selected Bibliography on Land Valuation Methods." Monograph #77–9. Cambridge, Mass.: Lincoln Institute of Land Policy, 4 November 1977.

Wolf, Peter. *The Future of the City: New Directions in Urban Planning*. New York: Whitney Library of Design, Watson-Giptill Publications, 1974.

TWO

NOTES ON BUYING AND SELLING THE CONTINENT

Balestier, Joseph N. *The Annals of Chicago*. 1840. Reprint. Chicago: Fergus Printing Co., 1876.

Billington, Ray Allen. *Westward Expansion*. New York: Macmillan Publishing Co., 1967.

Chamberlain, Samuel, and Moffal, David. *Fair Is Our Land*. New York: Hastings House, 1942.

Clawson, Marion. *Man and Land in the United States*. Lincoln: University of Nebraska Press, 1964.

Department of Housing and Urban Development. *The Influence of the Foreign Heritage on the American City*. Washington, D.C.: U.S. Government Printing Office, 1976.

Ellis, David M., ed. *The Frontier in American Development*. Ithaca, N.Y.: Cornell University Press, 1969.

Fein, Albert, ed. *Landscape into Cityscape*. Ithaca, N.Y.: Cornell University Press, 1968.

Gilbert, Martin. *American History Atlas*. New York: G.P. Putnam's Sons, 1977.

Hart, John Fraser. *The Look of the Land*. Englewood Cliffs, N.J.: Prentice-Hall, 1975.

Hoyt, Homer. *One Hundred Years of Land Values in Chicago*. Chicago: University of Chicago Press, 1933.

Jacobs, Wilbur R. *Dispossessing the American Indian: Indians and Whites on the Colonial Frontier*. New York: Charles Scribner's Sons, 1972.

Lange, Dorothea, and Taylor, Paul Schuster. *An American Exodus*. New Haven: Yale University Press, 1939.

Mayer, Harold M., and Wade, Richard C. *Chicago: Growth of a Metropolis*. Chicago: University of Chicago Press, 1969.

Moscow, Henry. *The Street Book: An Encyclopedia of Manhattan's Street Names and Their Origins*. New York: Hagstrom Co., 1978.

Pattison, William. *The Beginnings of the American Rectangular Survey System 1784–1800*. Department of Geography Research Paper no. 50. Chicago: University of Chicago Press, 1957.

Raines, Howell. "American Indians: Struggling for Power and Identity." *The New York Times Magazine*, 11 February 1979, p. 21.

Reps, John W. *The Making of Urban America*. Princeton, N.J.: Princeton University Press, 1965.

Reps, John W. *Cities on Stone: Nineteenth Century Lithograph Images of the Urban West.* Fort Worth, Tex.: Amon Carter Museum, 1976.

Sakolski, A.M. *The Great American Land Bubble.* New York: Harper & Brothers, 1932.

Sloane, Eric. *Our Vanishing Landscape.* New York: Ballantine Books, 1974.

Thomas, Dana L. *Lords of the Land.* New York: G.P. Putnam's Sons, 1977.

Vaughan, Alden T. *The New England Frontier.* Boston: Little, Brown & Co., 1965.

Waddell, Jack O., and Watson, O. Michael, eds. *The American Indian in Urban Society.* Boston: Little, Brown & Co., 1967.

THREE

PRIVATE RIGHTS VS. PUBLIC POWER

Ackerman, Bruce A., ed. *Economic Foundations of Property Law.* Boston: Little, Brown & Co., 1975.

Andrews, Richard N.L., ed., *Land In America.* Lexington, Mass.: D. C. Heath & Co., 1979.

Bosselman, Fred, and Callies, David. *The Quiet Revolution in Land Use Control.* Washington, D.C.: U.S. Government Printing Office, 1971.

Bosselman, Fred; Callies, David; and Banta, John. *The Taking Issue.* Washington, D.C.: U.S. Government Printing Office, 1973.

Hagman, Donald G. *Urban Planning and Land Development Control Law.* St. Paul, Minn.: West Publishing Co., 1971.

Healy, Robert G. *Land Use and the States.* Baltimore: Johns Hopkins Press, 1976.

Kolis, Annette. "The Taking Issue: Florida Law Authorizes Compensation for 'Unreasonable' Takings by State Environmental Agencies." *Urban Land,* May 1979, pp. 14–16.

National Resources Defense Council. *Land Use Controls in New York State: A Handbook on the Legal Rights of Citizens.* Edited by Elaine Moss. New York: Dial Press, 1975.

Planning Advisory Service. *Urban Growth Management Systems: An Evaluation of Policy-Related Research.* report nos. 309, 310. Chicago: American Society of Planning Officials, 1975.

Reilly, William K., ed. *The Use of Land: A Citizen's Policy Guide to Urban Growth.* New York: Thomas Y. Crowell Co., 1973.

Wiedl, Michael F. "Historic District Ordinances." *Connecticut Law Review,* Winter 1975–76, pp. 209–230.

FOUR

LAND AND TAXES

Arnold, Alvin L. *Tax Shelter in Real Estate Today.* Boston: Warren, Gorham & Lamont, 1979.

Berry, Brian J.L., and Bednarz, Robert S. "A Hedonic Model of Prices and

Assessments for Single-Family Houses: Does the Assessor Follow the Market or the Market Follow the Assessor?" *Land Economics,* February 1975, pp. 21–40.

Carbone, Robert, and Lai, Reinhard S. "Assessment of Urban Residential Properties: An Empirical Study of Pittsburgh." *Journal of Environmental Systems,* Fall 1974, pp. 207–216.

Chown, John, and Edwardes-Ker, Michael. *The Acquisition of Assets: Companies and Real Estate in Belgium, France, Germany, The Netherlands, United Kingdom.* London: Financial Times, 1974.

Cooperative Extension in New York State. "The Property Tax: Whither New York?" Mimeographed. Riverhead, N.Y.: Cooperative Extension Association of Suffolk County.

Cowing, Thomas G. "Real Property Taxes, Local Public Services and Residential Property Values: Comment." *Southern Economic Journal,* October 1974, pp. 325–329.

Dickstein, Dennis. "The Effect Property Taxes Have on Property Values: A Study of a Specific Situation." Cambridge, Mass.: Massachusetts Institute of Technology, 1974.

Hagman, Donald G., and Misczynski, Dean J., eds. *Windfalls for Wipeouts: Land Value Capture and Compensation.* Chicago: American Society of Planning Officials, 1978.

Harriss, C. Lowell. "Property Taxation: What's Good and What's Bad About It." *American Journal of Economics and Sociology,* January 1974, pp. 89–102.

Hyman, David N., and Pasour, E.C. "Real Property Taxes, Local Public Services, and Residential Property Values." *Southern Economic Journal,* April 1973, pp. 601–611.

International Association of Assessing Officials. *Assessing and the Appraisal Process.* 5th ed. Chicago: International Association of Assessing Officers, 1974.

King, A. Thomas. *Property Taxes, Amenities, and Residential Land Values.* Cambridge, Mass.: Ballinger, 1973.

Netzer, Dick. *Economics of the Property Tax.* Washington, D.C.: Brookings Institution, 1966.

———. "The Property Tax a Generation Hence." Mimeographed. New York: New York University, 1979.

Paul, Diane B. *The Politics of the Property Tax.* Lexington, Mass.: D.C. Heath & Co., 1975.

Roberts, James M. "Progress and Poverty's Continuing Challenge." *American Journal of Economics and Sociology,* July 1971, pp. 301–316.

Wendt, Paul F., and Cerf, Alan R. *Real Estate Investment Analysis and Taxation.* New York: McGraw-Hill, 1969.

FIVE

ZONING AND VALUE

Babcock, Richard F. *The Zoning Game.* Madison: University of Wisconsin Press, 1969.

Barnett, Jonathan. *Urban Design as Public Policy: Practical Methods for Improving Cities.* New York: Architectural Record Books, 1974.

Brambilla, Roberto, and Longo, Gianni. *An Appraisal: Traffic-Free Zoning.* New York: Institute for Environmental Action, 1976.

Bruhn, John A. "Zoning: Its Effect on Property Value." *Appraisal Journal,* October 1969, pp. 555–561.

Clarke, Frank J., and Rupnow, Roger F. *Zoning Problems in Atlanta: Two Studies of Policy, Practice and Community Acceptance and their Problem-Solving Applications.* Atlanta: Atlanta Urban Observatory, 1972.

Correll, Mark R.; Lillydalh, Jane H.; and Singell, Larry D. "The Effects of Greenbelts on Residential Property Values: Some Findings on the Political Economy of Open Space." *Land Economics,* May 1978, pp. 207–217.

Council of State Governments. *A Legislator's Guide to Land Management.* Lexington, Ky.: Council of State Governments, 1974.

Department of Housing and Urban Development, and Department of Agriculture. *The Message of Habitat: A Report to the Public on the United Nations Conference on Human Settlements.* Washington, D.C.: U.S. Government Printing Office, 1977.

Downie, Leonard, Jr. *Mortgage on America.* New York: Praeger, 1974.

Gottdiener, Mark. *Planned Sprawl: Private and Public Interests in Suburbia.* Sage Library of Social Research, vol. 38. Beverly Hills: Sage Publications, 1977.

Hamilton, Bruce W. "Zoning and the Exercise of Monopoly Power." *Journal of Urban Economics,* January 1978, pp. 116–130.

Lyman, Gregory A.; Meyer, Stephan J.; and Nelson, Ronald E. "Can Zoning Preserve Farmland?" *Practicing Planner,* September 1977, p. 18.

Maser, Steven M.; Riker, William H.; and Rosett, Richard N. "The Effects of Zoning and Externalities on the Price of Land: An Empirical Analysis of Monroe County, New York." *Journal of Law and Economics,* April 1977, pp. 111–132.

National Commission on Urban Problems. *Building the American City.* New York: Praeger, 1969.

Nelson, Robert H. *Zoning and Property Rights: An Analysis of the American System of Land-Use Regulation.* Cambridge, Mass.: M.I.T. Press, 1977.

Ohls, James C.; Weisburg, Richard C.; and White, Michelle J. "The Effect of Zoning on Land Value." *Journal of Urban Economics,* October 1974, pp. 428–444.

Perrin, Constance. *Everything in Its Place: Social Order and Land Use in America.* Princeton, N.J.: Princeton University Press, 1977.

Peterson, George E. "The Effect of Zoning Regulations on Suburban Property Values." Working Paper 1207–24. Washington, D.C.: Urban Land Institute, 1973.

Plosser, Charles. "A Study in the Effects of Residential Zoning Restrictions on Land Value." Urban Economics Report 78. Chicago: University of Chicago, 1972.

Real Estate Research Corporation. *The Costs of Sprawl: Detailed Cost Analysis.* Washington, D.C.: U.S. Government Printing Office, 1974.

———. "RERC Implements A New Approach to Land Use: 'The Transfer of Development Right.'" *Real Estate Report,* Spring 1974, p. 1.

Rose, Jerome G. *Legal Foundations of Land Use Planning.* New Brunswick, N.J.: Rutgers University Press, 1974.

Sagalyn, Lynne B., and Sternlieb, George. *Zoning and Housing Costs.* New Brunswick, N.J.: Rutgers University Press, 1972.

Schmid, A. Allen. *Converting Land from Rural to Urban Uses.* Washington, D.C.: Resources for the Future, 1968.

Scott, Randall W., ed. *Management & Control of Growth.* Washington, D.C.: Urban Land Institute, 1975.

Seymour, David R. "The Effects of Zoning Changes on Property Values." Washington, D.C.: Urban Land Institute, 1967.

Stull, William J. "Community Environment, Zoning, and the Market Value of Single-Family Homes." *Journal of Law and Economics,* October 1975, pp. 535–557.

Trillin, Calvin. "U.S. Journal: Mount Laurel, N.J." *The New Yorker,* 2 February 1976, pp. 69–74.

Whyte, William H. *Cluster Development.* New York: American Conservation Association, 1964.

Woodbury, Steven R. "Transfer of Development Rights: A New Tool for Planners." *Journal of the American Institute of Planners,* January 1975, pp. 3–14.

SIX

CLOSING THE DOOR TO DEVELOPMENT: NEW POWER, NEW PURPOSES

Babcock, Richard F., and Bosselman, Fred P. *Exclusionary Zoning: Land Use Regulation and Housing in the 1970's.* New York: Praeger, 1973.

Beach, Mark. *Desegregated Housing and Interracial Neighborhoods: A Bibliographic Guide.* Philadelphia: National Neighbors, 1975.

Berry, Brian J.L., and Hordon, Frank E. *Geographic Perspectives on Urban Systems.* Englewood Cliffs, N.J.: Prentice-Hall, 1970.

Briggs, Jean. "Home Sweet Suburbia." *Forbes,* 7 August 1978, pp. 55–60.

Bruner, John M. *The Effects of Racial Integration on Property Values and Real Estate Practices.* Los Angeles: University of California, 1970.

Coke, James G., and Liebman, Charles S. "Political Values and Population Density Control." *Land Economics,* November 1961, p. 354.

Conway, William C. "Fair Housing: Not Here You Won't." *Saturday Review,* 18 February 1978, pp. 23–24.

Danielson, Michael N. *The Politics of Exclusion.* New York: Columbia University Press, 1976.

Downs, Anthony. *Opening up the Suburbs: An Urban Strategy for America.* New Haven: Yale University Press, 1973.

Drury, Margaret Josephine. *Mobile Homes: The Unrecognized Revolution in American Housing.* 2nd ed., rev. New York: Praeger, 1972.

Effrat, M., ed. *The Community: Approaches and Applications.* New York: Free Press, 1974.

Galchus, Kenneth. "Property Values in an Integrated Neighborhood." *Real Estate Appraiser,* November/December 1972, pp. 15–20.

Hughes, James W. "Dilemmas of Suburbanization and Growth Controls." *Annals of the American Academy of Political and Social Science,* November 1975, pp. 61–76.

Hughes, James W., ed. *Suburbanization Dynamics and the Future of the City.* New Brunswick, N.J.: Rutgers University Press, 1974.

Huszar, Paul C. "Equity and Urban Growth: Real Property Value Appreciation in San Jose, California." *American Journal of Economics and Sociology,* July 1977, pp. 251–261.

Israel, Barry. "Increasing Interest Shown by Planners in Growth Control Techniques." *AIP Newsletter,* June 1974, pp. 9–11.

King, A. Thomas, and Mieszkowski, Peter. "Racial Discrimination, Segregation and the Price of Housing." *Journal of Political Economy,* May/June 1973, pp. 590–606.

Masotti, Louis H., and Hadden, Jeffery H., eds. *The Urbanization of the Suburbs.* Beverly Hills: Sage Publications, 1973.

Moss, William C. "Large Lot Zoning, Property Taxes, and Metropolitan Area." *Journal of Urban Economics,* October 1977, pp. 408–427.

Mullendore, Walter E., and Cooper, Kathleen M. "Effects of Race on Property Values: The Case of Dallas." *Annals of Regional Science,* December 1972, pp. 61–72.

Rose, Jerome G. "The Courts and the Balanced Community: Recent Trends in New Jersey Zoning Law." *Journal of the American Institute of Planners,* July 1973, pp. 265–276.

Rowan, Carl T., and Mazie, David M. "To Grow or Not to Grow." *Nation's Cities,* June 1975, p. 10.

Sternlieb, George. *The Tenement Landlord.* New Brunswick, N.J.: Rutgers University Press, 1966.

SEVEN

ACCESS TO LAND AS VALUE:
PUBLIC PRIORITIES AND PRIVATE PROFIT

Abouchar, Alan. *Transportation Economics and Public Policy: With Urban Extensions.* New York: John Wiley & Sons, 1977.

Adkins, William G. *Effects of the Dallas Central Expressway on Land Values and Land Use.* Bulletin no. 6. College Station, Tex.: Texas A & M College, 1957.

Ayers, F. Thomas, and Freiberg, Lewis. *The Impact of a New Transportation System on Rural Land Values: The Case of I-64 and Eastern Kentucky.* Monograph no. 3. Lexington: University of Kentucky, 1975.

Banham, Reyner. *Los Angeles: The Architecture of Four Ecologies.* New York: Harper & Row, 1971.

Boyce, David E.; Allen, Bruce; and Mudge, Richard R. *Impact of Rapid Transit on Suburban Residential Property Values and Land Development: Analysis of the Philadelphia Lindewold High-Speed Line.* Philadelphia: University of Pennsylvania, 1972.

Brown, Fred A., and Michael, Harold L. *The Impact on Land Value of a Major*

Highway Interchange Near a Metropolitan Area. West Lafayette, Ind.: Purdue University, 1973.

Chipman, William D.; Wolfe, Harry P.; and Burnet, Pat. *Political Decision Processes, Transportation Investment and Changes in Urban Land Use: A Selected Bibliography with Particular Reference to Airports and Highways.* Research report 7. Austin: University of Texas at Austin, 1974.

Davis, Frederick W. "Proximity to a Rapid Transit Station as a Factor in Residential Property Values." *Appraisal Journal,* October 1970, pp. 554–572.

Department of Transportation. *America's Highways 1776–1976: A History of the Federal-Aid Program.* Washington, D.C.: U.S. Government Printing Office, 1976.

———. *Highway Statistics: Summary to 1975.* Washington, D.C.: U.S. Government Printing Office, 1977.

———. *A Revised Estimate of the Cost of Completing the National System of Interstate and Defense Highways.* Washington, D.C.: U.S. Government Printing Office, 1977.

Dewees, Donald N. "The Effect of a Subway on Residential Property Values in Toronto." *Journal of Urban Economics,* October 1976, pp. 357–369.

Goldstein, Neil. "Westway—Worst Way." *Sierra,* February/March 1978, pp. 11–14.

Greene, Sheldon; Kirkpatrick, David; Madway, David M.; and Pearl, Richard. "Petition for Return of Railroad Lands." In *The People's Land: A Reader on Land Reform in the U.S.* Edited by Peter Barnes. Emmaus, Pa.: Rodale Press, 1975.

Holbrook, Stewart H. *The Story of American Railroads.* New York: Crown Publishers, 1947.

Langley, C. John, Jr. "Adverse Impacts of the Washington Beltway on Residential Property Values." *Land Economics,* February 1976, pp. 54–65.

Leavitt, Helen. *Superhighways—Superhoax.* Garden City, N.Y.: Doubleday & Co., 1970.

Lupo, Alan; Colcord, Frank; and Fowler, Edmund P. *Rites of Way: The Politics of Transportation in Boston and the U.S. City.* Boston: Little, Brown & Co., 1971.

Morlok, Edward M. *Introduction to Transportation Engineering and Planning.* New York: McGraw-Hill, 1978.

Mudge, Richard R. *The Impact of Transportation Savings on Suburban Residential Property Values.* Research paper 5259. Santa Monica, Calif.: Rand Corporation, 1974.

Poon, Larry C.L. "Railway Externalities and Residential Property Prices." *Land Economics,* May 1978, pp. 218–227.

Public Revenue Education Council. "This is Our Land—Millions of Miles of It." *House & Home Magazine,* August 1960. Reprint. St. Louis: Public Revenue Education Council.

Robinson, John. *Highways and Our Environment.* New York: McGraw-Hill, 1971.

Seyfried, Warren R. "The Centrality of Urban Land Values." *Land Economics,* August 1963, pp. 275–284.

Urban Design Concept Associates. "Preliminary Outline of Joint & Collateral

Development Complexes for the Maryland State Roads Commission Interstate System in Baltimore City." Mimeographed. Baltimore: Urban Design Concept Associates, 26 September 1968.

Urban Land Institute Research Division. *Joint Development: Making the Real Estate–Transit Connection.* With Gladstone Associates, economic consultants. Washington, D.C.: Urban Land Institute, 1979.

Warner, Sam B., Jr. *Streetcar Suburbs: The Process of Growth in Boston 1870–1900.* New York: Atheneum, 1962.

Wieand, Kenneth F., and Muth, Richard F. "A Note on the Variation of Land Values with Distance from the CBD in St. Louis." *Journal of Regional Science,* December 1972, pp. 469–473.

Wolf, Peter. "Land Investment Management Study Prepared for Sugarland Industries, Inc." Mimeographed. Sugar Land, Tex.: Peter Wolf, July 1970.

EIGHT

ENVIRONMENTAL REGULATION:
PUBLIC POWER CONFRONTS AND CREATES WEALTH

American Society of Civil Engineers. *Coastal Zone '78 Symposium on Technical, Environmental, Socioeconomic and Regulatory Aspects of Coastal Zone Management.* vol. 1. New York: American Society of Civil Engineers, 1978.

Anderson, Robert, and Crocker, Thomas D. "Air Pollution and Housing." Mimeographed. Lafayette, Ind.: Purdue University, January 1970.

Anderson, Robert, and Crocker, J.; and Crocker, Thomas D. "Air Pollution and Residential Property Values." *Urban Studies,* October 1971, pp. 171–180.

Bosselman, Fred; Feurer, Duane A.; and Siemon, Charles L. *The Permit Explosion: Coordination of the Proliferation.* Washington, D.C.: Urban Land Institute, 1976.

Cannon, James S. *A Clear View.* New York: Inform, 1975.

Chapman, Gail. "The CEQ Unleashed." *Sierra,* October 1977, p. 44.

Childress, Jim. "Actions of the 93rd Congress of Interest to Planning." *AIP Newsletter,* January 1975, pp. 29–33.

Christensen, Kathleen. *Social Impacts of Land Development: An Initial Approach for Estimating Impacts on Neighborhood Usages and Perceptions.* Washington, D.C.: Urban Institute, September 1976.

Cole, John N. *Striper: A Story of Fish and Man.* Boston: Little, Brown & Co., 1978.

Dornbusch, David M., and Barranger, Stephen M. *Benefits of Water Pollution Control on Property Values.* Washington, D.C.: U.S. Environmental Protection Agency, 1973.

Dorst, Stan J. "Environmental Challenges and Community Objectives." *Environmental Comment,* January 1975, pp. 1–3.

Evans, Brock. "The Sierra Club's 1977 Washington Wrap-Up." *Sierra,* February/March 1978, p. 26.

Ford, Henry II. "Blue Skies, White Elephants, and Red, Red Tape." *Finance,* March 1978, p. 9.

Frieden, Bernard J. *The Environmental Protection Hustle.* Cambridge, Mass.: M.I.T. Press, 1979.

Gruenfeld, Jay. "Environmental Impact Statements." *American Forests,* May 1977, pp. 18–19.

Hoch, Irving. *Urban Scale and Environmental Quality.* Reprint no. 110. Washington, D.C.: Resources for the Future, 1973.

Hornblower, Margot. "EIS: The Program That Grew and Grew." *American Forests,* May 1977, pp. 20–21.

Jaksch, John. "Air Pollution: Its Effect on Residential Property Values in Toledo, Oregon." *Annals of Regional Science,* December 1970, pp. 43–52.

Jester, Elizabeth. "Critical Areas Under Local Regulation: Connecticut's Inland Wetlands." *Environmental Comment,* October 1974, pp. 1–6.

Keyes, Dale L. *Land Development and the Natural Environment: Estimating Impacts.* Washington, D.C.: Urban Institute, April 1976.

"Land-Use Programs Snarl U.S. Industry Plans." *Oil and Gas Journal,* 21 November 1977, p. 53.

Lewis, Sylvia. "New York's Adirondacks: Tug of War in the Wilderness." *Planning,* September 1976, pp. 9–15.

Love, Sam. "Redividing North America." *The Ecologist,* August/September 1977, pp. 318–319.

McAllister, Donald M., ed. *Environment: A New Focus for Land-Use Planning.* Washington, D.C.: U.S. Government Printing Office, 1973.

McCahill, Ed. "Florida's Not-So-Quiet Revolution." *Planning,* March 1974, pp. 10–13.

McClaughry, John. "The New Feudalism." *Environmental Law,* Spring 1975, pp. 675–702.

McCloskey, Michael. "Nature and Cities." *Sierra,* April 1978, pp. 14–16.

McClure, Paul T. "Indicators of the Effect of Jet Noise on the Value of Real Estate." Santa Monica, Calif.: Rand Corporation, 1969.

The MacNeil/Lehrer Report. "Environment versus Inflation." Mimeographed transcript. New York: Educational Broadcasting Corporation and GWETA, 30 October 1978.

Muller, Thomas. *Economic Impacts of Land Development: Employment, Housing, and Property Values.* Washington, D.C.: Urban Institute, September 1976.

———. *Fiscal Impacts of Land Development: A Critique of Methods and Review of Issues.* Washington, D.C.: Urban Institute, 1976.

Oron, Yitzhak; Pines, David; and Sheshinski, Eytan. "The Effect of Nuisances Associated with Urban Traffic on Suburbanization and Land Values." *Journal of Urban Economics,* October 1974, pp. 382–394.

"Payoff for Business Initiative on the Environment." *Harvard Business Review,* November/December 1977, p. 8.

Polinsky, A. Mitchell, and Shavell, Steven. "The Air Pollution and Property Value Debate." *Review of Economics and Statistics,* February 1975, pp. 100–104.

Ramsey, David D. "A Note on Air Pollution, Property Values and Fiscal Variables." *Land Economics,* May 1976, pp. 230–234.

Reidel, Carl. "The Vermont I Know." *American Forests,* September 1977, p. 30.

Rhodes, Robert M. "Florida's Environmental Land and Water Management

Act Implements Article 7 of the Proposed American Law Institution Model Code." *AIP Newsletter,* January 1974, pp. 7–9.

Richardson, Dan K. *The Cost of Environmental Protection.* New Brunswick, N.J.: Rutgers University Press, 1976.

Ridker, Ronald G. *Economic Costs of Air Pollution.* New York: Praeger, 1967.

Ridker, Ronald G., and Henning, J.A. "The Determinants of Residential Property Values, with Special Reference to Air Pollution." *Review of Economics and Statistics,* May 1967, pp. 246–257.

Rooney, Robert F. "An Economic View of the Coastal Plan." *Cry California,* Spring 1976, pp. 3–9.

Schaenman, Philip S. *Using an Impact Measurement System to Evaluate Land Development.* Washington, D.C.: Urban Institute, September 1976.

Schaenman, Philip S., and Muller, Thomas. *Measuring Impacts of Land Development: An Initial Approach.* Washington, D.C.: Urban Institute, 1976.

Schultz, Charles. "Environment and the Economy: Managing the Relationship." *Challenge,* March/April 1978, p. 68.

Schumacher, E.F. *Small Is Beautiful: Economics as if People Mattered.* New York: Harper & Row, 1973.

Siegan, Bernard H. "Controlling Other People's Property Through Covenants, Zoning, State and Federal Regulation." *Environmental Law,* Spring 1975, pp. 385–474.

Strong, Douglas H. "The Sierra Club: A History." *Sierra,* October 1977, pp. 10–14.

United States Environmental Protection Agency. *EPA: Protecting Our Environment.* Washington, D.C.: U.S. Government Printing Office, 1977.

————. "Regulatory Agenda." *Federal Register,* 30 November 1978, pp. 56158–56171.

Vaughan, R.J., and Huckins, L. *The Economics of Expressway Noise Pollution Abatement.* Santa Monica, Calif.: Rand Corporation, 1975.

Vermont Natural Resources Council. *Vermonters on Vermont.* Montpelier, Vt.: Vermont Natural Resources Council, 1972.

Zube, Ervin H., ed. *Landscape Assesment: Values, Perceptions, and Resources.* Stroudsburg, Pa.: Dowden, Hutchinson & Ross, 1975.

NINE

THE CONSERVATION OF PRIVATE LAND:
HIDDEN VALUE IN OPEN SPACE

Association for Living Farms and Agricultural Museums. *Selected Living Historical Farms, Villages and Agricultural Museums in the United States and Canada.* Washington, D.C.: Association for Living Historical Farms and Agricultural Museums, Smithsonian Institution.

Boasberg, Tersh. "Federal Tax Problems Arising from Real Estate Activities of Non-Profit Preservation Organizations." *Urban Lawyer,* Winter 1976, pp. 1–53.

Brenneman, Russell L. *Private Approaches to the Preservation of Open Land.* New London, Conn.: Conservation and Research Foundation, 1967.

Burchell, Robert W., and Listokin, David. *Future Land Use: Energy, Environmental and Legal Constraints.* New Brunswick, N.J.: Rutgers University Press, 1975.

Conservation Law Foundation of New England. *Conservation Restrictions.* Boston: Conservation Law Foundation, March 1976.

———. *Gifts of Land for Conservation: Tax Advantages to the Land Owner.* Boston: Conservation Law Foundation.

Cooperative Extension Association of Suffolk County. *Farmland Owners Guide to Farmland Preservation.* Riverhead, N.Y.: Cooperative Extension Association of Suffolk County.

Coughlin, Robert E., and Plaut, Thomas. "Less-Than-Fee Acquisition for the Preservation of Open Space: Does it Work?" *Journal of the American Institute of Planners,* October 1978, pp. 452–462.

Fisher, Anthony C., and Krutilla, John V. *Valuing Long-Run Ecological Consequences and Irreversibilities.* Reprint no. 117. Washington, D.C.: Resources for the Future, 1974.

Gibbons, Boyd. *Wye Island.* Baltimore: Johns Hopkins Press, 1977.

Hayward, Philip. "Can rural America be saved?" *Preservation News,* February 1979, p. 6.

Hopple, Marcia. "Nature Preserves and Property Taxes." Mimeographed. Riverhead, N.Y.: Cooperative Extension Association of Suffolk County, 1979.

International Association of Assessing Officers. *Property Tax Incentives for Preservation: Use-Value Assesment and the Preservation of Farmland, Open Space, and Historic Sites.* Washington, D.C.: Property Tax Forum, 1975.

Krutilla, John V., and Fisher, Anthony C. *The Economics of Natural Environments: Studies in the Valuation of Commodity and Amenity Resources.* Baltimore: Johns Hopkins Press, 1975.

Lesher, W.G., and Conklin, H.E., eds. "Legislation to Permit Agricultural Districts in New York as Amended Through 1976." Mimeographed. Ithaca, N.Y.: Cornell University, November 1976.

Lesher, W.G., and Eiler, Doyle A. "Farmland Preservation in an Urban Fringe Area: An Analysis of Suffolk County's Development Rights Purchase Program." Mimeographed. Ithaca, N.Y.: Cornell University, March 1977.

Maryland Historic Trust. *Preservation Easements.* 2nd ed., rev. Department of Economic and Community Development. Annapolis, Md.: Maryland Historic Trust, 1977.

Matuszeski, William. *Less-Than-Fee Acquisition for Open Space: Its Effect on Land Value.* Philadelphia: University of Pennsylvania, 1968.

Morales, Dominic; Boyce, Byrle N.; and Favretti, Rudy J. "The Contribution of Trees to Residential Property Value: Manchester, Connecticut." *Valuation,* October/November 1976, pp. 26–43.

New York State Commission on the Preservation of Agricultural Land. *Preserving Agricultural Land in New York State: A Report to Nelson A. Rockefeller, Governor of New York.* Albany, N.Y.: State of New York, 1968.

Payne, Brian R., and Strom, Steven. "The Contribution of Trees to the Ap-

praised Value of Unimproved Residential Land." *Valuation,* October/
November 1975, pp. 36–45.

Proceedings of the Conference on Voluntary Preservation of Open Space. Potts-
town, Pa.: French and Pickering Creeks Conservation Trust, 1974.

*Selected Papers: Conference on Conserving the Historic and Cultural Land-
scape.* Washington, D.C.: Preservation Press, 1975.

Stokes, Samuel N., and Getty, Joe. "Rural Conservation." Information sheet
no. 19. Washington, D.C.: Preservation Press, 1979.

Sullivan, Peter. "Versatile Wetlands: An Endangered Resource." *Conservation News,* 15 October 1976.

Tsang, C. Steve, and Marshall, J. Paxton. "Procedure Employed to Determine
Use-Value of Agricultural Land in Virginia with Estimated Use-Values
for 31 Jurisdictions Authorizing Use-Value Taxation for the Tax Year
1977." Mimeographed. Blacksburg, Va.: Virginia Polytechnic Institute
and State University, September 1976.

Udall, Stewart L. *The Quiet Crisis.* New York: Holt, Rinehart & Winston,
1963.

Vineyard Open Land Foundation. *Looking at the Vineyard: A Visual Study
for a Changing Island.* West Tisbury, Mass.: Vineyard Open Land Foundation, 1973.

Warner, William W. *Beautiful Swimmers: Watermen, Crabs and the Chesapeake Bay.* Boston: Atlantic Monthly Press 1976.

Whyte, William H. *The Last Landscape.* New York: Doubleday & Co., 1968.

Wood, Robert C. *1400 Governments.* Cambridge, Mass.: Harvard University
Press, 1961.

TEN

PRESERVATION AND PROFIT

Advisory Council on Historic Preservation. *Report to the President and the
Congress of the United States, 1978.* Washington, D.C.: U.S. Government
Printing Office, 1978.

———. *Assessing the Energy Conservation Benefits of Historic Preservation:
Methods and Examples.* Washington, D.C.: U.S. Government Printing
Office, January 1979.

———. *The Contribution of Historic Preservation to Urban Revitalization.*
Washington, D.C.: U.S. Government Printing Office, January 1979.

Beeman, William Joseph. *The Property Tax and the Spatial Pattern of Growth
Within Urban Areas.* Research monograph 16. Washington, D.C.: Urban
Land Institute, 1969.

Costonis, John J. *Space Adrift: Landmark Preservation and the Marketplace.*
Chicago: University of Illinois Press, 1974.

Cowan, Eugenie C., ed. *Historic Preservation & the Law: The Metes and
Bounds of a New Field.* Conference sponsored by New York Landmarks
Conservancy and the Association of the Bar of the City of New York,
22–23 September 1978, New York City. Washington, D.C.: National Trust
for Historic Preservation, 1978.

Department of the Interior. "Sources of Preservation Funding." Mimeographed. Washington, D.C.: Heritage Conservation and Recreation Service, Office of Archeology and Historic Preservation, October 1978.

————. *Year-end Report: January 1979.* Heritage Conservation and Recreation Service Publication no. 10. Washington, D.C.: U.S. Government Printing Office, 1979.

"Environmental Laws and Property Taxes." Mimeographed. Riverhead, N.Y.: Cooperative Extension Association of Suffolk County, 1978.

Gamzon, Melvin A. "Adaptive use: An alternative for the 1980s." *The National Real Estate Investor,* January 1980, p. 30.

Goetze, Rolf; Colton, Kent W.; and O'Donnell, Vincent F. *Stabilizing Neighborhoods: A Fresh Approach to Housing Dynamics and Perceptions.* Boston: Boston Redevelopment Authority, November 1977.

Griffith, Thomas. "The Pacific Northwest." *Atlantic Monthly,* April 1976, pp. 46–93.

Haynes, Robert E., and Pribanic, Kenneth T., eds. *A Bibliography of Historic Preservation: Selected Publications of the Office of Archeology and Historic Preservation.* Washington, D.C.: U.S. Government Printing Office, August 1977.

Jandl, H. Ward; Lutz, Maricca J.; and Didham, Sarah. "Preservation and the Tax Reform Act of 1976." *Preservation News,* November 1977, pp. S1–S8.

Kettler, Ellen L., and Reams, Bernard D., Jr., eds. *Historic Preservation Law: An Annotated Bibliography.* Washington, D.C.: Preservation Press, 1976.

Knight, Carleton III. "Neighborhood revitalization: Is it a threat or a promise?" *Preservation News,* November 1978, pp. 8–9.

Nannen, Howard. *A Guide to the Financing and Development of Small Restoration Projects.* Hartford, Conn.: Hartford Architecture Conservancy, May 1976.

National Trust for Historic Preservation. *A Guide to Delineating Edges of Historic Districts.* Washington, D.C.: Preservation Press, 1976.

————. *A Guide to Federal Programs for Historic Preservation, 1976 Supplement.* Washington, D.C.: Preservation Press, 1976.

————. *Annual Report for 1977–1978.* Washington, D.C.: Preservation Press, 1979.

Nicholson, Sy. "Developers find profit in adaptive reuse projects, but lack of financing could stymie further growth." *National Real Estate Investor,* July 1977, p. 22.

Preservation League of New York State. *Economics and Historic Preservation: Five Case Studies in New York State.* Albany, N.Y.: Preservation League of New York State, 1976.

Rackham, John B. "Values of Residential Properties in Urban Historic Districts: Georgetown, Washington, D.C., and Other Selected Districts." Information sheet. Washington, D.C.: Preservation Press, 1977.

Raymond, Parish, Pine & Weiner, Inc. "The Impacts of Historic District Designation." Mimeographed. New York: New York Landmarks Conservancy, 16 November 1977.

Rettig, Robert B. "Case Studies of Increases in Property Values Following Historic District Designation." Mimeographed. Washington, D.C.: Planning Branch, National Register, National Park Service, Department of the Interior, 21 December 1977.

Reynolds, Anthony, and Waldron, William D. "Historic Significance . . . How Much Is it Worth?" *Appraisal Journal,* July 1969, pp. 401–410.

Reynolds, Judith, and Reynolds, Anthony. "Factors Affecting Valuation of Historic Property." Information sheet. Washington, D.C.: Preservation Press, 1976.

Shopsin, William C., and Marcus, Grania Bolton, eds. *Saving Large Estates: Conservation, Historic Preservation, Adaptive Re-Use.* New York: Society for the Preservation of Long Island Antiquities, 1977.

Soderberg, Lisa. "HCRS Historic Preservation Fund Grants: Potential Source for Local and Statewide Revolving Funds." *11593,* October, pp. 1–8.

Stipe, Robert E. Foreword to "Historic Preservation Symposium." *Wake Forest Law Review,* Spring 1976, pp. 1–281.

Tondro, Terry J. Introduction to "Symposium: Perspectives on Historic Preservation." *Connecticut Law Review,* Winter 1975–76, pp. 199–411.

Turner, Frederick Jackson. *The Frontier in American History.* New York: Henry Holt & Co., 1920.

Weber, Stephen F. *Historic Preservation Incentives of the 1976 Tax Reform Act: An Economic Analysis.* Department of Commerce, National Bureau of Standards Technical Note 980. Washington, D.C.: U.S. Government Printing Office, 1979.

ELEVEN

MIGRATION: THE CITY STRENGTHENS; SUBURBS IN TRANSITION; RURAL AMERICA AWAKENS

"Americans on the Move." *Time,* 15 March 1976, p. 55.

Anderson, Arnold C. "The Effect of Rapid Transit on Property Values." *Appraisal Journal,* January 1970, pp. 59–68.

Beale, Calvin L., and Fuguitt, Glenn V. "The New Pattern of Nonmetropolitan Population Change." Center for Demography and Ecology Working Paper 75–22. Madison: University of Wisconsin, 1975.

Beale, Calvin L. "A Further Look at Nonmetropolitan Growth Since 1970." *American Journal of Agricultural Economics,* December 1976, pp. 953–958.

Birch, David L. *The Economic Future of City and Suburb.* New York: Committee for Economic Development, 1970.

———. "From Suburb to Urban Place." *Annals of the American Academy of Political and Social Science,* November 1975, pp. 25–35.

Bowles, Gladys K. "Contribution of Recent Metro/Nonmetro Migrants to the Nonmetro Population and Labor Force." *Agricultural Economics Research,* October 1978, pp. 15–21.

Bradford, Calvin P., and Rubinowitz, Leonard S. "The Urban-Suburban Investment-Disinvestment Process: Consequences for Older Neighborhoods." *Annals of the American Academy of Political and Social Science,* November 1975, pp. 77–86.

Brodsky, Harold. "Residential Land and Improvement Values in a Central City." *Land Economics,* August 1970, pp. 229–247.

Carter, Luther J. "Research Triangle Park Succeeds Beyond its Promoters' Expectations." *Science,* 30 June 1978, pp. 1469–1470.

Casetti, E. "Urban land value functions: equilibrium vs. optimality." *Economic Geography,* October 1973, pp. 357–365.

Cose, Ellis. "Can America's Cities Survive?" *Current,* March 1978, p. 26.

Davin-Drabkin, Haim. *Land Policy and Urban Growth.* New York: Pergamon Press, 1977.

DeJong, Gordon F., and Sell, Ralph S. "Population Redistribution, Migration, and Residential Preference." *Annals of the American Academy of Political and Social Science,* January 1977, pp. 130–144.

Department of Housing and Urban Development. *The President's 1978 National Urban Policy Report.* Washington, D.C.: U.S. Government Printing Office, August 1978.

Downs, Anthony. "Squeezing Spread City." *The New York Times Magazine,* 17 March 1974, p. 38.

———. "Special Research Report." *The National Market Letter,* June 1974, p. 8.

Evans, Samuel III. "Industrial Parks Restudied." *Urban Land,* April 1972, pp. 14–21.

Flectwood, Blake. "The New Elite and an Urban Renaissance." *The New York Times Magazine,* 14 January 1979, pp. 16–20.

"Flight from Inner Cities Goes On." *U.S. News & World Report,* 11 September 1978, p. 49.

Forstall, Richard L. "Annexations and Corporate Changes Since the 1970 Census: With Historical Data on Annexation for Larger Cities for 1900–1970." In *The Municipal Year Book 1975.* Washington, D.C.: International City Management Association, 1975.

Frey, H. Thomas. *Major Uses of Land in the United States: 1974.* Agricultural Economic Report no. 440. Washington, D.C.: U.S. Government Printing Office, November 1979.

Frieden, Bernard J. "Location Preference in the Housing Market." *Journal of the American Institute of Planners,* November 1961, pp. 316–324.

Fuguitt, Glenn V., and Voss, Paul R. *Growth and Change in Rural America.* Washington, D.C.: Urban Land Institute, 1979.

———. "Population Growth in Rural America." *Environmental Comment,* February 1979, pp. 4–9.

Galchus, Kenneth E. "Property Values in an Integrated Neighborhood: Some Further Evidence." *Real Estate Appraiser,* March/April 1977, pp. 17–21.

Gelman, David; Lord, Mary; and Camp, Holly. "Government: Hitting Home." *Newsweek,* 8 May 1978, pp. 73–74.

"Golden Days Are Gone in Suburbia." *Business Week,* 5 September 1970, p. 34.

Gorton, Tom. "Railroads: An ace in the hole for rural America?" *Planning,* December 1978, pp. 18–19.

Gottlieb, Jerry R. "Industrial Park Appraisal in the 1970's." *Appraisal Journal,* October 1972, pp. 600–610.

Haar, Charles M., ed. *The President's Task Force on Suburban Problems.* Cambridge, Mass.: Ballinger, 1974.

Klaff, Vivian Z., and Fuguitt, Glenn V. "Annexation as a Factor in the Growth of U.S. Cities, 1960–1970." *Demography,* February 1978, pp. 1–12.

Leomides, James S., and Young, April L. "Provision of Public Open Space in Urban Areas: Determinants, Obstacles, and Incentives." *Journal of the American Institute of Planners,* July 1978, p. 287.

Levin, Charles L., and Mark, Jonathan H. "Revealed Preferences for Neighborhood Characteristics." *Urban Studies,* June 1977, pp. 147–159.

The MacNeil/Lehrer Report. "Saving the Cities: For Whom?" Mimeographed transcript. New York: Educational Broadcasting Corporation and GWETA, 22 September 1978.

Mazie, Sara Mills, ed. *Population, Distribution, and Policy.* vol. 5. Washington, D.C.: U.S. Government Printing Office, 1972.

Meadows, George Richard, and Call, Steven T. "Combining Housing Market Trends and Resident Attitudes in Planning Urban Revitalization." *Journal of the American Institute of Planners,* July 1978, pp. 297–306.

"The Mess in Mass Transit." *Time,* 16 July 1979, pp. 52–54.

"Migration: 'Rural Growth' is really urban sprawl." *Business Week,* 12 January 1976, p. 77.

Northam, Ray M. "Vacant Urban Land in the American City." *Land Economics,* November 1971, pp. 345–365.

———. *Urban Geography.* 2nd ed., rev. New York: John Wiley & Sons, 1979.

Otte, Robert C.; Zeimetz, Kathryn A.; and Frey, H. Thomas. "Everything You Always Wanted to Know About Urban Land Use Data." Mimeographed. Washington, D.C.: Department of Agriculture, Economic Research Service, 1 April 1977.

"Out of the Cities, Back to the Country." *U.S. News & World Report,* 31 March 1975, pp. 46–50.

Palmer, Lane. "Look Where America Is Growing Fastest." *Farm Journal,* January 1977, p. 53.

Regional Plan Association. *Growth and Settlement in the U.S.: Past Trends and Future Issues.* New York: Regional Plan Association, June 1975.

"Slowdown for 'Strip Cities': Reversal of Century-Old Trend." *U.S. News & World Report,* 7 March 1977, p. 39.

Sutton, Horace. "America Falls in Love with its Cities—Again." *Saturday Review,* August 1978, pp. 18–20.

Taylor, Thayer C. "Survey of Buying Power, Part II." *Sales and Marketing Management,* 29 October 1979, p. 5.

Thaler, Richard. "A Note on the Value of Crime Control: Evidence from the Property Market." *Journal of Urban Economics,* January 1978, pp. 137–145.

Thoryn, Michael. "Construction: Rising to the Challenge of a Changing America." *Nation's Business,* May 1978, pp. 81–82.

Tucker, C. Jack. "Changing Patterns of Migration Between Metropolitan and Nonmetropolitan Areas in the United States." *Demography,* November 1976, pp. 435–443.

"The Urban Impact of Federal Policies." *Practicing Planner,* December 1977, pp. 40–43.

Urban Land Institute. *Density: Five Perspectives.* Washington, D.C.: Urban Land Institute, 1972.

Vaughan, Roger J. *The Value of Urban Open Space.* Santa Monica, Calif.: Rand Corporation, 1977.

Wardwell, John M. "Equilibrium and Change in Nonmetropolitan Growth." *Rural Sociology,* Summer 1977, pp. 156–179.

Wendt, Paul F. *The Dynamics of Central City Land Values: San Francisco and Oakland.* Berkeley: University of California Press, 1961.

"Why More and More People Are Coming Back to Cities." *U.S. News & World Report,* 8 August 1977, pp. 69–71.

Witte, Ann D., and Bachman, James E. "Vacant Urban Land Holdings: Portfolio Considerations and Owner Characteristics." *Southern Economic Journal,* October 1978, pp. 543–558.

Woodward, Kenneth L.; Lord, Mary; Maier, Frank; Foote, Donna M.; and Malamud, Phyllis. "Saving the Family." *Newsweek,* 8 May 1978, pp. 63–68.

Yannacone, Victor John, Jr. "Limits on Development May Force Return to the Cities." *Appraisal Journal,* January 1978, pp. 128–131.

Zschock, Dieter, ed. *Economic Aspects of Suburban Growth: Studies of the Naussau-Suffolk Planning Region.* Stony Brook, N.Y.: State University of New York at Stony Brook, 1969.

TWELVE

LAND SPECULATION

Allen, James B. *The Company Town in the American West.* Norman: University of Oklahoma Press, 1966.

Apgar, Mahlon IV, ed. *New Perspectives on Community Development.* London: McKinsey and Co., 1976.

Burby, Raymond J. III, and Weiss, Shirley F. *New Communities U.S.A.* Lexington, Mass.: Lexington Books, 1976.

Campbell, Carlos C. *New Towns: Another Way to Live.* Reston, Va.: Reston Publishing Co., 1976.

"Change Comes to the 'Company Town.'" *U.S. News & World Report,* 6 December 1976, pp. 70–74.

Counter Information Services. *The Recurrent Crises of London: CIS Anti-Report on the Property Developers.* London: Counter Information Services, 1973.

Frasser, James. "Shift from Real Estate to Stocks?" *U.S. News & World Report,* 26 June 1978, p. 79.

General Accounting Office. *Getting the New Communities Program Started: Progress and Problems.* Washington, D.C.: U.S. Government Printing Office, 1974.

George, Henry. *Progress and Poverty: An Inquiry into the Cause of industrial depressions and of increase of want with increase of wealth.* New York: Modern Library, 1938.

Greenebaum, Mary. "Real Estate Funds May Be Getting Overpriced." *Forbes,* 25 September 1978, pp. 117–118.

Hayden, Dolores. *Seven American Utopias: The Architecture of Communitarian Socialism, 1790–1975.* Cambridge, Mass.: M.I.T. Press, 1976.

Henry, Rene A., Jr. *How to Profitably Buy and Sell Land.* New York: John Wiley & Sons, 1977.

Hine, Robert V. *California's Utopian Colonies.* New Haven: Yale University Press, 1966.

Holloway, Mark. *Heavens on Earth: Utopian Communities in America 1680–1880.* 2nd ed., rev. New York: Dover Publications, 1966.

Hoyt, Homer. *The Urban Real Estate Cycle: Performances and Prospects.* Washington, D.C.: Urban Land Institute, 1960.

"Income properties: Are they bound to rise in value?" *National Real Estate Investor,* June 1978, p. 32.

"Investing in Real Estate: Buying a Piece of Someone Else's Action." *Money,* February 1978, p. 74.

"Investing in Real Estate: How to Dig for Profits in Land." *Money,* December 1977, p. 60.

"Investing in Real Estate: Waiting Out Profits in Rental Property." *Money,* January 1978, pp. 36–38.

Jacobs, Jane. *The Death and Life of Great American Cities.* New York: Random House, 1961.

Knight, Rolf. *Work Camps and Company Towns in Canada and the U.S.: An Annotated Bibliography.* Vancouver, B.C.: New Star Books, 1975.

Leader, Susan. "The New Squeeze on Property." *Institutional Investor,* July 1978, pp. 89–90.

Lowry, Albert J. *How You Can Become Financially Independent by Investing in Real Estate.* New York: Simon & Schuster, 1977.

Maisel, Sherman J., and Roulac, Stephen E. *Real Estate Investment and Finance.* New York: McGraw-Hill, 1976.

Minard, Lawrence. "Real Estate: Why George Babbitt Should Be Smiling in His Grave." *Forbes,* 4 September 1978, pp. 41–46.

"Multi-use complexes increasing in numbers, scope and impact in downtown development." *National Real Estate Investor,* July 1976, pp. 24–30.

"New Towns Make Strong Pitch to Overcome Bad Publicity, Competition." *National Real Estate Investor,* August 1978, p. 38.

Norcross, Carl. "New Towns Under the Microscope: Living up to Promises?" *Urban Land,* February 1975, pp. 5–10.

Qadeer, Mohammad A. "Local Land Market and a New Town: Columbia's Impact on Land Prices in Howard County, Maryland." *Journal of the American Institute of Planners,* March 1974, pp. 110–123.

Ring, Alfred A., and Dasso, Jerome. *Real Estate Principles and Practices.* 8th ed., rev. Englewood Cliffs, N.J.: Prentice-Hall, 1977.

Ruff, Howard J. *How to Prosper During the Coming Bad Years.* New York: Times Books, 1979.

Schmid, A. Allen. *Converting Land from Rural to Urban Uses.* Washington, D.C.: Resources for the Future, 1968.

Sturm, Paul. "Mobil's Broad Acres." *Forbes,* 21 August 1978, pp. 31–32.

Train, John. "Investing in Land." *Forbes,* 20 March 1978, p. 104.

Tymon, Dorothy. *America Is for Sale.* Rockville Centre, N.Y.: Farnsworth Publishing Co., 1973.

Wiley, Robert J. *Real Estate Investment: Analysis and Strategy.* New York: Ronald Press Co., 1977.

THIRTEEN

RECREATIONAL LOTS AND SECOND HOMES: WHERE AMERICA PLAYS, IT BUYS AND SPECULATES

Allan, Leslie. *Promised Lands.* New York: Inform, 1978.

American Society of Planning Officials. *Subdividing Rural America: Impact of Recreational Lot and Second Home Development.* Washington, D.C.: U.S. Government Printing Office, 1976.

Carter, Luther J. *The Florida Experience.* Baltimore: Johns Hopkins Press, 1974.

"A Frosty Look at Sunbelt Subdivisions." *Changing Times,* September 1978, pp. 25–28.

"Investing in Real Estate: How to Swing a Second Home." *Money,* November 1977, pp. 58–61.

Mahon, Gigi. "Place in the Sun: Fortune Has Smiled Again on the Land Developers." *Barron's,* 17 April 1978, p. 4.

"Popular Delusions and the Madness in Maui." *Forbes,* 18 September 1978, pp. 105–106.

FOURTEEN

THE FEDERAL LANDS: PUBLIC WEALTH AND PRIVATE PRIVILEGE

"Adjacent Land Study: NPCA Surveys Superintendents About Threats to Parks." *National Parks and Conservation Magazine,* February 1978, p. 25.

Alderson, George. "Capitol Watch." *The Living Wilderness,* July/September 1975, p. 42.

Alstyne, Peter J. Van. "Utah wishes it hadn't scuttled statewide planning." *Planning,* December 1978, pp. 34–37.

"At least 170 National Park Service Units Endangered by Oil and Gas Rights." *National Parks and Conservation Magazine,* June 1978, pp. 22–23.

Bellows, William J., and Colacicco, Daniel. "Impact of C & O Canal National Historical Park on Land Values." Contribution no. 5155. College Park: University of Maryland, 1976.

Brockman, C. Frank, and Merriam, Lawrence C., Jr. *Recreational Use of Wild Lands.* New York: McGraw-Hill, 1973.

Brown, Charles; Kennedy, Doug; and Portnoy, Stuart. "Federal Land Policy Management Act: Its Implications for Administering the Public Domain." Mimeographed. Philadelphia: University of Pennsylvania, 1977.

Cantril, Albert H., and Roll, Charles W., Jr. *Hopes and Fears of the American People.* New York: Universe Books, 1971.

Chandler, Robert. *Public Opinion: Changing Attitudes on Contemporary Political and Social Issues.* New York: R.R. Bowker Co., 1972.

Church, Frank. "Whither Wilderness?" *American Forests,* July 1977, p. 38.

Clawson, Marion. *The Federal Lands Since 1956: Recent Trends in Use and Management.* Baltimore: Johns Hopkins Press, 1967.

Clawson, Marion, and Held, Burnell. *The Federal Lands: Their Use and Management.* Baltimore: Johns Hopkins Press, 1967.

Clawson, Marion. *The Economics of National Forest Management.* Washington, D.C.: Resources for the Future, 1976.

Department of the Interior, Bureau of Land Management. *Public Land Statistics 1977.* Washington, D.C.: U.S. Government Printing Office, 1979.

Department of the Interior, National Park Service. *Index of the National Park System and Affiliated Areas as of June 30, 1977.* Washington, D.C.: U.S. Government Printing Office, 1977.

Flavin, Peter T. *Mineral Resources: Geology, Engineering, Economics, Politics, Law.* New York: Rand McNally & Co., 1966.

Fraker, Susan; Lubenow, Gerald C.; and Cook, William J. "Preserving Alaska." *Newsweek,* 24 July 1978, pp. 43–44.

Frome, Michael. "No Home on the Range." *Field and Stream,* September 1974, p. 34.

Garrett, W.E. "The Grand Canyon: Are we loving it to death?" *National Geographic,* July 1978, p. 16.

General Services Administration. *Inventory Report on Real Property Owned by the United States Throughout the World as of June 30, 1974.* Washington, D.C.: U.S. Government Printing Office, 1974.

Goodwin, Richard H., and Niering, William A. *Inland Wetlands of the United States.* New London: Connecticut College, 1975.

Graham, Frank, Jr. *Man's Dominion: The Story of Conservation in America.* New York: M. Evans & Co., 1971.

Hagenstein, Perry R. "Changing an Anachronism: Congress and the General Mining Law of 1872." *Natural Resources Journal,* July 1973, p. 482.

Johnson, R. Roy; Carothers, Steven W.; Dolan, Robert; Hayden, Bruce P.; and Howard, Alan. "Man's Impact on the Colorado River in the Grand Canyon." *National Parks and Conservation Magazine,* March 1977, pp. 13–16.

Knetsch, Jack L. "Land Values and Parks in Urban Fringe Areas." *Journal of Farm Economics,* December 1962, pp. 1718–1726.

Laessig, Robert E.; Glaser, Edward R.; and Ricci, Paolo F. "A Retrospective Study on the Influence of a State Park: Lake on Land Value, From the Time of Land Acquisition to Reservoir Filling." *Decision Sciences,* October 1975, pp. 775–785.

McGee, Brian E.; Yegge, Hall; and Yegge, Evans. "Federal Coal Leasing: What a Difference a Year Makes." Mimeographed. New Orleans: 1977 Coal Lawyers Conference, 17–20 November 1977.

McPhee, John. *Coming into the Country.* New York: Farrar, Straus & Giroux, 1977.

Matthews, William H. III. *A Guide to the National Parks: Their Landscape and Geology.* Garden City, N.Y.: Natural History Press, 1968.

"National Parks: Success Is Causing a Crisis." *U.S. News & World Report,* 13 June 1977, p. 36.

Robbins, Roy M. *Our Landed Heritage: The Public Domain 1776–1936.* Lincoln: University of Nebraska Press, 1962.

Rosenkrantz, Barbara Gutman, and Koelsch, William A., eds. *American Habitat: A Historical Perspective.* New York: Free Press, 1973.

Sheils, Merrill, and Lubenow, Gerald C. "Profits in the Tundra." *Newsweek,* 21 August 1978, p. 62.

Sheridan, David. "Mining the Public Wealth: It's Time to Reform the Mining Law of 1972." *Sierra,* April 1978, pp. 10–13.

"The Shrinking Supply of Private Land." *U.S. News & World Report,* 20 February 1978, pp. 64–65.

Singer, Michael. "The Third Forest." *New West,* 17 December 1979, pp. 43–48.

Sontag, Susan. *On Photography.* New York: Farrar, Straus & Giroux, 1977.

Spring, Norma. *Alaska:* The Complete Travel Book New York: Macmillan Publishing Co., 1975.

Sternes, Richard. "Crime in the Outdoors." *Outdoor Life,* February 1978, p. 12.

Towell, William E. "Eastern Wilderness: Big 'W' or Little 'w'?" *American Forests,* April 1976, pp. 6–7.

Trueblood, Ted. "The Forest Service Versus the Wilderness Act." *Field and Stream,* September 1975, p. 16.

Voigt, William, Jr. *Public Grazing Lands.* New Brunswick, N.J.: Rutgers University Press, 1976.

Vrooman, David H. "An Empirical Analysis of Determinants of Land Values in the Adirondack Park." *American Journal of Economics and Sociology,* April 1978, pp. 165–177.

Wayburn, Peggy. "The Redwoods: Jobs and Environment." *Environment,* April 1978, pp. 34–39.

"Yellowstone: Park Service Discloses Ripoff Operations in Land of 'Old Faithful.' " *National Parks and Conservation Magazine,* August 1977, pp. 26–27.

FIFTEEN

FARMLAND: GEM OF THE NATION

Amato, Peter W. "Wisconsin hopes a new law will preserve its farms." *Planning,* January 1979, pp. 10–12.

Brown, Ralph J. "A Study of the Impact of the Wetlands Easement Program on Agricultural Land Values." *Land Economics,* November 1976, pp. 509–517.

Church, George. "The New American Farmer." *Time,* 6 November 1978, p. 92.

Cotner, Melvin L. *Land Use Policy and Agriculture: A National Perspective.* Economic Research Service Report no. 630, Department of Agriculture. Washington, D.C.: U.S. Printing Office, July 1976.

Dangerfield, Jeanne. "Sowing the Till." In *The People's Land: A Reader on Land Reform in the U.S.* Edited by Peter Barnes. Emmaus, Pa.: Rodale Press, 1975.

Department of Agriculture. *Our Land and Water Resources: Current and*

Prospective Supplies and Uses. Miscellaneous Publication no. 1290, Economic Research Service. Washington, D.C.: U.S. Government Printing Office, May 1974.

————. *Farm Income Statistics.* Statistical Bulletin no. 627, Economics, Statistics, and Cooperative Service. Washington, D.C.: U.S. Government Printing Office, October 1979.

Dideriksen, Raymond I.; Hidlebaugh, Allan R.; and Schmude, Keith D. *Potential Cropland Study.* Statistical Bulletin no. 578, Soil Conservation Service, Department of Agriculture. Washington, D.C.: U.S. Government Printing Office, October 1977.

Dill, Henry H., Jr., and Otte, Robert C. *Urbanization of Land in the Western States.* Natural Resource Economics Division, Economic Research Service, Department of Agriculture. Washington, D.C.: U.S. Government Printing Office, January 1970.

"Farmland Boom Starts to Slow Down." *U.S. News & World Report,* 10 April 1978, p. 77.

Frey, H. Thomas, and Dill, Henry W., Jr. *Land Use Change in the Southern Mississippi Alluvial Valley, 1950–69: An Analysis Based on Remote Sensing.* Agricultural Economic Report no. 215, Economic Research Service, Department of Agriculture. Washington, D.C.: U.S. Government Printing Office, October 1971.

Langford, Don A. "Agriculture in the seventies: a decade of turbulence." *Economic Perspectives,* September/October 1978, pp. 3–11.

Lee, Linda K. *A Perspective on Cropland Availability.* Agricultural Economic Report no. 406, Economic, Statistics, and Cooperative Service, Department of Agriculture. Washington, D.C.: U.S. Government Printing Office, July 1978.

Mize, Jim. "A Law That Cannot Meet its Objectives." *Virginia Municipal Review,* April 1979, p. 2.

Munger, James A. "Components of Rural Land Values in Northern Wisconsin." *Land Economics,* February 1964, pp. 87–91.

Otte, Robert. *Farming in the City's Shadow.* Agricultural Economics Report no. 250, Economic Research Service, Department of Agriculture. Washington, D.C.: U.S. Government Printing Office, February 1974.

Pasour, E.C. "Public Land Banking and the Price of Land: Comment." *Land Economics,* November 1976, pp. 559–564.

Pimentel, David, and Krummel, John. "America's Agricultural Future." *The Ecologist,* August/September 1977, p. 254.

Regional Science Research Institute. *Untaxing Open Space: An Evaluation of the Effectiveness of Differential Assessment of Farms and Open Space.* Washington, D.C.: U.S. Government Printing Office, April 1976.

60 Minutes. "The Grapes of Wealth." Mimeographed transcript, vol. 12, no. 5. Broadcast over the CBS Television Network, Sunday, 14 October 1979.

Wallace, Henry A. "Symposium on Iowa Land Value Appraisals: Comparative Farmland Values in Iowa." *Journal of Land and Public Utility Economics,* October 1926, pp. 385–392.

Zeimetz, Kathryn A.; Dillion, Elizabeth; Hardy, Ernest E.; and Otte, Robert C. *Dynamics of Land Use in Fast Growth Areas.* Agricultural Economic Report no. 325, Economic Research Service, Department of Agriculture. Washington, D.C.: U.S. Government Printing Office, April 1976.

CREDITS

PHOTOGRAPHS, MAPS, AND DIAGRAMS

Page

4   Photo by Dorothea Lange. Farm Security Administration Collection, Library of Congress.

8   Photo by Marion Post Wolcott. Farm Security Administration Collection, Library of Congress.

12   Reprinted with permission of Arlington House Publishers from *The Coming Real Estate Crash* by Cardiff and English. Copyright © 1979 by Gray Emerson Cardiff and John Wesley English.

13   Reprinted with permission of Arlington House Publishers from *The Coming Real Estate Crash* by Cardiff and English. Copyright © 1079 by Gray Emerson Cardiff and John Wesley English.

21   Rand Corporation, August 1978.

22   Rand Corporation, August 1978.

34   U.S. Dept. of Commerce, Bureau of the Census.

37   Clawson, Marion and Held Burnell. *The Federal Lands: Their Use and Management.* Baltimore: Johns Hopkins Press, 1957.

38   U.S. Department of Commerce, Bureau of the Census.

40   General Services Administration, No. 48–RST–7–25 in National Archives, American West #150.

42   Reprinted from *Man and Land in the United States* by Marion Clawson by permission of University of Nebraska Press. Copyright © 1964 by University of Nebraska Press.

44   Photo by J. Grabill, Library of Congress.

45   Reprinted from *Man and Land in the United States* by Marion Clawson by permission of University of Nebraska Press. Copyright © 1964 by University of Nebraska Press.

46   Photo by William H. Jackson, Library of Congress.

48   Photo by G.L. Clothier. Farm Security Administration Collection, Library of Congress.

48   National Archives, American West #180.

53   Library of Congress.

54   Library of Congress.

56   Kansas State Historical Society, Topeka.

59   Union Pacific Railroad Museum.

62   From *The Story of American Railroads* by Stewart H. Holbrook. Copyright © 1947, 1975 by Crown Publishers, Inc. Used by permission of Crown Publishers, Inc.

575

63   Harry T. Peters Collection, Museum of the City of New York.

65   The Beinecke Rare Book and Manuscript Library, Yale University.

68   Photo by J. Grabill, Library of Congress.

72   Photo by J. Grabill, Library of Congress.

72   Western History Collections, University of Oklahoma Library.

74   Library of Congress.

75   Library of Congress.

77   Photo by Lyntha Scott Eiler, U.S. Environmental Protection Agency/Documerica.

108   Photo by T.L. Gettings. Courtesy of the Rodale Press.

144   Photo by Charles O'Rear. U.S. Environmental Protection Agency/Documerica.

150   Peter Wolf.

163   Real Estate Corporation, Council of Environmental Quality, HUD, and the Environmental Protection Agency.

164   U.S. Environmental Protection Agency/Documerica.

166   Photo by Stan Wayman, *Another Chance for Cities.*

169   Photo by George Cserna.

173   Peter Wolf.

175   U.S. Department of Housing and Urban Development and the National Trust for Historic Preservation.

208   The J. Clarence Davis Collection, Museum of the City of New York.

210   Peter Wolf.

211   Peter Wolf.

213   From the Illinois Central Land Agency Collection.

214   *The Wall Street Journal.*

215   © Copyright Ed Nowak.

215   The New York Historical Society, New York City.

217   Photo by Marjory Collins, U.S. Office of War Information and the Library of Congress.

218   Channing Harris, Boston.

222   U.S. Department of Transportation, Federal Highway Administration.

224   Photo by Danny Lyon, U.S. Environmental Protection Agency/Documerica.

228   Photo by Franklynn Peterson, Black Star.

230   Photo by Joe Davi, City of New Orleans.

236   U.S. Department of Transportation, Federal Highway Administration.

239   Department of Transportation, *Highway Statistics Summary to 1975.* Washington, D.C.: U.S. Government Printing Office, 1977.

242   Washington Metropolitan Area Transit Authority.

246   City of Los Angeles.

256   Photo by Marc St. Gil, U.S. Environmental Protection Agency/Documerica.

259   Photo by Fred Ward, U.S. Environmental Protection Agency/Documerica.

265   Photo by Flip Schulke, U.S. Environmental Protection Agency/Documerica.

268   Photo by Danny Lyon. U.S. Environmental Protection Agency/Documerica.

274   The Bancroft Library, University of California, Berkeley.

280   Mohonk Mountain House, New Paltz, New York.

289   Diagram reprinted with permission of the Conservation Law Foundation of New England.

299   Association for Living Historical Farms and Agricultural Museums, Smithsonian Institution.

300   Old Sturbridge Village.

306   Group for America's South Fork, Long Island.

314   Vieux Carré Commission, New Orleans.

318   New York City Landmarks Commission.

318   © 1977 Nathaniel Lieberman.

337   U.S. Bureau of the Census, *Current Population Reports*, Series P-25, No. 640, November 1976.

338   U.S. Department of Commerce, Bureau of the Census.

340   U.S. Census of Population, 1970, and Conservation Needs Inventory, 1967.

341   U.S. Department of Agriculture, Economic Research Service.

342   Elizabeth Nomellini.

344   U.S. Bureau of the Census, *Current Population Reports*, Series P-25, No. 601 and No. 607.

345   Courtesy of The Conference Board.

361   Morrison, Peter A. *Current Demographic Changes in Regions of the United States.* Rand Paper Series P-6000, November 1977.

363   Regional Plan Association, New York.

364   *Ibid.*

365   *Ibid.*

370   Fuguitt, Glenn V.; Voss, Paul R.; and Doherty, J.C. *Growth and Change in Rural America.* Washington, D.C.: Urban Land Institute, 1979.

378   Library of Congress.

384   Photo by Russell Lee. Farm Security Administration Collection, Library of Congress.

388   Peter Wolf. Derived from Schmid, A. *Converting Land from Rural to Urban Uses,* Johns Hopkins Press, 1968.

391   Photo by Gene Daniels. U.S. Environmental Protection Agency/Documerica.

394   Photo by Russell Lee. Farm Security Administration Collection, Library of Congress.

395   *The Wall Street Journal.*

410   Photo by Russell Lee. Farm Security Administration Collection, Library of Congress.

424   U.S. Department of Housing and Urban Development, Office of Interstate Land Sales Registration. Published in *Subdividing Rural America: Impact of Recreational Lot and Second Home Development.* Washington, D.C.: U.S. Government Printing Office, 1976.

430   Photo by Fred Ward. U.S. Environmental Protection Agency/Documerica.

432   U.S. Department of Commerce, Bureau of the Census, *U.S. Census of Housing, 1970 Detailed Housing Characteristics,* 1972.

437   U.S. Department of Housing and Urban Development, Office of Interstate Land Sales Registration.

443   U.S. Department of Agriculture.

TABLES

CREDITS

401   Reprinted by permission of Times Books, a division of Quadrange/The New York Times Book Co., Inc., from *How to Prosper During the Coming Bad Years.* Copyright © 1979 by Howard Ruff.

402   *Ibid.*

403   *Ibid.*

405   Wiley, Robert J. *Real Estate Investment: Analysis and Strategy.* New York: John Wiley and Sons, 1977.

405   *Ibid.*

420   Warren E. Johnston, "Remote Recreational Subdivisions in Northeastern California." Published in *Subdividing Rural America: Impact of Recreational Lot and Second Home Development.* Washington, D.C.: U.S. Government Printing Office, 1976.

426   Reprinted from Allen, Leslie. *Promised Lands,* Volume 2: *Subdivisions in Florida's Wetlands* by special permission, © 1977 by Inform, Inc., New York.

427   *Ibid.*

428   Peter Wolf.

448   General Services Administration.

494   Dideriksen, Raymond I.; Hidlebaugh, Allen R.; and Schmude, Keith O. *Potential Cropland Study.* Statistical Bulletin No. 578, Soil Conservation Service, U.S. Department of Agriculture. Washington, D.C.: U.S. Government Printing Office, October, 1977.

495   Frey, H. Thomas. *Major Uses of Land in the United States: 1974.* Agricultural Economic Report No. 440. Washington, D.C.: U.S. Government Printing Office, 1979.

496   *Ibid.*

508   U.S. Department of Commerce, Bureau of the Census. *Statistical Abstract of the United States: 1979.* Washington, D.C.: U.S. Government Printing Office, 1979; *The Statistical History of the United States, From Colonial Times to the Present.* New York: Basic Books, 1976; and U.S. Department of Agriculture, Economics, Statistics, and Cooperative Service. *Farm Real Estate Market Developments,* annual.

521   *Indiana Real Estate Property Appraisal Manual,* State Board of Tax Commissioners, Regulation 17 (1968). In *Untaxing Open Space: An Evaluation of the Effectiveness of Differential Assessment of Farms and Open Space.* Washington, D.C.: U.S. Government Printing Office, April 1976.

INDEX

ABOUT THE AUTHOR

Peter Wolf, a land planner and land investment management consultant to individuals, communities, and corporations, is also an adjunct professor at the School of Architecture, Cooper Union, and serves as chairman of the Board of Fellows of the Institute for Architecture and Urban Studies, both in New York City. Educated at Yale, Tulane, and the Institute of Fine Arts, New York University, Dr. Wolf has lectured and published on a wide range of subjects connected to land use, land values, and planning. His recent book, *The Future of the City: New Directions in Urban Planning,* is a recognized guide for both laymen and professionals who seek an understanding of the recent evolution of American cities.

To support the research for *Land in America,* Dr. Wolf was granted a fellowship by the Graham Foundation for Advanced Studies in the Fine Arts and awarded an Accomplished Professional Fellowship in Design by the National Endowment for the Arts.